D0734495

JIMMY CARTER

THE LIBERAL LEFT AND
WORLD CHAOS

MIKE EVANS

A CARTER / OBAMA PLAN
THAT WILL NOT WORK

JIMMY CARTER

THE LIBERAL LEFT AND WORLD CHAOS

TIMEWORTHY BOOKS

P.O. BOX 30000 — PHOENIX, AZ 85046

Published by Time Worthy Books
P.O. Box 30000
Phoenix, AZ   85046

JIMMY CARTER: *The Liberal Left and World Chaos*
Copyright © 2009 by Time Worthy Books

Jacket Design: Lookout Design, Inc.
Cover Photo: Photo by Arnold H. Drapkin/Time Life Pictures/Getty Images

US   ISBN 13: 978-0-935199-33-8
CANADA   ISBN 13: 978-0-935199-34-5

*"Those who cannot learn from history
are doomed to repeat it."*

— PHILOSOPHER GEORGE SANTAYANA

*This book is dedicated to
a forgotten generation of innocent Iranians,
to those who loved America
and were betrayed by President Jimmy Carter.*

*It is dedicated to
those who have endured unspeakable hell
in Iran and who lost loved ones because of it.*

*It is especially dedicated to
Iranian military and diplomatic leaders who
so believed in America they refused to leave Iran...
and died for it.*

TABLE OF CONTENTS

ACKNOWLEDGEMENTS

MY DEEPEST GRATITUDE GOES TO the men and women who have agreed to interviews: Her Majesty Farah Pahlavi, wife of the former Shah of Iran; Ambassador Ardeshir Zahedi, a special thanks to Iran's last and most powerful ambassador to the U.S.; Valéry Giscard d'Estaing, former president of the French Republic; editorial journalist Samuel Segev; journalist and terrorism expert Charles Villeneuve; Dr. Parviz Mina, director, National Iranian Oil Company under the Shah; Dr. Abdol Majid Majidi, minister of Planning and Budget under the shah; Hubert Vedrine, adviser to President François Mitterrand and secretary general from 1991-1995; Benjamin Netanyahu, former prime minister of Israel; Israeli Prime Minister Ehud Olmert; Yitzhak Rabin, former prime minister of Israel; Shimon Peres, president of Israel; Uri Lubrani, former Israeli ambassador to Iran; former Israeli ambassador to the U.S. Dore Gold; Marvin Kalb, award-winning reporter for CBS and NBC; Dr. Alan Dershowitz, professor, Harvard School of Law; Israeli Mossad agent Eliezer Zafrir; General David Ivri, commander Israeli Air Force and ambassador to U.S.; General Yitzhak Segev; Dr. Ahmad Tehrani; and Lt. General Shapour Azarbarzin. I especially want to thank Israeli, French, and U.S. intelligence operatives (whose names must remain anonymous). They repeatedly told me the same thing which became the key to unraveling the Carter mystery.

This story began with late Israeli Prime Minister Menachem Begin and my talks with him during the Carter presidency. This book would not be complete without thanking many of the key people I interviewed over the years on this subject.: Dr. Reuben Hecht, senior advisor to Prime Minister Begin and my mentor; Yehiel Kadishai, personal aide to Prime Minister Menachem Begin;

Prime Minister Yitzhak Shamir; Major General James E. Freeze, assistant deputy director for Plans and Policy, National Security; General Jerry Curry, Department of Defense in the Pentagon; General George Keegan (retired), chief of Air Force Intelligence from 1972 to 1977; Lt. General Richard F. Schaefer (retired), deputy chairman of NATO Military Committee from January 1974 to June 1975; Isser Harel, former head of Israeli Intelligence and Security; Lieutenant General Moshe Ya'alon, former chief of staff, IDF; Mr. James Woolsey, former director, CIA; General Hugh Shelton, former chairman of the Joint Chiefs of Staff; General Yossi Peled, chief of the Northern Command, Israel; General Dani Yatom, head of Mossad, Israeli Intelligence Service; General Yaakov Amidror, former chief of IDF Intelligence; Lt. General Tom McInerney; Masoud Barzani, president of Iraqi Kurdistan; and the late General Robert "Dutch" Huyser, deputy commander in chief, United States European Command.

A special word of gratitude must go to Lanelle Shaw-Young, who has invested an enormous amount of time and work in this book from the beginning and throughout this entire project. The book would not have been possible without her contributions. I also wish to thank Arlen Young, who spent hours proofreading the pages of this manuscript. I am deeply appreciative to Pat Judd; to research assistant Dan Godzich, Washington, D.C.; Robert Baxter, research associate in Paris; to Ariel University; and especially to Dr. Ronen Cohen, who provided invaluable research information from Israel.

Finally, a book project of this magnitude demands a grueling work and travel schedule. I am deeply indebted to my beloved wife, Carolyn. Without her patience, compassion, encouragement, and sacrifice, there would be no possible way to have achieved this.

THE PRESIDENTIAL ELECTION was a public sounding-board for the much-touted failures of the Republican Party. He ran against a disgraced president and his policies; he ran in the aftermath of an unpopular war on a platform of "human rights"; and he won. His theme was "change," and that is what America and the world got. He kept his word, and change began. No, not Barack Obama, Jimmy Carter!

The first four years (2009-2012) of Barack Obama's presidency will likely be dominated by debate between the Republican and Democratic parties over Middle East policy, as it relates to the entire Middle East and especially the Persian Gulf states. It is there, in Israel, Iraq, Iran, Afghanistan, and Pakistan, that the epicenter of the War on Terror may be found, and it is from there that its ripples will continue to spread across the globe.

Jimmy Carter: The Liberal Left and World Chaos is immensely relevant and critically important in today's political climate. Why? The groundwork for this current miasma in the Middle East was laid while the Democratic Party, led by former President James Earl "Jimmy" Carter Jr., was in control. Jimmy Carter rejected the Nixon Doctrine and established the Carter Doctrine. It was all brought about in the name of change and hope and in response to Watergate and the Vietnam War.

Jimmy Carter: The Liberal Left and World Chaos outlines the failures of his administration in the Middle East. It contains substantive information gleaned from interviews with former French President Valéry Giscard d'Estaing, Harvard Law Professor Alan Dershowitz, and former Israeli Prime Minister Benjamin Netanyahu. I included a rare personal interview with the widow of the late

Shah of Iran, Her Majesty Farah Pahlavi, in her home outside Washington, D.C., former Iranian Ambassador Ardeshir Zahedi, members of the Shah's personal staff, and with Charles Villeneuve, one of the journalists on the Air France charter that carried the Ayatollah Khomeini back to Tehran following the Shah's departure. These are only a few of the individuals interviewed. They provide new insight into the Carter persona and how his policies had a profound effect on terrorism worldwide.

As I began to research details for *Jimmy Carter: The Liberal Left and World Chaos,* it became clear how the book would not only outline the life and times of the man who rose from peanut farmer to president; it would also give an overview of how Carter's policies have affected Barack Obama and the Liberal Left in America. One thing quickly becomes crystal clear: James Earl Carter Jr. is truly the epitome of the Liberal Left, the godfather of world chaos, and the ultimate enigma; Barack Obama is following closely in his footsteps.

Since his early days of politicking in the Deep South, Carter alternately cozied-up to and then excoriated the likes of Lester Maddox and George Wallace. It became impossible to determine if Carter espoused full-blown segregation or championed integration. More recently he has denigrated the policies and undermined the effectiveness of Republican presidents Ronald Reagan, George H.W. Bush, and George W. Bush. Is Mr. Carter pro-life or pro-abortion? Does he support the United States of America or the united organizations of terrorism that help fund his Carter Center and Library? His actions defy easy answers. *Jimmy Carter: The Liberal Left and World Chaos* provides the tools and insight to help understand his worldview and formulate an educated assessment both of his presidency and its consequences.

Is Carter perceived as liberal or conservative? The answer depends on the day and the circumstances. What day is it, and what are the circumstances? He set the bar early on even in his campaign for governor of Georgia with his penchant for straddling the fence, hopping down only as long and as often as it fit his own agenda.

It was Jimmy Carter who modeled for Barack Obama the intricate steps to the political "flip-flop hip-hop"—the mating dance of an aspiring Liberal Left president.

After his election Carter quickly distanced himself from the long-time Washington movers and shakers of his own party, replacing them with a cadre of like-minded "Good-Ole-Boys" from the South. Carter seems to have wanted a one-man presidency, where he carried all the weight of the country on his shoulders, eschewing the need for delegating authority. As a result, he was buried under the mountain of detail and triviality that surround the office of the nation's chief executive. On the one hand Carter has engendered the appearance of the smiling, good-natured Southern gentlemen; on the other, he has on multiple occasions reached for the sharp knife of rebuke; bullying and manipulating people and events to suit his purposes. Recently Carter ignored the wishes of Secretary of State Condoleezza Rice and met with HAMAS leader Khaled Mashaal.

To define the presidency of Jimmy Carter, one must look only at his legacy and the state of a nation inherited by Ronald Reagan: minor strongmen and clerics held the U.S. in derision; communism was proliferating in Syria, Angola, Ethiopia, Afghanistan, Vietnam, and in our own backyard…Cuba, El Salvador, Nicaragua, and Peru. In America inflation was rampant, interest rates were astronomical, gasoline was at a premium, abortion was legal, and prayer and Christmas celebrations on school campuses were illegal. Americans were being held hostage in Iran, and our armed forces had been decimated by Carter's policies. It is critical that Americans and newly elected President Barack Obama take a look back at Carter's policies in order not to make the same devastating mistakes Mr. Carter made while in the White House.

While the Liberal Left in America screams that the mess in Iraq and the War on Terror have been caused by the Republican presidency of George W. Bush, the truth is that the entire nightmare can be traced back to the liberal Democratic policies of the ultraliberal leftist Jimmy Carter. It was he who created the firestorm that destabilized our greatest ally in the Muslim world, the Shah of Iran, in favor of a religious fanatic, the Ayatollah Khomeini.

The chief of staff to the Senate Select Committee on Intelligence, William Miller, suggested that the U.S. openly support Khomeini and his Islamic Revolution. Miller was convinced that Khomeini would progressively pursue human rights reformations in Iran. A former naval intelligence officer and CIA operative during the Carter administration, who has asked to remain anonymous, related to me that the U.S. government wrote checks to Khomeini in increments of approximately $150 million. (This operative was directly involved in the operation of funding the cleric.) According to this gentleman, Khomeini's French operation was paid for by the U.S., including the Air France flight that returned the fanatical Islamic cleric to Tehran. He fully believes Khomeini left France for Iran because Carter stopped giving the cleric money. It is his opinion that Jimmy Carter should have been tried for treason for aiding and abetting an enemy of the United States.

Carter perceived Khomeini more as a religious holy man in a grassroots revolution than the founding father of modern terrorism. Carter's ambassador to the UN, Andrew Young, said, "Khomeini will eventually be hailed as a saint." Carter's Iranian ambassador, William Sullivan, said, "Khomeini is a Gandhi-like figure." Carter adviser James Bill proclaimed in a *Newsweek* interview on February 12, 1979, that Khomeini was not a mad mujahid, but a man of "impeccable integrity and honesty." Just as Carter administration officials pursued a relationship with Khomeini, so has Barack Obama stated that he wants to sit down without preconditions for talks with Iran's president and leaders from other rogue states.

In the midst of the turmoil in Iran or perhaps because of it, President Carter called for a summit on the French Republic island of Guadeloupe in the Caribbean. Invited to meet with Carter in January 1979 were French President Valéry Giscard d'Estaing, West German Chancellor Helmut Schmidt, and British Prime Minister James Callaghan. In his memoir, *Answer to History,* the Shah wrote:

"Giscard said they hoped to 'evaluate the situation of the world,' with special emphasis on events in the eastern Mediterranean and the Persian Gulf. I believe that during those meetings the French and West Germans agreed with the British and the American proposals for my ouster."

It was at Guadeloupe, according to d'Estaing, that Carter showed his hand in favor of the ouster of the Shah.

When Carter later sent General Robert Huyser to Iran as his special emissary to persuade the Iranian military leaders to acquiesce to the Shah's exile, Huyser represented not only the U.S. but the entire Western alliance. His counterparts in Iran agreed to the exile of Pahlavi only after Huyser produced copies of the record of the meeting in Guadeloupe.

Before General Huyser's death in 1997, I met with him in his home. During the meeting the general told me, "Jimmy Carter was responsible for the overthrow of the Shah." Huyser maintained Carter had "deceived not only the Shah, but me also."

On April 1, 1979, Khomeini declared the first day of the "Government of God." In July of that year President Jimmy Carter inked a top-secret document launching America on the path that would lead to the deaths of 2,974 innocent American civilians on September 11, 2001; another twenty-four individuals are still listed as missing. What was the document? It was the first order to send aid to the Afghanistan rebels fighting against the Soviet invaders. The aid would provide the weapons and know-how to train the rebels in terror tactics, lead to the creation of the Taliban, and give rise to the scion of a Saudi prince, a ruthless young man named Osama bin Laden, founder of the vile and violent al-Qaeda.

The Soviets wasted no time in seizing a golden opportunity to take advantage of the destabilization in Iran. On December 25, 1979, the USSR invaded Afghanistan. In 1980 Carter infused $30 million into the Afghan rebel cause. The ante was raised in 1981 to $50 million. It was generally thought that U.S. aid to the Afghanistan *Mujahedeen* was initiated in 1980 under the

Republican administration of Ronald Reagan. Not so. According to a document declassified on March 4, 2004, President Jimmy Carter signed a directive on July 3, 1979, approving covert assistance to anti-Soviet rebels in Kabul. The directive from President Carter favored supporting insurgent propaganda and other psychological operations in Afghanistan, establishing radio contact with the Afghan people through a third country, and providing appropriate support either in funds or non-military supplies.

Jimmy Carter has long exemplified the policies of the Liberal Left. This book chronicles Carter's rise from obscurity in Plains, Georgia, to become the most influential man in the world: president of the United States. It outlines how the man who admonished the American people not to speak ill of their country has become its most harsh and vocal critic. This book also reveals Carter's metamorphosis from "human rights advocate" to champion of some of the world's most murderous dictators.

Carter's policies and doctrines come into focus in terms of abandoning the Shah, ignoring warning signs of an imminent and disastrous revolution in Iran, bowing to Ayatollah Khomeini's demands for the release of the hostages, and allowing rampant inflation to plague the U.S. As president, Carter deserted not only the Shah to radical Islamic Revolution, he abandoned long-time ally Anastasio Somoza and Nicaragua to the Sandinista Guerillas and gave away the Panama Canal.

Despite their obvious differences in ideology, both the French and the Israelis were convinced the Shah would be overthrown, and the fanatical Ayatollah Khomeini would spell doom for the Iranian people. Cavalierly, the U.S. intelligence community rejected both reports as exaggerated. To further exacerbate matters, the CIA failed to investigate Khomeini's radically fanatical diatribes. Apparently, Khomeini's threats were not even taken seriously by the CIA, which had to scramble to even find copies of Khomeini's writings when the volcano of revolution erupted in Iran.

This book defines Carter's meteoric rise in national politics, his ability to portray himself as one who always sought the high ground while nursing a spitefully mean streak, and his skillful political demeanor based on hyperbole, insincerity, and sometimes utter sham.

President Jimmy Carter's ill-advised execution of human rights guidelines not only directly resulted in the ouster of the Shah of Iran but ultimately caused the loss of more than 600,000 lives during the Iran/Iraq War. These guidelines implemented rule by the mullahs and ayatollahs, were eventually responsible for Iraq's attack on Kuwait and *Desert Storm,* and spawned the Soviet incursion into Afghanistan, the rise of the Taliban, al-Qaeda, and Osama bin Laden. Finally, they led to the destruction of the two World Trade Center towers on September 11, 2001, with the deaths of nearly 3,000 innocent civilians.

According to leaders both in Israel and Iraq, the jihadists are looking for any microscopic evidence of weakness on the part of an American president. "If Islamic jihadists see weakness in the White House," they said, "the jihadists will strike us and the United States. The jihadists believe they ran the USSR out of Afghanistan, causing the fall of the Soviet Union through the power of Allah." Once the U.S. has been run out of Iraq, the jihadists opine, it too will fall. It would be the last "evil empire" to fall and would be the key to fulfilling the final prophecy of the Ayatollah Khomeini by establishing a worldwide caliphate, an Islamic global order.

These leaders are concerned that the world could slide into total chaos under the leadership of the Liberal Left in America. The Soviet Union would be motivated to reestablish itself as a world power, China would be emboldened to invade Taiwan, and Iran might be persuaded to launch an attack against Israel. Who would have the backbone to stop such aggression?

In the name of hope and change Liberal Democrat Jimmy Carter believed then, and still does, that evil really does not exist. Terrorist organizations are simply human rights movements, people are basically good, and America should embrace the perpetrators and castigate the victims. Here we now encounter the worst of Jimmy Carter's failed presidency: as a result of those above-mentioned shortcomings, the doors of worldwide terrorism sprang open.

Former President Jimmy Carter released yet another book on the Middle East on January 20, 2009, *We Can Bring Peace to the Holy Land*. The truth is, Carter's Liberal Left plan simply will not work. It is a prescription for chaos and will become yet another rallying point for radical Islamists. It is reminiscent of the former president's plan to remove the Shah of Iran from power. Consider the chaos that caused. Today the Iranians still feel they are under no compulsion to heed calls for a halt to nuclear activities because America has proven to be weak and ineffectual.

This latest Carter plan is no more and no less than the old Road Map for Peace Plan and the Shelf Agreement dressed up in "The Emperor's New Clothes," and every bit as transparent. It is not a "new" plan at all; it is the same tired, "old" plan to force Israel to return to 1967 borders, give Judea and Samaria to the Palestinian Authority, divide Jerusalem, and present East Jerusalem to the terrorists as the new capital of the Palestinian state.

Just as Carter ascribes altruistic acts to Hamas and Hezbollah, so his plan legitimizes terrorism and those who carry out such heinous attacks. It is reminiscent of the former president's plan to remove America's greatest Muslim ally, the Shah of Iran, from power. The Middle East today suffers from Carter's political machinations during his presidency.

Examine Carter's assessment of the problems in the Middle East. The finger always points to Israel. Carter has declared:

» Israel is an apartheid state that denies equal rights to Palestinians. (Over one million Palestinians enjoy equal rights under Israel's governance.)

» Israel wants to colonize Palestine. (Israel has annexed only those lands from which rocket attacks were launched against Israelis.)

» Israel is the obstacle to peace. If Israel would only return to its 1967 borders, the Palestinians would embrace peace proposals. (Carter's demand is ludicrous at best. Neither the treaty he co-authored at Camp David in 1979 nor UN Resolution 242 demand that Israel return to the 1949 Armistice line.)

» The West Bank clearly belongs to the Palestinians. (It is, in fact, a parcel of disputed land whose ownership is to be determined through negotiations between both parties, again according to UN Resolution 242.)

» Groups such as Hamas and Hezbollah are "freedom fighters" not bloodthirsty terrorists. He believes rocket attacks are not terror attacks and are justified by Israel's actions. He is the spokesman for the most radical of Islamists, and has continually fawned over such terrorists as Yasser Arafat, Khaled Mashaal, Bashar al-Assad, and others.

Furthermore:

» Carter is deaf to the fact that terrorist organizations and Arab countries repeatedly call for the destruction of Israel, which is specifically outlined in the Hamas Charter.

» Carter supports Hezbollah and meets with its leaders at every opportunity. (Hezbollah leader Hassan Nasrallah has said, "If the Jews gather in Israel, it will save us the trouble of going after them worldwide.")

» Carter believes the security fence erected by Israel is to keep the Palestinians within their territory. (In actuality, it was built to keep Palestinian terrorists out of Israel. Terror attacks have been reduced by 90 percent since its completion. Mr. Carter would have the fence torn down.)

» Carter supports the "right of return" for all Palestinians to Israel. (If that were to happen, Israel would become simply another Arab state, effectively wiping the nation off the map.)

» Carter barely gives basic lip service to the terror attacks against Israel. Jewish complaints are trivialized and anti-Semitism and bigotry ignored.

» Carter purports that pro-Israel supporters dominate the U.S. media. (The European media draws his approval for being "highly critical" of Israel.)

Mr. Carter has set the standard and provided the training for today's Liberal Left when it comes to shifting the focus away from terrorists and their deadly activities onto America's perceived wrongs. After all, if the former president appears in concert with terrorist leaders in the Middle East, it must surely appear to make their activities acceptable.

Jimmy Carter is among the number clamoring to change the worldview of these terrorists from that of mass murderers of the innocent to "insurgents" or "liberation movements." He is quick to indict the U.S. at every opportunity and equally quick to champion the downtrodden suicide bombers as—to be in sync with the Liberal Left—"martyrs."

While Carter's domestic policies—remember long gas lines and inflation?—were abysmal, consider his foreign policies. According to d'Estaing, it was Carter's wish that the Shah of Iran be forced to abdicate and flee his country. America lost a vital ally and Iran lost a leader who, we now understand, did much to hold the mad mullahs at bay, those who now daily plot the downfall and destruction of our nation. Once Jimmy Carter had abandoned the Shah, America's staunchest ally in the Persian Gulf region, Pandora's Box was opened and the demon of terrorism escaped. Islamic fanaticism inarguably has become one of the most important issues with which the West has to contend.

Once democracy was sought by the multitudes as the panacea for all ills. Now Islam appeals to the masses with its seemingly unlimited resources due to oil money, its global spread, and its message of world domination through intimidation. Khomeini's success against the Shah and the resulting Islamic Revolution became a model for other terrorists worldwide.

Now we face the likes of Osama, Hamas, and the specter of a nuclear holocaust that has spread around the world and stops at our shores. It is a battle that we fight in one form or another to this very day and perhaps will continue to fight for decades down the road. It might be added here that Mr. Obama was openly endorsed by the terrorist organization Hamas during his presidential campaign. In a radio interview by John Batchelor with Aaron Klein of *World Net Daily,* Hamas political advisor Ahmed Yousef said that he liked Mr. Obama and hoped that he would win the election.

Why does the life and presidency of Jimmy Carter matter in the twenty-first century? The same Liberal Left which accepted Carter's substance-starved campaign also bought into Obama's equally ambiguous rhetoric. Philosopher George Santayana said, "Those who cannot learn from history are doomed to repeat it." The United States paid an exceedingly high price for the years Carter practiced being presidential; what will President Obama cost Americans as he, like Carter, does his on-the-job training?

This book offers a brief review of the early years of Jimmy Carter and the events that shaped his liberal worldview, as well as a preview of how Liberal Left Democratic policies could create international chaos as did those of President Jimmy Carter.

ENTER STAGE LEFT: JIMMY CARTER

"Jimmy Carter would have been a profound priest
but not a profound president." (DR. AHMAD TEHRANI)[1]

JAMES EARL (JIMMY) CARTER JR. was born in Plains,
Georgia, on October 1, 1924. The son of a Georgia peanut farmer,
Carter would rise through the ranks of local and state politics to
become the thirty-ninth president of the United States. Along the
way, he would realize a number of "firsts." He was the first United
States president to have been born in a hospital, the first president
to graduate from the United States Naval Academy, the first native-
born Georgian to become president, the first president from the
Deep South, the first president to walk from the East Portico of the
Capitol Building down Pennsylvania Avenue to the White House,
the first (and only) president to be interviewed by *Playboy* magazine,
the first president to report an attack by a "killer" rabbit, and one
of only two presidents[2] to report a UFO sighting.

What is even more astounding about former President Jimmy
Carter is that he feels his short and arguably failed attempt at governing the United States has somehow endowed him with great
influence in the world arena. This is the same man in whose early

days of campaigning for the White House elicited the response, "Jimmy who?" Perhaps the better question would have been, "Jimmy? Why?" Even then Carter's duplicitous approach was evident. The ever-grinning Carter was an enigma, as Bill Moyers observed: "In a ruthless business, Mr. Carter is a ruthless operator; even if he wears his broad smile and displays Southern charm."[3]

Jimmy's father, James Earl Carter Sr., landed in Plains when his father, Alton, decided to move the family to the small town in southwest Georgia. "Mr. Earl," as Jimmy's father was known around town, was an astute businessman. His ventures in peanut farming, forestry, and a small grocery made him successful, if not rich. He was a well-known local figure and, like other farmers in Georgia and elsewhere, worked hard for his living. It is likely the elder Carter could well sympathize with author and poet, Andrew Nelson Lytle, who wrote: "A farm is not a place to grow wealthy; it is a place to grow corn."[4]

In his book *The Real Jimmy Carter*, Steven Hayward describes the area in which the future president grew into manhood: "Jimmy Carter [was] the first American president to be born in a hospital... about the only modern appurtenance in Plains.... There were few paved roads. Plains, with a population of about six hundred when Jimmy Carter was born, didn't get electricity for another ten years."[5]

Perhaps it was Carter's mother, the acerbic and outspoken Miss Lillian, who had the greater impact on the future president. Miss Lillian Gordy married James Earl Carter Sr. in 1923, the same year she completed her nurse's training in Atlanta. Jimmy, the eldest, was born in 1924. His three siblings, Gloria (1926), Ruth (1929), and Billy (1937) would all achieve some fame or notoriety, but none would reach quite the pinnacle as the eldest Carter. One of Miss Lillian's most famous quotes may have been the result of her exasperation with some of her offsprings' antics. Said the witty lady: "When I look at my four children, sometimes I say to myself, 'Lillian, you should have stayed a virgin.'"[6]

Some opine that it was Miss Lillian's defiance of typical Southern segregationist policies that would later influence Carter's stance on integration. Miss Lillian not only welcomed the Black population of Plains into her home through the front door, she nursed all equally, although that was illegal in the Deep South at that time. The Carter children were even allowed to play with the local Black children; unheard of in the South of the 1920s.

Lillian Carter was well-known around Plains for her social activism. Following the death of her husband, Miss Lillian, at the age of 68, applied to and was accepted by the Peace Corps. After receiving training she journeyed to India, where she spent nearly two years. Lillian Gordy Carter died of breast, bone, and pancreatic cancer in Americus, Georgia, in 1983; she was 85 years old. In fact, all three of President Carter's siblings died of pancreatic cancer.

After graduating from high School in Plains, Jimmy Carter attended Georgia Tech and Jackson State University. He received an appointment to the United States Naval Academy, from which he graduated with a B.S. degree in physics.

Following graduation he was assigned to a series of ships and diesel submarines in the Atlantic and Pacific fleets. (It is interesting to note that only President Dwight D. Eisenhower served longer in the U.S. military than President Jimmy Carter.) During this time, he was chosen by Admiral Hyman G. Rickover to participate in the Navy's nuclear submarine program. As president, Jimmy Carter asserted that the admiral had a "profound effect on my life, perhaps more than anyone else except my own parents." It was Rickover's question to the young Lieutenant Carter upon their first meeting in 1952 that prompted the president to give his autobiography the title, *Why Not the Best?* Shortly after his inauguration the new president invited Rickover to lunch at the White House. The admiral gifted the newly-elected president with a plaque that read: "*O God, thy sea is so great and my boat is so small.*"

In the summer of 1946 James Earl Carter Jr. married his sweetheart, Rosalynn Smith, following a one-year courtship.

Rosalynn was also a product of Plains. As a teenager she worked to help her widowed mother support her three siblings. Rosalynn once admitted that as a friend of Ruth Carter, she harbored a secret crush on big brother Jimmy, who was apparently oblivious to the adoring adolescent. That all changed when Midshipman Carter was home on furlough in 1945. Apparently, he was so smitten with the young Rosalynn Smith that before he returned to the naval academy, he announced his intention to marry her to Miss Lillian.

Shortly after his graduation the two were married, and for the first seven years of their marriage Jimmy and Rosalynn were a typical Navy family. Three of their four children, John William (Jack) Carter, James Earl (Chip) Carter III, and Donnel Jeffrey (Jeff) Carter, were born while Carter was still commissioned with the Navy; the fourth child and only daughter, Amy Lynn Carter, was born in Plains.

Lieutenant Jimmy Carter's aspirations of a Navy career were dashed with the death of his father in July 1953. He resigned his commission and returned to Georgia to take over the operations of the family farm. The young lieutenant was never to realize his dream of commanding a Navy nuclear submarine; the *USS Nautilus* (SSN-571) put to sea for the first time in January 1955.

While Jimmy Carter professed having become interested in politics at the young age of eight, he showed no real proclivity for political leadership during his high school years. His only stab at politics in college was an aborted run for class president during his freshman year. When asked about Carter's early political aspirations, an unnamed naval academy classmate replied, "He didn't show any signs of greatness, and I don't recall that he held any strong political or religious views.... I think we were all amazed when he became governor of Georgia, and positively astounded when he ran effectively for president." [7]

It was only after his father's death that Jimmy Carter followed his example and became active in the community. He served on several local boards, i.e., hospital, library, and etc., and eventually was appointed to the Sumter County Board of Education. It was his father's election to the state assembly and his encouragement of young Jimmy to get involved in public affairs that led to a run for the Georgia Senate.

When a new state district was drawn in 1962 that included the area around Americus and Plains, Jimmy Carter made the decision to run for the seat. He tossed his hat into the ring exactly three weeks before the primary election. When his opponent, Homer Moore, won the primary by 139 votes, Carter asked for a recount. After eliminating the "dead and imprisoned voters"[8] from the list, Jimmy Carter won the nomination of the Democratic Party. Kenneth Morris wrote that "tenacity rather than political acumen had catapulted Carter to office. It was a lesson he would never forget."[9] He defeated the Republican by less than 1,000 votes. In 1964 an unopposed Carter was elected to a second term in the Georgia State House.

Reg Murphy, an Atlanta newspaper reporter, said of Carter's years in the Georgia Senate:

> *"You just dreaded to see Carter coming down the hallway in a legislative session. You never could talk about substantive issues for him wanting to point out little picayune comma faults in stories…. Jimmy Carter…will never be human enough to overlook the faults in anybody else."*[10]

Jimmy Carter toyed with a run for the U.S. House of Representatives in 1966, but chose instead to run for governor of Georgia in an attempt to keep the state in the hands of a Democratic governor. In what proved to be one of the closest gubernatorial races in Georgia history, Jimmy Carter, Ellis Arnall, Lester Maddox, and James Gray each totaled more than 150,000 votes; Maddox and Arnall garnered enough votes to run for the Democratic nomination.

In a quirky finish, neither man won the election; Republican "Bo" Callaway captured the popular vote but not the majority.

The Georgia legislature was faced with deciding the winner. Rather than choose a Republican as governor, the legislature chose rabid segregationist Lester Maddox as governor of Georgia.

Carter's loss to Lester Maddox was apparently the catalyst that plunged him into depths of despair from which he emerged a "born-again" Christian. The term "born-again" was new to the majority of Americans even though Jesus, when speaking to Nicodemus in John 3:3 said, "'Most assuredly, I say to you, unless one is born again, he cannot see the kingdom of God.'"[11] Although Carter had been an active churchgoer and Sunday school teacher most of his life, it was at this crossroads that he felt something was missing. According to his sister Ruth Carter Stapleton, it was she who challenged Jimmy to make a total commitment to Christ. Jimmy's story differed in that he recalled being challenged by a Sunday sermon entitled, "If you were arrested for being a Christian, would there be enough evidence to convict you?" It was this challenge that laid the groundwork for Jimmy Carter's personal realization that his life was self-righteous and hypocritical and that change was needed.

Apparently the one thing Carter's born-again experience did not do was change him from a closet liberal to a died-in-the-wool conservative. Carter wrote, "A quotation from [German American theologian Paul] Tillich sticks in my mind: 'Religion is the *search* for the truth about man's existence and relationship with God.' Maybe our search will be fruitful."[12] A characteristic in modern liberal theology is that the *search* is more vital than the *discovery* of the truth.

Biographer Betty Glad wrote that Carter was "a kind of existentialist Christian."[13] Perhaps it was the definition of the word *existentialist* that caused Glad to characterize Carter in such a way. According to *Merriam-Webster's Online Dictionary*, an existentialist is one who practices existentialism: "A chiefly 20th-century philosophical movement embracing diverse doctrines but centering on analysis of individual existence in an unfathomable universe and the plight of the individual who must assume ultimate responsibility for acts of free will without any certain knowledge of what is right or wrong or good or bad."[14] Regardless of Carter's religious theology, his born-again characterization was enough to capture the attention of conservative Christians nationwide, and it certainly did not hurt his later run for the presidency.

Jimmy Carter spent the next four years planning his campaign to run for governor in 1970. By his own estimation, he gave some 1,800 speeches and shook hands with every Georgian that would stick a hand out. Despite his efforts Carter lagged behind in the polls. When he discovered that Georgia voters leaned toward the more conservative side, Carter morphed into a conservative. Using every card he had up his sleeve—such as the race card, innuendoes about his opponent's health, and charges of high living—Carter defeated Democrat Carl Sanders in the primary. Even pro-Carter Socialist Kenneth Morris, author of *Jimmy Carter, American Moralist*, called Carter's campaign against Sanders "blatant...the chicanery had been more than accidental; it had been systematic," and that his tactics "suggest a certain discrepancy beneath which may lurk something akin to viciousness."[15]

Bert Lance said of Jimmy Carter's campaign style:

Jimmy was a formidable campaigner. He was a moderate to the moderates, a conservative to the conservatives, and a liberal to the liberals. He was all things to all voters, a great trait to be able to project—and it got him elected."[16]

During his gubernatorial run Carter worked hard at his self-portrait of a blue-collar, conservative, good-ole-boy. Biographer E. Stanley Godbold said this of Carter's stand on racial issues during the campaign: "Carter himself was not a segregationist in 1970, but he did say things that the segregationists wanted to hear. He was opposed to busing. He was in favor of private schools."[17] Political Scientist Betty Glad added, "If you are really trying to accomplish good moral ends, you may have to be a low-life politician to get there. And he didn't probably like doing it that much, but he was willing to do it."[18]

What may have been one of Carter's most blatant campaign prevarications was his pledge to invite Alabama Governor George Wallace, the poster boy for segregation, to speak to the Georgia State Legislature. Imagine the surprise of the segregationist Georgia voters who had ardently supported Jimmy Carter when during his inaugural address, Carter stated, "I say to you quite frankly that the time for racial discrimination is over.... No poor, rural, weak, or black person should ever have to bear the additional burden of being deprived of the opportunity of an education, a job, or simple justice."[19] This was another "first" for Governor Jimmy Carter; he was the first Southern politician to publicly make such a sweeping, anti-segregationist statement.

What prompted the sudden about-face for Jimmy Carter? Is it possible that knowing he could not, due to term limits, succeed himself as governor of Georgia, Carter had already set his sights on a run for the presidency? Is it possible that he was, even at that moment, focusing not on his Georgia constituents but on the bigger picture of a nationwide audience?

Carter's inaugural address landed him on the cover of *Time* magazine[20] in a pose and with a hairstyle that was remarkably similar to the visage of slain President John F. Kennedy. This was a similarity that Carter himself was said to have fomented with photo ops of family touch football games in the backyard of his Plains home. The American public would be treated to more of Carter's "Kennedy obsession" with his courtship of Dean Rusk, secretary of state to both Kennedy and Lyndon Johnson.

Carter, never labeled "segregationist," was forced to share the State House with former governor and now Lieutenant Governor Lester Maddox. The two men quarreled publicly during the Carter administration and, in fact, had little good to say about each other. During the 1976 presidential campaign in which Maddox ran against Carter on the American Independent Party ticket, Maddox was quoted as saying that Jimmy Carter was "the most dishonest man I've ever met."[21]

Apparently, Maddox wasn't the only one to see that particular side of Jimmy Carter; author Gary Fink painted a rather disturbing picture of Carter's governorship. He said, "Carter usually claimed the moral and ethical high ground, [but] practiced a style of politics based on exaggeration, disingenuousness, and at times, outright deception."[22]

Upon reaching his objective to become governor of Georgia, Carter set out to reform the political structure of the state. He began by combining some 278 state agencies into twenty-two. Perhaps his most conflict-ridden strategy was to create three elite departments to handle administrative services, natural resources, and human resources. This plan would eliminate the need of sixty-two agencies. Carter also instituted strict zero-budgeting. Under his plan each agency had to defend every budgetary dollar requested.

Governor Carter introduced his "Adequate Program for Education in Georgia," a comprehensive education reform plan. It designated money to support vocational education, limit class size, and balance district funding. He was also responsible for the establishment of the state's kindergarten program.

Carter didn't stop with government and school reform; his next target was the state's judicial system. He took steps toward the formation of a unified court system, he championed the selection of judges based on a merit system, initiated a system for controlling judicial conduct, and oversaw a penal reform program.

To further distance himself from former segregationist Georgia governors, Carter broadened his appointment strategy. His own staff included more women and minorities, as did his appointments to Georgia boards, departments, and the judiciary. His penchant for forcibly pushing his reforms through the legislature caused one well-known politician to opine: "[Carter] reminds me of a South Georgia turtle who's been blocked by a log—he just keeps pushing,

pushing, pushing straight ahead, he doesn't go around here—until he finally gets a soft spot in the log and right on through he goes."[23]

Gary Fink described Carter's political style: "At times the governor could be absolutely ruthless. More than one Georgia legislator primly escorted influential constituents into the governor's office only to be bitterly chastised for opposing administration measures in their presence."[24] Carter showed such disdain for the Georgia legislature that by the end of his term as governor, he was held in low esteem by many. He would later adopt that same approach with the United States Congress.

Carter made one foray into the presidential arena in 1972 as he watched the ultra-liberal George McGovern capture the interest of the Democratic Party. Jimmy called a news conference in Atlanta, where he argued McGovern could not be elected president because of his liberal stance on foreign and domestic policy. When McGovern's nomination was solidified, in true Carter fashion he did an about-face and proffered himself as McGovern's running mate (an offer that was rejected). It is interesting to note that the Democrats did not hold Carter accountable for his attitude and, in fact, Carter received thirty votes on the vice-presidential ballot at the Democratic National Convention. Thus began Jimmy Carter's rise in the DNC's ranks. By 1974 he was chairman of the DNC's congressional and gubernatorial campaigns. Next stop: a presidential campaign for Georgia's ambitious peanut farmer.

Carter's aspirations for the presidency produced an added dimension to his governorship...trade missions overseas. With the backing of the Georgia-based Coca-Cola Bottling Company and its global outreach, Carter was able to meet with foreign dignitaries unavailable to other state leaders. This boon enabled Carter to get a step ahead of other presidential aspirants in the realm of foreign policy. During his term in office he made trips to Mexico, Brazil, Costa Rica, Argentina, Columbia, Asia, England, Belgium, West Germany, and Israel. It was during a trip to London that Carter met the men who would prove to be two of his most significant foreign policy mentors, David Rockefeller and Hedley Donovan (then editor-in-chief of *Time* magazine). Following their meeting, Rockefeller tapped Jimmy Carter as the Democratic gubernatorial representative for his Trilateral Commission. It was through his association with this Commission that Carter met his future national security advisor, Zbigniew Brzezinski.

Holly Sklar edited the definitive book on Trilateralism; she included information regarding the Commission's influence on the Carter run for the White House:

> *Brzezinski stressed as early as 1973 that the 1976 Democratic candidate "will have to emphasize work, the family, religion, and, increasingly, patriotism, if he has any desire to be elected." Samuel P. Huntington's 1975 Commission report on U.S. democracy seems to have been even more important in setting Carter's campaign strategy.... To become president, Huntington argued, a candidate should cultivate "the appearance of certain general characteristics—honesty, energy, practicality, decisiveness, sincerity, and experience."'*
>
> *His next piece of analysis was even more striking. After reviewing the political history of the 1960s and 1970s, Huntington summed up the experience by saying...the "outsider" in politics, or the candidate who could make himself or herself appear to be an outsider, had the inside road to political office.... Needless to say, Carter was an "insider" who campaigned as an "outsider."'...*
>
> *However, in all likelihood, an even more important result of Carter's trilateral ties was the inside track for favorable media coverage it gave him. As one journalist put it, this connection gave Carter "an opportunity to convince the corporate and media leaders that he was not a rustic yahoo but a man to be taken seriously." The media establishment did indeed take the Carter candidacy seriously.... Jimmy Carter, using a combination of charm, hard work, middle-of-the-road policy positions, and a keen sense of where power lies in the U.S., built his political career by gaining support,*

*first from the Establishment of his local area, and then from
the dominant sector of the national ruling class. Traditional
Democratic constituencies like labor, intellectuals, minorities,
ethnics, and big city machines provided support as time
went on, but the key to Carter's victory was the early
support given by upper-class groups centered in Atlanta and
New York, especially the latter's large financial and media
corporations.*[25]

Candidate Carter also sought out Frank Church after reading
the report from the Church Committee on U.S. Intelligence
Activities. In fact, Carter considered tapping Church as his running
mate. Instead, he chose another Church Committee member,
Minnesota Senator Walter Mondale. (Carter would, however, use the
Church Committee report on the CIA to decimate that organization
and cripple its ability to gather intelligence data that might have
averted the attack on the American Embassy in Tehran and saved
fifty-two Americans from suffering the indignities laid upon them for
444 days.)

The Coca-Cola Bottling Company and Jimmy Carter would
continue their association through his presidency and beyond.
In fact, the corporation has been a major contributor to the Carter
Foundation with representatives on the Foundation's board.

On another and lighter note: It was during his term as governor
that Mr. Carter stumped the panel on the popular game show
The New What's My Line. The panel neither recognized Mr. Carter
nor determined his occupation as governor of Georgia.

It was also as governor that Carter "'fessed up" to having
seen a UFO way back in 1969. He later said he did not remember
why he filed the report with the International UFO Bureau in
Oklahoma City. Apparently Carter determined that one of the Carter
kids made him do it.

The UFO sighting would later be eclipsed by the "killer rabbit"
attack during his presidency. It seems that while fishing in a pond
in Plains, the president encountered a rather berserk bunny.

the *Washington Post* picked up the story under the headline, "President Attacked by Rabbit." The animal, a large swamp rabbit that Carter described as "making strange hissing noises and gnashing its teeth,"[26] seemed determined to climb into the president's dinghy. The president valiantly fought off the invading rabbit with his oar. The episode soon became known as the "attack of the killer rabbit." One wonders, given Mr. Carter's penchant for spouting nonsense, if the rabbit weren't rabid, and if the former president weren't bitten by the mad bunny.

2

SEE CARTER RUN

"Let us assume that Jimmy Carter is an intelligent, decent, hardworking man...that he has appointed to his cabinet and sub-cabinet many men and women who are experienced and dedicated. How, then, can a president...with many advisers of high caliber, produce such an undistinguished presidency?"
(STEPHEN HESS, HISTORY NEWS NETWORK) [27]

"Jimmy Carter lacked Ford's calm personality, common touch, and shrewd political sense." (GENERAL ALEXANDER M. HAIG JR.)[28]

JIMMY CARTER MIGHT WELL have adopted the theme song for the popular sitcom *The Jeffersons*[29] for his presidential campaign; however, instead of moving on up to the East Side in New York City, Carter was intent on moving to Pennsylvania Avenue's most prestigious address. And he was determined not to get just a piece; Jimmy Carter was determined to get the whole pie.

As leader of the Democratic National Committee's congressional and gubernatorial campaigns, Carter kept a relatively low profile. He worked tirelessly in a behind-the-scenes capacity for the various candidates nationwide. His efforts, however, were not without merit; he made contacts that would stand him in good stead when he launched his own political campaign for the 1976 presidential nomination. It was a campaign based on the theme of "trust." Barack Obama launched his campaign with the theme of "hope."

New York Observer columnist Steve Kornacki outlined one major similarity between the two men who would be president:

> *Both men came along at exactly the right time. Carter's peanut-farmer-from-Plains simplicity and his oft-repeated promise that he "will never lie to you" were powerful political weapons after Nixon and his wiretapping, his plumbers, and his pardon from [Gerald] Ford. And Obama's message of hope—and his own life story—resonated with an electorate that, after these past eight years, feels utterly disconnected from its government and simply wants to believe in someone again."* [30]

One of his close associates in state government, Bert Lance, was the first to openly acknowledge Carter's ambitions in 1967. When Lance, who would later become Carter's director of the Office of Management and Budget, presented the governor with a set of coins representing the fifty states, he predicted, "This gift represents your dominion over one state as governor; but from what I've seen, at some point in the future you will have dominion over fifty states."[31]

Perhaps those words were the seeds planted in the mind of Jimmy Carter that germinated and burst forth from a fertile soil on December 12, 1974, when James Earl Carter Jr. announced his plans to run for the office of president of the United States. The soil into which those seeds fell had been well-tended and well-watered by three of Carter's state political aides, Hamilton Jordan, Jody Powell, and Peter Bourne. The three had confronted Carter with their impertinent plan to bypass the office of vice president and suggested instead that Carter tackle running for the highest office in the land.

Ostensibly, it was Hamilton Jordan who had thought longest and hardest about the plan because it was he who put down on paper a seventy-plus-page battle plan for capturing the White House. The plan covered everything from dealing with a possible run by Teddy Kennedy or George Wallace to media manipulation to campaign financing and everything in between. In addressing the George Wallace issue, Jordan made it clear that Carter had used Wallace to good effect during his campaign for governor. Said Jordan, "It is my guess that George Wallace resents you a little, as we used him effectively and beneficially in our campaign but refused to nominate him at the Democratic Convention. We should make every effort to court Wallace and gain his friendship and trust."[32]

Of Teddy Kennedy, Jordan opined, "Senator Kennedy will have a tremendous problem gaining the confidence and support of the majority of the American people and winning a national election." He went on to say, "Senator Kennedy can win the nomination much easier than he can win the election."[33] Jordan went so far as to say that Kennedy might even be shot were he to run for president. As it turned out, Carter had nothing to fear from Ted Kennedy; he took himself out of contention by announcing in late 1974 that he would not run in the 1976 presidential race.

Jordan's plan was relatively simple: 1) run as an alternative candidate to Governor George Wallace; 2) proffer yourself as the candidate with unimpeachable moral standards, a man of impeccable integrity, and one exuding Southern charm and confidence; and 3) capture the attention of the media—become their political darling.

Carter reached one of these milestones early in the campaign. Lawrence Shoup wrote in his book *The Carter Presidency*:

> *What Carter had that his opponents did not was the acceptance and support of the elite sectors of the mass communications media. It was their favorable coverage of Carter and his campaign that gave him an edge, propelling him rocket-like to the top of the opinion polls. This helped Carter win key primary election victories, enabling him to rise from an obscure public figure to president-elect in the short space of nine months.* [34]

Perhaps Carter's best assets were the fallout from Watergate and the resulting injury to the Republican Party, his self-painted portrait as an honest small-town American, and his own ability to ride the fence and address the issues evasively. On his chance of succeeding, reporter Jules Witcover wrote that Carter's was a "seemingly ludicrous proposition that the country should put itself into the hands of a peanut-farming, one-term governor of a Deep South state."[35] Carter's chances were thought to be so slim that his name didn't even appear on a Gallup Poll list of thirty-eight possible candidates.

Carter was to follow Jordan's manifesto with only one major exception: Jordan suggested that Jimmy Carter carefully select a few primaries in which to run; Carter ran in as many as feasible. With each passing primary, Jimmy Carter perfected his ability to dodge the issues and weave a perfectly evasive answer when cornered.

Carter's first major challenge in the campaign was (then, as now) in the state of Iowa. He launched a door-to-door attack throughout the state, ringing doorbells, shaking hands, and introducing himself to the Iowans. Although Carter was the choice candidate of only 4 percent of Democrats in January 1976, he captured 27.6 percent of the Iowa caucus votes and outdistanced opponent Birch Bayh. Political pundits vary on the importance of Iowa, but the truth is a win is a win is a win and another check mark in the "electability" column. An Iowa win was important because it propelled Carter to the head of the pack, providing momentum and giving him the impetus to achieve a much-needed win in New Hampshire just a month later. By March of that year he had gained a slight political advantage over Republican contender Gerald Ford.

The early primary wins were important in another way: news coverage. After those two important victories, Carter's face was plastered on the covers of *Time* and *Newsweek*, and the American public began to realize that Jimmy Carter was becoming a political force with which to be reckoned.

The Florida primary in early March pitted Carter against another rival. Just as Hamilton Jordan had predicted in his memo, George Wallace tossed his hat into the political ring and was Carter's major opponent. Carter and his "Georgia peanut gallery" of advisors developed a brilliant strategy for the defeat of Wallace in Florida. Having been soundly beaten in the Massachusetts primary, Carter was well-aware that a defeat in Florida would spell the end to his presidential aspirations. With that in mind he did what he does best; he straddled the proverbial fence. Carter portrayed himself as an alternative to the rabidly segregationist Wallace, and thus as the more mainline candidate of the Democratic Party.

Again, Carter's strategy proved to be one of brilliance. He won the Florida primary with 34.3 percent of the vote as opposed to George Wallace's 30.6 percent. Following his win in Florida, Carter, like the turtle in *Aesop's Fables*, began to slowly but steadily gather delegates as he knocked off his many opponents one at a time. By winning over George Wallace again in North Carolina, Carter removed his main Southern rival. Next to go was Senator Henry "Scoop" Jackson, who lost to Carter in Pennsylvania. Arizona Congressman Morris Udall was defeated in the Wisconsin primary. Toward the end of the campaign, Idaho Senator Frank Church and California Governor Jerry Brown entered the race as "ABC" candidates (Anybody But Carter).[36] It is ludicrous now to think that the "ABC" campaign was a result of the fact that many in the Democratic Party thought James Earl Carter Jr. too conservative for their ranks.

One of the conundrums of the Democratic race was the question of how a White, Southern candidate was able to capture the Black vote in the South. After all, this was the South of Lester Maddox, George Wallace, and John Bell Williams. During the primary in Florida, Carter captured 70 percent of the Black vote. Ninety percent of the Blacks in North Carolina opted for Carter. Even as far north as Roxbury, Massachusetts, Carter captured the hearts and minds of Black voters. Was it simply a hostile response to George Wallace's campaign? Was it due in part to the fact that Carter had added more Black employees to Georgia state offices than any other governor? Was it a response to endorsements from Rev. Martin Luther King Jr. and Andrew Young? Or, was it the votes of Black evangelicals who saw in Carter a man whose beliefs more closely resembled their own?

As campaigns go, Carter's was relatively blunder-free. The one serious gaffe attributed to him almost cost him the support of the Black community. When asked about integrating neighborhoods, Carter responded that he saw "nothing wrong with ethnic purity being maintained." He went on to explain that he had "nothing against a community that is made up of people who are Polish, or who are Czechoslovakians, or who are French Canadians or who are Blacks trying to maintain the ethnic purity of their neighborhoods."[37]

Reaction to Carter's pronouncement was swift and angry and centered almost solely on Carter's choice of the term "ethnic purity": "Jesse Jackson, director of Chicago's Operation PUSH, called Carter's views 'a throwback to Hitlerian racism.' Mayor Richard Hatcher of Gary, Indiana, declared: 'We've created a Frankenstein's monster with a Southern drawl, a more cultured version of the old Confederate at the schoolhouse door.' Added Civil Rights Activist Bayard Rustin of New York: 'He is only giving ammunition to those who would divide America. [He has] a big smile with no heart.'"[38]

It took two days for Carter campaign advisors to persuade him to withdraw his statement and offer an apology in some form. Carter finally admitted that his choice of words troubled him. Apparently, it was all the Black community needed to hear, and the apology was deemed suitable. Carter ultimately captured the Black vote in Pennsylvania.

It was widely reported that when Jimmy Carter announced to his mother, the redoubtable Miss Lillian, that he was going to run for president, she intoned, "President of what?" Jimmy Carter was about to prove to his mother and to the world that not only could he run, he could win the highest office in the land.

Carter's strategy for winning was simple and simplistic: straddle the fence on everything, thereby appealing to everyone; focus on values in an America sick-to-death of the Watergate fallout rather than focusing on the issues; and make use of the anti-Washington feelings consuming the nation. It was an approach that proved to be a winner for the man from Plains, Georgia.

Even before the Democratic Party nomination was awarded to Jimmy Carter, he made a bit of history: Carter asked the CIA to provide intelligence briefings. According to declassified CIA briefings, candidate Carter was especially interested in affairs relating to the Soviet Union:

> *CIA Director George Bush recommended to [President Gerald] Ford that as a first step he, Bush, should meet with Carter to discuss the ground rules and arrange for follow-on briefings, which would be delivered by intelligence professionals.*

> *CIA's session with Carter began about 1:00 p.m. and continued without interruption for a full six hours, adjourning about 7:00 p.m. The session included a current intelligence review of world trouble spots: Lebanon, Iraqi-Syrian relations, strains between Egypt and Libya, the Taiwan Straits, Rhodesia, the Cuban presence in Angola, and developments in Uganda. These subjects were covered in approximately 30 minutes. The bulk of the afternoon was devoted to a discussion of Soviet strategic programs and the status of the SALT talks.*

> *Carter was a very careful and interested listener and an active participant. All who were present remember that he asked a great many questions, often in minute detail. He was especially interested in the nature of the Intelligence Community's evidence, including satellite photography of deployed Soviet weapons.*"[39]

By the time the Democratic National Convention was gaveled to order at New York City's Madison Square Garden in July, 1976, James Earl Carter Jr. had the nomination firmly locked up. Carter easily won on the first ballot when Ohio's delegate votes (132) put him over the top. The months between his sweep of the DNC and the election proved to be harder than Carter imagined. Republican candidate Gerald Ford took Carter to task for his inclination to divert attention from the issues with his uninspired rhetoric.

During the presidential campaign, then-Governor Jimmy Carter met briefly with former classmate, Vice Admiral Stansfield Turner, in Atlanta. According to Turner, Carter took two minutes to relive their academy days; he then turned the conversation to naval preparedness. Carter wanted to know about the USSR and what strategy was in place to deal with a naval campaign against the Russians in a wartime situation. He wanted to know about staffing issues and if the Navy had sufficient seamen to properly handle any encounter. Carter also asked about the state of the naval fleet. Exactly thirty minutes after the meeting began, it ended. As Governor Carter showed the vice admiral to the door, he relayed to Turner that "in two days [he] would announce that he was running for the presidency.... That would be the last time I ever called him 'Jimmy.' From his inauguration...I have, of course, addressed him as 'Mr. President.'"[40]

September and October of 1976 were difficult months for Carter. Anti-abortionists took him to task for his opposition to an anti-abortion amendment to the Constitution. Then, in a typical Carter flip-flop, he angered pro-abortionists by assuming a more moderate position. What Carter managed to sidestep was the fact that he had penned the opening to a book, *Women in Need*, a pro-abortion tome, and that he had supported using abortion in Georgia's family-planning programs.[41] A meeting with a group of Catholic bishops during that period also proved not to be efficacious for Carter. His attempts to woo the Catholic vote were obscured by their concerns regarding his "born-again" brand of Christianity.

Carter's position on segregation also proved to be of some concern to the Catholics, many of whom vowed to vote Republican before casting a vote for Jimmy Carter.

Carter, it seemed, was destined to ride the aftermath of Lyndon Johnson's Vietnam and Richard Nixon's Watergate straight to the White House. Perhaps it was the promise of an evangelical with a deep religious faith that appealed to a war- and scandal-torn nation. Rev. Lou Shelton, head of the Traditional Values Coalition, anointed Carter, as did Rev. Pat Robertson, the host of a then little-known television program, *The 700 Club*.

Carter campaigned on the premise that the American people wanted not only to have faith in God but also faith in their elected officials and the government they represented. And again, Carter promised the American electorate he would never lie to them. Patrick Anderson, one of the individuals who wrote speeches for Carter, thought Carter "had been born again not only in a religious sense but in a political sense."[42]

While the majority of America's 30-million-strong white evangelicals supported Carter because of his unabashed faith, many were totally flummoxed by Carter's decision to sit for an interview with *Playboy* magazine, the unapologetically sexually explicit magazine of the day. It didn't help that Carter interjected his own biblical translation of the words of Christ and used euphemisms in the interview that many evangelicals found offensive:

> Because I'm just human and I'm tempted and Christ set some almost impossible standards for us. The Bible says, "Thou shalt not commit adultery." Christ said, "I tell you that anyone who looks on a woman with lust has in his heart already committed adultery." I've looked on a lot of women with lust. I've committed adultery in my heart many times....This is something that God recognizes, that I will do and have done, and God forgives me for it. But that doesn't mean that I condemn someone who not only looks on a woman with lust but who leaves his wife and shacks up

with somebody out of wedlock. Christ says [Carter trans-
lation], "Don't consider yourself better than someone else
because one guy screws a whole bunch of women while the
other guy is loyal to his wife. The guy who's loyal to his wife
ought not to be condescending or proud because of the
relative degree of sinfulness."[43]

The fallout from the *Playboy* interview was swift. The pastor
of Dallas' largest Southern Baptist church, Rev. W. A. Criswell,
swiftly endorsed Carter's opponent, Gerald Ford. It was, perhaps,
one of the biggest—if not the biggest—miscalculation in Carter's
campaign.

Also not to be overlooked was Carter's poor performance in
the first debate opposite Gerald Ford in Philadelphia in September.
Such a sound defeat for Carter was met with redoubled effort and
impressive preparation. In the second debate of the run-up to the
General Election, Ford committed what was, perhaps, the blunder
of all blunders. He stated that there was "no Soviet domination of
Eastern Europe."[44] The result was that according to pollsters Carter
defeated Ford in the two successive debates. Not to be outdone,
Gerald Ford renewed his efforts to paint Carter a fuzzy flip-flopper.
(And we in the twenty-first century thought that was a newly coined
expression.) On a whistle-stop tour through the state of Illinois, Ford
was quoted as saying: "Jimmy Carter will say anything, anywhere
to become president." At another stop, Ford quipped, "He wanders,
he wavers, he waffles, and he wiggles."[45] Ford's evaluation was
indicative of Carter's style.

In her volume *How Jimmy Won* Kandy Stroud wrote:

Carter established a broad-based appeal by selling himself
as both a liberal and a conservative, straddling issues with
the agility of a tightrope walker: for and against abortion;
for and against busing; for and against prayer in the schools;
for and against right-to-work laws; for and against big
business. Pummeling his audience with statistics, he con-
vinced them he understood complex issues well enough to be

president. But with his talk of compassion and decency and truth and love, he conveyed he cared first and foremost for what touched human beings." [46]

Ms. Stroud could have been writing about President Barack Obama's political campaign. Like Carter, expediency and audience were the order of the day.

Columnist George Will was quoted in the August 30, 1976, edition of *Newsweek* as saying, "Carter seems to believe that the way to keep knowledge pure is to keep it scarce."

The pollsters prognosticated a dead heat in the race for the White House. Depending on the day of the week or the poll, Carter and Ford were separated by the merest of percentage points. The general agreement among voters seemed to be that a vote for either would be a vote for the lesser of two inept candidates.

When the votes were tallied in the November election, Jimmy Carter had won by only 57 electoral votes and with 50.1 percent of the popular vote. The peanut farmer from Plaines, Georgia, had realized a long-time dream; he was officially elected president of the United States. Now he faced the greatest challenge of any political outsider: Could he ingratiate himself with Washington's political insiders...the men and women who were really in charge?

Only time would tell if the Jimmy Carter who delighted in proclaiming that he was not among the Washington elite could capture the political heart of the capital city as he had captured the imagination of American voters. Washington neophytes seem to appeal more to the general population than long-time D.C. insiders. This has been proven sufficiently beginning with Jimmy Carter. Carter had one term as a Georgia state senator and one term as governor before his election to the highest office in the land. He was followed in the White House by Governors Ronald Reagan, William Jefferson Clinton Jr., and George W. Bush—all Washington new-comers. George H. W. Bush (41st president) was the only president considered to be a Washington insider. He served in the House of Representatives, as an ambassador to the United Nations, as the director of the Central Intelligence Agency, as vice president under Ronald Reagan, and finally as president.

It is interesting to note that all of the presidents who succeeded Jimmy Carter had little to recommend them for the office other than their stints as governor. Ronald Reagan served as president of the Screen Actors Guild and one term as governor of California; Bill Clinton served as attorney general before serving two terms as governor of Arkansas; George W. Bush served one term as governor of Texas before being elected president. As with Carter, none served in Washington prior to becoming president. With the exception of James Earl Carter Jr. and George H. W. Bush all men served two terms as president.

A Carter win produced a boon for the Democratic Party and a critical blow to the Republican Party. To borrow a genuinely Southern expression, statistically the Democrats were in "high cotton." The Party controlled the Senate, state legislatures in all but four states; it boasted ownership of 38 state houses. The 1976 elections created another milestone when Albert Gore Jr. was elected as a representative in Tennessee and William Jefferson Clinton won the race for attorney general in Arkansas. "The rest," as they say, "is history."

3

JIMMY CARTER,
PRESIDENT AT LAST

"Electing Jimmy Carter president was as close as the American people have ever come to picking a name out of a phone book and giving him the job." (NATHAN MILLER) [47]

THE SINGLE TERM AS PRESIDENT for the peanut farmer from Plains, Georgia, has proven to be one of the most dreadful in political annals. Jimmy Carter's middle-of-the-road stance during the campaign had effectively accomplished not only his election but a chasm in the Democratic Party. His effectiveness at skirting the issues seemed to give Carter the idea that he could govern based on his image, not on substantive core ideals.

General Alexander Haig wrote of Carter's approach to politics in Washington:

> *Carter ran not so much against Ford and the Republicans as against the Washington establishment, and this made it inevitable that the Washington establishment would treat him as an antibody to be driven out of the system as quickly as possible.... He ran the administration like a nuclear submarine crew.... nobody talked back to this smiling,*

born-again Christian from the American heartland, who wore blue jeans on television when making presidential addresses....[48]

Almost immediately, Carter and/or his minions began to alienate the Washington establishment. At the inaugural dinner on January 20, 1977, Speaker of the House Thomas "Tip" O'Neill and his family were assigned seats usually reserved for the lowliest of guests—the table farthest from the president's head table. In fact, Carter and O'Neill reportedly had words even before the inauguration when Carter informed the Speaker that should he be thwarted in Congress, he would not hesitate to take his political initiatives directly to O'Neill's (or any other congressman's) constituency. O'Neill's attempts to educate Carter on the advisability of working *with* Congress and not against it proved to be useless. Carter's bullheadedness served only to estrange him from the very men and women with whom he would be expected to work during the next four years.

On January 21, 1977, Jimmy Carter's second day in office, he fulfilled one of his campaign pledges and managed to alienate all of the men and women who had dutifully served in the Vietnam War, as well as the loved ones of those who served and died on the battlefield there. President Carter signed a proclamation designed to pardon so-called draft dodgers who had left the country to escape induction into the armed services or who had failed to register for the draft. Carter's interpretation of the word *pardon* meant that "what you did, whether it's right or wrong, you're forgiven for it. And I [Carter] do advocate a pardon for draft evaders.... to bring about an end to the divisiveness that has occurred in our country as a result of the Vietnam War."[49]

Once he had attained the goal of the presidency, Carter began to transpose his campaign promises. He turned from those policies he had espoused on the trail to those he really intended to pursue; neither had any resemblance to the other. During the campaign Democratic Nominee Jimmy Carter touted himself as being tougher on communism than his Republican opponent Gerald Ford. After the election President Jimmy Carter leaned in the opposite and pro-Soviet direction. This tilt in foreign policy opened the door in Africa, Asia, and even in some Western countries for the advance of communism.

Following the advice of his personal pollster, Patrick Caddell, President Carter set out to systematically strip the presidency of its trappings of grandeur. He chose to be inaugurated in a business suit rather than the more traditional formal wear. After he was sworn in, he and his wife, Rosalynn, shunned the presidential limousine (creating quite a dilemma for the Secret Service) and walked down Pennsylvania Avenue from the Capitol to the White House. It was the first taste of what was to become the pauper's table of Carter's austerity program.

Ignoring the historical value of the presidential yacht, *Sequoia*, Carter apparently designated it as a useless trapping of the presidency and had it sold at auction. The yacht, built in 1931 for $200,000, was sold to the highest bidder for $270,000. The *Sequoia* had been the site of such events as:

> » Harry S. Truman's decision to bomb Hiroshima;

> » A base for Queen Elizabeth II on her U.S. visit during the Eisenhower administration;

> » Planning meetings with President John F. Kennedy during the Cuban missile crisis;

> » Meetings between Richard M. Nixon, Leonid Brezhnev, and Anatoly Dobrynin during the negotiations of the SALT I treaty;

> » Cabinet meetings during Gerald Ford's presidency; and

> » It was apparently aboard the Sequoia that Richard Milhous Nixon decided to resign as president of the United States.

Carter's austerity program came full circle in 2004 when the U.S. Congress appropriated a mere $2 million dollars to repurchase the historic vessel.

Carter called a halt to playing "Hail to the Chief" when he entered a venue; he limited the display of the presidential portrait; he abolished the office of White House chief of staff as he wanted to be available to anyone at any time; he stripped the White House staff of their accustomed limousines; and he actually carried his own luggage. Perhaps in an effort to hark back to a more genteel time and position himself as the president of the common man, he held his first nationally televised fireside address wearing a cardigan in imitation of President Franklin Roosevelt.

The president declared the White House to be "dry," meaning no liquor was to be served at State dinners; only wine would be allowed. His edict was also directed at Camp David and Air Force One. According to Bill Gulley, director of the White House military office, "'The Carters were the biggest liars in the world. The word was passed to get rid of all the booze...I said, 'Hide the booze, and let's find out what happens.' The first Sunday they were in the White House, I get a call from the mess [kitchen] saying, 'They want Bloody Marys before going to church. What should I do?' I said, 'Find some booze and take it up to them.' 'We never cut out liquor under Carter,' said Charlie Palmer, the chief of the Air Force One stewards. 'Occasionally, Carter had a martini'...or a Michelob light. Rosalynn...had a screwdriver.'" Of course, the president's brother Billy (of Billy Beer fame) was renowned for his drinking, and even Ms. Lillian preferred a shot of bourbon in the afternoon or a nip of brandy before bedtime.[50]

Carter had run for office as the "People's President" and, as such, eschewed those he considered to be money-lenders and influence-peddlers. After the debacle that was Watergate, he worked to absent himself from any situation that the American people might consider a compromise. Carter went so far as to avoid private conversations with the very congressional leaders he needed in order to achieve his campaign promises.

Charles Jones, a political scientist, wrote that Carter "was almost incapable of saying anything nice about members of Congress even as he traveled among their constituents."[51] Perhaps Carter himself overestimated his rapport with Congress when he titled a chapter of his memoirs, "My One-week Honeymoon with Congress." It is highly likely that Carter's "honeymoon" was even shorter than that if, in fact, there ever was a honeymoon.

Carter's foot-dragging approach to setting his (White) House in order following the election was of great consternation to many Washington political insiders. It took an entire month for the newly elected president to make his first cabinet appointments public. As director of the Office of Management and Budget, Carter chose close friend and fellow Georgian Bert Lance. Cyrus Vance was tapped as secretary of state, and shortly thereafter Michael Blumenthal, CEO of Bendix Corporation, was named treasury secretary and Congressman Brock Adams secretary of transportation.

To round out his team, Carter enlisted Charles Schultze, the former budget director under Lyndon Johnson, as chairman of the Council of Economic Advisors (CEA); Columbia Professor Zbigniew Brzezinski, national security advisor; CIT President Harold Brown, secretary of defense; Georgian lawmaker Andrew Young, UN ambassador; and Governor Cecil Andrus of Idaho, secretary of the interior. It was not until early January that the Carter cabinet would be entirely populated. At that time he finally named Theodore Sorenson (a Kennedy insider and conscientious objector during the Vietnam conflict) head of the CIA and James Schlesinger, the former defense secretary under Richard Nixon and Gerald Ford, as his assistant for energy. Sorenson's name was withdrawn before the Senate could vote on his nomination.

Having promised during his campaign to incorporate more women and minorities into high government positions, Carter was ultimately able to persuade only two women to join his cabinet: Patricia Harris (a former dean of Howard Law School) as secretary of Housing and Urban Development and Juanita Kreps (a Duke University VP) as Commerce secretary. For attorney general, Carter gave the nod to Griffin Bell. This appointment stirred early political controversy due to Bell's association with two segregated clubs and his decisions regarding desegregation issues.

Carter's choice to head the Central Intelligence Agency was Admiral Stansfield Turner, a former classmate and 1947 graduate of the U.S. Naval Academy. Turner, a Rhodes Scholar, had served as commander of U.S. forces in Japan and Korea and as commander in chief of NATO's Allied Forces, Southern Europe. He was president of the Naval War College for two years, 1972 to 1974.

Turner assumed the helm at the CIA in 1977 and began a purge that became known as the "Halloween Massacre." While budget cuts were responsible for some of the reductions in staff and operatives, the eradication of jobs was also due to a change from a paramilitary influence to the collection and analysis of data. Theodore Shackley, CIA chief of covert action, estimated that as many as 2,800 intelligence specialists fell victim to the drastic cuts.[52]

Stephen Hess, a senior fellow at Brookings Institute, wrote that Carter's governing style was one of "BOGSAT—the acronym for 'a bunch of guys sitting around a table.'" According to Mr. Hess, this format evolves when "a president lacks an overriding design for what he wants government to do.... his department chiefs are forced to prepare presidential options in a vacuum.... When direction is not present, they will go into business for themselves."[53]

Was it Carter's delay in settling on administration officials that set the tone for his entire tenure? His reluctance to appoint a true chief of staff left the impression that everyone—and no one—was ultimately in charge. It prompted a flurry of questions that remained unanswered even as Carter raised his right hand to take the Oath of Office on a cold January day: Who was in charge of running the White House? Who would see that authority was properly delegated? Who would handle the flood of paperwork to and from the Oval Office, and indeed, the White House as a whole? Who would oversee the president's schedule and protect him from the mundane issues that would bog down his daily activities?

The Carter cabinet was made up mostly of Washington outsiders, and that hampered his interaction with Congress. As part of his campaign rhetoric Jimmy Carter vowed to balance the budget during his first term. (As you will see in a later chapter that, too, was another promise not kept.) He determined he would not endorse agendas that contradicted his objectives. The Democrats in Congress had been the underdogs in Washington for eight years prior to Carter's win; having a Democrat in the White House, they thought, would mean approval and funding for some of the pet projects that had been denied by the Republicans. What Carter could not accept was that in Washington, D.C., it would be absolutely necessary to build coalitions, to create political capital, and to reach agreements with Congress.

Douglas Brinkley, author of *The Unfinished Presidency,* said: "Often he [Carter] wouldn't return phone calls of leading Senators. There was a kind of an abrasive attitude he had towards them. He never showed them respect. So they all eventually got bitter and turned on him."[54]

Perhaps one of the most telling comments that best describes Jimmy Carter's presidential style came from Congressman Dan Rostenkowski on PBS's *American Experience.* He related: "We were all invited down to the White House every other Tuesday. We walked into the private dining room on the first floor just off the East Room. We looked at the table, and there were these little finger-tip cookies, and...Tip O'Neill looked at me and he said, 'What's this?' And I said, 'Well I guess that's breakfast.' So the president walked in and shook hands with everybody. And O'Neill looked at the president and he said, 'Mr. President, you know, we *won* the election.'"[55]

Carter reveled in the response he evoked when he talked with Congress about balancing the budget. The Liberal Left was absolutely certain that once in office, Carter would gladly endorse the Party's pet spending programs. Not so! In his early days in office he showed no mercy when he vowed to veto a public works bill because it was so laden with pork. Carter demanded that the proposal be stripped of numerous planned projects. The supporters of the bill were aghast that their man in the White House had not conferred with them before making such a brash declaration. Such moves were not designed to engender camaraderie among the Democrats in power.

Just weeks into his administration it was obvious that Jimmy Carter was in over his head. He had incurred the wrath of Senator Ted Kennedy over his rejection of a national health insurance plan, disappointed many organizations to whom he had made campaign promises, dashed Congress' hopes that new programs and entitlements would be endorsed, and denied spending on urban programs to aid social programs. His former political rival, Gerald Ford, said, "Compromise is the oil that makes governments go."[56] Even after years of political involvement in local, state, and now national government, Jimmy Carter had not learned the lesson of compromise.

Carter campaigned on the promise of a new beginning and national healing following the Watergate scandal and America's ignominious withdrawal from a Vietnam War that divided the nation. In speech after speech he had promised a government "as good and decent and compassionate as the American people." However, Carter's very leadership style would be his undoing. Even his own vice president would divulge years later: "I never understood how Carter's political mind worked. Carter's got the coldest political nose of any politician I've ever met."[57]

Governor Carter's own critique of his first year in office in Georgia seems not to have made an impression on President Carter. He wrote: "If I have made one mistake, it has been in undertaking too many things simultaneously."[58] He seemed destined not to have learned from that leadership deficiency. Carter liberally flooded the halls of Congress with legislation. He sent reform bills for everything from campaign finance to welfare, from tax to health care. This un-prioritized influx of paper proved to be a real boondoggle on Capitol Hill.

Rather than becoming the elected "savior" of the American people, Jimmy Carter was rapidly becoming the "Judas goat." Just one hundred days after taking office, he was blindsided by inflation. The Dow had fallen 5 percent and continued to spiral to a 16-percent drop after his first year. This situation was further exacerbated by his choice for director of the Office of Management and Budget, Bert Lance.

One of Jimmy Carter's greatest disappointments during his first year in office was probably the scandal that surrounded Bert Lance. Lance's banking and business practices had come under close scrutiny. What began as a simple request from the new president to all of his appointees to fully disclose their financial holdings and to rid themselves of any that might be considered a conflict of interest resulted in the ultimate dismissal of Lance. Carter requested that Lance dispose of his assets in the National Bank of Georgia. Lance agreed to place some $3.3 million in stock in a blind trust which would be divested by the close of 1977. A deteriorating financial situation for Lance, however, forced him to seek the assistance of the president. The Senate Banking Committee began a comprehensive investigation of Lance's banking practices. A report released in August 1977 seemed to vindicate Lance of any wrongdoing. Carter praised both the findings of the committee and his appointee. Lance made it clear that with Carter's continued support he would remain in office.

According to an article in *New Yorker,* what Carter had missed in the report was the line that charged Lance with "unsafe and unsound banking practices." The article went on to say that the "report contained not a word that justified Carter's saying that 'my faith in the character and competence of Bert Lance has been reconfirmed.' Many people feel that in the end Lance will have to go."[59] Rather than retreating into the background, the Lance affair blossomed to include reports of free travel for presidential candidate Jimmy Carter, large overdrafts for selected friends and family, and undisclosed financial information. Shortly thereafter, the Senate Banking Committee reported to the White House that Lance was being referred to the Internal Revenue Service and the Justice Department (unreported campaign donation of free travel) for investigation.

After an appearance before the Senate committee conducting the investigation, Lance was finally persuaded to resign his post. Historians suggest that Carter's continued support of his old friend did great damage to the Carter administration by undermining public support for the president. Lance's departure, however, robbed the president of the one mature advisor on his staff.

Carter tackled the inflation problem by inveigling the Federal Reserve to increase the supply of money available and entreating it to lower interest rates. Public opinion polls taken in 1978, a year after Carter's inauguration, showed that Americans rated inflation above every other national problem.

Jimmy Carter had appointed G. William Miller as Federal Reserve chairman. Bruce Bartlett, in an article for *National Review,* wrote:

> Miller [whose background was that of lawyer, engineer, and corporate executive] didn't have a clue about monetary policy and only made the dismal inflation situation he inherited far worse.
>
> The consumer price index, which rose 4.9 percent in 1976, the year Carter was elected, jumped steadily to 6.7 percent in 1977, 9 percent in 1978, and 13.3 percent in 1979. At this point, Carter realized that he had made a serious error appointing Miller to the Fed. But he could not be fired, so Miller had to be induced to leave voluntarily. Consequently, Carter fired Treasury Secretary W. Michael Blumenthal,

who had been doing a fine job, in order to open the position for Miller, who left the Fed to replace him.

Under pressure from Wall Street Carter reluctantly appointed Paul Volcker to be chairman of the Federal Reserve Board in 1979. Volcker had been Under Secretary of the Treasury for Richard Nixon and was then serving as president of the Federal Reserve Bank of New York. However, it is naïve to think that Volcker was given a free hand by Carter. His inability to fully implement a tight-money policy is why the inflation rate fell only to 12.5 percent in 1980, despite a sharp recession that year.[60]

With the rise of inflation came a new word coined by economic pundits—*stagflation*. It was used to describe the rise of inflation combined with a sluggish business growth and an ever-increasing unemployment rate that topped 10 percent. It perfectly illustrates the economic melancholy that gripped the nation.

Carter's mismanagement of the economic crisis was to be repeated with the energy crisis facing the American public. The energy plan that was to liberate the U.S. from its dependency on foreign oil and eradicate waste of energy resources was developed in secret with little, if any, input from knowledgeable advisors or from his cabinet and without consulting Congress. Once again, Carter's penchant for trying to be all things to all people produced a contradictory and complex plan that proved to be of little value. Why Tip O'Neill took it upon himself to push the plan through Congress may never be understood; Carter was not so lucky in the Senate. His voluminous package was carved up like the proverbial Thanksgiving turkey and completely neutered. The final and lasting result of the president's work was the creation of the Department of Energy—a money-guzzling entity that produced not a whit of consumable energy.

Carter's disdain for the Old Guard in Washington plagued his entire four years in office. When he did make overtures, they were often stilted and clumsy attempts. He shunned the party circuit and refused to pander to the egos of the lawmakers in residence. From the days of Woodrow Wilson power-brokering—or exerting political pressure to achieve a specific end—was a tool used by numerous presidents. That particular tool was not in Carter's tool chest.

In their book, *The Presidency of James Earl Carter, Jr.*, Burton I. Kaufman and Scott Kaufman wrote:

> *There are certain parallels between [Woodrow] Wilson and Carter that permit a highly instructive comparison. Both leaders were progressive Southerners and devout Christians who believed in the gospel of service and considered political office a form of ministry. In contrast to Carter, however, Wilson had a clear sense of purpose...a better understanding of the negotiable and the expendable. Wilson...understood that flexibility and compromise on specific issues did not entail the repudiation of fundamental principles.*
>
> *Although Carter was by no means unaware of the realities of American politics and public life, in contrast to Wilson his progressive mentality seemed to blind him to the fact that...To rally support for his programs he needed to be a creative and flexible leader with a well-articulated sense of purpose that commanded broad respect. This latter requirement, in particular, would pose a stumbling block throughout his four years in office.*[61]

The disaster that was Jimmy Carter's domestic policy was only reinforced by his foreign policy. Carter's mixed signals to our allies and enemies alike plunged America into a worldwide maelstrom. Perhaps it was best summarized in a quote from Henry Kissinger: "The Carter administration has managed the extraordinary feat of having, at one and the same time, the worst relations with our allies, the worst relations with our adversaries, and the most serious upheavals in the developing world since the end of the Second World War."[62]

Carter even managed to insult Britain's jolly "Queen Mum," mother of the reigning monarch, Elizabeth II: "The Queen Mother had an active dislike for Jimmy who, when introduced to her, kissed her full on the lips. Rules of royal protocol state that you don't speak until spoken to when meeting a royal, much less kiss them. The Queen Mother's reaction? 'He is the only man since my dear husband died to kiss me on the lips!'"[63]

As bad as were Jimmy Carter's handling of domestic crises and his political and social gaffes, it was his mishandling of foreign affairs that ultimately sealed his fate in the 1980 election. Alexander Haig initially had high hopes for Carter's prowess in foreign affairs, but he was deeply disappointed as Carter fumbled his way through one untenable situation after another:

> [Carter]...never understood them [the Europeans], and they never accepted him. To the allies, he was an unknown quantity, a man inexperienced in foreign affairs, a figure from outside the Establishment who lacked personal knowledge in foreign leaders, a populist; when he was elected, they feared the worst... Some of Jimmy's "just plain Jimmy" theatrics... embarrassed the Europeans. Carter...abruptly decided in 1978 to reverse U.S. policy and not produce neutron weapons and deploy them in Europe.... Carter's decision came after the leaders of allied nations, especially Chancellor Schmidt of West Germany, had exposed themselves to great political risks in order to support the former U.S. desire to deploy the bomb.... Schmidt was deeply upset.... political considerations did not matter to the president in this case.[64]

His disastrous decisions would insure James Earl Carter Jr. a one-term presidency. Many of the decisions that would detrimentally affect the United States for decades to come were made during Carter's last year in the White House.

4

SHAPING THE ADMINISTRATION'S FOREIGN POLICY?

"Richard Nixon, that authority on presidential nobility, has denounced the Carter administration's treatment of the Shah of Iran as 'one of the black pages of American foreign policy.'"
(NEW YORK TIMES) [65]

AS JIMMY CARTER ENTERED the political battle that was the 1976 presidential campaign, America was still surfing the moderate wave of anti-Vietnam emotion. In fact, a group called the Institute for Policy Studies (IPS) seemed determined to infect every arena with liberal politics. The IPS network included many of what were labeled "alternative media outlets" which included the anti-war news disseminator the *Dispatch News Service,* the *Pacific News Service*, and blatantly liberal periodicals such as *Mother Jones* and *In This Time*. One of the fundamental purposes of the various network members was to affect foreign policy ideas and, in fact, that remains a stated goal today as evidenced by the following from the IPS website:

> *Since 1996 IPS has been working in the U.S. and in various international venues towards the broad goal of crafting a*

new kind of UN-centered, democratic and people-based internationalism. The project's work is in three major areas: the fight for peace with justice in the Middle East, defense of the United Nations against U.S. domination, and the challenge to U.S. unilateralism and military interventionism, especially in the wake of the September 11th terrorist attacks."[66]

With lawmakers firmly in the crosshairs, the IPS began a winning effort to lobby those supportive of the tenets of the organization. Having added the likes of Democrats Alan Cranston, Edward "Ted" Kennedy, John Conyers, George McGovern, Thomas Eagleton, and Republican Mark Hatfield to its ranks, the IPS targeted second-tier congressional staffers. It was a prudent move by the IPS, as a number of them were very opposed to the Vietnam war, and several were later elected to congressional seats. Ted Kennedy aides John Culver and Richard Clark, and Walter Mondale aides Toby Moffet and Richard Nolen were only four who were elected between 1964 and 1974. This served to further boost the lobbying efforts of the IPS.

The doctrine of the IPS came to be known as New Internationalism as outlined above in the quote from its own website. In order to persuade presidential candidate Jimmy Carter to implement the IPS doctrine, a campaign was launched at the 1976 Democratic National Convention. The group was determined that front-runner Carter adopt the platform penned by Marcus Raskin, an IPS founder. Raskin and his henchmen were able to wrest a promise from Carter that if elected president, he would cut spending by the military and contest the production of the B-1 bomber, among other things.

Perhaps the most contested area of Raskin's platform was that of human rights. The Liberal Left wanted a strong plank that supported leftist regimes and virtually ignored right-wing allies. This seemed to appeal to Carter as it fed his desire to see the world's poor elevated from abject poverty, disease, and war to a state of plenty. It appealed to Carter's crusade for morality, his sense of community, and his ongoing battle against elitism. To reach his goal Carter would have to rid Washington of former Nixon and Ford insiders and replace them with new names and new faces, all of whom, of course, were ardent supporters of the New Internationalism policies.

Had the Carter team determined early in his quest for the White House to hide behind the Foreign Assistance Act, Section 502B, in order to further their agenda in the area of human rights? The import of the document was that the U.S. was duty-bound to observe the values worldwide to which it professed to adhere at home. Congress superseded a presidential veto in 1976 to include Section 502B, a human rights statement, in the more wide-ranging International Security and Arms Export Control Act. Its detractors maintained that the inclusion of the rider was more representational; such symbolism, however, can be a weighty force in influencing public opinion. The document read, in part:

> *Sec. 502B. Human Rights.—(a) (1) It is the policy of the United States, in accordance with its international obligations as set forth in the Charter of the United Nations and in keeping with the constitutional heritage and traditions of the United States, to promote and encourage increased respect for human rights and fundamental freedoms for all without distinction as to race, sex, language, or religion. To this end, a principal goal of the foreign policy of the United States is to promote the increased observance of internationally recognized human rights by all countries.*
>
> *(2) It is further the policy of the United States that, except under circumstances specified in this section, no security assistance may be provided to any country the government of which engages in a consistent pattern of gross violations of internationally recognized human rights.*[67]

Congress took on the task of human rights in 1961 as a direct result of the Civil Rights Movement in the U.S. and the Nixon administration's foreign policy debacles. Both congressional leaders and many Americans felt that U.S. policy abroad should reflect its policy at home, thus the birth of the human rights movement. Members of the committee determined that human rights issues should be given precedence when determining foreign policy. A law was passed that established official prerequisite for the limitation or rejection of assistance for a nation or nations that repeatedly deny basic civil liberties for people. The law was an attempt to dissociate the U.S. from the unethical and abusive actions of beneficiaries of foreign assistance. Aid would no longer be dependent on a seeming pro-American stance; it would be given to those nations which valued human rights and self-determination.

The Foreign Assistance Act was made for Jimmy Carter. In her treatise on human rights, Clair Apodaca wrote:

> *There existed a coalition of those concerned with human rights, those that were looking for any reason to cut the foreign aid budget and foreign commitments, and those that simply wished to attack the Republican Party.*[68]

She very accurately described the Carter administration on all three points. What made it even more attractive to Carter's foreign policy team was a congressional amendment to the Act in 1976 that made the president responsible for the determination of which countries were guilty of abusing the human rights of its citizens. The escape clause giving the president more decision-making latitude was in the words "extraordinary circumstances exist which necessitate a continuation of security assistance for such country." This allowed the sitting president the leeway to determine what aid to which countries was in the national interest of the U.S. Such wording made it possible for Carter to launch his campaign against the Shah of Iran while simply ignoring other abusive regimes such as the one in Indonesia. Apodaca wrote:

> *Carter found that in the case of Indonesia in 1979, there was not a consistent pattern of human rights violations because*

*there was a plan to someday release the political prisoners.
So, in spite of the fact that approximately 100,000 people
were murdered and another 30,000 were still incarcerated,
Indonesia was not denied U.S. security assistance.*[69]

Effectively organizing Carter's team fell to IPS-supporter and
Carter running mate, Walter Mondale. Mondale's efforts resulted in
a team often referred to as the "Mondale Mafia," the core of Carter's
moralpolitik foreign policy aspirations. Mondale's protégés dotted
the new administration's landscape and would ultimately be responsible for Carter's abysmal foreign policy failures. Warren Christopher
was tapped as deputy secretary of state; Anthony Lake became the
head of Policy Planning at the Department of State; Paul C. Warnke
was named director of the Arms Control and Disarmament Agency
(ACDA).

When all of the new appointments were made, Carter had
surrounded himself with twenty-two first-timers. Two of the more
controversial appointments were Warnke who, upon taking
office, immediately scrubbed the agency's Verification and Analysis
Bureau (the agency that verified legitimate Soviet threats);
and Andrew Young, Carter's UN ambassador whose gaffes were
numerous. The left-wing bias regarding foreign policy grew with
each Carter/Mondale appointee.

Countries that were particular targets for human rights
violations were El Salvador, Nicaragua, South Korea, and Iran.
It seemed that Iran raised the ire of many of Carter's staff selections.
During the early organizational stages of the Carter transition team
and even prior to his being sworn into office, an in-depth report
on Iran was requested. John Dumbrell wrote in *The Carter
Presidency: A Re-Evaluation* that Walter Mondale and his aide,
David Aaron, had links to the U.S.-based Iranian resistance. They
were persuaded that Mohammad Reza Pahlavi, the Shah of Iran,
was not entitled to rule Iran and determined that he needed to
be restrained. Others in Mondale's fringe group simply wanted
the ruler deposed. According to Congressman David Bowen,

"Opportunists in the State Department were trying to out-Carter Carter."[70] Once in office, the president's Liberal Left supporters felt justified in redoubling efforts to remove Pahlavi from the Peacock Throne.

Apparently, it did not occur to anyone in the new administration that the U.S. must be prepared for what might happen were the Shah's monarchy to fail. And no one was prepared, least of all Jimmy Carter. Carter, however, was not alone in his inability to comprehend the state of affairs in Iran; other countries with strong ties to the Pahlavi monarchy, i.e., France, Britain, and Israel, either did not count the cost of an Iran without the Shah or simply waited too long to act.

In her memoir, *An Enduring Love*, Farah Pahlavi wrote of the Carter campaign:

> *During the whole of his campaign, Jimmy Carter had proclaimed the theme of human rights, the freedom of the people, which in reality has to be treated with caution, taking the economic and cultural context of each country into account. The Iranian opposition saw an ally in Carter for future struggles, and the rush of demands (on the Shah) in the spring of 1977 would doubtless not have been so great had another man been elected to the White House.*[71]

When Jimmy Carter took office in January 1977, he inherited the established Iran policies of numerous presidents before him, including Richard Nixon and Gerald Ford. The U.S. had, in 1953, backed a coup in favor of the Shah and against Prime Minister Dr. Mohammad Mossadegh. As prime minister, Mossadegh made a commitment to establish a constitutional monarchy, promote democracy, and nationalize the Iranian oil industry, then under the control of Britain. When Mossadegh ejected Anglo-Iranian Oil, the British determined that Mossadegh must be removed in any way possible and enlisted the aid of the United States to achieve the goal. Mossadegh believed that the United States would back his plan.

Kermit "Kim" Roosevelt Jr., grandson of Theodore Roosevelt and a CIA agent, covertly joined hands with the British and military forces loyal to the Shah in "Operation Ajax" to remove Mossadegh from office and restore the monarchy of Reza Pahlavi. (In a note of fancy, the CIA operatives chose as their theme song, "Luck Be a Lady Tonight" from the Broadway musical *Guys and Dolls*.) The coup attempt initially failed and the Shah fled to Rome. Kim Roosevelt was so determined to overthrow the prime minister that he ignored communiqués sent from CIA headquarters and launched a second successful coup.

Kermit Roosevelt dispatched U.S. Army General Norman Schwarzkopf Sr., who had from 1942-1948 trained and commanded the Iranian Gendarmerie, to Rome to try to persuade the Shah to adopt the "Operation Ajax" plan, but the Shah declined to commit to the CIA plot. Reportedly, the general carried several bags filled with millions in currency with which he paid members of the covert operation and enticed politicos, clerics, the media, and gangsters to support the overthrow of Mossadegh's government. After meeting with the Shah, the general advised President Eisenhower to approach the Shah to secure his cooperation. Pahlavi eventually agreed, but only after he was assured that both Britain and the U.S. were officially part of the plot to overthrow Mossadegh.

Manucher Farmanfarmaian wrote of the Shah's acquiescence to Kermit Roosevelt's plan:

> *A man whom I did not recognize appeared from behind the plane trees. He was dressed neatly in a dark suit...presented him [the Shah] with a document...the messenger was sent by Kermit Roosevelt and the document the Shah had signed appointed General [Fazlollah] Zahedi prime minister. Mossadegh's fall was imminent.*[72]

On August 19, Zahedi formally claimed the title "Prime Minister." The following day Mossadegh surrendered. The U.S. immediately stepped forward and promised Prime Minister Zahedi the funds necessary to untangle the Iranians from the ongoing oil disagreement with Great Britain, a total of approximately $150 million.

In 1977 Kermit Roosevelt approached the Shah to discuss his plans to write a book on the "Operation Ajax" plot. Asadollah Alam, the Shah's confidant, wrote of that audience:

> I reported that I've now examined the book and found it most undesirable. It portrays HIM [His Imperial Majesty] as a waverer, forced into various crucial decisions, for example the appointment of General Zahedi as Prime Minister, by pressure from Roosevelt. The man is...hoping to present himself as a hero. HIM said he had no idea the book contained so much nonsense.[73]

In an interview by Amir Taheri with the Shah's former son-in-law, Ardeshir Zahedi, he patently denies that the overthrow of Mossadegh was a direct result of CIA plotting:

> They (the U.S.) may have plotted that. But what is important is to ascertain whether Mossadegh fell because of American plotting or as a result of other factors. What I can say with confidence is that the fall of Mossadegh was not a result of any CIA plot. Victory, of course, has a thousand fathers while defeat is always an orphan. Had the August 1953 efforts to remove Mossadegh from power failed, there would have been no CIA "heroes" claiming the credit. There is a mass of evidence, including U.S., Iranian, British, and Soviet official documents and testimonies by people who played a role in the events that give the lie to the CIA operatives' claims.[74]

Manucher and Roxane Farmanfarmaian wrote of the Mossadegh affair:

> Had Churchill not won the election in England or had Truman run again in the United States; had Stalin not died or the Korean War not wound down when it did;

had Senator Joseph McCarthy been silenced just a bit sooner or Congress not been rocked by a Carter oil scare—history would have been different. Most bizarre of all, had the CIA not had an operative named Kermit Roosevelt... Mossadegh might have at last won. There are still many mysteries. The greatest is the resonant silence of the Soviet Union, which was fighting the United States and the rest of the UN on its eastern flank in Korea yet remained mute about Washington's flagrant activity on its southern border in Iran. History books ignore this detail, and the British archives on the subject are closed until 2050. No doubt there is much to hide.[75]

President Eisenhower remembered the joy with which the Shah returned to Iran following the coup:

The Shah is a new man. For the first time, he believes in himself because he feels that he is the king of his people's choice and not by arbitrary decision of a foreign power.[76]

On March 17, 2000, the Clinton administration gave the nod to Secretary of State Madeleine Albright to deliver a cleverly phrased apology to Iran for its role in the Mossadegh affair: "The United States played a significant role in orchestrating the overthrow of Iran's popular prime minister, Mohammad Mossadegh," Albright says. "The Eisenhower administration believed its actions were justified for strategic reasons. But the coup was clearly a set-back for Iran's political development and it is easy to see why so many Iranians continue to resent this intervention by America in their internal affairs."[77]

Just weeks later, President Clinton went one step (or perhaps two) further than his secretary of state. He spoke to a group assembled for a Millennial Evening in the White House East Room. Clinton all but grovelled at the feet of the mullahs controlling Iran:

I think it is important to recognize...that Iran, because of its enormous geopolitical importance over time, has been the

*subject of quite a lot of abuse from various Western nations.
And I think sometimes it's quite important to tell people,
look, you have a right to be angry at something my country
or my culture or others that are generally allied with us
today did to you fifty or sixty or one hundred or one hundred fifty years ago.... So we [the U.S.] have to find some way
to get dialogue—and going into total denial when you're in
a conversation with somebody who's been your adversary, in
a country like Iran...is not exactly the way to begin.*[78]

It is quite obvious to all but Albright and Clinton that the two
had chosen to ignore the indignities committed against the hostages
taken from the American Embassy and held for 444 days, or that
the Iranian-sponsored Hezbollah in Lebanon had murdered Dr.
Malcolm Kerr, William Buckley, and Lt. Colonel Robert Higgins,
Americans all.

Imagine the impact that Clinton's words had on the people in
Iran: A U.S. president was, for all practical purposes, apologizing not
only for his country, but for the actions of other countries. Clinton
went a bit overboard in describing Iran as "a true democracy" and
"one of the most stable countries" in the Middle East.[79]

Following the coup to unseat Mossadegh, an international
consortium was formed to oversee the petroleum industry in Iran.
Dr. Parviz Mina, director of National Iranian Oil Company, related
to me the breakdown of the members:

*Five major Americans [Mobil, Exxon, Gulf, Chevron,
and Standard Oil of California], seven independents,
British Petroleum, Shell, and Compagnie Francaise des
Petroles formed the group.... 40 percent belonged to British
Petroleum, 14 percent to Shell, 6 percent to the French
company.*[80]

Over time, Iran exported $5.2 million in oil daily to the world
market, the majority to Western Europe and the United States. The
country was second only to Saudi Arabia as the largest exporter of

crude. In 1971 the Shah hosted an OPEC conference in his country. He became an instant media target when he spoke in favour of OPEC's demanding the right to control production and oil prices. Pahlavi asked why the OPEC members should not get a higher price for their commodity in relation to rising prices for other commodities worldwide. Newspapers dubbed him a monster and began to blame the Shah for economic problems suffered by the West. According to Mina, the press used the fact that the conference was held in Iran to put pressure on the monarch.

By 1973 the Iranian National Oil Company (INOC) would rank 28th worldwide; in 1974 INOC had captured the third spot and would be on its way to an output of 6 1/2 million barrels daily. Iran in 1977 boasted an export figure of 270 million tons of oil products and had captured second place. The Iran-owned oil terminal on Kharg Island boasted the largest tanker port in the entire world.[81] The land of the Shah was a shining star in OPEC.

5

A CELEBRATION
CREATES CHAOS

*"The lavishness and the emphasis on Western taste turned out
to be a major mistake... we reporters didn't know that the
Persepolis indulgences would become a major milestone in the Shah's
eventual downfall.... We were there to cover a party."*
(B A R B A R A   W A L T E R S) [82]

ANOTHER EVENT IN 1971 would garner intense dislike
for Pahlavi. It began with a desire to pay homage to Cyrus,
the founder of the Iranian Empire, on its 2,500[th] anniversary; it escalated to what was likely the largest gathering of heads of state in
modern history. Such was the magnitude of the celebration that a
spokesperson for the Iranian government declared: "During these
unforgettable days, this august assembly will make Persepolis [the
site of the magnificent party] the centre-of-gravity of the world."[83]

Initially, the celebration was to have been a national event for
the Iranian people. It escalated to the point that multiplied-millions
of dollars were spent to create a field of sixty-eight fireproof tents
set on concrete slabs, with every possible amenity for the comfort
of the guests. Each tent was resplendent with silk and velvet walls,

gold-leaf furnishings, and with Persian carpets specially woven for the guests. China and crystal came from the French house of *Baccarat*. Escorts, male and female, were clad in French-designed dress. Guests were given a collection of gift products by *Elizabeth Arden* named after the Empress Farah. Mercedes 280-SEs transported visitors to and from the elaborate setting on the site of ancient Persepolis. The fact that cost was no object ignited the ire of many Iranians, few of whom even saw inside the "city."

The 500 guests ranged from Vice President Spiro Agnew to Emperor Haile Selassie; from kings and queens of Belgium, Denmark, Jordan, Morocco, Norway, Thailand, and Nepal, to Prince Rainier and Princess Grace of Monaco, Prince Philip and his daughter, Princess Anne of Great Britain; from Marshal Tito and Aga Khan to the socialite Charlotte Ford. Despite a tiff with Georges Pompidou, the president of France, the country was duly represented by its prime minister, Jacques Chaban-Delmas. Could it have been the French president's childish insistence that he be seated during the banquet higher up in the pecking order than any other French-speaking head of state that shaped France's future relationship with the Ayatollah Khomeini?

New York Times journalist Neil Farquhar wrote:

> *Historians tend to point to the estimated $200 million fete as the beginning of the end for the Shah, a breathtaking symbol of just how out of touch he was with ordinary Iranians, none of whom were allowed within miles of the place during the party.*
>
> *The festivities ignored centuries of Islamic rule in Iran, provoking scorn from Ayatollah Ruhollah Khomeini, patriarch of the revolution that toppled the Shah.*[84]

This was only another nail in what was to become Pahlavi's political coffin. With three groups in Iran swiftly aligning against him, the National Front, the *Mujahedeen*, and the clerics, the Shah would ultimately fall victim to Jimmy Carter's agenda of change.

Change for the sake of change is not always the most productive path to take, however. Once in office, Carter tackled the agenda that had been proposed by Nixon and National Security Advisor (and later Secretary of State) Henry Kissinger. Nixon's plan covered the next several decades. Kissinger believed:

> *It was dangerous for us to make the domestic policy of countries around the world a direct objective of American foreign policy.... The protection of basic human rights is a very sensitive aspect of the domestic jurisdiction of... governments.*[85]

Nixon adopted the purview that his administration would ignore a nation's human rights history if necessary to secure a geographical edge. He had to look no further than the strong U.S. ally, the Shah of Iran. Shah Mohammad Reza Pahlavi was the son of Reza Shah who had gained the Peacock Throne through a coup d'état against the ruling Qajar dynasty in 1921. His son ascended the throne after Reza Shah was ousted at the hands of the British and Russians. Mr. Kissinger, who enjoyed a close, personal relationship with the Shah, labeled Reza Pahlavi of Iran "the rarest of leaders, an unconditional ally."[86]

President Nixon then instituted what became known as the "Twin Pillar Doctrine." His approach was to establish American military substitutes in various regions, especially in Iran and Saudi Arabia, to deter the Soviet Union and provide protection for U.S. interests. Thus, it behooved Nixon to see that the Shah was adequately supplied with military arms. Following the debacle in Vietnam, Nixon determined to anoint proxies to act on behalf of the United States within their region. Iran received such a designation and was thus guaranteed access to U.S. arms in abundance.

Having Iran in his corner would give Nixon a deterrent against the Soviets in the Persian Gulf and would insure a virtual unending supply of Gulf oil. Pahlavi had no way of knowing that he was creating "a system capable only of defending itself but incapable of satisfying the people [of Iran]. This was its greatest weakness and the true cause of its ultimate defeat."[87]

Prior to a visit to Iran by President Nixon in May 1972, the Shah called on his friend and former son-in-law, Ambassador Ardeshir Zahedi,[88] who had left Iran for Montreaux, Switzerland. The Shah requested that Zahedi make a trip to Pakistan and Afghanistan before the president's arrival in Tehran in order to promote peace between the two neighbors. Zahedi's long-standing friendship with Pakistani Prime Minister Zolfaghar Ali Bhutto and Afghanistan Prime Minister Mohammad Musa Shafiq made him the logical choice for the mission. (Shafiq was executed by the Soviets after the Afghan invasion in 1978.) The Shah was most interested that these two countries coexist peacefully in order to deter Soviet expansion in the region.[89]

Zahedi, who had known Nixon since his days as vice president, provided the background for the president's visit to Iran and for what eventually became known as the "Nixon Doctrine." The ambassador was in New York for UN discussion regarding the Six-Day War. He and Nixon met for dinner at Club 21 in Manhattan. Zahedi remembered:

> *In those days nobody believed in a Nixon comeback, not even the Shah. On his return from a Vietnam trip in 1967, he stopped over in Tehran as my personal guest. I arranged an audience with His Majesty, which was supposed to be short but lasted several hours. I [invited] Mr. Nixon to dinner in my residence at Hesarak with Armin Meyer, then the U.S. ambassador in Tehran, and my deputy, Amir-Khosrow Afshar. When these two men left, we chatted until the early hours of the morning. We discussed the problems of the region, specifically Iraq, Oman, and South Yemen, which was on the verge of gaining independence.... I also arranged for Nixon to travel to Romania, especially as he had not been well-received by the Soviet leaders during a recent trip to Moscow. [The trip was arranged through my*

friend Corneliu Manescu who later became the UN Secretary General].

When Nixon became president in 1969, he was anxious to further develop his ties with Iran. He sent Elliot Richardson and Governor Harold Stassen to Tehran.

[The Shah made a reciprocal visit to Washington, D.C., accompanied by Mr. Zahedi].

When I look back at that visit, I think probably the most significant point which was made was related to China. At that time, Nixon's policy toward China had not yet been developed. Poland was acting as the go-between with China. I advised Secretary of State William P. Rogers to use Pakistan more as go-between; Rogers took that advice. (When Henry Kissinger went to China in 1971, he pretended to be in Pakistan.)

We raised a second point with Nixon and Rogers about Iraq...over close ties between Iraq and the USSR, especially when...Saddam Hussein came to power. Looking back, I can say that these events played an important role and were the roots of the policies that President Nixon and His Majesty developed in 1972. They wanted Iran to assure the security of the Persian Gulf and this was what the Nixon Doctrine was about.

American military sales to Iran began much before Nixon; but once Nixon and the Shah agreed on the role Iran should play in ensuring the security of the Persian Gulf, it was natural that Iran would receive the best military equipment. Nixon gave the Shah full assurance and carte blanche in that respect.[90]

Pahlavi was only too eager to ally Iran with the United States, and he was quite vocal about his vision for the Persian Gulf region: "My policy is honest and straightforward, and I have no hidden agenda," he told Nelson Rockefeller. "I say quite openly that I wish

Iran to play a role in the Indian Ocean. I have no objection to America being present; indeed, I shall actively defend your interests."[91]

In a memo to Secretary of State William Rogers and to Secretary of Defense Melvin Laird, Henry Kissinger forwarded the president's approval of a conversation Nixon had with the Shah. According to Kissinger, "The president has also reiterated that, in general, decisions on the acquisition of military equipment should be left primarily to the government of Iran. If the government of Iran has decided to buy certain equipment, the purchase of U.S. equipment should be encouraged tactfully where appropriate, and technical advice on the capabilities of the equipment in question should be provided."[92]

In an interview several years ago with Major General George J. Keegan, Air Force Chief of Intelligence from 1972 to 1977, he told me of documents secured near the end of World War II. The documents outline exactly what the Shah and Nixon were trying to prevent:

> *Russia's desire to dominate the Persian Gulf is long-standing and well-documented. In 1945 our boys managed to capture records of the German Foreign Office.... One of the files deals with the Soviet-Nazi Non-Aggression Pact signed by Hitler and Stalin in the late 1930s. Right there in black and white is the Soviets' clear statement of their desire to be the dominant force in the Persian Gulf.*[93]

Nixon was the beneficiary of President Lyndon Johnson's attempts to encourage the Shah to continue his efforts to modernize Iran, but at a steady pace. It was Johnson who declared Pahlavi a model monarch. "What is going on in Iran is about the best thing going on anywhere in the world," said Johnson.[94] The Shah was advised, however, not to overwhelm his people with an excessive number of proposed changes. When Carter took office, Iran was well-supplied with U.S. military equipment, it was decidedly pro-American, and it would relieve the U.S. of having an overt presence in the Persian Gulf.

During the five years preceding Carter's inauguration, the Shah of Iran had purchased some $10 billion in U.S. military matériel. The U.S. government's presence in the Persian Gulf region and its supply of oil from that area were contingent on the goodwill of the Shah. The United States looked to Pahlavi for the economic survival of Western industry, and he, in turn, relied on the United States for the arms and assistance to implement his vision for Iran's future. Failure on the part of either nation could cause unimagined economic and political upheaval.

Carter's Liberal Left leanings would dovetail perfectly with those inhabitants of "Foggy Bottom," the area in Washington where the State Department is located. The organization was composed of decidedly Left-leaning Arabists with views contrary to most Israel-supporting American presidents. Their grasp of foreign policy often tended to favor accommodation rather than confrontation. This was especially true during the late 1970s; the attitude at State was anti-Shah and anti-Iran. This divisive position would haunt American interests abroad for decades to come. It would open the door for the fanatical Ayatollah Khomeini and his Islamic Revolution.

By the mid '70s the Shah changed from an insecure young leader to one fully in control of Iran's bureaucracy. Pahlavi was working to drag the country into the twentieth century and was not seeking advice or direction, not even from his mentor, the United States government. How did the Shah make the transition from a retiring young man to the grandiose ruler?

Marvin Zonis writes in *Majestic Failure: The Fall of the Shah* that Pahlavi "relied on four principal sources of...support to maintain his capacity to act as Shah...the admiration he received from others [i.e., the people of Iran]...strength he received through a very small number of close personal associates...a life-long belief in a watchful and protecting God who had decreed his success in carrying out a divine mission...important diplomatic and personal psychological ties with the United States."[95] Perhaps there was one other well of adulation for the Shah that, when it had run dry, contributed to his unpopularity: the support of the mass media. It is likely that the failure of these five sources of support for Pahlavi led to his downfall.

The liberal media in America became obsessed with turning the Shah from the champion of modernization to the monster of human rights violations. One mass market paperback fiction writer of the times wrote a novel entitled *A Bullet for the Shah: All They Had to Do Was Kill the World's Most Powerful Man*. In an interview with a former U.S. joint chief of staff, I asked the question, "Who determines when wars are won or lost?"

He replied, "If you will commit not to divulge that I told you, I will tell you the truth." I affirmed my commitment to keep his identity secret. His response: "The media. Take Somalia. Why did we go there? We went there because of the media's obsession. Why did we leave? For the same reason! This is why we lost the Vietnam War and Cambodia." I was stunned at his revelation. However, in looking back over the life of the Shah of Iran it confirmed that he was riding high when Jimmy Carter took office. Three years later he was, as Henry Kissinger asserted, "a flying Dutchman looking for a port."[96] He was a ruler without subjects, a king without a throne, a man without a country, a long-time ally bereft of its partner, the United States.

Newly elected President Jimmy Carter was also the recipient of the years-earlier Richard Nixon–Henry Kissinger arms sale policies. It relegated the security of one of the world's richest regions into the hands of a monarch whose determination to bring social and economic change to Iran did not take into account the smoldering fire of Islamic instability that would soon explode.

The Shah had enjoyed a prolonged political association with the Republican administrations of presidents Richard Nixon and Gerald Ford. Under Nixon the Shah purchased vast supplies of military equipment, grew his army to the point that it had doubled the size of British forces, and increased his military budget from $293 million in 1963 to $7.3 billion in 1977.[97] The enormous amounts the Shah spent on the purchase of arms was a boon to the U.S. economy during the oil crisis of the Nixon presidency. Pahlavi was understandably wary of Carter, whose campaign platform stressed both human rights issues and a reduction in arms sales. The Shah was concerned that he would be viewed not as a progressive ruler but rather as tyrannical. This was of major concern because the Shah's regime had been criticized for the actions of its secret police, SAVAK, and had a long-standing and lucrative relationship with U.S. arms suppliers.

Asadollah Alam, appointed prime minister by the Shah in July 1962, was Pahlavi's personal confidant. Alam and the Shah had been classmates at the exclusive Swiss boarding school, Institut Le Rosey. He remained in office through major industrial and social reforms implemented by the Shah, sometimes referred to as the "White Revolution." Alam wrote of the Shah's concerns over Carter's election in his diary: "Who knows what sort of calamity he [Carter] may unleash on the world?"[98] He also wrote that Carter was "a political lightweight. He's managed to duck out of any clear statement policy issues."[99]

In September of 1976 Alam met with Ambassador Uri Lubrani, Israel's representative in Iran, and asked for his assistance to help improve the Shah's image with the American people. (It was Lubrani who co-authored, along with Reuven Merhav, a Mossad member, one of two reports which predicted the overthrow of the Shah within twelve months. Lubrani's report was so persuasive that Iranian Jews were cautioned to flee the country and seek refuge elsewhere.) Gholam Reza Afkhami, an advisor to Pahlavi, felt that, "No one could match Iran's power, Iran's culture, or Iran's history.... It's important to realize this in order to understand why [the Shah] did what he did... And also why everyone else in the world said that he was arrogant."[100]

Dr. Abdol Majid Majidi, Minister of Planning and Budget under the Shah, revealed to me that Pahlavi did, indeed, have a very good reason to be wary of Carter. He said of Carter's bid for the White House:

> At that time, the Democrats wanted to win in the election. Whatever could damage the Republicans, they were using; they were not thinking of America's interests in long-term or middle-term.... Carter was winning at any price, by condemning Iran and human rights.... All the speeches... were mentioning how they established human rights in Iran.... [Henry] Precht prepared a report describing the situation in Iran and what we should do in order to create stability and strengthen the Shah's position.... Precht said that he sent it to Brzezinski, who put it in the briefcase of Carter.... Two months after that day, Carter read that report... when it was too late.... [It was] a positive report for the president who was Jimmy Carter.... Two months after...Iran has really, literally deteriorated.[101]

Perhaps Carter felt that he could succeed where Mossadegh and others had failed. He would oust the Shah of Iran in favor of the religious cleric Ayatollah Ruhollah Khomeini.

6

CARTER'S POLICIES—
FOREIGN & DOMESTIC

"What might be called 'Carterism'—a sentimental,
neo-pacifist view of the world—has come to define the
core ideology of Democratic Party liberalism today."
(STEVEN HAYWARD) [102]

WHEN THE NEWLY ELECTED PRESIDENT began to form his cabinet, it quickly took the shape of a dovecote. Senator and presidential candidate Eugene McCarthy, the quintessential dove, lauded Carter's choices as "quite close to those I would have made myself." [103]

Carter liberally filled cabinet positions from both the Kennedy and Johnson ranks and with what some labeled "corporate liberals" such as Michael Blumenthal. One of the more controversial of Carter's appointments was Andrew Young as ambassador to the United Nations. Young entered the political scene during the Civil Rights Movement. His defense of the Black Panthers on an ABC program in 1970 was recounted in an article in *Commentary*. While never a member of the infamous group, Young was, nevertheless, enthralled with their ideology that the non-Western world was in need of liberation and that Blacks in America would play a significant role in achieving that objective. During the interview Young said, "If the white West is incapable of brotherhood with colored peoples, then this small body of colored peoples, Black people within the West, may be the revolutionary vanguard that God has ordained to destroy the whole thing."

Young was then asked by the interviewer, "Would you support the destruction of Western civilization if you were convinced that the rest of the world would be liberated?"

His reply: "I probably would."[104]

On Andrew Young's first trip to Africa as ambassador to the UN, he stepped off the plane onto the tarmac and greeted the assembled crowd with the Black Panther salute of a clenched fist. To further compound his political *faux pas* (plural), Young touted Cuban soldiers as providing stability in the region, hyped Soviet-trained guerillas as liberation forces, and denounced Britain as the inventor of racism.

His tendency to "shoot from the lip" landed Young in hot water again during the trials of Soviet dissidents Anatoly Scharansky and Aleksandr Ginzburg. When asked to comment on the fate of the dissidents, Young replied that there were "hundreds, maybe thousands of people I would categorize as political prisoners" in U.S. prisons. He added, "Ten years ago, I myself was tried in Atlanta for having organized a [civil rights] protest movement."[105]

Young's timing was abysmal! According to *Time* magazine, news of the release of Young's interview occurred just as Secretary of State Cyrus Vance handed a communiqué from President Carter to his counterpart, Soviet Foreign Minister Andrei Gromyko. TASS, the Soviet news agency, gleefully reported Young's statement as official proof that "political persecution is widespread in the United States."[106]

Young's ouster from the Carter circle came in September 1979. The ambassador had long pushed the Carter administration to allow him direct access to the Palestinian Liberation Organization (PLO).

It was Young's express desire to include the terrorist group in all Middle East peace talks. In a violation of specific United States policy, Young met secretly with the PLO's UN observer. The ever-vigilant Israeli government protested the meeting. Young's claim that the meeting was accidental was eventually refuted and his resignation tendered. While Young's lack of caution and self-control were responsible for his downfall, he was thought to be the perfect representative of Carter's true foreign policy and his liberal leftist leanings. This proved to be a correct assessment after Carter left office. The former president formed a "mutual admiration society" relationship with PLO head Yasser Arafat.

While revolution was bubbling beneath the surface in Iran and Carter insiders seemed determined to strip the Shah of power, the president was moving forward with other foreign policy initiatives that would have lasting repercussions—namely for the Panama Canal and for Israel.

Given his actions, it seems that Jimmy Carter entered the presidency determined to right what he saw as the wrongs of other administrations. As mentioned previously, Carter immediately began to fulfill his campaign promises. He pardoned almost all of the Vietnam War draft dodgers, who had either gone into hiding or fled the country to escape induction into the armed forces. He ended the production of the B-1 bomber and made good on his promise to rework federal agencies that were providing some of the same services. President Carter also announced that he would begin the process of cutting aid to foreign governments that were guilty of human rights violations.

Carter vowed to base his foreign policy decisions on moral issues. In an address to the UN he contended "that the United States has not only a legal right but a responsibility to speak out against human rights violations…[and that] foreign assistance was to be favorably linked to the human rights performance of the recipient country."[107]

John Dumbrell wrote:

For liberals, the policy promised a crusade against right-wing dictators (especially the military governments of Latin America), and embodied an atonement for Vietnam. For conservatives, the policy offered a lever against communism and its abuses—also a way, in Odom's words, "to really beat up morally on the Soviets."[108]

Carter's good intentions were insufficient to fully execute his planned foreign policy agenda. The actualities of relations between countries gave way to Carter's unpredictable and contradictory policies. At times, the president vociferously rebuked some violations of individual nations, while at other times he was strangely silent when flagrant cruelty was revealed in other countries. In Latin America, for instance, Carter targeted tyrannical right-wing regimes while ignoring the leftist rulers. As a result, he was forced to abandon his idealism in favor of a return to the Nixon policies he had initially eschewed.

Carter's greatest foreign aid/human rights debacle would occur in Iran, and all because, as Clair Apodaca pointed out, "Although foreign aid may have a humanitarian effect, the primary reason for its allocation is self-interest."[109]

Having assumed the reins of government, Carter immediately moved to breathe new life into the Middle East peace process and proposed a conference in Geneva that would bring Israel to the table with Arab states, the PLO, and possibly the Soviet Union. Israel was very much opposed to a conference that included the Soviets. Negotiations between Israel and her neighbors had taken a backseat to the presidential campaign and Carter's ultimate win. Seizing on the suggestions offered in a Brookings Institute report, the president chose to eschew former Secretary of State Henry Kissinger's slower methodology in favor of a multilateral technique.

Carter was quick to arrange trips to visit leaders in the region whose assistance would be invaluable. By his first anniversary in office, the president had logged trips to meet with Egypt's President Anwar Sadat, Jordan's King Hussein, President Hafez al-Assad in Syria and Israel's Prime Minister Yitzhak Rabin. Before President Carter could see his dream of another Geneva Conference complete with a Palestinian delegation come to fruition, Yitzhak Rabin lost an election to Menachem Begin. Unbeknownst to Carter, Sadat was already working secretly with Israel to establish an outline for talks. Eventually Carter would become an intermediary for the two nations.

Even though Carter had campaigned on a human rights platform, once in office his administration continued to support some countries where violations of even the most basic human rights ran rampant, i.e., the Philippines, Nicaragua, and Indonesia. Carter's selective human rights policies seemed to favor the leftist-leaning countries with infusions of money, arms, and positive press, while the more right-leaning countries received nothing except severe sanctions.

Carter's policies in Nicaragua, for instance, contributed to the unseating of a strong American ally, President Anastasio Somoza, in favor of a communist regime headed by Daniel Ortega. Under Somoza Nicaragua enjoyed free enterprise, religious freedom, an open press, and democratic elections. That ended when Ortega seized power. Somoza placed his confidence in an American president that he thought would never betray his people.

When Somoza penned his memoirs, entitled *Nicaragua Betrayed*, he listed a number of actions taken by the Carter administration that he felt were directly or indirectly responsible for the fall of Nicaragua to communism:

> *After one week in office, Mr. Carter cut off all military assistance.*

> *By Executive Decree, Mr. Carter prohibited the sales of military hardware to Nicaragua.*

An Israeli ship destined for Nicaragua and loaded with life-saving arms and ammunition was forced to return to Israel.

Mr. Carter successfully closed all markets where Nicaragua could purchase arms and ammunition.

Mr. Carter's representative on the International Monetary Fund twice blocked badly-needed standby credit for Nicaragua.[110]

Somoza also blamed Carter's policies for blocking financing for a hydroelectric dam project, instigating a boycott of shipping companies that resulted in Nicaragua's coffee crop not reaching foreign markets, closing U.S. borders to incoming beef exports from Nicaragua, and interfering with internal monetary policies. Somoza pointed out that Carter's Human Rights Commission was favorable to the Communist-supported Sandinista rebels. In addition, the IRS was instructed to accept as tax deductible donations made to the Communist Sandinistas; donations to Somoza's freedom fighters were declared invalid. (Shortly after the release of Somoza's book, he was assassinated. Coincidentally, several months later Somoza's co-writer, Jack Cox, and publisher, Larry McDonald, died aboard Korean Airlines Flight 007. It had been shot down by the Soviet Air Force.)

As a final indictment against Carter, Somoza wrote:

My country, my people, and I were betrayed. That betrayal does not rest with the American people, but with the president of the United States. My love for the United States and her people is as great as it ever was. My prayer is that those who now lead the United States will not betray humanity. If that happens, God help us all, for then it would be the entire free world, and not just Nicaragua betrayed.[111]

Another of Carter's perceived "wrongs that must be righted" involved renegotiating the Panama Canal Treaty. The U.S. purchased the land on which to build the Canal in 1903 following a revolution in Columbia. Estimates vary, but the consensus is that the waterway was completed at a cost of approximately $350 million dollars with a loss of lives to disease and hardship at well over 5,600 Americans. (This does not include the money spent by the French on an earlier attempt to span Panama; some 22,000 French workers died during that project.)

Carter responded to what he and other liberals saw as blatant empire-building and military expansionism (especially since the United States had some fourteen bases in Panama). In response to anti-American protests in the strategic tiny Central American country, Carter began his push to achieve what other liberal presidents before him had failed to do due to the opposition of conservatives in Congress.

By the time Carter took office in January of 1977, a military presence in Panama seemed to be of little importance, especially since the Canal could not handle the large tankers or aircraft carriers being built. It didn't seem to faze Mr. Carter that Panama was in the hands of Omar Torrijos' communist government. With a twisted sense of largess, the president seemed to feel that Torrijos with his ties to communist regimes worldwide merited the right of self-determination.

Carter's success in pushing the treaty through Congress would be yet another of his foreign policy debacles that would come back to haunt the U.S. In an article for the *American Daily*, Edward Daley wrote of the chicanery pulled on the U.S. Senate during the treaty negotiations. Daley alleges that Senator Dennis Deconcini authored a treaty containing paragraphs that allowed the United States to use military force to protect the Canal Zone, if necessary. Panamanian dictator Omar Torrijos objected to the inclusion of the paragraphs. Carter encouraged Torrijos to write his own amendment. Says Daley, "Knowing that the U.S. Senate would not accept the treaty with the Torrijos language, Carter presented [the treaty to the Senate] with the previous [Deconcini] version; [the Senate] ratified it without being aware that another version even existed. The two countries never actually agreed to the same treaty."[112]

In 1999 former President Jimmy Carter presided over the transfer of the Canal Zone from American to Panamanian oversight. It didn't seem to matter one whit to Carter that the U.S. had purchased the canal nearly a century prior, had maintained the canal, and had paid ridiculously excessive fees for the privilege of using its own property. It seemed to escape him totally that "communism" and "self-determination" were not mutually compatible terms. Panama was not the only country on which Carter set his sights; on his watch thirteen nations fell into communist hands and, some claim, with help from Mr. Carter.

With the end of U.S. involvement in oversight of the Panama Canal, it was no surprise that the ruling party in Panama awarded the Canal operations to Hutchison Whampoa Limited, a company based in Red China. According to Hutchison Whampoa's website, access to the Panama Canal is now controlled on both the Atlantic and Pacific ports by the Chinese. Also on its list of ports and related services are the Grand Bahamas Airport, the Freeport (Bahamas) Container Port, the Freeport Harbor Company (one of the largest cruise ship facilities in the Bahamas), the Buenos Aires container terminal, Ensenada International Terminal and Ensenada Cruiseport Village on the U.S.-Mexico border on the Pacific Ocean, as well as a terminal at the Port of Veracruz on Mexico's east coast and another terminal in the state of Michoacan on its Pacific coast. Hutchison Whampoa also boasts a terminal at the Port of Manta in Ecuador.

According to an article in BNet, Hutchison Whampoa is more than a Hong Kong shipping giant. Company chairman Li Ka-shing is an important cog in the economic machinery of the Chinese Communist Party and the PLA (People's Liberation Army), the unified military organization of the People's Republic of China. Li is a board member of the Chinese government's main investment arm, the China International Trust and Investment Corp., or CITIC, run by official PLA arms marketeer and smuggler Wang Jun.[113]

While the American people came to accept Jimmy Carter's give-away of the Panama Canal as inevitable, time has proven it to be an incredibly unwise move, especially as China's ring of control of ports just outside our borders has widened.

Many of Carter's domestic policies proved to be as precarious as his foreign policies. Despite his dovish leanings, the military budget claimed a large share of Carter's proposed budget. Rather than decreasing the budget as he had promised during his campaign, President Carter increased it by about $10 billion and proposed that the U.S. spend as much as one trillion dollars on its military.

When he took office, Jimmy Carter was determined to restore the faith of the American people in their government. Unfortunately for the president, the public's perception of his ability to keep his campaign promises waned early, even during his first year. Although his supporters were not quite ready to admit that Carter's campaign promises were not being fulfilled, early polls indicated that confidence in the newly entrenched president was decreasing. It seems that people began to wonder if the man from Plains, Georgia, could cope with the realities of Washington, D.C.

Inflation and high unemployment rates were a nemesis early on for the president, and he seemed to be unable to deal with either. Business leaders expressed concern over far-reaching legislation to overhaul Social Security and the national tax system, both a high priority for the president. When Carter's plan was finally sent to Congress, it contained a payroll tax increase of 300 percent over a ten-year period—the largest tax increase ever proposed by a president during peacetime. This alone raised red flags for the business community and increased its doubt about Carter's economic policies.

Carter's failure to disclose to Congress his proposals regarding additional tax increases sent a shiver through the business district. Already facing possible rises in Social Security taxes, the failure of Carter's complicated energy bill, and no information on tax proposals, business leaders focused on the possibility of higher taxes and interest rates, uncontrollable inflation, enormous budget deficits, and a looming recession. The stock market plummeted, and Americans at large were beginning to be concerned about the possibility of a recession.

Robert Lekachman, an economist, wrote of Carter's tax policies: "Perhaps the president's most outrageous act occurred last November when he signed into law an $18 billion tax reduction, the bulk of whose benefits accrue to affluent individuals and corporations."[114]

Critics of Carter economics referred to the burgeoning crisis as the "misery index." This so-called index was used to measure the effects of inflation, unemployment, and the prime interest rate. Frustration with the Carter administration was growing as these three indicators increased. Also growing was the concern over the energy crisis fueled by Carter's inability to work with Congress to resolve what would become a national emergency. Overall, Carter was beginning to look weak and ineffectual as a leader.

7

A CRISIS OF
CONFIDENCE

*"Carter's energy plan required four phone book-sized volumes to
spell out... The most significant result...was the creation of the
cabinet-level Department of Energy, which quickly came to have
a budget that rivaled the combined profits of the major
oil companies."* (STEVEN HAYWARD)[115]

IN JULY OF 1979 JIMMY CARTER FACED, perhaps,
one of his greatest domestic challenges as president. It was during
that month that the energy crisis Carter had tried desperately to
avoid exploded. The Organization of Petroleum Exporting Countries
(OPEC) announced yet another oil price increase, and gasoline
prices went through the roof. That was followed by purported
shortages nationwide. The result was long lines and short tempers
at the gas pumps. Gasoline that had sold for $14 per barrel rose to
$40 per barrel on the spot market. Prior to that time, the price of
OPEC oil had fluctuated between $2.50/barrel and $14/barrel.

I asked Dr. Mina, director, National Iranian Oil Company,
if it was correct to blame the Shah for the rise in oil prices.
"The whole OPEC was looking for that possibility of increasing
the...price of oil," said Dr. Mina. "One day OPEC should be able

to control prices and not leave it entirely in the hands of the international companies to decide what the price of [oil] should be.... naturally Iran was in favor of one day being able to control the prices. Because nowhere in the world was a commodity produced by a country and the price determined by someone else. It was natural for OPEC countries to say that we are producers of crude oil... we have to have a say in the price of the commodity like any other commodity."[116]

James R. Schlesinger, Carter's energy secretary, lit a match to an already volatile situation when he reported to Congress that the energy crisis and lack of Iranian oil imports were "prospectively more serious" than the oil embargo enforced by the Arabs in 1973.[117] Although covertly maintaining a diplomatic understanding with Israel, Iran had aided Egypt during the 1973 Yom Kippur War by providing crude. The Shah had also furnished transport planes and pilots to Saudi Arabia and evacuated wounded soldiers to Iran for medical care. (Perhaps it was this, as much as anything, that led Sadat to welcome the Shah to Egypt following the Islamic Revolution in Iran.)

Pahlavi refused permission to the Soviets to overfly Iran in military transports, but he did permit civilian airliners to deliver parts and supplies to the Arabs. While not engaged in actual warfare, the Shah allowed Iranian transport planes to ferry a Saudi battalion into battle and to evacuate wounded Syrians to Tehran for treatment.

Covertly and at a crucial time during the Yom Kippur War, Pahlavi returned a shipment of artillery shells and electronic equipment sold to him by the Israelis. The Shah, however, was averse to joining the 1973 oil stoppage and refused to use Iran's black gold as a bargaining chip against the U.S. or Israel. Following the 1973 conflict the Shah offered a multi-million-dollar loan to Anwar El Sadat that would enable the Egyptian leader to expand the Suez Canal, reconstruct Port Said, and erect a pipeline between Suez and Alexandria. This action negated the need for the Israeli line from Eilat to Ashkelon and would have allowed the Shah to halt or severely restrict the flow of oil. The Israeli government was able to compel the Shah to honor their past agreement and continue the flow of oil as usual.

As the oil embargo raged on, Carter's approval rating plummeted to 25 percent and he retreated to Camp David, surrounding himself with cabinet members and experts from whom he sought counsel. Following more than a week of meetings, Carter decided to address the American people. July 15, 1979, was the date the president chose to give his speech, which was later known as his "malaise" speech. In his address Carter chastised the American people for their overindulgence and dependence on foreign oil, and he laid out a six-point program to resolve the energy crisis that included a stringent conservation program:

> *"This nation will never use more foreign oil than we did in 1977—never.... The generation-long growth in our dependence on foreign oil will be stopped dead in its tracks right now.*
>
> *I will use my presidential authority to set import quotas. I'm announcing tonight that for 1979 and 1980 I will forbid the entry into this country of one drop of foreign oil more than these goals allow.*
>
> *I am asking for the most massive peacetime commitment... to develop America's own alternative sources of fuel—from coal, from oil shale, from plant products for gasohol, from unconventional gas, from the sun.*
>
> *I'm asking Congress to mandate...that our nation's utility companies cut their massive use of oil by 50 percent within the next decade.*
>
> *I will urge Congress to create an energy mobilization board which...will have the responsibility and authority to cut through the red tape, the delays, and the endless roadblocks to completing key energy projects.*

I ask Congress to give me authority for mandatory conservation and for standby gasoline rationing."[118]

Following his address Carter's approval ratings climbed, but it was not long before people began to surmise that there was nothing actually wrong with *them*; change needed to come at the top, in the White House. Roger Wilkins, a historian agreed: "When your leadership is demonstrably weaker than it should be, you don't then point at the people and say, 'It's your problem.'"[119] Just weeks later the president called for the resignations of his entire cabinet and ultimately accepted those of five members. What Carter considered his "crisis of confidence" paled by comparison to the events that would follow.

According to Henry Kissinger, national security advisor to Richard Nixon and secretary of state to both Nixon and Gerald Ford: "The Carter administration has managed the extraordinary feat of having, at one and the same time, the worst relations with our allies, the worst relations with our adversaries, and the most serious upheavals in the developing world since the end of the Second World War."[120]

While President Carter was busily pursuing the giveaway of the Panama Canal and courting Communist dictators in South and Central America, the underlying turmoil in Iran was at the point of near-eruption. The Carter administration had little, if any, reason to suppose that its policies would ultimately result in plunging Iran into the grasp of the Grand Ayatollah Ruhollah Khomeini; or did it?

As the poster boy for ambivalence, President Carter had sent mixed signals to the Shah regarding the actions Pahlavi was to take to preserve his leadership in Iran. The Shah had no idea whether or not Carter would support him if he took resolute measures to quell the rising tide of revolution. On the one hand, Carter seemed to support the Shah; while, in typical fashion, the president emphasized the need to avoid violence and promote human rights initiatives. The Shah was left wondering just what actions he should take in order not to offend Carter and his minions. This indecision would prove to be the beginning of the end of the Pahlavi dynasty in Iran.

In May 1977 Carter dispatched Cyrus Vance to Iran for a Central Treaty Organization (CENTO) meeting. Vance embarked with a 20-page classified memo. The document informed the secretary of state that he would be "the first senior civilian official of the Carter administration to talk with the Shah." It assured Vance that Pahlavi was "in a stronger position internally than at any previous time in his long [36-year] rule," that well-known terror organizations "have not caught the imagination of the populace, and except for the remote possibility of a successful assassination, are not an immediate threat to the Shah." The memo did not mention a possible opposition led by religious figures. It concluded, "We expect this stability to persist for the next several years."[121] After meeting with Vance, Pahlavi's opinion of the secretary of state was that he was "more a bureaucrat than a politician."[122]

The briefing paper also mentioned Carter's human rights project and gave Vance specific directions for its inclusion in discussions:

> *In discussing the priorities of President Carter, you will want to refer to the importance of human rights to the president personally and as an element of our national consensus. You could comment that we have noted steps taken by Iran to improve certain human rights practices and its image abroad and encourage further steps in this direction.*[123]

A CIA report delivered in August of 1977 seemed to support the State Department's evaluation of the situation in Iran. This intelligence organization purported: "The Shah will be an active participant in Iranian life well into the 1980s. There will be no radical change in Iranian political behavior in the near future." The CIA was convinced it was "looking at evolution, not revolution" in Iran.[124]

Manoucher Ganji, a historian, wrote of the reality of the situation faced by the Shah and his monarchy: "As it turned out, the United States offered no help. Instead it often spoke with multiple voices to a distraught Shah. From George Ball and Zbigniew Brzezinski to Cyrus Vance to Jimmy Carter and William Sullivan, each offered a different bit of advice."[125] In typical Carter fashion, he had again demonstrated his ability to straddle the fence and produce nothing substantive.

A January 7, 1978, article in *Etela'at*, an Iranian newspaper under the editorial control of Minister of Information Dariush Homayoun, sparked riots in the religious center of Qom. The article openly denigrated Khomeini: "He [Khomeini] was not truly Iranian; he had British connections; he led a dissolute life; and he wrote Sufic [mystical Persian love] poetry." The purpose of this article was unclear, but its effect was crystal clear. The seminary and bazaar in Qom closed, and 4,000 theology students and other Muslims demonstrated, calling for a public apology…the next day a communiqué from Khomeini began orchestrating the opposition's response.[126]

A meeting of what Ambassador Sullivan described as "An Eclectic Group of [Iranian] Oppositionists…Blaming USG via the Shah for Iran's Ills," drew this comment:

> *Except for the problem of fighting for the turn to speak, the group had a grand time. They were polite but pitiless in assailing USG [United States Government] policy and our puppet Shah…. [We] delivered our semi-official Embassy message that troops will be ready when the Shah leaves. Therefore, crowds should do nothing to provoke them. And meanwhile, we will use whatever influence we have to restrain [the Iranian] army. Moderate religious leaders had previously accepted this message graciously, as did several leading bazaaris. This group, however, reacted sharply.*[127]

By March 1978 the U.S. Defense Intelligence Agency produced a document entitled, "Iran: Religious-Inspired Opposition." It was clear that at least some in the Carter administration were beginning to look in a different direction regarding the opposition in Iran.

Although the report recounts the lengthy and comprehensive history of Shia Islam, it advises no action.

Homayoun later told a press conference in Tehran that the troubles in Qom were "extremely well planned." Rioters were being moved from city to city by private transport. He said there was evidence that Palestinian extremists were involved. Demands were being made for the rigid enforcement of Islamic law with the closure of cinemas, bars, and nightclubs. The agitators opposed television and the emancipation of women.[128]

Unlike those who attributed the Shah's downfall to his desire to modernize Iran, Eric Rouleau, a Middle East journalist for the French newspaper *Le Monde*, was of a different opinion. Rouleau wrote in an article on the revolt against the Shah:

> *The first signs of revolt passed unnoticed. The explosions of rage in the spring of 1978, first in Tabriz and then in Qom, were attributed to "obscurantist mullahs" hostile to the Shah's agrarian reform. The immense demonstrations by millions of Iranians, as well as the strikes in the administrations, factories, schools, universities, and oil fields, which paralyzed the state and in the last analysis caused the monarch's inglorious departure, were attributed to the fanaticism of the Iranian people.*
>
> *Rare were those who suggested that modernity is not necessarily synonymous with progress or well-being, or that the concepts of economic development current in the West, where quick material gain is often the only valid criterion, do not necessarily correspond to the true needs and interests of developing nations.*[129]

In April Ambassador Sullivan fired off a secret telegram to Secretary Vance. It was marked "NODIS" (No Distribution). He wrote, "I am becoming increasingly concerned by the evidence that Iranian authorities have decided to resort to heavy-handed means to discourage dissident political action."[130] Undersecretary Warren

Christopher responded to Sullivan's disquiet: "We share your concern about recent violence in Iran, including evidence of strong-arm tactics by the GOI (Government of Iran). We believe GOI should itself be concerned over widespread reporting in U.S. media of these indications of unrest in Iran." Christopher's memo advised Sullivan to discuss his fears with the Iranian prime minister.[131]

A telegram from Sullivan to Vance on June 19, 1978, indicated, "Lawyers have been at the forefront of the opposition movement in Tehran, and we can expect a renewed determination of this group to keep pressing for further change. They have told us privately that they will be monitoring court cases closely for evidence of improper procedure on the part of government officials, including prosecutors and judges."[132] Where were these same lawyers when Khomeini's revolutionaries began to execute their fellow countrymen after the Shah's departure, and why were they not present to represent those charged and condemned before kangaroo courts?

Late in 1978 the Carter administration received a lengthy shopping list for arms and communications devices from the Shah. Sullivan was concerned about the effects such a massive arms buildup would have on the general Iranian population and on the economy. The other side of the coin was the amount of money such sales poured into American coffers. Iran topped the list of buyers at over $4 billion annually.

In my conversation with Her Majesty Farah Pahlavi, I asked about the quantity of arms purchased by the Shah:

> *In those days when my husband was making a strong army much of the equipment was bought from America. We were buying also from Europe.... Then all the opposition people said, "The Shah loves these; it's like toys, a game, buying arms. He doesn't need it." But then, the Iraq/Iran War happened.*
>
> *If it were not for that army and for the trained military, especially pilots, we would have lost to Saddam Hussein in the first two days.... The Islamic Republic had assassinated*

many of our generals and military; many flew away from Iran, and some were in jail. They took the pilots out of jail; their families were held hostage so that they wouldn't fly away, but rather would fight against the invaders. Those who were against us must remember that.[133]

The Shah's arms list included F-14 and F-16 fighters, 707 tankers, P-3Cs, and other military supplies. Pahlavi was particularly interested in the purchase of the F-18, but his request was denied. Also on the list were crowd-control devices such as tear gas, ammunition, and riot gear. Ambassador Sullivan strongly opposed the sale of riot gear to the Shah. It was his opinion that such an infusion of equipment would only serve to encourage the Iranian military to consider a coup should the Shah be ousted. Both Sullivan and Cyrus Vance further pointed out that the British had already provided the necessary paraphernalia and instruction needed for crowd control. Some State Department heads, including Patricia Derian (Assistant Secretary of State for Human Rights and Humanitarian Affairs), Anthony Lake (Policy Planning), and Leslie Gelb (Political-Military Bureau), were fiercely opposed to the request. According to Sullivan, there were some who "were so strongly opposed to the Shah because of the human rights abuses of his regime that they wished to see him collapse no matter what the consequences for the United States or its allies."[134]

In order to appease the Shah Carter dispatched Zbigniew Brzezinski to Tehran for talks with him.

The Shah was confident in presenting his shopping list to the Carter administration; after all, Brzezinski had assured the king of continuing support:

The U.S. supports you without any reservation whatsoever, completely and fully in this present crisis. You have our complete support.... Secondly, we will support whatever decisions you take regarding either the form or composition of the government that you decide upon. And thirdly, we are not, and I repeat, not encouraging any particular solution.... it seems to me [you] have a problem of combining some gestures which would be appealing in a general sense with a need for some specific actions which would demonstrate effective authority.[135]

Now, *that* was certainly a clear-cut solution to the Shah's growing predicament! Pahlavi telephoned Sullivan for clarification of Brzezinski's vague advice. Sullivan also sidestepped the Shah with promises to contact Washington. When no answer was forthcoming either from Washington or Sullivan, the Shah concluded, "The fact that no one contacted me during the crisis in an official way explains about the American attitude.... the Americans wanted me out."[136] The Shah's former son-in-law and ambassador to the United States, Ardeshir Zahedi, told me of the Shah's frustrations with Sullivan. Pahlavi felt he was a victim of American hypocrisy. He was getting mixed signals from Sullivan and felt the American ambassador was not heeding Brzezinski's instructions.[137]

It was also in 1978 that Moscow issued a warning to the Carter administration regarding support of the Shah. Leonid Brezhnev, the Soviet Premier, cautioned:

It must be clear that any interference, especially military interference in the affairs of Iran—a state which directly borders on the Soviet Union—would be regarded as a matter affecting security interests.... The events taking place in that country constitute purely internal affairs, and the questions involved in them should be decided by the Iranians—the Shah has ruled with an iron will.[138]

Carter's Secretary of State Cyrus Vance responded halfheartedly that the U.S. "will continue to support the Shah in his efforts to restore domestic tranquility...and does not intend to interfere in the affairs of another country."[139] Carter's response sounded more like a death knell than encouragement from a supportive ally. When asked if the Shah could triumph, Carter muttered, "I don't know. I hope so."[140] Although the president, Brzezinski, and Vance realized that Iran was vitally important in maintaining security in the Persian Gulf area, they were single-minded in their determination to push the human rights agenda and to halt the sale of arms to the Shah. Vance wrote in *Hard Choices* that, "Neither the president nor I wished to use human rights as an ideological weapon but rather as a basic element of our foreign policy. We applauded and supported the measures the Shah was beginning to take to improve human rights; he had already begun to curb SAVAK...in its use of extralegal measures to control subversion."[141]

The debacle that would come in Iran following the Shah's departure would wreak havoc in the oil-rich Persian Gulf. It opened the door not only to the meteoric rise of Islamic fundamentalism but also for the Soviet invasion of Afghanistan. Almost overnight Afghanistan was converted from a neutral nation to a springboard for the Russians to move closer to the Indian Ocean.

Zahedi had also warned of the Soviet Union's intentions to subdue Afghanistan. Reportedly, the Shah wrote a letter to Carter warning him that Russia had definitely set its sites on Afghanistan and was moving on the region even then. Pahlavi asked for additional arms and supplies to meet the threat. By failing to sufficiently back the Shah in Iran and abdicating its position of strength in the region, the U.S. was unable to take overt steps to halt the forward progress of the USSR. Attempts to enlist needed allies in Egypt, Pakistan, and Saudi Arabia would still find the U.S. unprepared for the Soviet invasion of Afghanistan. It is difficult to understand how Carter's inner circle, and especially Brzezinski and Stansfield Turner, could have so completely missed the signs of instability and petulance emanating from Muslim leaders in Afghanistan even in the early days of the administration.

As Brzezinski wrote in his memoir, *Power and Principle*, "The longer-range strategic and political implications of the Iranian crisis came to be appreciated in Washington only gradually.... until [the seizure of the hostages]...the U.S. public was not overly aroused by a shift in power from a relatively unpopular Shah to a group of 'reformers.'"[142]

It is incomprehensible to think that the Ayatollah Ruhollah Khomeini could so mesmerize the majority of an entire nation with his persuasive rhetoric that the populace would blindly follow him. Khomeini had promised them what would be in American political terms "a car in every garage, and a chicken in every pot," and they believed him. Much like Jimmy Carter, Khomeini championed everyone but promised nothing in the way of programs to achieve his ends. Even though he emphasized "change," Khomeini offered no plan to implement changes.

Surely, that could not happen in America. Could someone rise up overnight and capture the hearts, minds, and will of the American people to the degree that they would be persuaded to vote him/her into office with little to establish credentials to govern this great nation? Think about it the next time you are tempted to blithely follow a leader because of his/her charisma, oratorical ability, and promises for hope and change. Or, is that what the American people did in November 2008?

CHAPTER

======== 8 ========

INDECISION SPAWNS
REVOLUTION

*"Khomeini's main attention was devoted to religious groups
associated with the National Front that were based in the United
States, Canada, France, Germany, and Britain, and it was these
groups which insured, until the time of the 1979 revolution,
that his pronouncements were properly circulated among
Iranians studying abroad."* (B A Q E R   M O I N) [143]

DURING THE SAME YEAR JIMMY CARTER attained
the White House, Iranian Islamic leader Ali Shari'ati died, thus
removing a huge potential rival to Ayatollah Ruhollah Khomeini and
solidifying Khomeini's support against the Shah in Iran. Shari'ati was
a French-trained sociologist of the same period as Khomeini and
contributed fuel to the fire of the Islamic Revolution when he
contended that:

> *All Shia's, irrespective of time and place, have the duty
> to oppose, resist, and even rebel against overwhelming odds
> in order to eradicate their contemporary ills...world
> imperialism, international Zionism, colonialism, exploita-
> tion, oppression, class inequality, cartels, multinational*

operations, racism, cultural imperialism, and gharbzadegi [loosely translated as being "besotted with anything Western"].[144]

Khomeini had been in exile since 1963, first in Turkey and then in Najaf, Iraq. His exile was the direct result of political protests against the rule of the Shah. He opposed what he referred to as the "Westoxication"[145] of the monarchy. He ranted against giving Iranian women the right to vote and called for the unification of the Muslim world. Khomeini spent a brief time under arrest in March 1963, but was soon back to his old fiery attacks against the Shah. He was arrested again in June of that year and spent two months in prison. In October 1963 he urged an embargo on parliamentary elections; that cost him eight months in prison and then deportation.

Moving from Turkey to Najaf, Khomeini found himself in an important center of Shia piety. It was there he established his reputation as an uncompromising opponent of Reza Pahlavi. Khomeini was to forever change the West's view of Iran and Shia Islam, and he would drastically change the future of one young revolutionary, Osama bin Laden.

A CIA memorandum states, "While in Iraq, Khomeini began working closely with the Islamic Terrorist Group *Mujahedeen-e-Khalq* (the People's Strugglers). In late 1972 Khomeini issued a religious declaration, or *Fatwa,* that enjoined faithful Shia to support the *Mujahedeen* and called for the devout to provide funds for their use. The money was raised from the *ulema* (Muslim scholars trained in Islamic law) and in the bazaars and funneled to Khomeini, who in turn gave it to the terrorists."[146] The Grand Ayatollah did, indeed, hold the strings of the purse filled with blood money from Libya and the PLO.

The CIA memorandum that documents this information, though severely censored with a black marker, also revealed that Khomeini had supplied funds for the *Mujahedeen* to target Americans:

The Mujahedeen embarked on a campaign of assassination of Americans to show their opposition to the Shah and to attract world publicity. In June 1973 two American Army officers were killed and in August 1976...three American employees of Rockwell International in Tehran.[147]

It was also in Najaf that Khomeini first made contact with PLO leader Yasser Arafat and enlisted his help to fight against his enemies: the Shah, the "Great Satan" (America), and the "Little Satan" (Israel). Arafat was more than willing to join forces with the Ayatollah. Although he did not personally meet the Shah until October 1969, Arafat had an axe to grind because the Shah had parted company with the PLO and its then-leader Ahmed Shukeiri in 1965 due to terrorist attacks on Israel and Jordan.

When the Shah finally met the militant Arafat in 1969, he was unimpressed with the diminutive terrorist. Arafat strutted into the room wearing a pistol and spouting lies about supposed PLO victories. The monarch told his aides following the meeting, "Arafat is no different from Shukeiri [the previous PLO leader]."[148] Pahlavi refused any further meetings with Arafat. Thus shunned, Arafat embraced Khomeini's determination to overthrow the Shah. In just months Arafat would take on the role of an active partner in the revolution by allowing young Iranians to train at his camps in Syria, Lebanon, Libya, and Iraq.

Arafat's notoriety would mushroom during the 1972 Olympics in Munich, Germany, when members of Black September, a militant extremist group with ties to Arafat's Fatah organization, would take eleven members of Israel's Olympic team hostage. After hours of negotiations between the leaders of the terrorist group and the German police, the eleven Israelis, five terrorists, and one German police officer would die during a bloody gun battle at the NATO air base in Firstenfeldbruck.

Arafat blithely swore that he was not responsible for the actions of the renegade arm of Fatah. However, Abu Daoud, the man who helped the terrorists scale the walls of the Olympic village on

September 5, 1972, refutes that assertion both in his memoir and in an interview with *Sports Illustrated*.

Daoud's book, *Palestine: From Jerusalem to Munich*, confirms "what many terrorism experts and Israeli officials long suspected... that the Black September organization, which Yasser Arafat and the Palestine Liberation Organization (PLO) always claimed was a renegade outfit, was in fact tightly controlled by Arafat. Even more shocking, however, was the allegation that [a top Arafat deputy, Mahmoud] Abbas...the man President George W. Bush has called a "man dedicated to peace"...provided the financing for the massacre."[149] [150]

Arafat and Khomeini were soon joined by the leftist organization headed by George Habash and other Marxist entities in Iran. (Habash was responsible for providing arms and aid to the *Fedayeen* (the more violent group which employed guerilla-style tactics), while Arafat underwrote the *Mujahedeen*. It was Habash who reportedly said of terrorist attacks against the Jews, "Killing one Jew far away from the field of battle is more effective than killing a hundred Jews on the field of battle...it attracts more attention."[151]) Proof of the alliance between Khomeini, Arafat, and Habash would reach SAVAK in July 1976. An agent seized a missive from Habash to Marxist leader Hamid Ashraf outlining the joint aims of the two groups. Letters from Habash to Iranian students in the U.S. also helped fuel the revolutionary fervor.

Another of Khomeini's closest advisors, Mustafa Ali Chamran, left Iran in 1957 to pursue a degree in physics at the University of California at Berkley. After finishing his degree in the U.S. Chamran moved to Lebanon, married a Palestinian woman, was indoctrinated in PLO goals, and later oversaw the training of Iranians in the PLO camps. His specialty was smuggling PLO terrorists and arms into Tehran. Chamran was repaid for his loyalty to Khomeini and his part in the revolution when he was named Khomeini's Minister of Defense.

Two events took place in Iran, both linked to the Shah and both spurring Khomeini and his followers to revenge. These two events essentially sealed the fate of the monarch. First, Ayatollah Hossein Ghaffari, a vocal critic of the Shah's regime, was allegedly tortured to death by Pahlavi's security forces. The cleric and Khomeini had corresponded during Khomeini's exile in Najaf; his death only added fuel to the Islamic revolutionary fires already burning in the Grand Ayatollah's chest.

Second, in October 1977 Khomeini's son Mustafa died of bulimia with heart complications, but antigovernment forces pointed the finger at the Shah's secret police, SAVAK, and Mustafa was proclaimed a martyr. This only served to further incite Khomeini's followers against the Shah. While there were various groups opposing the Shah's regime, i.e., leftists, the People's Mujahedin of Iran (MEK), Communists, and other groups, Khomeini had suddenly become the most popular opponent to Pahlavi's rule.

With the hope of improving the image of the United States as the benevolent superpower to the post-Vietnam world, Jimmy Carter created a special Office of Human Rights, and the Shah emerged high on the agency's target list. Having been very outspoken about the Shah's human rights record during his campaign, the newly elected president included that issue in his Inaugural Address:

> *"Our moral sense dictates a clear-cut preference for these societies which share with us an abiding respect for individual human rights. We do not seek to intimidate, but it is clear that a world which others can dominate with impunity would be inhospitable to decency and a threat to the well-being of all people."*[152]

Carter tapped Assistant Secretary of State for Near Eastern and South Asian Affairs Alfred L. Atherton to observe happenings in Tehran and to implement the president's human rights agenda. By the time Carter's actions and inactions had toppled the Iranian monarchy, Atherton had been appointed Ambassador to Egypt.

He was in residence in Cairo when the Shah fled his homeland and flew to Egypt.

Washington put pressure on the Shah to ease his control and allow more political freedom. This prompted the release of more than three hundred political prisoners, relaxed censorship, and overhauled the court system, which had the unforeseen side effect of allowing greater freedom for opposition groups to meet and organize.

Pahlavi was confident about the American commitment to Iran during an interview with *Kayhan International* in September 1977:

> *Relations between Iran and the United States are good and I do not think they could be otherwise.... When a new administration takes over, there are those who imagine everything will be changed. But it is only individuals who change; the long-term interests of a nation cannot change.... We will not accept anything less than a first-class position for Iran.... Iran must have a first-class status.*[153]

Time—and Jimmy Carter—proved the Shah very wrong.

Secretary of State Cyrus Vance was the first in Carter's administration to visit Iran. Vance was in the country for a meeting of CENTO (Central Treaty Organization) to discuss security in the region. While traveling with Vance, an "unidentified spokesperson" for the State Department leaked the information that the United States was pleased with the Shah's human rights efforts and was therefore willing to sell him AWACS aircraft.[154] In July, President Carter informed Congress that it was his objective to sell seven AWACS planes to Iran.

After months of congressional wrangling and intense debate, the sale was approved. The final package included an additional $1.1 billion in spare parts and technical instruction. The Shah, however, sorely missed the Nixon administration's willingness to provide an almost unlimited entrée to military equipment.

Shortly after Vance's return to the States Carter signed Presidential Decision Memorandum 13. Although the document did not specifically mention arms sales to Iran, the country was noticeably absent from the list of nations that would receive American arms largess. The Shah was decidedly disturbed that the new administration seemed not to value a long-standing liaison with his country. The document mentioned only Israel and the NATO allies: Japan, New Zealand, and Australia.[155] The Shah was mortified: "Does he [Carter] suppose that, strategically speaking, Iran is less significant than a country like New Zealand?"[156]

While the Shah's internal changes were making an impression on Carter, young men and women in Iran were swarming to radical Islam. Iran had never seen anything like this in its history. University students gathered at Islamic study centers to debate the imams of Shia Islam. Young women clothed themselves in the *chadors* (long black veils) that had been outlawed by the Shah. This new, radical Islam exploded on the campus of Tehran University in October 1977. A group of students calling for the isolation of women on campus rioted, leaving behind a trail of burned-out buses and broken windows.

On December 7, 1977, a charming and affable President Carter met with a small group of reporters. In such an intimate setting, there is an inherent danger of being altogether too frank. When asked about the rising instability of the Persian Gulf region, and whether the Shah could survive the upheaval, Carter succumbed to the temptation to be too forthright. His response, later deemed totally inappropriate, was:

> *I don't know. I hope so. This is something that is in the hands of the people of Iran. We have never had any intention and don't have any intention of trying to intercede in the internal political affairs of Iran. We primarily want an absence of violence and bloodshed, and stability. We personally prefer that the Shah maintain a major role in the government, but that is a decision for the Iranian people to make.[157]*

The president's words seemed to be filled with doubt that the Shah would be able to survive, and the press pounced. Carter's assessment only served to widen the chasm between him and Pahlavi and added fuel to the already-smoldering revolutionary fires burning in Iran. As is usual with any "blunder," planned or otherwise, damage-control steps were immediately taken. However, Carter's words spoken during his intimate moment with the press could not be recalled, and both Carter and the Shah would live to see the resulting calamity.

Initially, Jimmy Carter's attitude toward the Shah was more one of indecisiveness. He was at once impressed by the progressiveness of the Shah's programs and disturbed by reported human rights violations. The true turmoil that boiled just under the surface in Iran, fed by cassette tapes of sermons by Ayatollah Khomeini smuggled into the country, was difficult for the Carter administration to recognize. Neither did Carter understand that the casually spoken word in Washington could have a major and calamitous effect both on Pahlavi and the Iranian people halfway around the world.

Pahlavi's desire to see Iran dragged, sometimes kicking and screaming, into the twentieth century, to see the Iranian people with the advantages offered by Westernization, precipitated his downfall. He wanted to create a modern, industrialized nation that was productive, strong militarily and economically, and diverse culturally. Visionaries require a retinue of detail-oriented people around them to implement the vision and reach the goal. Unfortunately for the Shah, many of those with whom he surrounded himself were not averse to using any means to justify the end result. The outcome, of course, was unrestrained human rights violations. The poorer Iranian classes, seeking wealth, flocked into the cities where they encountered abysmal living conditions. Corruption proliferated, and inflation skyrocketed. Violence ran rampant, and the SAVAK did not hesitate to implement any method of torture to control it.

In an article published in *The New Yorker*, an unnamed Iranian official in Isfahan summed up the situation very succinctly; the summation was appropriate for any city in Iran:

> *Students have grown up under the Shah, and they don't know what things were like before development started. All they know is that the Shah promised that Iran was going to be like France or Germany. That isn't happening. The huge surge in population means that services are spread too thin and are constantly breaking down. There aren't enough telephones. It's impossible to buy a car. The schools are jammed. Housing is scarce. During the past three years, there has been a recession, especially in building, and many laborers are out of work. So the students are in a mood to reject everything that has happened. They are turning back to the old days and pursuing an idealized version of what things were like then. They are pushing the mullahs to go back and re-create the wonderful past. The mullahs see a chance to regain their prestige and power. The students provide them with a power base for putting pressure on the government to give them the consideration and importance they have been seeking for years. So the mullahs go along. That's the dynamic of trouble in Isfahan.*[158]

It is quite possible that had Jimmy Carter's advisors been more astute and less determined to see the Shah deposed, a lesson could have been learned from either of the two encounters that took place between the Carters and the Pahlavis—one in Washington, and the other in Tehran. Prior to the meeting in D.C., Carter received a briefing memo from Cyrus Vance. While the document failed to list "human rights" as a main objective of their meetings, an entire page was devoted to the topic. Outlined as the president's objectives were:

> *We should ensure that the Shah understands that your concern over human rights has a continued high priority, that we recognize the important positive actions he has taken in*

the last year, and that we would like to see programs continue.[159]

The Shah had, in fact, instructed his military courts to house political prisoners in better surroundings. He invited an entourage from the Red Cross to visit the prisons and inspect the facilities and handling of political detainees. The group reported that one-third of the prisoners had been tortured in some measure, but that such method had been forsaken. The Shah was convinced that once the findings of the Red Cross team had been published, the pressure on him would ease.

CHAPTER

$$====== 9 ======$$

A ROYAL VISIT
GONE AWRY

*"During the outdoor welcoming ceremonies at the White House
a surprising number of unruly anti-Shah demonstrators, almost all of
them Iranian students studying in the United States, massed outside
the gates chanting slogans such as 'Death to the Shah'—slogans that
would in a short time become quite familiar to Americans."* [160]

IN NOVEMBER OF 1977 the Shah and the Empress Farah
made a state visit to the White House. Using the freedom of speech
rights available to any citizen, or visitor for that matter, Iranian
students in the U.S. had been widely protesting the Shah's rule. As
the two leaders and their wives met on the South Lawn of the White
House, a group of the monarch's supporters were seated in bleach-
ers on the Ellipse beneath a banner that read, "Welcome Shah!"

In Lafayette Square on the north side of the White House,
some one thousand Iranian dissidents had gathered to protest with
shouts of angry anti-Shah slogans. As the two leaders greeted each
other, the protesters broke through police lines and charged
the Ellipse.

Ardeshir Zahedi remembered the state visit of the Shah and Empress quite vividly. He recalled the day before the White House reception:

> Several busloads of opposition activists were allowed to come to Williamsburg, which is a small place, for the overnight stay of state guests before the official program started the following day. I don't recall anyone carrying the picture of Khomeini in Williamsburg, but what I recall is that standard security rules were not observed by the Secret Service. These rules call for a distance of five hundred feet of separation between the crowd and the person who is the state guest. The Secret Service allowed the opponents to come very close, just a few meters from the Shah's living quarters.
>
> [The following day] a pro-Shah rally [was] organized in front of the White House.... a large crowd of pro-Shah demonstrators—maybe about 14,000 to 15,000 Iranians from all over the States—gathered in front of the White House.... The security people arranged things in a way that the Shah's supporters and opponents were one in front of the other. The clash between them could not be avoided.[161]

Mounted police were able to stop the riot but not before having to resort to the use of tear gas to quell the crowd. Standing downwind from the tear gas canisters, both leaders and their wives were victims of the acrid fumes. An account in *Time* magazine relates how the two men responded to the onslaught:

> Reeling slightly, the Shah sought refuge behind a white pocket handkerchief. The empress, standing behind him, fumbled in her purse for dark glasses. Vice President Walter Mondale and Secretary of State Cyrus Vance, eyes streaming, covered their faces. Only Carter, still speaking, refused to flinch. Tears rolled out of the president's eyes, but he made no move to wipe them. Recovering his composure when it was his turn to speak, the Shah thanked Carter for "your

very warm welcome," and the official party quickly retreated to the White House.[162]

The less-than-tactful Mr. Carter later toasted the Shah with, "There is one thing I can say about the Shah: he knows how to draw a crowd."[163]

Appalled by the turn of events, Ambassador Zahedi urged the Shah to return to Tehran, while members of the Carter administration implored him to reconsider. The Shah relented and calmly resumed his talks with the president.

The New York Times story the next day chose a photograph of the ceremony that showed the Shah speaking into a microphone while both President Carter and Mrs. Carter are seen on either side, tears streaming from their eyes. The headline read: "Clashes and Tear Gas Mar Shah's Welcome in Capital."[164]

Just in case anyone missed that headline, the *Times* ran an editorial the next day entitled "Tears and Sympathy for the Shah." The editorial stated that the tear gas "signaled the somewhat awkward nature of the occasion. A president committed to advancing the cause of human rights worldwide was offering a full-honors welcome to a ruler as close to an absolute monarch as exists these days." While the editorial pointed out "there has in fact been some progress on human rights in Iran in recent months," it went on to say, "the Shah's monopoly on decision-making creates vast inefficiencies. It also has created doubt that stability can survive his reign. Besides urging further attention to human rights, therefore, the United States has reason to urge institutional reform as well."[165]

The *Washington Post* Style section reported that the next day the Shah tried to smooth over the incident by saying, "It is true that it started out with tears in the morning, but it was the same last night after President Carter's remarks. There were tears of joy in my eyes knowing of the unshakable friendship between our two countries."[166] *Post* reporter Donnie Radcliffe snidely remarked, "On Tuesday at the White House the Shah had handed his handkerchief to Queen Farah as tear gas fired by DC police drifted up from the Ellipse. Yesterday, he kept it in his pocket, the same place; apparently, he kept his shopping list for several billion dollars worth of U.S. arms he wants to buy."[167]

The *Post* editorial page carried a story in the same edition. The writer noted:

> *The brief but ugly outbreaks of street fighting here during the visit of the Shah of Iran leave a number of reputations suffering severe bruises. The American authorities lost control of a crowd that was clearly spoiling for a fight.... When a foreign visit ends with a flood of casualties to hospital emergency rooms it's obvious that the hosts mismanaged the affair. Apparently the Carter administration was leaning over backwards to avoid any resemblance to the methods of the Nixon years. The result was to leave an inadequate contingent of Park Police, not even wearing helmets, facing the crowd as it prepared to rush them. For reasons still not clear, federal authorities never called in the Metropolitan Police. That was a serious mistake. The present tenant of the White House...would be exceedingly unwise to let Washington become known as a city where it is cheap and easy to disrupt public events.... Freedom of expression does not include the right to beat up the people who disagree....A riot on the Ellipse is not likely to persuade the Shah to relax police controls in Tehran.*[168]

A follow-up report two weeks later revealed that during the fracas on the Ellipse 96 demonstrators and 28 police were injured. According to the *Washington Post* story, Park Police were instructed "to leave their riot gear—helmets, face shields, riot sticks, and gas masks—on nearby buses. When the student attack occurred, just as the 21-gun salute for the Shah was sounded, the undermanned police were overrun.... The White House has denied recurrent rumors that it ordered the low-key profile...during the Shah's visit."[169]

The article further revealed that Attorney General Griffin Bell was asked to have the Justice Department hurriedly coordinate security for the remainder of the Shah's visit.

The event wreaked havoc in Iran when it was broadcast live on Iranian Television. Many in Iran, whether favorable or opposed to the Shah, were not accustomed to the liberty accorded the media in the United States and interpreted the use of tear gas during the ceremony as evidence that Carter lacked confidence in Pahlavi. The *Times* editorial only reinforced that perception.

Carter had to inform the king that arms sales would be curtailed, but he was able to hide behind the excuse of congressional pressure. Nevertheless, he boldly proclaimed that the military pact between the two countries was unwavering.[170] The president was able to applaud the Shah's move to allow more dissent and criticism of his government while, at the same time, seeking his support both of Israel initiatives and in curtailing oil prices. Overall, it was a successful trip: Pahlavi met Carter, and the AWACS deal that Carter had presented to Congress in July was finalized. It was, however, transparently obvious that the Carter administration was getting the elevator and the Shah was getting the shaft.

Zahedi explained his role in the final AWACS negotiations:

Lord Hartley and Lady Shawcross were houseguests in Washington. I discussed with Shawcross whether Britain may be willing to sell Iran their NIMROD air reconnaissance crafts....Shawcross, of course, was not in the British govern-ment and could not make a commitment, but I sent to His Majesty a message in Tehran which was not coded....I said to him that the UK may be willing to sell us these crafts.

Shortly after, some influential senators—Chuck Percy, Abraham Ribicoff, Jacob Javits—Howard Baker called me and said, "Don't rush it; after the recess the matter will be settled." That is how in the meeting of November 15...Carter announced he had agreed to sell Iran seven AWACS and asked Zbig to brief the Senate.[171]

The fact that the anti-Shah events happened at all in Washington, D.C., and especially during the monarch's visit added fuel to the opposition movement in Iran. The leaders asked themselves, "Could this have happened at the White House without President Carter's express knowledge and approval?" Obviously, the insurgents in Iran concluded that the answer was a resounding, "No," and at the least signaled Carter's lack of support for the Shah. The empress later wrote that an event such as that would not have happened during the Nixon administration; the rioters would have been held at bay. One of the protesters waved a placard with a picture of the Ayatollah Khomeini, and the visage of the fanatical cleric commanded the front page of the Washington Post. *This gave the empress pause for thought; she wondered how someone could equate Khomeini with liberty and moderation.*[172]

In her own mind, the empress questioned the motives of the demonstrators:

My God, if these people want democracy and freedom, why are they carrying the picture of this religious man? Many Iranians didn't know who Khomeini was. Then slowly the cassettes of Khomeini started with his speeches against the Shah and against the reforms. What happened is that the opposition was very well organized, and we were not; we were not politically organized to answer them. How could our people after what they had lived through go after a man like this and think that he could bring them happiness and a better life in Paradise?[173]

In December, while on a presidential jaunt that took him to Poland, India, and the Soviet Union, the president and Mrs. Carter made a brief stop in Tehran. The stop was, in essence, a reward for the Shah's assistance in urging the kings of Morocco and Jordan to persuade President Sadat to make peace with Israel. Again, Carter's Southern charm and hyperbole only exposed the fact that he did not fully grasp the undercurrents of revolution that were even then gripping Iran. During Carter's visit to Tehran, the Shah gave the president a "grocery list" of some $10 billion in arms supplies. The list contained the full gamut from ships to communication devices. Carter, on the other hand, was to alert the Shah of a new U.S. objective:

> To discuss the recent clashes between Iranian security author-
> ities and student/opposition politicians and to express our
> hope that these clashes do not portend a reversal of the
> encouraging human rights developments in Iran...We should
> indicate that the tough actions by Iranian security forces
> recently have created U.S. press, public, and congressional
> concern that the Shah has reversed the encouraging trend
> in the field of human rights. We should encourage him to
> continue the positive course in the relaxation in restrictions
> affecting human rights, which he embarked upon in early
> 1977.[174]

The Christopher memo, however, also reflected that the U.S. was aware the opposition forces in Iran were regrouping:

> Our analysis indicates that the so-called Iran Freedom
> Seekers Liberation Movement and various other opposition
> politicians who were prominent in the 1950s during the
> period of Prime Minister Mossadegh have attempted to form
> a broad but loose coalition of all opposition elements...from
> the far left to the far right...and to recruit students into this
> grouping. A broad-based effort of this nature, uncommon in
> Iran, may have reflected the new political openness in Iran
> in the past year.

According to the State Department, the Shah "would prefer that the issue not be raised, and if it is, will take the line that agitation by students and opposition elements is foreign-inspired or has foreign connections."[175]

No mention is made to Carter of possible Libyan or Palestinian connections to the terrorist groups at work in Iran.

According to Zahedi, rather than attend a banquet in the Shah's honor at the Iranian Embassy in Washington, Carter asked if he could pay the Shah a visit in Tehran. Zahedi replied that the Shah would be delighted. "That is how," stated Mr. Zahedi, "that the New Year's banquet came to be; it was not a state visit, only a courtesy call." Carter, however, was almost upstaged by King Hussein of Jordan. The Shah wanted the president and the Jordanian ruler to meet. Carter's advance group insisted that the king be invited to the dinner, which created yet another problem. If King Hussein were to attend the party, he would displace the president as the guest of honor and be accorded the seat at the Shah's right hand. The Jordanian ruler did join the guests that evening, but after dinner had been completed.[176]

During the banquet, the president raised his glass and praised Pahlavi: "Iran, whose destiny is so remarkably well guided by the Shah, is an island of stability in one of the more troubled areas of the world. That is a great tribute to you, Your Majesty, and to the great task that you are accomplishing in Iran, and to the respect, admiration, and love that your people bear you....There is no other head of state with whom I feel on friendlier terms and to whom I feel more gratitude."[177] The Shah was gratified by Carter's glowing words.

When I interviewed Her Majesty Farah Pahlavi in March 2008, I was shown her guest book with an inscription: "Thank you for all your wonderful hospitality." It was signed, "President Jimmy Carter" and "Rosalynn Carter." Princess Ashraf, Pahlavi's twin sister, put her impressions of the president on paper. She wrote, "I looked at his pale face. I thought his smile was artificial, his eyes icy—and I hoped I could trust him."[178] Yet again, it was apparent that neither Carter nor his advisors were fully apprised of the growing unrest.

The president seemed to waver between supporting the Shah because of his country's strategic importance in the region and his desire to make a human rights example of the Pahlavi regime. With the proper wise counsel, the Carter administration had every tool at hand to affirmatively sway the Shah's decisions and influence events in Iran. Rather than take decisive action to affect change early in his presidency, Carter waited until the situation was rapidly disintegrating and the ousting of the Shah a virtual certainty. By then, any word of praise or any expression of goodwill toward Iran's ruler only fed the flames of revolt and increased the enmity towards the United States. The Shah had the dubious distinction of being as much disliked by much of the American public as the Soviet leader, Leonid Brezhnev.

While the ultimate aims of different groups opposing the Shah were widely varied—some wanted a return to constitutional monarchy, others a Socialist/Communist government, and the imams and clerics an Islamic republic—it was the Ayatollah Khomeini who cunningly united these groups against the Shah by avoiding the specifics of what would happen beyond toppling the famed ruler from the Peacock Throne. As a result, opposition groups that would normally have been contending with one another instead grew more unified.

The dissenters were of the opinion that the Shah was nothing more than a puppet of the United States, one who moved at the bidding of the American leaders. The other side of the coin was that the same opposition felt that the U.S. was simply repeating a long-established pattern...a period of pressure on the Shah to enact reforms, then a time of retreat and acceptance of Pahlavi's resolve to retain absolute power. In a private setting with the president, National Security Advisor Brzezinski worked to convince Carter that to abandon Pahlavi would damage whatever good reputation the U.S. may have had worldwide.[179]

The Shah was bombarded by those in Iran who saw Carter's embrace of human rights as a signal to press the Shah for deeper changes. A group of lawyer-activists urged Pahlavi to enact new and more encompassing legal reforms. The Writer's Guild shouted for freedom of the press. One member of the Guild attributed their willingness to vocalize their demands was because "the government wouldn't dare jail all of us in the present climate of human rights."[180] Some attribute this remarkable feat of internal unity to Khomeini. Regardless of the instigator, it accelerated the revolution in Iran and later proved to be a deadly mistake, not only for the United States but for all Islamists.

Other new tactics were adopted by the dissidents, including a letter published by National Front leaders Karim Sanjabi, Dariush Foruhar, and Shapour Bakhtiar calling for the king to step down. The empress felt that "these people were acting in that way because they had the support of the United States, the new Carter administration."[181] Coinciding with the internal unrest fomenting in Tehran, a group of well-known Iranians dispatched missives to Kurt Waldheim, the UN secretary general, and President Carter to enlist their aid in promoting the institution of greater human rights in their country. Carter, with his human rights agenda firmly in place, was more than happy to comply.

In a personal interview, Samuel Segev, Middle East editor of *Maariv*, revealed to me that the military attaché in Tehran, General Yitzhak Segev (no relation), was certain the Shah would be ousted if the Carter administration continued with its policy. General Segev was convinced that U.S. interference was tying the hands of the Shah's military and making it impossible to act against the opposition.

General Segev, who was in Iran from 1977 through February 1979, expanded on the causes of the revolution during the interview. The general felt that Pahlavi had tried to expand democracy much too quickly; that he had tried to "take across Western ideas, in an area that was not ready for them. You can't form democracy," said

Segev, "in an area that lives as if in the Stone Age.... Carter pressured the Shah at every possible moment." Segev believed that Ambassador William Sullivan had no comprehension as to how different was the mentality of the Iranian people toward democratic ideals.[182]

According to Dr. Ahmad Tehrani, former Ambassador of Iran, the Shah's demeanor changed the year before he was forced off the throne when he was challenged by strikes, riots, and other turmoil:

> Let me say that the Shah had ruled Iran for more than forty years and knew how to take care of incidents like these.... but in 1978-1979, he did not take care of it. He was suffering from cancer. He would laugh and cry alternatively.... Now he's saying, "I love my people; I don't want to hurt my people," and the next day, he would say, "Shoot!"...suddenly he's sick.... Actually, there are so many reasons for the revolution: the financial situation, the social situation...but it's mainly because of pressure...and Carter's foolishness.[183]

Ambassador Zahedi voiced several factors he felt would have made a difference in the Shah's control of the situation in Iran:

> If His Majesty had not left the country, Khomeini would never have dared come to Iran, and the army would not have disintegrated. In less than two years, we had three changes of prime minister and government...followed by a military government with practically no power, and then to crown it all, came that demagogue, Shapour Bakhtiar, who destroyed all that remained and presented the country to Khomeini and his cronies as a gift on a gold platter. About Sullivan, I refer you to His Majesty's book, Answer to History. When he [Pahlavi] asks Sullivan when he should leave the country, Sullivan looks at his watch and says if he left sooner it would be better than later.His Majesty had problems within his own family. Some members had surrounded themselves with people of strong leftist inclinations. My beloved king was not influenced by them. Most important of all was his sickness, which had been kept secret from the Iranian people.... [His

*Majesty] should have told the truth about his own illness....
he was so loved by his people; they would have wept blood
instead of tears.The most important point is that I told His
Majesty point-blank, in the presence of the...queen, that if
he left the country, he would never return; it was a huge mistake to think that his wife or son could replace him. I tell you
that whatever the Carter administration intended to do at
that point would have been too little too late.*[184]

When asked if the Crown Prince or Empress Farah could have
succeeded his father on the Peacock Throne, Zahedi replied:

*His son could not have succeeded to the throne as he was not
of age....His wife could not have succeeded as this was
against the constitution, as well as the fact that this could
have provided ammunition for the opposition. Sadly, there
were many elements and people who were against her.*[185]

The Shah, who had placed the future of his monarchy squarely
in the hands of the U.S., was convinced, as he told Ford's Vice
President Nelson Rockefeller during a visit to Iran in May 1978, that
"the Americans and the Russians have divided the world between
them."[186] It was this that led not only the Shah and his supporters
in Iran but educated Iranians worldwide to determine that Pahlavi's
reign had ended because the U.S. wanted it to end. Khomeini had
overthrown the Shah of Iran because America had switched its
loyalties to the cold and calculating cleric; it is likely that without
some backing from the U.S., Khomeini would not have gained power
in Iran.

CHAPTER

10

AN AMERICAN
ALLY DEPOSED

*"Men and women in Iran broke old chains only to forge
new ones. They demolished the rule of one man and then
submitted to the tyranny of another."* (FOUAD AJAMI)[187]

*"The seeds of 9/11 were sown a quarter of a century ago
when Khomeini came to power. Khomeini's ascent to power
was aided by the policies of Jimmy Carter and his allies on
the political Left."* (DINESH D'SOUZA)[188]

IN AN ATTEMPT TO SOLIDIFY his position in the region,
Mohammad Reza Shah Pahlavi sought to align himself with his
neighbors as early as 1974. The Shah, who was able to move Iran
into a leadership role in OPEC during the Nixon-Ford administration, felt the time had come to move his country into a more central
position in the region. (In 1976 in a display of largess, Pahlavi gave
away nearly two billion dollars to countries such as Egypt, Jordan,
and Syria to help achieve his goal.) Pahlavi sent his trusted emissary,
General Gholam Reza Afkhami, to Cairo to research the possibility
of greater cooperation between Egypt and Iran. As a result of

Afkhami's hard work, Egypt garnered a state-of-the-art radar system and an opportunity for Egyptian pilots to see Iran's Phantom jets firsthand. It also paved the way for the first visit of an Iranian monarch to Egypt in twenty-three years. Sadat asked Pahlavi to intervene with Rabin over the Sinai oil fields.

The Shah's visit in Cairo led the monarch to inform Rabin that the Eilat-Ashkelon pipeline was in danger of being shut down in early 1975. Rabin sent his Foreign Minister Yigal Allon to Tehran for meetings with the Shah. The two men were able to reach an agreement that allowed the flow of oil to continue, albeit with a higher rate for transfer fees but with a lower price for the oil.

In May of that year, however, the Shah surprised Israel by siding with Sadat over Israeli withdrawal from the territories captured during the Six-Day war. This placed an inordinate amount of stress on Israel-Iran relations. Ambassador Uri Lubrani was informed that relations between the two countries would be deferred until Israel decided to acquiesce to calls for withdrawal at least from the Abu-Rudeis oil fields. Secretary of State Henry Kissinger was finally able to exact a commitment from Pahlavi that he would not stop the flow of oil to Israel. Even with this agreement, Rabin felt it necessary to return to Tehran for another secret visit with the Shah. Unfortunately, Rabin was unable to maintain his anonymity among the Jews in the region. Pahlavi, however, was able to assure Rabin that Israel's oil needs would be met.

While the Shah was also reaching out to Egypt and other Arab countries, he was determined to allow neither the Soviets nor Americans to establish bases in his area of the Persian Gulf. The fact that the Soviets defied an agreement to withdraw from Iran in a timely manner following World War II and created two republics within the territory occupied—Azerbaijan and Iranian Kurdistan—was very distressing to Pahlavi. It was not until UN intervention in 1946 that the Russians abandoned their territory in Iran. Perhaps that is why the Shah considered the USSR to be the most important threat to Iran; after all, the two nations shared a

1,240- mile border. For centuries the Russian agenda included securing a warm-water port facility and subverting any nation
considered to be pro-Western. Pahlavi felt the Russians had the
most to gain should Iran plunge into internal unrest. An April 1974
document from the State Department outlines the Shah's fears
regarding Soviet aggression:

> *The Shah believes Soviet activity in the Middle East indicates
> a continuing use of proxies such as Iraq and South Yemen to
> accomplish Soviet foreign policy goals. The Shah remains
> concerned by the potential for instability—and Soviet
> exploitation of it—in neighboring countries. He is concerned
> about radical movements in the Persian Gulf; Iraq's hostil-
> ity towards Iran.... He recognized the need for, and has been
> seeking, improved relations and cooperation with the more
> moderate Arab governments.... Establishing this coopera-
> tion is not easy because of long-standing Arab wariness
> toward Iran.*[189]

What Pahlavi may or may not have known was that the
Soviets began courting the PLO shortly after Israel's success during
the 1967 war. Soviet support for the terrorists was documented by
Russian General Ion M. Pacepa, a defector to the West in 1978.
In an article on *National Review Online*, Pacepa wrote:

> *Between 1968 and 1978...security forces of Romania sent
> two cargo planes full of military goodies every week to
> Palestinian terrorists in Lebanon.... [The shipments did not
> stop after the fall of the Shah]...in 1983 alone [the East
> German Stasi] sent $1,877,600 worth of AK-47 ammunition
> to Lebanon. According to Vaclav Havel [president of
> Czechoslovakia], Communist Czechoslovakia shipped 1,000
> tons of odorless explosive Semtex-H (which can't be detected
> by sniffer dogs) to Islamic terrorists—enough for 150 years.*[190]

In actuality, the Soviets extended an invitation to Arafat to set
up a PLO bureau in Moscow in 1974. General Pacepa wrote in his

memoirs that Arafat possessed "an incredible amount of fanaticism...of tangled oriental political maneuvers, of lies, of embezzled PLO funds deposited in Swiss banks, and of homosexual relationships, beginning with his teacher when he was a teenager and ending with his current bodyguards. After reading that report," said Pacepa, "I felt a compulsion to take a shower whenever [I] had just shaken his hand."[191]

Another Soviet counter-espionage defector from Poland, Colonel Michel Goleniewski, took aim at the Grand Ayatollah himself. The Russian exposed a CIA document from the early 1960s. The document reportedly revealed that "Khomeini was one of Moscow's five sources of intelligence at the heart of the Shiite hierarchy."[192]

Although the PLO was a vital ingredient in the overthrow of the Shah and the return of Khomeini to Tehran, it was, however, the signing of a peace treaty with the Kurds in Northern Iraq that may well have signaled the beginning of the end for the monarch. In allowing some ten thousand religious pilgrims the right to freely travel from Iran to Iraq, the Shah opened the door for the smuggling of Ayatollah Khomeini's fanatical and mutinous views across the border. It was through this pipeline that Khomeini's cassette tapes were transported into the hands of the opposition in Iran.

While the Shah was seen to be the principal patron of the Iraqi Kurds' struggle for independence and had supported the Kurds with arms and training, Iran's assistance came to a halt with the signing of the Algiers Accords between Iran and Iraq. During an OPEC meeting the two sides met and hammered out an agreement to end an ongoing dispute over borders, water, and navigation rights. The Shatt el Arab waterway was designated the defining border. On June 13, 1975, the two nations signed the treaty. Unfortunately for the Kurds, the Accords also meant the end of the Shah's support of the Kurdish rebels. Without that support the Kurds were powerless to provide any deterrent to Saddam Hussein's invasion of Iran.

Earlier in 1975 Secretary of State Henry Kissinger and Iran's Finance Minister Hushang Ansary had inked an agreement totaling $15 billion in purchases by Iran from the U.S. It was "the largest agreement of its kind ever signed by the two countries."[193] Such a massive sum of money was unfathomable to the vast majority of Iranians. This served to further distance the Shah from his people.

It was also in 1975 that the Shah established principals regarding private ownership of mining and industrial operations. Pahlavi gave the owners a period of three years to offer to the public 49 percent of the industries. This edict created a chaotic situation for the Shah. Wealthy industrialists were furious. They felt they were being forcibly stripped of their assets. Private citizens were equally disturbed at the thought of having to incur unwanted debt in order to purchase shares in the various companies. In his zeal to better the lot of the Iranian people, the Shah played right into the hands of what would become future President Jimmy Carter's human rights witch hunt by placing what appeared to be an unnecessary burden on the Iranian people.

With an agreement in place between Iran and Iraq, the Shah turned his attention to President Carter. In an attempt to mollify Carter's human rights agenda, the Shah ordered a sequence of liberalization policies. He permitted the reorganization of the National Front, an on-again-off-again, loosely organized political faction committed to "establish Iran's unequivocal sovereignty within and without; in other words...rule of law within, and political independence...without."[194]

In a note from Sullivan to the secretary of state, the ambassador commented that:

> *The GOI (Government of Iran) is continuing to feel its way through the circumstances which have resulted from its policy of liberalizing conditions for public airing of dissent. The decision to avoid the use of massive police action is encouraging.... If the dissidents opt for violent confrontation*

some nasty street fighting could erupt...and...turn into goon squads. We will continue to monitor carefully.[195]

The National Front had been inactive for a number of years. In its absence a generation of students had arisen who were devoted to radicalism and Islamic fanaticism. As an island of stability of what was increasingly becoming a turbulent sea of discontent in Iran, the National Front seemed content to protect the monarchy with the understanding that the "monarch reigned, but did not rule."[196] This seemed to be supported by the protest marches that crippled Tehran on December 10 and 11, 1978. A CIA assessment of Iran indicated:

> *The protest marches in Tehran...which brought out as many as a million demonstrators into the streets, were masterfully organized and controlled. The evidence suggests that local community leaders called dastehoardan, whose traditional functions include organizing religious processions, mobilized small crowds around local mosques and then moved these groups to join others from around the city.... The ability of these local community leaders to bring out large numbers of people in response to directives from members of the Islamic clergy gives the religious opposition in Iran an organizational strength which distinguishes it from any other group within the opposition....The Ayatollah Ruhollah Khomeini has served as the focal point for the loyalty of the religious opposition.... There is no evidence to substantiate the claim...that behind the pattern of events lies the guiding hand of "foreign elements," "leftists," or...the Tudeh party.... demonstrations in Tehran on the high holy days of Moharram...were the most impressive display of organizational ability thus far seen in the recent incidents of civil unrest in Iran.*[197]

The report went on to indicate that Khomeini had a strong following, particularly within the lower classes, urban centers, bazaar merchants and shopkeepers, and students who often chanted his name during rallies.

In a manifesto apparently drafted specifically for the December 10-11 marches, the Khomeini-inspired revolutionaries laid out their position. The document stated:

» Ayatollah Khomeini is our leader. Whatever he asks we will carry out. This march is a vote of confidence in Khomeini.

» The apparatus of the governmental dictatorship must be overthrown and power transferred to the people.

» The rule of Islamic social and individual justice must be established on the basis of the votes of the people.

» This is Human Rights Day. We ask for the human rights which our struggle has sought.

» The imperialism of East and West must be removed. The Iranian people will continue and extend their relations with other nations.

» People should not make money from money. The exploitation of human beings by others should be stopped. The collection of wealth in the hands of some people and the property of others should be redistributed.

» We salute the martyrs of the Iranian struggle.

» We demand release of all political prisoners and return of all who have left the country because of lack of freedom.[198]

The Embassy also asked the questions: Will the Shah call for martial law, and if so, how heavy-handed will the government be? And perhaps most importantly, would the opposition be able to unite sufficiently to be able to approach the Shah convincingly?

The State Department telegram concluded:

Situation...offers both danger and hope. Danger in that radicals will instigate violent incidents which will draw moderates' attention away from rather pleasant feeling of success and provoke severe military reaction. Hope in that opposition can get unified proposal ready to move forward to coalition government reasonably soon.[199]

Also in December the Shah approached National Front leaders Shapour Bakhtiar and Gholam Hossein Sadiqi (the Shah's first choice as prime minister) to pursue the idea of instituting a civilian government or a constitutional monarchy. The men also explored the possibility of military rule. Unfortunately, the National Front, unlike the exiled Khomeini, had no accessibility to a network by which to propagate its message across Iran.

Dr. Parviz Mina told me of his last visit to Tehran and his certainty that the Shah's monarchy would not survive:

When the plane took off it circled over Tehran. And I was looking down...on the northwestern side of the city...there was this famous avenue running from east to west...this street right from the beginning to the end was packed with people who were demonstrating against the Shah. I said, "By God, that's the end of it." That was the day I thought that he was...not going to survive.[200]

Waiting in the wings was the Ayatollah Ruhollah Khomeini, whose vendetta against the Shah of Iran began in 1963 when Pahlavi's forces successfully thwarted a religious movement headed by Khomeini and deported the fanatical cleric first to Turkey and then to Iraq. From that time Khomeini became obsessed with the overthrow of the Pahlavi monarchy.

It was Khomeini's ability to turn local mosques into cauldrons of revolutionary turmoil that was absolutely remarkable given the territorial nature of the mullahs and ayatollahs. Former Israeli Ambassador Uri Lubrani summarized his feeling about Khomeini's rise:

The religious establishment was the only organized body in Iran...in each village. If you ask about Khomeini having a

network, he had the best possible network in Iran. I tried to
touch base with the religious establishment in 1973;
they wouldn't talk to me. The Shah didn't have an agent
in each village, neither a policeman. Nobody was allowed
[by the Shah's government] to organize...only the religious
establishment.... add to that what Khomeini was disseminat-
ing from his exile first in Iraq and then in France, you'll see
that this big network was being fed with dissent
and sedition.... By the beginning of 1978 I began to have
forebodings...to feel uneasy...to look for more urgent
signs...of something brewing. I went to see my foreign min-
ister, Moshe Dayan, and told him of my concerns. I said,
"I have my forebodings...we ought to begin to phase out."
I knew at the end of the day...Israel will have no place in
Iran...the new regime will be an unfriendly regime to
Israel.[201]

In a move that in hindsight was likely one of the most imprudent decisions by the Shah, Pahlavi freed a number of pro-Khomeini mullahs from Iran's prisons in 1978. These disgruntled clerics bent on revenge gladly joined Khomeini's underground and were among the many whose mosques were made available to the radicals.

The network of mosques proved to be much more effective than the efforts of the National Front. Khomeini, however, was slow, methodical, and determined to seek revenge against his adversary, the Shah, no matter the time or cost in money or lives. The Grand Ayatollah recruited from the ranks of mid-level mullahs who whipped their followers into rabid, pro-Khomeini militants.

The Shah, of course, had charted his own path simply because he wanted the favor of his subjects, the Iranian people. He professed to be a pious Muslim; he made the required trips to pay homage at the various shrines. The Shah craved the favor of the clerics, and submerged himself in prayer. How could he openly declare war on the mullahs whose support he so actively sought?

Khomeini's charisma was especially appealing to the lower classes, the *mostazafin*...the dispossessed. They saw him as their savior; the one who would rescue them from their lives of toil. Ahmad Ashraf wrote of the Ayatollah: "Khomeini gave the masses a sense of personal integrity, of collective identity, of historical rootedness, and feelings of pride and superiority."[202] In their hysterical longing for the coming of the *Mahdi*, the risen one that would free the masses from privation, discrimination, and tyranny, some claimed to have seen the Ayatollah's face in the moon.[203] This would certainly be consistent with the Persian penchant for superstition, numerology, and dependence on "omens, symbols, prophecies, and revelations."[204]

It would be in the name of this *Mahdi* that a rogue Muslim fanatic and his faction in Saudi Arabia would seize the Grand Mosque in Mecca, seal the doors, and hold hostage the pilgrims inside the holiest of Muslim sites. The two-week siege would end only when French mercenaries and Saudi National Guard troops stormed the mosque. Hundreds were killed in the crossfire. This attack, though unsuccessful, was to be only a foretaste of the tactics Islamic fanatics were willing to use to achieve their goal...world domination through the return of the revered *Mahdi*. Khomeini was reputed by some to be the long-awaited redeemer of Islam.

Author Jahangir Amuzegar wrote of the mesmerizing Khomeini's appeal:

> He [Khomeini] spoke of such misty but universally popular goals as political and religious freedom, independence from pernicious foreign influences, social justice...the obligation to help the poor...the villainy of corruption, a need to conserve precious natural resources...and other goals.[205]

With his smooth rhetoric, Khomeini managed to ensnare leaders of *The People's Mujahedeen-e-Khalq* and the Marxist-inspired *Fedayeen-e-Khalq* ("freedom fighters" with strong ties to the PLO) and entice them to join his brand of Islamic Revolution.

It was the *Mujahedeen* with its thin veneer of Islam that endowed Khomeini with the venerable title of "Imam." The group joined hands with Khomeini, deeming the Shah to be too secular. The *Fedayeen* was more interested in launching a Marxist revolution akin to that of Fidel Castro in Cuba or Che Guevara in Latin America.[206] Both organizations had ties to the PLO. The Ayatollah had asserted he would be a "guide to the people."[207] Few realized that he would, instead, grip the reins of power in Iran and rule with an iron fist, squashing all opposition in his path. Khomeini managed to pull the wool over the eyes of the likes of intellectual James Bill, who described the tyrannical ruler as a man of "impeccable integrity and honesty, who has denied again and again that he will hold office."[208]

To fund his campaign to depose the Shah, Khomeini relied in part on both the PLO and Syria's Hafez al Assad. The Soviet defector, former General Ion Pacepa, also revealed that another source of funds to support this direct onslaught against the Shah came from the Soviet Union. Khomeini's fanatical influence on the mullahs in Iran was to be driven home to Pahlavi with powerful potency on October 9, 1977: twenty-plus students with covered faces rampaged through the University of Tehran, vandalizing classrooms, torching buses, and demanding that women be totally segregated from the male student population.

It was, however, during *Ramadan* (a Muslim month set aside for fasting and reflection) in August 1978 that large protest rallies erupted all across Iran. Curfew was imposed in some cities following days of mass rioting. The city of Abadan was the site of a mass murder said to have been staged by Islamic radicals. The doors of the *Rex Cinema*, hosting an Iranian film, were barred while the building was torched; 477 people died in the conflagration, including a number of children and their mothers. The clergy that directly supported Khomeini avowed that the fire was set by SAVAK, the Shah's secret police. Iranian police determined that followers of the Ayatollah were responsible for the murders of so many innocent people. In retrospect, this reeks of the tactics used by radical Islamic terrorists in countries such as Egypt, Algeria, and ultimately in the United States.

In Qom, the center of Islamic education in Iran, police fired into a group of rioters who were protesting a denouncement of Khomeini in the newspaper. Several clerics were killed in the melee. The Shah's attempts to suppress the rioting were rejected by his enemies and supporters alike. His enemies saw it as a weak attempt at appeasement, and his supporters just saw it as weakness, period. Khomeini saw it as the beginning of a tsunami that would sweep the Shah out of power. It was becoming more obvious that the threat to Iran was not from the communist Soviet Union, but from socio-economic, religious, and political sources.

Under the tutelage of his former son-in-law, Ardeshir Zahedi, the Shah was encouraged to offer up a scapegoat to appease the mobs of demonstrators. Zahedi, who had been appointed Ambassador to the United States, suggested such substitutes as Amir Hoveyda, and SAVAK heads Hasan Pakravan and Nematollah Nassiri. Zahedi assured Brzezinski, back in Washington, that he had the situation in Iran firmly in hand; obviously he was badly mistaken. Not even a counter demonstration organized by the ambassador could quell the unrest in his homeland.

In *Answers to History* Pahlavi wrote of the supposed role of the secret police:

> *The Western press...claims that bloodshed and death that marred our cities had nothing to do with terrorists but was the work of SAVAK agents.... If SAVAK had only been as effective as our enemies claimed, they would not have been out in the streets shouting vilifications.*[209]

Dr. Mina talked with me about SAVAK and its purpose in Iran as seen by the Shah:

> *One thing the Iranian people did not appreciate was the lack of freedom of political activity. There was absolutely no*

*other problem as far as individual liberty, religious liberty....
It was only political activity which was controlled .... the
reason that was being done was because...the Shah was
always afraid of the fact that Moscow would woo the inter-
mediaries of their own choosing, which was the Tudeh Party,
the communist party in Iran.... he was frightened against
communism.... It was the United States that encouraged
him to encourage the SAVAK.... But that secret police was
only fighting against communism.... That was one of the reasons that they [U.S.] helped the Shah to create this secret
police and then asked the Israelis to help Iran in training the
people in [SAVAK].*[210]

CHAPTER

11

ISRAEL, AN ALLY

*"[Khomeini asked,] 'What is this association between
the Shah and Israel? Is the Shah a Jew?'... Khomeini linked Israel
and America so intimately that there was virtually no distinction
between the two.... Israel and America are simply two points of evil
along a vast satanic continuum."* (MICHAEL A. LEDEEN)[211]

SEPTEMBER OF 1978 FOUND Ambassador Ardeshir Zahedi
and the crown prince on a visit to California. The ambassador
thought it good political training for young Reza to become completely familiar with the United States. While traveling, Zahedi was
contacted by the Shah, who asked him to return to Iran as quickly
as possible.

Zahedi remembers that visit vividly:

*I arrived in Tehran by nightfall, September 4.... Foreign
Minister Amir-Khosrow Afshar and a group of military leaders like Generals Oveissi and Nasser Moghadam...had come
to meet me.... I was surprised because my visit was supposed
to be confidential. They were all worried and pleaded with
me to talk firmly with His Majesty and encourage him to*

act.... Queen Farah, who had been informed [of my arrival]
by the guards, was waiting for me on the top of the stairs at
the main entrance hall. She warned me that His Majesty's
morale was very low and I had better avoid unpleasant
topics.... Queen Farah said, "The Shah was suicidal."

His majesty was suffering from depression.... When I saw the
Shah late that evening he was not in good shape. He had lost
weight and looked tired and depressed. As it was late,
I suggested [it would be better if I returned the next day....
he insisted that I stay].

I told the Shah about the gravity of the situation and
mentioned to him what I had heard from the generals and
others at the airport. We also spoke about corruption and
what people were saying about the royal family.... At that
time, I was not aware that the Shah had cancer.... only five
people knew he was gravely ill. I blame these people. If [the
Iranian people] had known the truth about the Shah's state
of health, he would have had a great deal of sympathy and
would not have been demonized by the opposition the way
he was.[212]

The queen, in fact, had shipped a quantity of personal and
household items to the United States. She was not alone;
many wealthy Iranians had moved to transfer large amounts of
money to Swiss, French, British, American, and Cayman Island
banking institutions.

Zahedi was informed by the Shah that martial law was
about to be declared by his newly appointed prime minister, Jafar
Sharif-Emami. Mr. Sharif-Emami, who had been prime minister in
1960-1961, was chosen because of his reputation for personal
integrity and because of his close links with religious leaders.[213]
On his appointment he was charged by the Shah to give priority to
Islamic traditions. As a gesture in this direction it was announced
that the new "Imperial" calendar introduced in 1976 had been
abandoned in favor of the traditional Islamic lunar calendar.

The new government of twenty-two included only five former ministers; among them were a former head of the Gendarmerie, General Abbas Gharabaghi, who became Minister of the Interior; and Mr. Amir-Khosrow Afshar, a career diplomat who became Foreign Minister.[214]

Emami and representatives of Ayatollah Shariatmadari agreed to a series of demands by the moderate opposition. Among those demands granted were:

» The religious meeting place (Hosseiniye) was allowed to reopen.

» The Bazargan-Minatchi human rights organization was allowed to register.

» Complete freedom of the press.

The prime minister agreed to try to push the following demands:

» Royal family to stay out of all business and generally be kept in tight rein.

» Speedy trials for those charged with corruption.

» Shah to reign not rule, and thus not interfere with daily government business. Shah would remain commander in chief of armed forces.[215]

The prime minister had begun his new administration with an attempt at appeasing the clerics, but the opposite effect was achieved. Sharif-Emami's moves only served to further enrage the radical mullahs. Emami, who served in the post of prime minister in the 1960s, was perhaps not the most auspicious choice by the Shah. He was seen by the Iranian people as the embodiment of the very dissolute system they were trying to overthrow. The ambassador strongly suggested to the prime minister that repeated changes in political direction only served to further destabilize the situation in Iran, and it was a necessity for any actions by the new government to be seen as honest and aboveboard. He also encouraged the Shah to relinquish the daily governmental tasks to his appointees and focus on maintaining the respect and confidence of the military.

The opposition to the Shah's government organized a series of demonstrations to begin on September 8. The Shah again called for Zahedi and sought his opinion about the course of action: Should he declare martial law or should he refrain? Zahedi advised him:

> "Majesty, you have named a government, now let them take their responsibility.... These huge crowds may decide to walk all the way up to the palace if they are left on their own." I insisted that the government must combine firmness with dialogue; otherwise His Majesty may face the same fate as Tsar Nicholas. We spoke more at length about the royal family and concluded that they should all leave the country. I called Princess Ashraf (the Shah's twin sister) that same night and told her to pack. Some royal family members were already outside the country.... [later] on my way back to Washington I called each one and told them not to return.[216]

All the while, the powers-that-be in Washington failed to recognize the danger of the downward-spiraling events in Iran. Carter, Cyrus Vance, and Brzezinski were all immersed in discussions with Sadat and Begin at Camp David. Zahedi was a bit surprised when Rosalynn was the Carter who received him at the White House for a debriefing on the situation in Tehran. It seemed obvious that the president had shoved the simmering pot that was Iran onto a back burner.

On September 8 marshal law was enacted and a curfew set in place. The next day demonstrations erupted in Iran. In an attempt to suppress a protest rally held in Jaleh Square in Tehran, troops fired into the crowd. Estimates placed the number of deaths at approximately one thousand; the Shah's government admitted to killing 122.

That bloody September day came to be known as "Black Friday." Houchang Nahavandi wrote of an interview with a participant in the riots:

Elements in the crown opened fire against the forces of orders, whose casualties were all due to bullet-wounds.... there were among the demonstrators Palestinians, who had entered the country with "genuine" false papers.... In July 1980 I received a first-hand account of the events... [by] someone who, in 1978, had been an activist in the revolutionary movement.... He was contacted by a group of "Islamic-Marxists," who assigned to him two armed Palestinians.... these two fired indiscriminately, not only at the soldiers, but also...into the crowd, simply to shed blood and create irreparable resentment.... Other armed men...lay in ambush...and opened fire in similar fashion.[217]

Zahedi requisitioned a helicopter and with Generals Oveissi and Khosrowdad flew over Tehran to observe the situation on the ground. (The ambassador sadly told me that both men were later butchered by Khomeini's henchmen.) He was in constant contact with the Shah in order to keep him informed of events. Zahedi also mentioned his thoughts on Ambassador Sullivan during those difficult days:

I learned that Ambassador Sullivan had gone to see Foreign Minister Afshar. He told Afshar he was getting negative noises from Washington about the situation in Iran, and "Ardeshir better return there quickly to fix it." I guess he wanted to get rid of me in order to have a free hand in Tehran.[218]

About that same time, State Department Appointee Henry Precht wrote that he had a "revelation":

The day after the massacre, I was taking my morning shower and the thought came to me that the Shah was indeed finished. This was a war between him and his people, and he could not prevail in such a war. When he might go, and how, I didn't know. Whether he would be able to make some compromise that would diminish his powers, I didn't know. But it was clear to me that the Iran of the future was not going to be the Iran of the past. The opposition elements would play a much larger role and the Shah a much smaller role, and we needed to adjust to that.[219]

An interview with the Shah by a *Time* magazine correspondent reveals the toll that the Jaleh Square incident and the imposition of martial law had taken on him:

The Shah was plainly an immensely saddened man. It showed in his face, which was grim and gaunt, and in his eyes, which were tired and melancholy. Even his dress, so often elegant, was somber. He wore a dark, formal suit, an unadorned white shirt and a narrow, conservative tie. There was little life and much caution in his voice. He answered questions after long and painful pauses.[220]

While the Shah was desperately trying to regain control in Iran, Khomeini had been in Iraq inciting revolution. Amir Taheri wrote in his book *The Spirit of Allah: Khomeini and the Islamic Revolution* of the ludicrous charges that Khomeini and his subversive network continuously directed at the Shah. Pahlavi was randomly charged with being a womanizer, a homosexual, a Jewish convert, a drug addict, and a Catholic. He was also labeled the "American Shah" and "Israel's Shah." Even the beautiful Empress Farah did not escape Khomeini's twisted defamation; she was maligned as an adulteress and linked romantically to none other than President Jimmy Carter.[221]

The term "Israel's Shah" was likely due to the fact that in 1957 Iran aided the Israelis by funding an oil pipeline from Eilat to the Mediterranean. In the summer of that year an Iranian representative met secretly with then Finance Minister Levi Eshkol and Minister of Trade and Industry Pinhas Sapir. At the end of the negotiations the three men signed an agreement that would permit the sale of Iranian oil to Israel for the now-paltry sum of $1.30 per barrel.[222] The Shah was eager to complete this transaction, as it would allow Iranian oil to circumvent the Suez Canal, which was under Egypt's jurisdiction. This was especially important, as some three-quarters of Iran's oil exports flowed through that strategic waterway.[223] The eight-inch pipeline, completed in approximately three months, was upgraded in 1958 to a sixteen-inch line.

It was also in 1957 that the Shah first asked Israel's Mossad to provide training for his secret police, *Sazeman-e Ettela'at va Amniyat-e Keshvar* (SAVAK). Some sources record that it was Mossad and American CIA agents who taught SAVAK the means of torture as an investigative tool.[224] My good friend, the late Isser Harel, was the head of Mossad when the Shah made his overture for assistance. The Israelis were not above using flattery with Pahlavi and compared him to Cyrus the Great, who was responsible for freeing the Jews from Babylonian captivity. Harel revealed: "The connection was very romantic, and I would say of great importance at that time.... [The Shah] wanted to play the part."[225]

In an interview in 1960 the Shah is said to have confirmed a long-standing association with the Israelis when he acknowledged, "Iran has recognized Israel long ago." (The Shah was speaking of the recognition afforded Israel by the Mossadegh regime in 1951.[226] Reportedly, that recognition came at the cost of a $400,000 bribe to Iran's then-Prime Minister Muhammad Sa'ed Maraghei. In March 1950 Israel had offered a consulate to Iran, although it was forced to work through the Swiss Embassy in Tel Aviv. Tehran then became an effective pipeline, not only for Jews wishing to escape Iraq and relocate to Israel, but also for oil sales to Israel.) Pahlavi's response so incensed Egypt's Gamal Abdul Nasser that he halted all political contact with Iran and launched a vitriolic crusade against the Shah and Iran.

Despite Iran's entente with Israel, the Shah believed that the Jews controlled the U.S. media and held enormous sway in

Washington, D.C.; therefore, he took great care not to antagonize the Israelis. The Shah's fears provided the Jews with a harvest of concessions from Iran.[227]

Because of Iran's large Jewish population, the largest in any other Middle Eastern country,[228] a number of very secretive meetings between Iranian and Israeli officials took place over the years prior to the Shah's ouster. These included Prime Minister David Ben-Gurion in 1961, Prime Minister Levi Eshkol, Prime Minister Yitzhak Rabin, Prime Minister Menachem Begin, and an invitation from the Shah to Prime Minister Golda Meir in 1972. Meir secretly flew into Tehran's Mehrabad airport for a meeting with Pahlavi. In some circles the Shah has been credited with trying to arrange a peace agreement between Meir and Anwar Sadat.[229]

Apparently, Iran viewed Israel as a strong deterrent to Soviet rather than Arab aggression in the Gulf region.[230] The Shah could readily visualize the possibility of a Russian dual flank operation against Iran through Iraq and Afghanistan and hoped that his covert relationship with Israel would serve him well. Gary Sick recounted that just "seven months after Begin's visit to Iran, the Israeli prime minister tried to convince Carter and Sadat at the Camp David talks that the Shah was finished."[231]

In our personal interview Samuel Segev, author of *The Iranian Triangle*, further suggests that Begin and Sadat tried to encourage Carter to issue a statement in support of the Shah. Segev said he found it "very odd that the president of the biggest country in the world...didn't understand...that the priority was to avoid, to prevent the fall of the Shah, and to get some stability in the region."[232] Each man, of course, had separate insight into the woes of the Shah; Begin had access to Lubrani's report on Iran, and Sadat was a close friend to the Iranian monarch.

Though Israel was not openly acknowledged by Pahlavi, the two countries continued to preserve amiable relations. Israel maintained a permanent mission in Tehran that housed, to all intents and purposes, an unofficial Embassy.

Israel's then-Chief of Staff Yitzhak Rabin first visited Iran in 1967. His trip was handled amidst great secrecy, and Rabin was whisked from place to place with little fanfare and clad in civilian clothes rather than his army regalia. Rabin, however, broke with tradition and signed his name in Hebrew when he visited the Tehran Mausoleum that housed the tomb of the Shah's father, Reza Shah.

Rabin was granted an audience with Reza Pahlavi and the two discussed such weighty matters as the possible repercussions of King Hussein's break with then-PLO leader Ahmed Shukeiri and Gamal Abdul Nasser's grip on the Arabian Peninsula and his influence in the Persian Gulf. Less than two months after his visit to Tehran Yitzhak Rabin would lead Israel's Defense Forces in a preemptive attack against Nasser's Egyptian army, which had amassed hundreds of tanks and tens of thousands of soldiers on the Egyptian-Israeli border. Given his Arab ties and his covert relationship with Israel, the conflict placed the Shah in a very difficult position. Tehran newspapers were openly and blatantly hostile toward Israel, but not the Shah's military leaders. Chief of Staff Bahram Ariana and his deputy General Feridoun Jam openly congratulated the Israelis on their victory over Egypt, Jordan, Syria, Saudi Arabia, Iraq, Kuwait, and Algeria.

The Shah, who was visiting Paris when the war began, stopped in Turkey on his way back to Tehran. During a press conference, the Shah called on Israel to withdraw from the territories captured during the six days of fighting. Expecting congratulations from the Shah for decimating Nasser's forces, Israeli government officials were stunned by the Shah's hard line and the fact that he halted joint endeavors with the Jewish nation. Pahlavi even went so far as to try to pressure President Lyndon Johnson to force Israel to relinquish the territory captured during the war, but Johnson refused.

Realizing that his efforts to snub Israel were futile, the Shah agreed to purchase another 6,000 Uzis from Israel and began to encourage King Hussein to establish ties with that country. (In 1965, the Shah sanctioned the purchase of a quantity of Uzi submachine guns to be used by his Royal Guard and the police.) Of course, oil would still flow between Iran and Israel, but now through a new 32-inch pipeline that was completed in December 1969.

According to one source, "In the aftermath of the Six-Day War, Israel transferred large amounts of oil from Iran to European markets via the Eilat-Ashkelon pipeline. In addition, Israel purchased a significant portion of its oil needs from Iran. Apparently, the two nations had numerous business transactions, although the extent of these dealings was never officially quantified."[233] The Shah shrugged off questions about oil sales to Israel by declaring he did not know the final destination of the oil once the tankers left their ports in the Persian Gulf. At the end of the Shah's rule, Iran's trade with Israel totaled approximately $400 million per year; and the Shah had purchased some $600 million in light weapons from Israel.[234]

CHAPTER

=== 1 2 ===

THE HANDWRITING
ON THE WALL

*"Man is a strange animal. He generally cannot read the
handwriting on the wall until his back is up against it."*
(ADLAI E. STEVENSON)

HAVING BEEN FUELED by the Iranian media following the
Six-Day War, hatred toward Israel and the Iranian Jews gained
momentum. Something as simple as a soccer match in Tehran in late
1968 opened the pus-laden sore of anti-Semitism. Swastika-painted
balloons floated over the stadium while an effigy of Moshe Dayan
was kicked and spat upon. The Shah could not believe his people
capable of such barbarism.

Iran and Israel still cooperated militarily, although one Iranian
navy commander put the cooperation in terms of its covert aspects:
"We couldn't have our ships running around the Persian Gulf with
Israeli (Gabriel) missiles onboard."[235] Not only did Israel sell arms
to Iran; it provided training for Iranian military officers, secret
police, and pilots, as well as instruction in intelligence-gathering.
This and more came to light when Khomeini's rogues raided the
Israeli Embassy in Tehran and published documents found inside.[236]

In the summer of 1972, Uri Lubrani was sent to Tehran as Israel's ambassador. Lubrani was to be the first Israeli to present his credentials directly to the Shah. After repeated attempts to gain an audience through Foreign Minister Abbas Ali Khalatbari, Lubrani determined he was being politely ignored by the monarch.

With information gained during his tenure, Lubrani repeatedly warned Israel's leaders of the imminent collapse of the monarchy in Iran:

> For years, at every opportunity we warned that there was an Iranian danger. That it was greater and more profound than any other danger facing Israel. Even more than the Palestinian issue. We said that it should be handled first. Not only in Lebanon, but in Tehran as well. Because from Tehran they send out tentacles to Berlin, to Saudi Arabia, to Argentina.[237]

Lubrani told me that it took weeks for him to muster up enough courage to put his thoughts and feelings down on paper. He had no proof that trouble was afoot; simply a gut feeling gained from talking to people in the bazaar, in the oil industry, and within the trade unions. He felt something very ominous but couldn't put his finger on what that might be. Lubrani was constrained by the knowledge that when an ambassador put his assessment in writing, it became an official, historical document. Finally, he wrote a memo that was distributed by Dayan to the Knesset. Lubrani suggested that Israel begin immediately to find an alternative source for the 95 percent of oil that was imported from Iran. Dayan had the Lubrani document paraphrased and forwarded to the CIA as being from a "usually reliable source." According to Lubrani, the CIA responded that the source didn't know what he was talking about. Nothing was expected to happen in Iran for ten or fifteen years.[238]

Lubrani chose to visit the bazaars, not because it was the place to shop, but because the bazaar was a place to "pray, to meet friends, to do business, to sit in a café. You can go there to catch up on gossip, can take part in an opposition rally. Without having to run all over town...the bazaar...is indispensable for earthly existence and, through prayer and offerings, also ensures [for the Shiite] his eternal life."[239]

When after five years as ambassador in Iran Lubrani was recalled from Tehran, Yosef Harmelin, former head of Shin Bet, Israel's security service, was appointed to replace him. When Harmelin was visited by General David Ivri, Israel's commander of the Air Force and the last senior officer to visit the country before the Shah was ousted, Ivri could sense the imminent collapse of the Shah's monarchy and that the protest movement had become a revolution in the making:

> *The strikes and demonstrations had spread over the country, oil production was barely adequate for local consumption... banks were closed, and there were serious shortages of basic food items. The Revolutionary Guards, trained in PLO camps in Lebanon and Libya, made their first appearance in the cities.*[240]

In a personal interview, general Ivri recounted the tension that could be felt in the streets of Tehran just weeks before the start of the revolution. The general had to be flown from location to location by helicopter due to the rioting and demonstrations in the streets. "The Army," said Ivri "was on strike."[241]

Israeli Prime Minister Yitzhak Rabin's second secret meeting in Tehran took place in 1974. He met with the Shah to present a proposal to trade land for peace. The two men spent two hours together, during which time each shared his personal analysis of the world situation, especially as it related to the Middle East and relations between Israel and Iran. Pahlavi called for Rabin to be more flexible in his dealings with Sadat and Hussein; at the same time, he refused to grant a billion-dollar loan for a number of projects to the Israeli prime minister.

By November 1978 the Israelis could clearly see the proverbial handwriting on the wall and began to evacuate all Israeli citizens who wished to depart the troubled country. November 6 saw the departure of 365 Israelis, the majority women and children. Although terrorists linked to the PLO had launched attacks on the El Al office in Tehran, the airline continued to operate flights in and out of Iran in order to accommodate as many Israelis as possible.

The Shah's major concerns, meanwhile, centered around three issues:

» Afghanistan—that the USSR would invade Afghanistan if Iran was weakened;

» Iraq—that Iraq would take advantage of a weakened Iran and invade;

» Khomeini—that the popular cleric would be successful with his call for an Islamic Revolution in Iran.

James A. Bill wrote "Iran and the Crisis of 1978"; his opinion paralleled that of Pahlavi:

> *Outside of Iran, there are three general opinions on the nature of the opposition to the regime. The Shah's opponents are said by some to consist of a small group of trouble-making Marxists supported in their treasonous activities by the Soviet Union and other radical regimes such as today's Libya. Others would maintain that Iranian opposition is dominated by a number of reactionary religious leaders who resent the Shah's modernization program, which emphasizes land reform and women's rights. A third position summarizes the Shah's problems in terms of an unholy alliance of these two extreme factions, which have joined forces with the sole aim of dismantling the present political system.*[242]

Pahlavi felt he could no longer count on the U.S. to remain a staunch ally under President Carter's administration. By 1977 the Shah was convinced that pro-Soviet Arab nations would unite and launch an attack against Iran. This fear prompted Pahlavi to spend billions on defensive weapons in an attempt to forestall an invasion by Soviet-backed Iraq. He knew that his armaments did not include anti-missile weapons that would help defend his country against Iraq's SCUD missiles. The Shah was concerned that Iraq possessed more armaments, including the Soviet-supplied SCUD missiles, than did Iran. The Iranian monarch felt compelled to arm his country against possible aggression from Saddam Hussein despite the signing of the Algiers Accords in 1975, which were intended to settle land disputes between the two countries.

In an interview with *Newsweek* in November 1977, the reporter asked Pahlavi about the accusations that the Shah's arms purchases represented *"la Folie des grandeurs"* (delusions of grandeur). The Shah answered:

> *It's not only U.S. unreliability as we witnessed in Vietnam, Cambodia, Laos, and during the India-Pakistan wars. It's also UN impotency. We have settled our differences with Iraq, but their military buildup continues.... I wonder how many of your editorial writers and congressmen realize that Iraq has more planes, tanks, and guns than we do—(even ground-to-ground SCUD missiles). Nor are we just in another state. Look at our borders. What would happen if what remains of Pakistan were to disintegrate? If we don't assume [our own] security in the regions, who will do it?* [243]

With the safety of Iran in mind the Shah approached Jimmy Carter about the purchase of Pershing missiles; the administration declined based on the fact that the Pershing was capable of carrying nuclear warheads.[244] In a move destined to cause enormous controversy, Iran turned to Israel for assistance. It came in the form of technology that partnered the two countries in the production of ballistic missiles.

The cooperation between Israel and Iran had begun when Israel Aircraft Industry founder, Adolf Schwimmer, secured a contract to overhaul Iranian airliners and American-made F-86 fighters. In order to gain entry into Iranian circles, Schwimmer sought the help of his friend and later business partner, Ya'acov Nimrodi. Nimrodi had spent twenty-five years in Tehran in various

Israeli governmental roles. (Much of his work during Israel's early years is still classified.) Through Nimrodi's influence Schwimmer was allowed access to Tehran's inner business circles. He was granted audiences with the Shah several times and hosted Iranian government officials and senior military men in Israel.

In my interview with Samuel Segev, the author related how Nimrodi described a trip to Israel for Iran's Chief of Staff General Bahram Ariana and General Hasan Toufanian. Ariana proved to be an advocate for Israel. He encouraged the Shah to collaborate with the Israelis. Ariana also encouraged the Shah to mediate a peace pact between Israel and Jordan's King Hussein. The king thought Israel's only interest was in securing the territory on the West Bank. Nimrodi escorted the two Iranians on tours of various industrial sites in Israel, leading Ariana to wonder if Iran might be allowed to manufacture 81 mm mortars for the Israelis.[245]

In 1976 Schwimmer outlined an elaborate proposal for technological advancement between the two countries. Shimon Peres, Israel's then-Minister of Defense under Yitzhak Rabin, presented the plan to the Shah. The two countries agreed to work together in a collaboration labeled *Project Flower* or "Tzur." The proposal included provisions for the production of a mid-range, surface-to-surface missile with the costs divided between the two countries. "The Flower project...involved the production of missiles with warheads weighing 750 kilograms...with a range of up to 300 miles. They were to be shipped through a Swiss company to central Iran for assembly and testing."[246] Also included in the agreement was the possibility of jointly building a new-and-improved version of France's Mirage 5 aircraft. Both countries agreed on secrecy for the project because each head of state feared interference from what was certain to be a Carter administration in the New Year.

During Shimon Peres' visit with the Shah, Pahlavi was perplexed as to exactly what the United States wanted of him, especially in regard to future dealings with the PLO. When I talked with Samuel Segev, he was able to give me insight into the Shah's feelings toward the PLO:

> I don't know what they want of me in Congress...to surrender to terror? We recently captured one hundred terrorists, and I have no intention of giving in to their blackmail. The Palestinians poison the atmosphere and do their best to subvert pro-Western governments in our region. Iraq still wants Kuwait and the Soviet Union is after Oman. I have no choice but to trust in Iran.[247]

At the same time, Pahlavi touted Sadat's role in the Middle East and his pro-Western leanings. Peres reassured the Shah that the agreement between Egypt and Israel was moving forward smoothly. The two men talked at length about the Shah's reservations over the upcoming U.S. election and the seeming finality of Jimmy Carter's presidential bid. The Shah, of course, again expressed his reservations about the tack that Carter's Middle East policies would take.

The collaboration of *Project Flower* brought Israel's Defense Minister Yitzhak Rabin and Iran's Procurement Chief Toufanian together to provide security for Iran against a Soviet and Iraqi offensive. One of the discussions during their meetings centered around the development of a submarine-launched missile, and concerns about India and Pakistan's nuclear arms race.[248] Toufanian was an old hand at procuring arms from Israel.

The election of Begin called a halt to the project for a time. It was reinstated in 1978, and according to NTI (Nuclear Threat Institute), "The following year Iran made a down payment for *Project Flower* by providing Israel with $280 million worth of oil. To support this project, a team of Iranian experts began construction of a missile assembly facility near Sirjan, in south central Iran, and a missile test range near Rafsanjan."[249] Both Iran and Israel chose to play their cards close to the vest regarding this issue and failed to inform their joint U.S. ally of the project. Assistant Secretary of State for Near Eastern Affairs Harold Saunders was forthcoming with his opinion about the Israel/Iran connection: "Israel built a lot of things for the Iranians that we [the U.S.] did not know about."[250] Khomeini's rise to power signaled the death of *Project Flower*.

Dr. Mina talked with me about another joint project between Israel and Iran:

> *We even invested in Israel in a special power plant which connected the Port of Eilat to Ashkelon in the Mediterranean. This power plant took the oil from the Gulf of Aqaba and delivered it to the Mediterranean Port of Ashkelon and also fed the refineries in Haifa. So, we were supplying oil for internal consumption, but at the same time they were using that pipeline for the export of our crude oil, which was a shortcut instead of paying a very high rate for tankers to go through the Suez Canal.*[251]

The Israeli Mossad held another card close: bringing together the Iranian and Chinese governments to discuss an underground war in Afghanistan against Soviet aggression. In September 1978 a high-level Chinese official, Qiao Shi, flew to Iran to meet with the Iranian secret police.[252] Having the Soviets in a quagmire in Afghanistan, similar to the U.S. situation in Vietnam, would siphon billions from the Russian economy. Whatever plans the two countries may have had to influence events in Afghanistan were upended when the Shah fled the country in January 1979.

After Begin assumed the position of Israel's prime minister, the Shah began to pull back from his support of the Jewish state. The Shah sided with the Arabs on the issue of the West Bank, and in a missive to government leaders called for the United States to compel Israel to reach an agreement with its Arab neighbors: "The Shah feels the U.S. should make every effort to bring about an early resolution to the Arab-Israeli situation. He is on record as opposing the Judaization of Jerusalem and supporting Israeli withdrawal from all occupied Arab territories and restoring the legitimate rights of the Palestinians."[253]

The Shah then instructed his procurement officer to hold back on covert Israeli/Iranian arms ventures. In other conciliatory moves toward his Arab brothers, Pahlavi denied Iranian participation in the celebration of Israel's twenty-second anniversary. He also forbade the Israelis an invitation to the festivities marking Persia's 2,500 years as an empire. It was this lavish celebration that incensed the American press. Pahlavi felt the response was because "the U.S. media was controlled by Jewish interests. He attributed any criticism of Iran in the American media as an Israeli effort to undermine him."[254]

Pahlavi also warned Israeli Foreign Minister Moshe Dayan that Soviet aggression would not bypass Israel and its Arab neighbors. During his meeting with Dayan, the Shah cautioned the tiny Jewish nation: "Israel would do well to take into account that these countries [Iraq and Syria], at the initiative and backing of Soviet Russia, would again make war on Israel."[255] Dayan suggested to the Shah that Iran and Israel normalize relations by changing the designation of the Iranian diplomatic mission in Tehran to an official Embassy. Pahlavi declined Dayan's suggestion for fear of inciting Iran's clerics. Pahlavi's generals sought Dayan's assistance to help the monarch understand the enormity of the threat Iran faced due to the Shah's inability to make critical decisions. Dayan was unsuccessful and concluded that Pahlavi was politically paralyzed.

The Shah's fears regarding the Soviets and the Iraqis would prove to be the least of his worries. It was not to be from countries outside Iran that his greatest challenge would come; it was to be the Ayatollah Khomeini who brought down the House of Pahlavi and the monarchy.

Khomeini's oratory was designed to create fear in the lower classes in Iran, those forced to do without while witnessing the overindulgence of the upper classes. He heralded what was seen as the Shah's complicity with Israel and the United States. The intellectuals, the political frontline in Iran, initially took a wait-and-see attitude, but it was not long before they joined forces with the oppressed and poverty-stricken and took to the streets in protest of the Shah's policies. With the help of PLO-supplied weapons, trained terrorists, and the murders of Iranian demonstrators as a means to incite the mobs in the streets, the mayhem spread. Yasser Arafat, head of the PLO, was hailed as a friend by Khomeini after the Ayatollah seized control of Iran. Arafat's reward was the Israeli Embassy in Tehran with a PLO standard flying overhead. Arafat quickly named a member of Fatah, Hani al Hassan, to head the mission.

The PLO leader was ecstatic. He saw the Iranian revolution as a way to reverse "the strategic balance in the Middle East against Israel and the United States." The Camp David Accords would be "merely ink on paper following the basic changes brought by the Iranian revolution, both in the region and our Islamic nation and in world strategy."[256] Arafat ridiculed speculation that Saudi Arabia's King Khalid, the UAE, or Kuwait might be exposed to the aftermath of Khomeini's revolution in Iran.

Henry Kissinger may have summed up what led to the Shah's downfall better than most in his book *White House Years*. Kissinger wrote of the 1953 coup that restored the Shah to the Peacock Throne:

> He [the Shah] never forgot that. It may have been the root of his extraordinary trust in American purposes and American goodwill and of his psychological disintegration when he sensed that friendship evaporating. On some levels excessively, even morbidly, suspicious of possible attempts to diminish his authority, he nevertheless retained an almost naïve faith in the United States.[257]

Ardeshir Zahedi thought Kissinger a "noble man...who understood that letting down an ally of three decades in his hour of need was a disgrace and not in the longer interest of the United States."[258]

It is possible that Kissinger had read the account of the Shah having reportedly told an aide, "As long as the Americans support me, we can do and say whatever we want—and I am immovable."[259]

The Shah had every reason to believe in the efficacy of the United States to Iran. After all, was it not the U.S. in conjunction with Great Britain that had removed Mossadegh and returned the Shah to power in 1953? Had not Dwight D. Eisenhower funneled $500 million to Iran between 1953 and 1957? Was it not the U.S. that aided Iran in expelling the Soviets following World War II? There was a long history of cooperation between the two nations, an international version of, "You scratch my back; I'll stake you to Iranian oil for companies in the U.S."

Various presidents paid cherished accolades to the Shah during his visits to the U.S.:

> *Dwight Eisenhower: "Under the courageous leadership of the Shah, the people of Iran met [the danger of a communist takeover]. In their efforts to restore economic stability, they received indispensable help from us.... Iran remains free; and its freedom continues to prove of vital importance to our freedom."*[260]

> *John F. Kennedy: "[The Shah is] a vital force in maintaining the independence of [Iran].... So when we welcome the Shah here we welcome a friend and a very valiant fighter."*[261]

Despite Kennedy's kind words, he was not so enamored of the Shah. He, like Carter, called for international reforms. So vitriolic was the U.S. position toward the Shah under Kennedy that Edward R. Murrow, Kennedy's appointee to oversee the United States Information Agency, cancelled a film on Iran simply because the Shah had ordered it shown throughout his country. Said Murrow, "Anything that pleases them so much as that can't be completely accurate reporting."[262] The Shah finally called on the head of the IDF Military Intelligence Branch, Chaim Herzog, for information as to why Kennedy seemed determined to ignore Iran's role in CENTO. Samuel Segev provided insight to the answer during our interview: He said Herzog explained to the Shah that Kennedy favored economic aid rather than arms supplies.

James A. Bill wrote, "Kennedy's doubts about the Shah were so strong that he even considered forcing his abdication in favor of rule by regency until his young son came of age."[263] Is it possible that Kennedy's view of Pahlavi was colored by a conversation he reportedly had had with Nikita Khrushchev in Vienna in 1961? The Russian strongman declared to the president that the Shah was no more than the son of a sergeant in the Iranian army. Khrushchev predicted that Pahlavi would suffer defeat, but not at the hands of the Soviets. The Russian's warnings were so unsettling to Kennedy that he ordered an analysis of the situation. The Intelligence Estimate concluded: "profound political and social change [probably revolutionary in nature] in one form or another is virtually inevitable."[264]

There are those who believe that Teymour Bakhtiar, SAVAK chief in Iran, was the one courted by Kennedy to attempt a coup against Pahlavi. Apparently the Shah was told of the plot and quickly removed Bakhtiar from his post. Perhaps Carter's desire to be compared to John F. Kennedy went deeper than imagined.

The Shah retaliated against Kennedy's rejection by appearing to court the Soviets and by giving hard-line interviews to U.S. newspapers.[265] Julius Holmes, U.S. Ambassador to Iran, outlined why the Shah was so upset by Kennedy's rhetoric:

> What really upset the Shah was what Kennedy had said in his speeches.... The U.S. was for "revolution"—that was the word.... The Shah interpreted these words to mean just one thing: we are going to support a revolution in Iran.[266]

The Shah's tough stance didn't last long. In mid-1961, in an attempt at appeasement toward Kennedy, Pahlavi named a leader in the opposition party and a clear favorite of the U.S., Dr. Ali Amini, as prime minister. It was U.S. support for Amini that caused the Shah to be increasingly suspicious regarding the U.S. Embassy's sympathy for the National Front in Iran. Dr. Ahmad Tehrani was also able to shed some light on the Shah's relationship with Kennedy during our interview:

The Shah was an extremely pragmatic man when he was talking to the leaders of the world. I was present and taking notes when he came to meet with President Kennedy. He [Pahlavi] had a profound knowledge of general politics of the world. Even before Kennedy won the election, (he was not particularly pro the regime in Iran)...he decided to meet the Shah privately. When the Shah was invited to Washington, I had a very good friend by the name of Jim Nichols. Jim was a speech writer and public relations man. He was extra-ordinarily impressed with the Shah and decided to help him with his speeches. We knew Kennedy did not see eye-to-eye with the Shah...and that is why we brought in Jim Nichols.... As far as I know, Kennedy was kind to the Shah.... The Shah's relationship with Nixon and Ford was the same. [With Carter] in the beginning it was not the same, but it became so that Carter decided to spend the New Year in Iran.[267]

Although he had made thirteen trips to the U.S., it may be that in the end Pahlavi had forgotten his earlier reception at the hands of U.S. presidents. He was reportedly ignored by Franklin D. Roosevelt when the commander in chief, in the company of Winston Churchill and Joseph Stalin, visited Tehran in November 1943 during World War II. The three men signed a declaration in support of "the independence, sovereignty, and territorial integrity of Iran."[268] However, Roosevelt did take time later to write a letter chastising the Shah for the lack of forestation (the planting of trees) in the country.[269] Harry S. Truman declined appeals for foreign aid; John F. Kennedy referred to Pahlavi as a despot. Jimmy Carter, with visions of grandeur as a reincarnation of John F. Kennedy, adopted his human rights stance against the Shah, greeted him warmly, and then set out to strip Pahlavi of his throne and country.[270] The Shah must have wondered at some point if Carter really was just another Kennedy clone.

In 1977 the American Embassy took steps to better report on opposition groups in Iran. As we discussed in other chapters, the U.S.

renewed contacts with moderate (and some not-so-moderate) politicians under the pretext of human rights. During the fall of 1977 both State Department and Embassy officials determined those contacts must be maintained regardless of the Shah's reaction. The contacts were often arranged through the aide of a former Iranian prime minister. The U.S. ambassador was informed that the U.S. government was well aware of the arrangements. This go-between was able to assist Embassy officials with better access to the more radical elements in both the bazaars and the clergy.[271]

The by-product of Carter's policy against the Shah was that the United States came to be seen as a capricious ally, one that could not be depended upon in times of crisis. Brzezinski, however, saw the necessity of this commitment. He felt that the only path for the U.S. was unconditional support of the Shah.

=== 13 ===

FOLLOW
THE BOUNCING
(GEORGE) BALL

"In a world in the midst of fundamental transformation, prudent statesmen are especially in demand. Disconnected idealists and visionaries like Adlai Stevenson, Eugene McCarthy, and, to a lesser degree, Jimmy Carter...fall short of statesmanship.... their wisdom is impractical.... The moral component of politics is sacrificed on the altar of political expediency."

(JAMES A. BILL) [272]

THE CARTER ADMINISTRATION seemed unable or unwilling to recognize or acknowledge that the Shah was in dire trouble. In fact, a CIA report from the late 1970s indicated that only two operatives were active in Iran. In his book *All Fall Down: America's Tragic Encounter with Iran,* author Gary Sick wrote: "U.S. intelligence capability to track the Shah's domestic opposition had been allowed to deteriorate to the vanishing point." [273] In fact, the State Department under Carter's administration was openly hostile to the Pahlavi regime, opposing not only the sale of conventional military weapons but also of ordinary riot gear. Meanwhile, Carter continued to vacillate between the priorities of demanding human rights concessions from the Shah and supporting a strategic American ally in the region.

In *Nest of Spies*, Amir Taheri wrote: "Khomeini's supporters also began to think of the 'new possibilities' that the expected rift between Tehran and Washington might offer. Ebrahim Yazdi, an Iranian-born American citizen representing the Ayatollah in the United States, wrote to him in Najaf in Iraq that 'the Shah's friends in Washington are out.... It is time to act.'"[274]

Liberal Princeton Professor Richard Falk described Khomeini's entourage of advisors as: "moderate, progressive individuals [with] a notable record of concern for human rights." Furthermore, Falk stated that an Iran under Khomeini's governance would "provide us with a desperately-needed model of human government for a third-world country."[275] Could he possibly have been any more wrong in his assessment? Carter's appointees were equally misinformed when making their evaluation of Khomeini.

During November 1978 Michael Blumenthal, Carter's Secretary of the Treasury, visited the Shah to discuss oil prices. He was deeply troubled by the Shah's appearance and reported back to Washington that the Shah seemed despondent and out-of-sorts. Pahlavi reiterated to the treasury secretary that he simply did not know what the Carter administration wanted him to do. Since the Mossadegh overthrow in 1953 the Shah had been under the protection of the American government. It was Blumenthal who suggested that the president approach George Ball to head an inter-agency task force on Iran. (Ball had been Blumenthal's mentor in the '60s.)[276]

Thus, former diplomat and Johnson Administration Undersecretary of State George Ball was engaged to do an independent and classified study on the Shah and make recommendations to the Carter administration. One political analyst penned, "Ball pops up, like a cork, every election year."[277] Ball was famous for being the prominent high official opposed to military escalation in Vietnam and a strong critic of Nixon's foreign policy. Ball believed the Shah to be "The son of a colonel in a Persian Cossack regiment, play-acting as the emperor of a country...."[278] Now the Shah's fate was in the hands of the man who viewed America's ally of thirty-six years in this manner.

Ball and Carter met for the first time in 1975 at a Lehman Brothers luncheon. James A. Bill said of Ball, "[He] came away from the session singularly unimpressed. Carter appeared naïve, overconfident, and absorbed by the minutiae of electoral politics. He seemed to avoid the substantive issues of politics and, in Ball's judgment, he lacked vision."[279] Although Ball and Carter were never able to establish a personal affinity, and his early opinion of Carter was less than positive, Ball agreed to take on the task. His report was given highly limited distribution in the Carter administration.

Ball suggested that the president restrict the Shah's power while State Department Appointee Henry Precht called upon the Shah to gracefully step down. Precht's opinion of the Shah was less than glowing: "Here we were depending on this autocrat to protect American interests in a very key part of the world, and it appears that he was some kind of nut! This job was going to be a lot more complex than I thought it would be."[280] How absurd! The future of the staunchest ally in the Persian Gulf region now lay in the hands of one man who thought the Shah an impostor and another who openly declared him "a nut!" Only Zbigniew Brzezinski persisted in warning the Carter administration that the Shah's overthrow would spell calamity for the United States. Neither Ball nor Precht were overjoyed with Zbig's stance.

In my interview with Marvin Kalb, the former network correspondent addressed the friction amongst the Carter administration:

> I can tell you that a lot of people, serious people in the [State] department, including Henry [Precht], were certainly aware of what was going on and there was a division...the split between Brzezinski and Vance...Iran was only one of the splits between the two of them, but it definitely was an important one. And that represented the views of those people in the department who knew a great deal about Iran, who

studied it carefully, who understood the increasing weakness of the Shah's position and the increasing strength of Khomeini's position and were trying to point this out to the U.S. government so that an intelligent American response could be orchestrated to meet this new set of challenges. The people at the White House were for the most part intent on supporting the Shah to the degree that they could because in their minds they were seeing it from a larger perspective. They were seeing it from a U.S.-Soviet perspective. They believed it was very important to keep the Shah in office as long as possible because he had always been a strong supporter of an anti-Soviet position. And a number of presidents...Ford, Nixon before, Kissinger, they all operated on an assumption that it was very wise to retain the closest possible relations with the Shah.[281]

Brzezinski strongly suggested that Carter send him to Tehran to try to help the Shah and expressed that desire in a meeting with the president and George Ball. Ball responded: "With all due respect, [this] is the worst idea I have ever heard."[282] Ball believed Brzezinski would reject any plan that suggested contacting Khomeini. Carter apparently agreed with Ball and nixed the Brzezinski trip. Zbig later admitted that he had made a mistake in agreeing to work with George Ball. Although initially very high on the former diplomat, Zbig reported that he "later wished I had listened to Cy [Cyrus Vance]. Ball's participation in our debates sharpened our disagreements while delaying basic choices...and his subsequent willingness to discuss what transpired within the White House and State Department with members of the press. Moreover...I violated a basic rule...one should never obtain the services of an "impartial" outside consultant.[283]

The Shah shared his confusion about the Carter administration's role in events in Iran:

The messages I received from the Americans continued to be confusing and contradictory. What was I to make of the administration's sudden decision to call former Under Secretary of State George Ball to the White House as an advisor on Iran? I knew that Ball was no friend, and I understood he was working on a special report concerning Iran. No one ever informed me what areas the report was to cover, let alone its conclusions. I read those months later in exile and found my worst fears confirmed. Ball was among those Americans who wanted to abandon me and ultimately my country.[284]

While formulating his report Ball met with Israeli Ambassador to Iran Lubrani. The two men and National Security Council member Gary Sick met at the Links Club in New York in the fall of 1978. Sick and Ball were most interested in Lubrani's sources for the report he had forwarded to Moshe Dayan. To counter their demands, Lubrani asked, "Do you have somebody in the entourage of Khomeini at Neauphle-le-Château? You know, this is where the next regime in Tehran is preparing to take office, in Neauphle-le-Château." Lubrani told me that Carter was to blame, not solely, but to some extent, for the current state of affairs in Iran.[285]

Ball's assessment of the Shah's precarious position was underlined by such inclusions in his report as:

The most desirable solution...would probably be for the Shah to remain as chief of state, retaining qualified command of the Army but entrusting the exercise of political power and decision to a civilian government.

Elements of the moderate opposition are proposing that the Shah abdicate in favor of the Crown Prince.... They hope to clear this scheme with Khomeini, since, were he to approve, it might relieve some of the current pressures.

We have...ample clout with the [Iranian] Air Force, which is the apple of the Shah's eye. We provide them with nearly all of their equipment, including $7.5 billion of highly sophisticated hardware now on order.

We should not delay in conveying our private views to the Shah that a transfer of power is indispensable and urgent.

The Ayatollah Khomeini, by his fanatical opposition to the Shah for more than fifteen years, has come to personify the revolt. The Iranian people view him as a legendary, almost sacred, figure, whose actions are beyond reproach.

We urgently need to open a disavowable channel of communication with him [Khomeini] or his entourage. If we are to undertake a more active role in political developments, we will at least need a means of passing messages or seeking private views.

We should also consult closely with the French at a very high level in an attempt to make Khomeini's visit to France as brief as possible and to limit the extent to which he and the shadowy group around him are permitted to manage events in Iran.

We should not...encourage the overthrow of an existing government until we are reasonably sure that the successor government would offer a better chance of stability.

Unless a man on a white horse should come riding on stage...we could hope for nothing better than the French Fourth Republic, without benefit of the French.

Never again should we transfer such vast military resources to an antiquated monarchy that rules largely by force without the consent of the people.

The Shah must announce unequivocally that he is transferring all civil power to a civilian government coalition.

We should use all our leverage with the military to persuade them not to resort to repressive measures to prop up a bankrupt regime detested by the people.[286]

Ball openly challenged former President Nixon's Twin Pillar policy and declared that the monarchy was on the "verge of collapse" because of it. He pontificated, "We have made the Shah what he has become. We nurtured his love for grandiose geopolitical schemes, and we supplied him with the hardware to indulge his fantasies.... his only chance to save his dynasty (if, indeed, that is still possible) and retain our support is for him to transfer his power to a government responsive to the people."[287] Ball proposed a Council of Notables and, with help from the State Department, prepared a list of possible members.

Of course, Ball's assessment of the Shah was most vividly expressed by his contemptuous statement regarding the monarch:

> *What an absurd, pathetic spectacle! The son of a colonel in a Persian Cossack regiment play-acting as the emperor of a country with an average per capita income of $250 per year, proclaiming his achievements in modernizing his nation while accoutered in the raiment and symbols of ancient despotism.*[288]

Ball expressed his disdain following the coronation ceremony of the Shah. He likened the affair to an operetta. He said he and his wife "waited expectantly for the empress to burst into an...aria, or the Shah to shuffle smartly into a soft shoe routine."[289] I can't help but wonder if Ball swallowed his contempt long enough to heap his plate with the Shah's caviar and drink his champagne.

Some of Ball's disdain for the monarch, Ambassador Zahedi believes, was due to a refusal on his part to set up an audience with the Pahlavi. When Ball, then Undersecretary of State under Lyndon Johnson, arrived in Tehran, Zahedi had arranged for him to meet with the ministers of finance and commerce. Pahlavi's schedule, however, did not permit a personal meeting with the undersecretary.[290] Apparently, Mr. Ball was not accustomed to being rebuffed by anyone for any reason.

Now, Ball filed his report with the Carter Administration and returned home in mid-December. He firmly believed that his recommendation to establish contact with Khomeini had been ignored.

Precht, however, had taken Ball's suggestion to heart. In a memo marked "Secret-Sensitive" Precht revealed a luncheon conversation with Yazdi, Khomeini's Iranian champion in the U.S. The two men talked of the possibilities of a new regime with the Shah as a figurehead, but Yazdi was uncompromisingly opposed to that. They spoke also about how a Khomeini-backed government might respond to oil sales and other issues. Precht wrote, "On parting, we agreed that neither of us would acknowledge that there had been any official contact between Khomeini and the U.S. government."[291] Precht was laying the groundwork for the "disavowability" defense suggested by George Ball.

President Carter's inaction following the release of the Ball report seemed to indicate his unwillingness to involve himself disproportionately in maintaining the Shah's monarchy. The indications were that he was more than willing to let the Iranians resolve their own internal crises and let the chips fall where they may.

The State Department seemed to be desirous of the Shah's overthrow. The general consensus among the department's hierarchy seemed to be that the religious leaders in Iran could not and would not participate in governing the nation should Pahlavi abdicate the throne. The Chief of Staff to the Senate Select Committee on Intelligence William Miller even suggested that the U.S. openly support Khomeini and his Islamic Revolution. Miller was convinced that Khomeini would progressively pursue human rights reformations in Iran.

As stated in the prologue of this book, a former Naval Intelligence officer and CIA operative during the Carter administration related to me that the U.S. government wrote checks to Khomeini in increments of approximately $150 million, essentially funding his French operation, including the flight that returned him to Tehran. My informant fully believes Khomeini left France because Carter stopped giving him money. It is his opinion that Jimmy Carter should have been tried for treason for aiding and abetting an enemy of the United States.

In an article for *Townhall.com*, Dinesh D'Souza wrote: "U.S. Ambassador William Sullivan even compared Khomeini to Mahatma Gandhi, and Andrew Young termed the radical cleric a 'twentieth-century saint.'"[292] This begs the questions: Was anyone in the Carter administration reading the memoranda being sent by the CIA? Was the CIA actually studying the information at hand? Or were they convinced that Khomeini was truly an old cleric with little chance of instigating a full-blown revolution in Iran?

When asked about Sullivan's lack of support for the Shah's monarchy, Her Majesty Farah Pahlavi replied:

> *Ambassador Sullivan...disliked the Shah for whatever reason; and he was not giving the proper advice or reports to President Carter. Dr. Brzezinski was saying at that time that the Shah should remain strong, but I think Cyrus Vance and Sullivan and Mr. Precht (the head of the Iranian desk), hated the Shah. I remember when Sullivan came to Iran, Mrs. [Ferdinand] Marcos sent a message to me.... She said in her message, "Marcos told me to tell you that wherever Sullivan goes, he creates a revolution." Now we know he was in touch with many opposition groups [in Iran].*[293]

Apparently, Sullivan did meet with such opposition leaders as Mehdi Bazargan, Nasser Minachi, Amir Entezam, and others who proved to be less than helpful to the ambassador. Bazargan, who would play a major role in Khomeini's Islamic Revolution, was a member of the Liberation Movement of Iran (LMI), a minor but decidedly scholarly and significant political faction committed to modernizing Shia Islam. Bazargan was deemed to be the guiding light of the organization that boasted such members as Ali Shari'ati and Sadegh Ghotbzadeh. Bazargan and members of this same group would travel to Paris in October 1978 to meet with Khomeini. Khomeini gave no indication to the leaders that he would cooperate, although John Stempel sent a telegram from the secretary of state in Washington to the U.S. Embassy in Paris that he was hopeful "some form of cooperation between in-country religious leaders and [the government of Iran] could help start the tension-reducing process."[294]

Ambassador Zahedi revealed to me he was totally unaware that the State Department even knew who Bazargan was. When he and Brzezinski met, the ambassador realized how upset the national security advisor was about events in Iran and how unsuitable he thought Bazargan was for consideration in any governmental position. Zahedi was told the Carter administration would back— 100 percent—any decision the Shah and Iranian people made, even if it did happen to be Bazargan.[295]

Sullivan's purpose to court Bazargan and position the U.S. interests for the downfall of the Shah was seen by many Pahlavi backers to be no more than a double-cross of the monarch, and ultimately brought the direst of results.

The Embassy Political Officer John Stempel was apparently privy to the meetings between Sullivan and opposition leaders. He sent a classified Memorandum of Conversation to the State Department on May 15, 1978.[296] Just who gave the political officer permission to approach the group has never been divulged. Stempel reported that the group was most interested in whether Carter's nosedive in approval ratings was due to his human rights policies. He wrote, "All the Liberation Front leaders insisted that the Shah must have been forced to liberalize, and they attributed this wholly to President Carter's human rights policy."

In September U.S. diplomat Charles Naas wrote to Victor Tomseth, the American Consul in Shiraz, Iran. Naas verified that several high-level Iranian officials had charged the U.S. was involved in demonstrations and were supporting the opposition in Iran.[297]

Stempel obviously was totally unaware of the clout held by Bazargan, and he was even more astounded to learn that his lowly translator, Mohammed Tavakoli, was a highly regarded member of the LMI. During Stempel's second meeting with the leaders on May 30, Tavakoli not only fielded questions but conversed with the other men as an equal. In less than a year Bazargan would be Khomeini's prime minister under the new Islamic Revolution. Tavakoli, it would be discovered, was actually Mohammed Tavassoli, a principal go-between of the Revolutionary Government and the U.S. Embassy. He would later become governor of Tehran.[298]

It was Cyrus Vance who proffered Tavakoli/Tavassoli's name to the Embassy in Tehran in a telegram to Sullivan. According to the U.S. ambassador, an "American academic expert recently gave [Department Office] the name of Mohammed Tavassoli, identifying him as person preferred by Khomeini group for contact with Embassy should that ever be desirable or practical." It listed a Tehran telephone number for Tavakoli.[299]

A telegram from John Stempel seemed to chastise Vance for revealing the identity of Tavassoli:

> *Tavassoli of [reference telegram] is individually known to us as Mohammed Tavakoli, with whom [political officer] Stempel has been in contact regularly since May 1978. He is not, [repeat], not a "Khomeini man" except in a limited sense. He is second-echelon LMI leader behind more prominent figures such as Bazargan...with whom we have also had contacts. LMI is, of course, most pro-Khomeini group in oppositionist galaxy. Tavassoli is somewhat disconcerted to have demonstrated to him that the Embassy knew who he really was.*[300]

This information presents any number of scenarios: Had the Embassy been talking to a Khomeini follower for months and were simply unaware? Was the CIA in contact with the Ayatollah through Tavassoli? Was the Carter administration actively seeking an open, yet disavowable, channel of communication with Khomeini?

Perhaps Ambassador Zahedi was absolutely right in being wary of the new U.S. ambassador in Tehran due to his previous postings in Laos and in the Philippines. He shared his reservations about Sullivan at the onset of his appointment to Iran. Zahedi said his intuitions were confirmed during a welcome party for Sullivan given by Ambassador Sidney Sober and former U.S. Ambassador Richard

Helms. Zahedi, then, went so far as to advise the Shah to reject Sullivan's credentials but was rebuffed by the monarch.[301]

Apparently Sullivan was not above trying to recruit members of the Shah's ministry in his search for damning information. Dr. Abdol, Majid Majidi, Minister of Planning and Budget, was approached by Sullivan at a party:

> *Sullivan [tried] from the very beginning to talk to me and get my personal views of the situation.... I couldn't give him clues to weaknesses or mistakes or anything.... [Sullivan] took me aside...and was trying to entreat me to talk to him as a sort of opponent of the Shah.... He was not like [former Ambassador Richard] Helms. Helms was willing to collaborate and work with Iran and support the Shah and the regime. Sullivan was not.*[302]

After having read some of the declassified CIA documents, I wonder if key administration personnel were paying attention to information coming in from Iran and Paris. One document dated November 20, 1978, is devoted to "The Politics of Ayatollah Ruhollah Khomeini." Among the points of the intelligence memorandum are these:

> *Ayatollah Khomeini has long been the central figure in the conservative Shia clerical opposition to the Shah. His influence is now so strong that neither other clerics nor civilian opposition leaders will take action he opposes.*

> *Khomeini is determined to overthrow the Shah and is unlikely to accept any compromise. He considers the Pahlavi regime to be corrupt, anti-Islamic, and controlled by the U.S.*

> *Khomeini's powerbase is composed of the Shia clergy, bazaar merchants, urban lower classes, and students. Senior military officers generally oppose and feel threatened by Khomeini, but junior officers and enlisted men presumably are more responsive to his Shia message.*

An Iranian regime under Khomeini's influence would be xenophobic [intolerant] and probably prone to instability. It would probably not be aligned with either the U.S. or USSR.[303]

Former CIA director Stansfield Turner summarized the situation very concisely in his book *Burn Before Reading*. He wrote:

While I think we in the CIA served the president well... we let him down badly with respect to our coverage of the Iranian scene. We had not appreciated how shaky the Shah's political foundation was, did not know that the Shah was terminally ill, did not understand who Khomeini was and the support his movement had.... As far as our failure to judge the Shah's position more accurately, we were just plain asleep.... It was egregious, though, that I did not insist on a thorough review of where the Shah stood.[304]

Marvin Kalb had another opinion about the downfall of the Shah:

The thing that is important to note here is the State Department experts were not advancing a specific policy option. They were fighting what they took to be an inordinate U.S. reliance upon the Shah at a time when they saw increasing weakness in the Shah's position. They were in effect saying to the conductor of the train about to go off the tracks, "Please be aware the tracks are unsteady, that your policy has a weak foundation, and you better think about a post-Shah Iran." But the White House...up until the end was not thinking in those terms. And that is why when the Shah finally had to leave, the U.S. was so surprised, struck dumb by the new situation they faced. They had been made aware of the new situation for a long time, but they simply did not buy into it.[305]

William Sullivan, appointed by Jimmy Carter in 1977, holds the dubious role of having been the last U.S. ambassador to Iran.

(He was the first ambassador appointed following the departure of Richard Helms during the Ford administration.)

In *Lifting the Veil: Life in Revolutionary Iran*, John Simpson and Tira Shubart wrote of Sullivan's introduction to and influence on U.S. policy in Iran:

> *Sullivan...had inherited a bureaucratic machine which was capable only of viewing the situation from one direction. His Embassy had become an office for selling equipment and weapons systems, and its political reporting role had been heavily reduced.... He faced hostility from Zbigniew Brzezinski's National Security Council, which tried to undermine his influence and that of the U.S. State Department.... Sullivan was reporting to an administration...concentrating on the Camp David negotiations...to the exclusion of almost everything else.*[306]

Right or wrong, Sullivan determined early during his stint in Iran that the Shah was incapable of making responsible decisions. Soon after his arrival in Tehran, Sullivan recorded his first impression of the Shah. He wrote: "The man to whom I presented my credentials certainly did not fit into the category of national leaders. He was not truly cast to be a leader of men or the nation in time of crisis."[307]

Uri Lubrani provided some insight on Sullivan's mind-set regarding the Shah:

> *Sullivan had little experience in Iran. He was very much reliant on Tony Parsons, the British ambassador...who was anti-Israel and whose wife was pro-Palestinian. He told Sullivan that this..."Lubrani doesn't know what he's talking about." Whom should poor Sullivan believe? Here you have Sir Tony Parsons...telling him straight from the horse's mouth...and Count Lubrani with his gut feelings. Obviously, he didn't take me seriously. But at that time the U.S. had thousands of officials in Iran...the foreign ministry, the Pentagon, information collectors.... I talked with the*

*American ambassador a number of times.... he relied on
access to Tony Parsons for information in Iran more than he
relied on the ambassador of Israel.*[308]

Sullivan saw the Shah at his best and his worst. In an audience
with the Shah in mid-1977 the ambassador related the Shah's
growing distrust of the CIA. Pahlavi felt the CIA had played a roll
in the demonstrations and protests that had gripped Iran. Sullivan
said of his conversation with the Shah:

> *He could understand the British intrigue to some extent,
> because there were those in the United Kingdom who had
> never forgiven him for nationalizing the oil industry.... What
> bothered him the most...was the role of the CIA. Why was
> the CIA suddenly turning against him? What had he done to
> deserve this sort of action from the United States?*[309]

Sullivan returned to Washington in June of 1978 for meetings
with administration heads. Secretary of State Vance was of the
opinion that Sullivan felt "the Shah faced a long, rough period
ahead, but that he should be able to weather the storm."[310] Vance
encouraged Sullivan to meet with opposition leaders to try to gain
more information, particularly about those planners and executers
of the anti-Shah protests. It was evident that the mullahs, led by the
wily Ayatollah Ruhollah Khomeini, were in the forefront. It was
becoming more obvious, at least to the Carter administration, that
two elements—the economy and religious forces—were leading and
fueling the marches in Iran. At the same time, it appeared the Shah
was beginning to suspect the U.S. was turning more toward the
opposition in an attempt to situate itself in the winning camp.

Contrarily, the Shah wrote of his interaction with Sullivan in
less-than-glowing terms:

> *He [Sullivan] said that he knew in September 1978 that
> I could not survive. He has told this [following his retire-
> ment] to the International Herald Tribune and anyone else
> who would listen. But he never told me. For the next four*

*months the only word I ever received from Mr. Sullivan was
reiteration of Washington's complete support for my rule. To
be more specific, the U.S. backed me 100 percent and hoped
I would establish law and order, as well as continue my program of political liberalization. For the balance of the year
I received numerous messages from various people in and out
of the Carter administration pledging U.S. support.[311]*

On December 29 Vance sent a telegram to Sullivan instructing
him to tell the Shah about various power-sharing possibilities and
to warn him that "in any case, it is our judgment that it will be
impossible to restore [Pahlavi's] absolute power."[312] According to
author William Shawcross, Sullivan was the messenger bearing the
news that the Shah was to leave his homeland for exile. Sullivan
painted himself in this episode as the savior of the Shah, even
offering to seek asylum for the monarch. Pahlavi's version differed
from Sullivan's.[313]

Did the duplicitous Sullivan think that by insinuating himself
with the Shah and removing him from Khomeini's path he might gain
an upper hand with the Ayatollah and his cronies? The same day
Sullivan dispatched a telegram to the State Department advising
that John Stempel had met with Richard Cottam, a former CIA
officer who had maintained ties with Iran's religious community over
the years. Cottam had met with Khomeini and formulated the
opinion that Yazdi had become the Ayatollah's chief of staff.[314]
How could such a plethora of information lead to such hindsight?

In 1977 Cottam, then a political science professor at the
University of Pittsburgh, testified before the House Subcommittee on
International Organizations. (The committee was on record in calling Iran "one of the major recipients of military cash sales from the
United States" and in declaring its "active interest in developments
that affect the human rights conditions in Iran.") In his prepared
statement Dr. Cottam addressed the human rights issue in regard to
its effect in Iran:

No one should expect that transition to a less repressive administration in Iran would be a smooth one. The Iranian public is bitterly polarized, the regime is vulnerable to charges of foreign sponsorship and control, and the opposition is mutually suspicious, divided, and incapable of serious cooperation. A strategy designed to encourage liberalization in this setting would be difficult but not impossible to devise. The regime has demonstrated responsiveness to pressure to move in a direction of controlled and gradualistic relaxation. The formula, easily stated but requiring artistry to execute, calls for the application of sufficient pressure to produce movement on part of the regime, but not so much as to encourage opposition elements to move so rapidly that the regime begins to see its survival as being in question. Administration policy thus far, unfortunately, has opted for the worst of both worlds. Initial statements concerning human rights encouraged a good deal of opposition activity in Iran.[315]

How had the information of this hearing so escaped Mr. Carter's attention?

Other nations were not so handicapped in intelligence gathering. While the U.S. was playing ostrich, Israel was openly voicing its reservations about the Shah's ability to maintain control in Iran. In fact, the Israelis were so convinced the Shah's fall was inevitable that Jews in Iran were warned to flee while there was still the opportunity.

In the book *Debacle: The American Failure in Iran*, authors Michael Ledeen and William Lewis outlined what they perceived to be the most basic problem in regard to the crisis in Iran: "The president [Carter] was notable for his absence. Carter never took an active role in the discussion, never gave any clear indication of the kind of solution he favored, and never put the question of Iran into the general context that would have aided the policymakers at lower levels in formulating options."[316]

14

THE DOWNHILL SLIDE
TO REVOLUTION

"Failure and weakness is the legacy of Jimmy Carter, a man who still demands that we lend our enemy the rope by which they have promised to hang us." (G L E N   R E I N S F O R D) [317]

AS OPPOSITION TO THE SHAH GREW in Iran and in an attempt to inhibit Khomeini's influence, Reza Pahlavi appealed to the president of Iraq, Saddam Hussein, to clamp down on the Ayatollah's activities. In my talk with Ardeshir Zahedi, he mentioned that Hussein offered to "liquidate" Khomeini should the Shah ask. "Saddam," said Zahedi "was happy to expel Khomeini who finally landed in Paris.... Letting him stay in Paris was a huge mistake. He became the darling of the media world...the media attention helped him become the unique opposition leader. As usually is the case, the more extreme and radical opinion gets the upper hand." [318]

In the late 1970s the worldwide media was controlled by its counterparts in three very powerful countries. In the United States *The New York Times* was the power media of record. In Great Britain the British Broadcasting Corporation (BBC) led the way; and then there were the newspapers and media sources in France.

It's difficult to imagine life as it was then—no Internet, CNN, CNBC, Fox Network, no iPhones, digital cameras, or text messaging. News was delivered via ABC, NBC, or CBS. What we referred to then as "mainstream" media was extremely powerful. In the 1960s this newly dominant media outlet introduced America to its first "television war." Night after night Americans ate their evening meal to the horrifying scenes of bloody and battered combat troops, body bags, and atrocities in Vietnam. According to the Museum of Broadcast Communications, the Saigon Bureau was the third largest after New York and Washington. It kept five camera crews busy the majority of the time. The result of the nightly bombardment of horror was revulsion and exhaustion. Eventually, Americans began clamoring for the troops to be brought home.[319]

It was the media that brought down the Nixon administration. A dazed and shocked nation watched as two Washington, D.C., reporters, Bob Woodward and Carl Bernstein, uncovered the Watergate scandal that led to the resignation of President Richard Nixon. America's media, largely Left in viewpoint and personnel, ruled the airwaves and front pages.

Just as the Ayatollah Khomeini became the darling of the media, so the Shah became the pariah. He and his monarchy bore the full brunt of media revulsion during the Carter years. *The New York Times* influenced decision makers, especially during the crucial months of 1978 and 1979. In France, Khomeini's country of choice during his exile, the press and television created a soft, fuzzy image of the Ayatollah. But perhaps the most damaging entity of all was the *British Broadcasting Corporation* (BBC), through its Persian language *BBC Persian Service* network. It became a primary voice for the Islamic Revolution. Pahlavi didn't stand a chance in the battle for public opinion with each of these powerful outlets as his foe. It is said that Bazargan expressed his appreciation for both the BBC and the French *Le Monde* following Khomeini's seizure of power.[320]

Iranian military leaders were very concerned with BBC broadcasts that were being aired from the island of Masirah, just off the Omani coast. The Shah had met with British Ambassador Anthony Parsons in an attempt to stop the broadcasts that were announcing to the Iranian people when planned demonstrations against the Shah were scheduled. The ambassador reminded the Shah's chief of protocol, Mr. Afshar, that the BBC was an independently owned and operated entity and not controlled by the British government.

The most curious and mysterious relationship between the media and the Shah was with the BBC was the only Western broadcaster to have a service that broadcast in the Persian language. The BBC Persian Service had been established during WWII to counterbalance the Nazi influence in Iran. In the 1950s BBC Persian Service was against the nationalization of Iranian oil, which at the time had been held by the Anglo-Iranian Oil Company (AIOC).[321]

At the beginning of the Shah's reign in 1953 the BBC Persian Service appeared to be a friend of his. In fact, early in the Iranian revolution, the opposition forces still viewed the BBC Persian Service with distrust. It took Abolhasan Bani-Sadr, later president of the republic and the same person who connected Paul Balta of *Le Monde* with Khomeini, to get the Ayatollah to trust the BBC. Bani-Sadr said later:

> *I suggested to Khomeini to give an interview to BBC, assuring him that they will broadcast exactly what he says, Khomeini rejected, saying, "BBC belongs to the British and it will not benefit us to give them an interview." I convinced him when I said all the other media you give interviews to are also all foreign, so what is the difference? Khomeini then accepted.*[322]

Soon the BBC Persian Service was broadcasting the ranting of the Ayatollah and other leaders of the revolution directly into Iran. In Iran this was very confusing to the Shah and his supporters.

It was well known that the BBC World Service, under which the BBC Persian Service fell, was funded by the British Foreign Office. The Foreign Office by the 1970s was claiming to have no control over the journalists. Friends of the Shah appealed a number of times to the Foreign Office and the BBC but to no avail.[323] In the meantime, the BBC Persian Service Broadcast had become a national event.

In Ehsan Naraghi's book, *From Palace to Prison, Inside the Iranian Revolution*, he reconstructs a dialogue between himself and the Shah regarding the BBC:

> *Shah: "We've stressed…that while respecting the BBC's right to freedom of expression, we considered that it was taking things too far…. The information that it was broadcasting about the situation in Iran was tantamount to instructions to the opposition on how they should behave from one day to the next."*

> *Naraghi: "It's true, Your Majesty, that the BBC has a very large audience in Iran. During the time when it broadcasts its evening program, from 7:45 to 8:30, I've noticed that the city looks completely different because so many people go home to listen."*[324]

To this day, the British Foreign Office has not opened up its files regarding this time period and the BBC Persian Service.[325]

The conversation regarding the BBC Persian Service led to another charge of bugging by Lt. General Azarbarzin. He was called into the Shah's suite following the meeting with Parsons and told:

> *"Destroying this station will create a political scandal…. You go ahead and make all preparations, and I'll give you confirmation in the morning at 9:00 AM." When I went to see the Shah, Ambassador Sullivan was ahead of me…. he had requested an emergency audience with the Shah at 8:30 AM …. After Sullivan had left, the Shah told me, "Don't take any action on what we discussed yesterday…. By the way, did you*

discuss   yesterday's   subject   with   anyone?"
I answered, "I do not discuss my missions with anybody."
The Shah said, "I am surprised, because Ambassador
Sullivan mentioned the words political scandal exactly as
I told you yesterday."[326]

General Huyser recorded that his Iranian counterparts were asking, "Why can't the big United States silence Khomeini? Cannot the U.S. silence the British Broadcasting's Farsi broadcasts?" Huyser said that "young and old alike carried transistor radios.... The BBC Persian Service was set up during World War II in order to help destabilize the regime of the Shah's father.... and the Shah himself probably had this in mind when they protested against the role of the BBC during this crucial period in the late 1970s."[327]

The New York Times in the 1970s was considered the "Gray Lady" of American print media. It claimed to provide, "All the news that's fit to print." With extensive Foreign Affairs coverage that was only rivaled by the *Washington Post, The New York Times* was mandatory reading for foreign policy analysts, professionals, and diplomats in the U.S. and abroad. It was also one of the morning papers on the desks of the television news producers at the three major networks of that day.

Many of the news stories on the national nightly news broadcasts came directly from the pages of the *Washington Post, The New York Times* and, occasionally, the *Wall Street Journal*. (It was, after all, Woodward and Bernstein who broke the Watergate scandal in the prestigious *Post*.) These three newspapers had nationwide circulation—making them the only "national" daily newspapers. When it came to an overseas story, no paper had more clout than *The New York Times*.

The Shah and his diplomats were not ignorant, uninformed individuals. They were aware of the sway held by the *Times*. Pahlavi's press office in Iran communicated frequently with news reporters stationed in Tehran, including the famous *Times*' correspondent, R. W. Apple. Unfortunately for the Shah, his attempts to generate goodwill yielded strange results.

When in May of 1977 Secretary of State Cyrus Vance visited Tehran for the CENTO meeting, he gave a speech to the assembly. Vance was quoted in the *The New York Times* by reporter Charles Mohr in an article headlined, "Vance, in Iran, Asserts Stability Depends on Rights." While Vance was actually speaking to the other four CENTO members—Britain, Turkey, Iran, and Pakistan— the article made Vance appear to be speaking solely to the Shah of Iran.

Vance was quoted as saying:

Each country's growth, prosperity, and stability sooner or later depends upon its ability to meet the aspirations of its people for human rights. The success of the nations of the world in mastering the economic and social problems of resource limits, population growth, and the environment will inevitably be linked to our success in promoting individual dignity.[328]

In the fourth paragraph of his article, Mohr instructed the reading audience what it should gain from Vance's speech:

Whether intentionally or not [wink, wink], the secretary's remarks seemed to have a special point when they were delivered in an ornate conference hall in the capital of this ancient monarchy. The Shah of Iran and his government have been criticized by some Iranian exiles and by foreigners for firm suppression of political opposition and for police surveillance of political activity.... The Shah was not present when Mr. Vance spoke today.... American officials indicated...the United States views the trends in Iranian civil liberties as "favorable".... and that any diplomatic or economic sanctions against the Shah were virtually out of the question.[329]

The article informed its readers that the Shah was "one of the largest customers of advanced American military hardware."[330] Reading this article made me pause to wonder if Mr. Mohr was quantifying the "U.S. soft-sell" with the real reason behind it; the U.S. pocketed a lot of money for the "military hardware" sold to the Shah. No, not to Iran, to the Shah. The writer is clearly indicating that the lack of U.S. sanctions is closely tied to the Shah's purchasing power.

It is also interesting to note that the word *sanctions*, brought up only by the reporter, was used against Pahlavi. Today, mention of sanctions applies to the country of Iran, not its leader, Mahmoud Ahmadinejad.

Iran's press office responded to the article in four days, as quickly as it could at the time. Iran's representative at the UN was Fereydoun Hoveyda. Hoveyda argued that it was unfair to immediately apply 1977 U.S. standards of human rights to developing nations. He pointed out, correctly, that "the political rights of women, about the lot of labor and...the situation of minority groups" was different in the U.S. in 1977 than it had been twenty-five or fifty years earlier. Then he enumerated Iran's achievements in land reform and its advancement in the rights of women. The piece was a brilliant public relations effort. It was torpedoed by a photo the editors placed in the very center of the op-ed. It showed Mr. Hoveyda dressed in a flamboyant military uniform bowing and kissing the hand of the Shah. The monarch was clad in a military dress uniform with ceremonial sword in hand.

A Chinese proverb tells us, "One picture is worth ten thousand words." The picture, with no caption, evoked striking imagery. In 1972 Francis Ford Coppola directed *The Godfather*. The Academy Award–winning movie portrayed the life of a Sicilian mob boss, the Godfather. One famous scene depicts minor members of the "family" kissing the Godfather's ring. The picture in *The New York Times* evoked memories of this scene in the movie. Hoveyda, who never mentions the Shah in his article of rebuttal, is obviously portrayed as the minion doing the bidding of the scary, egocentric strongman. Why did a newspaper the size of the *Times* not have a head shot of Mr. Hoveyda, a diplomat at the United Nations? Perhaps they did, but perhaps that picture would have more closely conveyed the message intended.[331]

Over the next few months articles and the editorial page of *The New York Times* repeatedly went after the Shah and the proposed U.S. sale of military aircraft.[332] Eventually, the administration weakened in its resolve to supply the planes to Iran. Finally, in a face-saving gesture to both Carter and itself, Iran withdrew its bid to buy planes.[333]

A favorable *Times* book review was a feather in the author's cap and indicated to readers that the literary tome was to be taken seriously. Seemingly, *The New York Times* seized every opportunity to castigate the Shah, even in something as innocuous as the newspaper's June 1977 tribute to *The Crowned Cannibals: Writings on Repression in Iran,* penned by Reza Baraheni. Reviewer John Leonard engaged in the "moral equivalence" doctrine so popular at the time. He drew such a comparison between events in the Soviet Union, Nazi Germany, and among America's allies. Leonard wrote:

> *First of all, the writer as witness of the Holocaust, of Stalinism, of the Shah and his thuggish SAVAK, is one of the few honorable callings in a bestial century.*[334]

This review might have been attributed to a seasoned publicist with a penchant for seizing the moment and linking his client's book to President Carter's human rights campaign; however, the *Times* piece was not the end. Another article entitled, "Publishing: Human Rights," also featured Reza Baraheni and his *Crowned Cannibals* book. The article tied the publishing of the book to a meeting in Belgrade to examine the effects of the Helsinki Accords: "Including the human rights section calling for freer exchange of people and ideas, several books are published here that cast light in the dark corners of literary freedom."[335] None of the other books were mentioned. It was simply another opportunity to denigrate the Shah in *The New York Times*.

During the crucial months of late 1978 and early 1979 leading up to the departure of the Shah, the *Times* ran a series of editorials along with their news stories. On November 6, 1977, the editorial read, "Suddenly, Iran No Longer Stable." It opened with the question, "How much more time for the Shah of Iran?" Previously, it had been only the anti-Shah protestors who demanded the Shah must go. Certainly no one in the U.S. government had been so crass as to utter those words aloud. Yet, here was the most influential foreign policy daily in the U.S. raising the question. The editorial ended by planting the idea: "Pressure on the Shah has mounted and many of his opponents have raised their sights from reducing his power to driving him from the throne."[336] Apparently that included *The New York Times* editorial board.

On November 8, 1978, and for reasons known only to the editorial staff, *The New York Times* took a step back. It noted that the Shah promised "that newly installed military rule will be brief and will be followed by free elections." It questioned, "Has it come in time?" but concluded, "so far, at least, they warrant continued Western support."[337]

Had the *Times* staff had a change of heart? Were they now proposing the monarch remain in power? By December 14, however, the editorial headline read: "On the Ropes in Iran." They gave the Shah a conciliatory nod by observing he "may yet weather the crisis. He has been a good ally; and as long as his rule remains plausible he is entitled to the respect and support that Mr. Carter has extended. But the Shah has gotten as he has given over the years, and the United States cannot be expected to leave all its stakes piled on one throne.... All the avenues require American contacts with the opposition."[338] It obviously did not explain how the U.S. could extend "respect and support" to Pahlavi and at the same time meet with the opposition. Iranians knew the Shah had returned to power with the help of the CIA in 1953. The U.S opening contacts with the opposition would have again been interpreted in Iran as a vote of no confidence in the Shah.

By December 29, 1978, while the Shah was trying to work out a government of national reconciliation, the *Times* published an editorial entitled, "The Ideal and the Real in Iran." While it praised the idea of the Shah staying in a figurehead role, it determined that: "The policy, however, has a serious flaw; it appears to be increasingly unrealistic." Oddly, the editorial concluded, "The United States should not, probably could not, encourage the Shah's departure." Apparently the Carter administration was expected to maintain its silence while *The New York Times*, on the other hand, was free to urge Pahlavi's ouster. The *Times* believed, "Every day, there seems to be more reason to doubt that present policy can prevent such an outcome."[339]

In September 1978, before fleeing to Paris from Iraq, Khomeini had been placed under house arrest. At that time, the Liberation Movement of Iran (a group which will play a prominent role later in this book) contacted the U.S. Embassy in Tehran and asked for its help in freeing Khomeini. The missive implied Khomeini wished to leave Iraq. The group's leaders also asked for a high-level meeting with U.S. officials and indicated they would unveil their strong religious connections at the meeting. The Embassy staff declined the request.[340]

In an aborted attempt to flee Iraq, Khomeini and his entourage became stranded at the Kuwait border when that country would not grant him entry, and he was then refused reentry into Iraq. Finally, the Ayatollah received permission to return to Baghdad where, on October 6, he was allowed, at the Shah's urging, to fly to France. The DST, the French secret service urged French President Giscard d'Estaing to turn Khomeini away. In a personal interview with d'Estaing, he seemed not to have realized just who Khomeini was when the cleric arrived in France:

> *No one knew in France exactly the name...and I heard he was here in Paris after the Interior Minister M. Christian*

*Bonair delivered me a note, the day after his arrival.
He [Khomeini] received a number of favors. He [Bonair] had
a personality who disembarked yesterday at the airport and
all his documents were in order saying he was coming from
Iraq.... Yes, Najaf... He was fleeing Iraq...and he was welcomed by a member of a small group who owns a house in
western Paris. He was driven there by his supporters. And
then we realized he was active in politics...and that he
was very important in the post-Shah regime. Then we
appointed a man from (French Intelligence) to check on
him.... We considered him...a sort of political refugee. And
you know in France, we accept political refugees.*[341]

Giscard then seemed to jump on the "downfall of the Shah"
bandwagon and agreed to provide asylum for the Ayatollah. Far
from halting his interference in Iran, Khomeini's exile only fired the
passions of the Islamic radicals in that country. His freedom to plan
and execute a revolution while under French protection would prove
to be the final straw for the Shah's regime.

A telegram from Ambassador Sullivan to the State Department revealed religious leaders close to Khomeini were urging
him to exercise caution and restraint because the civil unrest in
Iran was becoming unmanageable. The clerics were also alarmed at
surfacing rumors indicating that Khomeini was cooperating with the
Tudeh Party, the Communist opposition, and some Iranians were
beginning to believe the gossip.[342]

It was thought by some individuals that, as stated by Barry
Rubin in his book, *Paved with Good Intention*, the French allowed
Khomeini into the country because he was perceived as the future
leader of Iran.[343] Rubin also writes, "The CIA rented a villa near his
[Khomeini's] home. American Embassy political officers began to
meet occasionally with one of his advisors, Ebrahim Yazdi [leader
in 1968 of the U.S. branch of Muslim Students' Association of
America]."[344] Others in France went so far as to try to predict
when the Shah's end would come.

15

THE VORTEX OF
INDECISION

*"Defeat is always bitter, but losing without a fight is the
bitterest kind of defeat."* (ARDESHIR ZAHEDI)[345]

DESPITE THEIR OBVIOUS DIFFERENCES in ideology
both the French and the Israelis were convinced the Shah would be
overthrown and the alternative, the fanatical Ayatollah Khomeini,
would spell doom for the Iranian people. Cavalierly, the U.S. intelligence community rejected both reports as exaggerated. To further
exacerbate matters, the CIA failed to investigate Khomeini's radically
fanatical diatribes. Apparently, Khomeini's threats were not taken
seriously by the CIA, which had to scramble to even find copies of
Khomeini's writings when the volcano of revolution erupted in Iran.

The *Washington Post* addressed the lack of information about
the Ayatollah in an editorial printed on January 16, 1979:

*A great power should never be in the position the United
States is in, in Iran, of knowing so little about a figure—
Ayatollah Ruhollah Khomeini.... Until just the other day
the CIA could not lay its hands on some of Mr. Khomeini's
voluminous—and revealing—writings.... His mandate,*

he claims, arises from street demonstrations that make
him the only leader.... "Strongman" is a title he finds accept-
able.... Khomeini has strong anti-American tendencies....
it seems inescapable that he sees his political future in terms
that directly undercut American interests.... All this does
not mean that the United States should risk arousing Iran-
ian nationalism or his ire by working against Khomeini....
he gives every evidence of being bad news.[346]

In Iraq Khomeini's communication with his counterparts in
Iran was restricted, but France proved to be an open pipeline to
funnel information and revolutionary rhetoric directly to Khomeini's
information distributors. Every word, every hiccup, every move
Khomeini made was duly reported back to Iran through the BBC and
other international broadcasters. His was a cause all were rushing
to recount to the Iranian people.

In our conversation the empress questioned why Khomeini
was allowed so much freedom to wage his revolution from the
suburbs of Paris:

Khomeini is in Paris, why give him so much publicity? When
we were in the Bahamas, which was a small country and not
so important in international politics, we were told, "You are
not allowed to make any political comments." The French
said the same thing to Prime Minister Bakhtiar when he fled
to France. So why give him [Khomeini] so much publicity?
Every day he was on television; every day there was an
article in the newspapers. Maybe they thought that with the
movement in Iran, with the unrest in Iran, they'd better
take care of Khomeini. It is normal that each country thinks
of its own interests.[347]

Before his exile to Paris Khomeini's brooding countenance had
not been seen abroad in Iran and, in fact, it was forbidden to show
his visage on Iranian television. This was not the case in France.
During an interview on French television in 1978 Khomeini denied
that the Islamic Republic he touted would be run by the clergy.

His denial would prove to be as false as other assertions made by the glowering Ayatollah while on his journey to an iron-fisted rule in Iran.

David Pryce-Jones talked about "France's disturbing role in bringing about the Iranian Revolution" in a briefing delivered to the Middle East Forum:

> [Mr. Pryce-Jones declared the Iranian Revolution] "the most important revolution in modern times." France received Khomeini in 1978, when it was clear he was planning an insurrection against the Shah, and provided him lines of communication through which to mobilize demonstrations. This is the most dramatic example of the French penchant for harboring Islamic extremists.... they granted a safe haven to Haj Amin el-Husseini, the mufti of Jerusalem, returning him to the Middle East when he was wanted as a war criminal in 1945. He concludes that "twice now the world has been handicapped by French-harbored monsters—Haj Amin and Khomeini—who were fascists."[348]

From Paris, the City of Lights, darkness would slowly but surely engulf Iran. It was from Paris that Khomeini would declare himself the genuine leader-in-exile of the Iranian people. He took full advantage of the freedom to use the media for his purposes. The Ayatollah began to urge the workers in Iran—from oil workers to garbage haulers—to go on strike. Students were encouraged to riot in support of the working class. The strikes proved to be very efficient at creating dissention. One chronicler recorded:

> [On 9 September] about seven hundred workers at the Tehran oil refinery struck not just for higher wages but as a protest against the imposition of martial law and the massacre at Jaleh Square. Two days later...the strike had spread to the oil refineries of Isfahan, Abadan, Tabriz, and Shiraz. [Oil production dropped from over five million barrels per week to just under two million barrels per week]. On 12 September, four thousand print workers and other staff at two leading newspapers in Tehran walked out in

protest against the renewal of censorship ordered by General Oveissi, the military governor. On 13 September cement workers in Tehran went on strike, demanding higher wages, freedom for all political prisoners, and the ending of martial law.... But in October the situation was transformed.... 40,000 oil workers, 40,000 steel workers, and 30,000 rail workers had put down their tools within three weeks.[349]

Of the oil strikes, Dr. Parviz Mina, said:

"I think the strikes in the oil industry were organized by...the Mujahedin with the help of the clergy....That brought the oil industry to a standstill...created a shortage of products, shortage of income.... I was given the assignment to go and buy products.... I had to go to Saudi Arabia, to Bahrain, to Kuwait to buy petroleum products and ship it to Iran because the refineries were on strike.... We were exporting $5.2 million per day to the world market.... the majority was going to Western Europe and the United States.... I wish I knew why they [U.S. and Europe] didn't do [anything to stop that]. Not only didn't they do anything...they even helped the revolutionaries.[350]

The downside to Khomeini's call for strikes among the workers in Iran was that he failed to recognize "the radicals evidently are most active among the oil workers in southwestern Iran, where Ayatollah's injunctions to restore oil production...have proved difficult to implement because of the division among the striking workers."[351]

On September 10 President Carter wrote in his daily log that he had had an early morning meeting with Zbigniew Brzezinski and Gary Sick, NSC officer responsible for Iran. At the national security advisor's suggestion, Carter phoned the Shah and spent about five minutes talking with him. Sick recorded later that the Shah dominated the conversation and was firm in his pledge to restore order in his country and to continue to pursue democratic ideals. Following the telephone conference the president sent out a press release reiterating his commitment to the long-standing relationship between the U.S. and Iran.[352]

It was at this juncture that the CIA began to prepare a psychological report on Pahlavi. U.S. Embassy staff was asked to help in the preparation of the profile. Rumors that the Shah was suffering from depression abounded.[353] It is entirely possible the Shah was coming to grips with his cancer diagnosis and was overwhelmed with the unrest in his country. He was also wrestling with the fact that his teen aged son, Reza, was not of sufficient age to assume the responsibilities of the monarchy.

On November 11, 1978, a document from the secretary of state in Washington, D.C., was released to ambassadors and consulates around the world. It's subject? Iran. The assessment of the situation in Iran from Secretary Vance's point of view was that:

> [Relative quiet continues in Iran, broken by continuing sporadic disturbances in several provincial cities…. Embassy believes that current calm, with its various encouraging signs, is merely prelude to (unreadable) when opposition will try to mount serious disturbances to achieve aim of toppling Shah before end of December.
>
> Current encouraging signs include primary school attendance is virtually back to normal in Tehran, albeit more disrupted in the provinces; Tehran bazaar has been open for past two days, with Khomeini and mullahs [asking] shops to open up on December 2 to enable people to stock up.
>
> Some oppositionists seek our help in [unreadable] orderly evolution of power from the Shah to them. This last attitude can be expected to continue as there are realistic expectations of a move to a government and elections in the near future. If government were to continue for six months or more, however, we would see a good possibility of great desperation on the part of the opposition, leading to nastier attitude toward the U.S.[354]

Secretary Vance, who had been preoccupied in September and October 1978 with both the Camp David summit and SALT II talks in Moscow, returned to a State Department in conflict over how to handle the situation in Iran. Some underlings were convinced the Shah's monarchy had come to an end. These individuals were persuaded there were only two viable alternatives: a military solution or a British-style monarchy—a figurehead ruler under the control of a secular governing body. According to Vance:

> *They [State Department colleagues] made a strong case against U.S. support for a military government, pointing out that Ambassador Sullivan was opposed to increased military involvement in the political arena. The Iranian military...had shown no capacity to govern or to rally public support. Still, they saw the Shah as the only figure capable of leading a transition to a new regime.*[355]

Meanwhile, in Iran the Shah's government was pondering four different possibilities to resolve the crisis:

» The Shah would attempt to moderate his stance.

» The coming Islamic Revolution would be soundly crushed before it could be fully birthed (which many considered a total impossibility).

» The Shah would remove himself from Iran for an unspecified time, briefly abdicating in favor of a regent's council under the leadership of the Empress Farah. The empress would head the government until the crown prince reached his majority. Farah Pahlavi was convinced that this was the last proposal the Carter administration would consider.

» A military coup (favored by the CIA).

Pahlavi's naval commander, Admiral Kamilladin Habib Olahi, delivered a thirty-page proposal to the monarch outlining a military government. Olahi felt the revolution had advanced to the point where the king had to make a decision. (Pahlavi was concerned about a military move that would be against Iran's constitution.) Olahi was persuaded "the blame lay with Iran's allies—particularly the Americans and the British, who were giving him differing advice.... the Shah had depended on the counsel of foreigners. Now he was not getting it."[356]

The empress felt Pahlavi had begun to make arrangements for her to act as Regent as early as 1973. The Shah met with the prime minister and parliament members to deliver what Farah Diba felt was a governmental "last will and testament":

> I could die at any time. If this should happen when the crown prince is not of legal age to succeed me, authority will pass to the queen and the Regency Council. The armed forces should remain loyal to the queen and later to the young king. Orders can come from a woman or a young man; they should be obeyed. Our security and our lives depend on it.[357]

In late November President Carter asked Brzezinski to summon Zahedi to the White House for a meeting that also included Walter Mondale and Stansfield Turner. Zahedi was disturbed when the president insisted he return to Iran with a message for the Shah. The ambassador reminded Carter he served at the discretion of the Shah, to which the president replied that he, Carter, would fill the role of Iran's ambassador in Washington during Zahedi's absence. Carter particularly wanted Zahedi to reassure the Shah that he should not be concerned about the president's human rights push and to stand firm. He, Carter, would support Pahlavi in whatever decision he made regarding the situation in Iran. The ambassador returned to Iran in the days following the meeting and remained there until the Shah departed in January 1979.

Zahedi was appalled to learn that William Sullivan had summarily received copies of the White House confab but had failed to forward the information to the Shah. The Iranian ambassador wondered if, "by withholding that document, Sullivan may have hoped that my oral report to the Shah would carry less weight." Giving Sullivan the benefit of the doubt, he added, "I cannot be sure, of course, if that was his real intention."[358]

In December Carter dispatched a message to Sullivan from Camp David. In the missive, Carter asked the ambassador to meet with Pahlavi as quickly as possible. The president instructed Sullivan to convey to the Shah that:

» The indecision surrounding Iran's governance was detrimental to both the military and politicians.

» The resolution preferred by the U.S. was a moderate civilian government.

» The second choice of the Carter administration was a strong military junta to bring an end to the chaos and carnage.

» The last resort was a Regency Council that would oversee a military government.

» Lastly, Sullivan was to reconfirm support from the U.S., but with the understanding that Washington foresaw the loss of the Shah's absolute ruling power.

It was also in December that Carter approached Ardeshir Zahedi about lobbying for the post of prime minister of Iran. The ambassador explained he was more interested in being able to move about freely in order to try to help the Shah resolve the dilemma. Zahedi admitted, "What I was interested in was to be in contact with various actors and help find a solution for the crisis; if I accepted such a post, then I could have been accused of a conflict of interest."[359]

On December 23, 1978, a shot was fired that should have alerted the U.S. State Department, Carter, and Sullivan that the situation in Iran was becoming dangerous for American expatriates: Paul Grimm, "an American employee of Texaco who was on loan to the Oil Services Company of Iran...was ambushed and shot to death in Ahvaz while driving from his home to work.... Responsibility for the well-organized killing was claimed by *Mujahedeen* who, at the time of the slaying, were supporting Ayatollah Khomeini."[360] The CIA reported:

> *While Khomeini had in the early 1970s urged [his followers] to assassinate Americans, there is no evidence to suggest he was behind the attacks of December 23. In the aftermath of the double assassinations oil production plummeted.*[361]

Zahedi did, however, talk with military commanders in Iran such as General Gholam Reza Azhari, Joint Chief of Staff; General Gholam Ali Oveissi, Army chief and martial law administrator; General Abdul-Ali Badrei, commander of the Shah's elite guards corps; and, General Amir-Hussein Badi'ie, Air Force commander. The men expressed their frustration that the Shah seemed unwilling to allow them to crack down on the demonstrators and revolutionaries. Zahedi outlined a plan he proposed to the leaders during one meeting:

> *His Majesty would leave Tehran for the Persian Gulf naval base in Bandar-Abbas or else go on a pilgrimage to Mecca in order to give the military government a free hand to restore order. I proposed this plan to His Majesty and he first said, "Yes," but he changed his mind.*[362]

Zahedi felt the military was more than ready to go forward with the Shah as their commander. A plan to arrest the fanatical mullahs for agitation and plotting against the Shah and to imprison them at the sports complex near Tehran or in a temporary prison in southern Iran was also suggested, but it too was vetoed by Pahlavi, who Zahedi had apprised of his conversations with the various military leaders.

John Simpson and Tira Shubart wrote in *Lifting the Veil* of Sullivan's attempt to apprise the Carter administration of issues surrounding the demonstrations in Iran:

> *On 9 November...Sullivan broached the issues that had been raised by the demonstrators on the streets and by many journalists. His telegram entitled, "Thinking the Unthinkable," suggested that the Shah...might actually leave the country and Khomeini might return to Iran...choosing a leader who would be acceptable to the Iranian military.... The telegram was used as ammunition between the State Department and National Security Council and further eroded Sullivan's position in the bureaucratic infighting over Iran.*[363]

Zahedi found the telegram to be a misstatement of the facts as he knew them. He commented on Sullivan's tactics:

> *Let me be clear. I did not trust Sullivan's reporting. The Shah never intended to abdicate. He was prepared to leave the country temporarily. Even there, I strongly advised him against it. I told His Majesty he should not leave, and if he left, he would never come back.*[364]

The opposite view, that of a military coup, was espoused by Zbigniew Brzezinski; He fully supported a military solution, the iron fist approach, to the situation in Iran. Wrote Vance: "Zbig appeared to see a military coup, preferably in support of the Shah, as the only hope of protecting American interests. I strongly advocated a political solution...coupled with efforts to preserve the Iranian military as an institution. The iron fist [approach] was wrong on two counts: First, the Iranian Army...could not make it work. Second, support for the iron fist would be antithetical to what I believed the Carter administration stood for. The president refused to give American blessing to the iron fist."[365]

In his book, *The Making of Iran's Islamic Revolution*, Mohsen Milani wrote of the Shah's dilemma:

> *To weather the storm, the Shah had to act decisively. He either had to crush the growing movement or to relinquish*

some of his power and strike a deal with the moderate factions of the popular movement. He opted to do neither.

Contradictory counsel was offered to the Shah. On the one hand, William Sullivan and British Ambassador Anthony Parsons admonished him that their respective governments would not tolerate an iron-fisted approach and favored a peaceful resolution to the crisis. "Sullivan," Brzezinski wrote, "never explicitly urged the Shah to be tough." Some of his advisors...also urged the Shah to grant more concessions to the opposition. On the extreme other hand, the hawks, including General Gholam Ali Oveissi and Brzezinski pressured the Shah to rescind the liberalization and to begin a mass arrest of the more powerful members of the opposition. Brzezinski argued that, "the deliberate weakening of the beleaguered monarch by American pressure for further concessions would simply enhance his instability and eventually produce complete chaos."[366]

Zahedi felt the Shah did not have a proper crisis management team in place, and therefore allowed himself to be influenced by "his immediate family entourage and an incompetent government...with catastrophic results."[367] The ambassador arranged for the Shah to meet with what were considered to be political heavyweights to try to influence the ruler to relinquish the daily duties of running the government. The list included such names as former Prime Minister Ali Amini, Abdollah Entezam, and Gholam Hossein Sadiqi (Minister of the Interior under Mossadegh). Zahedi suggested the establishment of a Council of Notables to select a new prime minister. The new government elected by the Council would be responsible for handling the current crisis and for implementing reforms to calm the impending storm.

The "iron fist" resolution was, indeed, counter to everything Carter espoused as commander in chief. He was not in favor of a military crackdown that could result in a bloodbath in the streets of Tehran.

In my conversation with Her Majesty Farah Pahlavi, she confirmed the Shah's reluctance to approve military force against the people of Iran:

> *One of the French ministers wrote in his book that he had gone to see the Shah, and he told the Shah to remain in power. The Shah told him (which is true) that, "I don't want to keep my throne over the blood of my people." All of his life was dedicated to the Iranian people.*[368]

Pahlavi's former son-in-law, Ardeshir Zahedi, also reiterated the queen's observations concerning her husband:

> *The Shah was a real patriot and loved the Iranian people.... The Shah was kind-hearted and soft by nature and was horrified by bloodshed.... The Shah had always believed the Iranian masses loved him, and he could not bear seeing people turn against him with such vehemence.... His dream was to help Iran become the Japan of the Middle East, and he was in a hurry to make that wish become a reality. Many of the programs of today by the present regime are ideas and projects that the Shah started or foresaw.*[369]

Mohamed Heikal wrote of an encounter between the Shah and the Empress in a dispute over the demonstrations and riots that were happening throughout the country. The Egyptian journalist wrote that the empress tried to warn the Shah of events occurring outside the palace as reported to her by trusted friends and relatives. The Shah resorted to an old valet to confirm Farah Diba's claims. The valet, apparently in an attempt to placate the king, gave him a less than honest report on the situation. The empress' claims were perfunctorily dismissed by Pahlavi, and she fled his presence in tears. During the ensuing hours the Shah must have had a change of heart; he ordered his pilot to fly him over the city. The king was appalled at the sight below him: the streets of Tehran were overflowing with people protesting against Pahlavi. He returned to the palace and gave strict orders that no one—not even the empress—

was to be allowed inside his private quarters. He later relented and agreed to see Farah Diba in his chambers.[370]

Near the end of his life Pahlavi is said to have regretted acquiescing to the forces that were determined to relinquish Iran to Khomeini:

> I think the one mistake was to adopt this policy [of not spilling blood]...because then the opposition saw that now we were surrendering under duress and pressure and they decided they could go all the way.[371]

16

SPIRALING OUT
OF CONTROL

*"Those who can make you believe absurdities
can make you commit atrocities."* (VOLTAIRE)

EVENTS IN IRAN WERE ONLY BEGINNING a downward spiral. Without White House authorization Ambassador William Sullivan determined the reign of the Shah would have to end and began to communicate with leaders of the opposition to achieve that goal. Apparently, Sullivan felt that the Shah was losing his determination to remain in control. Through negotiations with leaders of Pahlavi's opposition, Sullivan amassed a list in excess of one hundred military men who would be certain to depart Iran with the Shah. It would then be up to the revolutionary organizers to choose their replacements. The more moderate elements in the revolution were expected to assure Sullivan that no revenge would be exacted from the military.[372] What an absolute absurdity for a U.S. ambassador to suppose that he had the authority to retire the top brass of a foreign army and ask a fanatical group of Islamic revolutionaries to submit a list of their replacements!

Was Sullivan's ambiguity regarding the Shah's situation in Iran only a reflection of that of President Carter? After all, it was Carter who proclaimed rather indecisively, "We have made it clear through my own public statements and those of Secretary Vance that we support the Shah and support the present government, recognizing that we don't have any control over the decisions ultimately of the Iranian people."[373] And while Sullivan was pursuing his agenda, the president had been in Guadeloupe pursuing an agenda of his own—seeking the backing of European leaders for the deposition of the Shah. Perhaps the president had not read Dante Alighieri's famous quote, "The hottest places in hell are reserved for those who in times of great moral crises maintain their neutrality."[374]

In November 1978 Leonid Brezhnev, the Soviet leader of the Communist Party, stepped into the fray with a warning to the U.S.: "I must be clear that any interference, especially military interference, in the affairs of Iran...would be regarded as a matter affecting security interests [of the USSR]."[375] (One of the Shah's major concerns was that civil strife in Iran would open the door for the Soviets to gain a foothold.) The typically milquetoast response from the U.S. State Department indicated that nothing would be done to interfere with Iran's internal affairs. In fact, it was a statement by President Carter at a December 1978 press conference that seemed to seal the Shah's fate. When asked if the Shah would prevail in Iran, Carter sidestepped with: "We [the U.S.] personally prefer that the Shah maintain a major role in government, but that's a decision for the Iranian people to make."[376] The press, foreign and domestic, reported the president's words and many interpreted them to mean that the U.S. government was standing ready to abandon Mohammad Reza Shah Pahlavi.

Following a November 1978 fact-finding mission to Iran by State Department insiders Stephen Cohen, George Griffin, and Carl Clement, they and Ambassador William Sullivan warned the Carter administration to steel itself for the likelihood that the Shah would no longer rule Iran and that his successors might be less than enamored of a U.S. presence in the country. Sullivan wrote that the State Department needed to make contingency plans for a transfer of power to a coalition government consisting of Khomeini follow-ers and the military. Was it possible that Sullivan was hoping to reach an accord with the opposition after the Shah left Iran? Was he simply waiting for the death rattle before stepping into the fray?

The *Washington Post* again took to its editorial page in late October to try to exonerate Jimmy Carter on his Iran policies with a rather one-sided viewpoint: "This administration inherited a deep American commitment to the Shah, and to his heady view of the importance of Iran in the strategic scheme of things…Jimmy Carter's support of Iran…has emphasized political liberalization…[which] involves a great gamble…. But the Shah…seems to be taking that gamble. At least for as long as he does, the United States has no good choice but to help see him through."[377]

Scarcely a month later, in early November, the *Post* cata-clysmically intoned, "The countdown [for the Shah's fall] has begun."[378] Not willing to place any blame on the Carter admin-istration for its failure to support a strong U.S. ally in the Persian Gulf, the *Post* declared, "The popular tendency to blame it all on Carter's civil rights policy is at best an oversimplification. In hind-sight, it was only a question of time before the system the Shah had built collapsed." In yet another attempt to absolve the president from any failure, the *Post* continued to build its case by declaring that it was not Jimmy Carter's crisis.[379] Apparently, either the *Post* editorialist did not know Mr. Carter as well as he thought he did, or he was unwilling to place blame where blame was due. The Shah, and therefore Iran, was abandoned to the fanatical element that supported the Ayatollah Khomeini.

According to Dr. Abol Majid Majidi, Carter sent Theodore Eliot Jr. to Paris in October 1978 to talk with Khomeini and his entourage. Majidi said Eliot "had tried to create a new relationship, but Khomeini didn't show any sign of willingness…. He was trying to facilitate a dialogue between Khomeini and the American government."[380]

All in all, the Carter administration was as busy juggling international conundrums as the mother of sextuplet toddlers is busy keeping them out of harm's way. The year had produced the Camp David Accords, Strategic Arms Limitation Treaty (SALT) talks, and top-secret advances to the Chinese government, as well as the turmoil in Iran. Unfortunately, the White House was slothful in closely following events in Iran. For instance, it seemed to have escaped the CIA and other agencies that the military was demoralized, defections were the order of the day, and it would be of little use to a coalition government. In an attempt to shore up the flagging Iranian military, Carter dispatched General Robert "Dutch" Huyser, deputy commander in chief of the U.S. European Command to Iran under Alexander Haig despite the misgivings of both Haig and Sullivan. Haig contacted Deputy Secretary of Defense Charles Duncan to express both his anger and concern over Carter's decision:

> *This is bad policy. It is also just plain wrong, and what you have in mind for Dutch Huyser is no job for a military man. You're sending the wrong man for the wrong purpose.*[381]

Haig's unease over sending Huyser to Tehran was overruled by a direct order from Jimmy Carter and the Joint Chiefs of Staff. Huyser was ordered to Tehran post-haste with an admonition from Haig:

> *Then you have to do what you have to do, Dutch. But watch yourself. You may end up destroying the Iranian military. And that would destroy any hope of a good outcome in Iran.*[382]

The Shah recorded that "as soon as Moscow learned of Huyser's arrival, *Pravda* reported, 'General Huyser is in Tehran to foment a military coup.' In Paris, the *International Herald Tribune* wrote that Huyser had not gone to Tehran to 'foment' a coup but to 'prevent' one."[383]

The Iranian generals, who would not attempt a coup while the Shah was on the throne, were awaiting the arrival of Alexander Haig and for some signal or some kind of guarantee from the U.S. that the Soviets would not invade Iran. But rather than send Haig to reassure his Iranian counterparts, his deputy, Dutch Huyser, was tapped for the mission. Huyser, for some unknown reason, did not notify the Shah of his arrival in Tehran as was customary; the Shah discovered he was actually in the country several days after Huyser's arrival.

Huyser's job was to inform the generals that Carter was in favor of democracy in Iran and to act as a morale booster. His orders were to try to persuade the military heads to remain in Iran and work with the U.S. According to former Israeli Ambassador to Iran Uri Lubrani, anyone who thought he could make a deal with the generals and not have made some arrangement with the religious establishment simply didn't understand the situation in Tehran.

General Huyser was soon to discover the truth in Lubrani's assessment: although a plan was supposed to have been in place for an eventuality such as an attempted overthrow of the Shah's government, these military leaders simply did not have a cohesive strategy to deal with the Shah's almost certain ouster by the Ayatollah's revolutionary forces. According to Lt. General Azarbarzin, former vice chief of the Iranian Air Force, Huyser set the generals to work to draw up a contingency plan, although no one in the palace or the Shah's chain of command had authorized the meetings.[384]

Reportedly, Sullivan was less than ecstatic at Huyser's arrival and tried to intervene with Washington. This is not surprising given Sullivan's list of generals he was trying to place on the last plane out of Iran before Khomeini's ultimate power grab. In Dr. Tehrani's estimation, Huyser's mission was totally compromised when shortly after his arrival in Tehran several top military officials defected to the revolution.[385]

Lt. General Azarbarzin told me why the generals were so opposed to a coup:

The military commanders [were] picked by the Shah and reported to him alone, not through the chain of command. They were not picked because they were the most competent, but because they were weak and loyal to the Shah. So, when the time came that they could have staged a coup, they were not capable of doing it; they were used to taking orders, not action.... The Air Force Cadets were neither officers nor non-commissioned officers nor enlisted men. They had a special contract that provided them pay higher than the colonels, special benefits, and paid education through a Ph.D. They were trained in the U.S. to run the most sophisticated technology. As part of their contract, once their service was over, they were to get a lump sum of money they could use to start their own business. For some reason, the chief of the Air Force decided to renege on the deal for six or seven cadets...against my advice. The chief went to the Shah and got his approval. Word got out...and morale sank. The cadets no longer trusted the military or the Shah.[386]

Empress Farah Pahlavi related in our interview that General Haig was concerned about Huyser's trip to Tehran:

I heard that after General Huyser met with President Carter, he went to Brussels when General Haig was there. General Haig told him, "I hope you go there to support the Shah." Huyser told him, "My instructions are otherwise." I wanted to write this in my book [An Enduring Love]; I called General Haig...to see if what I had heard was correct. He told me, "Yes, it is correct; and even more."[387]

Haig was not the only insider to admit the Shah had human rights problems within his country; however, the general felt that as ruler of Iran, Pahlavi was "an essentially benevolent despot,... a good friend of the United States, an implacable enemy of the Left, and an obstacle to the religious Right."[388] By turning a blind eye to the Shah's predicament, Carter allowed the door to swing open and aided Khomeini's takeover of Iran.

General Huyser was chosen as emissary because he had, over the years, built close relationships with a number of top-level Iranian military men. He had been a frequent visitor to the Shah's palace and had established a mutual respect and trust with the monarch. It had been Huyser to whom the Shah voiced his apprehension that he would estrange President Carter by not moving quickly enough to introduce sufficient changes to placate the administration's human rights policies.

Huyser wrote that President Carter had charged him

> ...to convey [President Carter's] concern and assurances to the senior military leaders at this most critical time. It was of vital importance to both the Iranian people and the U.S. government that Iran have a strong, stable government which would remain friendly to the United States. The Iranian military was the key to the situation.[389]

> I interviewed General Huyser at his home. With tears running down his face, he whispered, "They all died because of me." I asked him to explain.

Huyser said the generals in Iran trusted him. He was certain they could have saved the country from a revolution, "But I would not let them," said Huyser.

I asked if he believed Ambassador Sullivan, and Huyser answered, "No. He was lying to me all the time. Carter never really liked the Shah. He saw Pahlavi as a Republican invention. We never gave the generals a straight answer. We kept the Iranian brass in limbo until it was too late. They died believing in us."

> Carter promised that the U.S. would protect and provide all assets needed to shore up the [Shah's] government.... Carter had no desire to see a pro-Shah regime in power. He preferred the Ayatollah, whom he seemed to regard as a Gandhi-like figure. The comparison made sense to a point: the Ayatollah opposed the Shah, who had a terrible record

of human rights abuses. Gandhi was nonviolent. The Ayatollah was anything but.[390]

General Huyser was dispatched to Iran by President Carter to provide encouragement should a military solution be ordered by the Shah, or should the military decide to implement a coup. According to the general, the Iranian generals might have been persuaded to take up arms in defense of the monarchy, if—and only if—they had full military support from the U.S. Another of Huyser's aims was to encourage the more hard-line military men to accept Feridoun Jam, Bakhtiar's choice for defense minister. What proved to be even more difficult was to persuade Jam to agree to the appointment; he declined.

Ambassador Zahedi related his meeting to me, first with the Shah and later with some of the generals—Oveissi, Badi'ie, Toufanian, and Major General Manuchehr Khosrowdad—regarding Huyser's mission. The ambassador initially suggested to the Shah that Huyser either be arrested upon arrival or put on the same plane and sent back to the U.S. The Shah was in favor of waiting to see what Huyser had to say. The military men felt Huyser was encouraging them to disobey the Shah's orders. General Khosrowdad was so angry that he threatened to shoot Huyser on sight. Zahedi very delicately suggested they behave rationally, and that they also wait to see what Huyser proposed. Zahedi was saddened that Huyser's visit seemed to totally destroy morale among the Army leaders.[391]

The Shah's opinion of Huyser's mission was vastly different than that expressed by the general according to Pahlavi's memoirs. He felt that Huyser's interference had destroyed the Iranian army and decimated Bakhtiar's government. Pahlavi wrote that one of his generals, Ghara baghi, said of Huyser, "General Huyser threw the Shah out of the country like a dead mouse."[392]

Huyser's departure from Iran left General Philip C. Gast, chief of the U.S. Military Assistance and Advisory Group, in a leadership role. It was he who then maintained daily communication with both the Iranian military and Secretary of Defense Harold Brown.

Within just two short weeks Pahlavi had flown from Iran, Khomeini had strutted into Tehran a triumphant ayatollah, the Shah's army had crumbled in humiliation and disarray, and the Peacock Throne was barren. Haig tendered his resignation: "I felt I could not continue to serve the Carter administration."[393]

Huyser later recorded one of the ultimate ironies of his mission to Tehran. According to the general, he had the Iranian armed forces at his very command, yet was unable to complete the simplest goal: unloading an oil tanker.[394]

In the midst of the turmoil in Iran, or perhaps because of it, President Carter asked for a meeting on the French Republic island of Guadeloupe in the Caribbean. Although Carter prompted the meeting, ostensibly for him "and the leaders of Britain, France, and West Germany to talk informally about strategic and economic problems,"[395] the invitations were issued by French President Valéry Giscard d'Estaing to West German Chancellor Helmut Schmidt and British Prime Minister James Callaghan. Carter was concerned that a meeting called by the U.S. would upset other NATO leaders, i.e., Canada, Japan, and Italy.

In a briefing by Zbigniew Brzezinski prior to Carter's departure for Guadeloupe, Carter was to have told the assembled world leaders that "President Carter will reiterate his support of the Shah."[396] Apparently no one remembered to apprise Mr. Carter of that fact. In his book, *Le Pouvoir et la Vie*, d'Estaing recalls the meeting:

> *The President Jimmy Carter told us suddenly that the United States had decided not to support the régime of the Shah anymore. Without that support, that régime is now lost. I have kept in my mind the summary of the mission that Michel Poniatowski [French Minister of the Interior] had with the Shah on December 27 [1979]. He had found him with a clear mind but "sad, tired, and disillusioned."*

He thought the Americans would support him to the end. But in a week, the tide changed.... Jimmy Carter tells us what he sees coming. The military will take power and will bring order to the country. Its leaders are pro-West, and most of them have been trained in the United States. The Shah sees more clearly: speaking to Michel Poniatowski, he says "It is all about a powerful religious renewal, which has allowed a long fifty-years-old struggle between the Shiite clergy and our dynasty to turn into a test of forces." And it is the way things happen.[397]

Although not considered a "formal" meeting that required documentation, Carter's National Security Advisor Zbigniew Brzezinski did keep a journal of the Guadeloupe meeting. He recorded his impressions of one session on security issues in his memoirs, *Power and Principle:*

I must say that I was quite impressed by the discussion. It was a thoroughly stimulating and comprehensive review of the security situation, with Carter very effectively taking the lead and pressing the others to define their response to the perceived threat.... Giscard was clear, to the point, and quite decisive. Callaghan displayed good political sense, was quite vigorous, and spoke very sensibly.... [Schmidt] was the one who was most concerned about the Soviet nuclear threat in Europe and the least inclined to agree to any firm response.[398]

While Carter, Brzezinski, his deputy David Aaron, Vance, and other administration bigwigs were busily plotting the Shah's future, Pahlavi was seemingly adrift in a sea of indecision. Should he form a military government? Should he, as Brzezinski suggested, act decisively toward his opponents? Bombarded on every side to either step up to the plate or step down from the throne, the Shah addressed his Iranian subjects in tones that could only be described as conciliatory and apologetic. He acknowledged that he had digested the calls for revolution and was ready to make amends.

Pahlavi's remarks exposed his inner turmoil and struggles with what had become the proverbial handwriting on the wall: the monarchy was in its death throes and the Shah was in complete denial. Unable to make a clear-cut decision, the embattled ruler declared:

> *I commit myself to make up for past mistakes, to fight corruption and injustices, and to form a national government to carry out free elections.... I guarantee that after the military government, freedom and the constitution will be re-implemented.... Your revolutionary message has been heard.*[399]

During the meeting in Guadeloupe, the president also wrestled with the issue of the Shah and the Ayatollah: Should the U.S. make contact with Khomeini? Would it be beneficial to support a military coup? How long should the U.S. support Bakhtiar's interim government? Brzezinski detailed a telephone conference/meeting to which he was called the afternoon he arrived on the French island. The president was in deep conversation with Secretary of State Cyrus Vance. Vance was concerned that the Iranian military leaders would refuse to allow the Shah to depart Tehran and that massive bloodshed would follow that decision.

At the Guadeloupe summit Secretary Vance approached the president and asked that he "be authorized to open a direct channel to Khomeini in Paris." Vance's plan was to "do this through Ambassador Theodore Eliot, a very able, retired senior Foreign Service officer.... I wished Eliot to urge the Ayatollah to give Bakhtiar time to restore order before he returned to Iran.... The president rejected my recommendation.... After a long discussion on January 10...Carter decided to telephone French President Valéry Giscard d'Estaing to ask that the French government urge Khomeini to give Bakhtiar an opportunity to restore order, although he [Carter] agreed that the French should say this also represented American views."[400] The French leader agreed to contact the Ayatollah with Carter's appeal.

Brzezinski, who along with Secretary of Energy James Schlesinger and Deputy Secretary of Defense Charles Duncan favored military intervention, was appalled that Vance seemed determined to moderate the instructions that had been given to General Robert Huyser. Carter refused to allow that to happen. Wrote Brzezinski: "I was gratified by his [Carter's] firmness and dismayed that anyone at this late stage would actually wish to prevent what was clearly in the collective interest of the West."[401]

Another item on the agenda in Guadeloupe was whether or not the U.S. should reach out to Ruhollah Khomeini. While Ambassador to Iran William Sullivan seemed eager for that to happen, members of the Carter administration were reluctant to do so without the prior approval of the Shah. Various reports on the four-leader summit indicate that no conclusion regarding Khomeini was reached while on the island.

Giscard d'Estaing expressed his shock at Carter's lack of regard for a country that had been a close ally for decades:

> We were humanly shocked by the way Carter spoke because we knew at the end it would lead to the torture or the killing of the Shah. And he [Carter] was not embarrassed at all; no, no, he spoke very lightly of a man that we supported very strongly.... He [Carter] was a bastard of conscience, a moralist, who treats with total lightness the fact of abandoning a man that we had supported together. At least you need to have some emotion. And we didn't have any discussion.... No. No. It was, "We have decided." [We were shocked] by the lack of human consideration of the fate of the Shah. Because it was a man that we knew well. We worked with him, we had met with him and all that; so we could accept or understand that probably politically he cannot survive in Iran, or it would be very difficult; but it was some sort of anguish for us. Not someone who should be disgraced with one public gesture.[402]

The Shah was more astute than his so-called allies, however. In his memoir, *Answer to History*, the Shah wrote: "Giscard said they hoped to 'evaluate the situation of the world,' with special emphasis on events in the eastern Mediterranean and the Persian Gulf. I believe that during those meetings the French and West Germans agreed with the British and the American proposals for my ouster."[403]

The Shah continued: "About the same time French President Valéry Giscard d'Estaing sent a personal envoy to Tehran, a man very close to him [Comte Alexandre de Marenches]. He too advocated a 'political' solution to the crisis, a euphemism for accommodation and abstention from the use of force."[404]

Perhaps it was because, as Amir Taheri wrote in *The Spirit of Allah*, "the French were the first to be persuaded that a government under Khomeini would offer them a golden opportunity in Iran, Valéry Giscard d'Estaing...also began advising his Western allies not to try to prolong the Shah's regime."[405]

Mir Ali Asghar Montazam wrote of the Guadeloupe meeting in his book, *The Life and Times of Ayatollah Khomeini*:

> *The Guadeloupe summit...was the convenient opportunity he [Carter] found to agree with the three European leaders that the Shah was doomed.... all the allies needed was Iranian oil and stability in the region.... So, when General Robert Huyser, Carter's special emissary, arrived unannounced in Tehran about the time of Shapour Bakhtiar's becoming prime minister, he represented the entire Western alliance, not the United States only. The Iranian army commanders assented to the Shah's exile only after Huyser showed them the minutes of the allies' summit meeting in Guadeloupe.*[406]

C H A P T E R

17

THE FRENCH
CONNECTION

*"France recklessly encouraged a succession of Muslim leaders, who
proved to be implacably hostile to the West, from Gaddafi to Saddam
Hussein. It was the French who turned Yasser Arafat into a figure on
the world stage and tolerated his terrorists in their midst. And it was
the French who enabled Ayatollah Khomeini to launch his Islamic
revolution from a suburb of Paris."* (DANIEL JOHNSON)[407]

IT WAS WHILE IN FRANCE that Khomeini's speeches
and writings were the most prolific and where the planning for his
Islamic Revolution gained momentum. Khomeini, the usurper, gave
over one hundred media interviews during his short, four-month stay
in Neauphle-le-Château. His pronouncements were quickly
translated, printed, and sent to Tehran. According to Dr. Parviz
Mina, the French gave Khomeini every media advantage and
constantly covered his activities. "On the French news," said Dr.
Mina, "normally there are two special news programs, one at
1:00 in the afternoon and another at 8:00 PM And normally
international news takes up ten minutes or fifteen minutes....
During the time of Khomeini, every day, fifteen minutes they were
talking about Iran and Khomeini, every day...the media was given

the free hand.... [the French government] provided him security. I think all the facilities he needed is at his disposal."[408] The dour Ayatollah had been transformed overnight into a VIP, the darling of the liberal Western media, and France had become command central for the launch of his Islamic Republic.

France in 1979 boasted three major television outlets: *TeleFrance1 (TF1)*, *Antennae 2 (A2)*, and *France 3 (FR3)*; the latter two were owned by the government. *A2* was similar in style and content to America's Public Broadcasting System. The station set the tone for stories on "Journal 20h" (the 8:00 PM news), the equivalent of the NBC or CBS Nightly News. On October 10, 1978, mere days after Khomeini's arrival, he was pictured in a story on *A2*. The images showed Khomeini dressed in dark clothing and sitting tailor-fashion on Persian carpets. He was posed in a lush green garden surrounded by children. He was described as being a deeply religious man who abstained from worldly things.[409] The images were reminiscent of the beloved Indian leader Mahatma Gandhi, the champion of non-violence. Khomeini was clearly being modeled as a modest man compared to the extravagant Shah.

The most influential daily newspaper in France at that time was *Le Monde* or "The World." Though *Le Monde* was left-of-center, it was not as far left as the Communist *Libération*. On the other side of the coin was just slightly-right-of-center, *Le Figaro*. While French President Giscard d'Estaing was purported to be "Centrist," his views more nearly matched those of *Le Monde*.

Many in France thought journalist Paul Balta had been assigned by *Le Monde* to cover Khomeini; it was more apropos to say that Khomeini assigned him. Balta would tell the story years later of how he landed in Paris just after Khomeini arrived in exile at Neauphle-le-Château, a suburb of Paris:

While I was covering the Iranian revolution for Le Monde, *I came to Paris in November 1978. Abu Hassan Bani-Sadr, principal adviser to Khomeini and President of the Republic, told me that the Ayatollah, also called Imam,*

*wanted to meet me. To my surprise, he explained to me that
he had had my articles translated from the French press and
that Khomeini had said about me, "Who is he? He writes like
no other; he knows Islam and Iran. I want to see him."
I went to Neauphle-le-Château, where he lived in exile since
October 5. He shared his frugal meal with me: a large bowl
of soup, bread, fruit, and some cakes just for me. He said
that first he would ask me questions before answering mine.
Once done, he granted me an official interview, which it was
not customary.*[410]

Had the Shah established the same conditions for an interview, would Balta have been as kind to Pahlavi in his writings as he
was to Khomeini? For example, in a Khomeini biography/profile by
Balta for *Le Monde* on February 1, 1979, he wrote:

*A believer in jihad (in the original sense of the term, generally
translated as "holy war," it is the battle against oneself),
he (Khomeini) disciplines himself down to the smallest details
in daily activities and to an intense spiritual life. "He is an
example to all, and even his worst enemies can never contest
that," they say in Iran.*[411]

Did Balta later realize just how clever the Ayatollah had been
with him? He posed a question to Khomeini in January 1979:
"When you win [Not "if you win," but "when."], what will be the
status of the Iranian women?" Khomeini's answer: "Our women
fight like lions. They deserve our admiration. In the Islamic state,
they will have the status that they deserve."

Just weeks later Balta joined Khomeini's entourage on the
Air France plane that flew the triumphant Ayatollah to Tehran.
Delivering a significant speech to his adoring followers in Qom,
Khomeini returned the women of Iran to the Dark Ages.
Balta explained:

*He [Khomeini] outlined the main orientations of the future
Islamic Republic and proclaimed compulsory wearing of*

the chador—"veil"—which had been abolished by the Shah. At the conclusion of the ceremony, I expressed my surprise about the chador, but he replied to me: "I told you they deserve our admiration. It is always the case, but I added as in the Islamic state, they will have the status that they deserve."[412]

It was also in France, that most cosmopolitan of countries, that Khomeini received the makeover of all times. This son of an Indian fortune-teller was stripped of his past. His father became the leader of the Khomeini clan who, supposedly, was murdered by Pahlavi's father. Khomeini graduated from second-rate mullah to academic and renowned holy man. If he was the Eliza Doolittle, who was the Henry Higgins? What country (or countries) was so determined to unseat the Shah that it was willing to undertake the transformation?

Dominique Lorenz, a journalist for the French *Libération*, wrote that "having picked Khomeini to overthrow the Shah, [the Americans] had to get him out of Iraq, clothe him with respectability, and set him up in Paris; a succession of events which could not have occurred if the leadership in France had been against it."[413]

In France, Khomeini's Iranian visitors totaled more than one thousand per day, all of which the French blessed or, at the very least, turned a blind eye. The Ayatollah became the "Guru of Hate" as he shared his vitriolic dislike for the Shah with all who would listen and learn. These disciples, including a number from various American universities, were not coming just to sit at the feet of the "Teacher" and learn; their pockets, lined with money collected through the Bazaar, the commercial system in Iran, were empty when they left Khomeini's presence. Some estimates place the contributions at approximately twenty million British pounds.

The Ayatollah's compound was reportedly surrounded by representatives of covert agencies from the major powers: the CIA, Britain's MI-6, Russia's KGB, and the French intelligence organization, SDECE. One has to wonder why an unknown, uncultured, old cleric was the focus of such attention.

One visitor to Khomeini's château described the mesmerizing effect the Ayatollah had on his visitors:

> *He [Khomeini] started to speak in his deep, bass voice, and I never heard a voice as serene and moving. It was said that he caressed the ears of his listeners, in soft waves to put them in a trance state.... Here we had an Imam, with his long, grey beard and black turban of the Shiites...and here, all of these men representing the social and intellectual elite of Iran, listened in absolute silence, hanging on every word that fell from his lips with an attentive fascination.... Khomeini was always sure that the driving force of the revolution would be religious, and he was therefore destined to take the leadership role.*[414]

French journalist André Fontaine "compared Khomeini to John Paul II, heaping praise upon the [Ayatollah] without reserve. The philosopher Jacques Madaule, referring to Khomeini's role, asked if his movement did not 'open the gates of the future of humanity.'"[415]

Aiding Khomeini during his French exile was Abolhasan Bani-Sadr. Journalist Charles Villeneuve related to me that Bani-Sadr was responsible for supplying the cassette tapes filled with anti-Shah propaganda and dispatching them through the network that would insure their arrival in the mosques in Tehran.[416] The Iranian had resisted attempts by CIA operative Vernon Cassin (under the alias Guy Rutherford) to enlist him as a mole. Cassin's documents would eventually wind up in the hands of the militants who seized the American Embassy and would signal the downfall of Bani-Sadr.

In my interview with him, Giscard d'Estaing shed more light on the messages sent into Iran by the Ayatollah:

> *During his stay, the Imam was active. He sent messages to Iran to Tehran.... he used tapes...carried by followers to Iran...to Chayet, the man in charge.... we knew the Interior Ministry was still watching closely the activities of the Ayatollah. He seems to deliver violent messages.... we have*

political refugees, but they must abstain from violence. So we warned him...that we would not accept that [he] would go on sending messages.... But he went on...we had the tapes. The second time I was warned by our ambassador in Tehran that Khomeini had sent a message asking to kill the Shah.... five days later, we had confirmation that he sent another violent tape to Tehran saying the same thing, which was, "kill the Shah."[417]

CIA memoranda regarding Khomeini and the Shah seem to have either been deliberately ignored by the Carter administration or lost in the great governmental paperwork shuffle. One such memorandum flatly stated, "Khomeini is determined to overthrow the Shah and is unlikely to accept compromise.... Khomeini is anti-Communist, but his followers may be susceptible to Communist and radical penetration. He has cooperated in the past with Islamic terrorist groups."[418]

A CIA intelligence memorandum dated January 19, 1979, and released three days after the Shah's departure contained detailed information on Bani-Sadr and Sadegh Ghotbzadeh (Syrian-born leader of the opposition movement), including the fact that both men had ties to Palestinian commandos. Questions arise: Why was the memo released after the Shah's departure from Tehran? Did President Carter and administration officials have access to this information in the months prior to abandoning the Shah and permitting Khomeini to return to Tehran?

Early in 1977 Khomeini had begun to woo the military in Iran through his taped messages. The wily Ayatollah knew that to win the revolution he must first charm and disarm the military. He began to indoctrinate the troops with the message of the Shah's corruption and their own place as soldiers of Allah; as such, they were prohibited from shooting at their own brethren. He exhorted them to return to their homes, to the faith, and to service to Allah. Surprisingly, it was not SAVAK or the Shah's inner circle that stumbled onto

Khomeini's tactics; it was the Israeli mission to Tehran that had become apprehensive.

By fall 1977 the Ayatollah was giving the soldiers specific instructions as to how to achieve his goal. He encouraged them to desert their posts in numbers, reminding them it was their God-given right to take their arms with them. Ironically, the very day Jimmy Carter praised Iran as "an ocean of stability in a stormy sea," a battalion of five hundred soldiers abandoned their post in the Meshed region. Said one journalist, "The Ayatollah effectively disarmed the Shah's military before engaging it in final battle."[419]

In another ironic twist, the Shah found himself an unwitting accomplice of Khomeini's revolution. In his efforts to modernize Iran, the Shah had installed a costly direct-dial telephone system. It allowed Khomeini to pick up the phone in Neauphle-le-Château and have direct talks with his cohorts in Tehran.

It was this telephone system that Azarbarzin was certain the CIA had bugged. He cited one incident to support his theory:

The Shah asked me to bring General Nassiri back into the country; it seemed the Shah was considering putting him in as prime minister. Nassiri was then stationed as the Shah's ambassador to Pakistan. I ordered an aircraft at the airport, only told the crew where they were going once onboard. We flew to Pakistan at night and returned with Nassiri to a non-descript gate at the airport, and drove back to the palace. I had made arrangements and alerted the Imperial Guard that we would sneak Nassiri in through an unused entrance after midnight.

Usually Ambassador Sullivan arrived at the palace at 10:00 AM.... That morning...Sullivan arrived at 8:30 AM and asked to see the Shah. When they met Sullivan immediately began to explain that it was a mistake to name Nassiri...because the people demonstrating on the street were there because of Nassiri's actions as head of SAVAK.

> *Instead of making Nassiri the PM as planned, he was placed in jail to please the Iranian masses.*
>
> *On November 3, 1978, the Shah decided to create a military cabinet. His nominee was General Oveissi.... The Shah ordered General Oveissi to start selecting his cabinet members. On November 4 both British Ambassador Anthony Parsons and U.S. Ambassador William Sullivan had audiences with the Shah. They convinced him that people called Oveissi a butcher for the way he had put down protests in 1963.*[420]

The ambassadors suggested that the Shah appoint General Gholam Reza Azhari as prime minister. Was this just another attempt on the part of the U.S. and British governments to manipulate Pahlavi?

It seemed the Shah's government could do nothing to prevent Khomeini from attracting like-minded revolutionaries to his château outside Paris. In my interview with Samuel Segev, he confirmed that two of Khomeini's visitors in France were Farouk Kaddoumi, PLO department head, and a Libyan representative of Muammar al-Qaddafi. Khomeini was tendered arms and money in support of the revolution. Soon after, Radio Tripoli broadcast messages in Persian to Khomeini backers in Iran, and PLO terrorists were dispatched to Tehran.[421]

As the turmoil fueled by Khomeini's subversive methods in his country increased, the Shah tried appeasement measures to placate the rioters and strikers. He eased curfews, allowed processions to mark holy days, and ultimately succumbed to the pressure to put a new government in place. He chose Shapour Bakhtiar, a forthright critic of the monarchy, as the new leader. Ardeshir Zahedi urged General Oveissi to secure Bakhtiar's agreement that he would work with the army to restore order not undermine it, and Bakhtiar agreed.

At Bakhtiar's urging the Shah agreed to leave Iran for what was labeled "rest and recuperation." Empress Farah Pahlavi writes that even though Bakhtiar urged the Shah to leave, the Chief of Staff General Abbas Gharabaghi was opposed to the move and warned the empress that if the Shah left Iran, the army would collapse.

This evaluation was supported by Ambassador Lubrani. He dressed himself as a middle-class Iranian and went out among the rioters and demonstrators. He related that the soldiers simply stood by while women in the crowd placed carnations in the muzzles of their rifles. The army was effectively neutralized by the massive crowds of Iranians. The question then became: Had the Shah given the order to shoot into the crowd, would the army have complied?[422]

The Shah assumed that upon his return, he would become a constitutional monarch much like Queen Elizabeth II in England. Little did he know that once airborne, he would have caught his last glimpse of his beloved country, and that Iran would plunge back into the Dark Ages from which he had tried so hard to lead his people. Pahlavi was convinced the French government was ignoring Khomeini's clever plot to incite revolution in Iran.

From Paris, Khomeini had called upon the Iranian military to forestall any attempt by the Shah to promote a military coup. He had also urged the Iranian people to overthrow the Bakhtiar government, calling it illegal and illegitimate. The Ayatollah wrote:

> *"There is a possibility that the treacherous Shah, now about to depart, will commit a further crime, a military coup d'état. I have frequently warned that this is probable.... The courageous people of Iran know that there are only a few slavish and bloodthirsty individuals in the army, who apparently occupy important positions and whose identities are known to me, and that the honorable elements in the army will never permit these slaves of the Shah to commit such a crime against their nation and religion. In accordance with my God-given and national duty, I alert the Iranian army to this danger, and I demand that all commanders and officers resolutely prevent the enactment*

of any such conspiracy and not permit a few bloodthirsty individuals to plunge the noble people of Iran into a blood-bath. Iranian army, this is your God-given duty. If you obey these congenital traitors, you will be accountable to God, Exalted and Almighty, condemned by all humanitarians, and cursed by future generations.... The Iranian people... must recognize that a few treacherous members of the army cannot sully the army as a whole. The record and responsibility of a few bloodthirsty individuals is something separate from the army as a whole. The army belongs to the people, and the people belong to the army. The army will not suffer any harm as a result of the departure of the Shah.[423]

According to President Carter's memoir, *Keeping Faith*, President d'Estaing offered to deport Khomeini to halt the discord and stop Khomeini's rabble-rousing from French shores. Carter writes that "the Shah had thought it would be better to keep Khomeini there [France], instead of letting him go to Iraq or Libya or some place where he might orchestrate even more trouble."[424] A poll taken among the French people found that half [of those] questioned were "sorry that their government granted political asylum to the Ayatollah."[425]

18

ABDICATING TO A
RUTHLESS AYATOLLAH

*"Khomeini...insisted that, since his version of Islam was the only
true version, all Muslims should follow it.... Khomeini blithely allied
himself with anyone who could advance his cause.... [His] version
of Islam was unquestionably bloodthirsty."*
(M I C H A E L   A .   L E D E E N) [426]

PRIOR TO KHOMEINI'S ARRIVAL in France, Giscard had
dispatched his personal representative, Michel Poniatowski, to Iran
to meet with the Shah. Poniatowski reported back to Giscard that,
"[The Shah] understands nothing of what's going on; he thinks
Khomeini is without importance and he asks us to welcome him....
I don't want to; he should not be welcomed."[427]

Former Ambassador Zahedi agreed with Poniatowski:

*Every time His Majesty asked, I advised him to get Khomeini
out [of Paris]. Nothing changed. The prime minister [Jafar
Sharif-Emami] had influenced the Shah and none of us
managed to change his mind.*[428]

Giscard then sent his chief of secret services, Alexandre
de Marenches (who referred to Jimmy Carter as a "national and

international disaster"[429]) to interview the Shah and to confirm Poniatowski's impression. Marenches reported back to Giscard that the Shah appeared almost beaten and that the best thing to do would be to prepare in France for the aftermath of Khomeini's revolution.[430] According to Marenches, the Shah declined to use armed force against his people. Marenches replied, "Sir, in that case you are lost."[431] Uri Lubrani is of the opinion that France courted Khomeini as a way of "buying political influence...resting on their reputation of being a liberal country [that gave] political asylum to all sorts of renegades.... 'France is a whore,'" said Lubrani.[432]

General Huyser also pointed out that the United States should have learned how important it was not to abandon a friend. He assessed the Carter administration's lack of understanding:

> *The administration obviously did not understand the Iranian culture, nor the conditions that prevailed in the last few months of the Shah's reign. I believe that Washington should have recognized the seriousness of the situation early in 1978. If the real intent was to support the existing government, much could have been done to bolster the Shah's lagging confidence and resolve....*
>
> *The president could have publicly condemned Khomeini for his interference. He could have solicited the support of our allies, and in conjunction with them he could have given material support to the Bakhtiar government.[433]*

Unfortunately, the Carter administration did none of the things General Huyser suggested they might have done to ameliorate the situation. In fact, on January 4 Sullivan met with the Shah. His instructions from Vance were to "listen and report, but not encourage any line of action."[434]

On January 7 a *New York Times* editorial labeled the Shah as "The Friend That Failed," an interesting title given that reading the previous two years of the *Times* would have made Pahlavi seem more a burden to the U.S. than a close friend and ally. The editorial condemned the American penchant for sticking with its friends abroad as a "suicidal devotion" and that "such theories blind their devotees to all objective diplomatic reckonings."[435] The *Times'* strange reversal of standing up for human rights was considered noble, but at the same time the "real politick" of the Kissinger years was denounced. While devotion to principle was considered a weakness, the *Times* did not need to worry about such contradictions. In the end, "It was the Shah who failed in Iran, not the United States."[436]

One vastly important decision was reached by Carter on January 14, two days prior to the Shah's departure from Tehran. A meeting between Warren Zimmerman, the U.S. Embassy political advisor in Paris, and Ebrahim Yazdi, Khomeini's U.S. mouthpiece, was approved by the president. Meanwhile, Huyser was equally busy trying to persuade the military heads in Iran to open a line of communication with the Ayatollah. On that same evening, Khomeini stunned many in the Carter administration by telling a CBS reporter that a large number of the Iranian armed forces were loyal to his cause, and he would be the "strongman" in Iran.[437]

After the Shah's departure from Tehran on January, 17, 1979, a *Times* editorial sighed theatrically, "The Shah Departs, Finally." The question was posed: "Is there something to regret in this turn of events?" The editorialist felt compelled to answer the question for the readers: "Chiefly, that the Shah dallied too long before going."[438]

Zimmerman and Yazdi reportedly held several secret meetings in Paris during which they discussed topics related to possible Iranian military interference with Khomeini's plan to return to Tehran. Yazdi outlined three basic questions to which the revolutionaries wanted an answer. They were:

> *Would Khomeini's return trigger a military reaction or create such an uproar among the Iranian people that the military was forced to respond to the chaos?*

> *Would the upper echelon of the military insist on backing the Shah or would it acquiesce to Khomeini's leadership and transfer allegiance to the cleric?*

> *Did Americans working in Iran have the right to destroy what was described as "sophisticated military equipment" before departing the country? It was Khomeini's contention that the equipment fell under the auspices of the Iranian military.*

On a bitterly cold day, January 16, 1979, the Shah, who had ruled Iran for thirty-seven years, and his empress, Farah Pahlavi, boarded one of two planes destined for Egypt. Ironically, the two passenger jets were parked in front of the lavish and luxurious Imperial Pavilion where the Shah had often greeted kings and politicians who visited Tehran. The *Gulf News* reported his departure:

> *Two officers of the Shah's royal guard fell to their knees and tried to kiss the monarch's feet at Tehran's airport, but he motioned for them to rise, court sources said. Two other officers, standing face to face, held aloft a copy of Holy Quran and the royal couple passed beneath the impromptu arch to board the "Shah's Falcon," a royal Boeing 727....*

> *With tears in his eyes, Shah Mohammad Reza Pahlavi and Empress Farah Diba left Iran for Egypt and the United States, piloting his own jet on a journey many believe will end in permanent exile. His departure touched off jubilant celebrations throughout Tehran.*

> *"The Shah is gone forever," people chanted as millions poured into the streets of Tehran, showering each other with sweets and rose water, cheering and shouting with joy at what they saw as victory in a year-long, bloody uprising to topple the 59-year-old Shah.*[439]

On January 18, just two days after the Shah's departure from Tehran, President Jimmy Carter held a press conference. Did he momentarily forget his promise never to lie to the American people when asked if he had been in touch with Khomeini, was it just more of what George Ball would call "disavowability," or was Carter so out of touch with the various intrigues of his administration that he did not know the truth? Carter responded to the question with, "No, we have not communicated directly with Mr. Khomeini."[440]

During January 1979 meetings among the Carter White House operatives gained momentum, and it was reported that the Shah, while unenthusiastic that Bakhtiar would succeed, was ready to relinquish the reins of government to his hand-picked successor. As a result, administration insiders communicated to the Shah that he and his family were welcome to visit the United States home of Walter Annenberg in California or travel to Egypt at the invitation of Anwar Sadat. (Sadat had no regard for the fanatical Khomeini and felt he would only drastically harm Islam.) The Shah chose to spend a week in Cairo with Sadat and then travel on to Morocco for a two-week visit with King Hassan. It was in Marrakesh on February 11, 1979, that the Pahlavi family heard of the collapse of Bakhtiar's government. The next day, news of the slaughter of military officials reached the king.

Unfortunately, the Shah's stay in Morocco as a guest of King Hassan soon came to an end. Alexandre de Marenches contacted the Shah to inform him that King Hassan was in danger due to the presence of the Pahlavi family in Morocco. Khomeini's far-reaching hand was stirring the pot of unrest among students on the university campuses in that country, and the Shah was asked to leave.

The Shah requested that he be allowed to stay in Morocco, where he was able to maintain constant contact with his most loyal military contingent, the Royal Guard. He felt he could be called upon at any moment to return to Iran and resume the throne. King Hassan was forced to respond negatively to Pahlavi, and the Shah and his royal entourage departed Morocco. He was denied entry into France, which had clasped Khomeini to its bosom. Both Monaco and Switzerland, bastions of neutrality, also rejected a request to host the deposed monarch. Even the "Iron Lady" of Great Britain, Margaret Thatcher, declined to welcome the Shah and his family to England.

Two of Pahlavi's prominent acquaintances, Henry Kissinger and David Rockefeller, attempted to intervene on the Shah's behalf for asylum in Mexico. It seems that Khomeini's new government had withdrawn the royal family's passports. The Mexican bureaucrats were denying the Shah's entourage entrance into Mexico without some official documentation. Morocco had declined aid to the Pahlavi family because King Hassan did not want the Shah to be able to return to Morocco uninvited. Queen Farah was reduced to calling Prince Aga Khan, the UN High Commissioner for Refugees, and literally begging to be granted refugee status in order to secure proper passports for the king and his traveling companions.[441]

At that point, the Shah informed the Carter White House that he was ready to take it up on the offer of asylum at the Annenberg estate. William J. Daugherty, one of the U.S. Embassy employees who was later held hostage by the Iranians, wrote of the rescinding of the invitation:

> At a meeting of the Special Coordinating Committee (SCC— the highest level policy and crisis management group in the Carter White House) on 23 February the decision was made to inform the Shah that, while the invitation was still officially open, there were now serious complications. Specifically, the short-lived takeover of the American Embassy the previous St. Valentine's Day had some senior officials in Washington reconsidering the wisdom of hosting the Shah. The Shah's entry into the United States was poten- tially an inflammatory act and, with a deteriorating security situation in Tehran, there was still a very real threat to American interests and the remaining American officials and citizens. The risk to American lives at that time was serious, apparent, and exigent: U.S. intelligence personnel at one of the CIA's TACKSMAN intelligence collection sites had been

*taken captive days before, and American Ambassador
William Sullivan was at that moment in negotiations over
their release (the TACKSMAN sites were a cooperative effort
with the Shah's regime for monitoring the Soviet missile test
ranges). Manifestly, the entry of the Shah would no doubt
unleash severe and potentially uncontrollable repercussions
against these and other Americans in Iran.*[442]

In abandoning the Shah and Iran to the Grand Ayatollah
Ruhollah Khomeini, the Carter State Department had completely
overlooked Khomeini's tendency to refer to the United States as the
"Great Satan"—a superpower to be brought to its knees. Under
Khomeini's regime, blood would flow again through the streets of
Tehran and repression would reach new heights in the coming years
simply because multiplied tens of thousands of Iranians viewed the
Shah as a tool of the "Great Satan."

General Huyser was of the opinion that "the greatest potential
for disaster would be the early return of Khomeini. While a large
segment of the armed forces would remain loyal to the Shah, there
were quite a number who were pro-Khomeini, and even a few
communists. The armed forces were convinced that the return of
Khomeini meant the absolute finish of the Shah."[443]

Huyser's account differs from that of Cyrus Vance. Vance
wrote that Huyser found the generals confused and discussing the
advantages of contacting Khomeini. According to Vance's recollec-
tions, the generals felt that the "anti-communism of the military and
the religious leaders could give them common ground...[and that]
Khomeini would surely prefer to have a cohesive, effective
army...during the political transition to an Islamic republic."[444]

On February 6, 1979, General Huyser shared with Ambassador
Sullivan his fears of what a Khomeini government would mean for
Iran. It was Huyser's considered estimation, "If Khomeini took
control and formed an Islamic Republic, the country would drift
from right to left....if he took over completely and practiced what
he had been preaching, the country would disintegrate."[445]

Huyser's predictions, while true, didn't begin to paint the picture of the bloodshed that would occur in the ranks of the military in Iran. Stunned by the loss of the generals and hierarchy under the Shah, the rank and file of the Iranian security forces was cast adrift. The army was in total confusion. Khomeini was swift to deactivate the Shah's military and substitute his own, drawn from the revolutionaries that now surrounded him.

Khomeini instructed his followers in the ways of martyrdom as a means to disengage the Shah's troops:

> *You must appeal to the soldiers' hearts even if they fire on you and kill you. Let them kill five thousand, ten thousand, twenty thousand—they are our brothers and we will welcome them. We will prove that blood is more powerful than the sword.*[446]

General Alexander Haig, Supreme Allied Commander of NATO during the Carter administration, said of the ouster of the Shah:

> *It didn't take long for the world to realize that the Shah was an enlightened liberal next to the bloody reactionary regime that followed, and which executed more people in three months than the Shah had done in thirty years.*[447]

CHAPTER
19

ENGULFED IN
DARKNESS

*"A man will come out from Qom [Iranian holy city] and he will
summon people to the right path. There will rally to him people
resembling pieces of iron, not to be shaken by violent winds,
unsparing and relying on God."*

<small>(AN ANCIENT ISLAMIC PROPHECY)</small>[448]

MOHAMMAD REZA SHAH PAHLAVI'S JET was hardly
airborne on January 16, 1979, before Iranian newspapers screamed,
"Shah Raft!" or *"The Shah is Gone."* He had ruled over Iran from
the age of twenty-one; now he was leaving in ignominious defeat, not
knowing he would never return. Former Iranian Ambassador
Dr. Ahmad Tehrani summed up the Shah's feelings, perhaps better
than anyone, when he said, "The Shah never, ever believed the
United States would let him down. He believed Russia would do it,
he believed the British would do it, but not the United States or
France."[449]

In an interview with Houchang Nahavandi during a trip to
Poland and Czechoslovakia in early 1978, the Shah was certain he
was "irremovable." When asked what would happen to him should

the U.S. change its policy and forsake the monarch, Pahlavi answered, "The Americans will never abandon me."[450] That assumption would prove to be false, as Jimmy Carter was about to demonstrate.

Mohamed Heikal wrote of the Shah's stay at Aswan in Egypt:

The Shah comported himself as though he were still a head of state. He took advantage of a summit meeting between President Sadat and former President Ford to give voice to his grievances against the Americans. "Carter," he said, "had decided it [the Shah's ouster]. While he declared in public that he would support you to the end, at the same time, he was negotiating with the opposition behind your back." [The Shah] added that it was curious that the King of Morocco...offered to send troops to help him; the Americans, who were supposed to be allies, did not do so.[451]

Perhaps it was as Ardeshir Zahedi who suggested the Shah didn't think the radical cleric Khomeini could command change in Iran. He was certainly not the most influential Ayatollah at the time; that honor belonged to the leader of the Shiite world, Ayatollah Shariatmadari. Though not altogether pleased with the Shah, Shariatmadari was not clamoring for a regime change. Neither he nor the leading cleric in Najaf, Ayatollah Kho'ei, were pushing for the Shah's ouster.[452]

This was not the case with the ultra-radical Khomeini. A declassified document from the secretary of state to the U.S. Embassy in Iran detailed the situation:

There are...all strains of religious leadership....Those religious elements presently dominating the Iranian scene both organizationally and ideologically are committed to violence and obstruction as tools for attaining power. Ayatollah Khomeini has specifically called for the Shah's violent removal, and some of his followers in Isfahan and Shiraz have openly called for the death of the Shah.... Moderates such as Ayatollah Shariatmadari do not at this time feel capable of opposing Khomeini openly, though they reportedly still work for moderation within the religious movement.... Whatever the Shah wishes to do next, he must meet head-on the violent challenges to both his government and Iran's social fabric.... Many Iranians believe the Shah is not acting forcefully enough.... Some believe the Americans forced him to be restrained.[453]

Khomeini, as the world would soon see, boasted an underground network of fanatical mullahs, i.e., Ayatollah Mahmoud Taleghani and Mohammad Beheshti, who favored regime change. Khomeini's calls for an end to the Shah's reign were taken up by bands of radical hooligans who were only too happy to carry out the Ayatollah's wishes. Did Khomeini and his followers feel they had the backing of the Carter administration in their determination to destroy the monarchy?

I asked Lt. General Shapour Azarbarzin, former vice chief of the Iranian Air Force during the early days of the revolution, what Jimmy Carter could have done to prevent a revolution in Iran. He replied:

Carter could have called the Shah personally and told him it was okay to use strength to take control of the situation. Then, once order was restored, the Shah could have addressed the people from a position of strength. [I would have said] don't go through Sullivan, and Vance, and Huyser, and Brzezinski; this all just created confusion and signaled weakness.[454]

Shapour Bakhtiar, who was at the helm of the provisional government left by the Shah, pled with Ayatollah Ruhollah Khomeini to delay his arrival in Tehran for several months so that civil order might be restored. The determined Ayatollah adamantly refused. Gary Sick's description of the Ayatollah fit him perfectly:

Khomeini was the arch-type of the medieval prophet emerging from the desert with a fiery vision.... His God was

a harsh and vengeful deity...demanding an eye and tooth of
retribution.... Khomeini's philosophy had great tolerance
for pain, human suffering, and political chaos, but no toler-
ance for opposition. His opponents were satanic, and the
remedy was to "cut off their arms."[454]

Given its association with Israel, it would not have been beyond
the realm of possibility for Iran to seek the help of the Mossad to
stop Khomeini. However, Uri Lubrani who was stationed in Iran in
the 1970s has suggested that Israel might have considered backing
a military takeover in Iran, but the U.S. was slow to support such a
move. Perhaps, like the United States, Israel had chosen to take a
"wait and see" attitude regarding the situation in Tehran.

Meanwhile, both Ambassador William Sullivan and General
Dutch Huyser requested that the Carter administration reassess its
Iran policy. Sullivan also warned Carter that Khomeini's arrival in
Tehran would certainly mark the end of Bakhtiar and crush the
military. The ambassador was convinced the Iranian military was
"'a paper tiger' [and] the United States had been dealing with
'evaporating institutions,'"[456] prior to Khomeini's arrival in Tehran.
The men could see the strong possibility of a clash between the
military and the clerics. Huyser felt it incumbent to alert the
generals that the U.S. would not back a military junta should
Bakhtiar fail. Carter refused to allow Huyser and Sullivan to divulge
that information.

With the Shah's departure Khomeini's Paris entourage made
hurried preparations to get the Imam back to Tehran. Having
decided against the use of an Iranian airliner for fear of being
attacked by the Shah's Air Force, a jumbo jet was chartered from Air
France for a mere pittance of $3 million dollars plus an undisclosed
sum to cover the insurance premium for the aircraft. The crew that
manned the jumbo jet was comprised totally of volunteers.[457]

In his autobiography, *Keeping Faith*, Jimmy Carter purports
that on January 14, 1979, he contacted the French president to ask
that he not allow Khomeini's departure to Tehran:

I called Giscard d'Estaing quite early in the morning, asking him to contact Khomeini and to do everything he could to delay Khomeini's departure from France. Giscard was willing to cooperate. Said...he had no way to prevent Khomeini's leaving France, but could delay it somewhat. His government's only policy was to support the Bakhtiar government. Valéry said he has no relationship with the Iranian military, and that he believes a visit by the Shah to the United States would be a mistake. It would be much better if he would go to a neutral country for awhile before winding up here in our country. Later in the day, he called back. Giscard reported that Khomeini has no plans to leave Paris for the moment. He didn't know what "for the moment" means, but that Khomeini is afraid he might lose his life if he goes to Iran. Khomeini's final aim is to overthrow the Bakhtiar government.[458]

One of Khomeini's closest advisors, and coincidentally a naturalized U.S. citizen, Ebrahim Yazdi, was aboard the jet that carried the triumphant Khomeini back to Iran. According to Yazdi:

The civil airline in Iran arranged independently a flight from Tehran to Paris to bring Khomeini back. They called it the Revolutionary Flight. But we didn't trust them, because we knew that there was a possibility that the army might attack, or the army might force the aeroplane to land in some remote area. So, we didn't accept that. Instead, we chartered an Air France plane. In addition to that, we took with us more than a hundred and twenty journalists—reporters from all over the world. I have to confess that we took them as a human shield, so to speak. We knew that nobody would dare to shoot at such a plane, with so many reporters from so many nationalities.[459]

Fear of an attack on the Air France jet prompted Khomeini to leave behind his wife, daughter, and grandchildren, as well as the wives and children of his inner circle. Before departing Paris the

Ayatollah thanked the French government for allowing him to remain in France. Perhaps subtly, he was thanking the French for allowing him to wage an unhindered war against the Shah of Iran and to topple his government. Were the truth known, it is more likely that the government of France was happy to see the backside of his turban.

On the plane with Khomeini was a young ABC reporter, Peter Jennings. During the flight Jennings is said to have asked the Imam, "What do you feel [about returning to Iran]?" Khomeini replied, "Nothing." That was a strange answer from a man whose life had been consumed in recent years with the overthrow of the Shah and a triumphant return to Iran.

Bakhtiar, in an attempt to discredit Khomeini and persuade the Air Force cadets to support his government, sent a copy of the tape of the Ayatollah's response to the interview question. Unfortunately for the future of Bakhtiar and Iran, his plan backfired. The cadets remained faithful to Khomeini.

The Air France jet that bore the Grand Ayatollah Ruhollah Khomeini touched down in Tehran at precisely 9:33 AM on February 1, 1979, following a brief discussion on whether or not the airport should be reopened. It had been closed for five days due to demonstrations and riots. Lt. General Azarbarzin received a phone call from the Air Force chief instructing him to open the facility. Azarbarzin asked on whose authority he was to proceed, and he was told it was at the direction of Prime Minister Bakhtiar. When the Lt. General questioned the order, Bakhtiar personally ordered him to reopen the airport.[460] The Imam, who had slept for much of the $5\frac{1}{2}$ hour flight, was ending an exile that had lasted for more than fourteen years. There exists a photograph of Khomeini while on that historic Air France flight. While traveling through the night, Khomeini sat off by himself in a comfortable, first-class seat. The surviving photograph shows the Imam in a moment of self-satisfied meditation. A deep inner joy appears to emanate from his face.

At this moment, Ayatollah Khomeini was savoring the approaching moment when his life-long aspirations were finally to be realized.

In the photograph, his eyes have a distant look, as if he is peering into the past, or maybe into the future. He is 78 years old. He appears venerable, but by no means vulnerable. His trademark black turban sits atop his head, his visage is distinguished by a flowing white beard, and his dark eyes highlighted by thick eyebrows are fierce and piercing. The Imam's lips are pursed in a private smile, and his hands lie quietly in his lap, gracing the folds of his long robe. Perhaps he realized that, at last, his deal with the devil was about to produce his date with destiny. The photographer captured a moment of calm before the storm of frenzied public adulation broke upon him. Khomeini was now ready to receive his triumphant welcome and lead an Islamic Revolution that would shake the entire world. Khomeini stepped off the plane surrounded by his entourage and knelt to kiss the soil of Iran. Some say that his welcoming committee boasted several American officials.

There is a certain irony in the fact that Khomeini, despiser of all things American, the man who had referred to Jimmy Carter as "the vilest man on earth,"[461] was hustled into a Chevrolet Blazer for the trip to his first destination—the Behesht-e-Zahra Cemetery, the burial place of ten to twelve thousand who died during the revolution. According to a BBC report,[462] some five million Iranians lined the streets from the airport to the cemetery. Not even 50,000 Iranian police could control the massive crowd. They were so overjoyed at the sight of their returning Imam that, again, Khomeini had to be rescued by an American-made Air Force helicopter in order to complete his pilgrimage to the cemetery. Occupying the helicopter with Khomeini was the Shah's commander in chief of the Air Force General Amir Hussein Rabii.

Khomeini's progress was hampered by the disarray in the Iranian military following the Shah's departure. General David Ivri explained the confusion in the ranks:

*Some of them were not secure and they sent their families
abroad...with money.... deep inside they were afraid.... [After
Khomeini's arrival]. They were called to a meeting and told,
"You are fine. Stay in your positions." Everyone went home
calmly, and then they were caught in their homes.*[463]

The first act of the Ayatollah was to declare in no uncertain
terms that the caretaker government of Bakhtiar was illegal.
"If they continue," said Khomeini, "we will arrest them. I will shut
their mouths. And I will appoint a government with the support of
the Iranian people."[464] Ambassador William Sullivan, on the front
line in Tehran, could see signs of increasing instability. He felt the
Carter administration was not heeding his information until long
after it was presented. Sullivan was not surprised, therefore, when
Khomeini seized control of the government on February 11, 1979.
When Sullivan received a call from the White House on February 12,
giving him the go-ahead to encourage the Iranian military to keep
the revolution in check with the use of deadly force, if necessary,
it is said, "Sullivan declined, using colorful language."[465]

Ayatollah Khomeini had returned to bring his radical Islamic
rebellion to Iran. He believed this was the first step of his revolution
sweeping across the world. Khomeini's one, fervent desire was to see
the West, led by the United States, submit to the grip of radical Islam.
Soon, he felt the illegitimate state of Israel would be decimated.
He was certain all other religions would yield to his version of
Islam. Then a Muslim theocracy would be established in every
corner of the world. This was the Grand Ayatollah Khomeini's
vision of destiny. He informed the Iranian people that: "'This is not
the final victory, but only a prelude to victory." He called upon the
army to destroy its new sophisticated American weapons, and for the
people to strike and demonstrate against the Bakhtiar regime. As to
Carter's suggestion that he cooperate with Bakhtiar, he simply
declared that this had nothing to do with Carter."[466]

The day following Khomeini's arrival in Tehran, the Israeli
Embassy was ransacked and set afire. Several dozen Palestinians

among the rioters breached the walls of the building, tore the Israeli flag from its mooring on the top floor, and burned it. Cries of "Death to Israel! Long live Arafat! Israel get out!" could be heard from the mob. The Palestinian standard was then raised from the roof of the mission.[467] Israel's friends in the Shah's government turned a blind eye. General Yitzhak Segev, military attaché in Iran, called on a friend in the Iranian Air Force to afford them a military cargo plane to fly to safety. The contact, General Rabii, responded:

> *The Revolutionary Guards control the airport and I cannot help you. But if you find a plane, please evacuate me as well.*[468]

What influence Rabii may have had with Khomeini was short-lived. He was tried for "corruption on earth; war on God and the people of God; actions designed to weaken the country's independence and security; shaking the foundations of the country's system of government; defiling all that is sacred, whether religious or national, to the Muslim people of Iran and the world." Rabii was executed by firing squad on April 8, 1979. During the first year under Khomeini's rule, the Iranian armed forces saw their ranks dwindle by one hundred thousand troops. Even as Iran's military might faded, Saddam Hussein was building his Iraqi army and was stockpiling military supplies at an alarming rate.

It was left up to Israeli Mossad agents in Tehran to try to protect those Israeli attachés that remained in the city. Eliezer Tsafrir, a Mossad agent stationed in Iran recalled: "Israel was now the infidel enemy ("the Little Satan") and [I] had to evacuate 1,300 Israeli engineers, agronomists, and businessmen from Iran before they fell into the hands of the mullahs.... [The Iranians] intended to shoot first and ask questions later."[469]

Samuel Segev wrote of the harrowing escape from Iran of the thirty-three last remaining Israelis, including General Yitzhak Segev, Ambassador Harmelin, former Knesset member Mordechai Ben-Porat, and El Al employees:

The Israelis left the Hilton Hotel for the airport in a bus plastered with pictures of Khomeini. Two sixteen-year-olds, armed with Kalashnikov rifles and trained in Palestinian camps in Syria, served as bodyguards. Other armed youngsters...members of "the Imam Khomeini's Guards," subjected the Israeli passports to minute examination. They arrested the El Al and Kour Corporation representatives and one Israeli security man, charging that they were... Iranian Jews who were forbidden to leave the country. Harmelin...would not leave Tehran without the three men. After five hours...and at the personal intervention of... a leading member of the religious establishment, the three prisoners were freed and allowed to leave Iran. The Israelis took off on a Pan Am Flight to Frankfurt, arriving in Israel in a special El Al plane...bringing an end to twenty-five years of Israeli cooperation with the [Shah].[470]

THE EVOLUTION
OF REVOLUTION

"We do not worship Iran; we worship Allah. For patriotism
is another name for paganism. I say let this land [Iran] burn.
I say let this land go up in smoke, provided Islam emerges
triumphant in the rest of the world."
(AYATOLLAH RUHOLLAH KHOMEINI)

SOON AFTER HIS ARRIVAL IN TEHRAN Khomeini,
contrary to his in-exile rhetoric about retiring to Qom, comman-
deered the Refah girls' school as his nerve center and appointed
Mehdi Bazargan to head a new "Provisional Government."
Bazargan, who had been incarcerated several times by the Shah, had
met in late 1978 with a contingent from the U.S. Human Rights
Committee. The Iranian proffered five points that both he and the
Ayatollah felt essential to the future of Iran:

» The Shah must leave the country.

» The Shah must be replaced by a Regency Council.

» A liberal government acceptable to all must be established.

» Iran's current parliament must be disbanded.

» Iran must be allowed to have national elections.

The U.S. committee agreed to Bazargan's stipulations but balked when a mention was made of removing all references to the Shah from the country's constitution. In a later meeting the group also insisted upon the restoration of law and order within Iran. What no one was willing to admit was that only Khomeini could stop the runaway train of Islamic revolutionary fervor that gripped the country. In the end, the Ayatollah flatly rejected the proposals by the U.S., calling them a "joke, a compromise destined to abort the revolution."[471]

What would later come to light was the fact that Bazargan and members of his government, including Ebrahim Yazdi and Amir-Entezam, had met secretly on two occasions with American officials Robert Clayton Ames and George Cave (CIA), Bruce Laingen (Chargé d'Affaires), and Ron Smith (an energy specialist). Minutes of meetings taken from the American Embassy would be used to damage the reputation of Bazargan, Yazdi and Amir-Entezam, and would ultimately end in their being targeted by Khomeini's extremists.

Carter was so eager to establish relations with Khomeini's hand-picked prime minister that he gushed:

> *He and his predominantly Western-educated cabinet members cooperated with us. They protected our Embassy, provided safe travel for General Philip C. Gast, who had replaced Huyser, and sent us a series of friendly messages. Bazargan announced publicly his eagerness to have good relations with the U.S. and said that Iran would soon resume normal oil shipments to all its customers.*[472]

Clark Clifford, former secretary of state under Lyndon Johnson, had somehow managed to establish communications with Khomeini insiders and confirmed that initially Khomeini planned to leave the determination of Iran's future up to the people. Bazargan's appointment was a shrewd political movement by Khomeini, as it gave a false sense of security to the moderates in Iran whose vision of an "Islamic republic" may not quite have meshed with that of the Imam. Lt. General Shapour Azarbarzin, former vice chief of the Iranian Air Force during the early days of the revolution, related to me that the United States was committed to supporting Bazargan rather than the Shah's choice for prime minister, Shapour Bakhtiar.[473]

The moderate Bazargan's government would be used to quietly pacify the military and create a rapport with Khomeini. Ambassador Sullivan was dispatched to assure Bazargan that the Carter administration looked with favor on Khomeini's moves in Iran and would continue to furnish arms. Meanwhile, defections from the military were occurring at an alarming rate, and ultimately Chief of Staff General Gharabaghi declared that the armed forces had become a neutral factor. Bazargan's Provisional Government (PG) was ecstatic with the general's announcement.

As might have been expected, one of Bazargan's early moves as the new leader was to sever all ties with Israel, although the Israeli government attempted to establish a working relationship with Khomeini's regime. Though both countries espouse different ideologies and outlooks, it was a move designed to sooth the leftist revolutionaries, who felt Israel was a protégé of "The Great Satan," and the mullahs, who felt that Israel's very existence was offensive to Islam.

Khomeini was shrewd enough to couch his aversion to Israel in religious terms. He simply declared Israel a "cancer" that had to be removed, a usurper in the Middle East that despised the Koran and would destroy the Muslim holy book.[474] The fanatical new regime occupying Tehran saw Israel as "an illegitimate state and a usurper of Muslim land,"[475] and was "by its very nature against Islam and the Koran."[476] Khomeini's ultra-fanatical mullahs and clerics lectured that it was the responsibility of every Muslim to challenge Israel. By August of 1980 Iran's Foreign Ministry office demanded an end to the export of oil to nations that supported the Jewish State.

The truth is, both Israel and Iran are countries with vastly differing ideologies that will never mesh. Only one vision and one value system will survive. For Jews and Christians, there is only one answer: the long-awaited coming of the Messianic Age. For Muslims too there is only one solution to this age-old problem: a worldwide caliphate with all inhabitants bowing a knee to Allah. It is critical, therefore, for Israel to call attention to the probability that as soon as Iran's mad mullahs have full access to nuclear weapons not only Israel but the world as a whole will face an imminent attack.

In spite of the Ayatollah's rabid pronouncements against Israel, just months later the Israelis returned a number of tanks the Shah had sent to be repaired. Soon thereafter Ahmed Kashani visited Israel. Kashani, whose father, the Grand Ayatollah Abol Qassem Kashani, had a vital part to play in the nationalization of the Iranian oil industry in 1951, flew to Tel Aviv to discuss arms purchases and military teamwork between Iran and Israel. It seems that clandestine meetings between Israel and her Arab neighbors in the Middle East were acceptable, as long as it was kept under the radar. At one point Khomeini accepted a large shipment of arms from Israel. (Being supposedly unaware of the origin of the weapons, the Ayatollah could adopt a "laissez-faire" attitude.)

Menachem Begin's decision to accommodate the Iranians was in direct opposition to U.S. wishes to segregate Iran during the hostage crisis. Carter retaliated by withholding needed spare-parts shipments to Israel.[477] (After Ronald Reagan was elected to the White House, Israel and Iran continued to communicate regarding Iraq's nuclear threat. Both countries felt that each would be targeted if Saddam Hussein were to develop a nuclear warhead. In *October Surprise* Gary Sick wrote of meetings between officials of the two countries prior to Israel's attack on Iraq's Osirik reactor. According to Sick, "The officials reportedly agreed that in the event of an emergency, Israeli aircraft would be permitted to land at the Iranian airfield in Tabriz."[478]) General David Ivri recalled in a personal interview that the Iranians had attacked Osirik twice with

Phantom jets during the Iran-Iraq War. It accomplished little other than to encourage the Iraqis to reinforce the 30- to 40-meter thick walls around the facility.[479]

Various news reports stated that an Argentine "cargo plane crashed on the Soviet-Turkish border on July 18, 1981, revealing an arms deal between Israel and Iran—in direct defiance of the U.S. embargo on arms supplies to Khomeini's regime. The cargo was 360 tons of American-made tank spares and ammunition."[480] Sick also suggested that Israel sent "spares for F-4 aircraft, M-48 tanks, and M-113 armored personnel carriers, a total of $246 million" to Iran.[481] It is thought that Israel sent over $500 million in arms to Iran following the freeing of the U.S. hostages taken captive at the U.S. Embassy in Tehran.[482] It seems that Khomeini had few, if any, qualms about doing business with his arch foe, "The Little Satan."

Khomeini felt it was his divine duty to advance the cause of Islam. "Islam," he said, "is not peculiar to a country.... Islam has come for humanity."[483] For Khomeini, Iran was a launching pad for an Islamic Revolution that would engulf the entire world. His calling was to secure Iran for Islam and then spread the revolution. His ideology was one of world dominance, and his fanaticism strained ties with his Arab neighbors.

Even as Khomeini reassured the Shah's military leaders that they had nothing to fear from his newly established regime, the slaughter began. General Dutch Huyser had already departed Iran at this point, but he would tell me later that he was grief-stricken because he felt he had betrayed the Iranian generals. According to one observer:

> *Of the eighty top generals, more than seventy were tortured and executed, along with hundreds of lower ranking officers. By one estimate almost 75 percent of the Shah's senior officers were killed by the end of summer. The Bakhtiar government protested these often-grisly executions.... The executions, coupled with the appointment of mullahs as military prosecutors, totally demoralized the military and*

sent a signal that the real power lay with Khomeini and his Revolutionary Guards. The PG was equally powerless to stop the purge and arrest of some 15,000 to 30,000 civilian members of the Shah's regime.[484]

General Yitzhak Segev sadly recalled the mass executions of army generals following Khomeini's arrival in Tehran:

Some succeeded in running away and reaching America... most of them were executed.... The executions were merciless. They were brutal, not only for revenge purposes, but because...they were preventing the option of revolution against themselves [Khomeini's regime]. The first four were executed while I was still there.... [the executions] were broadcast live on television. Then, one at a time they killed hundreds of generals.... each general had a carpet placed beneath him...before he was shot in the head.... They executed the generals because they were connected to the old regime, and because they were a threat to the new regime.... There was total purification.[485]

One of those executed by Khomeini's kangaroo court was former Prime Minister Amir Abbas Hoveyda. Under Hoveyda's leadership in the mid-1960s Iran had filled the vacuum left by departing British troops from Persian Gulf bases by establishing two armored divisions that were outfitted with U.S.-made Patton M-60 tanks. He was also responsible for major expansions of the Iranian Air Force and Navy. Hoveyda, who had been placed under house arrest by Pahlavi, was a sitting target for Khomeini's revolutionary forces. Having been the Shah's prime minister for thirteen years, Hoveyda was a senior official in the monarch's government and, therefore, a prized catch. He was dragged out and tried in short order.

In his book detailing his tenure as president of France, Giscard d'Estaing wrote of his attempt to persuade Khomeini not to execute Hoveyda:

I decided to intervene personally with the Ayatollah Khomeini.... I asked someone to bring him a message. Some Iranian sources told me that after he received my letter... Khomeini wrote a letter to the prime minister. In his note he says: "His Excellency the President V. Giscard d'Estaing... has asked me to prevent the execution of Mr. Hoveyda. To the request of the French president, I would ask you to delay any action in this way." Unfortunately, the revolutionary court prepared its work very quickly, and Mr. Hoveyda was executed three days later, on April 7... after he was interviewed by a journalist from the French television.... Two days later the Tehran revolutionary court met during the night and allowed the execution of eleven persons from the old regime only half an hour after the verdict.[486]

Senators Jacob Javits and Henry Jackson, staunch supporters of Pahlavi, endorsed a resolution criticizing Khomeini's new government for its violent executions of those associated with the Shah's rule. James Bill wrote:

The resolution was triggered by the execution of a Jewish businessman named Habib Elghanian.... Javits and others immediately moved to condemn Iran in the strongest possible terms.... Elghanian had been one of twenty-nine executed May 7 to May 11, 1979...all had been targeted because of their close associations with the Shah's regime. Elghanian, who for years had been identified in U.S. Embassy reports as one of the three wealthiest individuals in Iran, was charged with corruption, capitalist exploitation, and treason for close political and economic associations with Israel. The Javits resolution...resolved that the Senate "expresses its abhorrence of summary executions without due process."... Senator Robert C. Byrd was especially supportive of the resolution, which he termed "very timely. For as we speak, the killing continues in Iran."... Senator Laughton [sic] Chiles added that "too many of us have stood

by too long and have been silent too long."... [Senator Abra-
ham] Ribicoff added that "the Shah was a proven and true
friend of the United States. The entire world should condemn
the excesses now taking place in Iran."[487]

One can only wonder why a nation of radical Islamists with
no thought of "human rights" was preferable to the regime of the
insecure and ailing Shah. Although the leaders of the Islamic
revolution boasted that between 60,000 and 100,000 had perished
as martyrs for their cause, the more realistic number of deaths in
Iran, as reported by Said Arjomand in *The Turban for the Crown:
The Islamic Revolution in Iran*, was "approximately three thousand
in the whole of Iran." Arjomand calculated the number from
September 1978 until the fall of the monarchy in February 1979.[488]

Shortly after assuming the role of leader in Iran, Khomeini
approved the erection of a training center on the site of what was
to have been Empress Farah University for Girls. Manzarieh Park
was to become the training ground for Iran's elite Revolutionary
Guards and for Shiite Muslim fundamentalist terrorists. Although
Khomeini later banned the training of Yasser Arafat's terrorists in
Iranian facilities, he apparently had no such qualms about using
North Koreans and Syrians as trainers. The camp was also the site
where the 15- to18-year-olds that would become the first line of
attack against Saddam Hussein's troops were instructed. Especially
singled out were those students who had flooded back into Iran
from the U.S. to serve as volunteers under the revered Ayatollah
Khomeini. They were often required to recount the decadence found
in America; the decadence that would be its downfall by the sword
of Islam.

The Ayatollah espoused and quoted the tenet of Islam that
declared, "Islam says: Whatever good there is exists thanks to the
sword and in the shadow of the sword! People cannot be made
obedient except with the sword! The sword is the key to Paradise,
which can be opened only for the Holy Warriors! There are hundreds
of other [Qur'anic] psalms and Hadiths [sayings of the Prophet]

urging Muslims to value war and to fight. Does all this mean that Islam is a religion that prevents men from waging war? I spit upon those foolish souls who make such a claim."[489] In Khomeini's Iran, training "with the sword" began at an early age.

On February 18, 1979, soon after Khomeini's arrival in Tehran, Arafat and a delegation of PLO bigwigs, sixty strong, jumped on the revolutionary bandwagon. Unannounced and uninvited, Arafat and his ragtag band flew into the not-yet-reopened Tehran airport. Upon entering Iranian airspace, Arafat's plane was met by a team of Phantom jet fighters. Arafat, whose experience with Phantoms had been limited to Israeli incursions over Palestinian territory, responded, "This is the first time Phantoms have been on my side."[490]

The group was met at the airport, welcomed to the city, and afforded posh housing commensurate with their long-standing opposition against the monarchy. Arafat went so far as to offer to send a contingent of PLO commandos to track down and eliminate the Shah.[491] Within days, Arafat had been presented the keys to the Israeli compound in Tehran, and the street on which the mission was located had been renamed Palestine Street. Arafat, who claimed responsibility for training and equipping thousands of Iranians, equated flying into Tehran with marching triumphantly through the gates into Jerusalem. He was lauded by Khomeini:

> The Iranian Revolution will repay the Palestinians for the help they gave us in overthrowing the Shah, and Iranian volunteers will take part in the struggle to end the Zionist conquest and to liberate Jerusalem.[492]

The PLO was allowed to establish bureaus in Iranian cities, but relations between Arafat and Khomeini were not cordial. Although Khomeini had rewarded the PLO with the Israeli Embassy in Tehran, by 1980 the Ayatollah was said to both dislike and distrust the PLO chairman based on Arafat's tendencies toward worldly pursuits. Arafat's "religious" tendencies would not surface until the end of the

Islamic Revolution. Khomeini felt that the PLO representatives in Iran were trying to incite an uprising between factions.

By 1985 Khomeini had overseen the establishment of fifteen terrorist training facilities in the country, including commandeering the ritzy resort hotel near Qom. The Afghans, Arabs, Southeast Asians, Irish, Americans, and Lebanese, as well as women terrorists trained in these facilities and were slated to become "the spearhead of the Islamic conquest of the world."[493]

While Khomeini was wary of Arafat, he declared his support for the Palestinian cause by naming August 17 Qods (Jerusalem) Day and calling on Muslims around the globe to march in support of their Palestinian brothers.[494] Arafat's favored-terrorist status was jeopardized when he began to align himself with the *Mujahedeen*. Khomeini saw that as a personal affront and refused to meet with Arafat during the Iran/Iraq War. The PLO terrorist departed Tehran with empty hands. Khomeini was quick to erase all references to the PLO from the Iranian media outlets.

Meanwhile, back in Washington and just after Khomeini's return to Iran President Carter's straddle-the-fence diplomacy had permeated the administration. Far from having studied the writings of Khomeini for any indication of his political leanings, the president's advisors were now playing catch-up and were trying to deduce what the events in Iran might mean for the region. Secretary of State Cyrus Vance urged Carter to reach out to the Ayatollah. This suggestion was supported by Ambassador William Sullivan and by Vice President Walter Mondale.

Egyptian journalist Mohamed Heikal wrote of Vance's attempts to contact Khomeini's Revolutionary Government to reassure them of four critical directives:

> » The Shah's reign was at an end.

> » The U.S. and Iran must remain allied against the Soviets.

» The Iranian Revolution and Khomeini's seizure of power were recognized by the American people.

» The U.S. wished to open a door of dialogue with Iran.

Upon hearing Vance's proposal, Khomeini, with Hafiz's communiqués regarding the Shah's arrival in the U.S. in hand, asked: "You mean he didn't talk about the Shah's arrival in the United States?"[495]

Vance would later write that the Carter administration was erroneously charged with the downfall of the Shah because of the president's human rights agenda.[496]

Dr. Majidi talked to me of his disappointment in the Carter administration's stance in Iran:

Even if someone would have told me that Americans are willing to help Khomeini and his group, I would have said, "Certainly, it's impossible." American long-term and short-term interests both require that America stand behind the Shah, behind Iran.... That was my idea, my philosophy, and my thinking; and I think was the same as the Shah's.... You never forget the [New Year's] speech of Carter...he talked of stability in the area of turmoil of the region. I think he was believing that; but he didn't have the guts to implement it and present it.... It's only how brave and how courageous to make the hard decision. Carter to my mind was not that person, and he didn't have the confidence in what he's doing and what he must do.[497]

Italian journalist Oriana Fallaci interviewed Khomeini shortly after the end of the Islamic Revolution in Iran. It was she who wrote: "[The] art of invading and conquering and subjugating [is] the only art at which the sons of Allah have always excelled.... Islamism
is the new Nazi-Fascism. With Nazi-Fascism, *no compromise* is possible. No hypocritical tolerance. And those who do not understand this simple reality are feeding the suicide of the West."[498]

Excerpts from her interview with Khomeini ran in the *Times* in October 1979. Fallaci, who came to believe "the Western world is in danger of being engulfed by radical Islam," wrote of her encounter with the Imam:

> *It did not take long to realize that in spite of his quiet appearance he represented the Robespierre or the Lenin of something which would go very far and would poison the world. People loved him too much. They saw in him another Prophet. Worse: a God.... Do believe me: everything started with Khomeini. Without Khomeini, we would not be where we are. What a pity that when pregnant with him, his mother did not choose to have an abortion.*[499]

CHAPTER

21

HAWKS VS. DOVES:
DOVES WIN

*"There seemed to have been at least four different U.S. centers
of decision-making during Iran's revolutionary movement: the
White House, the State Department, the National Security Council,
and the U.S. Embassy in Tehran.... All four centers made flawed
judgments about the Shah's regime and its opponents."*
(MOHSEN MILANI)[500]

THE TOPPLING OF THE SHAH'S monarchy would prove
to be a tactical catastrophe for the Carter presidency. Maybe the
calamity could not have been prevented under any circumstances;
perhaps the rise of Islamic fanaticism was preordained. In the
final analysis, however, is it just possible that the U.S. could
have done more to maintain stability in the region had the Carter
administration been infused with a mega-dose of backbone?

The failure of the U.S. to support the Shah's faltering
monarchy was of great concern to other allies in the region. Surely
the Saudis, responsible for an infusion of billions of dollars
annually into the American treasury market, must have questioned
how a staunch American ally like the Shah could have been allowed
to fall. The House of Saud must have wondered if its kingdom

would be the next domino in the Middle East to topple. Added to those questions was one of much larger import: What would the Carter administration do to prevent a recurrence of the ouster of the Shah from happening in the Kingdom? The concern stemmed from the fact that the Saudis, with the fall of Pahlavi, would take on the role of protectors of the shipping lanes in the Persian Gulf region.

Several countries were named by the U.S. Foreign Relations Committee as possible deterrents to attacks in the Persian Gulf; among them were Israel, Oman, Egypt, Kenya, and Somalia. Egypt was dismissed because of its weakness militarily and its instability. While Israel with its stable government and strong military would have been an excellent choice, Israel as a protector was dismissed out of hand because of the animosity of the Arabs toward the Jewish nation. The Carter administration felt it would be a direct affront to the Arabs and would potentially cause those nations to acquiesce to Soviet aggression in order to protect themselves from what they saw as an Israeli threat.

Is it more likely that, lacking central direction, the members of the inner Carter circle in Washington each had his own agenda and not the needs of U.S. allies in the Middle East in mind? There were those who wished to promote democracy in the region, while others were persuaded only a military coup was the answer to restoring stability.

The State Department was focused almost solely on the extraction of U.S. citizens from Iran. Some felt only a constitutional monarchy with a figurehead king akin to those of Sweden and Great Britain would resolve the disastrous situation. The priorities were as many and varied as the departments involved in the crisis. Of course, the administration's priorities had changed over the months. In November 1978 Carter declared his undying support of the Shah and his regime. By January 1980 the president was seeking advice on whether or not to approach the extremist Ayatollah Khomeini.

Zbigniew Brzezinski, one of the more hawkish of Carter's appointees, clearly favored top Iranian generals staging a military coup following the Shah's departure. However, with the lower ranks of the military in open rebellion and Iran poised to fall prey to fanatical Islam, what was Brzezinski to do? Should he woo Bakhtiar? The Generals? Bazargan? Amir Taheri writes that Zbig ultimately reached a decision: "Just weeks after the mullahs' regime was formed, Brzezinski traveled to Morocco to meet with Bazargan.... At the meeting, Brzezinski invited the new Iranian regime to enter into a strategic partnership with the United States."[501]

Brzezinski, most vocal in urging the president to withdraw support of the Shah, suggested Carter adopt a "wait and see" attitude toward Khomeini. It was all part of Brzezinski's so-called "Green Belt" strategy. This concept would see the establishment of a series of Islamic regimes designed to insure the destruction of the Soviet Union—a Godzilla versus King Kong scenario, with the most vicious monster surviving the clash. Brzezinski's vision, and Russia's nightmare, was played out in Iran with the brutal regime of Khomeini and in Afghanistan with the rise of the cruel and repressive Taliban.

In an attempt to assuage Khomeini and invoke Brzezinski's Green Belt philosophy, a long-forgotten memo from Dwight Eisenhower was produced. Eisenhower's report was a reaffirmation of Washington's commitment to defend Iran against Soviet aggression. It was all Carter needed to lift a ban on arms sales to Iran and supply the new revolutionary government with arms and materials. Going one step further, Carter declined to issue a visa to the deposed Shah that would have allowed him entry into the U.S. to obtain much-needed medical treatment.

Meanwhile Henry Precht, a Foreign Service officer and the State Department's "golden boy," was hard at work trying to enhance Khomeini's reputation within the administration. Precht had served as a liaison between the Embassy and U.S. military personnel in Iran from 1972 to 1976. Precht claims that one of his first visitors at the Iran Desk was an Israeli who warned him that the Shah was in big trouble. He was told that Henry Kissinger had just returned from a visit to Tehran. According to the story told Precht, the Shah believed the current unrest in Iran was too well-organized to be run by internal forces. Pahlavi felt that the CIA (who had helped him regain power in 1953) was behind it all. Precht's reaction: "I was dumbfounded. This was the man [Pahlavi] we were relying on to save our terribly important interests in Iran. He was a nut. This was the person I was going to have to deal with."[502]

Precht was adamant about forging ties with what he felt would be a liberal democracy under Khomeini. Precht's advisors suggested a number of ways to normalize relations, including a radio program and student and scholar exchanges. Although Embassy dispatches and CIA reports to the contrary were funneling into Precht's in-box, he failed to give credence to the fact that anti-American sentiment was growing.

Precht went so far as to make an appearance on a television show with Ebrahim Yazdi, the American-educated Khomeini advisor and representative in America, to discuss events in Iran. Yazdi's description of an Iran under Khomeini was akin to biblical descriptions of the Millennium...freedom for all, repression and torture for none, open elections, uncensored press, and cordial relations between countries. It was reminiscent of the old campaign promises of "a car in every garage and a chicken in every pot." Either Yazdi was a master at the game of smoke-and-mirrors, or he was totally mesmerized by the dark, hooded eyes of the Ayatollah.

Precht, in fact, circulated a memo that came to be known as the "Precht Doctrine." In essence, it said the Iranian people were tired of the resulting mayhem caused by the revolutionary process and were ready for a more sanguine leader like Bazargan. Precht was in favor of normalizing relations with Khomeini's hand-picked puppet as quickly as possible and defended the Ayatollah against his detractors. Ignoring admonitions to the opposite from American Embassy workers, Precht was adamant in his opinion that Khomeini was simply a figurehead for the more moderate forces that were actually in control in Tehran. He was convinced that

Khomeini, a religious man, had no knowledge of how to run a country nor a desire to do so. He felt the military would fall in line with the new, more moderate, Shah-less government. Precht was sure Iran would become a model country under Khomeini's auspices. UN Ambassador Andrew Young piped up with a comparison of Khomeini to those Blacks struggling in the American Civil Rights movement.

Just as Precht assumed his new duties as Iran Desk Officer, both Stempel and Sullivan left on vacation. Sullivan detoured through Washington to assure everyone at the State Department that things were copacetic in Tehran; the Shah's people had identified the key religious leaders and had paid them to keep quiet.[503] It had been rumored that the CIA was involved in paying hush money to the clerics, but Zahedi debunked that tale:

> *This was an entirely internal affair and did not concern the CIA. Due to the rivalry between Hoveyda, Amouzegar,[504] and Alam, the money paid to the clergy was stopped, so I can tell you very strongly that the CIA had no role to play and no money to pay. They want to have credit for something they did not do.[505]*

Following his stopover in D.C., Sullivan departed to Mexico for two months. His lengthy absence seemed to indicate that if the Carter administration was truly concerned about unrest in Iran, Sullivan's leave would have been shortened.

Sullivan returned to Tehran to find a memo from John Stempel on his desk. It was titled, "While You Were Away." It was subtitled, "...the place really didn't turn to crap, but it might have looked like it." The memo reflected the Carter administration's fervor to monitor human rights issues above that of the growing unrest that was roiling through Iran.[506] Sullivan indicated to the State Department that the Shah seemed determined to move Iran toward a more democratic government. The ambassador believed that "the United States policy on human rights has had only a peripheral bearing on the decision, and [should] refrain from claiming this as a 'victory' for the policy." He also warned that partisans of the Shah were "mindful of rumors that the U.S. wished to 'dump' the Shah or destabilize the country."[507]

Cyrus Vance saw the situation in Iran for what it was, chaotic and confused; however, his aversion to such violent instability set the course for cooperation with the Khomeini regime. His policies were dubbed by one observer as the "let's placate Khomeini policy."[508] Vance, the idealist, simply could not grasp the possibility that the new regime might refute American standards of justice.

It was to the credit of Cyrus Vance, however, that all non-essential American employees, dependents, and all Americans not attached to a U.S. government agency were ordered to evacuate Iran in late January 1979. The successful flight from Iran of some 45,000 Americans was accomplished without a single incident.

The walls of the American Embassy compound in Tehran were a testament to the long-time relations between the Shah and the American presidents who held office during his reign as monarch. Lining the stairway were photographs of Pahlavi and U.S. presidents from FDR to Jimmy Carter—eight in all. The photos represented decades of U.S./Iranian cooperation. So lengthy had been the relationship between the two countries that no one was prepared for the first attack on the U.S. Embassy in Tehran on February 14, 1979.

Shortly after 10:00 AM and under the cover of sniper fire, armed men breached the outer walls of the Embassy compound. The men, armed with everything from rifles to machine guns, opened fire inside the grounds. The Marines on duty tried to repel the attack with simple bird-shot in order to give Embassy staff sufficient time to destroy sensitive documents and coding devices. Ultimately, Ambassador Sullivan ordered the Marines to stand down.

Sullivan's staff assembled in the first-floor communications room while the Marine Guards flooded the lower floor with tear gas. It had little effect on the determined invaders, who eventually forced their way into the Embassy proper. The gunmen ransacked the East wing, smashing communications equipment and cutting off electricity and water. Sullivan's appeal to Khomeini's lieutenants went unanswered for over an hour. The siege was finally ended and Khomeini placed a group of "guards" outside the Embassy to provide protection for the staff. In order to safeguard classified documents housed at the Embassy, Sullivan had hundreds of boxes sent to the U.S. Within weeks, the documents were returned to the Embassy in Tehran. (The U.S. Ambassador to Afghanistan Adolph "Spike" Dubs was kidnapped the same day the Embassy was attacked. He was murdered in Kabul.)

Perhaps it was being held at gunpoint by members of the *Fedayeen* that prompted Sullivan to write a memo to the State Department titled, "A Comment on Terrorism in a Revolutionary Situation." The ambassador's memo outlined disquieting facts about the funding of various terrorist organizations:

> The [Fedayeen] is very well-trained. Instruction is received from the Popular Front for the Liberation of Palestine...the Popular Front for the Liberation of Oman...and the People's Democratic Republic of Yemen. SAVAK accusations of Cuban training were never confirmed. Early funds were obtained by robberies, stealing from parents, and salaries. In 1976 and 1977 large sums of U.S. currency were found on members and in [Fedayeen] safe houses. The money was allegedly provided by Palestinians and Libya.[509]

Sullivan also outlined *Mujahedeen* involvement:

> In 1975 the Mujahedeen infiltrated the U.S. Embassy... by using Iranian national employees. It collected information on various segments of the official U.S. community, especially those affiliated in some way with the Embassy. The [Mujahedeen] believed attacks on U.S. targets had greater impact than on Iranian ones. They attracted media attention, discredited the Shah, and contributed toward forcing the exodus of U.S. technicians.... Instruction is

received in Lebanon, Libya, and Syria from the Palestinian Liberation Organization, al-Fatah...and other rejectionist groups.... SAVAK claims of Mujahedeen training in Cuba were never confirmed.[510]

Unconfirmed SAVAK claims of terrorists being trained in Cuba was particularly revealing. It implied that the information regarding the PLO, Libya, and Yemen had been confirmed. The memo also revealed that Libya sent funds in excess of $100,000 to the *Mujahedeen* every three months.

Referring to Carter's foreign policy, renowned scholar Walter Laqueur wrote, "U.S. foreign policy has written off not only Iran but a far wider area.... the countries concerned would be therefore well-advised to come to terms with the Soviet Union as best they can.... It may also encourage the Russians to engage in a forward policy elsewhere, as the risks involved must now appear small or non-existent."[511] Before year's end Laqueur's prophetic words were to be proven true. Russia invaded Afghanistan. The Carter administration would have yet another concern: How would the invasion and America's subsequent reaction affect neighboring countries?

Prior to the overthrow of the Shah, Laqueur had warned of the mentality of the ruling party that would assume power following the Shah's expulsion. "No gifts of prophecy are needed to understand the next Iranian government," he said, "the next will rule the country more harshly than the Shah."[512] Again, time would prove Mr. Laqueur correct.

By April 1979 Shapour Bakhtiar could see the proverbial handwriting on the wall and fled Iran for Paris. Much like the Ayatollah whom he now battled for the soul of Iran, Bakhtiar released cassette tapes and pamphlets in an attempt to form a cohesive opposition to Khomeini. He became a target of one of Khomeini's fanatical lieutenants, Ayatollah Sadegh Khalkhali, for "making a campaign against Imam Khomeini."[513] The first attempt by assassin Anis Nakash to murder Bakhtiar failed. Not so the second; Bakhtiar paid with his life on August 6, 1991: "It was almost a perfect crime. Three well-dressed men walked into the suburban compound of Iranian exile Shapour Bakhtiar in broad daylight, passed through X-rays and metal detectors manned by 24-hour police guards, slit his throat, [murdered his secretary, Soroosh Katibeh] and disappeared."[514]

According to journalist and terror expert Charles Villeneuve, the plot to assassinate Bakhtiar came directly from the PLO:

> It's not at all the Iranians in SAVAK; that has to be known.... in the beginning all of the officers [or framework] of the Iranian revolution [was] developed in Beirut.... Khomeini asked the Palestinians...Arafat, Abu Jihad, Abu Mussa... the entire major Palestinian State, to supply them men to come and kill.... it is them who will come to try to kill Bakhtiar.... I was born in Beirut; I was raised there, so I talk with them and I become aware of all this business that is happening...all the anti-Westerners helped at the destabilization of the Shah. The Soviet Union also helped, if only in allowing the Palestinians to form the [framework]...of the Iranian revolution...because the Shah did not give money to Arafat. Arafat was a great racketeer. The entire Arafat system [was] based on a great deal of money.[515]

Slowly but surely Khomeini began to move his hand-picked mullahs into place in the moderate transition government. Fundamentalists soon began to seize power more openly. Dr. Parviz Mina related how shocked the National Front, the Tudeh (Communist) Party, and the Marxists were in Iran when they realized the mullahs had used them as a way to achieve their aims. They were even more shocked to realize they had been bested by a cleric. Khomeini's radical revolutionary forces exile or murdered the members of these groups and completely seized the reins of the country.[516]

Had the Tudeh Party leaders had access to a declassified State Department document, it would have shown what Khomeini's intentions were. The Ayatollah "expressed his conviction that the young malcontents who today claim communism will tomorrow rally to the Islamic government. 'Even supposing those who demonstrate with communist slogans are Marxists, they do not constitute a force in the face of thirty million Persians who are in revolt in the name of Islam.'"[517]

A March referendum gave the Iranian people only two basic choices for which to vote: "yes," they wished an Islamic Republic, or "no," they did not wish an Islamic Republic. Overwhelmingly, the people voted "yes," although few Iranians knew what Khomeini meant by "Islamic Republic." According to the Shah's assessment of the referendum:

> It was a grotesque farce. People over the age of fifteen voted. A green ballot meant one vote for the "Islamic Republic" and a red indicated a no-vote. Since this public election was held under the surveillance of the Guards of the Revolution, is it surprising that 98 percent of the voters cast green ballots? The Iranian media announced that the "Islamic Republic" had been voted on by approximately 23 million Iranians...nearly 18 million people were under fifteen years of age...that would make at least five million votes too many...and Iran...returned to the Middle Ages.[518]

Many political organizations inside Iran protested this election on the grounds that "it did not provide any opportunity for the people to express their ideas about the government's reform."[519] The new constitution drawn up by Khomeini's emerging Islamic Republican Party was vastly different from that proposed by the moderates. The core of the resulting document endowed Khomeini as the ruler of Iran for life, or *velayat-e faqih* (guardianship of the jurisprudent). The rule of law, of course, was Islam. Everything was permitted except when it was contrary to Islamic law; and almost everything, presumably, was contrary.

In a confidential memo from Bruce Laingen in Tehran to the State Department, he reported a meeting with Tehran lawyer, A. E. Lahidji. Laingen related some interesting observations regarding Khomeini:

*Khomeini currently controls the masses in Iran, and there is
little moderate intellectuals...can do to check Khomeini's
creation of a totally Islamic state. Khomeini...is becoming
increasingly isolated and surrounded by "yes" men. Most of
his advisors are weak...or opportunists.... Khomeini has
changed since [Lahidji] visited him in Paris. At that time
Khomeini told the moderates that the clergy should stay out
of politics. Lahidji said he and several other lawyers...had
written the original draft constitution along Western lines....
the religious leaders [in Qom] objected to the secular draft...
and when Khomeini returned the draft to the lawyers several
weeks later, it had been changed to give it a more Islamic
flavor.... Lahidji felt that Khomeini was behind the much
more Islamic constitution...and, in particular, behind the
idea of velayat-e-faqih. Absolute power corrupts absolutely,
and Khomeini has apparently decided he must run the country himself.... Khomeini has alienated all the moderate
groups.... Few clergymen are willing to make an open break
with Khomeini and face charges of weakening revolutionary
unity.*[520]

By summer's end in 1979 Khomeini's true vision began to be
revealed. Far from establishing the enlightened, democratic
government indicated by some U.S. State Department employees,
Khomeini, now the supreme leader of Iran, created a medieval
Islamic totalitarian state controlled by the mullahs and ayatollahs.
It was defined by intolerance, censorship, revenge, tyranny, vile
torture, and executions. Khomeini's murderous attacks against the
Shah's former officials had spread to include ethnic and religious
cleansing. Compared to Khomeini's regime, the Shah had been a
benevolent ruler.

Her Majesty Farah Pahlavi talked with me about the human
rights issue:

*What happened to those who cared so much for human
rights? How come when the Shah left, the Iranian people*

didn't have any rights anymore? What happened to the women?... Flogging, stoning, amputations, insults, all the killing of not only women, children, workers, intellectuals, and whoever even comes outside to demonstrate peacefully for their salaries.... the head of the bus drivers, they took him and they cut his palms.... They took his family to jail, his wife and his children of three or four in the jail. There is oppression which exists in the name of religion in Iran. What happened to those who cared?[521]

Rule by "scapegoat" seemed to be the order of the day under Khomeini. When his government or authority was challenged, he looked for a scapegoat. His first were the Kurds in Northern Iran. They were declared enemies of the Ayatollah and his Islamic Republic, and open-season was declared against the Kurdish population.

Although Khomeini was initially ambivalent about ties with the U.S., the fear of U.S. intervention and the return of the Shah plagued the Iranian people. That fear was, of course, fueled by the clerics. It was within the context of this domestic chaos that the bell which was the death knell for the Carter administration was sounded. It began innocently enough with what should have been a humanitarian act. After all, Jimmy Carter was the "human rights" president.

22

CANCER—INTERNAL
AND EXTERNAL

*"I think we should take Iraq and Iran and combine them
into one country and call it Irate."* (DENIS LEARY)[522]

IN 1974 DR. JEAN A. BERNARD, a French physician, had
been summoned to Tehran to treat an unidentified patient. He was
stunned to discover that his anonymous client was Mohammad Reza
Shah Pahlavi. The Shah's enlarged spleen and resulting bone marrow
tests revealed the presence of lymphocytic leukemia and *Walden-
strom's macroglobulinemia*, a condition of the blood.[523] Pahlavi,
who declined further tests because he wanted to keep his condition
a secret, opted instead for a medication to control the cancer.

The cancer that ravaged Pahlavi's body may have been the
catalyst for rumors of an assassination attempt in the summer of
1978. After a trip to a Caspian Sea retreat, the Shah was reportedly
sickly. While the illness was attributed to influenza, it is likely that
even then he was feeling the effects of the disease that would
ultimately claim his life.

While even the Empress Farah Pahlavi was kept in the dark
about her husband's cancer diagnosis, it is highly likely that the
closely guarded secret was known by the French government.

After all, Pahlavi was being treated by French doctors. The empress learned of the diagnosis on a trip to Paris in 1977. She writes:

> I can still feel the icy fear that filled me at that meeting [with the Shah's doctor]. Time has not erased it.... the first symptoms had appeared in autumn of 1973! This...added confusion to the pain: these doctors had been treating my husband for four years, but I had been kept out of the secret at his request.... I knew my husband's courage and willpower. He had wanted and still wanted to protect me from this ordeal.[524]

In an interview with *Le Figaro* magazine, Empress Farah talked further about the Shah's cancer and his mission to modernize Iran:

> It was because of the news of the illness that he wanted to build up a modern Iran so rapidly. It is a haunting fear: to disappear before completing one's work.[525]

The Shah and Empress Farah fled to Egypt in January 1979, and then traveled from Cairo to Morocco, the Bahamas, and Mexico. He was literally a man without a country, dependent on the good graces of former friends in high places. The Shah's physical condition soon worsened to the point that his physician believed he should be treated in New York City. The Shah was reluctant to travel to the U.S. When family members pressed him to follow the doctor's suggestion, the Shah replied that he'd "never gone where I'm not welcome."[526]

The Shah's twin sister, Princess Ashraf, not only urged her brother to seek treatment in the U.S., she privately petitioned the president to allow the Shah into the country despite her poor opinion of Carter. The princess believed her brother's monarchy had been abandoned by the United States and by Jimmy Carter particularly. In her missive to the White House, she wrote:

> One of the best-known traditions of the United States throughout the world has been its record of hospitality and

*refuge to those who are forced to leave their own countries
for political reasons.... I believe at one time that your government was concerned over the possible harm to American
citizens in Iran which might result from him being given
refuge.... I cannot believe that means could not be taken by
your country to assume the essential safety of the United
States citizens in Iran, rather than to submit to any such
blackmail.*[527]

Unfortunately for the princess and her royal brother, that was
exactly the case. The rabble-rousers in Iran were dictating the terms
of the relationship with the U.S. At the same time Khomeini's vile
henchman, Ayatollah Sadegh Khalkhali, had ordered the execution
of the Shah's family wherever they could be found. Princess Ashraf's
son, Shahriar Shafigh, was found in Paris on December 7, 1979.
He was gunned down by a sniper wearing a motorcycle helmet.

The president called on Secretary of State Warren Christopher,
Cyrus Vance's replacement, to respond to Princess Ashraf. His
answer was that the U.S. was thinking about her request. The Shah
interpreted Christopher's ambivalent answer as a "thanks-but-
no-thanks," which only reinforced his determination not to go
to New York for medical attention. Finally, friends and family
persuaded him to reconsider.

In the meantime the Carter administration, through National
Security Advisor Brzezinski, contacted Mehdi Bazargan in Iran to
seek his advice on admitting the Shah for treatment. Bazargan and
Ebrahim Yazdi agreed, "If it is a humanitarian matter, then we
agree. We still have time to settle our accounts with [the Shah]."[528]

On Friday, October 19, 1979, at a weekly foreign policy breakfast, President Carter relented and the decision was made to admit
Pahlavi to the United States for hospitalization. It seems some in the
Carter administration felt they owed the Shah some consideration,
given the treatment he had received at the hands of American
officials. Those present at the meeting, Vice President Mondale,
Cyrus Vance, Zbigniew Brzezinski, Secretary of Defense Brown,

and Carter's Chief of Staff Hamilton Jordan voted to admit the Shah. Carter asked the assembled group, "What are you guys going to recommend that we do when they take our Embassy and hold our people hostage?"[529] Others in the Carter staff relayed their concerns. If Pahlavi were allowed to enter the United States, many in Iran would see that as a move to return the Shah to the Peacock Throne in Tehran. It was suggested that Americans might even be taken hostage in retaliation.

Henry Precht, head of the Iran Desk, sent a communiqué to the American Embassy marked "Secret/Sensitive." The document posed three queries:

> What new circumstances justify a change of policy by the American government? What conditions do we need to find for the Shah to enter the United States? What precautions have been taken to defend the Embassy personnel? [Based on the possibility of a new government in Tehran, Precht answered his own questions]: We can alert this new government of our wish to answer certain outstanding questions, notably the status of the Shah; the intense pressures to welcome the Shah into the United States, pressure that we resist despite our traditional open door policy. In either of these scenarios, we propose changing our attitude towards the Shah in a positive direction around January 1980. Nevertheless, the risk of hostage-taking persists. Nothing should be done to admit the Shah without first substantially reinforcing the guard at the Embassy.[530]

Paralyzed with inactivity the Carter administration bandied about many solutions for the situation in Iran. They discussed everything from positioning a platoon of Marines and helicopters in the Azores for rapid deployment to putting the 92nd Airborne on alert. Carter also approved a plan to gain access to air and naval facilities on Diego Garcia, a British-controlled island. Evacuation of Americans was suggested but was nixed by Warren Christopher. It seems Ambassador Sullivan had not yet deemed the situation drastic enough to warrant such action. Another suggestion was to send the Iranian military leaders to Khomeini with hats in hand to pledge their conditional support. None of the suggestions were implemented.

As Brzezinski later wrote: "The Shah did not act; the military did not move; Washington never ordered a coup. Could Iran have been saved by a timely coalition?...did Washington have sufficient warning?... Should Washington...have triggered a military coup... without the Shah?" Brzezinski's summation was that effective remedies had not been proffered in Iran during the 1970s. One immediate result of that oversight was the darkness that became the Ayatollah Ruhollah Khomeini's regime [and ultimately, the takeover of the Embassy with the ensuing hostage crisis]; another was the blow to the American economy. Oil prices tripled because of the stoppage of Iranian oil production and an OPEC increase in the price of crude oil. These too contributed to the Carter election loss in 1980.

Another by-product of Khomeini's seizure of power in Iran was an income of some $76 billion from oil. Dr. Mina reported to me that most of the money was used to finance the terror groups that are now fighting against the U.S., i.e., Hezbollah, Hamas, and the Taliban. This included money, arms, and ammunition.

In September 1980, although no longer in power in Iran, another of the Shah's concerns was realized. Saddam Hussein acted upon the Shah's fear of a spreading Islamic Revolution and seized the opportunity to attack Iran. Uri Lubrani related a meeting he had had with Pahlavi. He asked the Shah why he spent so much on armaments rather than on education and economic development. The Shah's reply to the question surprised Mr. Lubrani. "I have to have a strong army in order to defend my country.... I'm going to be attacked by Arabs.... I know the United States will protect me if I'm attacked by the Soviet Union; that's why they have their [listening] posts north of Iran.... But they will not protect me when Iraq attacks me.... they were saying this is a regional conflict in which the

United States is not going to take sides. When that happens, I have to have a strong army to deal with it."[531]

No matter his fear of the Shah's past military, Hussein was not at all intimidated by the brooding countenance of Iran's ruling Ayatollah. He called Khomeini a "maniac playing prophet, when in truth he is nothing but a heretic working in the service of the U.S. and Israel." Not to be outdone in the slur department, Khomeini retaliated by referring to Hussein as "a criminal and enemy of Islam whose hand pokes out of an American sleeve and grasps the hand of Israel."[532]

In 1984 Khomeini entertained a delegation from the Islamic Conference Organization. The group traveled to Iran in an attempt to persuade Khomeini to call a halt to the Iran-Iraq War. Khomeini refused to entertain the suggestion of a cease-fire; instead, he wanted to know what punishment would ultimately be meted out to Hussein for starting the war. Another four years of death and destruction would pass before Khomeini was forced, due to a lack of ammunition, to "drink the poisoned chalice" and call a halt to the conflict.[533]

Empowered by his assault on the Shah and the success of his Islamic Revolution in Iran, Khomeini had set forth to spread his particular brand of Arab nationalism throughout the Middle East. Next on his list was Saddam Hussein's Ba'athist regime. His tactic of engaging the people had worked in Iran; why would it not work again in Iraq? The Ayatollah had begun to exhort the Iraqi people to rebel against Hussein's government. Iranian terrorists had attacked principal Iraqi leaders. Then Hussein invaded Iraq.

Khomeini saw the Iraq invasion as the perfect vehicle to bring the Ba'athist regime to its knees. The Ayatollah was forced to repair relations with other Persian Gulf states, reach out to the Europeans, and even contemplate talks with the dreaded "Great Satan." It was a setback to his hopes of uniting the Arab world under the banner of his Islamic Revolution. His only real success was the export of Hezbollah to Lebanon, and even that was tied more to the destruction of Israel than to a globe-encircling Arab state. Khomeini firmly believed Israel was simply a diversion instituted by the West to keep Muslims from uniting as one.

Lured on by the turmoil in Iran, seduced by visions of power, and backed by other Persian Gulf regimes, Hussein was determined to conquer his equally oil-rich neighbor. Like so many others Hussein may have thought the chaotic takeover in Iran, the execution of so many of the military hierarchy, and Khomeini's lack of experience in conducting warfare, would open the door to a swift and decisive victory for the Iraqis. He was as wrong as those who thought Khomeini was only interested in spiritual matters. Khomeini rallied the troops in Iran and somehow produced an effective war machine to repel the Iraqis.

It seemed the entire world sided with Saddam Hussein against Iran. In Iraq's corner were Saudi Arabia and Kuwait, which infused Iraq's coffers with billions in loans and grants. Support came primarily from the Gulf States that viewed Iran as the greater danger. Also involved in furnishing arms and other war materials to Hussein were Egypt, Jordan, the United States, France, the USSR, and the PLO. Iran's backing came from Syria, North Korea, Libya, and China...mostly in the form of missiles.

It took the United Nations Security Council two long years of death and destruction before that august body felt it incumbent to seek troop withdrawals. It would be another five years before the question of chemical warfare used by Hussein against Iran's troops and civilian population would arise.

Khomeini's newly instituted "Government of God" in Iran failed to draw the majority of the Arab world to his side; in reality, the opposite was true. Iran became abhorrent, friendless especially in the Gulf region, and squandered its most productive resource— oil revenues—by slowing oil production. At the same time Saddam Hussein was taking advantage of the chaotic situation in Iran to bolster his relationship with the U.S. There are those who believe the U.S. may have subtly encouraged the Iran-Iraq conflict because of what it surmised to be the benefits of such an encounter. Khomeini, who had outwardly shunned both Washington and Tel Aviv, was suddenly faced with the dilemma of how to hold off an invasion by Saddam Hussein without much-needed spare parts and arms from both the U.S. and Israel.

After eight long and bloody years, on August 20, 1988, an embittered Khomeini agreed to the UN Security Council Resolution for an immediate cease fire. In the aftermath, nothing was resolved between the two nations. Besides the horrific loss of human life, the toll to achieve this impasse was a cost of hundreds of billions of dollars and the disruption and wreckage of the oil fields in both countries. One major outcome of the war, however, was to produce a growing alliance between Iran and Syria and a slackening of the relationship between Khomeini and Arafat's PLO.

During those eight years of warfare between Iran and Iraq, statisticians place the death toll on both sides at 700,000 to 1,000,000 people, most of them Iranians. Baghdad resorted to the use of chemical weapons against the Kurds and Iranian troops, while Tehran conscripted children to act as human minesweepers in advance of Iranian troops.

Just as it had been in Afghanistan, Egypt was drawn into the conflagration as a U.S. surrogate by supplying technical assistance and arms for Saddam Hussein's battle against Khomeini. Sadat would pay the price for helping the Iraqi dictator by permitting the revival of the Muslim Brotherhood. The group had been banned by Gamal Abdul Nasser in 1954 when Sayyid Qutb, its leader, proclaimed Nasser's rule was a deviation from Islam and should be opposed. This was a contradiction of Sunni traditions to support the state and its leader. Fueling Qutb's passion was an ardent hatred of all things Western, especially of all things American. He viewed the United States as a spiritual vacuum, profligate, and antagonistic to Islam. Qutb felt Christianity was no match for Islam; Islam was a total system of laws, social codes, economic rules, and with its own form of government. He believed ultimately Islam would triumph.

Although Qutb was put to death in 1966 for treason, his was the forerunner of terrorist organizations such as al-Qaeda that continue to call for the violent overthrow of governments that oppose Islam, a call for jihad.

The Muslim Brotherhood found an ally in Anwar El Sadat. He used it as a tool against the Communists and Socialists who opposed his leadership. The Brotherhood would find a recruiting ground at the al-Azhar University in Cairo. Students from Muslim countries worldwide filled the halls of the famed learning center. Sadat lost their support when he signed the peace accords at Camp David. He was beset with calls for the return of control of Jerusalem to the Muslims and for Israel to be punished for the attack on the Osirik reactor in Iraq.

The Muslim Brotherhood saw the agreement between the two neighboring countries as an affront to Islam. Sadat was also castigated for backing his wife, Jehan, in a push to grant more privileges to Egyptian women, i.e., the right of divorce and the freedom to doff traditional Islamic dress. When Sadat withdrew his support of the Brotherhood, he would eventually pay with his life for what the extremists saw as his "treasonable acts or sins" against Islam. These were some of the same civil rights accorded women under the "Family Protection Act" passed under the Shah in Iran. According to Princess Ashraf, Pahlavi's sister, it like the one passed later in Egypt gave Iranian women "the most sweeping civil rights in the Islamic Middle East."[534]

Not having learned his lesson from the disastrous war with Iran, it took only two years for Saddam Hussein to again accost a neighbor—Kuwait. On August 2, 1990, Hussein's army invaded its neighbor and quickly seized Kuwait's rich oil fields. Tehran took advantage of Iraq's invasion of Kuwait to remind Washington and the Arab world that Iraq, not Iran, was the enemy in the region. Is it possible that Saddam Hussein would not have risen to such a position of power in the region had Carter found constructive ways to back the Shah's regime and not leave Iran exposed to the likes of Khomeini?

Under George H. W. Bush (41) the U.S. put together a coalition of Arab and European allies and soundly defeated Hussein. The Iranians acquiesced to the U.S. request to be allowed to fly over Iranian airspace and denied assistance to Hussein. By the end of the conflict with the U.S. and the Arab Coalition, Hussein's army had dwindled to one-third its size—down from nearly 1.5 million men— by the end of 1991. Iraq's arms budget also had dropped from slightly over $26 billion to less than one-tenth that amount.

Although forced to sit on the sidelines and not participate in the coalition due to Arab sensibilities, Israel quickly became a target for Saddam's SCUD missiles. Thirty-four missiles were launched into Israeli cities before Hussein was defeated. The warning from the U.S. not to retaliate was not well-received by the Israeli populace. For its cooperation in this, Israel was rewarded with a trip to the Madrid Peace Conference and coerced into signing yet another land-for-peace agreement with Arafat and his PLO. Nevertheless, peace is still elusive. While some sources indicate that since Madrid the Iranians have spent nearly $200 million annually to aid and abet terror groups in their fight to derail any peace process, the Israelis were compensated for their restraint by having a $10 billion dollar loan guarantee frozen! This was money Israel badly needed to provide housing for refugees, mostly Russian Jews. Historically the U.S. has been Israel's closest ally, but the lure of OPEC oil has been chipping away at America's dedication to that alliance.

Would Saddam Hussein have been bold enough to attempt either invasion—Iran or Kuwait—had Jimmy Carter not weakened Iran by failing to support America's strongest ally in the Persian Gulf region under the Shah of Iran? Would Saddam Hussein have tried to link the attack on Kuwait to Israel and its ongoing battle with Hussein's pal, Yasser Arafat and the Palestinian Liberation

Organization, had not Carter expressed his disdain for Israel and his support for Arafat?

Even today Carter continues to thumb his nose at the U.S. State Department. In April 2008 the former president again sidestepped the State Department's call for him not to meet with Hamas during a trip to the Middle East. In an interview on ABC television's *This Week with George Stephanopoulos*, Carter responded to the question of whether or not he should follow through with his plan:

Carter: "The State Department has not advised me against a meeting. I haven't heard that. But I've been in Africa and here in Nepal. They may have.

"But I've not confirmed our itinerary yet for the Syrian visit, but it's likely that I will be meeting with the Hamas leaders. We'll be meeting with the Israelis. We'll be meeting with Fatah.

"We'll be meeting with the Syrians, the Egyptians, the Jordanians, the Saudi Arabians, and with the whole gamut of people who might have to play a crucial role in any future peace agreement that involves the Middle East.

"As a matter of fact, I've been meeting with Hamas leaders for years. As a matter of fact, ten years ago, after Arafat was first elected president of the PLO and the Palestinians, we were monitoring that election, and I met with Hamas afterwards.

"And then, in January of 2006, we were the monitors there for the Palestinian election, and Hamas won the election. We met with them after the election was over.

Stephanopoulos: "Secretary Rice just said this week that it's hard to see what can be gained by you meeting with the Hamas leader because Hamas is an impediment to peace."

Carter: "Well, I'll be sharing what I find with Secretary Rice."[535]

The ever-arrogant Mr. Carter seems to think the end justifies the means. It's okay to defy the State Department and carry out his own agenda...so long as he shares his findings with Secretary of State Condoleezza Rice. The former president continues to forge ahead, much as he did while in office. The U.S. and its allies paid the price then. Will we continue to pay the price for Mr. Carter's strong will and apparent disregard for U.S. policies?

Following Barack Obama's election, Carter was quick to proffer his opinion of the new president's Middle East policy. He said that unlike his two predecessors, George W. Bush and Bill Clinton, Obama would "not wait for even a month after he is president to start working on the peace process.... I think it's a very important issue. I don't have any doubt in my mind that to find peace and human rights for the Palestinians and also for Israel would be a major factor in reducing the threat of terror."[536] Carter then offered to act as a mediator between Washington and Hamas, a role he seems to relish.

When asked if the U.S. economy would not take center stage for Mr. Obama, Carter reiterated that he too was faced with economic and energy crises during his term. Apparently he has forgotten that it was his own failure to properly handle the economic sector and his badly botched policies in the Middle East that cost him a second term. President Obama may be wise to seek counsel elsewhere.

CHAPTER
23

AMERICA HELD
HOSTAGE

"Our youth should be confident that America cannot do a damn thing....
America is far too impotent to interfere in a military way here. If they
could have interfered, they would have saved the Shah."
(GRAND AYATOLLAH RUHOLLAH KHOMEINI)[537]

IRAN WAS FREE OF THE SHAH but in the grip of diabolic revolutionary cleric Ruhollah Khomeini and his Islamic Republican Party. For the moment, Khomeini's dissenters had been silenced—or executed. However, unrest lay just beneath the surface. University students were forming demonstrations to protest the tack his revolution had taken. A far-from-happy middle class had become dejected and disheartened by the economic upheaval and the strict Islamic code that was being enforced. The political vanguard were crestfallen by the new constitution and the curtailing of civil liberties, and the more traditional religionists were appalled that Khomeini had been granted *velayat-e faqih* or rule-for-life status. Thrown into that mix was Mehdi Bazargan, hand-picked by the Ayatollah and in open rebellion against the constitution that would guide the new Islamic social order.

It is safe to say that if Jimmy Carter faced his worst domestic emergency with the energy crisis in July of 1979, he faced his worst foreign policy disaster in November 1979, and it was one of nightmare proportions. Not even the CIA was prepared for the events that unfolded.

A report on Iran to the House of Representatives stated:

CIA intelligence reporting on the Iranian international situation was minimal before late 1977. No reports based on contacts with the religious opposition had appeared during the previous two years, and there was absolutely no reporting on the internal situation based on sources within the opposition during the first quarter of 1978.

In sum, intelligence field reporting from Iran provided a narrow and cloudy window through which to observe the sweeping social and political changes underway.... During 1978 intelligence community analysts struggled to produce a National Intelligence Estimate (NIE) on Iran.... Clearly, policymakers were not served as well as they needed to be. Weaknesses in the intelligence community's performance in this case are serious.[538]

Perhaps sensing that his control was slipping, on October 28 Khomeini declared the beginning of a new purge of those who would defy him. Calling them traitors, he announced his opponents must be eradicated. Bazargan's control was almost non existent by this time; however, he was able to intercept the call for a massive protest march on the American Embassy on November 1 and divert the demonstrators.

Upon the Shah's arrival in New York City, the Ayatollah launched his fanatical diatribe against the U.S. He demanded the Shah be returned to Tehran to face criminal charges. Khomeini called for university and theology students to increase attacks against U.S. interests in Iran, especially what he called the "nest of spies" that inhabited the Embassy. He played on the fears of the Iranian people that the Carter administration would forcibly return the Shah to the Peacock Throne. His fictional scenario of the return of the Shah reached his desired end, and on November 4, 1979, a group of PLO-trained students and rabble-rousers from Qom, calling themselves "Students Following the Line of Imam" or SFLI, again attacked the American Embassy in Tehran. Their 32-year-old leader, nicknamed "Ayatollah Dollar" because of his reputation for dealing on the black market, led the assault.

The first line of attack on the Embassy was the most unexpected…a group of women engulfed in black chadors began to march around the Embassy's boundary with shouts of "Death to America." This diversionary tactic allowed another group of armed students to enter into the main offices through a basement window. Protected by a contingent of only thirteen U.S. Marines and a few Iranian policemen, the Embassy quickly fell to the SFLI. Soon, every American in the building had been bound, blindfolded, and paraded outside the Embassy. (Six Embassy officials eluded capture by taking cover in the Canadian and Swedish Embassies. They were later smuggled out of Iran using Canadian passports.)

In his book *All Fall Down,* Gary Sick writes, "According to one of the students who participated in the attack, the revolutionary guards had been alerted in advance and had cooperated by withdrawing their forces assigned to protect the Embassy."[539]

A *History News Network* article reported the frustration of at least one of the Marines on duty at the Embassy:

> *Years later one of the Embassy guards, former Marine Sgt. Rodney Sickmann, regretted that he'd been ordered not to fire so much as a tear gas canister at the Embassy invaders.* "Had we opened fire on them maybe we would only have lasted an hour," *he told* The New York Times *in 2002. But* "we could have changed history" *by showing that Americans could not be attacked with impunity. Instead the Embassy surrender showed that Americans were easy targets.* "If you look back, it started in 1979; it's just escalated," *Sickmann says.*"[540]

Secretary of State Cyrus Vance recalled the heroism of Elizabeth Koob and Political Officer Ann Swift. Ms. Swift locked herself inside the operations center at the Embassy in Tehran and for over two hours reported on the actions of the rioters attacking the compound. Vance wrote: "Swift said the remaining staff...was going to surrender before the mob began to harm the captives.... At 4:57 AM, phone contact with the Embassy ceased. [Kathryn] Koob, who was working in another building away from the compound, was still able to get through to the operations center by phone.... At 5:30 A.M...communications with Koob stopped. That was the final contact with the compound."[541] (Ann Swift and Kathryn Koob were the only two women held for the entire 444 days of captivity.)

In a separate building, other Embassy employees quickly began to shred documents, but they too were soon captured and driven outside to join the frenzied parade. The rampage of hatred that followed the taking of the Embassy mesmerized the American public. The SFLI conducted "press conferences" that were simply a means to parade their American captives before the world while enraged Iranians roared in the background. Anti-American slogans covered the walls of the Embassy compound. The world awaited the fate of the sixty-six individuals taken hostage.

One writer noted:

> *U.S. intelligence activities inside Iran during the previous twenty years had been directed primarily at the Soviet Union and entailed mostly the monitoring of missile tests from bases along Iran's northern border. The warehouse basement where the [hostage takers] initially stashed most of the hostages...had been built to house data-processing and communications equipment for those listening posts. Iran, as a staunch American ally, was not even a minor target for intelligence gathering. There is no better proof of this than the way the CIA was blindsided by the revolution. No one in Washington saw it coming.[542]*

Even CIA Director Stansfield Turner admitted the oversight in *Burn Before Reading*. Turner wrote that the news of the first so-called student incursion into the American Embassy in Tehran in February 1979 was "startling and totally unexpected."[543] Rather than learning from that brief debacle, the CIA snoozed and was once again caught off-guard on November 4, 1979.

Thomas L. Ahern, the CIA station chief in Tehran, was inside the Embassy when the walls were breached and captives taken. Ahern had been working to develop a relationship with Bazargan and the Revolutionary Council prior to the attack on the American compound. The bureau chief was taken captive along with the other hostages and held for the 444 days of infamy.

When CIA Director Turner received the second call about an Embassy incursion in the middle of the night, it was to summon him to an emergency session of national security advisors in the White House situation room. Why was everyone so stunned by the turn of events? Turner attributes it to the fact that the Shah had been a trusted friend of the U.S., and there was no reason to be caught "spying on friends."[544]

Faced with domestic challenges, Khomeini desperately needed a diversion for the Iranian people. The opportunity fell into his hands when President Carter granted permission for the Shah to travel to New York City for the removal of a gall stone. The news of the Shah's arrival on U.S. soil initially made little impact on the Ayatollah, other than his demand that Pahlavi's vast assets be uncovered and returned to Iran. In fact, Khomeini only urged student demonstrations at the hospital in New York and demanded that political asylum not be granted to the deposed and ailing king. Instead of Iranian students picketing outside the hospital, in the beginning only a group of American students arrived bearing placards that read, "Take Carter; we'll keep the Shah."[545] Empress Farah penned in her diary, "Will this start the Third World War?"[546]

Former Ambassador Zahedi lamented the other demonstrations outside the hospital: "The authorities allowed hostile anti-Shah crowds to come close to the hospital. They were yelling all day long. This was such an unbelievable move, and so un-American."[547]

Two visitors to the Shah during his hospital stay were former Ambassador to Iran Richard Helms and his wife Cynthia. An ailing Pahlavi told Helms:

> The real difficulty was caused by too precipitate liberalization.... The Americans and the British kept pushing me to be more liberal with my opponents. The changes were genuine on my part. But Iran is not ready for Western-style democracy.[548]

As soon as the Shah was declared well enough to leave the hospital, he and the empress were hustled to Lackland Air Force base in San Antonio, Texas. There they were virtual prisoners of the U.S. government. The empress requested and received permission to telephone a trusted friend, Kambiz Atabai, to ask if Carter had remanded them to prison. After two weeks confinement at Lackland, the Shah and Empress were allowed to fly to Panama at the invitation of General Omar Torrijos.

After a short stay in Panama, it was determined that the Shah again required surgery for the removal of his spleen. There were lengthy discussions between Carter's legal advisor, Lloyd Cutler, and the Panamanian government before Torrijos denied permission for U.S. surgeons to perform the operation in Panama. At her wits end, the empress telephoned her friend, Jehan Sadat in Egypt. Farah Pahlavi recounted the stress and frustration of those events during our interview:

> When we were supposed to go, after all the turmoil, from Panama to Egypt, President Carter had evidently talked to President Sadat and said to him, "Don't permit the Shah to come back." President Sadat told him, "Jimmy, I want the Shah here." When all this trouble started in Panama and we were very worried, Mrs. Sadat called me and said, "Come to Egypt. We will send you an airplane." We decided it was best

to go to Egypt because in those days there were some murmurs from the Iranian Islamic Republic to try the Shah for war crimes. At the last moment, the Americans sent some messages that they would give us an airplane. We had to rent an airplane for a lot of money. It was not an Egyptian plane; it was an American plane.

We stopped in Azores, and I am wondering why we are stopping in Azores. They told us that they wanted to ask permission for a route. An American plane asks before for the way to travel; they don't have to stop somewhere. The foreign minister of Portugal told me that when [the Portuguese] asked them, "Why are you staying here for such a long time?" they said, "We cannot tell you." It was Portuguese land! They had sent an ambassador to Washington asking, "Why did you keep the plane so many hours in Azores without telling us?" They were told, "This is something that is almost none of your business."

Later on, we found out that it was written, I think, by Mr. Salinger (ABC news bureau chief in Paris), or some other person, that the Carter administration was discussing with the Iranian Islamic Republic that if the Shah was taken back to Panama, they would release the hostages. The Iranian foreign minister could not gather the revolutionary committee because it was our New Year's holiday. So, we went to Egypt.

I felt very bad for the hostages and their families, and it was ridiculous for the Islamic government to say that America was supporting the Shah. The Shah could have been anybody; and for America to support him, it could have been anywhere. It didn't have to be in America. It was just an excuse.[549]

The empress, who had been appointed regent by her husband and who was forced by his illness to take charge of both the family and the large population of exiled Iranians, was also in actuality the caretaker of her son's future as Shah of Iran. She related the quandary surrounding her son, Crown Prince Reza Pahlavi, and his ascension to the Peacock Throne:

> I remember when my husband passed away and according to our [Iranian] constitution, the crown prince would have to come after his father at the age of twenty. It was in July and he was becoming twenty in October. I thought that in these three months something must be said; otherwise, the Iranian people in favor of us would think, "What's happened?" So, we decided that he would just give the message to the Iranian people that he would accept his duties according to our constitution. Then, Mr. Sadat called me and said that President Carter had called him and told him not to [let the crown prince make his statement]. Mr. Sadat told me it had put him in a very difficult situation. I said to Mr. Sadat, "I'm sorry, but we have sent some press releases that he is going to make a speech on the 31st of October 1980. So all the press knows. I cannot stop it now." Thank God, because if he had not done this press release, what could I have done? We were their guests. Thank God, I had sent the press release. When Mr. Sadat told President Carter what I said, I fancy President Carter smiled and said, "Farah did what she wanted."[550]

After the outbreak of the war between Iran and Iraq, the heir-apparent, Reza Pahlavi, informed the government in Tehran that he was willing to return to Iran as a fighter pilot. (The crown prince had trained at Reese Air Force Base in Lubbock, Texas, and was an accomplished pilot.) The young Pahlavi wrote to the chief commander of the Armed Forces in Iran, "I would like to offer my blood to save the inviolability of our dear native land." No one responded to his offer.

The Shah would succumb to the ravages of cancer just months after his return to Egypt. Zahedi talked of the almost circus-like atmosphere that surrounded the Shah during his final days…quarreling doctors, an Iranian general trying to persuade the

Shah to return to Iran to roust Khomeini, among other things. He also talked of the Shah's realization that he was dying. Zahedi made arrangements for the Pahlavi children to be brought to Cairo shortly before their father's death. It was Zahedi who performed the Muslim tradition of washing the Shah's body before it was transported to Kobbeh Palace Mosque prior to his burial.

The ambassador paid tribute to President Anwar El Sadat, who would accord the Shah dignity in death and a funeral worthy of a head of state. It was also because of Sadat's intervention that the empress, the Shah's sister Ashraf, and Mrs. Sadat were permitted to attend the Shah's funeral.[551]

Just fourteen months later, the empress would again join mourners behind another casket. This time it would be to comfort her friend Jehan Sadat following the assassination of her husband at the hands of Islamic militants.

The question remains: Did the wily cleric plant the seed that grew into the attack on the Embassy, or did he just take advantage of the situation? Whatever the circumstances surrounding the planned take-over, when it came to the cunning Khomeini's attention, he was not above using the Embassy seizure to his advantage.

The timing could not have been more perfect for him to unite all of the divided elements—Nationalists, Marxists, and Islamics— behind his banner of anti-American outrage. He could now launch the final stage of his planned Islamic Republic by purging pro-Westerners from Iran. With the new witch hunt in full force, it is little wonder the majority of Iranians remained silent regarding the assault on the U.S. Embassy.

Though the Ayatollah himself did not deign to visit the captured Embassy, he sent his son, Ahmad, to praise the students for their actions. Khomeini's callousness proved to be the straw that broke the backs of both Mehdi Bazargan and Ebrahim Yazdi. Bazargan resigned his post and Foreign Minister Yazdi was relieved of his duties. Khomeini and his own particular brand of Shia fundamentalism had Iran firmly in a stranglehold.

Dr. Ebrahim Yazdi, a product of American medical schools and a member of the faculty of Baylor College of Medicine in Houston following his last flight from Iran, later became a member of the Iran Freedom Party and a zealous adversary of the ruling clergy system. He now believes the clerics tainted Islam through their political activities, and religion was no longer truly the predominant force in Iran. Yazdi thinks a growing xenophobia (dislike of all things foreign) had been exacerbated by the nuclear proliferation in Iran, and that Ayatollah Ali Khamenehi (Khomeini's successor as Supreme Leader of Iran) and the mullahs used this issue to enrage the general population.

In an effort to gain the release of the captives immediately, President Carter approved sending an envoy to meet with Khomeini. Former Attorney General Ramsey Clark and William Miller, a former member of the foreign services, were dispatched to Tehran to attempt to negotiate with the hostage-takers. During a stopover in Turkey, the two were informed that Khomeini had taken a hard line and refused to allow any official in Iran to negotiate with a messenger from the U.S. government. Clark and Miller were forced to abort their mission and return home.

The American people were stunned at the barbaric behavior aimed at their fellow citizens by the Iranians. What followed the take-over of the Embassy was described by George Lenczowski as: "a saga of Iranian cruelty, duplicity, violation of diplomatic rules, and utter disregard of elementary human rights on the one hand," and he outlined the American response as one of "indecision, confusion, vacillation between the use of diplomacy and force to rescue the hostages, and of serious humiliation suffered by the U.S. government and military establishment."[552]

For six long months the hostages had endured treatment few Americans could even conceive. April 6, 1980, Easter Sunday, was a day of hope and prayers; prayers for the American hostages in Iran and their families, and hope that a negotiated release might soon be achieved. In fact, the hostages had been granted authorization to attend Easter services, and a group of American clergy flew from JFK in New York City to Tehran with what was purported to be a statement of understanding between the two nations.

Unfortunately, neither the messengers nor the message produced a favorable response from the Iranian captors. Negotiations came to a halt Easter weekend, and the Americans and Iranians were as divided as they ever had been.

Efforts to free the hostages included attempts to find an interlocutor to mediate a release. Carter's subordinates contacted an Argentine negotiator, Hector Villalon, and a French attorney, Christian Bourguet. Both Bourguet and Villalon had originally been hired by Iran to attempt to secure the extradition of the Shah. Taking a hint from Israeli Ambassador Abba Eban who disguised himself for a secret mission to Tehran in 1966, White House Chief of Staff Hamilton Jordan, 35, donned a grey wig, mustache, and dark glasses to portray a middle-aged man. In this disguise he flew to Europe for several clandestine meetings with these two mediators. In an attempt to spur on negotiations, President Carter wrote two letters to Iran's interim leader, Abolhasan Bani-Sadr.

The Carter team was amazed to learn from the Iranian news source, *Pars*, that the letters were said to have been addressed to Ayatollah Khomeini. In the letters Carter purportedly admitted to U.S. errors in judgment and that the president had called the capture of the hostages a "reasonable reaction of the youth of Iran."[553] While Carter denied having written to Khomeini, a Swiss intermediary confirmed that he, Carter, had corresponded with Bani-Sadr. Whether the letters were addressed to Bani-Sadr or to Khomeini, neither was swayed by the president's appeal.

Jimmy Carter and his foreign policy bunch also contacted Mr. Bazargan and Prime Minister Yazdi to seek their assistance in obtaining the release of the hostages. Neither man held sufficient clout in Khomeini's new Islamic Republic to be of any help to the Carter administration. Bazargan likened the Embassy crisis to a simple student sit-in that would end in a few days. Unfortunately for the president and his team, that proved not to be the case. The American captives were not released. With the sudden and unexpected departure of Bazargan and Yazdi, Carter had no friends in high places in Iran. America had plunged into the boiling cauldron that was Islamic fanaticism—Khomeini-style.

Despite the fact that the U.S. had agreed to furnish replacement parts for U.S.-made military equipment previously purchased by the Shah and was providing intelligence to Bazargan's government, the U.S. was now deprived of level heads that would provide access to Persian Gulf oil. A relationship that for decades had been friendly was now adversarial—and not just in the exchange of words. A deviously clever, manipulative fanatic was now in control of all decision-making in Iran, an old man who had labeled America "the Great Satan" and had no desire to negotiate with his sworn enemy.

What prompted Khomeini to dub the U.S. with that label? He "reached far back into Shia tradition for the symbol he needed for his revolution.... In Shiism, it is believed that Satan exerts his influence by acting within a person.... Khomeini applied the concept to the United States: Satan dwelled within the global superpower, directing its power toward Iran."[554] Thus America was "the Great Satan" and America's ally, Israel, was tagged "the Little Satan."

24

SLEEPING WITH
THE ENEMY

"The Iran-Iraq War would never have occurred had Jimmy Carter not toppled the Shah." (LOWELL PONTE)[555]

PRESIDENT CARTER'S FIRST RESPONSE to the hostage crisis was to resort to diplomatic channels to attempt to end the crisis. Later Carter would write that the government "asked the Algerians, Syrians, Turks, Pakistanis, Libyans, PLO, and others to intercede on behalf of the release of our hostages."[556] Arafat reportedly dispatched a top lieutenant, Abu Walid, to meet with Khomeini, but the Ayatollah refused an audience. The students holding the hostages ridiculed the delegation sent by Arafat with, "We told them we knew how to make a revolution and succeed. We knew how to defeat American imperialism. The Imam showed us the way. We did not need their advice how to conduct our revolutionary struggle."[557]

The PLO, of course, tried to take advantage of the hostage situation to improve their standing in the international community. Arafat demanded the United States grant recognition to the PLO, welcome an official PLO delegation to the nation's capital, and defer recognition of the Camp David Peace Accords between Sadat and Begin. That would put in deadly peril Carter's hopes of achieving a Middle East Peace in his time, so he declined Arafat's demands.

In the middle of November the jailers holding the hostages decided to show their commonality with what they saw as the oppressed minorities worldwide and released thirteen African-Americans and women. Khomeini was infuriated by Arafat's claims that the PLO had been instrumental in obtaining the release of the hostages and angrily condemned the terrorist organization for its attempts to insinuate itself into the good graces of the U.S. In July of 1980 hostage Richard Queen was released after being diagnosed with multiple sclerosis. The hostage-takers were left with fifty-two Americans, fifty male and two female prisoners.

By mid-November Carter had halted Iranian oil imports, Treasury Secretary G. William Miller had frozen $12 billion worth of Iranian funds in U.S. banks, and all shipments of military supplies to Iran were halted. This was followed by other, lesser sanctions against Khomeini's Islamic Republic. Carter's advisors suggested mining the harbors in Iran, halting the import of Iranian oil, petitioning the UN to impose sanctions on Iran, striking selective targets inside the country, and seeking the assistance of U.S. allies in bargaining with Khomeini.

The Iranians retaliated by threatening to withdraw all funds from U.S. banks. The president was now in the uncomfortable position of trying to decide what to do to secure the release of fifty-two Americans whose lives were now filled with daily humiliation, threats of execution, being blindfolded and paraded before cameras, and chained to the walls or bound and stretched out on cold, bare floors for hours at a time.

Meanwhile, Khomeini's regime repeated demands that the Shah be returned to Tehran and his wealth deposited in banks outside Iran be returned to the revolutionary government in Iran. Khomeini, the behind-the-scenes instigator, appeared to remain aloof from any negotiations with the Carter administration for the release of the hostages; that is, until it seemed that a resolution might be near. Whenever that occurred Khomeini would support the outlandish demands of the radicals and ruin any possible deal.

Within his own cabinet, President Carter was caught between a high-level dove/hawk combination. Secretary of State Cyrus Vance weighed in as the dove who wanted to make whatever concessions necessary to the Iranian fanatics in order to secure the release of the detainees. The hawk in the administration, Brzezinski, was ready and willing to mount a military operation in order to free the hostages. Carter, who stalwartly opposed any military intervention early on, sided with Vance. Although administration officials were able to inveigle both the UN Security Council and the International Court of Justice to issue calls for the release of the captives neither had any impact on Khomeini's government.

While Carter had his political eye focused on Iran, in December 1979 the Soviets marched into Afghanistan. Although the USSR had been clearing roads to the Afghan border, the Carter administration appeared to be shocked by the invasion. Determining that a harder line was needed against Soviet aggression, in typical fashion Carter jumped astraddle the fence. On the one hand he recalled the ambassador from Moscow; on the other hand, he instituted a grain embargo, but only on grain meant for animal consumption. He did not want to disenfranchise the Russian people.

Speculation by some has indicated that perhaps the Russian invasion was in direct response to Khomeini's Islamic Revolution in Iran. The Soviets may have been concerned that the fanaticism would spread into Afghanistan and from there into other mostly Arab countries on the southern border of the USSR.

Before the Soviet incursion began in 1979, the minority Shiites in Afghanistan (approximately 20 percent of the population) had relied on Iran under the rule of the Shah for encouragement and assistance. Once Khomeini seized power, Iranian revolutionaries tried to force the Afghan Shia to submit to the Ayatollah's oversight by eliminating the more moderate Shiites. The Afghan Shia population (mostly Hazara from the central region of Afghanistan and among the most economically deprived) refused to be dominated by Khomeini. In 1988 Iran successfully integrated eight of the Shia factions into the Unity Party (*Hizb-i-Wahdat*). Khomeini's Revolutionary Guards tried to force Shia clerics to submit to the oversight of the Ayatollah, but the clerics rebelled and joined with the Afghan Unity *Hizb-i-Wahdat*.[558]

Khomeini's anti-Communist Foreign Minister Sadegh Ghotbzadeh, a product of Georgetown University, was not impressed with U.S. support for the Afghan guerillas and was quick to condemn the Russians for their hostility. He suggested the Soviets and Americans had inked a secret agreement to conquer and divide the world between the two superpowers. Not to be outdone, Moscow accused Ghotbzadeh of being an undercover CIA agent. Amir Taheri notes: "It is significant that anti-Americanism was first propagated as a major theme of Muslim fundamentalism by young men and women from Islamic countries who had spent time in the United States as students or workers."[559]

Carter sent unarmed F-5 fighters to the Middle East; he engaged allies, Great Britain, Germany, Italy, and France, to bolster monetary support for Pakistan; and in a move designed to *really* challenge the Soviets in Afghanistan, he announced the U.S. would boycott the Olympics to be held in Moscow. Although encouraged to engage in dialogue directly with Brezhnev and to send Cyrus Vance to meet with his Soviet counterpart, Andrei Gromyko, President Carter decided against taking either step. It was also suggested Carter send Marshall Shulman, an expert on Soviet affairs, to meet with Brezhnev; but the president again refused.

The United States did, however, petition the UN Security Council to pass Resolution 461, which was built on the earlier Resolution 457, demanding the Islamic Republic of Iran release the hostages seized from the American Embassy. The Soviet Union, as expected, abstained. Vance was of the opinion the incursion into

Afghanistan was simply one symptom of a much more complex problem.

However vacillating Carter might have been in addressing this issue, in January 1980 he nevertheless publicly approved aid to the Afghan underground. This move prompted Anatoly Dobrynin, Soviet ambassador to the U.S., to liken Carter to a "bull in a china shop."[560] One prominent member of the resistance was none other than Osama bin Laden, the same man who spearheaded the attack on the World Trade Center in 2001. Bin Laden's presence was applauded by the CIA. As one writer related: "Delighted with his impeccable credentials, the CIA gave Osama free rein in Afghanistan, as did Pakistan's intelligence generals."[561]

What the CIA under the Carter administration apparently didn't know or chose to overlook was that young bin Laden was also influenced by Palestinian academic and spiritualist Abdullah Azzam. "Azzam's trademark slogan was, 'Jihad and the rifle alone: no negotiations, no conferences, and no dialogues.' This intoxicating message, breathtaking in its expansiveness, played an important role in the ideological formation of bin Laden, Ayman al-Zawahiri... and many other Islamic radicals."[562]

Azzam's teachings on jihadists and martyrs would influence the likes of al-Qaeda and its global following and would help found Hamas to balance Arafat's terrorist organization, the PLO. A local hero to Hamas, his likeness appears on posters dedicated to his prowess. He would, however, run afoul of al-Zawahiri, who decried a jihad that pitted Muslim brother against Muslim brother. The radical Azzam, though a fanatical foe of the U.S., saw nothing wrong with plundering U.S. mosques to fund his own brand of jihad.

The Soviet invasion of Afghanistan gave some members of the Khomeini regime pause for thought and brought a request that the U.S. give some indication it was willing to acquiesce to some of Khomeini's demands in order to precipitate a resolution to the hostage situation.

In his role as *faqih,* in early January 1980 Khomeini banned Muslim clerics from running as candidates in the upcoming presidential election. On January 25, 1980, Abolhasan Bani-Sadr was elected president of Iran. This Western version of an Iranian leader was exactly what Khomeini needed to bridge the gap between Bazargan and the soon-to-emerge, iron-fisted rule of Khomeini and his Revolutionary Guard. Bani-Sadr was destined for failure,[563] caught in the middle between the militant clergy and the more moderate elements. Bani-Sadr called for the hostages to be placed under legitimate government jurisdiction, while the mullahs demanded they remain under the control of the so-called students.

It seems ironic that the pilot who flew the Shah and his entourage from Tehran to Cairo later transported two Khomeini insiders, Abolhasan Bani-Sadr and Masoud Rajavi, to Europe when they fell out of favor with the Ayatollah. (The pilot later became a member of the *Mujahedeen.*)

Meanwhile, the Carter administration enlisted the aide of UN Secretary General Kurt Waldheim. Waldheim was given a checklist to present to Bani-Sadr on behalf of the State Department. The points included:

> » The acceptance of the government in Iran under Khomeini.

> » The acceptance of a UN resolution of any issues between the two countries.

Like a chess master contemplating his final checkmate, Khomeini sat back and watched the machinations. He only had to wait until April 24, 1980, when the U.S. launched an attempt to rescue the American captives under his control.

Carter's patience had run its full course by April. Obviously, sanctions were not effective. Negotiations had stalled. Only coercion in a threat to mine Iran's harbors elicited even a lukewarm response from the international community. Out of frustration, Carter opted for a military solution—*Operation Eagle Claw.* The logistics of such a rescue were astronomical, and in the final analysis it was probably doomed to failure from the outset.

As frustrated as Jimmy Carter was, Admiral Turner was more so. Although director of the CIA, Turner had been excluded from the planning meetings for the rescue operation. He challenged national security head Brzezinski, and was essentially told the CIA's help was not needed for a military operation. Turner advised Zbig of the foolishness of that assumption, and was finally admitted to the inner planning circle.[564]

As the preparations for an attempted hostage rescue escalated, the U.S. called on Israeli General Dan Shomron, who had commanded *Operation Entebbe*. General Yitzhak Segev recounted his thoughts on the plan to free the captives:

> *Every Friday Khomeini leaves the city.... bring in aerial resources, [grab Khomeini] and tell the Iranians if they want Khomeini back, they better release the hostages.... Everyone said I wasn't fair. [Segev warned about the dangers of using helicopters in the attempt:] When six helicopters were needed, we would take ten. A helicopter is a very delicate animal. Take it there, bring it around, every moment something breaks down. They needed six helicopters.... by the time they got there two had already broke down. They had no reserves. It was bound for failure...a huge mistake.[565]*

Not to be deterred, Carter forged ahead with the planned rescue. Completely shrouded in darkness, the aircraft carrier *Nimitz* plowed through the waters of the Arabian sea just southeast of Iran. Sitting on the deck of the huge nuclear-powered craft were eight Sea Stallion RH-53D helicopters. The rescue attempt would prove to be one of the most difficult operations of the newly launched U.S. Army Delta Force, members of which were aboard the Sea Stallions. The plan was dangerous and complex. Six helicopters were the bare minimum to accomplish the mission. The fuel range of each chopper necessitated a rendezvous for refueling in the middle of the desert, about 200 miles north of Tehran, a site codenamed *Desert*

One. Already en route to the desert location from a base in Oman were several C-130 transports loaded with fuel for the helicopters.

The plan was simple, but the execution was complex: Fly the Delta Force to a location near Tehran (*Desert Two*), storm the Embassy, free the hostages, and fly them out on C-141 transports under cover of Navy fighters. What the plan did not allow for was the fickleness of desert dust storms. Unfortunately, a serious error in judgment resulted in the removal from the helicopters of the very sand filters that might have meant the difference between success and failure. The filters, each weighing approximately 200 pounds, were discarded in an effort to give the machines greater lift capacity. It may be too that the Israelis, who closely monitor all Middle East events, including the weather, could have given the U.S. a heads-up regarding the approaching storm.

While the U.S. did not seek their assistance in planning and execution, the Israelis were totally aware through their monitoring posts of the operation taking place in the Iranian desert. The U.S. had failed to take the basic precaution of scrambling their transmissions between the *USS Nimitz* and the Delta Force. As the RH-53Ds were traversing the desert for their appointed refueling, the rogue sandstorm enveloped the aircraft. The resulting unrelenting sand, heat, and ensuing equipment malfunctions caused one helicopter to be abandoned in the desert. Another returned to the *Nimitz*, and a third reached the rendezvous point but was unable to continue to Tehran because of a hydraulic leak. With only five helicopters instead of the six needed, Colonel Charles Beckwith, who was in command, called a halt to the mission.

As the choppers refueled for the return trip to the *Nimitz*, one of the helicopters collided with a C-130 fuel transport and both burst into flames. Eight Americans, five Air Force crewmen in the C-130, and three Marine crewmen in the RH-53D, died in the horrific explosion. The survivors of the crash were quickly evacuated aboard the C-130s to an airfield on the island of Masirah off the coast of

Oman. The injured men were then transferred to a C-141 Medevac and transported to Ramstein Air Base in Germany.

Regardless of the failure of the mission itself, the actions and dedication of the men who attempted the rescue were heroic nonetheless: Sgt. John D. Harvey, Cpl. George N. Holmes Jr., Staff Sgt. Dewey Johnson, Major Richard L. Bakke, Maj. Harold Lewis Jr., Tech. Sgt. Joel C. Mayo, Capt. Lyn D. McIntosh, and Capt. Charles T. McMillan. Three of those who died share a common grave at Arlington National Cemetery, and all the men are honored on a remembrance panel inside that hallowed burial ground.

Marine Gunnery Sergeant John McClain offered his take on the rescue attempt:

> *Marine helicopters were designed to fly over ocean or desert and have a system known as EAPS, or "electro-static air-particle separators," which use high voltage and the static generated to separate dust and dirt from the air entering the engines. They "cost" eight or ten percent in power, but they allow "knap of the land flying" in combat conditions.*[566]

The Air Force helicopters are set up to land in permanent landing areas with concrete landing pads and runways. They have almost no "air cleaner" apparatus at all because it is not an issue if one does not fly close to the ground. They also didn't have the capacity for aerial refueling, so they are tied to a specific straight-line mission due to fuel restrictions. The entire reason the mission failed was due to the destruction of an engine on one of the choppers, caused by ingestion of sand and dust from the desert.

This failed attempt to rescue the Embassy hostages was not, in fact, the first hostage rescue as a result of Khomeini's Islamic revolution. The first was that of twenty-two American employees from one of two top-secret listening posts in Kapkan, Iran (Tracksman1 and Tracksman2). The technicians at the outpost were being held hostage by unfriendly local employees, who were demanding back wages be paid. In a clandestine plot, two American military men, Capt. H. F. Johnson and Col. T. E. Shaefer, commandeered an Iranian C-130, flew into the town, exchanged 30 million rials for the captives, and transported them to safety. Unfortunately, sensitive information-gathering equipment was left behind in the hands of hostile Iranians.[567]

The botched and deadly rescue mission to free the Americans held in Iran was a blow to Carter's presidency and to American prestige worldwide. Coupled with the hostage crisis and exacerbated by domestic issues such as energy and inflation, this was perhaps the final straw that would cost Carter his bid for a second term in office. Secretary of State Cyrus Vance suddenly resigned on April 28, 1980, in protest of Carter's botched mission. (He was replaced at the State Department by Senator Edmund S. Muskie.) According to Vance's personal papers, "he was opposed to the ill-fated hostage rescue attempt in Iran, and he sensed that the extensive use of force would make the U.S. dangerously vulnerable to further acts of hostility."[568] Vance was eerily prescient.

Andre Fontaine, editor-in-chief of the Paris newspaper, *Le Monde*, summed up the situation very succinctly from the European point of view:

> *That Uncle Sam was powerless to prevent the collapse of the imperial Iranian regime, in which he had invested so many dollars and hopes, struck Europeans the harder for the fact that at the beginning of 1979, at the Guadeloupe summit conference, the president [Carter] had still expressed great confidence about how the situation would evolve. Who would have supposed that, as we have learned he did, he would have gone so far as to push the Shah out himself—the same man on whom, during his visit to Tehran, [Carter] had heaped the most extravagant praise, even hailing him by the title (a deeply debatable one at that) of champion of human rights?*

The hostage affair ended by discrediting [Carter], even if European leaders were secretly relieved that "the Great Satan"...abstained from using force in so inflammable a region. That the richest and most powerful country on earth was unable to force a gang of frenzied revolutionaries to yield seemed a chilling illustration of America's decline.[569]

The revolution in Iran produced more than a change in leadership from that of the Shah to the inscrutable Khomeini. With the taking of the Embassy and the hostage crisis in Tehran following decades of favorable decisions toward Iran by U.S. presidents, both Democrat and Republican, America was faced with a massive failure in foreign policy orchestrated by Jimmy Carter. It would mark an immediate change in the balance of power in the Persian Gulf region and ultimately a change worldwide for Islam. The Shah, who had once held all of the power in Iran, would lose it all—his throne, power, acclaim from foreign entities—and would become a pariah, a man without a country, dependent on the hospitality of the few who would welcome him.

The horror for which no one in America seemed to be prepared engulfed Iran. The Shah was not the only Iranian to flee the country; he was joined by millions of his fellow countrymen. Europe and the United States were the recipients of many of these well-educated and technically skilled émigrés. They fled from what would become a massacre of vicious proportions and a reign of terror the likes of which the Iranian people had never seen or imagined under the Shah. Not only was Iran gripped in the iron fist of murder and mayhem, it was stripped of an entire generation of highly trained and competent young men and women—all at the whim of a fanatical old man bent on revenge.

CHAPTER

25

A PRESIDENCY
ABORTED

"The 1979 inflation rate is the largest increase in 33 years; rate stands at 13.3%, compared to 4.8% when President Carter took office.... Carter announces limited U.S. grain sales to USSR...Iowa farmers angry over grain embargo.... New gasahol program announced to appease farmers.... Exxon, Texaco, Gulf: no gasahol on its credit cards.... Grain embargo's effect on farmers a major political issue used by Carter challenger Senator Edward Kennedy.... 1979 wholesale prices increase highest in five years.... Kennedy challenges Carter to debate; Carter refuses."
(DAILY NEWS HEADLINES, 1979)[570]

IN THE MIDST OF THE HOSTAGE CRISIS abroad and the domestic crises at home, Jimmy Carter was trying to conduct a presidential campaign against his major opponent, Senator Edward Kennedy. Under the tutelage of the "Peanut Brigade," his loyal team of Georgia insiders that included Hamilton Jordan and Stuart Eizenstat, Carter set out to secure the Democratic nomination. Step one was to initiate a program that would combat the rampant inflation gripping the country. Carter's new economic plan included balancing the budget in 1981, adding a ten-cent tax on imported oil, and curtailing spending financed on credit. Carter acknowledged this plan would not bring change overnight, but it would eventually rein-in inflation.

A *Time* magazine article published after Reagan had defeated Carter in the election exposed Carter's budget machinations:

> *The 1982 budget that Jimmy Carter sent to Congress last week was a cold slap of reality for Ronald Reagan on the eve of his inauguration. The legacy of federal largesse that Reagan inherits is far worse than he had suspected, and the yawning budget deficit severely threatens his strategy to stimulate the U.S. economy by cutting taxes. Carter... was obviously trying to leave office with as small a deficit as possible, and he sometimes used mirrors to accomplish that. His revenue estimates, for example, include $13.1 billion from a proposed extra 10-cent-per-gallon tax on gasoline. Congress has often made it clear that it will not increase the tax on gas.... After looking over Carter's numbers, David Stockman, Reagan's budget chief, charged that "the relatively low deficit is entirely cosmetic and artificial.... Overall, Carter in his final budget was generous with the Pentagon and stingy with almost everyone else, where he had any choice in the matter."*[571]

Few had seen the efficacy of the president's program, and indeed, had rejected the idea that it would halt the rise of inflation. In fact, it was indeterminate as to whether Carter could even get this program passed through Congress. Amazed by the apathetic response to the president's proposal, Eizenstat had encouraged him to get out of the Rose Garden and into the mainstream of the American public. In other words, Carter needed to take his anti-inflation package directly to his constituents. According to Eizenstat, "You need not debate Kennedy or even campaign. The key is to get out and let the people know you are the general in charge."[572]

Held in the iron grip of the hostage crisis, Jimmy Carter had been able to do little overt campaigning for the nomination. He relied heavily on the First Lady and assigned her a politically active role. Rosalynn Carter registered her husband as a candidate in the New Hampshire primary and represented him during the 1980 primary period. She endeavored to persuade undecided delegates to vote for her husband over Kennedy.

Even with the urging of Stu Eizenstat, Carter did little to change his approach. His campaign strategy seemed to gain reinforcement when the president easily defeated Kennedy in his own little corner of the Northeast, New Hampshire. Was Carter so egotistical as to think that he could not be beaten by anyone in his bid for re-election? If so, the people in New York quickly proved the incumbent president wrong by giving Kennedy a clear primary victory. However, the dreaded polls that plague every candidate soon showed Kennedy lagging in key states, especially in the South.

As if to reinforce the Kennedy bid, the Carter administration erred colossally in the spring of 1980. Having met with his advisors, the president determined the U.S. should support a call for Israel to remove civilians from all Arab territories. Having abstained on this issue over the course of several votes, the president and his secretary of state now determined it was time to take a stand against "Israeli aggression." The only fly in the ointment were references in the UN resolution to Jerusalem. Carter was opposed to the inclusion of Jerusalem in the document and was assured by Vance that all references had been removed. Not so, as Carter found out after the vote had been registered and the resolution passed.

Jewish leaders in America were incensed by Carter's action. Their constituency retaliated by voting solidly for Kennedy in the New York primary. But according to a *New York Times* poll, the real reason New Yorkers voted so heavily for Kennedy was because they were disillusioned with Carter's leadership. In an article for *The New York Times,* columnist William Safire summed up the president's woes very succinctly: "The East wind that chilled the Carter candidacy this week [in New York] was made up of four I's—Inflation, Iran, Israel, and Ineptitude."[573]

The Carter political machine was convinced that Kennedy could not defeat the incumbent president and secure the nomination. However, they were shocked at what was revealed with each crack in the veneer of the Carter presidency: a large block of American people was fed up with Jimmy Carter's leadership. At the same time, Republican candidate Ronald Reagan was gaining ground on Carter in the polls. The real shock to the White House as the campaign progressed was the number of Democrats crossing party lines to vote in the Republican primaries. It wasn't just the Republicans who were enamored by the actor/governor-turned-presidential-candidate.

Turning up the heat on Carter, Kennedy squeaked out primary wins in Pennsylvania and Michigan. Kennedy was encouraged enough to promise to stay in the campaign through the June primary elections. The number of delegates pledged to Kennedy gave his supporters a secure bargaining point when the issue of the Party's platform later emerged.

Kennedy's small successes achieved what Eizenstat could not; it pried Carter from the confines of the Rose Garden and onto the campaign trail. The president's move from reclusive candidate to mainstream campaigner had the added bonus of taking the heat off his wife, Rosalynn, who had come under fire for her overt impact on the president and his administration. (In fact, during the general election the First Lady actively campaigned on the president's behalf against Reagan.)

The general malaise Carter encountered earlier in his presidency seemed to grip the entire Democratic Party during the 1980 run for the White House. Neither Carter nor Kennedy was a clear choice by the Party movers and shakers. The dissatisfaction prompted New York Governor Hugh Carey to recommend both men release their accumulated delegates and open the convention to new possibilities. Meanwhile, Reagan's lead over Carter in the polls was escalating.

Another nail in Carter's presidential coffin came in the form of a deepening recession. With a Congress that was less than enchanted with the president's policies, the administration now faced growing pressure to boost spending and to institute tax cuts. Jimmy Carter's running feud with Capitol Hill (which began almost as soon as he took office) resulted in a humiliating defeat for his proposed oil import tax. The president lobbied against suggested congressional increases in the defense budget and in family programs, but Congress ignored pressure from the White House and approved its budget plan. It was just one more humiliation.

Carter faced the Democratic National Convention with more minuses than pluses. Both foreign policy and domestic policy were in shambles, the economy was in total disarray, the hostage crisis was no closer to a resolution, U.S. allies were alienated due to events in Iran and Afghanistan, he was an outsider within his own party, and his approval rating was abysmal. Last, but certainly not least, Edward Kennedy was still in the primary race for his job.

Conciliatory moves were made to encourage Kennedy to drop out of the campaign. Kennedy resisted the overtures and openly snubbed the president's advances. One reason for Kennedy's resistance was that he felt an open debate with Carter was critical in order to settle the differences between them, but the president adamantly refused such an encounter. Kennedy remained in the fight until the Democratic National Convention in August, when he sadly withdrew as a candidate, having lost 24 of the 34 primaries he entered.

With the Party's nomination firmly in his grasp, Carter reached out to Kennedy in an attempt to heal the rift that divided the Democrats. Kennedy made a brief—and for him, uncomfortable—appearance at the convention but departed as quickly as possible. While watching the televised coverage of the convention, Republican candidate Ronald Reagan remarked, "If that's the best they can do in unity, they have a long way to go."[574] Perhaps the one thing reporters jumped on most quickly was Carter's gaff during his acceptance speech, when he was paying tribute to deceased

Democratic stalwart Hubert Horatio Humphrey. Carter mistakenly referred to him as "Hubert Horatio Hornblower."

As if the president didn't have enough problems with which to contend during the campaign, brother Billy Carter got himself into trouble with the Justice Department. It seems Billy had obligated himself to Muammar Qaddafi and the Libyans in return for a $500,000 loan. Billy had also sold himself to the Florida-based Charter Oil Company in a plan to help it secure tens of thousands of barrels of top-grade Libyan crude. A reduction in oil production quashed that deal and cost Billy millions of dollars. The Justice Department entered the picture when it was discovered Billy had not registered as a foreign agent—an individual doing business for a foreign entity—as legally required.

The Republicans quickly dubbed the entire affair "Billygate" and began to inquire how the president's brother came to be such a good friend to the Libyans. As the ripples spread from Billy's dabble in the pool of foreign intrigue, the White House revealed that Zbigniew Brzezinski had requested a meeting with Billy and a Libyan official in an attempt to secure the release of the American hostages in Iran. Once again, the Carter presidency suffered adverse effects as more information about Billygate came to light. The president was forced to acknowledge he had previously known of Billy's deal with Charter Oil and had known Billy was required to register as a foreign agent. These issues, in tandem with the other foreign and domestic issues surrounding the Carter White House, produced an air of distrust among Americans of Jimmy Carter's ability to run the country for another four years.

Prior to the Democratic National Convention, polls found Jimmy Carter at the new low of 21 percent. He had achieved what neither Truman nor Nixon on their worst days had achieved before him, the poorest rating ever. It appeared as though Ronald Reagan would run away with the election in November. Mr. Reagan, however, made some missteps in conducting his campaign that elevated Carter's standing in the polls. Reagan had the edge on economic issues, but Carter had the edge with war-related issues. Poll numbers reflected that voters felt Reagan was a stronger leader, but they felt Carter was less likely to engage in unwarranted conflicts.[575]

This was interesting considering that apart from domestic and foreign issues there was the real or perceived notion that Jimmy Carter possessed a mean streak. Carter's "meanness quotient" was troublesome to his campaign advisors, who were struggling to maintain what had been one of the president's best attributes: many Americans felt him to be a good man and impartial in his dealings with others.

Perhaps Carter's fear of defeat at the hands of his Republican adversary was enough to cause him to go for the throat of his opponent. Although Reagan responded with a sad shrug and lamented Carter's attacks, others in the GOP were more vocal. Gerald Ford called the president's statements "intemperate and totally misleading" and demeaning to the "office of the presidency," while Reagan's running mate, George Bush replied, "I'm appalled at the ugly, mean little remark Jimmy Carter made."[576] Carter's own staff realized he needed to tone down the mean-spiritedness and cautioned the president to rethink his tactics.

According to author and journalist Ron Kessler, Jimmy Carter was the most disliked president in modern history. He based his assertion on the way in which Carter treated underlings. The president treated White House employees with disdain. In an article for *Newsmax* Kessler wrote:

"When Carter first came here, he didn't want the police officers and agents looking at him or speaking to him when he went into the office," Nelson Pierce, an assistant White House usher, told me for my book Inside the White House. *"He didn't want them to pay attention to him going by."*

"We never spoke unless spoken to," said Fred Walzel, chief of the White House branch of the Secret Service Uniformed Division.

"Carter came into the cockpit once in the two years I was on with him," James A. Buzzelli, an Air Force One flight engineer, told me. "But [Ronald] Reagan never got on or off without sticking his head in the cockpit and saying, "Thanks, fellas," or "Have a nice day." He was just as personable in person as he came across to the public."[577]

Kessler writes of Carter's refusal to keep the briefcase that held instructions in the event of a nuclear attack with him at his home in Plains. The military person responsible for the "nuclear football," as it was called, was forced to stay in Americus, Georgia, ten miles distant. Had the U.S. come under nuclear attack, the president could not have responded instantly. The aide would have been required to travel the ten miles to Carter's residence. Bill Gulley, who oversaw the White House military office, suggested installing a mobile home near the Carter residence, but the president vetoed the suggestion.[578]

Carter is small in stature and apparently small-minded, as well. As chief executive, he was said to be temperamental, suspicious, and a micromanager of the first order. He even went to the unprecedented length of determining who on his staff could use the White House tennis courts, even when he was away on Air Force One. Charles Palmer, Chief Steward on Air Force One, described Carter as one who savored "the power of the presidency." Palmer reported that it was he who most often was charged with delivering the requests to the president. No one else wanted to endure Carter's wrath.[579]

One unidentified Secret Service agent said, "Carter had the ability and didn't know how to use it. His biggest problem was he had a chip on his shoulder."[580] If the stature of a man is measured by how he treats those under his authority, Carter fell seriously short.

Carter's meanness was further evidenced in the political matchup with Ronald Reagan. The president labeled the former California governor a racist as well as a warmonger. In a speech delivered on October 2, 1980, Carter alleged: "The actions that you take [in this election] will...literally decide the lives of millions of people in our country and indeed throughout the world....You'll determine whether or not this America will be unified or, if I lose the election, whether Americans might be separated, black from white, Jew from Christian, North from South, rural from urban, whether this nation will be guided from a sense of long-range commitment to peace, whether our adversaries will be tempted to end the peace for which we all pray."[581]

During October 1980 circumstances were such in Iran that it was thought Khomeini might be willing to barter for the release of the hostages. Economic hardship brought about by the sanctions imposed after the Embassy takeover, a slowdown in oil production, isolationism, and the threat of war with Iraq gave hope that the powers-that-be in Tehran (Khomeini) might be willing to sit down at the bargaining table.

While the Carter administration was pursuing an end to the hostage crisis, conspiracy theorists were having a field day. Whispers of attempts by Ronald Reagan to engage the Khomeini radicals in a deliberate plan to detain the Americans until after the election plagued the Reagan camp. Gary Sick, the White House aide for Iran during the Carter presidency, expanded the theory into a full-blown exposé in his book *October Surprise: America's Hostages in Iran and the Election of Ronald Reagan*. The only problem with the "theory" was that it was apparently false. In 1992 the Committee on Foreign Relations released a House report that debunked the entire conspiracy theory. The House Committee found there was no reliable evidence to support what became known as the "October Surprise." Furthermore, it was thought that several key witnesses might have lied on the witness stand while giving sworn testimony.[582]

26

CRUSHED BY THE
ECONOMY

"Carter tried 'voluntary' wage and price controls. They didn't work. He tried credit controls. They didn't work. He kept oil-price controls mostly in place and created a vast new bureaucracy—the Energy Department—that has since wasted tens of billions of dollars without creating a single drop of new energy."[583]

AS MUCH AS THE CRISIS IN IRAN was a focal point in the campaign, so was economics. It was Ronald Reagan who said during a 1980 presidential campaign speech, "A recession is when your neighbor loses his job. A depression is when you lose yours. And recovery is when Jimmy Carter loses his."[584] As the Republican candidate, he promised the American people a healthy economy, a balanced budget, to restore America's military might, and to reduce taxes.

In reality, Carter's bungling produced the worst period of economic disaster ever to grip the American people up to that time. The bare facts are appalling considering the acceleration rate of inflation under the Carter administration:

» The purchasing power of the American dollar…[was] worth 55 cents in 1977; by 1980 it had shrunk to 41 cents.

» In 1977 the index of consumer prices, according to the Bureau of Labor Statistics, stood at 181.5; it hovered at 246.8 in 1980.

» In 1977 average unemployment amounted to 6.991 million; in 1980 it stood at 7.637 million.

» According to Treasury Department statistics, during the same period federal unemployment insurance taxes, which obviously increase the cost of labor, rose from $92.61 billion to $139.27 billion.

» According to the Bureau of the Census statistics, the number of Americans living in poverty amounted to 24.7 million in 1977 and 29.27 million in 1980.

» According to the Office of Management and Budget and the Treasury Department, federal outlays soared from $409 billion in 1977 to $590.9 billion in 1980, budget deficits went from $53.6 billion to $73.8 billion, and the federal debt went from $709 billion to $914 billion.[585]

On September 21, 1979, the League of Women Voters invited President Carter, Republican candidate Ronald Reagan, and Independent candidate John Anderson to a debate. Carter, fearing Anderson's presence would hurt his own campaign, chose not to attend. The LWV threatened to place a vacant chair to signify Carter's decision not to attend. Ultimately, the decision was made not to follow through with that threat, but that did not halt the proliferation of political cartoons and jokes about the absentee debater.

Although he had resisted the idea of a debate with Reagan and, in fact, declined to attend the first presidential debate, Carter finally acquiesced and the two men faced each other on October 28, 1980. Moderated by respected newsman Howard K. Smith, the two candidates touched on topics that included the American captives in Iran, nuclear arms treaties, nuclear proliferation, and of course, economic issues.

When questioned regarding nuclear proliferation and the SALT treaty negotiations, President Carter's rambling discourse prompted Governor Reagan to reply, "I know the president's supposed to be replying to me, but sometimes I have a hard time connecting what he's saying with what I have said or what my positions are. I sometimes think he's like the witch doctor that gets mad when a good doctor comes along with a cure that will work."[586] It was Carter's response on the nuclear arms issue during the debate that became the butt of late-night television comedians' jokes. When given the opportunity to have the last rebuttal, the president replied:

> *I had a discussion with my daughter, Amy, the other day before I came here, to ask her what the most important issue was. She said she thought nuclear weaponry—and the control of nuclear arms.*[587]

According to one source, the crowd was so rowdy that following the president's answer, someone yelled, "Are you sure you weren't talking to your dog?"[588] At the end of the debate, those in attendance were reluctant to name a winner. One disgruntled attendee declared John Anderson, a distant third party candidate, the winner. He was not invited to the event.

The crowning comment from Ronald Reagan came during his summation at the end of the debate. The affable Reagan addressed the crowd and asked:

> *Next Tuesday all of you will go to the polls, will stand there in the polling place, and make a decision. I think when you make that decision it might be well if you would ask yourself, are you better off than you were four years ago? Is it easier for you to go and buy things in the stores than it was four years ago? Is there more or less unemployment in the country than there was four years ago? Is America as*

respected throughout the world as it was? Do you feel that
our security is as safe, that we're as strong as we were four
years ago?[589]

Polls following the debate declared Reagan the winner. James
Baker, an advisor to the Reagan campaign, thought the challenger
needed only to exit the debate neck-and-neck with Carter. Many
thought Reagan had exceeded that expectation. He was able to
redirect the attention of the American people back to the issues
that had most plagued Carter from the beginning of his presidency.
He exposed the soft underbelly of the incumbent.

Just days before the election the Carter administration heard
from the Iranians holding the American hostages. The Iranian
government had dictated the terms on which they would free the
captives: 1) return of the late Shah's wealth, 2) cancellation of
all U.S. claims against Iran, 3) release of Iranian assets frozen in
the U.S., and 4) an American guarantee of noninterference in
Iranian affairs.[590] Would this be the shot-in-the-arm Carter's
campaign needed?

Carter's advisor, Hamilton Jordan, suggested the president
release a statement to the American people regarding a possible
hostage release. Carter advised a nation already leery of a
last-minute deal for a hostage release that: "We are within two days
of an important national election. Let me assure you that my
decisions on this crucial matter will not be affected by the
calendar.... I wish that I could predict when the hostages will return.
I cannot."[591]

Carter's announcement had the diametrical opposite effect for
which he had hoped. Many voters who had been "undecided"
jumped ship to the Republican Party.

On Election Day, November 4, 1980, James Earl Carter Jr.,
the 39th president of the United States, lost his bid for a second term.
Reagan won by a landslide (51 percent to Carter's 41 percent) and
carried a number of congressional candidates into office with him.

Carter's was the most ignominious defeat since Franklin Roosevelt won over Herbert Hoover in 1932.

In a move that angered and frustrated House Speaker Thomas P. "Tip" O'Neill Jr., Carter chose to concede the election to Ronald Reagan *before* the polls closed on the West Coast. This move likely cost several Democrats running for congressional seats wins in close races. Said a furious O'Neill, "You guys came in like a bunch of [expletive deleted], and you're going out the same way."[592] The *Nation* questioned Carter's concession: "One wonders if the president entertained the idea of conceding even before the polls opened."[593] A well-known politico, Daniel Patrick Moynihan, commented that Herbert Hoover had won more electoral votes than the man from Plains.

Carter, in his book *Keeping Faith*, pointed to two events he felt most influenced voters against his presidency: the hostage situation in Iran and the influx of illegal immigrants from Cuba. Carter wrote:

> *Although many of the emigrants were good citizens, we were soon to discover that some were mental patients and criminals.... I sympathized with the plight of the refugees, but they were coming in illegally, and I was sworn to uphold the laws of the land.... I could only keep the number to a minimum and struggle to process the refugees in accordance with the laws of the United States. We treated the new immigrants properly and humanely, but it was costly in political popularity.[594]*

Jimmy Carter's final days in office were spent pursuing his post-election, pre-retirement agenda. A proposed jobs bill was so embroiled in debate that it had to be shelved. Carter was successful in lobbying Congress to enact environmental legislation. One of the president's proposals was for the establishment of a toxic waste fund to the tune of $1.6 billion. The other was the Alaskan Lands Bill, which increased the span of national park lands and wildlife refuge areas. The Bill was not widely acclaimed by all Alaskans:

The Anchorage Times complained about "locking up" the mineral resources of Alaska, making the riches of the national parks accessible only to "butterfly chasers" and backpackers.... Tom Snapp, editor of a Fairbanks weekly paper, wrote, "We were supposed to be taken in as a state on an equal basis, but we're not going to be allowed to develop the way other states develop their resources...to develop Alaska meant to take the resources as the base of an economy that could expand, providing jobs, livelihoods, and material comfort for all those who wanted to live in the state...." [While some conservationists lauded Carter's signing of the bill], "President Carter has now replaced Teddy Roosevelt as the greatest conservation president of all time." [Others took him to task]. Congressman Don Young complained that "Alaskans have been slanderously portrayed as land rapists by the preservation lobby and the president has chosen to believe this image."... At a rally in Fairbanks, citizens burned Carter in effigy.[595]

Carter's most ardent pursuit, however, was a renewed effort to secure the release of the hostages before Ronald Reagan took office. Carter sent Warren Christopher and a small contingent of State and Treasury Department officials to Algiers for face-to-face negotiations with an Algerian team representing the Khomeini government.[596] The Iranians were relentless in the pursuit of the Shah's assets, purported to be stashed in American banks. In a move seemingly designed to further insult the United States, Khomeini's negotiators demanded a total of $24 billion dollars be transferred to a bank in Algeria. On the heels of the ridiculous stipulation, the Iranians distributed a synopsis of their demands.

The U.S. retaliated by printing a summation of its own correspondence with the rogue nation. The deadlock between the two countries seemed insurmountable until January 15, 1981. Just days before Carter was to leave office, Iran capitulated and agreed to Carter's demands to pay off loans owned to U.S. banks. In marathon sessions new drafts were produced, new documents drawn, and the Bank of England was approved as the repository of escrow funds. Shortly after 4:00 AM on Inauguration Day, January 20, 1981, the Carter administration relinquished $7.977 billion to the Iranians. According to one source, the transfer required fourteen banks and the participation of five nations acting concurrently.[597]

Could it have been Ronald Reagan's unwavering challenge to the Iranian regime that tipped the scales? Reagan openly referred to those holding the Americans as "criminals." Was it his no-nonsense tone that moved the Khomeini crowd to action? Reagan's message to the Iranians, delivered by Edwin Meese, leader of the transition team, was: "'The Iranians should be prepared that this country will take whatever action is appropriate' and they 'ought to think over very carefully the fact that it would certainly be to their advantage to get the hostages back now.'"[598] Perhaps, the Iranians finally understood Newton's Third Law as applied by Ronald Reagan: for every action there is an equal and opposite reaction.

As a final insult to President Jimmy Carter, the Iranians refused to release the hostages until after President-elect Ronald Reagan was sworn in as 40th president of the United States. Headlines around the world screamed, "Tehran Releases U.S. Hostages after 444 Days of Captivity."

The release of the hostages proved to be Ronald Reagan's first triumph over a fanatical regime, and no shots were fired. One of Carter's own resentfully admitted, "We probably would not be getting the hostages out now if Carter had been reelected."[599]

Ronald Reagan wrote of the Carter administration's treatment of the Shah in his autobiography, *An American Life*:

> *Our government's decision to stand by piously while he [the Shah] was forced from office led to the establishment of [a despotic regime in Tehran that was far more evil and far more tyrannical than the one it replaced. And as I was to learn through personal experience, it left a legacy of problems that would haunt our country for years to come.*[600]

Reagan's Attorney General Edwin Meese also wrote of the Carter administration's inability to corral Libya's Muammar al-Qaddafi:

In the late 1970s, in his role as would-be challenger to the United States, Qaddafi decided to extend the coastal claims of Libya to the waters where [U.S.] maneuvers were conducted. The entire Gulf of Sidra, extending up to one hundred miles from Tripoli and Benghazi, was proclaimed...off-limits to our forces. The Carter government, unfortunately, had meekly rescheduled our maneuvers to stay out of the prohibited area.[601]

With Carter's milquetoast response, Reagan was later forced to confront an ever more defiant Qaddafi following a Libyan attack on April 5, 1986, in Berlin that killed an American soldier and a Turkish citizen, and wounded some two hundred bystanders, including fifty servicemen. On April 15, 1986, President Reagan ordered a retaliatory strike against the Libyan strongman. The president addressed the American public following the air raid: "We believe that this pre-emptive action against his terrorist installations will not only diminish Colonel Qaddafi's capacity to export terror, it will provide him with incentives and reasons to alter his criminal behavior."[602]

Secretary of Defense Caspar Weinberger disclosed that U.S. F-111's were forced to add an additional nearly one thousand miles to their route due to the fact that France declined a request for the planes to overfly French territory.[603] The U.S. lost two American servicemen during the attack. Reagan later related, "As tragic as the loss of life was, I don't think they were lives lost in vain. After the attack on Tripoli, we didn't hear much more from Qaddafi's terrorists." Would the Libya ruler have been as ruthless if Carter had defied him earlier? Would Qaddafi have been so determined to sponsor terrorism had he been warned of the consequences of his actions?

As I reflect on Carter's inability to lead this country, it is obvious that his was a flawed administration doomed to mediocrity. Carter was an intelligent man, but not a cunning politician. A lack of long-range planning and his penchant for straddling the fence hamstrung his staff on many occasions. He was an unabashed champion of human rights but lacked the negotiating skills to achieve efficacious results. President Carter was an unyielding micro-manager but without the skills to adequately manage. He quickly discovered that being the leader of the free world in no way compared to managing a peanut farm in Georgia. His reactions seemed to be knee-jerk rather than thoughtfully formulated for success.

Carter insider Jody Powell made a statement regarding the negotiations for the release of the hostages. He said, "The more that gets clarified, the more there is that needs to be clarified."[604] That could easily have been the summation of the entire Carter presidency.

Or perhaps it was Sean Hannity who best described Carter's tenure in *Deliver Us from Evil*:

> *Carter's failure to act with conviction, coupled with his liberal view of the world, helped create a geopolitical mess that Ronald Reagan would spend much of the 1980s trying to correct.*[605]

George Bush's (41) Secretary of Defense Robert Gates participated in a meeting with National Security Advisor Zbigniew Brzezinski during the Khomeini takeover in Iran. Gates divulged details of the meeting. According to Mr. Gates, Brzezinski outlined the U.S. stance regarding the ouster of the Shah and Khomeini's new Islamic Revolution very succinctly: Acceptance of the revolution; recognition of Khomeini's government; supplies of arms contracted by the Shah delivered to Khomeini; and a future working relationship. Carter allowed the American Embassy in Tehran to be overrun by terrorists, Americans to be taken and held hostage for 444 days. Rather than take a stand against Khomeini's radicalism and defend

America's long-time ally Reza Pahlavi, Carter assumed the mantle of passivity, and his inaction proved deadly.

One must ascertain that the U.S. government had done some horrible injustice to the Iranian people or to Khomeini in particular. Not so! Negotiators in our national capital had gone above and beyond the call of duty to negotiate, conciliate, and establish trust. Carter and Brzezinski bent over backwards, exposed their vulnerable underbelly, and groveled like wounded animals to Khomeini's representatives, only to be challenged with further demands of, "Give us the Shah, and then just maybe we'll consider talking with you." Even Carter could not stomach such a move.

Iran, on the other hand, has never been punished for its capture and incarceration of 52 American citizens for 444 days. Other than being labeled a terrorist state, the Iranian government has had absolute freedom to fund and fuel terrorism on many fronts. It has had the liberty to import the materials to build centrifuges in order to acquire the materials needed to construct nuclear weapons, and it has been free to kill Americans in countries around the world. Why? President Jimmy Carter did not have the intestinal fortitude to face down the Khomeini regime. Instead, we begged, pleaded, cajoled, and ultimately paid off the Ayatollah and his gang of thugs. In so doing, we presented a face to the world that said, "We're weak and ineffective. Come and get us."

27

CAMP DAVID PEACE ACCORDS: THE BEGINNING

"Time and again, the U.S. has given in to Arab blackmail.
Carter is pushing Israel and trying to get them to
endanger their own security." (HERSCHEL AUERBACH,
National Vice President, Zionist Organization of America)[606]

ALTHOUGH WARNED by a senior CIA official that he should pay more attention to the disquieting events in Iran, Jimmy Carter responded, "Let's deal with one subject at a time."[607] The subject that so captivated Carter was the Camp David Peace Accords and Carter's determination to bring Anwar Sadat and Menachem Begin to the table to sign a treaty.

While President Carter has been widely touted and honored as the engineer of the treaty between Israel and Egypt, there were certainly others involved in getting the two sides to sit down together. It has already been noted that Romanian leader Nicolae Ceauçescu played a part in the process, but let's look back at the other forces that came into play prior to Camp David.

In June 1976, during the only major address on the Middle East during his presidential campaign, Jimmy Carter stressed that a precondition to peace in the region must be a change in Arab attitude toward Israel. (Unfortunately nothing has changed since the Carter years. Principals are still demanding that the Arab countries recognize Israel's right to exist prior to negotiations, and Arab leaders continue to refuse.) Carter emphasized that such a change must be reflected by tangible and concrete actions, and not just empty words. Among the necessary alterations must be:

» Recognition of Israel.

» A signed peace treaty.

» Diplomatic relations with Israel.

» Open borders.

» An end of the economic boycott.

» An end to hostile propaganda against Israel.[608]

In his speech, Carter specifically addressed the Palestinian problem:

There ought to be territories ceded for the use of the Palestinians. I think they should be part of Jordan and be administered by Jordan. I think that half of the people of Jordan are Palestinians. That would be my preference.[609]

Once ensconced in the Oval Office, however, Carter's Middle East policy contrasted sharply to his pre-election discourse. Then-Israeli Prime Minister Yitzhak Rabin considered the American leader to be openly hostile to Israel, and the Israeli leader's suspicions of Carter only grew stronger after the two men met in Washington in March 1977. The Israeli prime minister, though toughened by years of anti-Israel sentiment, was nevertheless stunned by Carter's about-face. Rabin's anger grew exponentially later that month when Carter spoke in Massachusetts. The president urged a "homeland for the Palestinians."[610]

Shortly after that speech, President Carter launched a series of meetings with various Arab leaders. In April 1977 he met separately with Egypt's Anwar Sadat and Jordan's King Hussein I. In May he traveled to Geneva to meet with Syria's autocratic leader, President Hafez Assad. At the time, Carter thought Assad would staunchly support an initiative for peace in the Middle East; however, he wrote of the meeting in his book *Keeping Faith*:

> *"'It was a very interesting and enjoyable experience. There was a lot of good humor between us, and I found him to be very constructive in his attitude and somewhat flexible.'"* This was the man who would soon sabotage the Geneva peace talks by refusing to attend under any reasonable circumstances, and who would, still later, do everything possible to prevent the Camp David accords from being fulfilled.[611]

The meeting with President Assad took place one week before Israel was to hold crucial parliamentary elections. In fact, on May 17, 1977, the Israeli electorate sadly disappointed the Labour Party by inducting Menachem Begin's Likud Party into power, a first since the rebirth of the nation of Israel in 1948. Begin's election roiled the waters in Washington, Paris, Cairo, and Damascus. Leaders wondered just how the upheaval would affect Israel's policies. Begin tried to reassure them that he would continue the search for peace in the region, and as a measure of encouragement appointed Moshe Dayan, a Labour member, as his foreign minister.

The appointment signaled a major shift in Israel's priorities. Both Begin and Dayan thought Jordan's King Hussein I too weak to be an effective partner in peace and incapable of reaching a compromise with Israel. The new focus would become not Jordan but Egypt. Their opinion was based on meetings between Hussein and Israeli leaders before and after the 1967 Six-Day War. One meeting was held in London in September 1968. Present were then-Israeli Prime Minister Levi Eshkol and Foreign Minister Abba Eban. Moshe Dayan was invited to join those in attendance, but Dayan refused. Instead, Eshkol sent his deputy, Yigal Allon, to join the group in London.

King Hussein I was accompanied by his prime minister and confidant, Zeid Rifai. During that meeting, the monarch readily admitted he lacked the courage to conclude a separate peace agreement with Israel. He suggested a most impractical option: that Israel talk to President Gamal Abdul Nasser of Egypt. Nasser's instruments of war had been fully replaced or restored by the Soviet Union, and he had adopted the slogan: "What has been taken by force will be returned by force."[612]

In his zeal to decimate Israel, Nasser requested the Soviets appoint a Russian Air Force general to command the Egyptian Air Force; Moscow refused. The USSR had no desire to be directly involved in a conflict with Israel lest the U.S. adopt the same policy with the Israeli army. The wily Russians instead requested they be allowed to act as Egypt's agent in all diplomatic negotiations with the U.S. aimed at resolving the Arab-Israeli conflict. In a move designed to insure that the PLO fell under the Soviet umbrella in the Cold War, Nasser secretly took Yasser Arafat to Moscow.[613]

Nasser's successor, Anwar El Sadat, wished to reverse course and sought to end Egypt's diplomatic dependence on the Soviet Union. In 1973, prior to the beginning of the Yom Kippur War, Sadat petitioned Moscow to supply Egypt with ground-to-ground SCUD missiles. The Soviets were prepared to meet his request, but only if Soviet officers were allowed to be responsible for the missile launches; Sadat refused the condition.

It was Dr. Henry Kissinger who exercised his brilliant diplomatic skills and persuaded Sadat to expel the Soviet military and civilian experts from Egypt. Sadat then began his move toward the U.S., a position that was cemented when the Egyptian president paid an official visit to Washington, D.C., in November 1975 and was invited to address Congress. The precarious marriage between Egypt and the USSR had been severed; the divorce was final.[614]

During the remaining years of the Nixon administration, both Egypt and Israel were comfortable with the Kissinger diplomacy. However, in the summer of 1976 Israel began to search for a more direct approach to Egypt through Morocco's King Hassan II. After Morocco's independence in 1956, Israel's Mossad established a secret presence in that important North African Arab country. The initial intent was to smuggle Moroccan Jews into Israel. In March 1961 the young king determined to expand his relationship with Israel due to opposition from radical elements opposed to his ascension to the throne. Since these young rebels were supported by Egypt and Algeria, King Hassan II sought an alliance with Israel, particularly in the field of domestic security. Israel, in turn, sent Mossad agents to train the king's bodyguards and Moroccan security agents, who were faced with thwarting repeated attempts by Egyptian and Algerian agents to break into the Moroccan embassies in Rabat and Cairo.

In February 1963 Algeria and Egypt (both members of the Soviet Bloc) attacked Morocco. Mossad director General Meir Amit flew to Morocco and secretly met with King Hassan at his head-quarters near Marrakech. Amit presented the monarch with a complete file on Egyptian involvement in the conflict and provided full details about the activities of the Moroccan opposition leaders hiding in Cairo. Amit reassured the king: "We can and want to help you." Hassan accepted Israel's offer without hesitation.[615] From that time, Israeli/Moroccan relations expanded dramatically, especially in the fields of security and intelligence, training Moroccan pilots and armored officers, and in blossoming economic relations.

The summer of 1976 found Prime Minister Rabin seeking a more personal and direct contact with the Moroccan monarch. Rabin knew that Sadat was, at least publically, committed to an overall settlement to the solution of the Palestinian problem. The Israeli leader also knew that there was always a sizeable gap between public rhetoric and a real solution. Wanting to probe the possibility of a separate Israeli-Egyptian settlement, Rabin knew his foot-in-the-door with Hassan was the Mossad. By that time, General Yitzhak Hofi, a respected member of the forces that captured the Golan Heights during the Yom Kippur War, was in charge of Israel's security organization. Since replacing Amit, Hofi had cultivated a relationship with Hassan based on trust. When Hofi suggested a meeting with Rabin to the king, he immediately agreed.

Rabin adopted a disguise, flew to Paris, and met with General Ahmed Dlimi of the Moroccan Secret Service. The two men boarded a special *Mystere 20* Royal Moroccan plane and flew to Fez. So it was that Rabin made history as the first Israeli prime minister to meet with King Hassan II. After two encounters, Rabin left Hassan with only two questions to put to President Sadat:

> » What would Egypt give in return for Israel's total withdrawal from Sinai?
>
> » What would Egypt give in return for a partial Israeli withdrawal?[616]

Sadat declined to respond, fearing Rabin lacked the daring to deliver on his promises. Following Begin's election and Dayan's appointment, Sadat changed his mind in June 1977. One reason for Sadat's about-face was Jimmy Carter; the Egyptian president felt Carter didn't understand how embarrassing it would be for Egypt to invite the Soviets back into the Arab-Israeli peace process.

Although after his election Begin wished to meet with Sadat, he did not want to rely only on Carter's negotiating skills to make that happen. He sent General Yitzhak Hofi to Morocco in an attempt to pressure Sadat for an answer to his two questions. When Hofi met with the king in Ifrane, the beautiful winter resort city high in the Atlas Mountains, he was surprised to see Sadat's confidant and senior cabinet minister, Muhammad Hassan el-Tuhamy. His presence was sufficient proof that Sadat was at last willing to explore a separate peace agreement with Israel. The meeting set the precedent for further discussions between Tuhamy and Dayan, none of which were arranged by Jimmy Carter.

Not surprisingly, the king had been very concerned about the growth of Islamic radicalism in the Arab world, and especially in

Egypt. In view of his concerns, he urged the Israelis to also establish contact with the Saudis. Hassan knew of Israel's secret relationship with Jordan, and he thought it well past time to include other moderate Arab countries in this secret inner circle. In 1976 the king tried to arrange a clandestine meeting between Rabin and Saudi Crown Prince Fahd, soon to become King of Saudi Arabia. Although Fahd knew of Morocco's dealings with Israel, he felt it was too soon to meet with an Israeli leader.[617]

After introducing Tuhamy and Hofi, the king left them to talk privately. During this first meeting, Hofi found Tuhamy stiff and uncompromising. The Egyptian diplomat further alienated the Israeli by adamantly championing the known extremist positions. Hofi complained to Hassan. By the following morning, Tuhamy had apparently been advised to find common ground for a meeting between Sadat and Begin.[618]

That was the beginning of a real breakthrough for Israeli-Egyptian relations. Begin and Dayan were pleased with the outcome of Hofi's meeting, so much so that Dayan flew to Marrakech in August 1977 for a personal meeting with King Hassan. This followed Secretary of State Cyrus Vance's trip to Israel and the Arab countries to investigate reconvening the Geneva Peace Conference, but this time with Carter pressing strongly for Soviet participation. It was Vance's trip that convinced Begin and Dayan that Carter was determined to dispense with the Kissinger diplomacy, at least in two major areas:

» Kissinger had wanted to reduce Moscow's role in the Arab-Israeli peace process; Carter wanted more Russian participation.

» Kissinger favored a step-by-step diplomacy; Carter wanted an overall settlement that included Syria, the most radical and pro-Soviet country in the Arab world.

From their first meeting, King Hassan and Dayan found common ground: the monarch thought Dayan "an Israeli hero and legend," and Dayan described Hassan as a "liberal autocrat."[619]

The king's report to Sadat was glowing, and he recommended that the Egyptian president meet with Prime Minister Begin. The outcome of Hassan's effusiveness was a secret meeting between Moshe Dayan and Muhammad Hassan el-Tuhamy at Skhirat, a royal palace south of Rabat, in September 1977. After introducing the two gentlemen, the Moroccan leader remarked that should Israel and Egypt find common ground for resolving their age-old conflict, Carter would have to be informed of that development in order to include the U.S. in the peace process.[620] The consensus by both leaders was to maintain the secret channel and prevent Carter's direct involvement.

The meeting between Dayan and Tuhamy lasted some four hours. When asked by Tuhamy for a commitment from Israel for a complete withdrawal from the Sinai, Dayan refused to comply. He felt he was simply an envoy of Begin's and was not able to commit to anything without first reporting to the prime minister. The two men agreed to meet again in Morocco within two weeks under the auspices of King Hassan.

Before leaving Morocco, Dayan and the monarch agreed on a date for a meeting between him and Begin—November 20, 1977. Begin was to make a stopover in Morocco on his way home from an official visit to London. Not only would the meeting between the King of Morocco and the prime minister of Israel be an historic event, but also it would prove the courage and vision of the three primaries, Sadat, Begin, and Hassan. Sadat had decided he was ready to ignore the decisions made by the Arab contingent at the 1974 Arab Summit, including the decision neither to recognize nor establish a separate peace with Israel.

Dayan reported the outcome of his meeting with Tuhamy to the prime minister and then flew to New York to head the Israeli delegation to the UN General Assembly. While meeting with Cyrus Vance, Dayan was handed a working paper that was to serve as a basis for an American-Soviet decision to reconvene the Peace Conference in Geneva. The contents of that paper included a clause relating to Palestinian representation. Both Carter in Washington and his cohorts in Moscow proposed that the PLO be represented by "junior" officials and not the organization's top guns. Bolstered by recent meetings in Morocco, Dayan boldly rejected Vance's paper, sensing that Sadat would do the same.

Ignoring Israel's objections, the Carter and USSR proceeded to call for the Geneva Peace Conference to be reconvened on October 1— with Palestinian representation. Of course, the documentation announcing the conference failed to mention the PLO directly; it simply mentioned the need to establish a Palestinian homeland and called for a total withdrawal by Israel to its 1967 boundaries.

Begin was not informed of the contents of the joint statement until shortly before its release, when U.S. Ambassador to Israel Sam Lewis delivered a copy of the document to the prime minister's residence. Begin's shock was so great he had to be rushed to the hospital. Begin was not the only one stunned to learn of this turn of events; all of Israel and the American Jewish community were appalled as well. It appeared as if Carter was showing his true colors by running roughshod over Israel and moving toward an imposed resolution to the Arab-Israeli conflict.

Syria and the PLO, on the one hand, were overjoyed by the American and Soviet statement. On the other hand, Sadat was surprisingly silent, but the Egyptian government-run media denounced the move by the two superpowers. Rather than directly denounce the U.S., however, the media attacked the Soviet Union for yielding to American pressure and for now identifying the PLO by name.

After a six-hour emergency meeting of Sadat's cabinet on October 3, 1977, Egyptian Foreign Minister Ismail Fahmy personally handed Cyrus Vance a message from Sadat to Jimmy Carter. Although the contents of the note were not divulged, the Egyptian media soon left no room for speculation: Sadat objected to what he saw as Carter's decision to impose a renewed Soviet role in the Middle East peace process.[621]

Neither did Carter escape the ire of U.S. congressional leaders. It was obvious he had not considered the long-range implications of his move, and he was eventually forced to alter his stance. On October 5 Dayan and Vance met in Washington. A heated, six-hour debate that included Carter ended with the release of an amendment to the original draft. The most notable change regarded PLO representation at the Geneva Conference. Rather than have independent envoys, the Palestinians would become part of a joint Arab League delegation. An agreement was reached to split the Geneva conferees into several subcommittees following the opening session of the meeting. Also contained in the amended text was the notation that the Palestinian issue would be discussed only between Israel and the joint Arab delegation. The changes were approved by Begin and the Israeli cabinet.

Though an agreement had been reached, clarification of the terms was still a sticking point between Israel and the U.S. Israel declared that the PLO representatives would be chosen from the West Bank and Gaza, areas under Israel's control. The U.S. argued that the emissaries should also come from "outside the territories now occupied by Israel," thus leaving the door open for the inclusion of future PLO members in peace negotiations.[622]

Despite the amended version of the joint statement, Israel remained opposed to the very principle of the Geneva Peace Conference, and most especially with Soviet participation. Mid-October brought a delegation of American Jewish leaders to the White House to meet with Carter. The mission protested what appeared to be a heavy-handed move by the U.S. to join the Soviet Union in forcing a resolution on Israel, a move totally contrary to Carter's promise before being elected president.[623] On the same day, the Hashemite Kingdom of Jordan stepped forward in support of the Dayan-Vance amendment to the joint statement. According to King Hussein I, the Palestinians in the West Bank and Gaza were better able to speak for their cause than the PLO. Now, all ears were tuned to Egypt and President Sadat, waiting to hear about a possible meeting between him and Begin.

While all the intrigues and schemes were taking place in Washington, Tuhamy made three secret trips to Rabat to seek additional clarifications from Israel. Meanwhile, Carter was wooing Sadat to gain his support for the amended statement regarding the Geneva meeting. On October 21 and 23, Carter sent Sadat two hand-penned messages regarding the amendment. It was obvious he did not understand Sadat's reluctance to become embroiled again with the Soviet Union. Carter urged the leaders— Sadat, Begin, and other Arab heads of state—to ignore "procedural arguments" and attend the Geneva Peace Conference.[624]

At the end of October Sadat made a trip to Romania, where he mentioned his desire to meet with Begin to the Romanian leader, Nicolae Ceauçescu. Upon his return to Cairo in early November Sadat proposed the establishment of a "working group" that would study the subjects on the agenda for Geneva. Israel didn't understand Sadat's motive and mistakenly suspected that Ceauçescu was behind the move. In actuality, Sadat's ploy was to gain time and remove the U.S. and the Soviet Union from the position of joint-chairmanship at the conference.[625]

Additionally, Sadat stunned his security council by announcing his decision to go to Jerusalem. Only Foreign Minister Fahmy obstinately opposed this move by Sadat, but the Egyptian leader seemed equally determined and ready to pay the price for his actions. Carter was not apprised of Sadat's intentions until the very last moment. And though the U.S. president congratulated the Egyptian leader for his courage, he still unyieldingly insisted that the Geneva Peace Conference would go forward as planned—with Soviet participation.

Scottish poet Robert Burns aptly described the outcome of Carter's manipulations when he wrote:

> *The best laid schemes of mice and men*
> *Go often askew,*
> *And leaves us nothing but grief and pain,*
> *For promised joy!* "[626]

In other words, Carter's plan to stack the deck against Israel with his insistence on including the Soviets in any Middle East peace talks and then force her to the bargaining table yet again failed to come to fruition.

Sadat dropped his bombshell to the Egyptian parliament on November 9:

> *In order to seek a settlement, I am ready to go to the end of the world. I am prepared to go even to Israel, to the Knesset, and talk to its members in an effort to make peace. I am ready to do that, if I can save the life of even one single soldier. But Israel should understand that any agreement should include a total Israeli withdrawal from all territories and the establishment of an independent Palestinian state.*[627]

The day after Sadat's jaw-dropping announcement, Begin and Dayan met with members of the U.S. Congressional Armed Services Committee, led by Congressman Melvin Price. Begin advised Price:

> *When you meet with President Sadat tomorrow, you can tell him that should he come to Israel, we shall welcome him at Ben Gurion Airport in the most official manner. The prime minister of Israel will accompany him to Jerusalem, and Sadat will be able to address the Knesset.*[628]

Sadat informed Price and the delegation that, should he be invited to Israel, he would go. From that point, events escalated. The Soviets were critical of Sadat's resolve, which they saw as an attempt to exclude them from peace negotiations; King Hassan congratulated Sadat for his courageous decision; the Saudis remained aloof and silent; and Sudan and several Persian Gulf States, including the Shah of Iran, supported Sadat's decision.

The Shah, who had been an ally of both countries, had encouraged Yitzhak Rabin to open channels of communication, not only with the secret service in Morocco but also with King Hassan II. After Begin's election, Dayan traveled to Tehran to meet with Pahlavi, who urged Israel's prime minister to meet with Sadat.

Michael David Evans and
Empress Farah Pahlavi

Michael David Evans and former French
President Valery Giscard d'Estaing

Michael David Evans and former
Prime Minister Menachem Begin

Iranian Ambassador Ardeshir Zahedi with
whom Dr. Evans had extensive interviews.

Michael David Evans and former
New York City Mayor Rudy Giuliani

Michael David Evans and former
Prime Minister Rabin

Ayatollah Ruhollah Khomeini's compound outside Paris – Neauphle-le-Chateau)

Michael David Evans outside gate at Neauphle-le-Chateau

Michael David Evans at Neauphle-le-Chateau

Michael David Evans, Michael Evans II, and Israel President Shimon Peres

Michael David Evans and former Prime Minister Benjamin Netanyahu

Michael David and Carolyn Evans with Benjamin Netanyahu and his father on the anniversary of his brother Jonathan's death during the raid on Entebbe in Uganda.

Michael David Evans and former
CIA Director James Woolsey

Michael David Evans and
Prime Minister Ehud Olmert

Michael David Evans celebrating the Feast
of Tabernacles with Chief Rabbi of Israel.

Michael David Evans and Iraqi Kurdistan
Prime Minister Nechirvan Barzani

Temple Mount in Jerusalem

Michael David Evans, Michael Evans II,
and Foster Friess on Kotel (Western Wall.)

Michael David Evans and Iraqi Kurdistan
President Massoud Barzani

Michael David Evans stands at the border
between Iran and Iraq

Michael David Evans with Marines in Beirut
the day before the Marine barracks
were bombed by terrorists at 6:45 AM
October 23, 1983.

Michael David Evans with the Egyptian Army
in Saudi Arabia during Operation
Desert Storm

Michael David Evans at the Royal Palace
for the Madrid Peace Conference

Michael David Evans, former chief of staff
Lt. General Moshe Ya'alon,
Mayor Ron Nachman (Ariel, Israel).

In actuality, neither Begin nor the Shah trusted Carter, and both were convinced he did not understand the mechanics of Middle East politics.[629]

Even though the White House welcomed—at least outwardly—Sadat's decision to go to Jerusalem, Carter continued to push for a Geneva-type conference. And, he insisted the Soviets be involved in any resolution to the Israeli-Egyptian question.[630] Reality, however, trumped the U.S. president's wishes. Sadat was very wary of both Carter's insistence on Russian participation and the Dayan-Vance amendment to the original joint statement regarding Geneva. In 1972 the Egyptian president had fought to expel the Soviets, and thus their influence in his country. Now he simply wanted to create a framework whereby Israel and Egypt could dialogue together without oversight by the U.S. and the USSR. He wanted to deny the two countries total control of the meeting. After discussions with Sadat, Israel reversed its initial rejection of the group the Egyptian leader had established to study the topics to be discussed at the Geneva Peace Conference.[631]

Sadat's presence in Jerusalem dropped into the Arab world like a match into a tinderbox. Sudan came out in support of the visit, Libya called for a severance of relations with Egypt, and French Prime Minister Raymond Barre told Hafez al-Assad of Syria that Sadat shaking hands with Begin was akin to French Prime Minister Maréchal Pétain[632] shaking hands with Adolf Hitler. Assad permitted the Syrians to demonstrate against Sadat in Damascus and other Syrian cities. Iraq voiced its disdain with Sadat for shaking hands with the "arch-terrorist, Begin." The PLO accused Sadat of abandoning the Palestinian cause. The Soviets reacted as expected, by arguing that the Egyptian president was striving to exclude the Soviet Union from discussions regarding the Arab-Israeli question. The Russians refused to attend the Egyptian-sponsored meetings of the working group in Cairo scheduled in mid-December of 1977.[633] As usual, the UN sided with the USSR.[634]

On December 9 Cyrus Vance made another trip to Cairo and Jerusalem. His mission was to inform Begin that Israel's Sinai concessions were not sufficient and Israel would be required to make similar concessions to the Palestinians. Vance reiterated that U.S. participation in the meeting of the so-called "working group" in Cairo did not mean Carter was prepared to abandon the Geneva Peace Conference.

Begin simply ignored Vance's argument and asked him to arrange a meeting with Carter in Washington in order to present his plan for Palestinian administrative autonomy in the West Bank and Gaza. Just days later, Begin flew to Washington, where Carter rejected Begin's proposal. Carter countered with a plan to deploy a UN force in the Palestinian Territory for a five-year period, after which joint rule would be implemented by the Israelis and Jordanians. Begin, likewise, rejected Carter's outline.[635]

Plagued by uncertainty, Begin flew to Ismailiyah to unveil his Palestinian plan to Sadat, who rejected it just as Carter had. He did, however, accept Begin's proposal as a basis for negotiations. Like a bride with a new husband, Sadat hoped to change Begin's mind shortly after the "I do's" were repeated.

Just before leaving for a trip to Egypt, Saudi Arabia, and Iran in late December, Carter held a press conference in Washington. He told the amassed reporters that he had never supported the creation of a Palestinian state. (I wonder what Arafat thought of that.) Carter said he believed the Palestinians should be tied to Jordan: "This is my priority, but whatever is accepted by Begin and Sadat will be accepted by me also."[636]

During a Carter trip to Aswan, Egypt, in early January 1978, he thoroughly disheartened Sadat by revealing he didn't believe the Egyptian leader would be able to achieve a peace agreement with Israel. Meanwhile, Carter continued to explore ways and means to persuade King Hussein I of Jordan to join the peace process, despite Israel and Egypt's objections to his inclusion.

Sadat was appalled by Carter's statement that he had never supported the creation of a Palestinian state. He was correct in thinking it would be misinterpreted in the Arab world as a softening of Sadat's insistence on an independent Palestinian state. Sadat implored Carter to modify his verbiage regarding the U.S. position, and Carter complied. In briefings to Congress and in discussions with Persian Gulf states, the U.S. began to emphasize two points:

» The U.S. recognizes Israel's security needs. However, the U.S. also believes that instead of an exclusive Israeli military presence in the West Bank and the Gaza Strip, the parties should explore also a UN presence, or a joint Israeli-Jordanian military presence.

» In order to prevent a one-sided Israeli annexation of the West Bank and the Gaza Strip, the U.S. insists that Israel give a public assurance that the future of these territories be decided after a transition period of five years.

Begin then requested that Carter stop in Jerusalem on his jaunt through the Middle East, but Carter refused.[637] The prime minister saw Carter's refusal as a tilt toward Egypt motivated by two factors:

» Strengthening Sadat would also strengthen the American presence in the Arab world, especially in the Persian Gulf.

» Since the 1973 Yom Kippur War, Egypt had received financial assistance from Saudi Arabia totaling $11 billion. Should this assistance stop because of Arab opposition to Sadat's position, Egypt would certainly turn to the U.S. for compensation.[638]

Sadat too was uncomfortable with Carter's interference in what had begun as silent efforts by Morocco's King Hassan II in cooperation with Egypt and Israel. He was also wary of the president's efforts to involve the USSR and Jordan in the peace process. Sadat had identified his first priority as settling the

Palestinian question. Once that was accomplished, he would then turn to the Sinai negotiations. Carter, however, believed the opposite: return the Sinai to Egypt and then discuss the Palestinian question. The Morocco meetings prior to Carter's involvement had produced a meeting of the minds on the question of whether or not to include Jordan in the discussions: both Middle East leaders felt that Jordan's King Hussein I should remain on the sidelines, at least for the moment.

Begin and Dayan were not at all in agreement on the proposed Palestinian resolution, but they were united in their opposition to a joint Israeli-Jordanian presence in the West Bank and Gaza.[639] As the weeks and months passed with no determination, both Begin and Sadat became discouraged and impatient. Sadat decided to turn to Carter and Europe for assistance. He even asked Shimon Peres, the Chair of the opposition Labour Party in Israel, for help, but to no avail.

The Egyptian president suggested to Carter that he invite both sides, along with the five permanent members of the UN Security Council, to a secluded place to try to hammer out an agreement. His idea of seclusion was onboard an American ship in the Mediterranean. Carter accepted his suggestion, but rather than a ship at sea Carter chose Camp David, a rustic 125-acre mountain retreat in the hills of Maryland. Both men agreed, and after thirteen days of intense negotiations the Camp David Accords were signed.

Jordan's King Hussein I awaited an invitation to Camp David in London, while wondering why neither Sadat nor Begin wanted him present in the meetings. The invitation was never issued. After the Camp David Accords and the Israeli-Egyptian Peace Treaty were signed, the question of why Carter was not more insistent on bringing Jordan into the process remained. After all, Carter rarely missed an opportunity to impose his will and ideals on others. He failed simply because neither Sadat nor Begin would bend on that issue or on the issue of including the Soviets. He did not understand that he couldn't force acquiescence on these two seasoned leaders.

Many believe it was Carter's blinder-mentality and his determination to isolate himself and the other participants in the debate that led in part to the downfall of the Shah of Iran. Rather than let Egypt and Israel continue their clandestine talks under the auspices of Morocco's King Hassan II, Carter felt impelled to become involved and thereby impose his will on these two countries. He devoted his time and energy to a situation where he was very likely not needed and ignored the Iranian crisis. Thereby, Jimmy Carter betrayed the Shah of Iran, and America is still paying the price for that betrayal today.

28

THE ABCs OF MIDDLE EAST POLICY: ARAFAT, BEGIN, CARTER, AND SADAT

"Carter's animus against Israel has been confirmed from many reliable quarters. His Secretary of State, Cyrus Vance, once revealed that if Carter had won a second term, he intended to sell Israel down the river." [640]

DR. LAURENCE J. PETER, formulator of the "Peter Principle," is credited with saying, "Political success is the ability, when the inevitable occurs, to get credit for it." [641] This has proven to be true of what many thought of as Jimmy Carter's shining moment in the White House: the Camp David Peace Accords.

Jimmy Carter has often been credited with orchestrating the Camp David Peace Accords. He is certainly due some credit, but he cannot claim total responsibility for the peace agreement between Israel and Egypt. It was, in fact, my dear friend Prime Minister Menachem Begin who made the first overture to Anwar El Sadat through a third-party intermediary—Nicolae Ceauçescu of Romania. In a private conversation that I had with Menachem, he related that he first envisioned a meeting with Sadat while on a trip to Romania. Begin intimated to Ceauçescu that he would like to meet the Egyptian president. (Begin had repeatedly called on Arab leaders to meet with him.)

It was Ceauçescu who finally relayed Begin's wish to Sadat while the Egyptian leader was visiting Bucharest. Since the Israeli prime minister was unfamiliar with Sadat, he wanted Ceauçescu's opinion. "'Begin,' Ceauçescu assured him, 'wants a solution.' Sadat pressed the question: Was Begin honest, and was he a strong enough leader to deliver it? The Romanian's answer was 'yes' on both counts. That was sufficient for Sadat."[642] Following the Romanian leader's input and the involvement by King Hassan of Morocco, Sadat confirmed he was agreeable to a meeting with his Israeli counterpart. Sadat confirmed his commitment in a speech to the Egyptian parliament that was broadcast on American television: "I am willing to go to the ends of the earth for peace," he said. "Israel will be astonished to hear me say now, before you, that I am prepared to go to their own house, to the Knesset itself, to talk to them."[643]

Menachem Begin's immediate response was an invitation to Sadat to visit Jerusalem and to address the Knesset. The invitation was issued through the American ambassador. In a speech broadcast directly to the Egyptian people, Begin said:

> "Citizens of Egypt, this is the first time that I address you directly, but it is not the first time I think and speak of you. You are our neighbors and will always be. For the last twenty-nine years, the tragic and completely unnecessary conflict continued between your country and ours. Since the time when the government of King Farouk ordered to invade our land, Eretz Yisrael, in order to strangle our newly restored freedom and democracy, four major wars have taken place between you and us. Much blood was shed on both sides, many families were orphaned and grieved in Egypt and in Israel.... You should know we have come back to the land of our forefathers. It is we who established independence in our land for all generations to come. We wish you well; in fact, there is no reason whatsoever for

hostilities between our people.... Your president said two days ago that he was ready to come to Jerusalem to our Knesset in order to prevent one Egyptian soldier from being wounded. I have already welcomed this statement, and it will be a pleasure to welcome and receive your president with the traditional hospitality... you and we have inherited... from our common father, Abraham. I, for my part, will be ready to come to your capital, Cairo, for the same purpose: No more war, but peace, real peace, forever.[644]

I asked Prime Minister Begin if he was really that eager to go to Egypt. With a smile and a twinkle in his eye, he replied he really would like to see the pyramids built by our ancestors. He jokingly said he would not ask the Egyptians for compensation.

Sadat's recompense for his overture to Israel was separation from many of his own Arab countrymen. Algeria, Iraq, Libya, Syria, and South Yemen condemned the trip to Jerusalem and seemed determined to "work [through] the frustration of the results of President Sadat's visit to the Zionist entity."[645] The leaders declared they would refuse to attend Arab League meetings held in Egypt and would freeze relations with the nation. Sadat retaliated by severing ties with all of the countries. When Sadat issued an invitation for a conference in Cairo to promote unity, a humiliated Sadat received positive responses only from the U.S., Israel, and the UN.

Sadat further alienated the Islamic Egyptian rank-and-file with his plans for a gala to honor Islamists, Christians, and Jews. The backlash was immediate and vocal. Sadat opted for a massive festival *The New York Times* depicted as a "bunch of beautiful people [who] created their own island of conspicuous opulence in a sea of Egyptian poverty.... Over 400 partygoers from the United States and Europe enjoyed what was probably the most extravagant social affair Egypt has seen since the...overthrow of King Farouk.... white-uniformed policemen, some with automatic rifles, shooed away curious Egyptians from a nearby village." The ticket price was a mere $2,500, calculated at nine years' salary for an Egyptian worker.[646]

The animosity of the Arab world toward Israel and the disdain for Sadat following his overture to Begin was perhaps best explained by Boutros Boutros-Ghali, an Egyptian minister of state for foreign affairs, diplomat, and UN secretary general:

> "'The fierceness of the Arab reaction against Sadat's initiative,' he explains, 'stemmed from a deep-rooted fear that if you so much as began to talk to Israel, half the battle was lost because dialogue implied equality, while the facts indicated an immense imbalance between the two sides.' Even for him (Boutros-Ghali), a sophisticated scholar married to a Jew, the very fact of stepping on Israeli soil for the first time came as a shock: 'Israel seemed as strange to me as a land in outer space. For decades it had been the enemy, the cancer in the body of the Arab world, which we had to do all in our power to destroy.'"[647]

How did Jimmy Carter actually become known as the negotiator of peace between these two leaders, especially when warned by his own advisors not to become embroiled in the Middle East impasse? In an attempt to court Jewish voters during the presidential campaign, Carter stressed the necessity of strong ties with Israel. He supported Israel's call for "defensible borders." This phrase generally refers to the areas recovered during the Six-Day War in 1967. Carter vowed not to acknowledge the Palestine Liberation Organization (PLO) until he was certain the organization's leaders were ready to recognize Israel's right to exist.[648]

Once elected, however, Carter reacted typically; he flip-flopped. Still averring he would strongly support Israel, Carter nevertheless decided to exert his considerable power as president of the United States to resolve the age-old Arab-Israeli discord, even if that placed him at loggerheads with Israel and with his Jewish constituency.

The president's position toward the region was particularly swayed by a document published by the Brookings Institution's 1975 Middle East Study Group:

In the summer of 1974, the Brookings Institution of Washington D.C., invited a group of distinguished Americans, scholars, diplomats, and public figures, to consider how the United States could help in the achievement of a settlement in the Middle East. The report was very influential in the formulation of the Middle East policy of the Carter administration in 1977, and one of the members of the study group, Professor Zbigniew Brzezinski, was appointed Assistant to the President for National Security Affairs.[649]

As an evangelical Christian, Carter was interested in the country where Christ was born, walked, died, and rose again. As a politician, it is likely Carter saw what many after him also perceived: a lasting legacy of having been the man who was able to achieve peace in the Middle East. One can only speculate that he also may have viewed the Palestinians as being beneficiaries of his human rights crusade.

Soon after taking office President Carter ran afoul of Jewish leaders in the U.S., many of whom had voted for him, as well as Israeli leaders. The sanctioning of a Palestinian homeland and a proposed meeting with Hafez al-Assad of Syria created an aura of distrust of Carter's motives. Yitzhak Rabin and his Labor Party were concerned Carter's actions would endanger the Israeli government and usher in Menachem Begin's more hawkish Likud Party. Rabin's fears were realized when, on May 18, 1977, Begin won the chair of prime minister. A stunned Jimmy Carter feared any attempt at launching a peace initiative had just collapsed.

Carter dispatched Brzezinski and Vice President Mondale to meet with American Jewish leaders in an attempt to retain their support, but his efforts were soon overshadowed by two events. In July 1977 Carter's decision to block Israel's sale of twenty-four *Kfir* (in Hebrew "Lion Cub") fighter/bombers to Ecuador, under the guise of restricting the sale of arms to third-world countries, further troubled our staunchest Middle East ally. (Carter's control over the sale was due to the fact that the *Kfirs* were powered by engines built in the U.S.) It was, however, Carter's proposed deal with Saudi Arabia that caused the most unease: the president offered sixty F-15 aircraft to the Saudi government.

The package deal sent to Congress for approval included the sale of fifty F-15s and F-16s to Israel, as well as fifty F-5Es to Egypt. The Israelis were understandably concerned that the passage of such a deal would tie future sales of additional arms for Arab countries. Begin took a hard-line stance, ready to quash the deal rather than see Israel's sworn enemy supplied with the very weapons that would make the tiny nation even more vulnerable. Israeli Foreign Minister Moshe Dayan explained Israel's position: "Even if we have to absorb the punishment [estrangement from the U.S.], we will continue to oppose the deal."[650] Congress finally approved the sale, but with conditions attached. The Saudis were to receive aircraft with limited range and offensive capabilities lest the delicate balance in the region be tipped against Israel.

Shortly after his election as prime minister, Menachem Begin flew to Washington, D.C., to meet with President Carter. Begin was squarely on the right in Israeli political circles. The Likud Party had captured the Knesset under Begin's campaign strategy of a territorialist platform, and he was the first leader of Israel to refer to the West Bank as Judea and Samaria.

The diminutive prime minister was welcomed to Washington, D.C., with all the ruffles and flourishes Carter could summon as president of the United States. Perhaps it was designed to flatter the elder statesman; perhaps it was meant to soften the old hard-liner. As the prime minister reiterated Israel's stand on Jerusalem, Judea, Samaria, and the Gaza Strip, Carter bristled and Cyrus Vance must have seen any hope of reaching an agreement evaporate.

During the meeting with Carter, as related in the following article by Yehuda Avner, Begin asked his aide to unroll a map of the region as he explained the reasons for his decision not to relinquish the territory in question:

> "Mr. President," he said, "I wish to tell you something personal...about my generation.... To my generation of Jews these eternal bonds are indisputable and incontrovertible truths.... They touch upon the very core of our national being....We were a helpless people, Mr. President.... We lost a third of our people in one generation—mine.... No one came to our rescue. We suffered and died alone.... Now we can defend ourselves." [He pointed to the map]. "The Syrians sat on top of these mountains.... They shelled our towns and villages from the tops of those mountains, day and night." [Begin's] finger now hovered over Tel Aviv.... "Here live a million Jews, twelve miles from that indefensible armistice line. And here, between Haifa in the north and Ashkelon in the south, live two-thirds of our total population...whosoever sits in these mountains"—his fingertips tapped the tops of Judea and Samaria—"holds the jugular vein of Israel in his hands.... Mr. President," continued Begin.... "This is our map of national security.... It is our map of survival.... Today, our menfolk can defend their women and children. In the past they could not. Indeed, they had to deliver them to their Nazi executioners. We were tertiated, Mr. President... Tertiated, not decimated. The origin of the word decimation is one in ten. When a Roman legion was found guilty of insubordination one in ten was put to the sword. In our case it was one in three—tertiated!"[651]

During the course of the encounter with Begin, Carter found him to be less rigid than he imagined. The talks also helped to assuage the fears of Jewish leaders regarding Carter's Middle East policies. Not even the genial conversations were enough to remove the key divisions between the two, however, which were the disposition of the "occupied" territories and the building of settlements in those areas.

Soon after returning to Jerusalem, Begin revealed that new housing construction was to begin on the West Bank. Washington and Israel traded harsh words over the proposed building. Carter declared the project to be both unlawful and an impediment to any peace process. One constant remained during this exchange: Carter was intent on reviving the Geneva Peace talks. So determined was the president that he sent Cyrus Vance to Moscow to meet with Soviet Foreign Minister Andrei Gromyko in order to gain Soviet support for a Geneva initiative.

Anwar Sadat, who in 1972 had expelled 5,000 Soviet military advisors and 15,000 air combat personnel from Egypt, was less than enchanted with Carter's machinations. He preferred not to have the Soviets play any role in Middle East peace talks. Sadat had no desire to face Syria, Iraq, and the USSR across the bargaining table, as all had a vested interest in gaining superiority in the region. Begin, who felt he also was being pressured unfairly by Washington, was as appalled by Carter's move as was Sadat.

Carter's endeavors to rally support for his Geneva plan were met with rejection. Meanwhile, Begin and Sadat continued to communicate behind the scenes, although it was clear to both men that the process was similar to a field strewn with land mines. Sadat demanded Israel return to the 1967 borders. Begin, on the other hand, could agree to the return of the Sinai within a five-year timetable but would not budge on the border issue or on Palestinian self-determination.

The White House finally concluded that its intervention was needed between the two leaders. A trip to Egypt by Cyrus Vance produced only the promise that the Egyptian and Israeli foreign ministers would meet with Vance in London. Then the president issued an invitation to both Menachem Begin and Anwar Sadat to visit him at Camp David and engage in further peace talks.

Both men accepted the president's invitation. The National Security Council's Middle East expert, William Quandt, summed up his feelings: "We're here for group therapy. What are we doing?"

asked Quandt. "My impression was, from everything I had read, that Begin and Sadat could not stand one another, and that this was going to turn out to be a disaster."[652]

On September 5, 1978, the two men arrived at Camp David. Carter, who had established a greater rapport with Sadat than with Begin, was disheartened by the initial session. Both leaders were intransigent regarding the 1967 boundary issue. It was Sadat, however, who had the most to lose. He had already lost face with other Arab leaders by his insistence on negotiating with Begin; he could not afford to leave Camp David empty-handed.

The real issues at stake between the two parties meeting at Camp David were: implementing a peace treaty between the two countries; a military step-down in the Sinai, and the elimination of Israeli settlements in the area; the disposition of the West Bank and Gaza; and an agreement regarding a return to 1967 borders and the Palestinian right of self-determination.[653] It is interesting to note here that Israel's population is approximately 2 percent of the Middle East, and it occupies one-sixth of one-percent of the land mass.

Former Israeli Ambassador Dore Gold talked with me about Carter's role at Camp David:

> *Carter came in after Israel and Egypt had been meeting several times...and after the Sadat visit, and he tried to affect the Israel/Egyptian negotiations. Some believe Carter was more pro-Palestinian than Sadat because he did not want Israel and Egypt to reach a separate deal; he wanted the Egyptian/Israeli negotiations to include the future of the West Bank and Gaza.... Peace with Egypt was not a result of Jimmy Carter; it was despite him.*[654]

Sadat's fellow-countryman Boutros Boutros-Ghali wrote of his exhilaration "of sharing a ringside seat at a tense, fascinating, and fateful diplomatic process"...at Camp David: "Cyrus Vance was careful. Zbigniew Brzezinski, the special presidential assistant for national security affairs, was eager. Begin was pompous...Dayan was surly. And President Carter," he notes with obvious disapproval, "appeared without a necktie."[655]

Neckties aside, the men continued the work to hammer out a compromise that would be agreeable to both. Finally, Carter offered a document to Sadat that the Egyptian president found acceptable. It included a reference restoring the Sinai to Egypt. Begin unequivocally rejected the proposal; he would not contemplate dismantling settlements in the Sinai.

Sadat packed his bags and prepared to leave the U.S. In an emotionally charged confrontation, Carter prevailed upon the Egyptian president to return to the negotiating table. Sadat agreed. In an effort to break the stalemate, Israel's Defense Minister Ezer Weizman proffered the idea that Israel relinquish its airfields in the Sinai in return for U.S.-built bases in the Negev. As the incumbent facing a rapidly approaching election, Carter was amenable. He was determined to hammer out an accord between the two men and was counting on this agreement to bolster his presidency.

Brzezinski wrote of an encounter with Carter in mid-November. Carter was pessimistic about the progress in Israel and Egypt reaching an accord. In response to Brzezinski's, "How are things?" the president responded morosely, "Lousy." Carter felt that negotiations were collapsing and that neither principal player was as interested in reaching a peace pact as was the president.[656]

29

JIMMY CARTER,
CAMP COUNSELOR

*"The president added that 'by getting them [Begin and Sadat]
to Camp David, away from the press and out of the glare of publicity
and away from their own political constituencies, I think I can bring
them to understand each other's positions better.' The mountain-top
retreat was so isolated…. Begin would joke that he felt like he was
in a concentration camp."*[657]

HOW DID JIMMY CARTER VIEW HIS ROLE at Camp
David? Was he an interested bystander? Was he a catalyst? Was he
an intermediary? Carter perceived his role to be that of an agent of
change. Certainly he had a vested interest in the signing of a peace
agreement between Israel and Egypt. Carter could achieve two
major goals at Camp David: the salvation of his presidency and a
huge political step toward stability in the Middle East. He felt his
job was that of a skilled chef.

All of the ingredients for a successful banquet were on the
table; all Jimmy Carter had to do was mix them correctly. His recipe
was one of infinite delicacy. He had to carefully balance the relationship between the U.S. and OPEC (Organization of the Petroleum
Exporting Countries), between the administration and the Jewish

lobby, between the Middle East countries and U.S. corporations—a teaspoon here, a pinch there, maybe turn the fire up a notch. He also had to incorporate a heaping helping of his desire to win a second term in office. Carter mixed and measured the ingredients. The results: the *pièce de résistance and* the showpiece of his administration—the Camp David Accords signed and sealed.

Meanwhile, Menachem Begin was being pressured by the Knesset to surrender the Sinai settlements in exchange for a peace treaty with Egypt. When Begin conceded, the last major impediment had been eliminated. After thirteen days of deliberation, Carter's dream of a Middle East Peace Agreement in the form of the Camp David Accords had been realized. The official signing ceremony at the White House was all Carter had hoped it would be...and Carter, basking in the media coverage, was the man of the hour.

Eric Silver wrote of the Camp David triad in *Begin: The Haunted Prophet*, that Carter was certainly not neutral as an intermediary.[658]

Jimmy Carter wrote of the two men, "Sadat seemed to trust me too much, and Begin not enough."[659] In an interview with *Time* magazine, Carter explained further, "I would not even try to deny that I was pro-Sadat. He was completely open, courageous, generous, far-sighted. He was willing to ignore details to reach an ultimate goal of peace that was beneficial to him and to Egypt."[660]

Silver expounded on the negotiation strategy of the two men:

Sadat showed [Carter] some of his cards in advance...he succumbed to Sadat's charm. Sadat's demands were no less extreme than Begin's, but he left the haggling to his aides. It made it easier to sustain the pose of the reasonable and courageous man of peace. Begin, by contrast, was the most intransigent of the Israeli negotiators, scrutinizing every word and punctuation mark, beavering day and night.... throughout the negotiations, Begin beseeched Carter not to present Egyptian proposals as made-in-America.[661]

In 1995 I wrote of a meeting with Menachem Begin in my book *Save Jerusalem*. Chapter 2 recounted a meeting that I had with my dear friend:

> *I once asked Prime Minister Begin to speak to the controversial subject of the Israeli settlements in Judea and Samaria, what Israel's opponents called "the occupied territories." He began by sharing about his first meeting with President Carter.*
>
> *Begin responded: "We were in the cabinet room and President Carter asked me a question. But, in that question, he made a statement that was very negative. He said the settlements were illegal. I had prepared a counter question I wanted to pose to him.*
>
> *"It was a prepared improvisation. One day Winston Churchill was interviewed in his study. He said, 'I'm preparing my improvisations for question time in the House of Commons. Hard work!'*
>
> *"So, I had asked our Israeli Embassy in Washington to prepare a list of American cities that were named after Israeli cities in the Bible: Bethlehem, Shiloh, Hebron, and Bethel. Then I showed President Carter my list; it was very long. The American people love the Bible, and I asked him if he could imagine that the governor of Pennsylvania would proclaim that anyone could live in the city of Bethlehem, Pennsylvania, except Jews. President Carter agreed that such a man, if he did such a thing, would be guilty of racism.*
>
> *"Why? Because it was Bethlehem of Pennsylvania! Pennsylvania is in the United States, and the United States is a free country. So, I pointed out that I was governor of the state in which the original Bethlehem, and the original Jericho, and the original Shiloh were located. Did he expect me to say that everybody could live in those cities except Jews?*

"*Of course, he didn't. It would be absurd. Jews must have the right to settle in these places as much as anyone else.*

"*This land we occupy is Eretz Israel, the land of Israel, since the days of the prophet Samuel, three thousand years ago. We had a downfall later, but even the Romans called us 'Judea' until after the Bar-Kokhba revolt in the second century.*

"*Then, because the Jewish resistance had been so fierce and heroic and because the Emperor Hadrian had suffered such severe casualties, he decided to try to delete all memory of the connection between the people and that land. The Romans had done it with Carthage, why not here? So he renamed the area Syria et Palestina, using the name of our ancient enemies, the Philistines.*

"*So the word 'Palestine' came into all languages. Thus the preamble to the British mandate after World War I used these words: 'recognition having been given to the historical connection between the Jewish people and Palestine.' So, in spite of Hadrian, nobody forgot that it was our land. Every intelligent person understands that Palestine is a misnomer for the land of Israel.*

"*So we have a right to live in Judea and Samaria, and we will live there. That does not mean we want to evict even one Arab from his village or town. We never wanted to do that.*

"*For us living there today, there is an ever more pressing need for settlements. That is our national security. Without Jewish settlements in those hills, the PLO could easily hide in them and descend into the plain to kill our people whenever they liked.*"

I followed that question up with another for Mr. Begin; I asked if he was ever criticized for quoting the Bible. Mr. Begin replied:

"*When we face our various problems, we should always strive to live by the Bible. That is true for all humanity.*

This is the book which has kept the Jewish people alive; that is my belief. I am proud to quote from the Bible in substantiation of our rights. If anyone brings it up, I tell them I plead guilty to quoting the Bible on matters of public policy; I don't apologize.

"Ben-Gurion had a wonderful saying. He was my opponent, of course, but it was a wonderful saying when he addressed the British Royal Commission. He said, 'Some people say that the mandate is our Bible, but it is not. The Bible is our mandate.'

"You know something? Every time you read the Bible, you find something new. Every Saturday night a group of sages gather at my house and we study the Bible together. Every time, we find something new. The book which has been studied for thousands of years by great rabbis, professors, and sages still yields something new every time you study it. It's wonderful."

Lastly, I asked Prime Minister Begin about his thoughts on a Palestinian Arab state in the West Bank (Judea and Samaria.) He answered:

"You know, there are 22 sovereign Arab states from the Persian Gulf to the shores of the Atlantic Ocean. I would like every man with a molecule of feeling of justice to ask himself: should the Arab people have 22 states and the Jews none?

"If the Arabs occupied 22 sovereign states, we would be trapped on a narrow plain between the hills and the Mediterranean. They would get up there in those hills with the Soviet-made missiles they're already using, and they would make a hostage of every child in Israel. They haven't abandoned their plan to 'liquidate the Zionist entity' as they like to call us. No nation in the world would agree to that.

"I would like to remind the Free World nations that wish us to agree to it anyway that the PLO is an alliance with the Soviet Union. Judea and Samaria would be a Soviet base in no time if we let them have a Palestinian state there. You can reach Bethlehem in two-and-one-half hours flying by jet from Odessa in the southern Ukraine. It would be better than Afghanistan for them.

"From Samaria, they could move south, east, west, wherever they liked. Is that what the Free World wants: a Soviet base in the heart of the Middle East?

"That is why President Carter said he was opposed to a Palestinian state. Some European countries are so thirsty for oil and petrodollars they would rather surrender. It would not be the first time they surrendered to pressure. It happened in the thirties and brought disaster on the world. Do we want to repeat that disaster?

"A Palestinian state is a mortal danger to Israel and a great peril to the Free World. We never agreed to a Palestinian state at Camp David. What we agreed to was autonomy as a way to solve the problem of the Palestinian Arabs. With autonomy they can elect their own ministers of council to deal with daily affairs, and we shall not interfere at all.

"This would be a great historic change for them. Under Turkish, British, and Jordanian occupation they lived under the whip. The only thing we want to retain is the matter of security. It we do not, the PLO will come in....

"The Camp David agreement calls for security for Israel and autonomy for the Arab inhabitants. This agreement should be carried out by all of us."[662]

Following Khomeini's revolution in Iran, Yasser Arafat charged that the U.S. had cast the Shah in the role of enforcer of the Accords. He believed, "The Shah was to control Iraq, Saudi Arabia, and the Gulf States so that the Iraqi army...remained tied to the

Persians.... Since the revolution in Iran, Iraq can now throw its army fully into the battle against the Zionist enemy.... Iran's new chief of staff regards his country now a confrontation state against Israel."[663]

A former U.S. Ambassador to Egypt, Hermann Eilts, believed that Anwar Sadat had two great disappointments regarding the agreement. Sadat had accepted Carter's word that he could provide support from the Saudis, but that support was never realized. Secondly, Sadat believed that the halt to Israeli settlements would be permanent; Begin insisted it was only a three-month moratorium.[664]

In 1978 Menachem Begin and Anwar El Sadat were nominated for the Nobel Peace Prize; Jimmy Carter was not. Golda Meir, in her own inimitable way, commented on the nomination of the two peace-seekers:

> *"I'm not sure in the end whether Begin and Sadat will get the Nobel, but for certain both should get the Oscar."*[665]

Despite Meir's reservations, the two brave statesmen won the Nobel Peace Prize. At the awards ceremony in Stockholm, Sweden, the presentation read, in part:

> *The Norwegian Nobel Committee has awarded the Peace Prize for 1978 to Anwar El Sadat, President of Egypt, and Menachem Begin, Prime Minister of Israel, for their contribution to the two frame agreements on peace in the Middle East, and on peace between Egypt and Israel, which were signed at Camp David on September 17, 1978....*
>
> *The award of the Prize to the President of Egypt, Anwar El Sadat, and the Prime Minister of Israel, Menachem Begin, is moreover historical in the wider sense, in that we only know of one previous peace agreement between Egypt and Israel. This, as Israeli scholars have revealed, took place some 3,000 years ago; it was the peace concluded between King David's son, wise King Solomon, and the Egyptian Pharaoh....*

May I express the hope that this Nobel Peace Prize ceremony, enacted in our small and wintry country, tucked away near the Arctic Circle, may provide an enduring reminder to the world that it was here that representatives of Egypt and Israel shook hands as they celebrated the greatest of all victories—conciliation and lasting peace based on respect for human rights and human dignity.[666]

In reality, the Camp David Accords were worth little more than the paper on which they were written. They were, in fact, labeled by one writer "a misty penumbra of formulational ambiguity."[667] Key issues between the two countries had been glossed over, and neither leader seemed willing to offer further compromises. In March 1979 Carter traveled to Egypt and to Israel to confer with Sadat and Begin. The result of the trip was, finally, a signed peace treaty between the two nations.

Despite the fact that the Palestinians were a central theme of the Middle East peace initiative, and that Carter wanted to include them in the now-defunct Geneva conference; they were not represented in the talks between the Israelis and Egyptians. Nevertheless, Yasser Arafat and his Palestinian Liberation Organization, as well as other self-styled terrorist groups, failed to bolster the position of the Palestinian people by continuing attacks against the Israelis:

> » February 1978: A bomb planted on a bus filled to capacity exploded in Jerusalem; two were murdered, forty-six injured.

> » March 11, 1978: A Fatah terrorist murdered Gail Rubin, niece of U.S. Senator Abraham Ribicoff, on the Tel Aviv beach.

> » March 11, 1978: PLO terrorists seized a bus on the coastal road, killing thirty-five men, women, and children.

> » March 17, 1978: PLO terrorists launched Katuysha rockets on the Western Galilee, killing two and wounding two.

> » June 2, 1978: A PLO terrorist bombed a Jerusalem bus, killing six and wounding nineteen.

» August 20, 1978: PLO terrorists attacked El Al crew members in the London airport, killing a stewardess and wounding eight.

» December 21, 1978: PLO terrorists launched a Katuysha rocket, killing one and wounding ten in Kiryat Shmona.[668]

By the time William Jefferson Clinton assumed office as the 42nd president of the United States, Yasser Arafat was a household name and had become a major player in the game of Middle Eastern Russian roulette.

One can only wonder how a fanatical terrorist like Arafat could achieve the position of viable "peace partner" with Israel. Perhaps the answer can be found in advice that Arafat received from dictator Nicolae Ceauçescu: "In the shadow of your government-in-exile [PLO], you can keep as many operational groups as you want, as long as they are not publicly connected with your name. They could mount endless operations all around the world, while your name and your 'government' would remain pristine and unspoiled, ready for negotiations and further recognition."[669] It was not surprising then to learn that while Arafat groveled at Khomeini's feet, he was busily cheering on the Soviets in Afghanistan and providing assistance to Syria in its assault on Lebanon.

So massive was the Soviet support of the PLO that, when in 1982 Israel invaded PLO bunkers in Lebanon, it took 4,300 trucks to transport the war matériel to Israel. The trucks were said to be laden with "5,630 tons of ammunition; 1,320 [Soviet] armored vehicles including...tanks; 1,352 anti-tank weapons; 82 artillery pieces, 215 mortars; 62 Katuysha rocket launchers; 196 anti-aircraft guns; and 33,303 small arms. These arms had been supplied by the Soviet Union and Warsaw Pact countries Red China, North Korea, and Vietnam."[670]

Given the PLO support for the Soviet-backed regimes in the area, it is no wonder that, because of his agreement with Israel, Sadat was increasingly isolated by his Arab neighbors. King Hussein of Jordan implemented economic sanctions against Egypt, and Saudi Arabia simply gave the Egyptian leader the silent treatment.

In 1981, during a military parade, a group of gunmen charged the dais on which Sadat sat with a number of foreign dignitaries. Two grenades exploded near the stands as automatic gunfire raked the area. By the time Sadat's bodyguards responded to the assault, Anwar El Sadat lay mortally wounded. He died within hours. Eleven members of the official entourage were killed, including the ambassador to Cuba, the Irish minister of defense and four U.S. military liaison officers. There are many who believe, myself among them, that Anwar Sadat's murder was tied indirectly to his overtures to Israel.

President Ronald Reagan said of Sadat, "America has lost a great friend, the world has lost a great statesman, and mankind has lost a champion of peace."[671]

C H A P T E R

30

BLOWBACK: THE LIBERAL LEFT'S LEGACY OF TERRORISM

"You should not be concerned that I am biased. I am much more harsh with the Israelis.... I have a permanent, unassailable commitment to do what I can for the Palestinians."
(JIMMY CARTER TO YASSER ARAFAT)[672]

THE TERM "BLOWBACK" was apparently coined by the CIA to describe "the unintended consequences of covert operations."[673] Ironically, its first usage has been traced back to the 1953 *coup d'état* in Iran. "Blowback" ideally describes the events that have transpired since Jimmy Carter and his administration first conspired to oust the Shah of Iran.

The Old Testament prophet Hosea lamented, "For they have sown the wind, and they shall reap the whirlwind."[674] During his tenure in office, James Earl Carter Jr. sowed to the wind; America and Israel are not the only nations worldwide that continue to reap the whirlwind. Carter's "liberation" of Iran from the Shah set in motion events that have resulted in untold death and destruction for the past twenty-eight years.

Mohammad Reza Pahlavi and Ruhollah Khomeini, despite their disparities, had similar visions for Iran: a primary leadership role in the Gulf region. The two men had vastly different ideas on how to achieve that dominance. Khomeini espoused the theory that only a theocracy with not only the Iranian people but the Muslim world as a whole, firmly under the iron fist of Islamic radicalism, would suffice. The Shah's vision was the diametrical opposite; he felt that a modernized and democratic Iran backed by strategic alliances with the West would afford his country the respect and admiration he sought from the nations in the region.

Khomeini, though outwardly advocating a coalition with other Arab countries in the vicinity, in reality wanted only to dominate through his own brand of radicalism. In order to begin his march beyond the boundaries of Iran, however, Khomeini had to first subdue the Persian influence and replace it with a maniacal devotion to fundamentalist Islam. The Ayatollah knew too that he would have to eradicate all traces of the Western influence from Iran.

For the West in general and the Carter administration in particular, the loss of a major ally in the Gulf region was a devastating blow. Perhaps Khomeini never intended to completely sever ties with the United States; only the Ayatollah knew with certainty. Whatever his plan, it was thwarted by a few purported "Iranian students" who made the determination to attack the U.S. Embassy on November 4, 1979. When the dust settled and Khomeini assessed the situation, he was left with little choice but to back the students and forever lose any hope of an ongoing alliance with America. Rather than a future ally, Washington had become a menace. The Iranian revolutionaries now saw the U.S. through Khomeini's eyes—"The Great Satan" that must be defeated.

For the Carter administration and future U.S. relationships in the Persian Gulf region, "Iran's location at the perimeter of the Arab world, its economic and military ties to Israel, its oil and its traditional enmity with Iraq and the Soviet Union, made it next to irreplaceable."[675] With the Shah's departure, Israel lost a strategic, though understandably covert, ally as well. The Israelis had a difficult time following Khomeini's power play, but they did make several tries to restore relations between the two countries. Then-General Ariel Sharon was in favor of sending Israeli troops into Iran to preserve the Shah's monarchy.[676] Sharon would later warn American leaders not to allow Khomeini's rabid rhetoric to invalidate Iran's strategic importance in the Persian Gulf.

Many in Israel's upper echelon had clung to Prime Minister David Ben-Gurion's periphery doctrine. This doctrine, as defined by Ben-Gurion, "held that the improbability of achieving peace with the surrounding Arab states forced Israel to build alliances with the non-Arab states of the periphery—primarily Iran, Turkey, and Ethiopia—as well as with non-Arab minorities such as the Kurds and the Lebanese Christians."[677] A note in Ben-Gurion's diary reveals his mindset about this attempt at an alliance: "We are in historic times, and this opportunity for action will not repeat itself. Elias has notified me of Turkey's agreement in principle to a meeting of the two prime ministers. If the Arabs find out about this, the whole thing will explode, and then the Americans will interfere as well."[678]

Having already lost the support of Haile Selassie in Ethiopia, Israel was anxiously searching for ways to shore up the Shah's regime. Prime Minister Menachem Begin, under whom Sharon served, was as hawkish as his general. He believed that the fanatical arm of Islam responded only to a show of force and strength greater than its own. Begin feared that with the loss of Iran as an ally, Iraq would become a major player in the Middle East and pose a deadly danger to Israel. The prime minister was right on target.

This periphery doctrine, coupled with the treaty signed by Israel and Egypt, would continue to skew Israel's view of Iran and Iraq into the 1980s. The Israeli government continued to view Iran favorably. The author of *Khomeini and Israel* wrote of Defense Minister Yitzhak Rabin's unchanged opinion that Iran was "Israel's best friend and we do not intend to change our position in relation to Tehran, because Khomeini's regime will not last forever."[679] In that assumption Israel was wrong; in many cases dead wrong, as Yasser Arafat began to court Saddam Hussein, who then funded PLO suicide bombers and encouraged attacks on Israel.

From the moment Ayatollah Ruhollah Khomeini stepped from the plane onto Iranian soil in 1978 and, on April 1, 1979, (April Fools day) declared his Islamic Republic, he had given little thought to Israel. Instead, he was emboldened and determined to begin the spread of fanatical Islam using a network of terrorist organizations. According to the Council for Foreign Relations, today Iran supports such proxy groups as Hamas and Palestinian Islamic Jihad[680]; and Brookings Institution reports that another sub-contractor, Hezbollah in Lebanon, has been responsible for killing more Americans than any other single global terrorist group.[681]

I could fill page after page with terror attacks that have implicated Iran or Iranian proxies since the taking of the American hostages in 1979. Below are just a few instances:

Iran's proxies have attempted to infiltrate and/or smuggle arms and explosives into France, Germany, Saudi Arabia, Tunisia, and Turkey, to name a few.

Kidnappings and murders:

> *William Buckley, American, kidnapped and murdered by Iran's Revolutionary Guards; Peter Kilburn, librarian, American University, Beirut, kidnapped and murdered; Michel Seurat, French writer, kidnapped and murdered by hostage-takers; Colonel William Higgins, American officer assigned to the UN in Lebanon, kidnapped and executed by Iranian agents; Professor Hitoshi Igarashi, Japanese translator of Salman Rushdie's Satanic Verses, stabbed to death; Ettore Capriolo, Italian translator, survived being stabbed; William Nygaard, the Norwegian publisher of Rushdie's book, barely survived an assassination attempt in Oslo in 1993; Hikmet Cettin, a Turkish journalist, murdered.*

Iran has been linked to bombings worldwide:

> *1983 U.S. Embassy in Beirut (sixty-one killed, 120 injured);*
> *U.S. Marine headquarters in Beirut (241 killed, 80 seriously*
> *injured); series of Paris bombings in 1986; 1989 bombings*
> *in Mecca (scores injured); Amia Jewish Center, Buenos Aires*
> *(95 killed, 230 injured); 1996 bombing outside the Khobar*
> *Towers in Saudi Arabia (20 murdered, nearly 400 wounded).*

Hijackings and airline explosions:

» 1983—Air France 747—plane destroyed at Tehran's Mehrabad Airport.

» 1985—TWA Boeing 727—U.S. Navy diver, Robert Dean Stethem, severely beaten and later executed by hijackers.

» 1987—Air Afrique DC-10—French passenger murdered.

» 1988—Kuwaiti 747—landed at Mashhad, Iran; two passengers murdered.

» 1988—Pan Am Flight 103 exploded in midair over Lockerbie, Scotland, 270 passengers from 21 countries perished.[682]

Iran and 9/11:

> *The 9/11 Commission report linked Iran to at least facilitat-*
> *ing the travel plans of the 9/11 terrorist/murderers by not*
> *stamping their passports.[683] There is also evidence that Iran*
> *assisted al-Qaeda when that organization was forced to*
> *withdraw from Afghanistan in 2001 and has, in fact, allowed*
> *that rogue group to continue to operate from within Iran's*
> *borders.*

In July 1979 President Jimmy Carter inked a document launching America on the path that on September 11, 2001, would lead to the deaths of 2,974 innocent civilians; another twenty-four individuals are still listed as missing. What was the document? It was the first order to send aid to the Afghanistan rebels fighting against the Soviet invaders. The aid would provide the weapons and know-how to train the rebels in terror tactics; lead to the creation of the Taliban; and give rise to the scion of a Saudi prince, a ruthless young man named Osama bin Laden, founder of the vile and violent al-Qaeda.

In 1980 the Afghan rebels were aided by a $30 million infusion from the Carter administration. The ante was raised in Carter's 1981 budget to $50 million. It marked a rise in significant aid for the resistance from international sources.[684] It was generally thought that U.S. aid to the Afghanistan *Mujahedeen* was initiated in 1980. Not so; according to a document declassified on March 4, 2004, President Jimmy Carter signed the directive on July 3, 1979, approving covert assistance to anti-Soviet rebels in Kabul.

The directive from the president favored supporting insurgent propaganda and other psychological operations in Afghanistan, establishing radio contact with the Afghan people through a third country, and providing support either in funds or non-military supplies.[685] In December 1979 the CIA would begin shipping what would be described in a Carter directive as "lethal" arms to Pakistan for distribution to the Afghan rebels. According to CIA officer Charles Cogan, "the first arms, which were mainly.... 303 Enfield rifles, arrived on the 10th of January, and of course this was done in collaboration with the Pakistanis."[686]

It was not only the Liberal Left under Carter that supplied funds to the *Mujahedeen*, but also the liberal Church in America. Islamic *Mujahedeen* warriors were invited to address the churches where they were applauded for their "spiritual courage in the common fight against Marxism and godlessness."[687]

Although seemingly caught off-guard by the Soviet invasion of Afghanistan, Carter's national security advisor was prepared to put forth a strategy to defeat the Russians. In a memorandum to the president Zbigniew Brzezinski suggested: "Our ultimate goal is the withdrawal of Soviet troops from Afghanistan. Even if this is not attainable, we should make Soviet involvement as costly as possible."[688] In fact, the Afghanistan invasion would be the beginning of the end of the entire Soviet empire. In the years since the Afghan invasion, it has become even more obvious that fanatical Islam, not communism, is now the greater challenge. While areas such as Ethiopia, South Yemen, and Southeast Asia were once assaulted by communism, Islam is making direct inroads and supplanting what former Secretary of State Cyrus Vance thought would be a communist stronghold.

Perhaps the pertinent question is this: Was the Carter administration caught off-guard, or was it a ploy to divert attention from the truth? In an interview with National Security Advisor Brzezinski in *Le Nouvel Observateur*, he confirmed that the intervention in Afghanistan actually began nearly six months before the invasion in the form of arms to the *Mujahedeen*, or resistance fighters. Brzezinski responded to the interviewer's question regarding arms supplies:

> *According to the official version of history, CIA aid to the Mujahedeen began during 1980; that is to say, after the Soviet army invaded Afghanistan, 24 Dec 1979. But the reality, secretly guarded until now, is completely otherwise. Indeed, it was July 3, 1979, that President Carter signed the first directive for secret aid to the opponents of the pro-Soviet regime in Kabul. And that very day, I wrote a note to the president in which I explained to him that in my opinion this aid was going to induce a Soviet military intervention.*[689]

American intervention in Afghanistan goes much farther back in Afghan history. In 1956 the United States denied requests from the government in Kabul to supply arms and approve loans to aid the country. With this rejection, the Afghanis turned to the Soviet Union for aide. The USSR was more than willing to lure the country into its communist stronghold by investing in vast projects of tactical importance to the Soviets, i.e., highways, port facilities, military installations, and pipelines to carry natural gas. It was the gas line that would be the only really successful project of the decade. Estimates are that the Russians had loaned the Kabul government in excess of a billion dollars, an enormous amount of money in the late 1950s and 1960s, and at such exorbitant interest rates that Afghanistan would never be able to crawl out from under Soviet control. By the early 1970s the Russians had become Afghanistan's biggest loan holder.

In 1973 King Zahir Shah, who to his credit had tried to implement democratic principles in Afghanistan, was overthrown when a group of officers declared a government by the army and ended the rule of the monarchy. The group chose the king's cousin, Mohammad Daoud, a former foreign minister, as their figurehead. His reign as head of the government was short-lived; he and his family were murdered in 1978. It was this latest uprising in Afghanistan that brought to power the communist and pro-Soviet People's Democratic Party of Afghanistan. The new president, Nur Muhammad Taraki, was simply another figurehead for Hafizullah Amin. Amin, thought to be pro-American and perhaps even a CIA operative, was kept under surveillance by Brezhnev's minions.

An uprising in Herat, Afghanistan, in March 1979 resulting in the murders of several Soviet "advisors" led Taraki and Amin to request assistance from the USSR. The rebellion of an Afghan army unit and the attempt to gain control of the fortress of Balahisar in the midst of Kabul led the Soviets to suspect collusion with the CIA. It was, however, a later request for two or three battalions of troops which paved the way for a full-fledged Soviet offensive by the end of 1979. Even in Herat, the influence of the heretical Khomeini was felt. Khomeini followers in Iran were supportive of the uprising in Afghanistan.

Following the incursion, Carter administration insiders were of the opinion that Taraki and Amin had never asked for Soviet assistance even though both had suggested to the Russians that a small infusion of troops might be needed. By that time, however, neither man was able to confirm nor deny the allegations; Taraki had supposedly been smothered to death while asleep and Amin was killed when the Soviets marched into Kabul. Nothing Carter had learned in office prior to the Russian invasion had prepared him for the kind of Soviet aggression he saw in Afghanistan. In the end, historians will judge whether it was the loss of Afghanistan to the Soviets or the loss of Iran to Khomeini, or a combination of both, that hampered Carter's bid for reelection.

In a declassified top-secret memorandum signed by Gromyko, suspected U.S. interference is recorded simply as "foreign support." Gromyko writes that such interference was "threatening the achievements of the April [Afghan] revolution and the security interests.... in accordance with the provisions of the Soviet-Afghan treaty of 1978, the decision was made to send the necessary contingent of the Soviet Army to Afghanistan."[690]

The Carter administration and the world were to witness the Soviet invasion of Afghanistan on December 24, 1979. Days before the CIA had reported Soviet activity near Kabul. On Christmas Day, Russian transport planes dropped into Afghan airports nationwide and disgorged highly trained troops. Within days, the Russians had some forty thousand troops on the ground. The number would climb to over 85 thousand within just weeks.

A group of elite Soviet forces attacked the presidential palace in Kabul and assassinated Prime Minister Hafizullah Amin. It lay to rest the Soviet claims that the prime minister had issued an invitation to the Soviets to move into Afghanistan. A later announce-ment regarding Mr. Amin's fate indicated that the leader had been executed for so-called "crimes against the state." Foreign minister Andrei Gromyko justified the Soviet's actions by accusing the CIA of trying to undermine Muslim areas inside the USSR, and especially in the Hindu Kush mountain region. He cast his vote in favor of the invasion at a Politburo meeting on December 12, 1979.[691]

Apparently the Soviets felt the move was a necessary one in the Cold War between the two world superpowers. The Americans had unlimited access to the Persian Gulf through their association with the monarchy in Iran. Pakistan also was favorable to the U.S. and was, in fact, aiding in preparing Arab guerillas for war against the ruling Afghan regime of Taraki. A U.S. presence in the region led the Russians to feel more than justified in intervening in Afghanistan.

While the Carter administration was apparently blindsided by the invasion, the French apparently had inside information. The story is told that Count de Marenches advised *Newsweek* reporter Arnaud de Borchgrave to go to Kabul if he wished to find the scoop of the decade. De Borchgrave took the Count's advice and found himself in Kabul three weeks before the Soviet invasion on December 24, 1979.[692]

Radio Kabul was replete with announcements that a group of Afghan soldiers had staged a *coup d'état* in order to reinstate a former leader, Babrak Karmal. It was not at all difficult for intelligence sources to discover that so-called Radio Kabul was broadcasting from the Soviet side of the Afghanistan border.

Brzezinski suggested to Carter that shipments of funds and arms as well as technical instruction be continued to the Afghan resistance. In a December 26, 1979, memo to the president, the national security advisor wrote:

> As mentioned to you a week or so ago, we are now facing a regional crisis. Both Iran and Afghanistan are in turmoil, and Pakistan is both unstable internally and extremely apprehensive externally. If the Soviets succeed in Afghanistan and [words blacked out] the age-long dream of Moscow to have direct access to the Indian Ocean will have been fulfilled.... Accordingly, the Soviet intervention in Afghanistan poses for us an extremely grave challenge.[693]

Brzezinski was overjoyed as he told *The Guardian,* "that the Russians had been drawn into what he saw as his cleverly baited trap. The day Soviet forces crossed the border he wrote to Carter, saying: 'We now have the opportunity to give the USSR their

Vietnam War.'"[694] Brzezinski saw the Afghan invasion as a precursor to undermining the Soviets and the total disintegration of the USSR. President Carter believed that the Muslims in Afghanistan and other Middle East countries would prove to be effective American allies against the spread of communism.

In 1998 Brzezinski granted an interview to the French weekly, *Le Nouvel Observateur*. Brzezinski confirmed to the French reporter what had long been suspected: the U.S. had offered aid to the Afghan rebels before the Russian invasion, not after. Among his admissions during the interview, Brzezinski confirmed the U.S. had overtly increased the chances that the Soviets would push into Afghanistan by providing aid to the Afghan rebels. Said the former national security advisor:

> *"It was July 3, 1979, that President Carter signed the first directive for secret aid to the opponents of the pro-Soviet regime in Kabul. And that very day, I wrote a note to the president in which I explained to him that in my opinion this aid was going to induce a Soviet military intervention.... That secret operation was an excellent idea. It had the effect of drawing the Russians into the Afghan trap."* [When asked by the French journalist if he regretted having armed future terrorists Brzezinski, in his own inimitable, pompous rhetoric, summed up U.S. covert intervention in the region with]: *"What is more important in world history? The Taliban or the collapse of the Soviet empire? Some agitated Moslems or the liberation of Central Europe and the end of the cold war?"*[695]

The national security advisor was supported in his theories by those in Washington who had withstood the CIA disgrace of the 1960s and 1970s. These men were certain that U.S. support of the Afghan rebels fighting the USSR would be totally gratifying.

President Carter was incensed at the Soviet actions, and at Leonid Ilyich Brezhnev, General Secretary of the Communist Party of the Soviet Union, for the cavalier way in which he confirmed the invasion of Afghanistan. Accessing the hotline to the White House, Brezhnez announced that the foray into Afghanistan had been for the good of the people to protect them from outside aggression.

Just months earlier, Carter had traded the traditional, if somewhat comical, greeting of hugs and kisses with the Soviet leader in Vienna. Now, he felt that he had been forced to assume the role of the fool. Soon after taking office, Jimmy Carter rejoiced over the fact that he felt America was "free of that inordinate fear of communism, which once led us to embrace any dictator who joined us in our fear."[696] He reversed that opinion the moment the Russians crossed the border into Afghanistan. Said Carter: "This action of the Soviets has made a more dramatic change in my own opinion of what the Soviets' ultimate goals are than anything they've done in the previous time I've been in office."[697]

Carter was somehow able to overlook the fact that for years the U.S. Navy had patrolled the Indian Ocean and Pakistan was firmly under U.S. control. He nimbly sidestepped knowledge of the informal but effective "Safari Club," a group of influential leaders whose expressed purpose was to embark on covert operations for the CIA in order to assist the West in Third World countries. (Club meetings were held in Saudi Arabia, France, and Egypt.) The men involved, including Kamal Adham of Saudi Arabia (also an advisor to King Faisal), King Hassan II of Morocco, Anwar Sadat of Egypt, French intelligence head Count Alexandre de Marenches, and the Shah of Iran, would undertake anti-Communist missions for the U.S. The Soviets obviously saw the major threat in the region coming not from the Afghans but from the Western-controlled (U.S.) entities.

Another area in which the Safari Club was of assistance was in Somalia. The tiny country became a Soviet client in the 1960s, with the Russians providing loans to arm and train the Somali army. The USSR provided Somalia with a "substantial number of T-34 tanks, armored personnel carriers, MiG-15 and MiG-17 aircraft, small arms, and ammunition. Approximately 300 Soviet military advisers deployed to Somalia to train the army, and about 500

Somali pilots, officers, and technicians received training in the Soviet Union. Until Mohamed Siad Barre seized power in 1969, Somalia's Western orientation and small amounts of United States and West German aid to the Somali police force limited the impact of Soviet military assistance. After the coup, however, Somalia's President Siad Barre embraced scientific socialism and the Soviet Union became Somalia's major supplier of military matériel."[698]

When Barre severed ties with the Soviets in 1977 the Shah had pled with the U.S. State Department to support the Somali leader. Seeing that the U.S. was lukewarm at best regarding Barre's regime, Pahlavi bolstered the Somali leader by providing small arms a nd ammunition. Egypt too, at the suggestion of the Safari Club, provided outdated Soviet war matériel to Barre's troops.

When Jimmy Carter took office in January of 1977, his new team members Cyrus Vance and Andrew Young campaigned for a lighter hand in the region that included Somalia and Ethiopia. Unfortunately for Carter and U.S. interests, the Soviets had adopted more blatantly hostile methods. While Ethiopia was torn by internal revolution, the Russians recruited the Somalis and aided them in planning an invasion of the Ogaden Desert region of Ethiopia. In spite of the pending military incursion, Carter halted the sale of arms to Ethiopia under the same guise as he abandoned the Shah of Iran, human rights issues. The Soviets were overjoyed at the turn of events and Carter's sanctimonious stance. The USSR simply provided the matériel that Carter had declined to supply.

Writing for the *National Review*, Robert D. Kaplan summed up Carter's tactics in the sub-Sahara this way:

> *Had Carter promptly armed the Somalis he might have moderated the behavior of both [its leader] Mengistu, and the Soviets in the Horn. His decision not to do so made for a policy that was more sanctimonious than virtuous.... as the example of Ethiopia shows, when it comes to dealing with brutal regimes, [Carter's] instincts are not to be trusted.*[699]

The haunting outcome of U.S. policies in Somalia and Ethiopia would be the bloody ambush in Mogadishu: 18 U.S. Marines dead and 84 wounded.

31

UNDER THE
MICROSCOPE

"Not only has Carter palled around with Yasser Arafat, Kim Jong-Il,
Fidel Castro, and the Chinese oligarchs, he has always bristled at
those who dared label his buddies 'terrorists' or 'dictators.'"
(G I L   T R O Y) [700]

WHEN JIMMY CARTER'S PURPORTED ROLE as an anti-
war president is placed under the microscope, one has to look only
as far as his own commentary to discover the flaw in casting. In his
last State of the Union address on January 23, 1980, Carter notified
the listening audience that an "attempt by any outside force to gain
control of the Persian Gulf region will be regarded as an assault on
the vital interests of the United States of America, and such force will
be repelled by any means necessary, including military force."

Despite the above evidence, to the contrary Carter soon
adopted the role of dove and accused President George H. W. Bush
(41) of being the warmonger. In 1990 Carter deliberately tried
to circumvent President Bush's endeavors to gain UN Security Council consent to take action to free Kuwait from the grip of
Saddam Hussein. Carter sent letters to every head of state

represented on the Security Council, imploring them to deny the resolution. Carter urged the leaders to support the Arab League, instead of the move to liberate a sovereign nation that had suffered an unprovoked attack from a neighboring strongman. Not surprisingly, the former president tried to tie the conflict to the Palestinian issue. (Money speaks loudly; not always sensibly, but loudly.) Of course, Carter has been very vocal about the Iraq conflict, and equally vocal in his denunciation of President George H. W. Bush.

President Bush (41) learned, as did Bill Clinton after him, that Jimmy Carter had (and still has) his own agenda; and it often does not resemble that of the sitting president of the United States. Carter's alliance with Yasser Arafat embellished his persona in the Arab world but damaged his standing with the Bush (41) administration.

Carter further strained relations with the president when, on November 19, 1989, he wrote a letter to members of the UN Security Council and a number of world leaders urging them to enter into negotiations with Saddam Hussein before liberating Kuwait from the grip of the Iraqi dictator. He suggested that members of what would become the coalition to liberate Kuwait not assume the role of lemmings and blindly follow the Bush administration over what Carter saw as the edge of a cliff. It was a call for the rest of the world to abandon Kuwait to Hussein and to turn a blind eye to U.S. efforts to stop the Iraqi dictator. President Bush was incensed at Carter's interference. According to historian Douglas Brinkley, Bush thought Carter's tactics violated the code of ethics for a former president.[701]

Operation Desert Storm gave Jimmy Carter another opportunity to partake of what seems to have become a favorite pastime: Israel bashing. In a January 2, 1991, opinion piece for *The New York Times*, Carter wrote:

> *"'Linked' or not, there is no way to separate the crisis in the Gulf from the Israeli-Palestinian question. Following a settlement with Iraq, either through peace or war, even greater*

pressure will emerge within the international community to convene a peace conference. United Nations resolutions on the Middle East, from four decades ago to the present, have been given a new vitality and will not go away again. Now is a propitious time for Israel to come forward with a genuine peace initiative, and President Bush and congressional leaders should do everything possible to encourage such a move.[702]

So, Saddam Hussein invades neighboring Arab country Kuwait, ravages the nation, sets fire to its oilfields, rapes and pillages the population, and it's purported to be Israel's fault. Such mental machinations totally disregard logic.

Once Jimmy Carter had abandoned the Shah, America's staunchest ally in the Persian Gulf region, Pandora's Box was opened and the demon of terrorism escaped. As the prophet Hosea predicted, the whirlwind had been unleashed. Islamic fanaticism has inarguably become the most important issue with which the West has to contend. Once democracy was sought by the multitudes as the panacea for all ills; now Islam appeals to the masses with its seemingly unlimited resources due to oil money, its global spread, and its message of world domination through intimidation. Khomeini's success against the Shah and the resulting Islamic revolution became a model for other terrorists worldwide.

In 1982 Iran scored a logistical victory when Revolutionary Guard troops were moved into Lebanon. When both Israeli and American troops were forced to withdraw, as were the Italian and French, Lebanon was destined to become a hotbed of terrorist activities. Israel and America became the main targets of Syrian-backed and Iranian-funded Hezbollah. The plan: to wage war against Israel, America's staunchest ally in the Middle East. Major General Ataollah Saleh, an Iranian, declared, "The Americans will run away, leaving their illegitimate child [Israel] behind, and then Muslims will know what to do."[703] Khomeini then set his sights on the Iraq holy city of Karbala, and from there marching on to liberate Jerusalem.

Riding the wave of Khomeini and his predecessors, a new president in Iran, Mahmoud Ahmadinejad, is utilizing every opportunity. Following the death of the Grand Ayatollah in June of 1989, Ali Akbar Rafsanjani, a former student of Khomeini's and dedicated to his cause of establishing an Islamic Republic, became president of Iran and successfully served two terms. His successor, Ali Mohammad Khatami-Ardakani, won a landslide victory in 1997 and served until replaced in 2005 by Tehran mayor Ahmadinejad.

It appears that under Ahmadinejad's regime Iran is returning to the tactics of Khomeini. Ahmadinejad seems to have embraced the Ayatollah's dream of Iran as the primary leader in the Persian Gulf region. Khomeini had foreseen a time when Islamic revolutionaries would embrace his ideology, unseat American-backed leaders, and form Islamic republics based on Khomeini's interpretation of the Koran. Unlike the Shah, who based his monarchy on the belief in a strong armed forces and a U.S. ally, the Ayatollah believed his version of fanatical Islam and his fervor would be sufficient to defeat any adversaries, inside or outside Iran. It is also possible that the formidable Ayatollah had visions of routing Saddam Hussein in Iraq and joining the two countries into one dominant Islamic power.

Perhaps Ahmadinejad was "channeling" the late Ayatollah Khomeini when he passionately declared the UN Security Council had little, if any, control over Iran's nuclear pursuits. Ahmadinejad has asserted that the resolutions passed by the Security Council are worthless and, in his words, "illegitimate." That could be due in part to the fact that the United States is responsible for having given Iran the technology and equipment to implement the nuclear cycle and ultimately produce a nuclear bomb. Yes, Washington is responsible. During the reign of the Shah, Richard Nixon's Secretary of State Henry Kissinger negotiated the sale of nuclear equipment to Iran. Why should Ahmadinejad not mock warnings of sanctions against Iran, just as Khomeini did? Why? The country threatening the sanctions is the U.S., the very country that, along with its allies, was responsible for bolstering Iran's nuclear program as early as the late 1960s.[704]

With Ahmadinejad's threats falling on their ears, our European "allies" are breaking all speed records to assist the U.S. in confronting Iran and halting its nuclear ambitions, aren't they? Of course not! As it did during the hostage crisis in 1980, NATO has turned a blind eye and deaf ear to America's pleas for help despite the diminutive dictator in Iran threatening to "wipe Israel from the map," sponsoring global terrorism, and continuing to thumb his proverbial nose at the Nuclear Non-Proliferation Treaty. I wonder just what our NATO allies *will* do, and when?

Ahmadinejad's utter contempt for the UN Security Council in particular and the world in general was never more apparent than in March and April 2006. In March the Security Council insisted Iran halt the enrichment of uranium; in April Ahmadinejad proclaimed a major advancement in his country's enrichment program. Did his actions anger the Europeans? Not! It only encouraged them to offer Iran's president a list of incentives, one of which was the possibility of talks with the United States.

The proffered enticements included wording closely resembling that of Jimmy Carter when, in his 1981 State of the Union address, he made an offer to Khomeini, the mad mullah of Tehran: "We are prepared to work with the government of Iran to develop a new and mutually beneficial relationship."[705] The latest, almost identical offer to Iran's government came from international envoy Javier Solana. In typical fashion Ahmadinejad responded not by decreasing but by increasing the enrichment of uranium.

In an article for *The Wall Street Journal*, Bret Stephens offered this observation:

> *For three years, the administration has deferred to European and UN diplomacy while seeking to build consensus around the idea that a nuclear-armed Iran poses unacceptable risks to global security.... Today, the international community is*

*less intent on stopping Tehran from getting the bomb than
it is on stopping Washington from stopping Tehran.*[706]

Of course, none of this has fazed the super-egotistical Mr.
Ahmadinejad. He was not deterred from sending an eighteen-
page letter to President George W. Bush (43) in which he urged the
president to convert to Islam.

Amir Taheri suggests the letter not be dismissed out-of-hand.
According to Taheri, Ahmadinejad is simply following the lead of the
Prophet Mohammad:

> *To some in Washington, Ahmadinejad's epistolary exercise
> may look like another of his quirks. But it is based on a long
> historic tradition and fits into a framework of religious prac-
> tice developed by Muslims over the past fourteen centuries.*
>
> *Prophet Muhammad himself initiated the practice of writing
> letters to "the rulers of the world." In 625 AD, having con-
> solidated his position in Medina and established a secure
> power base for his rule, the prophet decided it was time to
> call on "the infidel" to abandon their faith and submit to
> Islam. Accordingly, he dictated three letters: to Khosrow
> Parviz, the Persian King of Kings, a Zoroastrian; and to
> Emperor Heraclius of Byzantium and the Ethiopian monarch
> Negus, who were Christians.*
>
> *The prophet's offer to the three recipients of his letters was
> simple: convert to Islam and secure a place in paradise or
> cling to your beliefs and face the sword of Islam.*[707]

In his epistle to the president, Ahmadinejad issues a veiled
warning, nay threat: "Those with insights can already hear the
sounds of the shattering and fall of the ideology and thoughts of the
liberal democratic systems."[708] Rather than give proper credence to
the Iranian president's letter, the Bush administration chose to ignore
the threats contained therein. Having done so, at some point the
president of the United States, whether Democrat or Republican and
regardless of ethnicity, will be confronted by the question: Do the

non-Muslims of the world prefer freedom of choice or living under the dictates of a mullah-controlled society?

Ahmadinejad seems to have adopted the motto of his hero, Ruhollah Khomeini, who said: "America cannot do a damn thing."[709] The Iranian leader has succeeded in thwarting any efforts made by the U.S. to sanction Iran because of its nuclear program. It seems, all too often, that the Liberal Left is determined to assist Mr. Ahmadinejad in his attempts to discredit the sinister United States by giving him the benefit of the doubt. Iran, the liberals believe, has justifiable complaints against the "Great Satan." After all, in some minds 9/11 was caused, not by a fanatical hatred for all things American, but by the failure of the U.S. to empathize with the privation and hopelessness in Third World countries. "Along these lines," wrote David Limbaugh, "is it any surprise that Obama... thinks we are at fault for not trying hard enough to meet Iranian tyrant Mahmoud Ahmadinejad halfway?"[710]

As a side note to Ahmadinejad's flaunting of world opinion, four former American Embassy hostages identified the Iranian president as one of the prison guards during the 444 days of captivity under Carter. In a *New York Times* article published in 2005, intelligence officer William J. Daugherty said:

> *"I recognized him right off. When you're in a situation where your life is in jeopardy, where you know your family is going through hell because of what you're in, and your country is being humiliated, you don't forget the people who cause it."... Another former hostage, Kevin Hermening...a Marine guard at the Embassy, remembered Mr. Ahmadinejad as an interrogator and "higher-ranking security official."*[711]

These identifications were categorically denied by Iranian officials.

Unfortunately, the actions of President Jimmy Carter set a precedent with Iran that still proves true today: Rather than call his bluff, the U.S. cowers behind a group of allies which are as toothless a tiger as can be found on the planet. Also, thanks in large part to Carter, the world is again being challenged by what may be the best student to emerge from Khomeini's *madrasas* (Islamic schools), Mahmoud Ahmadinejad.

The global reach of the Carter-blessed Khomeini is not restricted to Iran. In a treatise by Gen. (Ret.) Moshe Ya'alon, he writes, "According to Iranian Supreme Leader Ali Khamenehi and Iran's Syrian partners, the Second Lebanon War [August 2006] was launched by Hezbollah—Iran's proxy—as a hostile probe of U.S. reflexes via the engagement of Israel, which for Iran and Syria is a direct extension of Washington in the Middle East."[712] It is apparent that Tehran wishes to neutralize America's influence in the Middle East as a major step in the plan to defeat Western civilization. Foremost in that effort is the funding, training, and arming of Hezbollah in Lebanon, and not just with pistols and ammunition.

Not only does Iran directly support Hezbollah, but also it supplies Hamas with funds, arms, and training. For years Lebanon has played host to about 250 members of the Islamic Revolutionary Guard Corps, the elite of the Iranian military, and is best at training other terror units. It is obvious to me that Iran has a long-term plan to take control of the Middle East region by using proxies: Hamas, Hezbollah, and Palestinian Islamic Jihad, not to mention Muqtada al-Sadr's Shiite Mahdi Army in Iraq. Would the spread of such terrorist entities have been assured had Jimmy Carter worked with the Shah to correct human rights issues rather than against the monarch?

Ahmadinejad is equally determined to destroy Israel. Recalling Khomeini's earlier rhetoric, in October 2005 he declared, "This regime that is occupying Qods [Jerusalem] must be eliminated from the pages of history."[713] Despite Ahmadinejad's hateful proclamation, Persian Jews continue to live in Iran. The Iranian Jews were content to remain there following the establishment of the State of Israel (only about eight thousand emigrated), but the safety of the Jewish population is no longer guaranteed under the radical regime of Mahmoud Ahmadinejad. According to available research:

> *The Islamization of the country has brought about strict control over Jewish educational institutions. Before the revolution, there were some twenty Jewish schools function-ing throughout the country. In recent years, most of these have been closed down. In the remaining schools, Jewish principals have been replaced by Muslims. In Teheran there are still three schools in which Jewish pupils constitute a majority. The curriculum is Islamic, and Persian is forbidden as the language of instruction for Jewish studies. Special Hebrew lessons are conducted on Fridays by the Orthodox Otzar ha-Torah organization, which is responsible for Jewish religious education. Saturday is no longer officially recognized as the Jewish Sabbath, and Jewish pupils are compelled to attend school on that day. There are three synagogues in Teheran, but since 1994 there has been no rabbi in Iran, and the bet din [rabbinical court of Judaism] does not function.*[714]

Rather than being the savior of Iran and the champion of human rights that the Carter administration had hoped for, the Ayatollah Khomeini instead became the personification of Islamic terrorism, a man whose cruelty and hatred knew no bounds. It was Khomeini who, during the Iran/Iraq conflict, is said to have ordered hundreds of thousands of plastic keys from Taiwan. According to an article by Marcos Aguinis in the Argentine newspaper, *La Nacion*, these cheap bits of plastic were presented to some 450,000 children as the keys to the gates of paradise. These unsuspecting youngsters between the ages of twelve and seventeen were then dispatched to the front lines to be used as minesweepers. One Iranian soldier described the scene: "The kids destroyed the mines with their bodies. It was an almost enthusiastic race...each and every child wanted to be the first to explode."[715] Of course, not all died; sadly, some were maimed beyond belief. I cannot begin to fathom the unspeakable horror of using children in such an inhumane way in an attempt to achieve military superiority.

Would the Iran/Iraq conflict that elicited this heinous murder of children even have occurred had it not been for Jimmy Carter's determination to see the ouster of the Shah? Would Saddam Hussein have attained such power in Iraq? Would Kuwait have been invaded by the determined Saddam, triggering *Desert Storm*? Lastly, will the power vacuum left by Saddam Hussein be filled with another of the likes of the Grand Ayatollah Ruhollah Khomeini or his apt pupil, Mahmoud Ahmadinejad?

Perhaps Edward Daley summed it up best in an article for *The American Daily*:

> *Jimmy Carter's misguided implementation of human rights policies not only indirectly led to the overthrow of the Shah of Iran but also paved the way for the loss of more than 600,000 lives, Iran's rule by Ayatollahs, the Iran-Iraq War, Iraq's invasion of Kuwait and Desert Storm, the Soviet invasion of Afghanistan, the Taliban, al-Qaeda, Osama bin Laden, and the destruction of the World Trade Center towers on September 11, 2001.*[716]

In July 2008 the Taliban was once again rearing its ugly head in Parachinar, Pakistan, a town near the Afghan border. This is the same strategic point of land called Parrot's Beak from which the American-backed *Mujahedeen* carried out incursions against the Russians during the Cold War. This area became the focal point of a struggle between Sunni Muslims and Shiites. The constant fear of attack kept the Shiite villagers in their homes, creating a shortage of food and sending the price of flour to as much as $100 for a sixty-six pound bag.

The Pakistani army handled the situation very effectively. Its leaders signed a peace agreement with Pakistani Taliban leader Baitullah Mehsud that would keep the troops inside their barracks. Fearing for their lives, Shiites from the vicinity of Parachinar fled to

Peshawar looking for safety in the homes of family. Where might these people be today had Jimmy Carter not sanctioned the first payments to Osama bin Laden and his Afghani cohorts?

Second only to Carter's policies during his administration leading to 9/11 are the actions of the Clinton administration. In the late 1990s John O'Neill, a counter-terrorism expert for the FBI, repeatedly warned of his rising concerns about the possibility of terror cells planted inside the United States. O'Neill was sent on assignment to Spain; during his absence, a communiqué sent to the FBI in New York was intercepted by agent Jack Cloonan. His response to the memo detailing bin Laden's plan to train pilots in the U.S. was to crumple it and toss it away. He questioned how the FBI would interview the tens of thousands of Muslim students in America.[717] It would be one of the many threads that would ultimately be unraveled *after* the horrific events of 9/11. Lawrence Wright supposes in his book, *The Looming Tower,* "O'Neill was a flawed and polarizing figure, but there was no one else in the bureau...who might have taken the morsels of evidence the CIA was withholding and marshaled a worldwide dragnet that would have stopped 9/11."[718]

Another group of bin Laden disciples led by Khalil al-Deek, a U.S.-trained computer specialist, were arrested and tried in Amman, Jordan, for plotting to attack American and Israeli tourist sites in that country. Among the targets were the Radisson Hotel, Mount Nebo (famed as the site where God allowed Moses to see the Promised Land), and landmark churches at Madaba and Bethany on the Jordan River. The plot was foiled. The Radisson was targeted again on November 9, 2005, as was the Grand Hyatt Amman and the Amman Days Inn. Sixty were killed and 115 wounded in the attack; al-Qaeda claimed responsibility for the bombings. The West must take heed; both Jordan's King Abdullah and Egypt's Hosni Mubarak have warned of the danger of the formation of a Shiite-dominated area that would take in Iran, Iraq, and Lebanon.

Former President Carter presents himself as a neutral, third-party arbitrator, and especially in Middle East affairs. The good works Carter proposed to do through The Carter Center and his legacy of the Carter Library have, however, been tainted by those with whom he has chosen to align himself. These same allies have strained Carter's credibility in other arenas, as well.

═══ 32 ═══

THE FOUNDATION
FOR DISASTER

*"For decades it [Israel] had been the enemy, the cancer in the body
of the Arab world, which we had to do all in our power to destroy."*
(B O U T R O S   B O U T R O S - G H A L I) [719]

SOME CHARGE ANWAR EL SADAT'S assassination to his
association with Jimmy Carter and his subsequent support of
U.S. policies in the Middle East. Sadat had helped, at Zbigniew
Brzezinski's behest, in raising an army of mercenaries to aid the
Afghan rebels in their fight against the Soviets (with the assistance
of the covert Safari Club). Perhaps Sadat thought his support of the
Afghan jihad would help pacify those Muslims who faulted him for
signing the peace accords with Israel in March 1979. He was
ostracized by Saudi Arabia, Syria, the Palestinians, Iraq, and other
fellow Arab nations. These actions served to push Sadat further
toward Washington and the Carter administration and, in fact, he
made Egyptian airfields available to American cargo planes
transporting supplies to the *Mujahedeen* in Afghanistan through
Pakistan. As Carter's term of office drew to a close, Sadat had
opened the door to allow Special Forces instructors to train Egyptian volunteers being dispatched to Afghanistan.

Sadat had been handsomely rewarded by the U.S. to the tune of $1.5 billion in loan guarantees for signing the peace treaty with Israel. His complicity in Afghanistan poured another $2 billion into Egypt's coffers and allowed Sadat to indulge in purchases of advanced weapons that included the F-16 fighter. Unfortunately for Sadat, this largess, which included CIA-trained personal security forces for the Egyptian president, could not prevent his assassination in Cairo in October 1981. Sadat's last months in office were dominated by ferreting out his adversaries—real or imagined—and killing or imprisoning them. Unfortunately, he was unable to stop a small but determined group of Islamic fanatics from planning and executing his assassination. Even his CIA-trained guardians led by William Buckley were unable to protect him from the determined assassins. (Buckley would later be kidnapped by Hezbollah operatives and allowed to die in captivity.) It was the peace accords between Egypt and Israel that really cemented these various Islamic splinter groups, galvanizing them to action.

Spurred on by the signing of the peace accords with Israel and incensed by what they saw as Sadat's corrupt financial practices, the group felt justified in murdering him in the midst of a parade celebrating the 1973 October War anniversary. As the parade of predominately Western-manufactured armaments rolled past Sadat's reviewing stand and Mirage jets roared over the crowd, Egyptian Army Lieutenant Khalid al-Islambouli walked calmly forward. As Sadat, surrounded by foreign dignitaries, rose to salute the lieutenant, members of the murderous group began to spray the reviewing stand with assault rifles, tossing grenades at the Egyptian leader. When the smoke from the attack cleared, Anwar El Sadat and eleven others were slain, twenty-eight were wounded.

Earlier in the day Sadat's wife, Jehan, had implored him to don a bulletproof vest for the parade. Sadat declined with, "When God is ready to take me, he'll take me." Mrs. Sadat countered, "Okay, but you don't have to help."[720]

The small but lethal group responsible for the assassination was inspired by rogue Sheikh Omar Abdel-Rahman. Members of the group were arrested following Sadat's murder, forced to strip, and then subjected to humiliating interrogation by Egyptian police. The men were incarcerated in tiny, stone prison quarters and forced to listen to the shrieks of other prisoners. Both Dr. Ayman al-Zawahiri, a member of a prominent Egyptian family, and Sheikh Omar were arrested and interrogated. Sheikh Omar stood trial with the planners and executors of Sadat's assassination. The blind sheikh was acquitted but is said to have felt Sadat's murder was permissible under Islamic law.

Rahman was later arrested, tried, and convicted of planning the first World Trade Center attack in 1993. He remains behind bars at Butner Medical Center, Butner Federal Correctional Institution, Butner, North Carolina.

Dr. al-Zawahiri joined Rahman in his determination to return Egypt and all Muslim countries to an Islamic caliphate. Dr. al-Zawahiri was convinced Egypt could and would become the center of jihad against the Western world. He believed it would signal the beginning of the end for America and Israel.

Zawahiri received his battlefield indoctrination in the military hospitals in Peshawar, Pakistan, during the Soviet invasion of Afghanistan. The doctor treated the multiplied thousands of Afghanis who had fled to Pakistan to escape the Russians. Many had been victims of land mines planted by the invading army. After his tenure in Pakistan, Zawahiri returned to Egypt even more radical than when he left the country. He is said to have written about the Afghan *Mujahedeen* that the war was "a training course of the utmost importance to prepare the Muslim *Mujahedeen* to wage their awaited battle against the superpower that now has sole dominance over the globe; namely, the United States.[721]... Then history would make a new turn...in the opposite direction against the empire of the United States and the world's Jewish government."[722]

Sadat's successor, Hosni Mubarak, picked up the reins of government and continued to partner in the region with the United States. Although fanatical Islamists in Egypt refused to recognize Jimmy Carter's brokered peace agreement with Israel and sporadically engaged in murder and sabotage, Mubarak has been able to maintain control of the government in Cairo and remain tied to established U.S. policies. Yet, it was Mubarak's alliance with the United States that elicited calls for his assassination. In fact, Sheikh Rahman and his fanatical group reportedly planned to kill the Egyptian president during a trip to New York City.

Carter, however, had not yet learned a truth about the Muslim religion: Politics and religion have a record of blending about as well as oil and water. Jay Tolson, *U.S. News* columnist, wrote of Islam's impact on politics and religion:

> *As the foundation for moral reasoning for most Muslims, how could Islam not have an influence on the laws and institutions of a predominantly Muslim nation? The question is how direct or exclusive that influence should be. And to resolve that, Muslims will have to arrive at a clearer consensus on what shariah means—whether it is a broad set of ethical principles set forth in the sacred texts or a fixed legal code that can be imposed directly on society. Islamists and puritanical literalists tend to think the latter. And that is probably why most Muslims find the Islamist program unacceptable and even frightening.*[723]

Both Sheikh Rahman and Dr. Zawahiri fall into the "frightening and unacceptable" category. It was Rahman, the blind cleric who incited Muslims to "kill Americans wherever you find them; destroy their embassies, sink their ships, shoot down their planes."[724] While Rahman received a life sentence, the U.S. has offered a $25-million reward for the arrest of Dr. Zawahiri for his affiliation with al-Qaeda.

It is highly probable that the virulent hatred for the United States was born during the aftermath of Sadat's assassination in the prisons of Egypt. Those arrested following Sadat's murder were subjected to brutal forms of interrogation, and the leaders were targeted more frequently than the other prisoners. The prison became a cauldron of anti-Americanism. The detainees began to hold Washington responsible for all assaults, real or imagined, against Islam. It was in this Cairo hell-hole that Sheikh Rahman and Zawahiri began to plot to bring America to her knees. Rahman's plans would culminate in the backrooms and front parlors of his followers in Little Egypt, a quarter in Jersey City with an exceptional view of Rahman's target: the World Trade Center.

Rahman, on the U.S. terror watch list, traveled freely across the United States spewing his own brand of Islamic fanaticism and Jew-hatred. It was he who called his American hosts "descendants of apes and pigs who have been feeding from the dining tables of the Zionists, communists, and colonialists."[725] Thankfully, Rahman's overall plan to attack major New York City landmarks, including the UN Building, was aborted.

It is unfortunate Carter's cabinet members were not endowed with prudence, foreknowledge, or special insight into what its actions might unleash on the world. Could it have been such foresight that led Rudyard Kipling to write in 1888, "For the North, guns always—quietly—but always guns."?[726] Could he have possibly known that nearly one hundred years hence the policies of first Jimmy Carter, then Ronald Reagan, as well as the ruling junta in Pakistan would supply the weapons necessary to raise a *Mujahedeen* army to fight the Russians in Afghanistan? Could Kipling have unknowingly prophesied the mayhem that would arise from decisions made by men as yet unborn?

When Brzezinski flew into Islamabad, Pakistan, in January 1980, he was very likely unaware of Kipling's words. With Afghanistan on its border *to the north*, the country of Pakistan had become the supply base for arms and fighters pouring across the border into the Afghan guerilla army. Just four months prior to Zbig's trip to Pakistan, U.S. sources were concerned Pakistan's economy was so bad, President Zia al-Haq would not be able to retain his position of power in order to aid the guerillas waging jihad in Afghanistan. Although the economic situation was so disturbing that Zia had asked for the due dates on all Pakistan loans to be moved forward, he adamantly refused to reduce expenditures on the nation's nuclear program. Brzezinski's meeting with Zia did, however, produce the directive that would regulate all members of the alliance fighting the Soviet invasion of Afghanistan:

> *All arms supplies, finance, and training of the fighters must be provided through Pakistan and not directly from the CIA.... Zia placed three absolute conditions for allowing shipments of arms.... First, the countries concerned—the U.S., Egypt, Saudi Arabia, China, and eventually Britain, France, and even Israel—were to maintain absolute silence about the shipments.... Second, arms and other war supplies were to be shipped to Pakistan by the fastest available means.... Third, the shipments by air...were to be limited to two planeloads per week.*[727]

Israel's participation in the Soviet-Afghan war would prove to be detrimental. Many of the trained volunteers for the Muslim army dispatched to aid the Afghanis were Palestinians. These resistance fighters became the foundation for Hamas, the terrorist organization that now inhabits Gaza and the West Bank and whose vendetta against Israel is ongoing and deadly.

All of the safeguards imposed by Zia did not prevent cases of assault rifles and other matériel from disappearing from the warehouses along the docks in Karachi. These supplies, including CIA training books, were often commandeered by volunteers headed for Afghanistan as well as local Pakistani troops.

According to Phil Gasper, writing for *The World Traveler*:

> *The CIA became the grand coordinator: purchasing or arranging the manufacture of Soviet-style weapons from Egypt, China, Poland, Israel, and elsewhere, or supplying*

their own; arranging for military training by Americans, Egyptians, Chinese, and Iranians; hitting up Middle-Eastern countries for donations, notably Saudi Arabia, which gave many hundreds of millions of dollars in aid each year, totalling probably more than a billion; pressuring and bribing Pakistan—with whom recent American relations had been very poor—to rent out its country as a military staging area and sanctuary; putting the Pakistani Director of Military Operations, Brigadier Mian Mohammad Afzal, onto the CIA payroll to ensure Pakistani cooperation.[728]

Ultimately, these arms, ammunition, and CIA manuals would end up in the hands of rebels and fanatics in the Palestinian Territory, and as far afield as Bosnia and the Philippines. These young jihadists would become today's international terrorists, birthed from the warrior-womb of Afghanistan. It would be these revolutionaries, trained and hardened on the battlefields of Afghanistan, who would return to Egypt and invest time and effort in overthrowing first the government of Anwar El Sadat and then attempting the overthrow of his successor, Hosni Mubarak. These same revolutionaries would provide the training for the next generation of terrorists that would attack Western interests around the world. One of the most well-known would be Mohammad Atta, leader of the nineteen hijackers responsible for the attack on the World Trade Center and the Pentagon on 9/11.

One of the key players in funneling money to the Afghan rebels was the son of King Faisal of Saudi Arabia. Turki, the youngest of Faisal's progeny, attended Lawrenceville School in New Jersey. Upon completion of his courses at the ritzy prep school, Turki enrolled at Georgetown University, where he met fellow classmate and future president of the United States William Jefferson Clinton. (Some sources say that Clinton tutored Turki for a test on ethics.)

Shortly after the Russian invasion of Afghanistan, Turki traveled to Pakistan to witness the Soviet aggression firsthand. He was appalled at the incursion into Afghanistan and returned to

Saudi Arabia more determined than ever to get monetary aid into the hands of the ragtag band of rebel soldiers fighting the Russians. Turki and the Carter administration became allies in channeling funds to the Afghan warriors through the Pakistani Inter-Services Intelligence (ISI) organization. The Saudis would eventually send billions of dollars to the ISI for the Afghani fighters. Of course, Saudi Arabia paid special attention to its own, Osama bin Laden, who had joined the Afghan cause. ISI Chief General Akhtar Abdel Rahman Khan felt a very strong message would be sent to the Soviets if the Afghani rebels could win a major war waged by the freedom fighters.

When historians study the presidency of James Earl Carter Jr., they will find that the "human rights" president did, in fact, set the United States on the road to events that would provide the basis for today's War on Terrorism. It would produce the likes of Osama bin Laden, the Taliban, al-Qaeda, the 1993 World Trade Center attacks, the devastating attacks on the World Trade Center in 2001, and the invasion of Iraq. (According to FBI records, it was Osama bin Laden who helped finance Rahman's vitriolic ranting against America.)

There were other by-products of the Soviet-Afghan war. One was predicted by the U.S. Drug Enforcement Agency: the upswing in heroin imports from Afghanistan to the United States. In the mid-1970s little heroin was imported from Afghanistan, but 1980 saw an almost 40 percent surge in heroin imports. It was a boon for the CIA-created Afghan warlords, whose power and wealth were derived from the drug market.[729]

Another by-product of the war was a clandestine program code-named SOVMAT. Under the auspices of the CIA and fronted by counterfeit conglomerates, weapons were purchased from such unlikely sources as Bulgaria (KINTEX), Israel, Egypt, and even from Afghan guerillas for testing by the U.S. military. A decided edge was gained when late-model Soviet war matériel could be tested and compensatory measures taken to neutralize Russian tanks and missiles. Regrettably, some of the war machinery developed as a result of SOVMAT later found its way into the hands of such entities as Iran's Revolutionary Guard.

President Carter and his administration had achieved what no other president before him had accomplished: With the assistance of Anwar El Sadat of Egypt and Zia al-Haq in Pakistan, he had gone to battle against the Soviets using Afghanistan as a surrogate. He needed to recruit only one other anti-Soviet leviathan: China. This endeavor would require absolute diplomacy to maintain the balance of power between the two Asian superpowers. Carter was faced with the conundrum of whom to send to the Far East as his official emissary. Would it be the stalwart, brusque Brzezinski? No; Carter selected Defense Secretary Harold Brown, the picture of discretion.

In January 1980, while Brzezinski was in Pakistan, Brown was winging his way to a meeting with China's Vice Premier Deng Xiaoping. The somber and reserved Brown was the perfect choice for the task. Brown was able to keep his own counsel and thereby reveal nothing to the media regarding the purpose of his foray to Asia. With his first meeting in Beijing, Brown was satisfied his Chinese counterparts had done their research as diligently as had he. Following four days of lengthy discussions with Vice Premier Deng, Brown was able to relay at a press conference only that the talks did not center around arms sales, but that the issue of sharing technology was on the agenda. Although the Chinese and the Americans danced around the subject of arms for Afghanistan, it is thought Chinese weapons were in the hands of Afghans as early as mid-1979.

Brown returned from Beijing with the message that the Chinese were willing to consider cooperating but were not yet willing to commit to an outright alliance. He was, however, able to secure permission for U.S. supply planes to traverse Chinese airspace on flights to arm the Afghan *Mujahedeen*. Soon thereafter, and despite China's history of ignoring human rights issues, Congress conferred upon the Chinese government the status of most-favored-nation. The U.S. agreed to sell specific technological materials that had both military and civilian uses. This was followed in May 1980 by a fourteen-day visit from the Chinese vice-premier for security, which resulted in agreements to sell China transport planes, helicopters, and radar to be used for air defense.

One of the grand covert operations to come from this quasi-alliance between the U.S. and China was the construction of two electronic listening posts in the northern province of Xinjiang near the border of Afghanistan. This move would prove to be of critical importance when the Islamic Revolution, spurred by the Ayatollah Khomeini, rendered the listening posts in northern Iran useless to the United States. The outposts in China would continue to give the U.S. the capability to monitor the Russians. As for China, having the Soviets stuck in an unwinnable war in Afghanistan was a win/win situation: Beijing would gain international significance while the Soviet Union would soon crumble.

The effects of the war in Afghanistan would not end with the Russian withdrawal. The aftermath was the carnage of over a million lives lost and had turned that country and its neighbors, Iran and Pakistan, into an opium-growing area comparable to Columbia in South America. It prompted the U.S. investment of over $100 million dollars, much of which is suspected to have come from the CIA's infamous "Black Budget." This so-called "Black Budget" had been established by Franklin D. Roosevelt as a means to fund the Manhattan Project, the development of the atomic bomb.[730]

In *Unholy Wars*, John K. Cooley issued a warning:

> *When you decide to go to war against your main enemy, take a good, long look at the people behind you whom you chose as your friends, allies, or mercenary fighters. Look well to see whether these allies already have unsheathed their knives— and are pointing them at your own back.*[731]

CHAPTER

33

JIMMY CARTER: APOSTLE OR APOSTATE?

"The Carter Center, which has done much good in the world, could have been a force for peace if Jimmy Carter were as generous in spirit to the Israelis as he is to the Palestinians."

(DR. ALAN DERSHOWITZ) [732]

THE JURY IS STILL OUT on Jimmy Carter's legacy. Is he, as some say, an apostle for peace; or is he, as others avow, an apostate; a traitor to this country and to the ideals he once espoused? Is the real Jimmy Carter the unselfish worker for Habitat for Humanity and founder of the Carter Center? Or, is the real Jimmy Carter the outspoken critic of American policies in nations around the world?

As president of the United States, Carter's main thrust was in the arena of human rights. Once he left office, Carter began to search for ways to establish a reputation as a layman devoted to bettering the lives of those who are victims of social discrimination. One of his first projects was the establishment of The Carter Center, an organization dedicated to: "Creating a world in which every man, woman, and child has the opportunity to enjoy good health and live at peace."[733]

The Center joined with Emory University in a program committed to the advancement of human rights and the relieving of suffering worldwide. Founded as a non-profit, non-partisan organization, the Center's peace mission statement touts it as also being non-governmental. It is dedicated to conflict resolution and democratic principles. The Center's website lists its impartiality and record of success as one of its main achievements and backs that claim with an impressive list of accomplishments.

The Carter Center health programs are designed to teach peoples worldwide how to improve their health through training. It establishes public health programs and drug distribution centers, teaches farming techniques, institutes disease control measures, and works to improve the conditions for the mentally ill in countries around the world.

In 1984 Jimmy and Rosalynn Carter united with Habitat for Humanity, a Christian-based organization that builds homes for the homeless worldwide. Those chosen to inhabit the homes must work hand-in-hand with the organization to provide "sweat equity" as part of the program. Each year the former president and First Lady donate a week of their time to work alongside other Habitat for Humanity volunteers in cities across America and in countries around the world. These "Jimmy Carter Work Projects" have benefited cities in such states as Mississippi, California, Georgia, Michigan, New York, Florida, and Texas. The Carters have implemented projects in India, Mexico, Africa, The Philippines, and South Korea. The first Carter project with Habitat was the renovation of a six-story building in New York City in order to provide homes for some nineteen families.

According to the Habitat for Humanity website, "Volunteers work with future homeowners to build or renovate houses, which are then sold to partner families at no profit, with no interest charged on the mortgage. The money from the sale of each house goes into a revolving Fund for Humanity, to support future projects."[734]

In his book *Our Endangered Values*, Carter wrote of his association with Habitat:

> *This has become a surprisingly well-known aspect of our post-White House years, although we just send out some fund-raising letters and lead a group of volunteers for one week each year to build homes somewhere in the world. We have done this for more than twenty years.... This has been an enjoyable and heartwarming opportunity for us and many others.*[735]

There is something to be said for a former president who will don overalls, take hammer in hand, and undertake manual labor for the betterment of mankind. President Jimmy Carter had learned the lesson of servitude, but not necessarily the lesson of attitude.

After Carter left the White House in 1981, his attitude toward the newly elected Reagan was one of intense dislike. Carter's biographer, Douglas Brinkley, quoted Carter as saying, "Allowing Ronald Reagan to become president was by far my biggest failure in office."[736] Carter continued to share his opinions regarding the Reagan presidency with all who would listen. He admonished the new president for what Carter felt was warmongering. Carter criticized Reagan's policies in Africa and continued to travel to nations around the world to consult with leaders and dictators alike. The former president's critics are many and vocal about what they see as his critical attitude and his interference in politics.

Since leaving office President Jimmy Carter has vied for the questionable prize of "Worst President." He has tried to push that moniker off on succeeding presidents, but it keeps coming back to bite him. Perhaps a summation of the Carter presidency by Senator Eugene McCarthy says it all: "Mr. Carter quite simply abdicated the whole responsibility of the presidency while in office. He left the nation at the mercy of its enemies at home and abroad. He was the worst president we ever had."[737]

The Claremont Institute in a book review of Steven F. Hayward's book, *Malaise Forever*, wrote of the Carter presidency:

> *Whether Carter was our first pacifist president or simply a Guinness Book narcissist is up for discussion. What seems beyond dispute is that Carter was the worst president of the modern era....as an ex-president, Carter is a menace now more than ever...behind the genial eccentricity is a tiny monster.... It was Carter's pacifism that allowed the fall of the Shah...it was Carter's pacifism that encouraged the Soviets to invade Afghanistan...Carter's pacifism...shaped the modern Middle East and helped Islamic fascism survive its infancy. This is a much more dire legacy than the simple corruption of Democratic ideology.*[738]

In the mid-1980s Carter's lot began to improve, some think chiefly because of his association with Habitat for Humanity and for his championing of world health issues. So great was his resurrection that Democratic Party candidates began to seek a "Carter endorsement." (This was especially true of 1988 presidential candidate Joseph Biden.) Carter and Carter Center directors were tapped to monitor elections in Zambia, Haiti, the Dominican Republic, Nicaragua, and Panama. *Nation* magazine observed, "It is as if Carter had decided to take the most liberal and successful policies of his failed administration—human rights, peacemaking, and concern for the poor—and make them the centerpiece of a campaign for his own political resurrection."[739] Unfortunately, Carter was unable to demonstrate the kind of self-discipline and good manners associated with former White House residents.

As I mentioned previously, the good works Carter proposed to do through The Carter Center and his legacy of the Carter Library have, unfortunately, been tainted by those from whom he has chosen to receive donations. These same allies have strained Carter's credibility to its limits in many areas.

For instance, the former president represents himself as a neutral, third-party arbitrator, especially in Middle East affairs. Despite his role as intermediary at Camp David, Carter has, in recent years, made statements that might be construed as anti-Semitic. He has become a harsh and outspoken critic of Israel and has favored Israel's enemies over the only democratic society in the Middle East.

The Carter Center bestowed an air of authenticity on the Palestinian elections held in the West Bank in 1996. It was this "election" that crowned Yasser Arafat as president of the Palestinian Authority, a position he held until his death in 2004. In 2005 Hamas won seventy-six of the 118 seats in the Gaza Strip, a distinct threat to the U.S.-endorsed government of Mahmoud Abbas, Arafat's successor. In June of 2007 the Associated Press reported Carter informed the attendees at a human rights convention in Ireland that "the Bush administration's refusal to accept Hamas'...victory was 'criminal.'"[740] This is the same organization that has killed hundreds of Israelis in suicide bombing attacks and claims responsibility for the murders of many Americans on foreign soil.

In April 2008, when Carter defied the State Department in order to meet with Hamas representative Nasser al-Shaer in Gaza, former Deputy Undersecretary of Defense Jed Babbin classified Carter as a "shill for Hamas." Babbin went on to say of Carter:

> *You have a former president of the United States being a useful idiot for a foreign terrorist organization...he's now recommending that we have direct negotiations with Hamas.... I called him a useful idiot, which was Lenin's term for people who are so dumb that they do the bidding, inadvertently, of their enemies. And that's exactly Carter's role.... this guy is clearly not doing anything for the good guys.... This man is a loose cannon. He is off on his own...detour here. And he's going to do some considerable damage.... he is going to paint the issue that you can get away with murder and America will come and...talk to you.*[741]

Just as Carter believed Khomeini would be good for Iran and democracy, so Carter believes Hamas will be good for the Palestinian Territory and Middle East peace.

It is ludicrous to think that Hamas will suddenly consent to the three conditions established by the world community regarding Israel: recognize Israel's right to exist, repudiate violence, acknowledge past agreements. One writer outlined very succinctly why such nonsensical posturing would fail:

> *First, so long as Hamas does not renounce violence and actively work to oppose it, violence will continue, whether perpetrated by Hamas or by Islamic Jihad and others with Hamas' blessing. Without a renunciation of violence "solidifying the cease fire" and "restoring law and order" are meaningless. It would allow violence to resume at any time. Second, so long as Hamas does not recognize Israel, it will not deal with Israel—pragmatically or otherwise. In Hamas' view, dealing with Israel means making demands on it, which Israel has no reason to fulfill. Third, the endorsement of the Beirut Resolution is meaningless because it is contingent upon Israel accepting the "right" of "Palestinian refugees" to return to their "homes" in Israel—which Israel can never accept without forfeiting its character as a Jewish state. Sure "Palestinians" would accept these "benchmarks." They'd be happy to see Israel agree to commit national suicide.[742]*

When asked to define the downside of talking to Hamas, Dr. Michael Ledeen of the American Enterprise Institute responded:

> *It leads Hamas and other evil people to believe that the American government is willing to make deals.... it teaches them...just keep on killing people and the Americans will eventually show up in some form or another and give us what we want.... Hamas is now, effectively, an extension of Iran. And you remember how Jimmy Carter negotiated with Iran.... you've got to defeat Iran.[743]*

When asked about the refusal of Israel's leadership to meet with Carter, Ledeen replied:

The person [President Shimon Peres] who met with him is someone who holds a ceremonial position with no authority.... the people with real authority [Ehud Olmert] wouldn't talk to him...so they snubbed him.... he's [Carter] one of the world's most outspoken anti-Semites at the moment. He's wandering around saying terrible things about Jews and Israelis.[744]

Ambassador Dore Gold related his own dismay at Carter's trip to Israel:

Jimmy Carter was saying that what Israel is doing to the Palestinians is genocidal, and even worse than the murder of 800,000 Tutsis in Rwanda in 1994...worse than the murder of 800,000 innocent people.... So I went on Israeli Radio in Hebrew and said, "Anyone who charges Israel with genocide against the Palestinians, who says we are worse than the way the Tutsis in Rwanda were treated by the Hutus is not—and should not—be legitimized by the State of Israel. We should not meet with him."[745]

In a recent interview with Alan Dershowitz, I was allowed a look at the manuscript for a not-yet-published book. In the chapter entitled, "The Case Against Jimmy Carter," Professor Dershowitz wrote: "Carter's 'humanitarianism' seems to go in one direction only. His latest 'humanitarian' intervention has taken the form of support for Hamas."[746]

The former president has not shirked on his own writings as supported by the publication of yet another book on the Middle East released in January 2009. It is hoped that Carter's book, *We Can Bring Peace to the Holy Land,* will not be as controversial and error-riddled as his previous *Palestine: Peace not Apartheid,* released in 2006.

In this latest book, Carter declares that the U.S. must seize the moment, this matchless time in history to achieve a lasting peace in the Middle East. He offers what he calls a "bold and comprehensive plan"[747] to achieve that goal.

The latest plan, however, is no more and no less than the old Road Map Plan or the Shelf Agreement dressed up in "The Emperor's New Clothes," and about as transparent. It is not a "new" plan; it is the same tired "old" plan to force Israel to return to 1967 borders, give Judea and Samaria to the Palestinian Authority, divide Jerusalem, and present East Jerusalem as the new capital of the Palestinian state.

It would seem that someone who "has been a student of the biblical Holy Land all his life...has studied the complex and interrelated issues of the region's conflicts, and has been actively involved in reconciling them"[748] would understand the prophetic implications of the strategy he is trying to impose on Israel.

Carter undertakes the task of educating the public on why peace attempts by others have failed or fallen far short. Of course, those failures are blamed on everyone else. Mr. Carter assures his readers that the time to move forward is now under the leadership of a *new* Democratic president. He believes President Barack Obama is *the one* to take the Carter plan and run with it, thereby achieving what other, unsuccessful presidents following after him failed to accomplish. The truth is: Carter's Liberal Left plan simply will not work. Just as Carter ascribes altruistic acts to Hamas and Hezbollah, so his plan legitimizes terrorism and those who carry out such heinous attacks. It is a prescription for chaos and will become yet another rallying point for radical Islamists. It is reminiscent of the former president's plan to remove the Shah of Iran from power. Consider the chaos that caused. The Iranians still today feel they are under no compulsion to heed calls for a halt to nuclear activities because America has proven to be weak and ineffectual.

During the Carter Center's two-day forum of "international human rights activists" in December 2008, Carter determined it was the "persecution of the Palestinians...and lack of U.S. commitment to resolve the Arab-Israeli conflict [that remained] one of the most volatile issues in the Muslim world."[749]

Carter's press secretary, Deanna Congileo, did not rule out meetings with terror organization leaders of both Hezbollah and Hamas during the trip. However, Mr. Carter was shunned by the leadership of the Shiite Muslim group Hezbollah: "I understand that some of the leaders of Hezbollah have said they were not going to meet with any president or former presidents of the United States."[750]

Carter has not limited his poll-watching to the Middle East. He inserted himself into the elections in Nicaragua in 1990. Daniel Ortega succumbed to pressure from the international arena and held the first democratic election in his country since the Sandinistas wrested control in 1979. Carter, who had held long and cordial discussions with Ortega and who had hosted the Nicaraguan strongman at a Habitat for Humanity event in New York City, was certain that his good friend would have no difficulty maintaining his stranglehold in the Central American country. Carter was equally certain that the Reagan-Bush administration was totally wrong to believe that the majority of Nicaraguans would favor the less restrictive Contras over Ortega.

Much to the surprise and chagrin of the former president, Daniel Ortega lost the election to the people's choice, Violeta Chamorro, by a decisive margin of 55 to 41 percent. This was a devastating blow to Jimmy Carter and his liberal friends in the United States. Carter was certain his support of Daniel Ortega and his propensity for the Sandinistas was more than enough to spur the group to victory. In fact, early exit polls did, indeed, seem to indicate that Ortega and the Sandinistas were enjoying a huge lead over Chamorro and the Contras. It simply didn't occur to Carter that the pollsters were gleaning false information fired by fear of retaliation had the voters been truthful about how their votes would be cast.

Then there was South Korea. Shortly after Jimmy Carter announced his intentions to seek the office of president of the United States, he made his first mention of that strategic country. Carter thought the United States should pull its troops out of Korea. It was Vice President Walter Mondale who, after only one week in office, actually made the announcement in Tokyo that American troops would be pulled out of the Korean peninsula. This was Carter's decision alone; he did not deign to seek the counsel of China, North Korea, South Korea, or the USSR. Apparently, the new president was intent on making good on his campaign promises without seeking proper counsel and without giving thought to the consequences of his actions.

While in the White House, President Carter established a cordial relationship with North Korean dictator Kim Il Sung. It is thought by some historians that Carter's attitude toward and treatment of South Korean leader Park Chung Hee contributed to his assassination and the resulting military coup. Chalk up another catastrophe to Carter's human rights campaign.

It was Carter who lifted the ban on traveling to both North Korea and Cuba, and in a speech on May 22, 1977, shamed Americans for an "inordinate fear of communism." It seemed that as president, Carter was determined to do everything in his power to aid the Soviets in their quest to conquer as much of the world as possible. Within days of Carter's speech, Castro sent troops to Ethiopia.[751]

It soon became obvious that Carter's approach to the Cold War and Soviet aggression was, "I'm in your way? Oh, excuse me." Contrast this with Ronald Reagan's approach, "I'm in your way! Turn around and go home or deal with me!"

His relationship with Kim Il Sung didn't end when Carter left the White House. In 1994 North Korea began the process of removing spent fuel rods from its nuclear reactors, a forerunner to making weapons-grade nuclear material. The Clinton administration was adamant that North Korea stop its nuclear program, turn over the spent fuel rods, and permit UN inspectors back into the country.

Carter felt it incumbent that he travel to North Korea with or without approval of the Clinton administration. The former president was certain, it seems, that he was the only one who could avert a war. As he told historian Douglas Brinkley, "Kim Il Sung's invitation to talk was something I couldn't turn down; it was perhaps the only hope left before war commenced."[752] In other words, Carter was convinced he was indispensible.

President Bill Clinton was reportedly appalled at the outcome of Carter's visit with the North Korean dictator. Carter took it upon himself to emasculate Clinton's offer. He simply let it be known to Kim Il Sung that the only requirement for an agreement was that North Korea halt its nuclear program; in return, the U.S. would agree to hold further talks.

Despite North Korea's reputation for having the most abominable human rights record in the world Carter, the champion of human rights, fawned over Kim. In fact, he told his fellow congregants at a church back in Plains that the North Koreans look upon Kim "as almost a deity, as a George Washington, as a Patrick Henry, as a worshipful leader all rolled into one."[753] This was the same Kim who was reputedly responsible directly or indirectly for the deaths of between 1.5 and 3 million North Koreans in concentration camps or due to starvation.[754]

In 2006 North Korea announced its first test of a nuclear bomb. The government in Pyongyang persisted in its declaration that the pursuit of nuclear capabilities was only to provide electricity. The test prompted former President Carter to write an opinion piece published by *The New York Times*. In the article, Carter came down squarely on the side of the North Korean dictator Kim Jong-il, son of the former despot. According to Carter:

> *Beginning in 2002, the United States branded North Korea as part of an axis of evil, threatened military action, ended the shipments of fuel oil and the construction of nuclear*

power plants, and refused to consider further bilateral talks. In their discussions with me at this time, North Korean spokesmen seemed convinced that the American positions posed a serious danger to their country and to its political regime.

Responding in its ill-advised but predictable way, Pyongyang withdrew from the Nuclear Nonproliferation Treaty, expelled atomic energy agency inspectors, resumed process- ing fuel rods, and began developing nuclear explosive devices.[755]

Carter, the former U.S. commander in chief made no mention in his essay of the secret nuclear pursuits by North Korea that were responsible for sanctions levied against Pyongyang:

Washington's pledge of no direct talks could be finessed through secret discussions with a trusted emissary like former Secretary of State Jim Baker, who earlier this week said, "It's not appeasement to talk to your enemies."

What must be avoided is to leave a beleaguered nuclear nation convinced that it is permanently excluded from the international community, its existence threatened, its people suffering horrible deprivation, and its hard-liners in total control of military and political policy.[756]

Of course, Carter's rule by vacillation still haunts us today. His Middle East capitulation to the Ayatollah Khomeini and the Islamic Revolution drove the Shah from Iran, robbed the U.S. of a valuable ally, and drove oil prices still higher. It was President Carter who eased the U.S. into decontrolling the cost of oil. Oil prices then, as now, were predicated on panic and speculation. Rather than confront the trend head-on, Carter installed a wood stove in the White House and donned a cardigan to showcase his energy-saving plan.

James Woolsey, Jimmy Carter's undersecretary of the Navy (and Bill Clinton's CIA director) today is not alone in his conviction that America must end its reliance on Middle Eastern oil.

Mr. Woolsey's "forlorn quest...goes back decades...the U.S. can't cut itself off from all oil imports or turn itself into an 'economic hermit,' but we can destroy oil's monopoly."[757] Would that Mr. Carter had seen the handwriting on the wall before casting his lot with Khomeini. Perhaps we would not be fearful of skyrocketing oil prices and short supplies.

3 4

AND THE
ANSWER IS...

*"Jimmy Carter is an evil man. It is painful to label a past president
of the United States as a force for darkness. But it is dangerous
to let a man like Jimmy Carter stalk around the globe cloaked in
the garb of American royalty, planting the seeds of Western
Civilization's destruction."* (BENJAMIN SHAPIRO)[758]

MORE THAN TEN YEARS REMOVED from the White
House, Jimmy Carter's persona as a peacemaker had fallen under the
scrutiny of James Petras, author and sociology professor at New
York's Binghamton University. According to Petras, Carter was
"a hard-nosed defender of repressive state apparatuses, a willing
consort to electoral frauds, an accomplice to U.S. Embassy efforts
to abort popular democratic outcomes, and a one-sided mediator."
Petras described Carter's interference in 1990 in Haitian politics as
being no different from his support of other ruthless regimes: "Every
time Carter intervenes, the outcomes are always heavily skewed
against political forces that want change. In each case, he [Carter]
had a political agenda.... In Haiti Carter used that moral image
again to impose one of the worst settlements imaginable."[759]

The Haitian "political forces that want change" were those people who were tired of having their necks under the boots of coldblooded despots.

Carter's interference in Cuba and his overtures to Fidel Castro in 2002, much against the wishes of President Clinton, is legendary. A statement from Senator George Allen sums up Carter's trip very succinctly:

> It was amazing and disappointing for many of us to learn of Mr. Carter's visit to a Cuban biotechnology facility and his acceptance, at face value, of the assurances of communist Cuban officials there that the facility is engaged solely in medical and humanitarian pursuits.... The words and actions of Mr. Carter at this facility are a breach of trust, and it is made even worse in that the individual involved in that breach is one in whom the American people once placed the ultimate trust and responsibility of the presidency.[760]

President Bill Clinton was dismayed at Carter's behavior. He ultimately shunned the returning Carter and, in fact, refused to invite him to the White House for a debriefing. Carter, undeterred, traveled to Washington anyway and was received by a low-level Clinton administration staff member. Cuba aside, Clinton and Carter teamed up in 2008 to promote a fledgling organization, the New Baptist Covenant. The new coalition is designed to give the more moderate Baptists a stronger national voice.

Two well-known Baptists have rejected this coalition and refused to meet with the organization. Mike Huckabee, 2008 Republican presidential candidate, former governor of Arkansas, and Baptist minister, declined to attend the meeting after hearing Carter make disparaging remarks about President Bush. Some leaders such as Richard Land, president of the Southern Baptist Convention's Ethics and Religious Liberty Commission, also declined the invitation. Land said, "This is a meeting that [at the time was] called by two former Democratic presidents—one of whom [had] a wife who [was] a major candidate for the Democratic nomination for president—and the meeting [was] held less than a week before Super Tuesday. Coincidence? I think not."[761]

Clinton and Carter were joined at the first meeting of the New Baptist Covenant by former Vice President Al Gore. This liberal political trinity has been anointed to tackle such issues as "HIV/AIDS, promoting evangelism, fighting poverty, reforming the criminal justice system, and other social issues."[762] Morris H. Chapman, president of the Southern Baptist Convention Executive Committee, dismisses the former president's worries about the world having a harmful view of Baptists. Chapman wrote to the *Baptist Press*: "He [Carter] has been one of the most vocal critics of Southern Baptists, using 'fundamentalist' as a pejorative and drawing a caustic comparison between Ayatollah Khomeini's rise to power in Iran and the resurgence of conservative leadership being elected in the SBC."[763]

Of course, Jimmy Carter's pro-Arafat and pro-Palestinian leanings are legendary. Never was that more obvious than in Carter's most recent book, *Palestine: Peace not Apartheid*. According to Carter's assessment (one, I might add, that is held by the world at large), Israel is the crux of the problem. Never mind that Israel has endured decades of terror attacks from Lebanon, Syria, and Gaza, worthless peace agreements, and a desire by its Arab neighbors to see it "wiped off the map." None of this moves Mr. Carter. In his world Yasser Arafat was the poor, pitiful, put-upon Palestinian president sorely abused by the Israelis.

In a question-and-answer session with Benjamin Netanyahu during the Middle East Peace Conference in 1991, I asked if there had ever been any discussions regarding giving the Jews in the Middle East the same rights as those enjoyed by the Arabs, i.e., the privilege to settle in other territories. Mr. Netanyahu replied with a closer definition of apartheid than that found in Mr. Carter's book:

If Arabs desire to live among Jews, as they do and they have a right to do, Jews should have the right to live among the Arabs. The fact is that no Jews are allowed to live in Jordan or Saudi Arabia, and that is the kind of conception, an apartheid peace if you will, that we cannot tolerate and that no one should tolerate in the closing part of this century.[764]

In his exposé of all Israel's wrongs, Carter contends that the Palestinians have never been granted much sought-after autonomy. As with other avowals in his book, this one is decidedly wrong. Mona Charen, in a *National Review* article, disputes Carter's claim:

In December 2002, pursuant to the Oslo Accords, Israel (unwisely) gave nearly complete autonomy to the Palestinians in the disputed territories and even gave the Palestinian security forces weapons. In return, the Palestinians were supposed to prevent terror attacks against Israel. Not only did the PA fail to prevent terror attacks, it organized and carried them out.[765]

Harvard Law professor Alan Dershowitz outlined a litany of errors in Carter's book. In particular, Dershowitz soundly refutes Jimmy Carter's declaration that the Palestinians, not the Israelis, have long been in favor of a two-state solution. Said Professor Dershowitz:

Carter repeatedly mentions Security Council Resolution 242, which called for return of captured territories in exchange for peace, recognition, and secure boundaries, but he ignores the fact that Israel accepted and all the Arab nations and the Palestinians rejected this resolution. The Arabs met in Khartoum and issued their three famous "nos": "No peace, no recognition, no negotiation," but you wouldn't know that from reading the history according to Carter.[766]

Dershowitz summed up the content of the Carter book quite succinctly. He was quoted in the *Pittsburgh Post-Gazette* as saying: "Carter's book is so filled with simple mistakes of fact and deliberate omissions that were it a brief filed in a court of law, it would be struck and its author sanctioned for misleading the court."[767]

Following the release of the book, fourteen members of the Carter Center's Board of Councilors resigned. The departing group included several prominent Jewish businessmen from the Atlanta area. In a letter to the former president, the fourteen men and women cited inaccuracies in the Carter book among other inequities as their reason for tendering their resignation. The letter read, in part:

> The Carter Center has always played the useful and constructive role of honest broker and mediator between warring parties. In your book, which portrays the conflict between Israel and her neighbors as a purely one-sided affair with Israel holding all of the responsibility for resolving the conflict, you have clearly abandoned your historic role of broker in favor of becoming an advocate for one side.... [you wrote] "that it is imperative, that the general Arab community and all significant Palestinian groups make it clear that they will end the suicide bombings and other acts of terrorism when international laws and the ultimate goals of the Road Map for Peace are accepted by Israel." In this sentence you clearly suggest that you are condoning violence against Israelis until they do certain things (p.213). Your use of the word "Apartheid," regardless of your disclaimers, has already energized white supremacist groups...[and finally] it seems that you have turned to a world of advocacy, including even malicious advocacy. We can no longer endorse your strident and uncompromising position. This is not the Carter Center or the Jimmy Carter we came to respect and support. Therefore, it is with sadness and regret that we hereby tender our resignation from the Board of Councilors of the Carter Center, effective immediately.[768]

One of those who resigned was Dr. Kenneth W. Stein. Dr. Stein, a noted Mid-East academic, described *Palestine: Peace not Apartheid* as being "replete with factual errors, copied materials not cited, superficialities, glaring omissions, and simply invented segments."[769]

Even ultra-liberals Democratic Speaker of the House Nancy Pelosi and DNC Chairman Howard Dean issued statements in opposition to Carter's divisive language. Pelosi said: "It is wrong to suggest that the Jewish people would support a government in Israel or anywhere else that institutionalizes ethnically based oppression, and Democrats reject that allegation vigorously."[770]

Dean followed suit with:

> *While I have tremendous respect for former President Carter, I fundamentally disagree and do not support his analysis of Israel and the Israeli-Palestinian conflict. On this issue President Carter speaks for himself, the opinions in his book are his own, they are not the views or position of the Democratic Party. I and other Democrats will continue to stand with Israel in its battle against terrorism and for a lasting peace with its neighbors.*[771]

In Abraham Foxman's review of the Carter book, he questioned Mr. Carter's goals:

> *It is not the goals that Carter seeks that are so troubling—he calls for a two-state solution, with Palestinians and Israelis living securely in two states, which, of course, is the policy of Israel—but his obsession with blaming Israel for these goals not being achieved... He unjustly encourages Israel-bashers around the world. The legitimizing factor of being able to quote a former president of the United States and winner of the Nobel Peace Prize cannot be over-estimated.... this gives comfort to the extremists on the Palestinian side who are reinforced in their extremism.... In the end, it is the Palestinians themselves who are hurt by such a biased approach.... they become even further entrenched in their illusions about weakening Israel and the need not to change.*[772]

How did Jimmy Carter's worldview become so skewed against Israel? Is it possible the huge sums donated to the Carter Center and Library by Arabs have colored his ability to be neutral?

Annual reports from the Carter Center website[773] are replete with donations from such notable and wealthy Arabs as His Majesty Sultan Qaboss bin Said Al Said of Oman, Jordan, members of Saudi Arabia's royalty, Sheikh Zayed bin Sultan Al Nahyan, and organizations in the United Arab Emirates. Tens and hundreds of thousands of dollars have also reached Carter Center coffers from the Kuwait Fund for Arab Economic Development and His Royal Highness prince Moulay Hicham Ben Abdallah of Morocco. Interestingly, corresponding amounts from Israeli sources are not noted.

The Carter Center and Jimmy Carter Library boast among their most generous founders various members of Middle Eastern royalty. Agha Hasan Abedi's name appears on the Carter Center list. Abedi, a banker and the founder of Bank of Credit and Commerce International was involved in a banking scandal of gigantic proportions in 1991. (It was Mr. Abedi's BCCI, a bank that was under written by the Saudi royal family and fiercely anti-Semitic, that salvaged the Carter family peanut farm in the late 1970s.) Journalist Rachel Ehrenfeld wrote of BCCI's ideological objective: "[to build] the best bridge to help the world of Islam, and the best way to fight the evil influence of the Zionists."[774] Just how far will former President Carter go to keep Arab funds flowing into the Carter Center coffers? Apparently, the donations from this cash cow have been sufficient to blind him to human rights issues in the world of Islam.

Perhaps Carter's blinders were firmly in place in 1979 when an article that appeared in the *Washington Post* revealed (according to a State Department memo) that Dr. Brzezinski had asked the CIA to "prepare a comprehensive study on Islamic movements in all parts of the world."[775]

The memo continued:

Such a comprehensive study is long overdue, but it is regrettable that it should have leaked in this fashion. It is bound to interfere with the Embassy's efforts to foster a productive dialogue with right-wing religious elements in Egypt. There is no sector more sensitive in Egypt than the orthodox Muslim Right, the residuum of the former Muslim Brotherhood movement that plagued Egypt in the 1940s and 50s. It is still politically powerful.[776]

According to an Egyptian Embassy official:

In this past year and a half some contact could be made by political section officers with Omar Talmansky, editor of the Brotherhood Monthly, Al Dawa.... This contact has had to be carefully and discreetly nurtured.... Nothing will frighten them off so much as the implications that these exchanges are part of a covert CIA program to "study" Islamic Movements.[777]

For a year and a half the Carter administration had been reaching out to the Muslim Brotherhood, the very organization that fought so strongly against Anwar El Sadat and the Camp David Accords between Egypt and Israel signed at Carter's urging. This organization would ultimately become the Egyptian Islamic Jihad. In 1981 its members would successfully assassinate President Sadat, giving rise to one of al Qaeda's wiliest leaders, Ayman al-Zawahiri, and the events of 9/11. Jimmy Carter paid a high price for choosing militant terrorists over two staunch American allies, Reza Pahlavi and Anwar Sadat.

Before his death, His Majesty King Fahd of Saudi Arabia presented the Carter Center with a gift of $7.6 million and is listed as a "founding" member; his nephew, Prince Alwaleed Ibin Talal, contributed at least $5 million. (It was Ibin Talal who offered then-New York Mayor Rudolph Giuliani a donation of $10 million dollars following the 9/11 terrorist attacks. Giuliani refused the offer after Ibin Talal blamed the attack on close ties between the U.S. and Israel.) The Saudi Fund for Development appears frequently on the donor list for the Center. According to an article in *FrontPage Magazine.com*, ten of Osama bin Laden's brothers promised the former president a $1 million donation for the Center.[778]

Is there anything wrong or underhanded about Carter accepting money from Arab sources to fund his Center and Library? No; but what has come to the fore is Carter's penchant for being a mouthpiece of anti-Semitic political rhetoric. Carter has urged the United States to fund Hamas, an avowed terrorist organization whose name is on the U.S. list of terrorist organizations. The Hamas Charter specifically targets Israel: "Israel will exist and continue to exist until Islam will obliterate it, just as it obliterated others before it."[779] In a *New York Times* opinion piece, Jimmy Carter attacked Ariel Sharon and, in essence, blamed him for Palestinian ills. He seemed to strongly suggest that Prime Minister Sharon bore the brunt of the responsibility for suicide bombings in Israel.[780]

In a March 2007 statement to the UN Human Rights Council, Carter wrote: "The singular focus on the violations committed by Israel, while failing to address with the same vigor serious human rights abuses in many other parts of the world, has been counterproductive."[781]

Counterproductive? Why not call a spade a spade, or in this case a terrorist a murderer? These heartless killers must not be exalted as revered "freedom fighters." Why not list the human rights abuses of today's Iran, Saudi Arabia, Libya, and Syria? It simply exposes once again Carter's anti-Semitic bent.

Although the Carter Center's mission statement declares it to be "nonpartisan" and "neutral," can that be a true statement if the organization is funded by Arab money? That raises another question: Why is an organization that focuses on "human rights" devoid of representation in Saudi Arabia, one of the world's greatest abusers of human rights?

Yet, it was supposedly Jimmy Carter's "decades of untiring effort to find peaceful solutions to international conflicts, to advance democracy and human rights, and to promote economic and social development,"[782] that won a nod from the Nobel Peace Prize committee in 2002. The award, however, was not without controversy, which is par for just about anything associated with the former president. One member of the committee was quite vocal in his assertion that awarding the prize was a slap in the face to President George W. Bush's administration. "[The award] should be interpreted as a criticism of the line that the current administration has taken," Chairman of the Nobel Committee Gunnar Berge said. "It's a kick in the leg [translated "a slap in the face"] to all who follow the same line as the United States."[783] However, one must wonder how awarding the Nobel Peace Prize to Carter seems to those who have been dispossessed because of his liberal policies? Sean Hannity answered that question well when he wrote, "To those who suffer under the despotism born of his appeasement, Carter's Nobel Peace Prize must seem a cruel joke."[784]

Bad judgment is not something that infiltrated the Nobel Committee just this year; it dates back to 1994 when the noble Nobel members thrust greatness upon a terrorist by the name of Yasser Arafat. Unbowed and unrepentant, Arafat accepted his portion of the "peace" prize then quickly returned to his lair in the Palestinian Territory to mastermind attacks against Israel. Perhaps it is fitting that both Yasser Arafat and Jimmy Carter received this prestigious award. After all, as historian Douglas Brinkley wrote: "There was no world leader Jimmy Carter was more eager to know than Yasser Arafat, the master logistician and survivor of byzantine Middle East politics.... Carter felt certain affinities with the Palestinian."[785]

Carter and Arafat met the first time in Paris at the Hotel de Crillon for a ninety-minute session. According to a euphoric Carter, "He [Arafat] has done everything possible these last months to promote the [Middle East] peace process. He's explored all the possibilities to make progress toward a total peace settlement."[786] Arafat welcomed Carter with open arms. Why not? After all, Arafat was engaged in dialogue with the man Anwar Sadat considered a brother; the man who was the highest-level American to have met with him. It mattered not that Carter was a *former* president; it mattered that he was sympathetic to the Palestinian leader.

Israel's leaders were appalled at Carter's fawning over Yasser Arafat, the man who just days before had been kissing up to Saddam Hussein in Baghdad. During his visit to Iraq, Arafat had spewed his hate-filled rhetoric designed to enrage the Arab world against Israel. Furthermore, he had threatened Israel with attacks using Baghdad's al-Abed missiles. (In 2007 Jimmy Carter was interviewed on *Al-Jazeera* Arab television. During the interview, the former president admitted: "Well, I don't really consider, I wasn't equating the Palestinian missiles with terrorism."[787] Perhaps that is why Arafat's threats from Baghdad were of so little concern to Mr. Carter.)

Despite Arafat's record of murderous terrorist activities, Carter chose to embrace him. In fact, he went so far as to assist Arafat with writing a generic speech to be delivered to Western audiences. Carter's advice to Arafat was to try to drum up as much sympathy as possible from world leaders and to show Israel in as bad a light as possible, as often as possible. He gave the PLO leader specific samples, sympathetic illustrations that could be changed or embellished to suit the audience in question.[788] This aid from Carter came regardless of the fact that in 1980, Arafat bawled, "Peace for us means the destruction of Israel. We are preparing for an all-out war, a war which will last for generations."[789]

Carter's jibes at America and American presidents are legendary. Brinkley wrote of Carter's ridicule of President Ronald Reagan during a meeting in Cairo in 1984. Carter lambasted Reagan as a warmonger rather than a diplomat. He decried Reagan's willingness "to use American battleships to shell the villages around Beirut."[790]

In a 2002 meeting with Castro and other Cuban officials, Carter purportedly intimated Undersecretary of State John Bolton was lying about the development of biological weapons in Cuba. Carter ridiculed that idea, and in so doing lent credence to the Cuban dictator's regime.

Carter's penchant for taking U.S. leaders to task on the world stage also flouts credibility. Perhaps Carter's own words are his greatest indictment. At the close of what has come to be known as his "Malaise Speech," Carter challenged the American people with these words:

> *I will do my best, but I will not do it alone. Let your voice be heard. Whenever you have a chance, say something good about our country. With God's help and for the sake of our nation, it is time for us to join hands in America. Let us commit ourselves together to a rebirth of the American spirit. Working together with our common faith we cannot fail.* [791]

It would benefit Mr. Carter to meditate on these words. Perhaps he should adopt a form of the carpenter's motto as his own. Rather than measure twice, cut once—the former president would benefit by thinking twice and speaking once. Better yet, he might adopt the motto, "Silence is golden."

How is looking back at the presidency of Jimmy Carter relevant today? It is pertinent for several reasons: In his book, *Palestine: Peace Not Apartheid*, Carter has effectively rewritten history. He used his voice to seemingly eradicate decades of Arab terrorism against the Jews in Israel; castigate the media, which he claimed is excessively pro-Israel; accuse the American government of catering to Israel; accuse Israel of unwarranted aggression against the PLO and opposition to a peace initiative; and demand ridiculous sacrifices from Israel.

At a literary festival in Wales in May 2008, Carter numbered Israel's nuclear arsenal at "150 or more." A BBC report covered the former president's lapse:

The U.S., a key ally of Israel, has in general allowed the country's policy of "nuclear ambiguity," neither confirming nor denying the existence of its assumed arsenal.... Former Israel military intelligence chief Ahron Zeevi-Farkash [said] he considered Mr. Carter's comments "irresponsible." *... During the press briefing, Mr. Carter...criticized [Israel's] domestic and foreign policy. "One of the greatest human rights crimes on earth is the starvation and imprisonment of 1.6 million Palestinians."*[792]

Mr. Carter frequently overlooks the fact that there are some 1.6 billion (yes, billion) Muslims worldwide; there are 13.2 million (with an "m") Jews worldwide. The Middle East Policy Council website reports that "one of every five human beings is a Muslim."[793] If those figures are anywhere near correct, and I assume they are, the question becomes: Why are 1.6 billion Muslims allowing their brothers, the Palestinians, to starve? Why have the Palestinians become the poster children for Arab hatred against the Jews? Why does Jimmy Carter not take the Muslim countries to task?

Carter has carried his Liberal Left political invective far beyond his presidency. He seems to have forgotten he still represents the United States, even though he doesn't rise every morning and trek downstairs to the Oval Office. Jimmy Carter's popularity seems to be at its height among those despots whose hatred of America is legendary. He is a man who considers himself to have been an ideal president and whose term was simply "unfinished."

Time magazine reporter Lance Morrow characterized Jimmy Carter as "a psalm-singing, global circuit rider and moral interventionist who behaved...as if the election of 1980 [and Ronald Reagan's win] had been only some kind of ghastly mistake."[794]

That leads us back to the original question: is James Earl Carter Jr., an apostle or an apostate? If you ask the folks at Habitat for Humanity or the people who have been helped through the Carter Center, he is definitely the apostle of human rights. If you ask reputable historians, Carter is a man whose record as president is likely the worst; his accomplishments more negative than positive.

Despite that, Carter has inserted his opinions in countries around the world, and in so doing has managed to regularly and repeatedly speak ill of those elected by the majority of Americans to conduct business on their behalf. Only time will determine if Jimmy Carter is the worst ex-president, but the current consensus of opinion is that, at the moment, he holds exclusive rights to that moniker. Under the presidency of James Earl Carter Jr. America became non-confrontational, non-threatening, and weakened. *National Review* columnist Jay Nordlinger summed it up very succinctly when he wrote of Carter's speech at the Democratic National Convention in 2004:

> *"You can't be a war president one day and claim to be a peace president the next," [Carter told the gathered crowd]. Of course, sometimes the only way to be a peace president is first to be a war president, as the most valuable presidents have always known. Because some presidents allow threats to gather, other presidents have to make war—or at least be tougher.*[795]

In an article for the *Guardian*, a British newspaper, Jonathan Freedland quotes Carter's "rose-colored glasses" review of his own presidency. Carter says he took some "revolutionary" steps while in office and is pleased that he did:

> *We established human rights as the basis of our foreign policy, whereas in the past our government had been in bed with every dictator on earth if they supported our economic framework. [Apparently Carter doesn't consider the likes of North Korea's Kim Yong-il, Hugo Chavez, Fidel Castro, Robert Mugabe, or China's Hu Jintao to be particularly dastardly dictators. He obviously doesn't consider the millions of Arab dollars flowing into the Carter Center and Library to be in support of his "economic framework."] We normalized diplomatic relations with China [and thereby supported*

Jintao, one of history's most murderous regimes]. We brought peace to the Middle East between Israel and Egypt. We kept the peace with the Soviet Union. We told the truth. We kept our country at peace; we never dropped a bomb; we never launched a missile.[496]

It helped Carter's self-image to have labeled the hostage rescue attempt in Iran a "humanitarian" effort rather than a military endeavor. It did not, however, provide comfort to the families who lost loved ones during that mission. Freedland wrote of Carter's certainty that the next president could change the course of America in the time it would take to recite his Inauguration Day speech. That speech, according to the former president, would reassure the American people that the U.S. "would never again torture a prisoner...never again attack another country unless our security is directly threatened."[797]

Carter says the only clout he has is "moral authority." Perhaps the former president sees himself more a Gandhi than a failed politician, more a Martin Luther King than a weak and pacifist former leader who only made America weaker in the eyes of her enemies. One unnamed senior Democrat said of Carter, "He is indifferent to political timing, part of his self-image as a holy man, but often undermining the causes he pursues."[798]

It is easy to see why Carter would appeal to those Europeans who pursue pacifism at any cost. However, "the former president's peculiar combination of rectitude and starchy pride can be a little irritating, as it was three decades ago when he lectured us on energy independence and then blamed our 'malaise' for our failure to heed him."[799]

Has former President James Earl Carter Jr. become a unifying force for peace, as he hoped he might; or has he become the divisive, sanctimonious, pacifist many see? Discord and wrangling still dog his steps, even after nearly thirty years down the road from the White House. It is the sound of "meaningless noise like a loud gong or a clanging cymbal."[800] It grates on one's nerves.

Jimmy Carter's liberal leftist policies during his administration and his outspokenness against things American since departing 1600 Pennsylvania Avenue should leave no skepticism regarding his past performance. It should, in fact, be a red flag to every American: Don't take the Carter road ever again.

A LIBERAL BY ANY
OTHER NAME...

"At the heart of liberalism is the naive belief that people are basically
good. As a result of this belief, liberals rarely blame people for the
evil they do. Instead, they blame economics, parents, capitalism,
racism, and anything else that can let the individual off the hook."
(D E N N I S   P R A G E R)[801]

THE FRENCH CALL IT LAISSEZ-FAIRE, but Americans
have a much more provocative name for the freethinking, non-
interventionist, broadminded faction. We call it the Liberal Left.
For years it has dominated the Democratic Party, whose lack of
moral clarity has driven such issues as abortion-on-demand, school
children compelled to undergo sensitivity training on the homosexual lifestyle, pornography disguised as the National Endowment
for the Arts and funded by Congress[802]; and political correctness—
not truth—touted as the voice of the people.

Abraham Lincoln said of right and wrong, "It is the eternal
struggle between two principles...throughout the world."[803]
Where did our Founding Fathers (oops, that is no longer politically
correct; now we call them "Framers of the Constitution") go wrong?

Where did we lose our way? It is my strong belief that America set off down the wrong road under the direction of a man whose strong Bible beliefs were hijacked by his liberal tendencies...James Earl Carter Jr., the 39th president of the United States. Just as Judas betrayed Jesus to further his own agenda, so Jimmy Carter betrayed America's allies in order to do the same. From Iran to Afghanistan, from Panama to Israel, from Egypt to Central America, Carter left broken relationships, shattered allies, and scores of victims as surely as if he had pulled the trigger or piloted the airplane. Even today, he continues to court America's enemies as if they were close, personal friends.

As we have seen early in Jimmy Carter's administration, he took aim at America's closest ally in the Middle East, the Shah of Iran. Carter seemed determined to undermine the regime of the Shah, who was attempting to modernize his country, provide educational opportunities, and free women from repression. The election of a Democratic president was the perfect opportunity for the Liberal Left to rid itself of past agreements with what was deemed dictatorial rulers. Jimmy Carter's White House tenure only proved that the Liberal Left had coined its own very selective definition of "dictatorial."

Samuel Segev, Middle East editor of the newsmagazine *Maariv*, reiterated in our interview that he thought Jimmy Carter lost Iran for the United States. Carter's cardinal mistake was in not knowing the mindset of the region:

> *Jimmy Carter...democratized the Middle East...and did not understand the mentality and political set-up of the people in the region. They are not yet prepared [for democracy]. They were teaching democracy according to American standards or European standards...or according to Israeli standards. Islam is an exception; not even Turkey is as democratic as Israel.... Carter wanted to impose a set of values that were not understood.*[804]

Due to Carter's policies and lack of understanding, America no longer has a strong ally in the Persian Gulf region. Carter's insistence on deposing the Shah served only to usher in the more despotic rule of Ayatollah Ruhollah Khomeini and his rabidly fanatical Islamists. The former president's dislike for what he saw as the Shah's repressive monarchy was a major factor in Carter's decision to destabilize Pahlavi's regime in favor of a fanatical Islamic cleric.

The monster that arose from the depths of Islamic fundamentalism as a result of the acts of an egocentric president has replicated itself in Afghanistan, Iraq, Algeria, Kosovo, Gaza, Pakistan, Lebanon, and Syria, just to name a few. Now there is only the Iran of the Ayatollah Khomeini and the succession of terrorists bent on the destruction of the nation that helped elevate him to power. The practice of coddling America's enemies has continued with subsequent Liberal Left politicians such as Bill Clinton, Howard Dean, Al Gore, and Senators John Kerry, Hillary Clinton, and Barack Obama.

Carter removed the cork in the genie's bottle, he inserted the key into Pandora's Box and he freed the enemies whose singular goal today is the destruction of America. Under Carter's tutelage it has become preferable to form pragmatic partnerships with terrorist organizations. No, the Liberal Left fails to understand that these radicals hate everything and everybody associated with "The Great Satan," America. The terrorists who targeted the World Trade Center and the Pentagon on 9/11 did not stop beforehand to inspect the voting credentials of those murdered. They did not ask for voter registration cards to determine Republican or Democrat. They didn't even ask for nation of origin. People were murdered simply because they were in the World Trade Center Towers in New York City, New York, U.S.A.

Jimmy Carter's interference in Egypt backed Anwar El Sadat into the proverbial corner. Sadat was pressured by the Carter administration to implement policies that would birth a radical Islamic movement, produce the likes of Dr. Ayman al-Zawahiri, Sheikh

Omar Abdel-Rahman, and ultimately result in the two attacks on the World Trade Center Towers. It was this incursion in Egypt's political system that fueled the destabilization of Sadat's regime and finally led to his assassination at the hands of Muslim extremists.

One move in Egypt that would certainly be outlawed by the Liberal Left in America was to prohibit mullahs from venerating suicide bombers and spouting rhetoric that would incite terrorism. The outcome of the ban was that terrorism in Egypt under Sadat's successor, Hosni Mubarak, declined dramatically between 1998 and 2002.[805] The results are both good and bad. According to Peter Beinart, "Most of Egypt's remaining Osama bin Ladens are in jail." [However, the emergency law passed in Egypt in 1981 has opened the door for fundamentalist Islamic clerics to impose], "unprecedented control over Egypt's educational system and cultural life.... Saudi Arabia has done something similar, handing over its schools to militant clerics in an effort to buy them off. To preserve themselves today, the regimes are sowing the seeds of a theocratic future."[806]

Of course, the American government will not follow the Egyptian method of terrorist control, but must we tolerate with equanimity the antics of a former president who travels around the world courting the very terrorists who would destroy our nation? Since leaving office Carter has continued to spread his particular brand of liberalism worldwide, especially in the countries and camps of the very terrorists who wish to destroy both America and Israel. Benjamin Shapiro wrote of Carter's last visit to Gaza:

> *Jimmy Carter met with leaders of the terrorist group Hamas. He embraced Nassar al-Shaer, the man who has run the Palestinian education system, brainwashing children into believing Jews are the descendants of pigs and dogs. He laid a wreath at the grave of Yasser Arafat, the most notorious terrorist thug of the 20th century. Then he had the audacity to offer to act as a conduit between the Palestinian Arabs and the Israeli and U.S. governments.... Carter is a notorious anti-Semite and an even more notorious terrorist-enabler.[807]*

In May 2008 Hamas spokesman Fawzi Barhoum admitted to the press that France and parliament members of the European Union had met with his organization and had spoken of a desire to establish a relationship with the terrorist organization. Barhoum talked of the Jimmy Carter meeting with Hamas leaders and said he was hopeful Carter would urge EU members to reveal their wishes to support Hamas. Bernard Kouchner, French foreign minister, verified that Paris politicos had made contact with Hamas; however, according to Kouchner, "We are not the only ones to have them. We are not charged with any kind of negotiation."[808]

In an article in the French newspaper *Le Figaro*, it was reported that a French diplomat had met in April in Gaza with deposed Hamas Prime Minister Ismail Haniya and Mahmoud al-Zahar, Hamas chief in Gaza. Al-Zahar heads what is commonly known as the Hamas military operation and is thought to be even more radical than Khaled Meshaal, who directs Hamas from Syria. In March 2007, al-Zahar rallied the Hamas faithful with a call to "liberate Palestine." He said, "Our final goal, which will be achieved, is that Islam will enter every house and will spread all over the world."[809]

Barhoum reported a meeting with "a delegation from France, the government, and from Italy and Norway and from the EU parliament and from Carter. All of these are supporting Hamas, and they have a plan to support Palestinian rights and interests." He called Carter "a very important and serious person. We think meeting with us will encourage others who are already sending messages to us."[810]

Carter, of course, ignored the U.S./Israeli plan to isolate Hamas, an organization on the U.S. designated terrorist list, and visited with Meshaal against direct opposition from the State Department.

If the United States were to adopt the stance that any and all inducements for terrorism must be eliminated, the sitting president would be forced to deal with Jimmy Carter and his pandering to the various terrorist organizations. The U.S. would also have to formulate a method whereby it would deal singularly with every type of terrorist—domestic and foreign. It is imperative that every nation worldwide adopt a policy whereby the response to terrorism is uniform, whether the threat comes from a terrorist organization or a misguided former head of state. Of course, if the Liberal Left controls both the Congress and the White House, Mr. Carter would be free to continue his courting dance with world terrorists.

In 2002 Carter wrote an article for the *Washington Post* entitled "The Troubling New Face of America." Within the article, Carter referred to "a core group of conservatives who are trying to realize long-pent-up ambitions under the cover of the proclaimed war on terrorism." He pronounced an indictment against the American government for what to him is the reprehensible "support [for] almost every Israeli action in the occupied territories." Mr. Carter berated President Bush for sidestepping policies imposed on Israel and for siding with the Jewish state, our one true ally in the Middle East. His complaint is one frequently heard by Israel's staunchest enemies. Apparently, Carter is as determined as the wealthy Muslim contributors to the Carter Center to see Israel erased from the pages of time. No attack on Israel or its citizens is heinous enough to evoke an angry denouncement from the former president.

In a speech at the Democratic National Convention in 2004, President Carter continued to undermine the sitting president when he denigrated George W. Bush for not force-feeding the PLO's desired concessions down Israel's throat. How remiss is President Bush for not seeing eye-to-eye with Jimmy Carter and his dear friend, the late Yasser Arafat? Carter's virtuous side was exposed for all to appreciate when he officiously pontificated, "We cannot be true to ourselves if we mistreat others." In his opinion, the mistreated would include Khaled Meshaal, murderous leader of Hamas, who is responsible for numerous suicide bombing attacks against Israel; Syrian President Basher al-Assad, head of a terrorist state; North Korean strongman Kim Yong-il; and the list goes on.

Mr. Carter has set the standard and provided the training for today's Liberal Left when it comes to shifting the focus away from terrorists and their deadly activities and onto America's perceived wrongs. After all, if the former president appears in concert with terrorist leaders in the Middle East, it must surely make their activities acceptable. As Norman Podhoretz wrote on *CommentaryMagazine.com*, "Hitler, Mao, and Pol Pot also had their apologists who saw them as 'nationalists' with 'legitimate grievances.'"[811] This was never more obvious than the meetings between the former president and Hamas leaders in April 2008. Fox News reported:

> *Hamas official Mushir Masri, in a fiery speech Friday to thousands of Hamas supporters in Gaza, said the meetings with Carter were proof that Hamas was not a terrorist group, but a national liberation movement.*[812]

In January 1995 this same organization was named a terrorist group by the U.S. government. Having received this classification, it then became unlawful to have business or financial dealings with Hamas. Are former presidents exempted from this law? In August 2003, following a terrorist attack in Jerusalem (that claimed the lives of twenty people, four of whom were U.S. citizens) for which Hamas claimed responsibility, the U.S. Treasury Department's Office of Foreign Asset Control labeled Khaled Meshaal and Musa Abu Marzouk "specially designated global terrorists."[813] With this designation it was, and still is, prohibited to conduct *any* transactions with them.

Why, then, did Carter defy the Bush administration and meet with Hamas? In an *Associated Press* interview, Secretary of State Condoleezza Rice told reporters that President Carter had been "explicitly warned...against meeting with members of Hamas." Rice contradicted Carter's assertions that he never got a clear signal from the State Department. "I just don't want there to be any confusion.... The United States is not going to deal with Hamas and we had certainly told President Carter we did not think meeting with Hamas was going to help."[814] Again, I ask the question: Are former presidents above the law? Though Carter has never been particularly interested in appeasing the Israeli government, he did manage to find time to visit a few victims of Hamas rocket attacks on the village of Sderot just before he met with Meshaal, the man responsible for lobbing those rockets into the middle of the Israeli town.[815]

During his four years as president of the United States, Carter did not so much act as he did react. Had Carter been a chess player, his reactions to dangerous world situations could well have ended his game and put this nation in checkmate after only two moves. Reagan's UN Ambassador Jeane Kirkpatrick very succinctly summed up Carter's liberal game strategy and its future impact in her book, *Dictators and Double Standards*:

> *While Carter was president there occurred a dramatic Soviet military buildup, matched by the stagnation of American armed forces, and a dramatic extension of Soviet influence in the Horn of Africa, Afghanistan, southern Africa, and the Caribbean, matched by a declining American position in all these areas. The United States never tried so hard and failed so utterly to make and keep friends in the Third World. As if this were not bad enough, in one year, 1979, the United States suffered two other major blows—in Iran and Nicaragua—of large and strategic significance. In each country, the Carter administration not only failed to prevent the undesired outcome but actively collaborated in the replacement of moderate autocrats friendly to American interests with less friendly autocrats of extremist persuasion.*[816]

Comatose is the state in which the Liberal Left leaders have most often found themselves. For instance, Carter shilly-shallied over the Soviets and the Shah of Iran; Clinton turned ostrich when confronted with terrorism. Rather than take a strong stand, each man adopted the tactics of appeasement to the detriment of the United States. Whether one chooses the quotation from Edmund

Burke ("All that is necessary for evil to succeed is that good men do nothing.") or from Albert Einstein ("The world is a dangerous place, not because of those who do evil, but because of those who look on and do nothing."[817]), there is one absolute: evil will flourish if not met head-on and conquered. Jimmy Carter was absolutely right in his assessment: the American people had suffered a "crisis of confidence"[818] during his White House tenure—not in the nation—but in its leadership.

In her address to the Republican National Convention in 1984, Kirkpatrick put her finger precisely on the problem when she declared:

> *The Carter administration's motives were good, but their policies were inadequate, uninformed, and mistaken. They made things worse not better. Those who had least suffered most. Poor countries grew poorer. Rich countries grew poorer too. The United States grew weaker...the Soviet Union grew stronger.... Those were the years the Ayatollah Khomeini came to power in Iran.*[819]

Ronald Reagan believed that three liberal entities—what he called the Iron Triangle—were at work to hinder the progress of freedom: special interest groups, the liberal media, and the liberal Democrats.[820] Perhaps the thought process of the liberal media has best been described by Dennis Prager, a popular and respected conservative radio talk show host. In his column titled, "What makes a Liberal?" Prager gives this definition:

> *At the heart of liberalism is the naive belief that people are basically good.... A second naive liberal belief is that because people are basically good, talking with people who do evil is always better than fighting, let alone killing them. "Negotiate with Saddam," "Negotiate with the Soviets," "War never solves anything," "Think peace," "Visualize peace"—the liberal mind is filled with naive clichés about how to deal with evil.*

*Indeed, the very use of the word "evil" greatly disturbs
liberals. It shakes up their child-like views of the world,
that everybody is at heart a decent person who is either mis-
understood or led to do unfortunate things by outside forces.*

*[Prager concluded:] For the liberal, right and wrong are
dismissed as unknowable, and every person chooses his or
her own morality.... Hence the liberal attempt to either erase
the Judeo-Christian code or at least remove its influence
from public life. Nothing could provide a better example of
contemporary liberalism than the liberal battle to remove the
Ten Commandments from all public places. Liberals want
suggestions, not commandments.*[821]

Carter's four years in the highest office of the land has had
a lasting effect, not only in the United States but worldwide. As
mentioned in previous chapters, the president approved the
emasculation of the CIA, essentially gifted China with the Panama
Canal, allowed the USSR to extend its poisonous tentacles of communism into countries worldwide, deceived our closest ally in the
Persian Gulf region—the Shah of Iran, and opened the door to the
fanatical Islamic fundamentalism that plagues the world today.

In order to win the war on terrorism, enemies must first be
identified. It seems more obvious with his every trip abroad that
the U.S. is harboring a snake in its bosom in the guise of a former
president. No other American president sitting or retired has caused
the stir that has Jimmy Carter. Our enemies are not only those
radical Muslims who embrace jihad and the despots that fund them,
they are also the Liberal Left which supports the tenets and doctrines
of the terrorist organizations. Sun Tzu, a Chinese general and
military strategist in 400 BC said, "Keep your friends close and your
enemies closer."[822] Those of us who do not support those rogue
regimes and dictators must constantly defend America's right to
stand behind Israel, her friend, as well as maintain a presence in the
Persian Gulf in the midst of our enemies.

Why Jerusalem has become such a focal point for radical Islam?

In apocalyptic writings, Jerusalem is portrayed as the capital of Islam. Bassam Jirrar, a Hamas member, said, "Islam began in Mecca and Medina and will end in Jerusalem." The subjugation of Jerusalem is apparently necessary for an Islamic takeover of the known world. It is the conquest of the city of God that enflames an irrevocable global jihad.

According to Islamic literature, the failure of Muslims to conquer the world is directly tied to the fact that Jerusalem remains in the hands of the Jews. A resounding defeat of the Jews and the fall of Jerusalem would signal the beginning of an unbeatable Islamic empire worldwide. This is not a new idea; twelfth century Muslim imam Ali Ibn Tahir al-Sulami proclaimed that Jerusalem was the key to success for military victories against the West.

The emphasis on Jerusalem has resulted in it becoming the powder keg on which rests the future of the Middle East. Apocalyptic writings of recent years have made Jerusalem the focal point of Islamic fanaticism. The most hateful and violent terrorist groups have adopted the destruction of Jerusalem as their mantra. The end result could well be what Israeli Major General Farkash called "A global jihad tsunami."

The recurring land-for-peace initiatives are as effective at deterring these radical Islamists as a drop of water on a California wildfire. The fanatics who are so hell-bent on reclaiming Jerusalem want, not East Jerusalem, but all of Jerusalem. They will not rest until they see the Jewish people wiped from the face of the earth. They have not factored into their equation Jehovah God, the Defender of Jerusalem.[823]

I believe the first action that must be taken is a rehabilitation package calling for the dismantling of the UN-maintained refugee camps. The Palestinian Authority needs to be dissolved and absorbed into the Hashemite Kingdom of Jordan. Jordan needs to be given economic incentives to stabilize the Palestinian territory, including the formation of a police force, army, schools, infrastructure, and hospitals. The Arab League and the world community need to provide resettlement, employment, and housing for the refugees. This would be similar to what happened to the Jewish refugees throughout Europe and the Arab world in 1948.

Secondly, I would do everything to help Jordan grant citizenship status to West Bank Palestinians until the late 1980s. The Palestinians do not need more land; they need a life free of fanatical Islamic kindergarten camps that continue to instill hatred for the Jews into children at an early age. They do not need to have the refugee dilemma fueled and fed by radical Islamists who use it as a recruitment tool. Arab countries must be as willing to incorporate Palestinian refugees into their societies as Israel and America have been.

Jerusalem can no longer be used as appeasement bait. President Obama needs to sign the Jerusalem Embassy Act recognizing Jerusalem as Israel's capital and then relocate the Embassy from Tel Aviv. We must stop using the offer of East Jerusalem as a capital for a Palestinian State to pacify Arab rage.

I am reminded over and over of the scripture in Psalm 83:2-5 (NKJV):

> *For behold, Your enemies make a tumult; and those who hate You have lifted up their head. They have taken crafty counsel against Your people, And consulted together against Your sheltered ones. They have said, "Come, and let us cut them off from being a nation, That the name of Israel may be remembered no more." For they have consulted together with one consent; They form a confederacy against You.*

The Bible says in Isaiah 62:6-7 (NKJV):

> *I have set watchmen on your walls, O Jerusalem; They shall never hold their peace day or night. You who make mention*

of the Lord, do not keep silent, And give Him no rest till He establishes, And till he makes Jerusalem a praise in the earth.

Muslim extremists hate everything Western: the freedom to speak out; freedom of the press, the freedom to worship as we wish, the freedom for women to choose. Former Speaker of the House Newt Gingrich wrote, "Politically correct secularists cannot understand that we are participants in a global civil war between... the irreconcilable wings of Islam. While the irreconcilable wing must be fought militarily, this is also a cultural, political, and economic war.... This war is not primarily about terrorism; it is about an Islamist insurgency against the modern world."[824]

Carter is among the number clamoring to change the worldview of these terrorists from that of mass murders of the innocent to "insurgents" or a "liberation movement." He is quick to indict the U.S. at every opportunity, and equally quick to champion the downtrodden suicide bombers or, to be in sync with the Liberal Left, "martyrs."

... I S S T I L L
A L I B E R A L

"God who gave us life gave us liberty. Can the liberties of a nation
be secure when we have removed a conviction that these liberties
are the gift of God? Indeed I tremble for my country when I reflect
that God is just, that his justice cannot sleep forever."
(T H O M A S J E F F E R S O N)[825]

"Men must be governed by God or they will be ruled by tyrants."
(W I L L I A M P E N N)[826]

T H E O L D T E S T A M E N T P R O P H E T I S A I A H warned those
who were determined to change the definition of evil:

> *What sorrow for those who say that evil is good and good*
> *is evil, that dark is light and light is dark, that bitter is sweet*
> *and sweet is bitter.*[827]

The very basis of the Liberal Left belief system is an
unwavering assurance that evil is non-existent. Liberalism says
that mankind is essentially good; and because of that innate
goodness, people should not be held accountable for their actions.

Children are no longer taught there are consequences for their actions and are stunned later in life to find themselves challenged or punished for lying, cheating, stealing, or committing adultery. It becomes a matter of, "I did not have sex with that woman,"[828] rather than facing reality and telling the unvarnished truth. Liberalism, rather than making the guilty pay for their crimes, finds a way to justify the evil and make excuses for the evildoer.

It's time to face the facts: these are terrorists, not insurgents or liberators; for many, the only "choice" is abortion, not life; and those who have sex with underage girls are not "spiritual husbands," they are pedophiles.

The great anathema of those of the Liberal Left is religion. After having lost the election in 2004 to George W. Bush, the party of the Liberal Left tried a new tactic—religion. Freethinking minister Jim Wallis happily offered to instruct Democratic candidates in the skill of formulating responses in an attempt to appear to believe in God. In an interview, Wallis acknowledged his plan to "help the Democrats get religious language so they can win an election." He happily castigates the Religious Right for being so narrow-minded as to think that such issues as abortion and gay rights may not be God's perfect plan for mankind.[829]

Our first president, George Washington, said, "Let us with caution indulge the supposition that morality can be maintained without religion.... Reason and experience both forbid us to expect that national morality can prevail in exclusion of religious principle."[830] John Adams said, "Our Constitution was made only for a religious and moral people. It is wholly inadequate for the government of any other."[831] Perhaps that is why the Liberal Left is fighting so deliberately to remove all things religious from this country: prayer in schools, "under God" from the Pledge of Allegiance, "In God We Trust" from our coins. This is why liberal secular humanists have now forced an entire country to celebrate a holiday labeled "X-mas" and hail the Easter bunny rather than the risen Savior.

What Pope Benedict XVI said of relativism could well be applied to today's definition of liberalism:

Having a clear faith, based on the Creed of the Church, is often labeled today as a fundamentalism. Whereas, relativism, which is letting oneself be tossed and "swept along by every wind of teaching," looks like the only attitude (acceptable) to today's standards. We are moving towards a dictatorship of relativism which does not recognize anything as for certain and which has as its highest goal one's own ego and one's own desires.[832]

Those who practice liberalism have a tough time envisioning ethical issues clearly, and most of them are moral relativists. They deny there is an unconditional definition of good and evil or right and wrong. In their opinion, man is attaining perfection, human nature is on an upward course toward spiritual enlightenment, and the idea of original sin is old-fashioned. This is the moral equivalent of, "If it feels good, do it." It's the Starbucks generation of instant coffee, instant tea, instant gratification, and all at a very high price.

The secular humanist/moral relativist spouts such platitudes as, "Murderers, rapists, and child molesters, are a product of society and should be coddled and rehabilitated not confined." Or, "When law enforcement gets tough with the criminals, minorities are targeted." How about, "Let's do away with the death penalty because it is 'cruel and unusual' punishment"? Tell that to the families of the victims of Richard Speck, Ted Bundy, John Wayne Gacy, Charles Manson, David Berkowitz (Son of Sam), or the most internationally known mass murderer of them all, Yasser Arafat.

It was these moral relativists who glorified Arafat, bestowing on him the Nobel Peace Prize rather than the prison cell he so deserved. After all, it was Arafat the terrorist who was responsible for ordering the cold-blooded murders in Khartoum of Ambassador Cleo Noel and his *chargé d'affaires* G. Curtis Moore; and the murder on the cruise ship, *Achille Lauro*, of Leon Klinghoffer, a disabled American tourist. Mr. Klinghoffer's bullet-riddled body, still strapped in his wheelchair, was then tossed overboard off the coast of Egypt. Not once during Arafat's numerous visits to the Clinton White House was any mention made of arresting the murderous PLO leader for his crimes against humanity. Would that Clinton had displayed the audacity of former New York Mayor Rudolph Giuliani.

When the UN celebrated its fiftieth anniversary in 1995, a long list of world leaders and dignitaries were invited to a concert by the New York Philharmonic at Lincoln Center. Mayor Giuliani spied the PLO leader and his entourage heading for a private box in the concert hall. Giuliani dared to take a strong stance and ordered the terrorist and his minions out of the building.

The Liberal Left was appalled by the mayor's move. While regular New Yorkers applauded the mayor, disdain for Giuliani's actions poured from the pages of the ultra-liberal *New York Times*: "The proper role of New York, as the UN's home city, is to play gracious host to all of the 140 or so world leaders present for the organization's gala 50th birthday celebrations."

Giuliani's response to the brouhaha: "I would not invite Yasser Arafat to anything, anywhere, anytime, anyplace. I don't forget."[833] Unfortunately, the Liberal Left had amnesia where Arafat was concerned. The Clinton White House (which had worked so tirelessly to present Arafat to the American public as a revered statesman) was harsh in its criticism of Giuliani, whose position was called "an embarrassing breach of international diplomacy."[834] While the moral relativists might have forgotten Arafat's death count, Giuliani had not. As Giuliani took the moral high road, the Liberal Left was in a fit of high dudgeon that Arafat, the innocent international statesman, could be so embarrassed in a public setting.

At the Harvard graduation ceremony in 1978, Alexander Solzhenitsyn summed up the Liberal mind-set. Solzhenitsyn characterized U.S. politicians as becoming gripped with paralysis when faced with terrorism on an international scale and compared the battle against it as a spiritual war. Solzhenitsyn asked the Harvard audience these questions:

> *How did the West decline from its triumphal march to its present sickness? Have there been fatal turns and losses of direction in its development?*
>
> *[Then answered:] It does not seem so. The West kept advancing socially in accordance with its proclaimed intentions, with the help of brilliant technological progress. And all of a sudden it found itself in its present state of weakness.*
>
> *This means that the mistake must be at the root, at the very basis of human thinking in the past centuries. I refer to the prevailing Western view of the world, which was first born during the Renaissance and found its political expression from the period of the Enlightenment. It became the basis for government and social science and could be defined as rationalistic humanism or humanistic autonomy: the proclaimed and enforced autonomy of man from any higher force above him....*
>
> *This new way of thinking, which had imposed on us its guidance, did not admit the existence of intrinsic evil in man nor did it see any higher task than the attainment of happiness on earth. It based modern Western civilization on the dangerous trend to worship man and his material needs.*[835]

Stating his opinion was a risk, for Solzhenitsyn suddenly found himself a pariah. It transformed him from media darling to outcast. Once adored by the Liberal Left, he became repugnant simply because he had openly declared his belief in God. But Solzhenitsyn, long held captive for his beliefs, knew one must take a stand against evil or lose all self-respect.

My good friend Bishop Keith Butler wrote about morality in the political arena in his book *Reviving the American Spirit*. Keith wrote:

> *I believe that there's no such thing as "good government" without a moral basis to it.... When the moral quality of*

those in governmental positions is off-track, damage results.... Things are off-track when you need police protection in public schools...when half of the married couples in the nation...are divorced...when every year more than a million babies are aborted.... Where moral principles are the basis for action, good results follow.... Good ideas are brought to fulfillment by good management. The overall conditions of society improve.... You can't legislate morality...but you can legislate morally. You can legislate with integrity and a clear conscience. You can legislate with the goal of serving the good of the people who elected you. You don't have to be religious to be moral...all you need is common sense.[836]

Many, if not all, secular humanists despise Christian beliefs. I wonder if these practitioners of secularism even understand the meaning of Natan Sharansky's "town square test?" Sharansky asked:

Can a person walk into the middle of the town square and express his or her views without fear of arrest, imprisonment, or physical harm? If he can, then that person is living in a free society. If not, it's a fear society.[837]

Daily, Christians seem to lose more ground in the battle to articulate their opinions without fear of retribution from the Liberal Left. The Judeo-Christian principles upon which this nation was founded have given way to the pursuit of multiculturalism. How did this happen? New York University Professor Carol Iannone gave her answer:

Quite simply, it happened because America lost its grasp of its own historic character and embraced "diversity" as a national goal. In the name of equality and nondiscrimination we invited mass immigration from every part of the globe and made no demands on the newcomers to become Americans. In fact, we gave up our American core, adopted multiculturalism, and declared all cultures equal. We invited the new groups to celebrate themselves while we cravenly permitted libelous denigration of our own past. Like fools we prated that diversity is our strength, when common sense and all of history tell us that strength comes from unity.

Absolute nondiscrimination meant we no longer enforced standards, made judgments, distinguished between good and evil, friend and foe. We grew lazy, stupid, and careless— about our borders, about national security, even about previous terrorist attacks against us. We worried over our "hate crimes" and "racial profiling," while men resided in our midst who seethed with murderous fury even against our children and plotted our destruction.... The truth is that the idea of America is nothing if it is not rooted in a sense of identity, of peoplehood, of belonging. As C.S. Lewis might put it, it's...the sentiments we Americans refused to convey, the beliefs we refused to impart, the legacy we have so ignobly betrayed.[838]

In his allegorical tales, *The Chronicles of Narnia*, C. S. Lewis wrote of how the citizens of the mythical Narnia lost their way. David Kupelian, in his book, *The Marketing of Evil,* told of this phenomenon in Lewis' masterpiece, *The Last Battle:*

The inhabitants of Narnia throw away their cherished civilization—losing both their lives and their world itself—by falling for a shabby ruse perpetrated by a few cunning and unprincipled characters...you can't help but thinking, "This isn't even a very clever con game...it's easily seen through from a thousand different directions"...nevertheless, as the con men ruthlessly play on the doubts and fears of the Narnia folk, their lies take hold, and the light of civilization goes out.

[Kupelian asks:] Haven't we in America done exactly the same thing?...We've traded Western civilization for vain delusions, cheap thrills, and laughably illogical doctrines. Like the townsfolk in The Emperor's New Clothes, we all know the king is wearing no clothes...but we play along

out of fear and intimidation...of being labeled "judgmental," "racist," "bigoted," or "homophobic." We quietly allow our minds to be twisted as we surrender our former beliefs and bequeath an unknown country to our children and grandchildren.... Millions residing here are not loyal to American values...the nation is divided and segregated... America literally has been invaded, and we are at war.[839]

I repeat the questions that I asked in my book *The Final Move Beyond Iraq*:

Are we better off today than we were in 1963 when, following a suit filed by Madalyn Murray O'Hare, the U.S. Supreme Court in an eight-to-one decision voted to ban "coercive" prayer and Bible-reading from public schools in America? Are our schools safer? Are fewer kids on drugs? Are fewer kids engaged in promiscuous sex? Are fewer crimes committed by school-age children?[840]

I penned the answer to that question in my book *The American Prophecies*:

We have rejected the foundation of our culture that has traditionally held us together—God and the Holy Scriptures—and as our culture drifts away from that center, we...no longer hear His voice. As a nation, our innocence is being drowned. Things are falling apart. In our halls of justice, in our pulpits, and in the political arenas, those who would speak for God not only lack the conviction to be effective, they are being systematically silenced because of a perverted interpretation of "separation of church and state." First Amendment rights are denied to those who would speak for God, while those who fight for self, special interest, and immorality are passionately intense...as the "spirit of the world" takes over.... We have witnessed this spirit being more active in our world than ever before through the "isms" of Fascism, Nazism, Communism, and terrorism—the greatest threats to human liberty we have ever faced.[841]

The American public was stunned in the 1960s by the murders of President John F. Kennedy, his brother Robert F. Kennedy, and civil rights leader, Dr. Martin Luther King. It was the first taste of terrorism on American soil. It was the precursor of events that would thrust this nation into an ongoing battle between light and darkness, good and evil, and life and death. It signaled the end of national innocence enjoyed by preceding generations. America progressed, if you wish to call it that, from the clean-cut *Ozzie and Harriet* to Archie Bunker's bigoted, beer-guzzling, boorish character in *All in the Family*; from *Leave it to Beaver* to *Beavis and Butthead*. Music has deteriorated from dulcet tones with understandable words to screaming harpies jumping about on the stage like banshees released from the halls of hell.

Art has degenerated from that of the likes of Claude Monet or more recently, Thomas Kinkade, to that of Andres Serrano's federally-funded photographs of a crucifix submerged in his urine; or Artists Space, a National Endowment for the Arts-funded gallery which required patrons to tread upon an American flag on the floor as part of the exhibit, "What is the Proper Way to Display a U.S. Flag?" There are other NEA exhibits that are too profane to mention, paid for with our tax dollars. Jeff Jacoby of the *Boston Globe* wrote of the NEA:

> *The NEA consistently rewards novelty over quality. Its grant recipients are often distinguished by little more than intolerance toward traditional standards and art forms. Artistry, beauty, and craftsmanship are routinely rejected in favor of radical politics, victim chic, and anger.*

The family has been bombarded with the vulgar and profane for so long, we hardly shuddered when Bea Arthur as the character *Maude* underwent an abortion in 1972; or when the first television movie about open homosexuality, *That Certain Summer,* also aired in 1972; or when Steven Bochco introduced nudity and profanity-laced dialogue on the television series *NYPD Blue*.[842]

Today, condoms can be freely dispensed to students on campus, but it is illegal to give a Bible to a student on school property. And under the guise of "news" we are bombarded with pictures of same-sex couples in states (such as California and Massachusetts) happily kissing each other after being declared legally "married."

I wrote in *The Final Move Beyond Iraq*:

> *The hippies of the 60s have become the establishment against which they once railed. Even now they run the culture, the media, the educational system, the courts, the arts, and...they are still self-destructing. From the public and private sector, from mainstream Hollywood to the public schools, from Washington politics to local judges, from the arts to the sciences, they are self-destructing.*[843]

Not all is gloom and doom, however. Roman orator Cicero proclaimed, "While there is life; there is hope." Perhaps even more appropriate would be the words of the apostle Paul, "Awake, you who sleep, arise from the dead, and Christ will give you light" (Ephesians 5:14, NKJV). The good news is that while America has sown to the wind, it can escape the whirlwind. How is that possible? Like the prophet Isaiah who, when faced with God's holiness in Isaiah 6:5, cried, "Woe is me, for I am undone! Because I am a man of unclean lips, and I dwell in the midst of a people of unclean lips." The writer of II Chronicles 7:14 (NKJV) in the Old Testament had the answer to Isaiah's predicament, and ours, within his grasp. It lies in humility, prayer, repentance, and restoration: "If My people who are called by My name will humble themselves, and pray and seek My face, and turn from their wicked ways, then I will hear from heaven, and will forgive their sin and heal their land."

Integrity is an essential ingredient; the determination to do the right thing must triumph over apathy. Perhaps the ancient Chinese philosopher Confucius said it best: "To put the world right in order, we must first put the nation in order; to put the nation in order, we must first put the family in order; to put the family in order, we must first cultivate our personal life; we must first set our hearts right."

George Barna, a respected pollster, released a study which indicated that professing Christians in America are little different in thought and actions than non-believers. Said Barna:

> For years we have reported research findings showing that born-again adults think and behave very much like everyone else. It often seems like their faith makes very little difference in their life. This new study helps explain why that is: Believers do not train their children or act any differently. When our kids are exposed to the same influences, without much supervision, and are generally not guided to interpret their circumstances and opportunities in light of biblical principals, it's no wonder they grow up to be just as involved in gambling, adultery, divorce, cohabitation, excessive drinking, and other unbiblical behaviors as everyone else.[844]

Many churches today have become hotbeds of liberalism, little more than Left-embracing political action committees. Numbers of these organizations find shelter under the National Council of Churches banner which includes the Evangelical Lutheran Church in America, Presbyterian Church (USA), United Church of Christ, United Methodist Church, Disciples of Christ, Episcopal Church, as well as a number of Baptist Churches that have broken away from the Southern Baptist Convention.

Rather than conforming to God's Word, liberal churches have conformed the Word to meet their beliefs; thus, anything goes. One can find a church to fit whatever that person wishes to believe...and if not, start their own. The alternatives are mind blowing: liberal or conservative, ethical or amoral, high-energy or contemplative, noisy or quiet, racist or all-encompassing, Jew-lovers or Jew-haters, Christ-honoring or Satan worshippers, mainstream or bizarre.

We learned in 2008 that former presidents are not above establishing their own religious organization; Jimmy Carter and Bill Clinton founded the New Baptist Covenant. This should not have surprised anyone, as Carter had relinquished his membership in the Southern Baptist Convention in 2000. According to Carter, he and Clinton were attempting to bring Baptists together "in the spirit of serving Christ without recrimination and without animosity and without criticizing each other." Sounds good on paper!

Little, if anything, was done to disguise the Liberal Left influence on the organization with such events as a "Stewardship of the Earth" luncheon hosted by Al Gore, speakers Tony Campolo, Marian Wright Edelman, and Bill Clinton. Just for the sake of parity a couple of border-line Republicans, Lindsey Graham and Chuck Grassley, were invited.

Given Carter's growing messianic complex, it is no wonder that in his view, Christ passed up a wonderful opportunity, when tempted by Satan, to establish the perfect example of secular leadership for the former governor/president. In his book *Keeping Faith*, Carter contemplated Satan's offer of world leadership if Christ would only turn from God. According to Carter:

> *What a wonderful and benevolent government Jesus could have set up. How exemplary justice would have been. Maybe there would have been Habitat projects all over Israel for anyone who needed a home. And the proud, the rich, and the powerful could not have dominated their fellow citizens. As a twentieth-century governor and president I would have had a perfect pattern to follow. I could have pointed to the Bible and told other government leaders, "This is what Jesus did 2000 years ago in government. Why don't we do the same?"*[845]

The great theologian Francis Schaeffer attempted to warn the Church of its destructive downward path in his book *The Great Evangelical Disaster*:

> *Most of the evangelical world has not been active in the battle, or even been able to see that we are in a battle. And when it comes to the issues of the day the evangelical world*

most often has said nothing; or worse has said nothing different from what the world would say. Here is the great evangelical disaster—the failure of the evangelical world to stand for truth as truth. There is only one word for this—namely accommodation; the evangelical church has accommodated to the spirit of the world.[846]

Theology Professor David F. Wells of Gordon-Conwell Theological Seminary asked the question:

Why is it that with more than a third of the nation's adults in 1990 claiming a born-again experience and many more beyond that claiming allegiance to Christian values, the society moves on oblivious to its religious citizens, reshaping laws and policies as if they are not there?"

With frightening clarity, Wells answers his own question:

They [professing Christians] are not there.... Whatever follies the Marxists committed...they always had the wisdom to know that if they yielded their worldview, they yielded their reason for existence. Evangelicals are not quite so wise.[847]

The darkness that has seeped into the Church, even when espoused by former presidents, must be exposed to the Light; evil must be revealed and named as such. Fortunately, there is still time; the cry from Revelation 3:20 (NKJV) can still be heard: "Behold, I stand at the door and knock. If anyone hears My voice and opens the door, I will come in to him and dine with him, and he with Me."

When Joshua stood before Israel, he knew what made a nation great; not its government, not its leaders, not a constitutional mandate, but rather, a people committed to godly living. Joshua challenged the children of Israel to make a choice, so must we heed his words:

And if it seems evil to you to serve the Lord, choose for yourselves this day whom you will serve.... But as for me and my house, we will serve the Lord" (Josh. 24:15 NKJV).

A line has been drawn in the sands of time; we must either step across the line and take up the banner of truth, or we will perish in the choking, swirling whirlwind. We must abandon liberalism or be caught in the crush of the multitudes on the road that leads to destruction.

THROUGH THE LOOKING GLASS: THE FUTURE OF THE LIBERAL LEFT

"To this day he [Carter] still doesn't know how much he doesn't know." (MICHAEL SCHOENFELD)[848]

"The true agenda of the Left is...control of the society by a small elite group. They are a patient lot and willing to achieve their goals over a long period of time through seemingly minor and incremental changes in the laws and attitudes of the nation." [849]

ONLY TIME WILL TELL IF PRESIDENT Barack Obama proves to be even more liberal and left than was Jimmy Carter. During the election campaign, Obama stated one of his first goals as president would be to sit down and negotiate with the rogue leaders of such countries as Iran and Syria. The despotic heads of those countries and others like them are looking for any microscopic evidence of weakness on the part of an American president.

In an article for *American Thinker*, Bruce Walker compared the two Democrats:

Carter promised change and hope.... Millions of Americans listened. They trusted Carter to be "'different.'"... He was an idealist who was not wedded to failed ideals of the past.... Carter supported on "human rights" grounds the overthrow of the Shah.... He pursued domestic policies which called for privation instead of growth. Carter [who promised he would never lie] lied about firing U.S. Attorney David Marston, who had been investigating corrupt Pennsylvania Democratic congressmen.... Carter...was "surprised" that communism was aggressive and malignant.... Carter seriously seems to have considered that...Moscow was no great threat to America, and that the proliferation of virulently anti-American dictators around the globe was in our long-term best interest.... Barack Obama seems cut of identical cloth.... He rejects anti-Semitic, anti-American supporters only when nudged to do so.... It certainly seems as if Obama feels himself morally superior to those in politics today, much like Carter did thirty years ago.... Obama, like Carter, is an utter and complete Democratic partisan.... Jimmy Carter never tried to "govern from the center" or "seek bipartisanship." He could easily have passed tax cuts or defense spending increases. He did not want to. Barack Obama never sought bipartisanship. He embraces leftism completely. They are the same: Barack Obama is our next Jimmy Carter.[850]

The world could slide into total chaos under the leadership of the Liberal Left in America. The Soviet Union would be motivated to reestablish itself as a world power and, in fact, has already tested the resolve of both America and the world by invading its neighbor, Georgia. China would be emboldened to invade Taiwan, and the Arab League might be persuaded to launch an attack against Israel. Who would have the backbone to stop such aggression? Obama, who proudly proclaims he had no part in the war in Iraq? There are concerns in the Middle East that should the U.S. pull out of Iraq, Iran would launch a Khomeini-style revolution in Iraq such as the one that happened during the Carter presidency. Would President Obama take the side of the aggressor nation rather than go to battle to protect the rights of the downtrodden? President Obama may have to learn quickly what other leaders already know: "Without national security, nothing else matters."[851]

General David Petraeus, U.S. Central Command, Multi-National Forces in Iraq, expressed his concern that the U.S. would withdraw troops precipitously, leaving Iraq open to the vultures that are waiting along the borders to descend and lead the country into a maelstrom of murder and reprisals. Advances against al-Qaeda would be lost, Iran would stand to gain control over Iraq's large oil reserves, and the Taliban resurgence in Afghanistan could spread into Iraq. American credibility in the world, already strained, would be shattered, as would Obama's smug campaign promise to restore confidence in the U.S. abroad. All of this could well happen while Barack Obama is in the White House. During the campaign, he avowed:

> *Let me be clear: there is no military solution in Iraq, and there never was. The best way to protect our security and to pressure Iraq's leaders to resolve their civil war is to immediately begin to remove our combat troops. Not in six months or one year—now.*[852]

Barack Obama took one Carter-like step early in his campaign. He added former Carter National Security Advisor Zbigniew Brzezinski to his own list of advisors. Brzezinski, of course, got himself into trouble early in his role as advisor when "he published an essay in the summer issue of the journal *Foreign Policy*, defending a controversial new book about the power of the 'Israel Lobby' in American politics. 'It is a tremendous mistake for Barack Obama to select as a foreign policy adviser the one person in public life who has chosen to support a bigoted book,' said Harvard Law professor Alan Dershowitz, one of the most visible critics of the [Stephen] Walt and [John] Mearsheimer volume, titled *The Israel Lobby*."[853]

One of Zbig's first jobs as advisor was to defend Mr. Obama's plan, if elected to the highest office in the land, to meet with Iran, Syria, and Venezuela: "What's the hang-up about negotiating with the Syrians or Iranians?" asked Brzezinski. "What it in effect means is that you only talk to people who agree with you."[854] People who agree with you? It would be interesting to know just exactly what it is on which President Obama thinks he, Ahmadinejad, Chavez, and Assad agree.

Remember, it was Mr. Obama who said early in the campaign that he wanted to sit down with Iran's president for talks. One question that might be put to Barack Obama: How do you expect to accomplish what seasoned veterans of "talking with the enemy" have not been able to do? How can you top what Britain, France, and Germany have already tried? What is it you plan to give away in order to best Europe's most gifted negotiators? Carter gave away the Panama Canal and Iran; perhaps we don't *really* need Alaska or Hawaii, do we?

It has been proven time and again that offering unprecedented concessions to the enemy is ineffective. In a *Jerusalem Post* article, Barry Rubin explained:

> *If the other side won't give anything…merely offer more. And if the other side takes those concessions, pockets them, gives nothing in return and continues its behavior, this merely proves you have to give still more.*

> *Here's more evidence why that's wrong. Former US Marine Col. Timothy Geraghty was Marine commander in October 1983 when suicide bombers attacked the barracks of US peacekeeping forces in Beirut, killing 242 Americans. He now reveals that a September 26, 1983, U.S. intelligence intercept showed Iran's government ordering the attack through its embassy in Lebanon. The timid response to that operation set a pattern leading directly to the September 11 attack.[855]*

Making concessions didn't work for Carter, Reagan, or Clinton, and it won't work for Barack Obama. It will only further endanger Americans at home and abroad.

During the campaign Obama continued to surround himself with people whose anti-Israel leanings were suspect. One such individual is Robert Malley, whose Syrian-born father is said to have "loathed" Israel and who became a close confidant to Yasser Arafat. Malley has written a number of op-eds that are scathingly opposed to Israel. He often blames Israel for any perceived failure to reach a Middle East peace settlement with her enemies. Malley's rhetoric has proven to be rich fodder for the PLO and for anti-Israel militants worldwide.

Another man from whom Obama sought advice was Joseph Cirincione, President of the Ploughshares Fund. Listed in "Discover the Networks," a guide to the Liberal Left, the Fund is defined as: "'a public grant-making foundation that supports initiatives to prevent the spread and use of nuclear, biological, and chemical weapons and other weapons of war, and to prevent conflicts that could lead to the use of weapons of mass destruction.' It also opposes America's development of a missile defense system."[856]

Cirincione is said to have decidedly anti-Israel leanings. Ed Lasky, writer for *American Thinker,* concurs. He wrote that Cirincione was "another in a disconcertingly long line of Obama advisors who seemingly have an anti-Israel bias and who would be very willing to apply American pressure on our tiny ally to disarm itself in the face of its mortal enemies."[857]

Days before the 2008 election, the leader of one rogue state endorsed Obama according to an AFP article in *YNetNews:*

> *Iranian parliament Speaker Ali Larijani said Wednesday that Iran would prefer Democrat Barack Obama in the White House next year. Larijani also dismissed any idea that the US would attack Iran. "We are leaning more in favor of Barack Obama because he is more flexible and rational, even thoughwe know American policy will not change that much," Larijani said at a press conference during a visit to Bahrain.[858]*

Now, why do you suppose both a terrorist organization and a terrorist state would support one candidate over another? Could it have been the knowledge that one candidate is likely to be more left, more liberal, and more willing to sacrifice Israel than the other? And yet, it is eerily apparent that despite his circle of anti-Israel advisors, the media and voters see Barack Obama as a staunch supporter of that tiny nation in the midst of a sea of detractors.

Unfortunately, Mr. Obama did not fare as well with al-Qaeda's second-in-command, Ayman al-Zawahri. He chose a racial slur to describe the president-elect.

> *Speaking in Arabic, al-Zawahri used the Arabic term "abeed al-beit;" the literal translation means "house slaves."*
>
> *"America has put on a new face, but its heart full of hate, mind drowning in greed, and spirit which spreads evil, murder, repression and despotism continue to be the same as always," the deputy of al-Qaida chief Osama bin Laden said.*
>
> *"Be aware that the dogs of Afghanistan have found the flesh of your soldiers to be delicious, so send thousands after thousands to them," he said.*
>
> *Al-Zawahri did not threaten specific attacks, but warned Obama that he was "facing a Jihadi (holy war) awakening and renaissance which is shaking the pillars of the entire Islamic world; and this is the fact which you and your government and country refuse to recognize and pretend not to see."*
>
> *He said Obama's victory showed Americans acknowledged that President George W. Bush's policies were a failure and that the result was an "admission of defeat in Iraq."*[859]

Perhaps it would make more sense if Mr. Obama were to tackle the question of just how he's going to keep these Islamic terrorists at bay, or how he's going to formulate a plan to deal with the likes of Iranian President Mahmoud Ahmadinejad, whose sole focus is to bring America to her knees, or more correctly, on her face in obeisance to Islam.

Obama's campaign strategist David Axelrod took a relatively unheard-of candidate and thrust him onto the political stage with complete success. He gave his front-runner a nebulous message of "hope and change." The media fawned over him as if he were, indeed, the savior of the world.

Writing of media bias, David Limbaugh said:

> *The media's deification of Obama is largely responsible for the perception that the candidate is superhuman.... we can chalk up the media's irrational exuberance to their eagerness to have someone of like mind—someone sufficiently socialistic and appeasement-oriented—back in the Oval office.... What's more difficult to stomach is their reckless obliviousness to their own closed-mindedness, intolerance, unreasonableness and conceit.*[860]

In another Carter-likeness: "Mr. Obama appears determined to undertake a radical change in the way Washington does business with the outside world; changes that could have the same disastrous consequences for America and the rest of the world as did Mr. Carter's policy."[861]

Also like Mr. Carter, early on in his campaign President Obama tasted the political efficacy of straddling the fence, and he has mastered the ability to backtrack. During a speech to the American-Israel Public Affairs Committee (AIPAC) in June 2008, Obama modified some of his earlier statements "under the guise of 'clarification'...Yes, he is still in favor of meeting with Iran's leaders, but only at the suitable levels and at a place and time of his choosing. He favors a withdrawal of American troops from Iraq, but it must be gradual. He prefers diplomatic and economic pressure, but says the military option should be left on the table. In short, the Democratic candidate has shifted toward the center."[862] After all, center is where the votes are, and as his predecessor Jimmy Carter learned, one must be willing to do or say anything to achieve election to the highest office in the land.

How committed is Obama to Israel's security? He promised the members of AIPAC a "Palestinian...state that is contiguous and cohesive, and that allows them to prosper...[and] Jerusalem will remain the capital of Israel, and it must remain undivided...[but that the final solution for Jerusalem] must be negotiated between the two parties [Israelis and Palestinians], an agreement that they can both live with." How can this be, when the Palestinians have demanded again and again that Jerusalem must become the capital of the Palestinian state?

Reports have also surfaced that during his visit to Israel in 2008, Barack Obama embraced the Peace Initiative adopted at the 2007 Arab League Summit in Beirut. The E.U. and Russia also backed the Initiative which calls for Israel to withdraw to 1967 borders and execute UN Security Council resolutions 242 and 338. Israel would be granted full recognition and relations with all Arab and Muslim states normalized. The international community supports this plan. There have been calls from some quarters for President Obama to appoint a special envoy to oversee yet another peace initiative which would strip Israel of land and offer little in return.

Barack Obama developed an impenetrable mask as presidential candidate. Behind that façade stands the real persona of the man who would lead. Throughout his early political career, he joined forces with numerous anti-Israel activists. In his formative years and with a myriad of churches from which to choose, he aligned himself with Rev. Jeremiah Wright Jr. Wright's stance regarding Israel and the Jews became well-known during Obama's campaign. The pastor, a Black Muslim sympathizer riddled with anti-Semitism, led a church whose officers accepted and backed his anti-Israel practices. His diatribe following 9/11, an event Wright labeled as "chickens coming home to roost," was particularly offensive and provoking. He insinuated the horrific assaults were godly revenge for America's many failures at race relations.

In his now-famous discourse, "Confusing God and Government," Wright sermonized:

> The United States government has failed the vast majority of her citizens of African American descent.... Think about this, think about this. For every one Oprah, a billionaire, you've got five million blacks who are out of work. For every one Colin Powell, a millionaire, you've got ten million blacks who cannot read. For every one Condoleezza Rice, you've got one million in prison.[863]

Plausibility failed when candidate Obama avowed he and his wife sat in a pew at Trinity United Church of Christ for twenty years and were not influenced by the malicious proclivity of Rev. Wright toward racism, crudeness, and anti-Americanism.

Rev. Wright also openly supported Louis Farrakhan, Supreme Minister of the Nation of Islam. Farrakhan has labeled the Jews "bloodsuckers." A *New York Times* article included a statement from a sermon delivered by him that defined his opinion of Israel:

> "Now that nation called Israel never has had any peace in forty years and she will never have any peace because there can be no peace structured on injustice, thievery, lying, and deceit, and using the name of God to shield your gutter religion under His holy and righteous name."[864] Remember that Obama referred to Wright as his "spiritual mentor, his moral compass, and his sounding board. He was the man who gave Obama the term, 'The Audacity of Hope.'"[865] It makes one wonder: for what exactly does Barack Obama hope?

On foreign policy issues, Obama's call to eradicate nuclear weapons worldwide would leave the West and Israel at the mercy of unscrupulous, hate-filled leaders in countries such as Iran and Syria. Those nations would simply go farther underground and continue the secret production of nuclear arms. A part of Israel's firewall against the launch of a globally inclusive attack is its nuclear arsenal. Obama's plan would effectively disarm Israel, while making it impossible to police the Irans of the world. Has he considered the danger of beating our collective swords into plowshares? That would leave the world even more vulnerable to those who don't follow suit, who instead keep their swords at the ready.

As was Carter, Obama has been compared to yet another former president, John F. Kennedy. The comparison is flattering but limited: "JFK was a seasoned political veteran. When he announced his presidential candidacy in January 1960, Kennedy had already represented Massachusetts in Congress for thirteen years, first in the House of Representatives and then in the U.S. Senate.... Kennedy benefited from the new, 20th-century media environment, with looks and grace that easily won out over Nixon's sweaty lip and grim demeanor.... The Illinois senator is promoting a vaguer version of JFK's 'New Frontier.'"[866]

Unlike Carter, Obama captured the endorsement of Kennedy's brother, Senator Ted Kennedy. He was also endorsed by JFK's daughter, Caroline Kennedy Schlossberg, who was then named to Obama's committee for selecting a running mate. Obama, however, has not yet landed on the cover of *Time* posed as President Kennedy. Carter won that prize during his second campaign for the White House.

When elected, Barack Obama lacked hands-on experience in executive leadership and national security, and like Carter he has no shortage of self-esteem or egotism. His record as a senator was patently unexceptional, except for his record of missed votes. While running for office, Mr. Obama and his fellow senator/opponents were present for roll-call votes five of the first ninety days of 2008. Regardless of their absenteeism, all candidates were paid in full— $165,000 per year. Dick Morris asked the question: "Would you still get paid if you took a year or two off to compete for another job?"[867] Accusations have been made that his frequent absences coincided with votes on the more difficult issues, i.e., calling for Iran's Revolutionary Guard to be named a terrorist group.

Unfortunately, Obama's accomplishments have been too few. He burst on the national scene at the 2004 Democratic National Convention with a rock star-like celebrity. The day before he was to deliver the keynote address, he and a friend, Mary Nesbitt, met. She remembered:

> *We were walking down the street late in the afternoon, and the crowd was building behind us, like it was Tiger Woods at the Masters. "Barack, man, you're like a rock star." [Obama replied] "Yeah, if you think it's bad today, wait until tomorrow." "What do you mean?" "My speech," Obama said, "is pretty good."*[868]

In June 2008 Obama took his massive campaign entourage, enough to fill a twenty-car motorcade, through the streets of Amman, Jordan, and went on a whirlwind tour of the Middle East and Europe. The adoration of the assembled masses would have done any Hollywood megastar proud. The size of the entourage was eclipsed only by the media attention garnered by the *candidate* for the Democratic nomination. It seemed that not only had Mr. Obama removed the word "presumptive" from before "nominee," he had also removed the word "candidate" from after "presidential." He was moving through foreign destinations—Afghanistan, Iraq, Jordan, Israel, and Germany, to name a few—with all the ease, aplomb, and expectations of a chief executive. In Afghanistan he and Hamid Karzai sat before a fireplace for their "fireside chat." (That too is reminiscent of Mr. Carter's fireside chats, complete with cardigan.)

The only disappointment of the well-planned and executed trip was a denial from the Germans for "President-elect" Obama to speak at the Brandenburg Gate, the site of Ronald Reagan's famous and effective "tear down this wall" speech in 1987. It was also in

Berlin that John F. Kennedy made his equally noted *"Ich bin ein Berliner"* speech. Such audacity, and so early in the campaign!

In answer to Obama's request, German Chancellor Angela Merkel said through her spokesperson:

> *"It is unusual to hold election rallies abroad. No German candidate for high office would even think of using the National Mall (in Washington) or Red Square in Moscow for a rally because it would not be seen as appropriate."* Merkel later added: *"If the candidate—or any other candidate is elected, then (he) is welcome to speak as president before the Brandenburg Gate."*[869]

Addressing the crowd in Berlin and uplinked to news media around the world, Obama declared his candidacy as the globalist president, the candidate of the New World Order: "People of Berlin—people of the world—this is our moment. This is our time."[870] Obviously ignoring the admonition in the poem, "Mending Wall," by Robert Frost ("Good fences make good neighbors"[871]), Obama spoke of the need to tear walls down:

> *The walls between old allies on either side of the Atlantic cannot stand. The walls between the countries with the most and those with the least cannot stand. The walls between races and tribes, natives and immigrants, Christian and Muslim and Jew cannot stand. These now are the walls we must tear down.... We know they have fallen before. After centuries of strife, the people of Europe have formed a Union of promise and prosperity.*[872]

When followed to its most far-reaching conclusion, this seems to be a simple call for a communist world. Obama's starry-eyed followers prefer to believe that, as president, he will be able to resolve all of the world's problems with a swish of the pen. Unfortunately for Mr. Obama, these problems have plagued the planet since time immemorial: wars, hunger, fear, greed, paucity, and disease. His speech in Berlin and his egomania simply opened the door for a myriad of questions regarding an Obama presidency:

» Where will America be after four (or even eight years) of Liberal Left leadership?

» What will President Obama concede to our enemies in order to assuage his ego?

» Does he understand there are people who hate America simply because the American people are free to choose?

» How far left and how "global" will Obama take our country?

» What will happen to Social Security and to the myriad of baby boomers just entering retirement age?

» How high will taxes be raised on capital gains (up to 28 percent, says Dick Morris[873]), inheritances, and Social Security?

» Will anything be done to control the influx of illegal immigrants, or will the Liberal Left throw wide the door and create an even greater burden on taxpayers?

» Will medical care become so difficult to acquire that millions are left uncovered?

» How vulnerable will we be to terrorism? Will Obama, like Jimmy Carter, be such a pacifist that terrorist regimes worldwide will not hesitate to ply their trade on our shores?

» Will Obama abandon our allies in the Middle East, as Carter abandoned the Shah of Iran?

» Just what is Barack Hussein Obama's agenda for the citizens of the United States of America?

During the campaign, Obama was accused of elitism. Will he further embrace what has been called the "conceit of the elite?" And just what does that mean? The political definition of "elitism" as applied to Barack Obama means a person "out of touch with the common people. The implication is that the 'elitist' person or group thinks they are better than everyone else, and therefore put themselves before others. It could be seen as a synonym for snob. An elitist is not always seen as truly elite, but only privileged."[874]

Only time will paint the true portrait of Obama: Will he truly grasp the plight of the middle- and lower-class men and women across racial lines who struggle to make ends meet? Or will the opposite be true: In an attempt to create a classless society, will he drain the wallets of those business owners and entrepreneurs who provide jobs and wages for American men and women?

Obama's choice for his vice president just prior to the Democratic National Convention, Senator Joe Biden, was another feather in the cap of the Liberal Left. According to the *National Journal Online*:

> *[Biden's] composite liberal score of 94.2 placed him as the 3rd most-liberal senator in 2007, two ticks behind Barack Obama, who was the most liberal senator last year with a score of 95.5.*[875]

David Freddoso pointed out that "Obama represents the merger of two of the worst aspects of Democratic politics...60s radicalism and corrupt Chicago machine politics. With the addition of...Biden to the ticket, Obama has added to his [ticket] an epic amount of Beltway cluelessness and arrogance unsupported by anything except frequent flier miles and Delaware's love for a chuckle-headed fellow with a big smile.... For Obama, it is all about politics and words, elections and poses...Joe is the perfect running mate on a perfect ticket for a party betting on wind to solve the energy crisis."[876]

It is also interesting to note that for the first time in sixty-eight years, the Democrats and the majority of American voters chose two men who have no military experience. That may prove to be problematic for a world filled with Osama bin Laden wannabes, an awakening Russian bear, and enough global hotspots to rival hell. Given the fact that Dick Cheney was castigated by the Dems for having received five deferments during the Vietnam War, I wonder why Joe Biden escaped the same scrutiny. He is only a year younger than Cheney and received the same deferments for education as did the former vice president.

In an article for *World Net Daily*, Ilana Mercer introduced an interesting note about President Obama:

> *When Barack Obama looked Americans in the metaphoric eye and told them he was not and was never a Muslim he had...been worshipping at the Trinity United Church of Christ for twenty-odd years.... On the Muslim matter...in Islam, the father's faith determines that of a child.... [According to] Daniel Pipes, a scholar of the Middle East and Islam...Obama's patrilineal ties to Islam—Muslim father and grandfather—make him a Muslim by birth. And "only Muslim children are named Hussein."...the young Obama would have had to "learn about Islam for two hours each week in religion classes."...for a few formative years, Obama had a moderate "Muslim upbringing."... To claim, as Obama has, that he has always been Christian and had never practiced Islam is, then, not quite so.... Christian doctrine decrees that embracing Jesus Christ as personal savior is the only road to redemption...Obama disagrees. He...says, "There are many paths to the same place.' Is that Christianity?... Hussein's a hip hybrid: not quite Muslim, not quite Christian...he'll be the first post-American president in a post-Christian America.*[877]

In an article for *National Review Online*, Mark Krikorian defined a "post-American." The same definition could be applied to a "post-Christian." He wrote:

> *"Let me be clear what I mean by a post-American. He's not an enemy of America—not Alger Hiss or Jane Fonda or*

Louis Farrakhan. He's not necessarily even a Michael Moore or Ted Kennedy. A post-American may actually still like America, but the emotion resembles the attachment one might feel to, say, suburban New Jersey—it can be a pleasant place to live, but you're always open to a better offer. The post-American has a casual relationship with his native country, unlike the patriot, "who more than self his country loves," as Katharine Lee Bates wrote. Put differently, the patriot is married to America; the post-American is just shacking up.... [post-Americans] are those who have moved beyond America, "citizens of the world," as the cliché goes— in other words citizens (at least in the emotional sense) of nowhere in particular.[878]

As with questions regarding any occupant of the White House, only time will tell how the liberal Mr. Obama and his social conscience will fare. Obama has already embraced the "global is good" theme, endorsed in his speech in Berlin in July 2008.

An editorial in *National Review* stated the obvious in July 2008: "Obama may or may not be a left-wing radical. He is certainly a utopian radical. And if that makes him a better man, it also makes him a worse statesman."[879]

How *has* Barack Obama handled the challenges that faced him as the forty-fourth president? In short, the American people had no earthly idea what Barack Hussein Obama would do when he arrived at 1600 Pennsylvania Avenue. More questions than answers remained: Should Iran launch a nuclear attack against our allies in the Middle East, will Mr. Obama have the courage to open the briefcase and enter the code for retaliation? Or would he, like Jimmy Carter, refuse to keep that "nuclear football" in close proximity at all times? If America were to be attacked again by fanatical Muslim terrorists, how would Mr. Obama respond? Only time will tell just how much an Obama presidency would echo that of Jimmy Carter's. It is obvious their worldviews and lack of moral clarity are more than similar; in fact, it is eerily parallel. Another comparison between the two men is that Obama, like Carter, had "undeniably slim"[880] Washingtonian credentials and no hands-on foreign policy experience.

I pray when challenged by those who wish only to see America's destruction, and he will be, that he will stand firm and consider the security of America first and foremost. Is the Obama who refused to salute the flag of this country during a rendition of the National Anthem truly a "citizen of the world" as he seemed determined to portray himself in Berlin in July 2008? Will he consider the U.S. above other Western nations, or will he sell this country down the river as Jimmy Carter seemed determined to do during his administration?

Questions continue to abound: Will Obama assume the "human rights" mantle from his mentor Jimmy Carter and jeopardize U.S. allies in every region of the world? Just what *is* his "backbone quotient"? Carter gave away the Panama Canal and abandoned Iran to Islamic fundamentalists. Will Obama give Israel away and then abandon America to her enemies? Will America become the frog in the pot of cold water? Have we become so complacent that when the fire is ignited, America will perish without a fight?

Only time will reveal the answer to all of these imponderables. Now we can only pray that Barack Hussein Obama will be more a John F. Kennedy than a Jimmy Carter; that he will be cast more in the mold of a Ronald Reagan than a William Jefferson Clinton.

There were some very telling indicators in the early days of the Obama administration about the governing style of the president: he is liberal to the core, matching the voting record of the likes of John Kerry, Ted Kennedy, and Joe Biden; and he sports an all-inclusive worldview that supports not only the entry of illegals but would afford privileges which would require an even greater tax burden on American citizens.

Like his political role-model, Jimmy Carter, Barack Obama is captivating, eloquent, amiable, and unruffled. Obama spoke little during his campaign of his political viewpoint. It has been said of Carter and Obama that they seem "cut of identical cloth.... Obama quickly corrects statements which show how he truly feels.... It seems that Obama feels himself morally superior to those in politics today, much like Carter did thirty years ago.... Barack Obama has never sought bipartisanship. He embraces leftism completely... Barack Obama is our next Jimmy Carter."[881]

Yet another noted collegian, James W. Ceaser, professor of politics at the University of Virginia, wrote:

> *The candidate whose path to the presidency most resembled Obama's was Jimmy Carter; he too used an intensely personal and inspirational appeal to compensate for a thin resume. Having courted the public with flattering rhetoric— promising "a government as good as the American people"—Carter came a cropper as president.*[882]

Charles Krauthammer, in his summation on the Fox News Channel on election night, summed up Barack Hussein Obama better than any other commentator:

> *Here's a man nobody had heard of a few years ago...and who created himself. He beat the Clinton machine ...with the force of his intelligence and charisma I don't think anybody has seen since Pierre Elliot Trudeau did in Canada...and he carried himself all the way to the presidency. I think it's that force of personality...it's also what makes him opaque and unknown. Which way will he go as president, nobody knows. Because we really still don't know who he is, and we'll discover that after he occupies the Oval Office. We really don't know who he is and what he believes, but we know of his intelligence and ambition.*[883]

It is still not too late to learn from the Carter White House, and perhaps we can avoid the plethora of mistakes made by former President Jimmy Carter. Should we decide to play ostrich, to forget the past, and not hold Mr. Obama accountable, our reward could very well be the whirlwind of destruction.

WE CAN HAVE PEACE IN THE HOLY LAND

"Those who think 'negotiations' are a magic answer seem not to understand that when A wants to annihilate B, this is not an 'issue' that can be resolved amicably around a conference table."
(THOMAS SOWELL)[884]

ON JANUARY 20, 2009 JIMMY CARTER announced a new plan for peace in the Middle East and appealed to President Barack Obama to implement that plan.

Jimmy Carter met with Barack Obama just days before the inauguration. It was Carter's stated hope that he would be able to sway Obama about what the former president called an "unnecessary war" in Gaza. Carter has long been a vocal proponent of establishing an ongoing relationship with Hamas' terrorist leaders. It appears his influence has already made inroads in Obama's Middle East policy plans.

The *Guardian* newspaper in Britain reported, "The incoming Obama administration is prepared to abandon George Bush's doctrine of isolating Hamas by establishing a channel to the Islamist organization, sources close to the transition team say."[885] The question then becomes: Will Barack Obama keep his campaign promises to stand with Israel, or will he march to the beat of Jimmy Carter's drum?

President Obama indicated prior to his inauguration his intention to halt the violence between Israel and Hamas. He told ABC's George Stephanopoulos that "working through the politics of this requires a third party that everyone has confidence [in].... to see a fair and just outcome.... [The] Obama administration, if we do it right, can provide that kind of interlocutor."[886]

During a CBS interview, Obama reiterated his determination to include Iran in any peace talks. "We are going to start on Day One.... we're going to have to involve Syria.... we're going to have to engage Iran...." The need to engage Iran[887] stems only from the fact that Hamas is a useful weapon in Iran's arsenal.

Three days after his inauguration, and during his first visit to the State Department on the day Hillary Clinton was sworn in as Secretary of State, President Obama called for Israel to open the Gaza border with "appropriate monitoring" to ease food and medicine shortages. He reiterated his plans to pursue a lasting peace agreement between Israelis and Palestinians.

Obama outlined his plan to send new envoy George Mitchell to the Middle East. Mitchell said the conflict "demands our maximum effort no matter the difficulties, no matter the setbacks. The key is the mutual commitment of the parties and the active participation of the United States government."[888]

Secretary of State Clinton added, "Nowhere is a robust diplomatic approach needed more."[889]

Said the President, "Let me be clear: America is committed to Israel's security. And we will always support Israel's right to defend itself against legitimate threats. No democracy can tolerate such danger to its people, nor should the international community...."[890]

President Obama lauded Egypt for its part in negotiating an end to fighting in the region. But, he emphasized the need to stop arms smuggling between that country and Gaza. He said, "Just as the terror of rocket fire aimed at innocent Israelis is intolerable, so, too, is a future without hope for the Palestinians."[891]

He implored both Israel and the Palestinian Authority to encourage the world community to monitor the points that provided access for Hamas to smuggle arms into Gaza. "It will be the policy of my administration to actively and aggressively seek a lasting peace between Israel and the Palestinians, as well as between Israel and its Arab neighbors," he said.[892]

Obama's ideology seems to dovetail perfectly with Carter's proffered plan:

» A Palestinian state overseen by an international peacekeeping force.

» A return to pre-1967 borders and total withdrawal of Jewish settlers from the West Bank.

» A divided Jerusalem with joint control over the Old City.

» The right for Palestinians to return to Gaza and the West Bank and to be compensated for any perceived losses.

» The recognition by both Israel and the Palestinians of the right of the other to live in peace. (This is contrary to the Hamas charter which states, "Israel shall exist and will continue to exist until Islam will obliterate it....".[893]

» A specific time limit for the culmination of this plan. (Carter suggests September 2009.)

Obama considered the appointment of former Senator George Mitchell as envoy to the Middle East. Mitchell has openly stated his expectations of negotiations regarding Israel:

"I think there has to be an immediate cessation of violence on both sides, a recommitment to the principles to which they have already agreed, both at the summit to which you referred in October of 2000 in Sharma al-Sheikh in Egypt— the summit that occurred in the same place the previous year, September of 1999 and agreements going back to Oslo in 1993; a recommitment to those principles."[894]

Hillary Rodham Clinton's appointment as secretary of state is fraught with uncertainty. After all, "In 1998, she accompanied Bill Clinton to Gaza, on the first such visit of a U.S. president.... She caused a sensation when she endorsed the idea of a Palestinian state, going further than her husband's stated policies."[895] Perhaps of greater concern is whether or not she will be influenced by the millions Bill Clinton has received in donations from Arab countries such as Saudi Arabia, Qatar, Oman, Dubai, and Kuwait.

Only time will tell if President Obama's cabinet, agenda, and initiatives truly embrace Israel as a partner in the Middle East, or if he, too, will follow in the footsteps of Jimmy Carter and abandon Israel to the radical terrorists that surround them.

Carter refers to Jews again and again as "radicals," another word for terrorists. He called former Israeli Prime Minister Menachem Begin a "radical" and then went on to describe him as the "most notorious terrorist in the region." Of course, he said the British said that, not him. Carter describes Likud Party leader Benjamin Netanyahu as a "key political associate and naysayer"[896] who was strongly opposed to Israel relinquishing control over the Sinai. Carter wrote of, "Prime Minister Benjamin Netanyahu and Ehud Olmert with whom I later had heated arguments about the subject."[897]

It appears that Jimmy Carter is revising history. The Benjamin Netanyahu I know was attending college during the Camp David meetings. In fact, when I recommended him to Begin for a government job, the prime minister did not even know who Benjamin was. I have no idea how Carter was so aware of Benjamin Netanyahu's political ideology; he was selling furniture to help fund his schooling.[898]

The subtitle of this book is *A Carter/Obama Plan That Will Not Work*. The foundation of my plan is that Jerusalem be recognized as the indivisible capital of Israel.

The former president writes that Begin agreed to divide Jerusalem. I found that to be astonishing...especially since Mr. Begin had given me a copy of the letter he wrote to Carter on

Sept. 17, 1978. In the letter he wrote, "Dear Mr. President.... On the basis of this law, the government of Israel decreed in July 1967 that Jerusalem is one city indivisible, the capital of the State of Israel."[899] According to Begin, Carter informed him that the U.S. government did not recognize Jerusalem as Israel's capital. Begin told me he responded, "Excuse me sir, but the State of Israel does not recognize your non-recognition."

Carter states that Prime Minister Begin agreed to a freeze on building Jewish settlements. Begin told me he had not agreed to a total freeze; he only agreed not to build new settlements for three months, during the negotiations.

Carter gives the impression that he and Begin were close friends by saying that Begin and Sadat visited him in Plains to reaffirm the personal commitments each had made to the other. I found that quite humorous; Mr. Begin told me he had refused to meet with Carter when the president traveled to Jerusalem. At that time, he was no longer prime minister but was outraged that Carter had misrepresented the events during their meetings.

Carter, like most of the Palestinian population, has a propensity for rewriting history. He claims in his book, "public opinion polls in the Arab world will reveal that the United States will be seen as a greater threat than Iran."[900] Every Sunni leader with whom I've met has told me he is terrified at the thought of a Shia state. In fact, the Gulf States are scrambling for nuclear arms to protect its territory.

Saudi Arabia has built a four-hundred-mile wall between its country and Iraq. The leaders believe the Shia revolution in Iran will spread virally into Iraq and throughout the Middle East. A nuclear Iran presents a horrifying scenario to neighboring leaders and, indeed, the world.

Carter states in his book, "Palestinian land is being restricted by Israeli settlements and the wall."[901] How can the land become Palestinian if there was no Palestinian language, culture, or history prior to three decades ago? I posed a question to Dr. Hanan Ashwari, the spokesperson for the PLO (or should I say PTO—Palestinian

Terrorist Organization) during that period:

> **Mike Evans:** *"Dr. Ashwari, I am an American evangelical Christian. What is the logic in the term 'land for peace' as a guarantee for peace, when the Arab world started three wars against Israel when the Arab world had Judea and Samaria?"*

> **Dr. Hanan Ashwari:** *"I find the reference to Judea and Samaria as being in extreme bias and therefore offensive. I am a Palestinian Christian . . . and I am a descendant of the first Christians in the world. Jesus Christ was born in my country, in my town. Bethlehem was a Palestinian town—"*

> **Mike Evans:** *"A Jewish town."*

> **Dr. Ashwari:** *"I will not accept this offensive implication on Christianity…nor will I accept a distortion of my religion."*[902]

In Carter's new book, *We Can Have Peace in the Holy Land, A Plan That Will Work,* he describes Sderot as a ghost town. He recalls that the thoroughfares were empty, as were parks and public buildings. During the Israel/Gaza conflict in early 2009, I went to the town of Sderot and met with Mayor Eli Moyal. When I mentioned the repeated Hamas rocket attacks to him, he told me that there had been over 7,500 missile strikes in his little town. Despite that, the people were out and about talking with neighbors. Mothers were pushing their babies in strollers down the sidewalks and children were playing. The streets were decidedly not empty.

I looked around the mayor's office, which is actually a bunker, as is the police headquarters. Even the playground equipment in Sderot is made of concrete and can act as bunkers in the event of a rocket or mortar attack. Mayor Moyal talked with me about Jimmy Carter's support for Hamas and its alleged democracy.

It seems that Carter wants to bring terrorist states such as Iran and Syria and groups such as Hezbollah and Hamas to the bargaining table and make them partners in the peace process. It would allow multitudes of Palestinians, many of whom are Hezbollah and Hamas fighters, to launch tens of thousands of Iranian missiles in hopes that Israel will be forced to invite them into the Bible Land, divide the city of Jerusalem, and give Judea and Samaria to the Palestinians. Israel would be forced to return the Golan Heights to Syria, another terror state.

Mr. Carter's view of the Palestine Liberation Organization is simply that it is a "human rights" movement. He calls the most infamous terror organization, an organization that was established to "liberate the homeland of the Palestinian people." He refers to the Israelis as "militants" or "terrorists," the same way he referred to Menachem Begin.

When was the last time you saw an Israeli strap a suicide bomb to his or her body and blow up innocent Palestinians? In Carter's worldview, the real victims are the terrorists. He pens, "We pursued the concept of non-violent resistance of Hamas leaders and gave them documentation and video presentations on the successful experiences of Mahatma Gandhi, Dr. Martin Luther King Jr., and others."[903]

In Carter's warped view, the real terrorists are the Jews. He views all Jewish refugees as an obstacle to peace. He claims that he brought peace to Egypt and Israel. He describes Prime Minister Menachem Begin, my dear friend, as a "radical" or terrorist. Carter goes on to say the British described Begin as "one of the most notorious terrorists in the region, beyond comprehension."[904]

Mr. Carter claims that in a meeting with Begin in March the prime minister failed to refute the president's proposal that Israel return to pre-1967 borders. He tells of how Begin failed to respond to the introduction of such issues as illegal settlements and withdrawal from the West Bank. Begin's memories of those meetings were far different than the president's, according to the prime minister's secretary, Yehiel Kadishai.

I was told by Mr. Begin that at the Camp David meetings Carter promised he would oppose a Palestinian State. "A Palestinian state is a mortal danger to Israel," Begin said, "and a great peril to the free world. And we never agreed to a Palestinian state at Camp David. What we agreed to was autonomy as a way to solve the problem of the Palestinian Arabs."[905] Begin said he had gone to Camp David to make peace with Egypt. An American statesman told the prime minister that the government of the United States did not recognize Jerusalem as the capital of Israel. Begin answered, "Whether you do or do not recognize Jerusalem, it is the capital of the State of Israel."

On March 17, Begin wrote to Carter stating the above facts. Begin asked Carter to explain to him exactly where the capital of Israel was. Carter did not respond. "If Jerusalem is not the capital of Israel," Begin asked, "where is it? Jerusalem is the center of the power of government, the Supreme Court." Carter reiterated, "We don't recognize Jerusalem as Israel's capital." Begin responded, "Excuse me, sir, but the State of Israel does not recognize your non-recognition."

Carter's plan is simply to embrace the Quartet which believes Israel will live happily ever after with the Arab world by simply giving terrorist regimes its land. I am reminded of the question I asked Benjamin Netanyahu at the Madrid Peace Conference: "For human rights not to be biased, Jews would have the same freedom as Arabs regarding settling in territories if they chose to do so, be it Riyadh of Amman, etc. Has there been any discussion on that?"

Netanyahu replied, "On the question of individual rights of Arabs and Jews, there is no symmetry now. That is, if Arabs desire to live among Jews, as they do and they have a right to, Jews should have the right to live among Arabs. The fact is that no Jews are allowed to live in Jordan or Saudi Arabia, and that is the kind of conception, an apartheid peace if you will, that we cannot tolerate and that no one should tolerate in the closing part of this century."[906] It was Jimmy Carter who in a previous book accused Israel of being an apartheid state.

"On the land-for-peace issue," I asked Netanyahu, "the aggressors throughout history have given up territory such as Germany, Poland, and France; what territories have the Arabs been willing to give up for peace?"[907] The answer is obvious: none!

Why the Arabs aren't willing to solve the refugee crisis is the root of the problem. Israel has solved the Jewish refugee crisis. Every refugee crisis in the world has been resolved except that concerning the Palestinian refugees. The Arab League does not want this issue resolved. It has learned that the Arab countries would rather support the use of the bullet than the ballot. In order to justify an army, one must have an enemy. Israel, the Zionists, makes a perfect enemy as long as there is a Palestinian crisis. It prevents the terrorist organizations in the region from turning on other Arab countries.

Carter legitimized Yasser Arafat in 1993 by writing his speech for the signing of the Peace Accords at the Clinton White House. In 1993, the first terrorist attack rocked New York City's World Trade Towers on February 26. Arafat gave his message in Arabic and stated, "I do this for the 'peace of the brave.'" It was translated incorrectly; in Arabic, the phrase was "I do this for the blood of the martyrs."

The former president has a way of lionizing Palestinian militant leader Marwan Barghouti, whom he calls the "most intriguing player in the Middle East."[908] This is a man Carter fully supports. Barghouti is one of the most sinister terrorists in the world. He has been accused of thirty-three counts of murder and sentenced to five life sentences plus forty years. He has run for the office of president in the Palestinian National Authority.

Jimmy Carter writes of "The Elders," a group seen as key to the solution of the Middle East crisis. Mark Steyn wrote of this organization, "The initiative stems from an idea formulated by British entrepreneur Sir Richard Branson and musician Peter Gabriel to create a world council of elders to tackle issues such as conflict, AIDS, and global warming. A 'world council of elders' is just what we primitive global village tribesmen need to put the village in order."[909] Jimmy Carter and the Carter Center are heavily involved with this endeavor. For Israel to be asked to embrace the ideals of this organization is mad.

The only book outside the Koran on which the Islamic world agrees is *The Protocols of the Learned Elders of Zion*. This work of fiction which many embrace as truth inspired the pogroms in Russia. It is a bestseller in the Middle East and supports the rampant theory of a Zionist conspiracy of the Jews gaining control of the entire world. In truth, the real problem is Jew-hatred. It is being fed and fueled by Islamic bigotry. Carter believes that a Palestinian state with an international security force devoid of Israel defending itself, Israel returning to pre-1967 borders, a divided Jerusalem with East Jerusalem as the capital of a Palestinian state, permission for millions of Palestinians living in Lebanon to return to the West Bank, East Jerusalem and Gaza, would bring peace.

I believe the only solution for peace is moral clarity. Jerusalem must not be auctioned off. It is the legitimate capital of Israel— the oldest capital in the world, but not heralded as such. It dates back to the days of King David. The Hashemite Kingdom of Jordan must move its police and military into the Palestinian Territory and establish a rule of law. It must build hospitals, schools, roads, and housing, annexing the Palestinian Territory into the Hashemite Kingdom, of which it was a part before Israel was attacked.

The Arab League must move the project forward in association with the U.S., the EU, and the rest of the world. Refugee camps in Lebanon need to be closed and the Arab world should absorb the refugees as other nations have done in the past. The terrorist organizations operating in Palestinian Territories, including al-Qaeda, need to be completely eradicated. This is the formula for peace in the Middle East.

Carter's final plea in his book is for President Barack Obama to "shape a comprehensive peace effort between Israel and the Palestinians.... then use persuasion and enticements to reach these reasonable goals with the full backing of other members of the International Quartet [Russia, the UN, the EU, and the United States] and the Arab nations."[910]

Carter vows in his book that his only interest and focus is finding the key to elusive peace in the Middle East and helping to implement the policies to achieve it. One can only hope that Mr. Carter's "peace plan" does not dovetail with his human rights initiatives in Iran during the reign of the Shah. His idea of a democratic society does not necessarily echo the definition as penned by Mr. Webster. Could it be that Jimmy Carter's ideals are formulated by the number of zeros before the decimal point on the contribution checks to the Carter Center given by various Arab millionaires?

CHRONOLOGY OF
JIMMY CARTER'S PRESIDENCY

1977

JANUARY 20
Inaugurated President

FEBRUARY 2
*Signs Emergency Natural Gas
Act; "Fireside Chat"*

MARCH 30
*Soviet Union rejects SALT II
proposals*

APRIL 4
Meets with Sadat in Washington

APRIL 6
Signs Reorganization Act

APRIL 18
*Addresses nation on energy
(second address)*

JUNE 30
Halts B-1 bomber production

JULY 19
Meets Begin in Washington

AUGUST 4
*Establishes Department of
Energy*

SEPTEMBER 7
Signs Panama Canal Treaty

SEPTEMBER 21
Bert Lance resigns

SEPTEMBER 27
*Agreement with Soviet Union on
SALT II*

OCTOBER 5
*Signs International Covenant on
Human Rights*

NOVEMBER 19
Sadat visits Israel

1978

MARCH 16
*Senate ratifies first Panama
Treaty*

SEPTEMBER 4
Begins Camp David Summit

SEPTEMBER 17
Signs Camp David Accords

OCTOBER 13
Signs Civil Service Reform Act

DECEMBER 15
*Announces normalization of
relations with People's Republic
of China*

1979

JANUARY 16
Shah leaves Iran

JANUARY 19
Deng Xiaoping visits Washington

FEBRUARY 1
Khomeini returns to Iran

MARCH 8
Trip to Egypt and Israel

MARCH 26
Egyptian-Israeli Peace Treaty signing

APRIL 5
Address to the nation on energy

JUNE 18
Signing of SALT II Treaty in Vienna with Brezhnev

JULY 3
Cancels energy speech; begins meetings at Camp David on state of the administration

JULY 15
Address to the Nation—the "malaise" speech

JULY 17
Announces cabinet and senior staff changes

AUGUST 15
Andrew Young resigns as Ambassador to the United Nations

OCTOBER 17
Department of Education established

OCTOBER 20
Decision to admit the Shah to the United States for medical treatment

NOVEMBER 4
American Embassy in Teheran overrun

DECEMBER 27
Soviet invasion of Afghanistan begins

1980

JANUARY 4
Address to the nation on Soviet invasion of Afghanistan; sanctions announced

JANUARY 20
First caucuses held in Iowa

JANUARY 21
State of the Union Message outlining "Carter Doctrine"

FEBRUARY 20
Decision to boycott 1980 Summer Olympic Games in Moscow

MARCH 14
Anti-inflation program announced; balanced budget sent to Congress

APRIL 11
Decision to attempt hostage rescue mission

APRIL 21
Vance resigns as Secretary of State

APRIL 24
Rescue mission fails

JULY 16
Republicans nominate Ronald Reagan

JULY 22
Carter statement on Billy Carter's relations with Libya

AUGUST 13
Democratic Convention nominates Jimmy Carter

SEPTEMBER 22
Iraq invades Iran

OCTOBER 28
Carter-Reagan debate

NOVEMBER 4
Reagan defeats Carter in election

DECEMBER 2
Carter signs Alaska Lands Bill

DECEMBER 7
Carter warns Soviets against military intervention in Poland

DECEMBER 11
Carter signs Superfund Bill to clean up toxic waste dumps

1981

JANUARY 16
Final terms for release of American hostages negotiated

JANUARY 20
12 noon—Ronald Reagan inaugurated as president 12:20 PM EST—hostages released in Teheran

JANUARY 21
President Reagan sends Carter to Germany to welcome hostages home

MIDDLE EAST TIMELINE: 1978-1980

IRAN 1978

January 9—*The Shah gave a public statement in support of President Sadat's Middle East peace initiatives. He declared Egypt is doing "precisely what we believe is right."*

January 11—*Iran lifted its trade boycott on Italy and Denmark imposed for attacks on Iranian missions in both countries.*

January 30—*A Ministry of Education official sentenced to execution by firing squad for selling Iranian secrets to the USSR was granted a stay of execution.*

February 19—*Street battles lasting over twelve hours erupted in Tabriz; six were killed and 125 injured.*

February 21—*The death toll of the rioting in Tabriz rose to nine; an opposition religious party claimed more than 100 rioters were killed by police.*

March 5—*The Shah announced he was in negotiations with the Netherlands and West German governments to buy frigates and submarines.*

March 6—*The Iranian ambassador and his staff were recalled from East Berlin. The East German government refused to prosecute Iranian students who raided the Embassy and destroyed documents.*

April 5—*A U.S. firm reportedly signed a contract to construct a harbor at the Chah Bahar Naval Base in southeast Iran.*

April 12—*The USSR and Iran agreed to build a 488-km section of the 1,420-km gas pipeline from Kangan to Astara.*

May 9—*Serious rioting occurred in Qom and Tabriz.*

May 10—*The Iranian Ministry of War and the British Government-owned Millbank Technical Services agreed to construct a small-arms ammunition factory in Isfahan.*

May 11—*Serious rioting spread to Tehran; thousands of demonstrators, after being harangued by religious leaders, marched through the bazaar area. Police threw tear gas and fired over the heads of the crowd; about 100 civilians were reported to have been injured. The Shah postponed visits to Hungary and Bulgaria planned for May 12.*

August 1—*Anti-government demonstrations in ten Iranian cities resulted in seven deaths and the arrest of 115 people.*

August 10—*In a press conference in Nowshahr, on the Caspian, the Shah stated his plan to restore free political activity, starting with elections in June 1979, was irreversible, even if violence resulted. Iranian papers had reported anti-government riots in Tehran, Isfahan, and Shiraz.*

August 11—*Martial law was declared in the city of Isfahan after riots lasted all day. The Information Ministry said four people had been killed and 66 injured. The riots were led by orthodox Muslims protesting against the government's liberalization program.*

August 13—*Martial law was extended to the towns of Najafabad, Shareza, and Homayunshahr in Isfahan province.*

August 15—*The Shah announced an amnesty for 62 political detainees and 649 other prisoners to mark the 25th anniversary of the fall of Dr. Mossadegh.*

August 16—*Unrest spread to Tehran when the bazaar was closed by the religious-dominated Shopkeepers Association. Troops were out in the streets suppressing disorders. Demands were being made for the rigid enforcement of Islamic law with the closure of cinemas, bars, and night clubs. The agitators opposed television and the emancipation of women.*

August 20—*A cinema in Abadan was targeted with four incendiary bombs at each of the four corners; 430 were killed.*

August 27—*The Shah dismissed the government of Mr. Jamshid Amouzegar and appointed as Prime Minister Mr. Jafar Sharif-Emami. The move was prompted by the disorder in the principal cities.*

August 28—*Prime Minister Sharif-Emami announced all casinos and gambling clubs would be closed.*

August 29—*China's Chairman Hua Kuo-feng arrived in Tehran for a four-day visit. He praised the Shah's leadership, called for increased cooperation between the two countries, and condemned the "aggression and expansionism of the big powers."*

August 30—*Chairman Hua Kuo-feng and the Shah discussed security and political developments in the Gulf and the situation in Afghanistan.*

August 31—*Fighting between security forces and Islamic rioters in the city of Mashhad caused two deaths. In Tehran a bank was set on fire.*

September 6—*A terrorist attack was made on a police station in Tehran; one policeman was killed.*

September 7—*A demonstration against the Shah in Tehran was estimated at 100,000 strong.*

September 8—*Tehran and eleven other Iranian cities were placed under martial law. Violent demonstrations in the capital caused 58 deaths according to official figures; unofficial estimates ranged up to 250. The casualties resulted principally from troops firing on the crowds;*

in addition, over 100 cases of arson were reported in which banks, cinemas, police stations, shops, and other buildings were destroyed.

September 10—*Troops fired on demonstrators defying a martial law ban on public processions in the city of Qom. In Teheran nine members of Parliament walked out in protest against the loss of life in the suppression of disturbances there. Prime Minister Sharif-Emami appealed for a vote of confidence affirming his faith in the Constitution and in the principles of Islam; he claimed the disturbances were caused by extremists abusing the measures of liberalization which the Shah had introduced in August.*

September 11—*In the cities of Mashhad and Qom demonstrators were fired on by the army. Five deaths were reported.*

September 17—*An earthquake destroyed the city of Tabas in the province of Khorassan. The first estimate of the number of people killed was 11,000. The introduction of martial law in twelve cities was approved by Parliament. A government spokesman said the situation was returning to normal.*

September 18—*Empress Farah visited the area around Tabas, which had been devastated by earthquake. The official estimates of deaths rose to between 15,000 and 18,000.*

September 20—*The Shah visited Tabas and was gladly received by survivors of the earthquake.*

September 26—*The British Ambassador in Tehran, Sir Anthony Parsons, reaffirmed British support for the Shah.*

October 1—*Colonel Mortexa Zamanipoor, a police station commander, was assassinated in Mashhad while taking his son to school.*

October 2—*The government declared an amnesty for all persons engaged in "anti-state" activities. It included students abroad and exiles, including the Shi'ite Moslem leader, Ayatollah Khomeini.*

October 3—*The government promised to meet in full the demands of striking bank, telecommunications, and oil-refinery workers.*

October 6—*Opening the new session of Parliament, the Shah declared progress towards democracy would "certainly continue." He intended to extend the liberalization process further.*

October 8—*In Tehran the police clashed with university students.*

October 9—*Rioting in the cities of Amol and Babol on the Caspian Sea cost the lives of three individuals.*

October 11—*In Tehran journalists staged a lightning strike against military censorship. Troops fired on students outside the university; three were reported killed.*

October 13—*The Minister of State for Executive Affairs, Mr. Manouchehr Azmoun, announced the government had accepted the demands of striking journalists for lifting censorship.*

October 16—*Shops and businesses throughout the country were closed in mourning for the rioters killed in Tehran in September.*

October 17—*Rioting continued in the provinces; Tehran remained quiet.*

October 19—*Ayatollah Khomeini, the spiritual leader of the Shi'ite community and the principal opponent of the Shah, said in an interview in Paris that he was prepared to urge his followers to armed rebellion to establish an Islamic Republic.*

October 22—*In riots in Hamadan and Bushehr at least six people were killed by police fire.*

October 23—*The government announced that on October 26, the Shah's birthday, 1,451 prisoners would be released, including 1,126 political detainees. The Minister of Justice, Mr. Mohammad Baheri, said those released would be fully compensated for their detention and were entitled to return to their former jobs.*

A press interview given in Paris by Ayatollah Khomeini was criticized by Iranian opposition leaders as likely to

cause a split. Particular objection was taken to the Ayatollah's demand for the abolition of the monarchy.*

October 24—*The Leader of the Opposition in the Lower House of the Majlis bitterly criticized the British Foreign Secretary, Dr. Owen, for supporting "alien and anti-Iranian policies" in his recent statement of support for the Shah.*

The U.S. Deputy Defense Secretary, Mr. Charles Duncan, arrived in Tehran for confidential talks on the subject of a possible reduction in Iranian arms contracts with the U.S..

October 26—*The Shah's 59th birthday celebrations were marred by street rioting in Tehran and other cities.*

October 27—*Five deaths and scores of injuries were reported in worsening anti-government violence in many areas. In Isfahan tanks and armored cars were used to quell the riots.*

October 29—*The government dismissed or forcibly retired 34 senior officials of SAVAK, the state security and intelligence organization.*

Young men set fire to a cinema in Tehran. Eight persons were killed in clashes in 37 provincial towns.

October 30—*Karim Sanjabi, leader of the opposition National Front Party, met in Paris with Ayatollah Ruhollah Khomeini. The Ayatollah had told a French newspaper that he favored the replacement of the Shah by an Islamic Republic; Mr. Sanjabi was believed to prefer a reformed monarchical system. No statement was issued after the meeting.*

October 30—*Workers at the Abadan refinery went on strike.*

October 31—*Further widespread strikes halted the flow of oil. The strikers, who demanded an end to martial law and the release of all political prisoners, brought to a standstill oil wells and natural gas plants. Troops opened fire on students outside the university, vehicles were set on fire in the streets, and banks and government buildings were attacked.*

November 5—*Mobs set fire to large areas of Tehran. Banks, cinemas, night clubs, hotels, and liquor stores were targeted. The British Embassy was set on fire. The U.S. Embassy was attacked but the rioters were beaten off by heavily-armed troops.*

The Prime Minister, Mr. Jafar Sharif-Emami, offered his resignation, which was accepted.

November 6—*The Shah broadcast to the nation on radio and television to announce he had appointed a military government. It was headed by General Gholam Reza Azhari, Chief of Staff of the Armed Forces since 1971. In a later broadcast General Azhari called on religious leaders to cooperate with him to restore order and security and to combat corruption.*

In Paris Ayatollah Khomeini declared the only solution was the abdication of the Shah and the establishment of an Islamic Republic. He called on the army to disobey orders to confront the rioters.

November 8—*The military authorities arrested Mr. Amir Abbas Hoveyda, Prime Minister for most of the preceding thirteen years. An official announcement said he was being held under a martial law regulation which provided for the indefinite arrest without trial of any suspect.*

November 9—*Shia Muslim religious leaders rejected the military government's invitation to collaborate and urged the faithful to continue struggling against tyranny and injustice.*

The prime minister announced a commission had been set up to investigate the financial affairs of the Shah's family.

November 11—*Dr. Karim Sanjabi, leader of the opposition National Front, was arrested in Tehran.*

November 12—*General Boghrat Jaffarian, the governor of the province of Khuzestan, in which most of the oil industry is concentrated, warned oil workers to abandon their strike under threat of dismissal.*

November 14—*Troops opened fire on rioters in the bazaar quarter of Tehran. In the oil-producing areas some workers returned to work; refinery output was normal.*

November 22—*The government of General Azhari was given a vote of confidence.*

November 24—*Troops in Shiraz were reported to have killed fifteen persons in suppressing anti-monarchist riots.*

November 26—*Severe rioting was reported at Gorgan. A document published by striking employees of the Central Bank purported to show that in the two months ending in mid-October about $2,500 million had been sent out of the country by people in high positions, including politicians, members of the royal family, and generals.*

November 28—*General Gholam Reza Azhari announced in a broadcast that all processions would be banned in the Shi'ite mourning month of Muharram, starting on December 3. At the same time he promised his government planned to abrogate all laws that did not conform to Islamic principles and that future laws would be drafted "with the guidance of the great ayatollahs."*

December 1—*Large numbers of Muslims, defying both the curfew and the ban on public demonstrations during Muharram, were out on the streets in Tehran. Troops opened fire and dispersed the crowds; no figures for casualties were reported.*

December 3—*Violent rioting in Tehran.*

December 5—*In a strongly-worded statement, the Ministry of Information denied reports the Shah intended to abdicate and hand over power to a Regency Council acting for his son.*

December 6—*Ayatollah Khomeini declared in a press interview near Paris that he would not be bound by restrictions imposed by the French government.*

December 7—*Large numbers of foreigners crowded the airport at Tehran in an attempt to leave. The numbers who had left over the past ten weeks were estimated at 8,000, including 5,500 Americans.*

December 10—*A demonstration whose numbers were estimated at a million was mounted in Tehran, calling for an Islamic constitution, an end to dictatorship, and presenting anti-American slogans. Similar demonstrations were held in Mashhad, Tabriz, and Isfahan.*

December 11—*A further demonstration, estimated at the same size as on the previous day, took place in Tehran. In Isfahan crowds attacked the headquarters of SAVAK, the secret police, and five people were killed by troops' fire; all the cinemas in the city were reported to have been burned down.*

December 12—*Further violence in Isfahan resulted in an estimated ten deaths; liquor stores, restaurants, hotels, the town hall, and five banks were attacked and seriously damaged.*

December 14—*Ayatollah Khomeini issued a statement from his French exile rejecting proposals for the formation of a Regency Council to rule until the elections of June 1979.*

The prime minister banned all demonstrations and threatened severe measures against strikers.

December 18—*It was reported from Tabriz that an army unit was recalled to barracks after some troops refused to obey orders. This was the first instance reported of insubordination in the army.*

December 21—*The Majlis (Parliament) was adjourned until January 14.*

December 23—*An American and two Iranians were shot and killed in Ahwaz. The American, Mr. Paul Grimm, was deputy head of the Oil Service Corporation of Iran.*

December 25—*Dr. Gholam Hossein Sadiqi, who had been charged by the Shah with examining the possibilities of forming a civilian government, asked for more time. To facilitate his task he reportedly obtained concessions from the Shah over the lifting of press censorship and legal action against former ministers accused of corruption.*

December 26—*There were violent clashes on the streets of Tehran, in particular between troops and students.*

December 27—*The government imposed rationing gasoline and paraffin. Iran Air was grounded by a strike declared as total and indefinite; Pan American Airlines suspended flights to Tehran.*

December 29—*Dr. Gholam Hossein Sadiqi announced he had failed to form a government. The Shah asked Shapour Bakhtiar to attempt the task.*

December 30—*British, American, and other foreign-owned buildings were attacked by crowds in four provincial capitals. In Ahwaz, Shiraz, and Mashhad offices of the British Council were attacked, and in Tabriz the American Consulate; the Turkish Consulate General in Tabriz was totally destroyed by fire.*

The Shah's 92-year-old mother was flown to San Francisco for medical treatment.

December 30—*General Gholam Reza Azhari tendered his resignation as prime minister in order to make way for a political solution.*

December 30—*Dr. Shapour Bakhtiar, the prime minister designate, said in an interview with French television the Shah would leave Iran "on holiday" a month after the new government took office and would nominate a council to exercise power in his absence. He would not abdicate nor give up the command of the armed forces, but he would probably be absent for "at least eighteen months."*

1979

January 16—*The Shah and his family have left for Egypt. In Iran, streets are crowded with joyous people shouting, "Shah raft! Shah raft!" (The Shah is gone.)*

February 1—*In the spirit of a new freedom for Iran, Prime Minister Bakhtiar has allowed the Ayatollah Khomeini to return. Millions greet Khomeini, who calls for expelling all foreigners from Iran.*

February 11—*Khomeini has been demanding Bakhtiar's resignation. Youthful Khomeini supporters seize weapons and take control of the streets. Bakhtiar goes underground and will resurface in Paris in July. U.S. citizens who have been working in Iran begin to leave, joining many wealthy Iranians who for weeks have been emigrating.*

February 14—*In Kabul, Afghanistan, extremists kidnap and kill U.S. Ambassador Adolph Dubs.*

February 22—*The U.S. announces its aid to Afghanistan will be drastically cut.*

March 10-20—*Afghan army officers in the city of Heart mutiny and are crushed.*

March 20—*In Moscow, President Taraki of Afghanistan requests Soviet troops. He is told by Brezhnev that Soviet forces "would only play into the hands of our enemies—both yours and ours." Brezhnev advises Taraki to go slow with social reforms and to seek broad support for his regime. He advises Taraki to remove Prime Minister Amin. He promises Taraki military equipment.*

March 26—*President Anwar Sadat of Egypt and Prime Minister Menachem Begin of Israel sign a peace treaty in Washington.*

July 3—*President Carter signs a directive for secret aid to the opponents of Afghanistan's government. National Security Advisor Zbigniew Brzezinski tells Carter this aid will draw the Russians into a disaster—a Soviet-style Vietnam War.*

July 16—*In Iraq, President Hassan al-Bakr resigns and is replaced by the acting president, Vice President Saddam Hussein.*

September 16—*In Afghanistan, squabbling within the Taraki regime results in Taraki's death. Vice President Hafizullah Amin takes power.*

October 9—*Amin announces his predecessor, Taraki, died from "a severe and prolonged illness."*

November 4—*The U.S. has informed the Khomeini regime in Iran that the Shah of Iran, Reza Pahlavi, has come to the U.S. from Mexico to receive medical treatment. Pahlavi has serious illnesses, including cancer. About 3,000 Iranian youth invade the U.S. Embassy in Tehran and take 53 Americans and others hostage. They demand the U.S. send the Shah to stand trial.*

November 1-31—*Afghans have been fleeing to Iran and Pakistan and organizing resistance against the "atheistic" and "infidel" communist Amin regime. President Amin launches a successful military force against anti-government forces in Paktria Province, obliterating a few villages. He also attempts to appease his detractors by promising more religious freedom and to repair mosques. He begins distributing the Koran, refers to Allah in speeches, and describes his revolution as "totally based on the principles of Islam."*

November 20—*According to the Muslim calendar, it is the beginning of a new century. Juhayman bien Seif al Utaybi believes the Mahdi is coming. Approximately 200 of heavily armed Sunni followers, with an appointed Mahdi, seize the Grand Mosque in Mecca in an attempt to overthrow the Saudi government, which they believe is corrupt and in league with the devil.*

November 21—*The Carter administration believes the siege at Mecca was instigated by the Ayatollah Khomeini. Khomeini accuses the U.S. and Israel of orchestrating what he describes as the despicable horrors at the Grand Mosque. A wave of anti-American demonstrations and attacks on U.S. Embassies follow; the first in Pakistan on this day.*

November 25-30—*Saudi Shiite youths rebel in the eastern region along the Persian Gulf. The government institutes a new black-out and sends in the Saudi National Guard to quell the uprising.*

December 4—*Carter responds to the anti-American demonstrations with what would come to be called the "Carter Doctrine." It was intended to demonstrate U.S. strength and commitment to the Persian Gulf nations vital to the interests of the U.S. U.S. negotiators flew to Oman to discuss establishing a military base and an increased American presence in the Gulf.*

The Saudi Press Agency issues a statement by Prince Nayef that the "purge of renegades" from the Grand Mosque has been accomplished. The official number of dead was set officially at 26; observers estimate the toll was more than 1,000 dead.

December 10—*In response to the attack on the Grand Mosque, Carter moved the carrier* USS Kitty Hawk *and a battle group from the Philippines to the Persian Gulf. The Soviet military begins to assembly troops numbering 75-80,000 along the Afghan-Soviet border.*

December 24—*The Soviet Union sends troops into Afghanistan.*

December 27—*Soviet KGB agents in Afghan uniforms storm the presidential palace in Afghanistan and kill President Amin and 200 guards. The USSR describes Amin as an agent of "U.S. imperialism."*

December 31—*Carter tells ABC News the Soviet invasion of Afghanistan has "made a more dramatic change in my own opinion of what the Soviets' ultimate goals are than anything they've done in the previous time I've been in office."*

1980

January 1—*The Kamal regime in Afghanistan says it invited Soviet troops into the country because of the aggressive actions of the enemies of Afghanistan.*

January 3—*Carter wins approval from Congress to lift the ban on military aid to Pakistan, Afghanistan's neighbor. India is displeased; Prime Minister Indira Gandhi suggests that the U.S. is meddling in Afghanistan.*

TASS, the Soviet press agency, denigrates Carter for describing the Soviet troops in Afghanistan as an "invasion." According to TASS, it "breaks all records of hypocrisy and lies."

January 4—*Carter announces a grain embargo against the Soviet Union and a permanent American naval presence in the Indian Ocean.*

January 9—*Saudi Arabia beheads 63 Muslim extremists for their part in the siege of the Grand Mosque. The leader, Juhayman, is executed, but not before his writings against Saudi Arabia reach Egypt. They will lead to the assassination of Anwar Sadat and will impress Osama bin Laden.*

January 19—*China announces it will not resume talks with the Soviets.*

January 23—*In his State of the Union message, President Carter introduces what is called the Carter Doctrine.*

January 27—*Six U.S. diplomats sneak out of Iran using passports provided by Canada.*

January 29—*The UN General Assembly passes resolutions 104-118 calling for an immediate withdrawal of Soviet troops from Afghanistan.*

January 31—*U.S. Embassy hostages become world news.*

Carter believes a Soviet success in Afghanistan would endanger the oil fields in the Persian Gulf region.

February 1—*A Defense Department report on the Persian Gulf region concludes U.S. forces cannot stop a Soviet thrust into northern Iran and the U.S. should consider using tactical nuclear weapons in any conflict there.*

Senator Ted Kennedy says Carter has created a "war hysteria" in the U.S.

February 14—*West German Chancellor Helmut Schmidt criticizes the U.S. for failing to consult its allies before responding to Soviet intervention in Afghanistan.*

March 21—*President Carter calls for a U.S. boycott of the Summer Olympics in Moscow.*

April 2—*Ayatollah Khomeini advocates a Shia uprising against Saddam Hussein in Iraq.*

April 5—*Price of crude oil has doubled in the last twelve months...from $15.85 per barrel to $39.50 per barrel.*

April 7—*The U.S. severs diplomatic ties with Iran and imposes economic sanctions.*

April 24—*The U.S. attempts to rescue the hostages from the Embassy in Tehran. Due to weather conditions the mission is aborted, but not before eight U.S. servicemen are killed.*

April 25—*Khomeini cites divine intervention in the hostage rescue failure and warns that any further attempts will endanger the captives.*

April 26—*Carter vows to pursue a hostage release by every avenue available.*

April 27—*Government troops attack student demonstrators in Kabul, killing more than fifty students.*

May 22—*Japan imposes a freeze on export and service contracts with Iran due to the hostage crisis.*

June 25—*An assassin attempts to kill Syrian leader Hafez al-Assad.*

June 27—*Carter signs a bill requiring 19, and 20-year-old males to register for the draft in response to the Afghanistan invasion.*

July 1—*President Saddam Hussein campaign in rural Iraq.*

July 3—*Syria makes association with the Muslim Brotherhood a capital offense.*

July 14—*Billy Carter discloses payments from Libya and his ties with the government of Libya. (Two weeks later President Carter admits he had given Billy classified information regarding Libya.)*

July 22—*Lebanese journalist Riad Taha is assassinated; Syria is accused of the murder.*

July 23—*In Paris a former prime minister and opponent of President Hafez al-Assad is assassinated.*

July 26—*Reza Pahlavi, the Shah of Iran, dies in Egypt of cancer at the age of sixty.*

September 1-31—*The Afghan army is reduced from 80,000 to approximately 32,000 due to desertions.*

September 17—*Saddam Hussein declares Iraq's 1975 agreement with Iran is null and void.*

September 20—*Iran calls up military reservists to defend the country against an Iraqi invasion.*

September 22—*Saddam Hussein launches a land and air invasion against Iran.*

September 23—*Carter pledges not to intervene in the Iran-Iraq conflict and urges the Soviet Union and other nations to do the same.*

September 26—*Soviet Chairman Brezhnev calls on Iran and Iraq to negotiate a settlement.*

October 9—*Iranian officials report victories along the front with Iraq; Iraq denies the report. Khomeini tells the Iranians to drive the invaders back into Iraq and punish the Ba'ath Party regime for its crimes.*

October 15—*An estimated 900,000 Afghanis seek shelter in Pakistan.*

October 29—*Equipment failures result in the permanent postponement of another Carter hostage rescue mission.*

November 4—*Republican candidate Ronald Reagan wins a landslide electoral victory against President Jimmy Carter. He captures the votes in every southern state except West Virginia and Georgia.*

MAP OF THE MIDDLE EAST

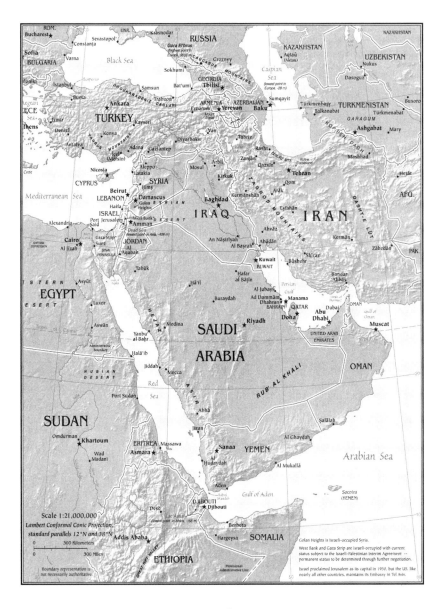

GLOSSARY OF NAMES

A

Aaron, David: Ambassador to the Organization for Economic Co-operation and Development (OECD) in Paris during Clinton administration; helped set up the negotiations for the Camp David peace agreement between Israel and Egypt.

Abbas, Mahmoud: Chairman of the PLO Executive Committee since November 11, 2004, after Yasser Arafat's death.

Abdel-Rahman, Omar: Blind Egyptian Muslim leader; currently serving a life sentence in the U.S. His prosecution grew out of investigations of the World Trade Center 1993 bombings.

Abdallah, Moulay Hicham Ben: Grandson of the late King Muhammad V and nephew of King Hassan II; a member of the Alawi dynasty, which has ruled Morocco since the 17th century.

Abdullah, bin Abdul Aziz Al Saud: Current king of the Kingdom of Saudi Arabia and head of the House of Saud; succeeded to the throne and assumed the title of king upon the death of his half brother, King Fahd on August 1, 2005.

Abedi, Agha Hasan: Founded the Bank of Credit and Commerce International (BCCI) in 1972. BCCI, at one point the seventh largest private bank in the world, collapsed in 1991 after extensive pressure from the federal government of the United States. It was involved in providing extensive finances to the government of Pakistan, at the time facing U.S. economic sanctions due to its nuclear program. Deceased.

Adams, Brock: Member of the House of Representatives (1965-1997) and Jimmy Carter's secretary of transportation. Deceased.

Adams, John: Second U.S. president; term of office 1797-1801.

Adham, Kamal: Political and intelligence advisor to two Saudi Kings; outstanding Saudi businessman; brother-in-law to Saudi King Faisal, who treated him like a favorite son. When Faisal became king in 1964 he appointed Adham to be head of the country's intelligence agency, a post he held until 1979. Deceased.

Afkhami, Gholam Reza: Professor of Political Science at the National University of Iran (1978), secretary general of Iran's National Committee for World Literacy Program and Deputy Minister of Interior.

Afshar, Amir-Khosrow: Deputy to Ardeshir Zahedi; former son-in-law to the Shah of Iran.

Afzal, Mian Mohammad: Pakistani Director of Military Operations.

Agnew, Spiro: Governor of Maryland and then Vice President under Richard Nixon (1969); resigned from office (1973) after having been formally charged with extortion, bribery, tax fraud, and conspiracy. Deceased.

Ahern, Thomas L.: CIA station chief, Tehran (late 1970s); developed intelligence sources within Mehdi Bazargan's administration.

Ahmadinejad, Mahmoud: Sixth and current president of the Islamic Republic of Iran; became president (on August 6, 2005) after winning the election by popular vote.

Alam, Asadollah: Prime Minister of Iran (1963-1964); confidant of and advisor to the Shah; Imperial Court minister; UN representative; founded Mardom Party. Deceased.

Albright, Madeleine: Sworn in as 64th secretary of state (1997), the first female secretary of state, and the highest-ranking woman in the history of U.S. government.

al-Assad, Bashar: Second son of President Hafez al-Assad; was studying ophthalmology in London when his older brother and heir apparent Basil was killed in a car accident. Bashar came into power in 2000 after the death of his father.

al-Assad, Hafez: President of Syria (1971-2000); succeeded by son, Bashar al-Assad; joined ranks with the U.S.S.R.; helped launch Yom Kippur War against Israel in 1973; sent terrorists to Lebanon. Deceased.

al-Deek, Khalil Said or Joseph Adams: after 1996 had dual U.S.-Jordanian citizenship; came to U.S.A. to study computer science. He worked as computer engineer and Charity Without Borders staffer. The Charity was discovered to be an al-Qaeda organization used to funnel money overseas and wasn't shut down until after September 11, 2001.

al-Haq, Zia: Pakistani general and later president in power from 1977 until his death in 1988, probably an assassination, in an aircraft explosion.

al-Hassan, Hani: Leader of the Fatah organization and member of the Palestinian Authority Cabinet and the Palestinian National Council; was replaced in April 2003, and was slated to act as Arafat's national security advisor.

al-Islambouli, Khalid: Arranged and carried out the assassination of Egyptian president Anwar Sadat during the annual "6 October 1973 victory parade" in 1981. Immediately after assassinating the president, he was captured, tried and found guilty. Publicly executed by firing squad.

Alinsky, Saul: Generally considered the father of community organizing; often credited with laying the foundation for the grassroots political organizing that dominated the 1960s. Alinsky and the current generation of Alinsky inspired/styled activists (especially Barack Obama) have been attacked as advocates for a quiet Socialist revolution merely using the language of social change, organizing, and empowerment as euphemisms for the traditional Marxist vocabulary. Deceased.

Allen, George: Former U.S. senator from the Commonwealth of Virginia (2001-2007); the son of former NFL head coach George Allen.

Allon, Yigal: Israeli politician and a commander of the Palmach; acted as prime minister and foreign minister of Israel, as well as being a member of Knesset. Deceased.

Amit, Meir: Director of the Mossad from 1963 to 1968; born in Palestine during the British mandate, he fought for the Haganah during the 1948 Arab-Israeli War. In a recent interview, Amit assessed the current problem of Islamic terrorism. He said he views the conflict as World War III, a widespread attempt to impose Islamic beliefs across the world.

Al-Nahyan, Zayed bin Sultan: Principle architect of United Arab Emirates (UAE); the ruler of Abu Dhabi and president of the UAE for over thirty years (1971-2004). Deceased.

al-Qaddafi, Muammar: De facto leader of Libya since a 1969 coup. Although he holds no public office or title, he holds several honorifics.

Al Said, Qaboss bin Said Sultan: Current ruler of Oman; seized power upon the death of his father, Said Bin Taimur; began the task of revitalizing his country. The political system which Qaboss established is that of an absolute monarchy.

al-Shaer, Nassar: Former Education Minister of the Palestinian National Authority serving as a member of Hamas. After the Hamas takeover of the Gaza Strip, all Hamas ministers in the PNA government were dismissed, including Shaer.

al-Zahar, Mahmoud: Co-founder of Hamas and a member of the Hamas leadership in the Palestinian-occupied Gaza Strip; served as foreign minister in the government of Prime Minister Ismail Haniya.

al-Zawahiri, Ayman: Physician and Founder of al-Qaeda; the second and last "emir" of Egyptian Islamic Jihad; under worldwide embargo by the UN 1267 Committee as a member or affiliate of al-Qaeda, with a $25-million reward offered for his capture.

Ames, Robert Clayton: CIA agent killed in an explosion of a bomb in a car that crashed through the Embassy gates in Beirut, Lebanon, killing 63 people, including 17 Americans, six CIA agents. Eventually, the terrorist group Hezbollah claimed responsibility for the attack.

Amin, Hafizullah: Second president of Afghanistan during the period of the communist Democratic Republic of Afghanistan. On December 27, 1979, members of the Russian KGB OSNAZ (Alpha Group) assassinated him, and Babrak Karmal became president.

Amini, Ali: Prime Minister of Iran (1961-1962); Minister of Finance; negotiator, Oil Consortium Agreement (1954); ambassador to the U.S. (mid-1950s); organized royalist opposition group in Paris (1979).

Amir-Entezam, Abbas: Deputy prime minister of Iran, spokesperson (1979); member, Liberation Movement. Favored normalization of relations between Iran and Ayatollah Ruhollah Khomeini's government. Imprisoned November 4, 1979.

Amouzegar, Jamshid: Prime minister of Iran, (1977-1978); economist; Minister of Health; Minister of Finance; led Resurgence Party; criticized for allowing opposition to unite behind Khomeini.

Anderson, John: Previously a member of the Republican Party, U.S. representative from Illinois, and an Independent candidate in the 1980 presidential election.

Andrus, Cecil: Governor of Idaho a combined 14 years (1971-1977 and 1987-1995) and Secretary of the Interior (1977-1981) during the Carter administration. Served as governor longer than anyone else in Idaho history.

Anne, Princess: Only daughter of Queen Elizabeth II of England. Only member of the British Royal Family to have competed in the Olympic Games.

Annenberg, Walter: After his father's death in 1942, Annenberg took over the family businesses and purchased additional print media as well as radio and television stations. During his lifetime, it is estimated Annenberg donated over two billion dollars to charitable organizations.

Ansary, Hushang: Had a distinguished career in his native Iran where he served as Minister of Economic Affairs and Finance and as Ambassador to the United States. Resident of the United States since 1979 and citizen since 1986.

Apple, R. W. : Correspondent and editor at *The New York Times* for more than 40 years. Deceased.

Arafat, Yasser: Former president, Palestine Liberation Organization (PLO); first to recognize Khomeini's Islamic Republic; first to visit Tehran under Khomeini; trained revolutionaries in PLO camps; Islamic Republic supported Arafat's intifada against Israel with arms and terrorists. Deceased.

Aram, Gholam Abbas: Minister of Foreign Affairs, Iran (1959-1960, 1961-1964); Served as diplomat in Japan, India, U.S., and other countries; Minister of Foreign Affairs.

Ariana, Bahram: Appointed Chief of the Great Generals Army Staff by Mohammad Reza Pahlavi and served in that post for four years. Dismissed from the directorship (1969), and after a short time he was retired. Deceased.

Arnall, Ellis: Ran against Jimmy Carter in Georgia governor's race (1966).

Ashraf, Hamid: Marxist leader of the Fedayeen in the late 1970s.

Ashraf, Princess Pahlavi: Twin sister of Mohammad Reza Pahlavi, the last Shah of Iran and the Pahlavi Dynasty; currently resides in France.

Atabai, Kambiz: Official spokesperson for the Empress Pahlavi.

Atherton, Alfred L., Jr.: Assistant Secretary of State for Near Eastern and South Asian Affairs, U.S. State Department (1974-1978); ambassador to Egypt (1979-1983); implemented Jimmy Carter's human rights policies. Deceased.

Atta, Mohammad: Known associate of al-Qaeda and the leader of the nineteen hijackers who perpetrated the September 11, 2001, attacks. He personally participated in the hijacking of American Airlines Flight 11, the first plane to crash into the World Trade Center.

Axelrod, David: Political consultant; best known as a top adviser to Barack Obama, first in Obama's 2004 campaign for the U.S. Senate in Illinois and as strategist for Obama's 2008 presidential campaign.

Ayers, William Charles (Bill): Professor of education at the University of Illinois at Chicago, known for his work in education reform. While a radical activist during the political upheavals of the 1960s, Ayers went underground for eleven years as a co-founder ofthe violent and radical Weatherman group.

Azarbarzin, Shapour: Lt. General; Deputy commander in chief of Operations of the Imperial Iranian Air Force.

Azhari, Gholam Reza: Prime Minister of Iran (1978); Chief of Staff Iranian Armed Forces; appointed to restore law and order; failed in his mission.

Azzam, Abdullah: Highly influential Palestinian Sunni Islamic scholar and theologian; also famous as a teacher and mentor of Osama bin Laden. He was assassinated by a bomb blast in November 1989.

Aziz, Khalid bin Abdul: King of Saudi Arabia; from the time of the assassination of King Faisal in 1975 until his own death of a heart attack in 1982; feared Khomeini would spread Islamic revolution to Saudi's Shiite population; supported Iraq in war against Iran.

B

Babbin, Jed: Former United States Deputy Undersecretary of Defense; served during the first Bush administration and is the author of political books.

Badi'ie, Amir-Hussein: General; Iranian Air Force commander.

Badrei, Abdul-Ali: General; commander of the Shah's elite guard corps.

Baker, Howard: U.S. Senator from Tennessee (1967-1985), was Senate Majority Leader (1981-1985) and White House Chief of Staff under Ronald Reagan (1987-1988). Known in Washington, D.C., as the "Great Conciliator."

Baker, James A., III: Has served in senior government positions under three United States presidents. The 61st Secretary of State (1989-1992) under President George Bush. Served as the 67th Secretary of the Treasury (1985-1988) under President Ronald Reagan, served as White House Chief of Staff to President Reagan. Mr. Baker's record of public service began (in 1975) as Undersecretary of Commerce to President Gerald Ford.

Bakhtiar, Shapour: Prime Minister, Iran (1978-1979); National Front leader; promoted democratic system; served as Shah's final prime minister; fled to France to escape Khomeini; founded National Union to overthrow Khomeini. Assassinated in Paris (1991) by Khomeini's sympathizers.

Bakhtiar, Teymour: Iranian general; the founder and head of SAVAK (1958-1961), until he was dismissed by the Shah. (In 1970), after the Iranian Revolution, he went into exile and was assassinated in Paris (in 1991) by Khomeini's sympathizers.

Bakke, Major Richard L.: Crewman on the abortive 1980 mission to free American hostages in Iran. Deceased.

Ball, George W.: Undersecretary of State, U.S. State Department (1961-1966) under John F. Kennedy and Lyndon Johnson; appointed by Carter to scrutinize Iranian crisis and recommend a plan of action; suggested Shah's monarchy would fail and the U.S. should contact Khomeini.

Balta, Paul: An expert on Euro-Med issues, journalist and writer; former Director of the University Paris III Sorbonne.

Bani-Sadr, Abolhasan: First president of Iran following the (1979) Iranian Revolution and the abolition of the monarchy; soon fell out with Ayatollah Khomeini. Khomeini reclaimed the power of commander in chief on June 10, 1981.

Barhoum, Fawzi: Hamas spokesman.

Barre, Raymond: French centre-right politician and economist; served as prime minister under Valéry Giscard d'Estaing from 1976 until 1981. Barre was probably the only French politician to have reached such high levels of responsibility without having ever been an official member or leader of any political party. Deceased.

Barre, Mohamed Siad: President of Somalia (1969-1991). Prior to his presidency, he was an army commander under the democratic government of Somalia. Deceased.

Bayh, Birch: U.S. Senator from Indiana (1962), reelected in 1968 and 1974. Deceased.

Bazargan, Mehdi: Prime Minister, Iran (1979); supported Mohammad Mossadegh; opponent of Shah; founded National Resistance Movement, renamed Liberation Movement of Iran (LMI); joined Khomeini's revolutionary council; assisted cleric during his Paris exile; helped coordinate Islamic Revolution in Iran; campaigned for secular government in Iran; resigned after Embassy takeover; later elected to first *Majlis* (national legislative body) in Iran.

Beckwith, Charles: Retired Army Colonel; led the abortive 1980 mission to free American hostages in Iran. Deceased.

Begin, Menachem: Prime Minister of Israel (1977-1983); signed Camp David Accords with Anwar El Sadat (1979); directed Israel's attempt to remove PLO from Lebanon; received Nobel Peace Prize (1978); retired from public life (1983). Deceased.

Beheshti, Mohammad Hosseini: Cleric; associate of Khomeini; organized internal revolt against Shah under Khomeini's direction; Revolutionary Council member; Chief Justice of Supreme Count (1980-1981); killed by Mujahedeen bomb.

Bell, Griffin: Another of the Carter Georgia connections, born in Americus, Georgia. Appointed the 72nd U.S. Attorney General in the Carter cabinet, serving until 1979.

Benedict XVI, Pope: 265th and reigning Pope, by virtue of his office of Bishop of Rome; spiritual head of the Roman Catholic Church and, as such, Sovereign of the Vatican City State.

Ben-Gurion, David: First Prime Minister of Israel; immigrated to Palestine from Russia in 1906, and became a major leader of Paole Zion with Yitzhak Ben-Zvi. Deceased.

Ben-Porat, Mordechai: Deputy Speaker of the Knesset (1965); deputy secretary-general of the Labor Party (1970-1972); and a member of Israel's United Nations mission in 1977. In 1982 he was reelected to the Knesset on the list of Telem, the party founded by Moshe Dayan. In 1983 he established the Movement for Social Zionist Renewal. He joined the Likud in 1988.

Bentsen, Lloyd, Jr.: Four-term United States senator from Texas (1971-1993) and the Democratic Party Nominee for Vice President in 1988 on the Michael Dukakis ticket. He also served in the House of Representatives from 1949 to 1955. Deceased.

Berge, Gunnar: Norwegian politician for the Labour Party. He was member of the Storting (1969-1993), Minister of Finance (1986-1989), Minister of Local Government and Regional Development (1992-1996), as well as Minister of Nordic Cooperation (1992-1996).

Berkowitz, David: Known as the .44 Caliber Killer and the Son of Sam, an American serial killer and arsonist. Shortly after his arrest in August 1977, Berkowitz confessed to killing six people and wounding seven others in the course of eight shootings in New York City between 1976 and 1977. He has been imprisoned for the crimes since 1977.

Bernard, Dr. Jean A.: French physician.

Bernstein, Carl: American journalist who, as a reporter for the *Washington Post* along with Bob Woodward; broke the story of the Watergate break-in (1972) and consequently helped bring about the resignation of U.S. President Richard Nixon.

Bhutto, Zolfaghar Ali: President of Pakistan (1971-1973) and Prime Minister (1973-1977). Deceased.

Biden, Joseph, Jr.,: Senior U.S. Senator from Wilmington, Delaware; President Barak Obama's Vice President (2009-2013).

Bill, James: Arrived at the College of William and Mary in 1987 to take over as director of the newly-founded Wendy and Emery Reves Center for International Studies; recently honored by the College as he formally retired.

Bin Laden, Osama: Founded Al Qaeda (1988) to consolidate the international network he established during the Afghan war; son of a billionaire Saudi businessman, he became involved in the fight against the Soviet Union's invasion and occupation of Afghanistan. Al Qaeda committed its most devastating attack on the World Trade Center in New York City on September 11, 2001. Nearly 3,000 people were killed in the attack. Whereabouts unknown.

Blumenthal, Michael: U.S. Secretary of Treasury (1977-1979). Traveled to Iran (in 1978) to discuss ways to relieve pressure on the Shah's monarchy, and informed Carter administration officials of Shah's seeming depression and lethargy. Deceased.

Bolton, John: Served in several Republican presidential administrations. Interim Permanent U.S. Representative to the UN (2005-2006) on a recess appointment and resigned in December 2006 when his appointment would have ended.

Bork, Robert: Conservative American legal scholar who advocates the judicial philosophy of originalism. He formerly served as Solicitor General, acting Attorney General, and judge for the United States Court of Appeals for the District of Columbia Circuit. In 1987 he was nominated to the Supreme Court by President Ronald Reagan, but the Senate rejected his nomination.

Bourguet, Christian: Leftist French lawyer, associate of Sadegh Ghotbzadeh prior to revolution in Iran, with Hector Villalon was go-between for U.S./Iran negotiations to release Embassy hostages (1980), and helped prepare the extradition papers that Iran sent to Panama in its effort to capture the deposed Shah.

Bourne, Peter: Special Assistant for the President for Health Issues under Jimmy Carter, resigned in 1978 after charges were brought that he signed a fraudulent prescription and after rumors of his use of cocaine.

Boutros-Ghali, Boutros: Egyptian diplomat; the sixth Secretary-General of the United Nations (1992-1997).

Bowen, David R.: Served as U.S. Representative from Mississippi (1973-1983).

Boxer, Barbara: Democratic politician and the current Junior U.S. Senator from the State of California, first elected to the U.S. Senate in 1992, becoming one of the first two female Jewish senators, along with Dianne Feinstein.

Brezhnev, Leonid: Chosen chairman of the Presidium of the Supreme Soviet in 1960, with Khrushchev's support, returned to the Secretariat after three years. In 1964 his group succeeded in ousting Khrushchev from power, whereupon Brezhnev immediately took over as first secretary of the party's Central Committee. In 1966 his title was changed from first secretary to general secretary. Deceased.

Brown, Harold: Secretary of Defense (1977-1980), informed administration of possible military coup in Iran following visit in 1979, and may have aided in first Embassy take-over on February 14, 1979.

Brown, Jerry: Current California Attorney-General and former Governor (1975-1984). Unsuccessfully sought Democratic nominations for president (1976, 1980, 1992).

Brzezinski, Zbigniew: U.S. National Security Advisor (1977-1981), hard-liner, pro-military solution in Iran, collided with Secretary of State Cyrus Vance over Iranian crisis, established talks with Provisional Government under Khomeini prior to Embassy take-over, and assisted in planning failed rescue mission.

Buckley, William: Lieutenant Colonel, CIA Station Chief at the U.S. Embassy in Beirut. Died in 1985 after fifteen months captivity of illness and torture.

Bundy, Ted: American serial killer, who murdered numerous young women across the United States between 1974 and 1978. After more than a decade of vigorous denials, he eventually confessed to thirty murders, although the actual total of victims remains unknown. Executed in 1989.

Burke, Edmund: Anglo-Irish statesman, author, orator, political theorist, and philosopher. Served for many years in the British House of Commons as a member of the Whig party. Deceased.

Bush, George W.: Forty-third U.S. president from 2001-2009. Initiated the War in Iraq (2003) and saw the greatest economic crisis in America in the last year of his second term. There have been no terrorist attacks on American soil since September 11, 2001.

Bush, George H. W.: 41st U.S. president from 1989-1983. Campaigned in 1980 for the presidency and lost, but became Vice President under President Ronald Reagan. Had been Director of the Central Intelligence Agency.

Butler, Bishop Keith: Founding pastor of the nondenominational Word of Faith International Christian Center (WOFICC) in suburban Detroit. Detroit City councilman and the only Republican elected to the council since before World War II.

Buzzelli, James A.: Retired Air Force Colonel, a member of the Air Force One flight crew for President Jimmy Carter and during President Ronald Reagan's first term. Deceased.

Byrd, Robert C.: U.S. Senator (1956-present), traveled to Iran as Senate Majority Leader, urged Shah to appeal to Iranian people through television and radio broadcasts but the Shah declined.

C

Caddell, Patrick: American public opinion pollster and a political film consultant; worked for Democratic presidential candidates George McGovern in 1972, Jimmy Carter in 1976 and 1980, Gary Hart in 1984, Joe Biden in 1988, and Jerry Brown in 1992.

Callaghan, James: Prime Minister of the United Kingdom (1976-1979) and leader of the Labour Party (1976 to 1980). Callaghan is the only person to have served in all four of the Great Offices of State: Prime Minister, Chancellor of the Exchequer, Home Secretary, and Foreign Secretary. Deceased.

Callaway "Bo": Businessman and former politician from the state of Georgia, he served as Secretary of the Army (1973-1975) and as Gerald Ford's first campaign manager in 1976.

Campolo, Tony: American pastor, author, sociologist, and public speaker known for challenging Evangelical Christians by illustrating how their faith can offer solutions in a world of complexity. With his liberal political and social attitudes, he has been a major proponent for progressive thought and reform in the Evangelical community.

Capriolo, Ettore: Translated Salman Rushdie's novel, *The Satanic Verses*. After a *fatwa* was issued by Ayatollah Ruhollah Khomeini, he was beaten and stabbed on 3 July 1991 at his home in Milan but survived.

Carey, Hugh: Democratic member of the House of Representatives (1960-1974) serving seven terms, part of the time acting as deputy whip. In 1974 Carey was elected governor of New York, a post to which he was re-elected in 1978.

Carter, Amy Lynn: One of four children of Jimmy and Rosalynn Carter, born October 19, 1967.

Carter, Billy: Jimmy Carter's brother, born in 1937. Deceased.

Carter, Donnel Jeffrey (Jeff): One of four children of Jimmy and Rosalynn Carter, born August 18, 1952.

Carter, Gloria: Jimmy Carter's first sister, born in 1926. Deceased.

Carter, James Earl (Chip), III: One of four children of Jimmy and Rosalynn Carter, born April 12, 1950.

Carter, James Earl, Sr.: Father of Jimmy Carter, grocer and peanut framer. Deceased.

Carter, Jimmy: 39th U.S. President from 1977-1981. Sought to improve human rights worldwide, limited sale of arms to Third World countries, abandoned Shah of Iran to Islamic revolutionaries, mismanaged Embassy hostage crisis and rescue attempt, facilitated Camp David Accords between Israel and Egypt, lost second bid for the presidency to Ronald Reagan.

Carter, John William (Jack) : One of four children of Jimmy and Rosalynn Carter, businessman and politician who unsuccessfully ran for the United States Senate in Nevada in 2006, born July 3, 1947.

Carter, Lillian: Jimmy Carter's mother, wife of James A. Carter Sr. Deceased.

Carter Stapleton, Ruth: Sister of Jimmy Carter and was known in her own right as a Christian evangelist; born in 1929. Deceased.

Carter, Rosalynn (nee Smith): Wife of Jimmy Carter; they were married in 1946.

Carter, Ruth: See Carter Stapleton, Ruth.

Cassin, Vernon: Under the pseudonym Guy Rutherford tried unsuccessfully to recruit future Iran Prime Minister Bani-Sadr as CIA informant.

Castro, Fidel: Cuban guerrilla leader; became that country's 22nd president and ruled from January 1959 until his retirement in February 2008.

Cave, George W.: Political Officer, U.S. Embassy, Iran (1958-1961); Commercial Officer, U.S. Embassy, Iran (1973-1976); CIA Station Officer, Iran (1979); CIA expert on Iran; briefed Bazargan's government on Kurds, Russian economy; records of meetings helped topple Bazargan as Khomeini's prime minister.

Ceauçescu, Nicolae: Leader of Romania (1965-1989); a revolution and coup removed him from power. Deceased.

Cettin, Hikmet: Turkish journalist; murdered.

Chaban-Delmas, Jacques: Served as prime minister under Georges Pompidou (1969 to 1972). Deceased.

Chamorro, Violeta: Nicaraguan political leader and publisher; the 48th President of Nicaragua (1990-1997), when she unseated Daniel Ortega. Chamorro left politics after her term.

Chamran, Mustafa Ali: Close advisor to Khomeini; repaid for his loyalty and his part in the revolution when he was named Khomeini's Minister of Defense. Deceased.

Chapman, Morris H.: President of the Southern Baptist Convention Executive Committee.

Chávez Frías, Hugo Rafael: Current President of Venezuela; promotes a political doctrine of democratic socialism and Latin American integration.

Chiles, Lawton M., Jr.: Politician from Florida; in a career spanning four decades, he never lost an election; served in the Florida House of Representatives (1958-1966), the Florida State Senate (1966-1970), the United States Senate (1971-1989), and as the 41st Governor of Florida from 1991 until his death in office in the last month of his term.

Christopher, Warren: Deputy Secretary of State under Jimmy Carter; sworn in as secretary of state in 1993; also served as deputy attorney general in the Lyndon Johnson administration.

Church, Frank: U.S. Senator from Idaho reelected three times (1957-1981). Deceased.

Churchill, Winston: British politician known chiefly for his leadership of the United Kingdom during World War II; Prime Minister of the United Kingdom (1940-1945) and again (1951 to 1955). A noted statesman and orator, Churchill was also an officer in the British Army, a historian, a Nobel Prize-winning author, and an artist. Deceased.

Cirincione, Joseph: President of the Ploughshares Fund, a public grant-making foundation focused on nuclear weapons policy and conflict resolution; previously served as vice president for national security and international policy at the Center for American Progress in Washington, D.C., and for eight years as the director for non-proliferation at the Carnegie Endowment for International Peace.

Clark, Ramsey: U.S. Attorney General (1967-1969); represented the Carter administration in attempts to establish relations, first with Bakhtiar and later with Khomeini. He is also known for his role as defense attorney in the trials of Saddam Hussein.

Clark, Richard: U.S. Senator from Iowa (1973-1979); following a loss for reelection, he was appointed by Jimmy Carter as Ambassador at Large and U.S. Coordinator for Refugee Affairs in 1979.

Clement, Carl: State Department official; served in the Bureau of Human Rights.

Clifford, Clark: 9th Secretary of Defense under Lyndon Johnson (1968-1969); was consulted as well by Presidents John F. Kennedy and Jimmy Carter. Deceased.

Clinton, William Jefferson, Jr.: 42nd U.S. president from 1993-2001.

Clinton, Hillary: President Barack Obama's choice for United States Secretary of State. Junior U.S. Senator from New York; candidate for the Democratic nomination in the 2008 presidential election, but dropped out of the race. She is married to Bill Clinton, the 42nd President of the United States, and was the First Lady of the United States (1993-2001).

Cloonan, Jack: Twenty-five-year veteran of the FBI; internationally respected security expert.

Cogan, Charles: Director of CIA operations in Afghanistan; head of the CIA covert aid program to Afghanistan.

Cohen, Stephen: Deputy Assistant Secretary of State for Human Rights and Security Assistance, U.S. State Department (1978-1981); with George Griffin and Carl Clement, traveled to Iran to assess political crisis; determined Shah would not retain crown.

Conyers, John: Entered the U.S. House of Representatives in 1964, representing the State of Michigan; he is the second-most senior member of the House. He is also one of the fourteen founding members of the Congressional Black Caucus.

Cottam, Richard: Political scientist and Iranist (1925-1997; joined the CIA in 1953); joined the faculty of the University of Pittsburgh in 1958, and spent the rest of his professional career at the university until his retirement in 1990. Deceased.

Cranston, Alan: U.S. Senator from California and four times the Senate Majority Whip. Served four six-year terms in office (1968 to 1993). An unsuccessful candidate for the democratic presidential nomination in the 1984 election. Deceased.

Culver, John: U.S. Senator from Iowa (1975 to 1981); earlier served ten years in the House of Representatives.

Cutler, Lloyd: Attorney who served as White House Counsel during the Democratic administrations of Jimmy Carter and Bill Clinton; also served as counsel in Bill Clinton's administration. Deceased.

Cyrus the Great: Persian Emperor; the founder of the Persian Empire under the Achaemenid dynasty. The empire expanded under his rule, eventually conquering most of Southwest Asia and much of Central Asia, to create the largest state the world had yet seen. Cyrus left a lasting legacy on Jewish religion (through his Edict of Restoration), human rights, politics, and military strategy, as well as on both Eastern and Western civilizations. Died in battle.

D

Daley, Richard: Served for twenty-one years as mayor and the undisputed Democratic boss of Chicago and is considered by historians to be the "last of the big city bosses." He played a major role in the history of the Democratic Party. Deceased.

d'Estaing, Valéry Giscard: French center-right politician who was President of the French Republic (1974-1981) and a proponent of the United States of Europe. Having limited his involvement in national politics after his defeat, he became involved with the European Union.

Daoud, Mohammad (Khan): Commonly known as Abu Daoud, the leader of Black September, the Palestine Liberation Organization splinter group that carried out the 1972 Munich massacre at the Olympic Village. Assassination in 1978 as a result of a revolution led by the Marxist People's Democratic Party of Afghanistan (PDPA).

Daugherty, William J.: One of the U.S. Embassy employees held hostage by the Iranians; later an associate professor of government at Armstrong Atlantic State University in Savannah, Georgia.

Dayan, Moshe: Israeli military leader and politician; the fourth Chief of Staff of the Israel Defense Forces (1953–1958); became a fighting symbol to the world of the new State of Israel. Until 1964, he served as the Minister of Agriculture. Deceased.

Dean, Howard: Politician and physician from the U.S. state of Vermont, and former chairman of the Democratic National Committee, the central organization of the Democratic Party at the national level. Served as governor of Vermont when Richard A. Snelling died in office. He was subsequently elected to five two-year terms.

de Marenches, Alexandre: Head of the Service de Documentation Extérieure et de Contre-Espionnage (SDECE, France's external intelligence agency) (1970-1981). Deceased.

DeConcini, Dennis: U.S. Senator from Arizona (1977-1995); sponsored the critical amendment to the Panama Canal Treaty of 1977 that allowed the Senate to come to a consensus on returning to Panama the control of the Panama Canal.

Derian, Patricia: Assistant Secretary of State for Human Rights and Humanitarian Affairs, U.S. Department of State (1977-1981); refused to approve sale of tear gas for riot control to Iran; overruled by every other department and agency head.

Dershowitz, Alan: Professor of Law at Harvard Law School; known for his extensive published works, career as an attorney in several high-profile law cases, and commentary on the Arab-Israeli conflict.

Dlimi, Ahmed: Moroccan General under the rule of Hassan II. After General Mohamed Oufkir's 1972 assassination, he became King Hassan II's second-hand man. He died in January 1983, officially in a car crash, but allegations were made he was assassinated.

Dobrynin, Anatoly: Soviet Ambassador to the U.S. during the terms of six U.S. Presidents (Kennedy, Johnson, Nixon, Ford, Carter, and Reagan). After his long term as ambassador, he returned to Moscow, joining the Secretariat of the Communist Party of the Soviet Union.

Dohrn, Bernadine: Former leader (with husband Bill Ayers) of the radical leftist organization Weather Underground; an Associate Professor of Law at Northwestern University School of Law and the Director of Northwestern's Children and Family Justice Center.

Donovan, Hedley: Former editor-in-chief of *Time* magazine. As editor-in-chief for fifteen years beginning in 1964, he was responsible for the content of all Time Inc. publications, including *Time, Life, Fortune, Sports Illustrated, Money,* and *People.* Deceased.

Dubs, Adolph "Spike": United States Ambassador to Afghanistan (1978-1979); killed in an exchange of fire after a kidnapping attempt.

Duncan, Charles, Jr.: American entrepreneur, administrator, and statesman; best known for serving as U.S. Secretary of Energy on the Cabinet of President Jimmy Carter (1979-1981). He had previously served as Carter's United States Deputy Secretary of Defense during the Iranian Revolution.

E

Eagleton, Thomas: Became U.S. Senator from Missouri in 1968; a Democratic vice presidential nominee on the ticket with George McGovern in 1972. At McGovern's request, Eagleton withdrew from the race when it became known he had earlier suffered several bouts of physical and mental exhaustion, for which he had been hospitalized.

Eban, Abba: Elected Vice President of the UN General Assembly (1952); elected to the Knesset (the Israeli parliament) as a member of Mapai. He served under David Ben-Gurion as Minister of Education and Culture (1960-1963), then as deputy to Prime Minister Levi Eshkol until 1966. Through this entire period (1959-1966) he also served as president of the Weizmann Institute in Rehovot. Served as Israel's foreign minister (1966-1974), defending the country's reputation after the Six-Day War. Deceased.

Edelman, Marian Wright: American activist for the rights of children; president and founder of the Children's Defense Fund.

Eilts, Hermann: American Ambassador to Saudi Arabia and Egypt who assisted Henry Kissinger's Mideast shuttle diplomacy effort and worked with Egyptian President Anwar el-Sadat throughout the Camp David Accords. Deceased.

Einstein, Albert: German-born theoretical physicist; best known for his theory of relativity and specifically mass-energy equivalence, $E = mc^2$. Einstein received the 1921 Nobel Prize in Physics. Deceased.

Eisenhower, Dwight D.: 34th U.S. president from 1953-1961; during the Second World War he served as Supreme Commander of the Allied forces in Europe. Deceased.

Eizenstat, Stuart: President Jimmy Carter's Chief Domestic Policy Adviser and Executive Director of the White House Domestic Policy Staff (1977-1981); Bill Clinton's Deputy Treasury Secretary, Undersecretary of State for Economic, Business, and Agricultural Affairs; and also served as the Undersecretary of Commerce for International Trade at the International Trade Administration (ITA) (1996-1997).

Elghanian, Habib: Multimillionaire, a plastics manufacturer; was convicted of spying for Israel in a 1979 summary trial in Iran. Executed by firing squad.

el-Husseini, Haj Amin: A Palestinian Arab nationalist and a Muslim leader in the British Mandate of Palestine; the Grand Mufti of Jerusalem (1921-1948), and played a key role in resistance to Zionism. In 1937, wanted by the British, he fled Palestine and took refuge successively in Lebanon, Iraq, Italy, and finally Nazi Germany, where he met Adolf Hitler in 1941. He asked Germany to oppose, as part of the Arab struggle for independence, the establishment of a Jewish national home in Palestine. Deceased.

Eliot, Theodore L., Jr.: Inspector General, Foreign Service, U.S. State Department (1978); named covert emissary to Khomeini to coordinate with transition government (1979); mission endorsed by William Sullivan without White House approval; Carter cancelled trip.

Elizabeth II, Queen of Britain: Queen ruling sixteen independent states and their overseas territories and dependencies; she is resident in and most directly involved with the United Kingdom, her oldest realm. She ascended the thrones of seven countries in February 1952, on the death of her father, King George VI.

Elizabeth, Queen Mother: Full name: Elizabeth Bowes-Lyon. Queen consort of King George VI from 1936 until his death in 1952. Before her husband ascended to the throne, she was known as the Duchess of York. Deceased.

el-Tuhamy, Mohammad Hassan: Confidant to Egyptian President Sadat and senior cabinet member.

Emanuel, Rahm: Democratic member of the United States House of Representatives since 2003, representing Illinois's 5th Congressional District. Emanuel was chair of the Democratic Congressional Campaign Committee for the 2006 elections. After the Democratic Party regained control of the House, he was elected as the next chairman of the Democratic Caucus. He is the fourth-ranking Democrat in the House, behind Speaker Nancy Pelosi, Leader Steny Hoyer, and Whip Jim Clyburn. On November 6, 2008, Emanuel accepted an offer from President-elect Barack Obama to become the White House Chief of Staff in Obama's administration.

Entezam, Abdollah: A diplomat, he was one of the most prolific politicians of the 20th century; close to the Shah of Iran. His many roles included chairman of the Iranian Oil Company, secretary of state, and ambassador to Germany. Deceased.

Entezam, Amir: Spokesman and Deputy Prime Minister in the Interim Cabinet of Mehdi Bazargan in 1979. In 1981 he was sentenced to life imprisonment on charges of spying for the U.S., a charge critics suggest was a cover for retaliation against his early opposition to theocratic government in Iran.

Eshkol, Levi: Third Prime Minister of Israel from 1963 until his death from a heart attack in 1969; the first Israeli prime minister to die in office.

F

Fahd, King: King of the Kingdom of Saudi Arabia, (1982-2005); head of the House of Saud as well as Prime Minister. Fahd suffered a debilitating stroke November 29, 1995, after which he was unable to continue performing his full official duties. His half-brother, Abdullah, the country's crown prince, served as de facto regent of the kingdom and succeeded Fahd as monarch upon his death on August 1, 2005.

Fahmy, Ismail: Former Egyptian Foreign Minister; resigned in 1977 because he opposed President Anwar el-Sadat's visit to Jerusalem. He died after suffering a heart attack. Mr. Fahmy, a career diplomat, was appointed foreign minister after Egypt fought Israel in the 1973 Middle East War. He was also deputy prime minister from 1975 to 1977.

Faisal, King: King of the Kingdom of Saudi Arabia (1964-1975); he is credited with rescuing the country's finances and implementing a policy of modernization and reform. Assassinated.

Faisal, Turki: Saudi Arabia's ambassador to the United States (2005-2006); he is the youngest son of the late King Faisal by Princess Effat Al-Thuniyyan, brother of Foreign Minister Saud al Faisal, and a nephew of the present King Abdullah.

Falk, Richard: Professor, International Law, Princeton; human rights activist; met with Sullivan in Iran and Khomeini in Paris; praised the Ayatollah's ideology; believed him to be humane.

Farouk, King: The tenth ruler from the Muhammad Ali Dynasty and the penultimate King of Egypt and Sudan, succeeding his father, Fuad I, in 1936; overthrown in the Egyptian Revolution of 1952, and was forced to abdicate. He died in exile in Italy.

Farrakhan, Louis: Supreme Minister of the Nation of Islam (NOI) as the National Representative of Elijah Muhammad; also well-known as an advocate for African American interests and a critic of American society.

Fonda, Jane: American actress, writer, political activist, former fashion model, and fitness guru; has served as an activist for many political causes, one of the most notable and controversial of which was her opposition to the Vietnam War.

Ford, Charlotte: Fashion designer and consultant; has written books on etiquette and shopping. Her father was a former chairman of the Ford Motor Company, which was founded by his grandfather Henry Ford.

Ford, Gerald R.: 38th U.S. president from 1974-1977; succeeded Richard Nixon following Watergate scandal. Deceased.

Foruhar, Dariush: Minister of Labor, Iran (1979); Founded National Party of Iran; backed Mohammad Mossadegh; Minister of Labor under Khomeini's regime; forced into hiding by Islamic activists.

Frost, Robert: An American poet; highly regarded for his realistic depictions of the rural life and his command of American colloquial speech. Deceased.

G

Gacy, John Wayne: American serial killer; convicted and later executed for the rape and murder of thirty-three boys and young men between 1972 and his arrest in 1978, 27 of whom he buried in a crawl space under the floor of his house, while others were found in nearby rivers.

Geraghty, Col. Timothy: Former U.S. Marine commander in October 1983 when suicide bombers attacked the barracks of American peacekeeping forces in Beirut, Lebanon, killing 242 Americans.

Gandhi, Mahatma: Major political and spiritual leader of India and the Indian independence movement; pioneer of *Satyagraha*, resistance to tyranny through mass civil disobedience, which led India to independence and inspired movements for civil rights and freedom across the world. Deceased.

Gast, Lt. Gen. Philip C.: Head of the U.S. Military Assistance Advisory Group (MAAG), Iran (1978-1979); worked with General Robert Huyser during his last mission to Iran in 1979.

Gelb, Leslie H.: Director of Policy Planning and Arms Control for International Security Affairs at the Department of Defense (1967-1969). Robert McNamara appointed Gelb as director of the project that produced the controversial Pentagon Papers on the Vietnam War. Served as an assistant secretary of state in the Carter Administration (1977-1979).

Ghaffari, Ayatollah Hossein: Opposed Shah's regime; linked to Khomeini during exile in Najaf; reportedly tortured to death by SAVAK in 1974.

Gharabaghi, Abbas: Minister of Interior, Iran (1978); Chief of Staff of Iranian Armed Forces; ordered his troops into their barracks rather than fight Khomeini's take-over of Iran.

Ghotbzadeh, Sadegh: Director of National Iranian Radio and Television (1979); Foreign Minister, Iran (1979-80); personal aide to Khomeini during Paris exile; tried to negotiate release of Embassy hostages; arrested after falling from favor in Khomeini's Islamic Republic; executed September 1982.

Gingrich, Newt: Speaker of the United States House of Representatives (1995-1999); during his tenure he represented the public face of the Republican opposition to Bill Clinton.

Ginzburg, Aleksandr: Russian journalist, poet, human rights activist, and dissident. Between 1961 and 1969 sentenced three times to labor camps. In 1979 Ginzburg was released and expelled to the United States along with four other political prisoners and their families as part of a prisoner exchange. Deceased.

Giuliani, Rudolph: Served two terms as mayor of New York City; ran for the U.S. Senate in 2000 but withdrew due to being diagnosed with prostate cancer. Giuliani ran for the Republican Party nomination in the 2008 U.S. presidential election but withdrew on January 30, 2008, and endorsed John McCain.

Glad, Betty Carter: Biographer and political scientist; Olin D. Johnston Professor of Political Science at the University of South Carolina.

Glick, Caroline B.: Deputy managing editor of the *Jerusalem Post* and the senior fellow for Middle East Affairs at the Center for Security Policy.

Gold, Dore: Former Israeli diplomat; also served as president of the Jerusalem Center for Public Affairs as well as an advisor to former Israeli Prime Minister Ariel Sharon.

Goleniewski, Michel: Officer of Polish Military Intelligence and a spy for the Russian government during the 1950s. After his defection in 1961, he worked for the CIA. Deceased.

Gore, Albert, Jr.: American environmental activist, author, former journalist; served two terms as vice president under President Bill Clinton. Ran unsuccessfully as the Democratic presidential candidate twice (1988 and 2000).

Griffin, George B.: Director, Bureau of Intelligence and Research, U.S. State Department (1977-1981); traveled to Iran (November 1978) to determine gravity of crisis.

Graham, Lindsey: American politician from South Carolina; member of the Republican Party, he is currently the senior United States senator from that state.

Grassley, Chuck: Senior U.S. Senator from Iowa; a member of the Republican Party.

Gray, James: Ran against Jimmy Carter in 1966 Georgia Governor's race.

Grimm, Paul: First American to die during Islamic Revolution, December 23, 1978; worked for Oil Services Company of Iran.

Gromyko, Andrei: Chairman of the Presidium (1985-1988); earlier, Russian Foreign Minister for twenty-eight years. Deceased.

Guevara, Che: Known as Che Guevara, El Che, or simply Che; an Argentine Marxist revolutionary, politician, author, physician, military theorist, and guerrilla leader. Deceased.

Gulley, Bill: Director of the White House military office under Jimmy Carter.

H

Habash, George: Palestinian freedom fighter. A Palestinian Christian, who founded the Popular Front for the Liberation of Palestine and was the organization's secretary general until 2000. He held a firm belief that Palestine must be liberated by all possible means, including through violence. Violently opposed to the Oslo Agreements. Deceased.

Hadrian, Publius Aelius: Emperor of Rome from 117 to 138 AD; he attempted to root out Judaism, which he saw as the cause of continuous rebellions; prohibited the Torah law, the Hebrew calendar, and executed Judaic scholars.

Haig, Alexander M., Jr.: U.S. Deputy Assistant to the President for National Security Affairs, (1970-1973); Assistant to the President for National Security Affairs (1973-1974); Commander-in-Chief, U.S. European Command (1974-79); Supreme Commander, Allied Forces in Europe (1979); U.S. Secretary of State (1981-82); openly opposed President Carter's handling of the Iran crisis.

Haniya, Ismail: Senior political leader of Hamas and former prime minister of the Palestinian National Authority; he was dismissed from office on June 14, 2007, by Palestinian President Mahmoud Abbas.

Harel, Isser: Israeli spymaster; directed the abduction from Argentina of Adolf Eichmann and became a member of Haganah's intelligence department. When Israel became independent in 1948, Harel was the first head of Shin Bet, Israel's internal intelligence agency. In 1952 he also became head of Mossad, the foreign intelligence agency. Deceased.

Harmelin, Yosef: Director of Shin Bet; Israel's security service (1964-1974); later served as chairman of an oil company; Israeli ambassador in Iran and South Africa; and the supervisor of the security establishment in the office of the state comptroller. Deceased.

Hermening, Kevin: Former American Embassy hostage, a Marine guard.

Harris, Patricia: Secretary of Housing and Urban Development, becoming the first Afro-American in Jimmy Carter's cabinet; later in 1979, she was named secretary to the larger cabinet post of Housing, Education and Welfare. Deceased.

Harvey, Sgt. John D.: Crewman on the abortive 1980 mission to free American hostages in Iran. Deceased.

Hassan II, King: King of Morocco from 1961 until his death in 1999; he was the eldest son of Mohammed V, Sultan, then King of Morocco, and his wife Lalla Abla bint Tahar.

Hatcher, Richard: First African-American mayor of Gary, Indiana, on January 1, 1968; served in that role until 1987.

Hatfield, Mark: Governor of Oregon (1959-1967); he was elected to the U.S. Senate, serving until 1996. Consistently voted against military appropriations; voted to end the war in Vietnam. Also served as chairman of the Appropriations Committee.

Havel, Vaclav: Czech writer and dramatist; he was the tenth and last president of Czechoslovakia (1989-1992) and the first president of the Czech Republic (1993-2003).

Hee, Park Chung: General and leader of the Republic of Korea (1961-1979); he has been credited with the industrialization of the Republic of Korea. Assassinated.

Hefner, Christie: Chairman and Chief Executive Officer, Playboy Enterprises, Inc.; *Playboy* magazine founded by her father, Hugh Hefner; as of this writing has announced she will step down January 31, 2009.

Helms, Richard: CIA Director (1966-1973); U.S. Ambassador to Iran (1973-1977); knowledgeable regarding Iran's domestic and foreign relations; believed U.S. interests were tied to Shah; unpopular in Iran due to CIA history; replaced by William Sullivan (1977).

Henry, Patrick: Prominent figure in the American Revolution; known and remembered for his "Give me Liberty, or give me Death!" speech.

Heraclius, Emperor: Byzantine Emperor; ruled the Roman Empire for over thirty years, from 610 to 641.

Hermening, Kevin: A Marine, at twenty-one was the youngest hostage of those held at the American Embassy in Iran.

Herzog, Chaim: Sixth President of Israel (1983–1993), following a distinguished career in both the British Army and the Israel Defense Forces. Deceased.

Higgins, Colonel William: U.S. Marine Corp Colonel captured in 1988 while serving on a UN peacekeeping mission in Lebanon; held hostage, tortured, and eventually murdered by his captors.

Higgins, Lt. Colonel Robert: Captured by Iranian-sponsored Hezbollah in Lebanon; assassinated in 1984.

Hiss, Alger: U.S. State Department official involved in the establishment of the United Nations; he was accused of being a Soviet spy in 1948 and convicted of perjury in connection with this charge in 1950. He was found guilty on both counts of perjury and received two concurrent five-year sentences, of which he eventually served forty-four months. Deceased.

Hitler, Adolph: Austrian-born German politician who led the National Socialist German Workers Party, more commonly known as the Nazi Party; Chancellor of Germany (1933–1945) and Führer of Germany (1934–1945). Deceased.

Hofi, Yitzhak: Director of Mossad from 1974 to 1982; he headed the Northern Command of the IDF during the Yom Kippur War in 1973. He was acting chief of staff for a brief period in 1974, before retiring from the military and taking the post of director of Mossad.

Holder, Eric: Former Judge of the Superior Court of the District of Columbia, United States Attorney and Deputy Attorney General of the United States. He was one of three members of Obama's vice-presidential selection committee. On December 1, 2008, Obama announced Holder would be his nominee for attorney general in the incoming administration. He is the first African-American attorney general of the United States.

Holmes, Cpl. George N., Jr.: Crewman on the abortive 1980 mission to free American hostages in Iran. Deceased.

Holmes, Julius: Served in the U.S. Army during World War I; Foreign Service Officer; U.S. Vice Consul in Marseille, 1926; U.S. Consul General in Hong Kong, (1959-1961); U.S. Ambassador to Iran, (1961-1965). Deceased.

Homayoun, Dariush: Minister of Information, Iran (1977-1978); Minister of Labor and Social Welfare, Iran (1979); tapped by Shah to introduce liberal tone to government; held responsible for article in *Ettelat at* that denigrated Khomeini, causing riots in Qum, events thought to be beginning of revolution and Pahlavi's resignation.

Hoover, Herbert Clark: 31st U.S. President from 1929-1933; lost a bid for a second term to Franklin D. Roosevelt. Deceased.

Hoveyda, Amir Abbas: Prime Minister, Iran (1965-1977); that country's longest tenure as prime minister; founded Iran Novin party; arrested in 1978; executed by Islamic revolutionaries.

Hoveyda, Fereydoun: Influential Iranian diplomat, writer, and thinker; Iranian ambassador to the United Nations 1971 to 1979. Deceased.

Huckabee, Mike: Baptist minister, politician, and a political commentator for Fox News Channel; a member of the Republican Party, he served as governor of the U.S. State of Arkansas (1996-2007) and was a Republican candidate in the 2008 presidential primaries. Exited the race on March 4, 2008.

Humphrey, Hubert Horatio: 38th U.S. Vice President , serving under President Lyndon B. Johnson; twice served as a United States senator from Minnesota, and served as Democratic Majority Whip. In 1968, Humphrey was the nominee of the Democratic Party in the United States presidential election but narrowly lost to the Republican nominee, Richard Nixon. Deceased.

Huntington, Samuel P.: An American jurist, statesman, and revolutionary leader from Connecticut; a delegate to the Continental Congress, where he signed the Declaration of Independence as Governor of Connecticut.

Hussein I, King: Ruler of Jordan from the abdication of his father, King Talal, in 1952, until his death in 1999.

Hussein, Saddam: Iraq President (1979-2003); President Ba'ath Party, Iraq (1979-2003); Chairman of Revolutionary Command council, Iraq (1979-2003); arch-rival of Shah in Persian Gulf; aligned with Soviet Union; attacked Islamic Republic of Iran September 1980; attacked Kuwait in 1991; and overthrown by U.S. and coalition forces in 2003. Executed for crimes against his countrymen.

Huyser, Gen. Robert "Dutch": Deputy Commander-in-Chief, U.S. Forces in Europe (1975-1979); sent to Iran in January 1979 to enlist the Iranian military to support Bakhtiar's government.

I

Iannone, Carol: Conservative writer and literary critic; she has published extensively in conservative and neoconservative publications. She espouses traditionalist Roman Catholic ideology in her work.

Ibin Talal, Prince Alwaleed: Commonly known as Prince Al-Walid; a member of the Saudi Royal Family and an entrepreneur and international investor. He is ranked by *Forbes* as the 19th richest person in the world.

Igarashi, Hitoshi: Japanese translator of Salman Rushdie's novel *The Satanic Verses*. After Ayatollah Ruhollah Khomeini issued a *fatwa* calling for his death, he was stabbed to death by an unknown person on July 11, 1991.

Ivri, David: Israeli Ambassador to the United States (2000-2002); the ninth commander of the Israeli Air Force. In 1999 he was appointed first director of the National Security Council.

J

Jackson, Henry "Scoop": In 1941 at the age of twenty-eight, he entered U.S. Congress as its youngest member and representing Washington State; served under nine presidents. Never lost an election. Deceased.

Jackson, Jesse: Civil rights leader, politician, minister; in 1984 and 1988 sought presidential nomination of Democratic Party and lost each time.

Jam, Feridoun: Head of Iranian Imperial Army Corp (1969-1971); left army because of some professional conflicts with the Shah; retired from the Army in 1973. Deceased.

Javits, Jacob K.: Member U.S. House of Representatives (1947-1954); Senator, (1957-1981); condemned executions in Iran under Khomeini's regime; his comments triggered anti-American demonstrations in Iran. Deceased.

Jefferson, Thomas: 3rd U.S. President from 1801-1809.

Jennings, Peter: Canadian-American journalist and news anchor; the sole anchor of ABC's *World News Tonight* from 1983 until his death in 2005 from complications of lung cancer.

Jihad, Abu: Appointed official deputy of Arafat, his second and closest ally; assassinated in his house in Tunis by Israelis 1988.

Jintao, Hu: Paramount Leader of the People's Republic of China; holding the titles of General Secretary of the Communist Party of China since 2002, President of the People's Republic of China since 2003, and Chairman of the Central Military Commission since 2004.

Johnson, Captain H.F.: Commandeered an Iranian C-130 in a 1979 clandestine plot; flew into the town of Kapkan, Iran; exchanged 30 million rials for American hostages at an advance listening post, and transported them to safety.

Johnson, Lyndon B.: Member, U.S. House of Representatives (1937-1949); Senator (1949-1961); Vice President (1961-1963); 36th President (1963-1969); became president following John F. Kennedy's assassination in 1963; bolstered Iran as a U.S. ally.

Johnson, Staff Sgt. Dewey: Crewman on the abortive 1980 mission to free American hostages in Iran. Deceased.

Jones, James: President-elect Barack Obama's selection for United States National Security Advisor. He previously served as Supreme Allied Commander Europe (SACEUR) (2003–2006), commander of the United States European Command (COMUSEUCOM) (2003–2006), and as the 32nd Commandant of the Marine Corps (July 1999–January 2003). Jones retired from the United States Marine Corps on February 1, 2007, after forty years of service.

Jong-il, Kim: Leader of the Democratic People's Republic of Korea; he succeeded his father Kim Il-sung in 1994; commands the fifth largest standing army in the world.

Jordan, Hamilton: White House Chief of Staff (1977-1981); aided Carter in Panama Canal Treaty approval; secretly negotiated for release of Embassy hostages; offered the Shah in return for their release.

K

Kaddoumi, Farouk: Key figure in the PLO and after 1973 headed its political department in Damascus, Syria. Upon Arafat's death, Kaddoumi constitutionally succeeded him to the position of Fatah chairman.

Kalb, Marvin: Award-winning reporter for CBS and NBC News for thirty years; was the last newsman recruited by Edward R. Murrow to join CBS News. His work at CBS landed him on the Nixon administration's "enemies list."

Kamel, General Hussein: Son-in-law and second cousin of Iraqi leader Saddam Hussein; he defected to Jordan to help the UN Special Commission (UNSCOM) and the International Atomic Energy Agency IAEA inspection teams assigned to look for weapons of mass destruction in Iraq.

Karmal, Babrak: Third President of Afghanistan (1979-1986) during the period of the communist Democratic Republic of Afghanistan; best known of the Marxist leaders. Deceased.

Karzai, Hamid: President of Afghanistan since December 7, 2004; became a prominent political figure after the removal of the Taliban regime in late 2001.

Kashani, Abol Qassem: Prominent Twelver Shi'a Muslim cleric and former Parliament Minister of Iran. Deceased.

Kashani, Ahmed: Son of the Grand Ayatollah Abol Qassem Kashani; played a vital part in the nationalization of the Iranian oil industry in 1951, discussed arms purchases and military teamwork between Iran and Israel.

Ka-shing, Li: Asia's richest and most influential investor; his fortune is centered on conglomerates Cheung Kong and Hutchison Whampoa; real estate developer, cell phone provider, retailer, major supplier of electricity to Hong Kong, and the world's largest operator of container terminals.

Katibeh, Soroosh: Secretary to exiled Shapour Bakhtiar; both were murdered (1991) with PLO suspected of the crimes.

Keegan, George J., Jr.: Major General; Assistant Chief of Staff, Intelligence; Headquarters U.S. Air Force (1972-1977). Deceased.

Kennedy, Edward: Elected to office in 1962; represents the state of Massachusetts. Younger brother of John and Robert.

Kennedy, John F.: Member, U.S. House of Representatives (1947-1953); Senator (1953-1960); 35th President of the United States (1961-1963); assassinated in office; pushed Shah for reforms in Iran; refused military aid to Shah; reportedly supported deposing of Shah.

Kennedy, Robert F.: U.S. Attorney General (1961-1964); a U.S. Senator from New York from 1965 until his assassination in 1968.

Kerr, Dr. Malcolm: Born in Lebanon, a student of the Middle East; taught at the University of Beirut. Deceased.

Kerry, John: Serving his fourth term as the Junior U.S. Senator from Massachusetts; as the presidential nominee of the Democratic Party, he was defeated in the 2004 presidential election by the Republican incumbent, President George W. Bush.

Khalatbari, Abbas Ali: Iran Foreign Minister; executed with regime change.

Khalidi, Rashid: American historian of the Middle East; is the Edward Said Professor of Arab Studies at Columbia University and the director of the Middle East Institute of Columbia's International and Public Affairs. Khalidi has been accused of having ties to the Palestinian Liberation Organization, based on his work for Wafa in the late 1980s.

Khalidi, Mona: Wife of Rashid Khalidi and president of the American Action Network, or AAAN, a "non-profit, grassroots, community-based organization working to improve the social, economic, and political conditions of Arab immigrants and Arab Americans" in the Chicago Metropolitan area.

Khalkhali, Sadegh: Chief Justice, Revolutionary Court, Iran (1979-1980); blatantly executed members of Shah's regime without due course; elected to Majlis (1980).

Khamenehi, Ali: President, Iran (1981-1989); disciple of Ayatollah Khomeini; opposed Shah; member Revolutionary Council; sought to export revolution; succeeded Khomeini as "supreme religious authority."

Khan, Aga: Prince Karim Aga Khan IV is the 49th Ismaili Imam becoming the present Aga Khan IV, tracing his lineage to Ali, cousin of Muhammad, and his wife Fatima, Muhammad's daughter.

Khan, Aktar Abdel Rahman: Pakistani Inter-Services Intelligence chief who supervised a variety of political and military operations (1980-1988); killed along with President Zia Al Haq in a mysterious plane crash.

Khatami-Ardakani, Ali Mohammad: Moderate leader; elected Iran's president in 1997 with an overwhelming majority and re-elected in 2001. Replaced in 2005 by Tehran Mayor Mahoud Ahmadinejad.

Kho'ei, Ayatollah: Prominent Twelver Shi'a Muslim cleric and former Parliament Minister of Iran. Deceased.

Khomeini, Mustafa: The elder son of the founder of Islamic Republic of Iran; died in 1977 under questionable circumstances.

Khomeini, Ruhollah Ayatollah: Emerged as leader of Iran's Islamic Revolution; overthrew monarchy; established Islamic Republic; religious leader with an iron fist; kept Iran subjugated under Islamic revolutionary law until his death in 1989; succeeded by Ali Khamenehi.

Khosrowdad, Manuchehr: Brigadier General; the Shah's Aide de Camp. Executed.

Khrushchev, Nikita: First Secretary of the Communist Party of the Soviet Union from 1953 to 1964 following the death of Joseph Stalin and Chairman of the Council of Ministers from 1958 to 1964. Party colleagues removed him from power in 1964, replacing him with Leonid Brezhnev. Deceased.

Kilburn, Peter: Librarian, American University, Beirut. Deceased.

King, Martin Luther, Jr.: Elected president of the Southern Christian Leadership Conference in 1957; youngest person to receive the Nobel Peace Prize at the age of thirty-five. Assassinated April 4, 1968.

Kirkpatrick, Jeane: American ambassador and an ardent anticommunist; after serving as Ronald Reagan's foreign policy adviser in his 1980 campaign and later in his cabinet, the longtime Democrat-turned-Republican was nominated as the U.S. ambassador to the United Nations. Deceased.

Kissinger, Henry A.: U.S. Assistant to President Nixon for National Security Affairs (1969-1974); Secretary of State (1974-1977); extensive contacts with Shah; accompanied Richard Nixon to Iran in 1972; aided and supported the military build-up in Iran.

Klinghoffer, Leon: Retired, wheelchair bound appliance manufacturer from New York; murdered by Palestinian terrorists in the hijacking of the cruise ship *Achille Lauro* in 1985.

Krauthammer, Charles: Pulitzer Prize-winning syndicated columnist and commentator; appears regularly as a commentator on Fox News and as a weekly panelist on *Inside Washington*.

Koob, Elizabeth: U.S. Embassy employee in Tehran at the time of the students' attack in 1979.

Kouchner, Bernard: French politician, diplomat, and doctor; co-founder of Doctors Without Borders (MSF) and Doctors of the World. Currently the French Minister of Foreign and European Affairs.

Kreps, Juanita: Economist and Duke University professor; became the first woman director of the U.S. Stock Exchange in 1977. She was named Secretary of Commerce in the Carter cabinet, serving until 1977.

Kurtzer, Daniel: Considered by President Barack Obama for the appointment as his administration's presidential envoy to the Middle East. Former American Ambassador to Egypt (1997-2001) and Israel (2001-2005).

L

Lahidji, A. E.: Iranian lawyer.

Laingen, L. Bruce: Chargé d'Affaires, U.S. Embassy, Iran (1979); sought to establish direct contact with Khomeini; taken hostage with other Embassy employees; spent most of 444 days in solitary confinement.

Laird, Melvin: U.S. Secretary of Defense (1969-1973) under Richard Nixon; earlier, U.S. Representative from Wisconsin, re-elected eight consecutive times.

Lake, Anthony: Foreign policy advisor to several Democratic presidents; National Security Advisor under Bill Clinton (1993-1997).

Lance, Bert: Appointed by Jimmy Carter as Director of the Office of Management and Budget. Allegations of financial irregularities forced his resignation in 1977.

Ledeen, Dr. Michael: An expert on U.S. foreign policy; a former consultant to the NSC and to the U.S. State and Defense Departments.

Lee, Spike: Emmy Award-winning and Academy Award-nominated American film director, producer, writer, and actor; noted for his films dealing with controversial social and political issues.

Lenin, Nikolai: Russian revolutionary; a communist politician, the main leader of the October Revolution, the first head of the Russian Soviet Socialist Republic, and from 1922 the first *de facto* leader of the Soviet Union. Deceased.

Lewis, Maj. Harold, Jr.: Crewman on the abortive 1980 mission to free American hostages in Iran. Deceased.

Lewis, Samuel: Retired career diplomat; Director of the State Department's Policy Planning Staff for the Clinton Administration during 1993 and 1994. During his last overseas assignment as ambassador to Israel, Lewis was a prominent actor in Arab-Israeli relations, participating in the 1978 Camp David Conference.

Lincoln, Abraham: 16th U.S. President from 1861-1865; assassinated while in office.

Lubrani, Uri: One of the world's leading experts on Iran; has had a long and distinguished career in the service of the State of Israel. His posts have included Head of Mission to Iran, Government Coordinator for Lebanese Affairs, Coordinator of the Rescue of Ethiopian Jews, chief negotiator for the release of Israeli hostages, and ambassador to several countries, including Ethiopia and Uganda.

M

Maddox, Lester: Ran against Jimmy Carter in Georgia governor's race in 1966. In one of the closest races in that state's history, Maddox was declared governor by the legislature; Lieutenant-Governor under Jimmy Carter. Deceased.

Majidi, Dr. Abdol Majid: Minister of Planning and Budget under the Shah of Iran.

Manescu, Corneliu: Foreign Minister of Romania (1961-1972); former Romanian diplomat with a reputation for integrity, who became a courageous opponent of Nicolae Ceausescu, his country's dictator; president of the United Nations General Assembly (1967-1968). Deceased.

Manson, Charles: An American criminal who led the "Manson Family," a quasi-commune that arose in the U.S. state of California in the late 1960s. He was found guilty of conspiracy to commit the Tate/LaBianca murders, whose members carried out at his instruction. On May 23, 2007, he was denied parole for the eleventh time.

Maraghei, Muhammad Sa'ed: Prime Minister of Iran (1943-1944) and again (1949-1950); born in Maragheh, he studied at University of Lausanne and first became prime minister after the fall of Ali Soheili's cabinet. Deceased.

Marcos, Mrs. Ferdinand (Imelda): Widow of Ferdinand, President of the Philippines (1965-1986); former First Lady; an influential political figure.

Mariam, Mengistu Haile: Most prominent officer of the Derg, the military junta that governed Ethiopia from 1974 to 1987; President of the People's Democratic Republic of Ethiopia from 1987 to 1991.

Marston, David: Prominent Philadelphia lawyer and author; forced out of his position as U.S. attorney in 1978 in a public dispute with U.S. President Jimmy Carter; an appointee of Carter's predecessor, Gerald R. Ford he had obtained convictions of political leaders from both parties in Pennsylvania when Carter authorized his removal.

Marzouk, Musa Abu: Deputy Chief of HAMAS's Political Bureau based in Damascus, Syria; his activities include directing and coordinating terrorist acts by HAMAS against soldiers and civilians in Israel and the West Bank and Gaza.

Masri, Mushir: Hamas official; Palestinian Legislative Council Deputy.

Mayo, Tech. Sgt. Joel C.: Crewman on the abortive 1980 mission to free American hostages in Iran. Deceased.

McCain, John: Senior United States Senator from Arizona and Republican Party nominee for president of the United States in the 2008 election; he lost to Barack Obama.

McCarthy, Eugene: Member of the House of Representatives (1949-1959), U.S. Senator from Minnesota (1959-1971); he was later considered as Lyndon Johnson's running mate in 1964, but fellow Minnesota Senator Hubert Humphrey was chosen. Deceased.

McGovern, George: Representative and U.S. Senator from South Dakota; he ran for the presidency in 1972, losing to Richard Nixon.

McIntosh, Capt. Lyn D.: Crewman on the abortive 1980 mission to free American hostages in Iran. Deceased.

McMillan, Capt. Charles T.: Crewman on the abortive 1980 mission to free American hostages in Iran. Deceased.

Meese, Edwin: 75th U.S. Attorney General (1985-1988) under Ronald Reagan.

Mehsud, Baitullah: Leading tribal militia leader in Waziristan who, while he is sympathetic to both the Taliban and Al Qaeda, is primarily tribally oriented. The Pakistani military has officially claimed that military operations against Mehsud are continuing.

Mengistu, Haile: The most prominent officer of the Derg, the military junta that governed Ethiopia from 1974 to 1987, and the President of the People's Democratic Republic of Ethiopia from 1987 to 1991. Mengistu fled to Zimbabwe in 1991 at the conclusion of a long rebellion against his government and remains there despite an Ethiopian court verdict finding him guilty *in absentia* of genocide.

Meshaal, Khaled: Palestinian exile; the "political leader" of Hamas politic bureau from Syrian branch and leader of Hamas since the assassination of Shaykh Amad Yassin in 2004.

Meir, Golda: 4th Prime Minister of the State of Israel (1969) after serving as Minister of Labour and Foreign Minister. Deceased.

Merkel, Angela: Chancellor of Germany; the first female chancellor of that country; considered by *Forbes* magazine to be the most powerful woman in the world at the present time. In 2007 she became the second woman to chair the G8 after Margaret Thatcher.

Meyer, Armin: Career diplomat in the administrations of Presidents Kennedy, Johnson, and Nixon. Deceased.

Miller, G. William: Appointed as Chairman of the Board of Governors by Jimmy Carter in 1977; appointed Secretary of the Treasury (1979-1981). As Treasury chief, he became a key advocate for the $1.5 billion loan guarantee program that saved Chrysler and thousands of jobs there. Deceased.

Miller, George: Congressman and Chairman of the House Education and Labor Committee; a leading advocate in Congress on education, labor, the economy, and the environment. He has represented the 7th District of California in the East Bay of San Francisco since 1975.

Miller, William: Chief of staff to the Senate Select Committee on Intelligence.

Mina, Dr. Parviz: Managing Director of the National Iranian Oil Company; chosen by the Shah of Iran to institute an international oil consortium (INOC after 1979) to oversee Iranian oil production.

Minachi, Nasser: Iran's Minister of Information and National Guidance; reportedly had close links with the CIA. He was arrested by revolutionary guards, but the ruling Revolutionary Council ordered his release.

Moffett, Toby: U.S. Representative from Connecticut (1974-1983); an unsuccessful candidate for the U.S. Senate that year.

Moghadam, General Nasser: Fourth and last chief of SAVAK; succeeded General Nematollah Nassiri, who was arrested by the Shah's order in 1978. Moghadam was executed under Ayatollah Khomeini's order.

Mohammad VI: King of Morocco; enthroned July 23, 1999, just hours after the death of his father.

Moin, Baqer: BBC journalist and author; described as "a specialist on Iran and Islam and is head of the BBC's Persian Service" and is "BBC's Central Asia specialist."

Mondale, Walter: Appointed as Minnesota Senator in 1964 to fill the vacancy caused by Hubert Humphrey, who resigned to run for the presidency; later was elected to run with Jimmy Carter as vice presidential candidate. Unsuccessful democratic nominee for presidency in 1984.

Moore, G. Curtis: American diplomat; assassinated during a terrorist attack on the United States Embassy in Khartoum, Sudan (1973).

Moore, Homer: Georgia politician; ran against Jimmy Carter in 1962 primary election race for a Georgia Senate seat. Moore won the election but lost to Carter on a recount.

Moore, Michael: Academy Award-winning American filmmaker, author, and actor. Moore is a self-described liberal who has criticized globalization, large corporations, gun ownership, the Iraq War, U.S. President George W. Bush, and the American health care system in his written and cinematic works.

Morris, Dick: An American political author, newspaper columnist, and commentator; previously worked as a pollster, political campaign consultant, and general political consultant; became an adviser to the Bill Clinton administration after Clinton was elected president in 1992.

Mossadegh, Mohammad: Prime Minister, Iran (1951-1952; 1952-1953); lawyer and land owner; exiled for opposing Reza Shah's coronation; as member of Majlis, called for nationalization of British-controlled oil industry; responsible for National Front coalition; overthrown by CIA-initiated coup under the direction of Kermit Roosevelt; served three years in prison.

Moyers, Bill: American journalist and public commentator; White House Press Secretary in the Johnson Administration (1965-1967).

Moynihan, Daniel Patrick: American politician and sociologist; member of the Democratic Party, he was first elected to the United States Senate for New York in 1976 and was re-elected three times (in 1982, 1988, and 1994). Deceased.

Mubarak, Hosni: President of Egypt since October 14, 1981; succeeded Anwar Al Sadat, following Sadat's assassination.

Mugabe, Robert: President of Zimbabwe; has served as the head of government since 1980, as Prime Minister (1980-1987), and as the First Executive President since 1987.

Murrow, Edward R.: American journalist and television and radio figure; first came to prominence with a series of radio news broadcasts during World War II. Murrow resigned from CBS to accept a position as head of the United States Information Agency, parent of the Voice of America, in 1961. Deceased.

Muskie, Edmund S.: U.S. Secretary of State (1980-1981); filled Cyrus Vance's post following his resignation over the failed mission to rescue Embassy hostages. He also served as Governor of Maine, as U.S. Senator, and ran as a candidate for president of the United States. Deceased.

Mussa, Abu: Deputy military head of PLO operations room in Lebanon (1977-1982).

N

Naas, Charles: Retired American career diplomat posted to Iran shortly before the U.S. Embassy hostages were taken.

Nakash, Anis: Hezbollah operative; reputed assassin, arrested and sentenced to life in prison but was released by the French in a prisoner exchange with Iran.

Nasser, Gamal Abdul: Second President of Egypt from 1956 until his death in 1970. Along with Muhammad Naguib, he led the Egyptian Revolution of 1952, which removed King Farouk I. Deceased.

Nassiri, Nematollah: SAVAK Chief (1965-1978); held key position in overthrow of Mohammad Mossadegh; as SAVAK head, responsible for harsh treatment of dissidents; executed by revolutionaries.

Nesbitt, Mary: Managing Director of the Readership Institute at the Media Management Center and Associate Dean for Curriculum and Professional Excellence at the Medill School, both at Northwestern University.

Negus: Ancient Ethiopian monarch; a Christian.

Netanyahu, Benjamin: The 9th Prime Minister of Israel (1996-1999) and Chairman of the Likud Party. He is the official leader of the Opposition in the Knesset.

Nichols, Jim: Speech writer and public relations man.

Nicholas II, (Romanov) Tsar: Ruled from 1894 until his abdication in 1917. His rule ended with the Russian Revolution, in which he and his family were first imprisoned then later executed by the Bolsheviks in 1918.

Nimrodi, Ya'acov: Israel's military attaché; reportedly helped organize and encourage the rebellion of Kurdish tribesmen against Iraq, the Shah's main political and military rival in the region. The chief government agent for Israel's burgeoning arms industry.

Nixon, Richard M.: Member, U.S. House of Representatives (1947-1950); Senator (1950-1953); Vice President of U.S. under Dwight D. Eisenhower (1953-1961); 37th President of the U.S. (1969-1974); resigned from office during Watergate scandal; formulated "Twin Pillar" doctrine; liberally sold arms to Shah.

Noel, Cleo: U.S. Ambassador to Sudan; killed by the Black September Palestinian terrorist organization.

Nolen, Richard: An aid to Walter Mondale.

Nygaard, William: Norwegian publisher; responsible for publishing the Norwegian edition of Salman Rushdie's novel *The Satanic Verses*. Ayatollah Khomeini issued a *fatwa* against Salman Rushdie and his publishers. On the morning of October 11, 1993, Nygaard was shot three times and left for dead outside his home, but after several months of hospitalization he recovered.

O

Obama, Barack: Junior U.S. Senator from Illinois and Democratic Party in the 2008 presidential election. He is the first African American to be a major party's nominee for and to become the President of the United States.

Obama, Michelle: Lawyer and the wife of President Barack Obama. After completing her formal education, she worked for a law firm, on the staff of the Mayor of Chicago Richard M. Daley, for the University of Chicago, and for the University of Chicago Hospitals.

O'Hare, Madalyn Murray: Best known for the lawsuit which led to a landmark Supreme Court ruling and ended the practice of daily prayer in American public schools; later founded American Atheists. She was murdered in 1995 along with her son and granddaughter.

Olahi, Kamilladin Habib: Admiral; the Shah of Iran's Naval Commander.

O'Neill, John: A top American anti-terrorism expert; worked as a special agent and eventually Assistant Director in the Federal Bureau of Investigation until late 2001. Deceased.

O'Neill, Thomas P. "Tip", Jr.: Served thirty-four years in the House of Representatives, representing two congressional districts in Massachusetts. Speaker of the House (1977-1987) when he retired. Deceased.

Olmert, Ehud: 12th Prime Minister of Israel; became the interim prime minister on 14 April 2006 but had been exercising the powers of the office as acting prime minister, since they were transferred to him on 4 January 2006 after Ariel Sharon suffered a severe hemorrhagic stroke. Announced his retirement following allegations of corruption.

Ortega, Daniel: President of Nicaragua; for much of his life, he has been an important leader in the Sandinista National Liberation Front.

Oveissi, Gholam Ali: Chief of Staff, Iran (1975-1978); Military Governor of Tehran (1978); Minister of Labor, Iran (1978); favored military suppression of revolutionary opposition; exiled to Paris (1979); executed 1984.

P

Pacepa, Ion M.: Russian General; defected to the West in 1978.

Pahlavi, Ashraf: Princess and twin sister of Shah; delegate to UN Human Rights Commission; supported women's rights.

Pahlavi, Farah Diba: Agriculture student before wedding the Shah; mother of heir to Peacock Throne, Reza Pahlavi; promoted health, education, and culture as queen; exiled with Shah (1979).

Pahlavi, Mohammad Reza: Shah of Iran (1941-1979); ascended to throne following invasion of Iran (1941); courted U.S. assistance to offset Soviet influence in Persian Gulf region; attempted to modernize Iran through his "White Revolution;" built up Iran militarily with aide from U.S.; overthrown by Ruhollah Khomeini's Islamic Revolution (1979). Deceased.

Pahlavi, Reza: Shah of Iran (1925-1941); backed Nazis during World War II, replaced by son Mohammad Reza with assistance from Great Britain and Soviets. Deceased.

Pahlavi, Reza Cyrus: Crown Prince of Iran; declared Reza Shah II following death of his father. Resides in the U.S.

Pakravan, Hassan: SAVAK Chief, Iran (1961-1965); succeeded by Nematollah Nassiri; imprisoned and executed by Khomeini's revolutionaries.

Palmer, Charles: Chief steward on Air Force One during the Carter presidency.

Parsons, Anthony: Assigned to Iran as Ambassador in 1974; came to the United Nations as Britain's permanent representative in 1979. Deceased.

Parviz, Khosrow: King of Persia of the Sassanid (or Sassanian) Dynasty; grandson of Khosrow I. He is also called Chosroes II or Khosru II.

Pelosi, Nancy: First female and first Italian-American Speaker of the U.S. House of Representatives. Since 1987 she has represented the 8th Congressional District of California.

Percy, Charles: U.S. Senator from Illinois (1967-1985); active in the areas of business and international affairs. During the early 1970s he clashed with President Richard Nixon and criticized the U.S. conduct of the war in Vietnam.

Peres, Shimon: Ninth (and current) President of the State of Israel; previously served twice as prime minister of Israel and once as acting prime minister; has served in twelve cabinets during a political career lasting over sixty-six years.

Perle, Richard: American political advisor and lobbyist; Assistant Secretary of Defense under Reagan administration and worked on the Defense Policy Board Advisory Committee from 1987 to 2004. He was Chairman of the Board from 2001 to 2003 under the Bush administration.

Pétain, Maréchal: Prime Minister of the Vichy government of France in 1940; formed a new government and asked the Germans for an armistice; in effect, surrendering. Petain had become a legendary war hero for successfully repelling a German attack on the French city of Verdun during the First World War. When Paris was finally liberated by General Charles de Gaulle in 1944, Petain fled to Germany. He was brought back after the war to stand trial for his duplicity. He was sentenced to death, which was then commuted to life in solitary confinement. He died at ninety-five in prison.

Philip, Prince: Duke of Edinburgh; married Queen Elizabeth of England in 1947.

Pierce, Nelson: Assistant White House usher during the Carter administration.

Pompidou, Georges: President of the French Republic (1969-1974); Prime Minister under de Gaulle. Deceased.

Poniatowski, Michel: Polish Prince and French politician; founder of the Independent Republicans and a part of the government of President Valéry Giscard d'Estaing. Poniatowski served as Minister of Health (1973-1974) and Minister of the Interior 1974-1977. Deceased.

Pot, Pol: Leader of the communist movement known as the "Khmer Rouge;" the Prime Minister of Cambodia (1976-1979), having been *de facto* leader since mid-1975. Deceased.

Powell, Jody: Press secretary to Jimmy Carter.

Pakravan, Hassan: Well-known diplomat and minister in the Pahlavi pre-revolutionary government of Iran; not only notable for his political involvement with the Mohammad Reza Shah government and SAVAK, but also his relationship with Ayatollah Ruhollah Khomeini. Deceased.

Precht, Henry: U.S. Embassy Political Officer, Iran (1972-1975); Iran Desk Officer, U.S. Department of State (1978-1979); alerted Carter administration of instability in Iran; favored a coalition government.

Price, Melvin: Longtime member of the United States House of Representatives, representing the State of Illinois; he served as the chairman of the United States House Committee on Armed Services between 1975 and 1985. Deceased.

Pryce-Jones, David: conservative British author and commentator.

Q

Quayle, Dan: American politician and a former Senator from the State of Indiana; 44th Vice President of the United States under George H. W. Bush (1989–1993).

Quandt, William: Staff member on the National Security Council (1972-1974, 1977-1979); was actively involved in the negotiations that led to the Camp David Accords and the Egyptian-Israeli Peace Treaty.

Queen, Richard: Vice Consul at the U.S. Embassy in Tehran. On November 4, 1979, he was among the sixty-six hostages taken in the Iran Hostage Crisis. He was released for health reasons and later diagnosed with multiple sclerosis. Deceased.

Qutb, Sayyid: Egyptian author, socialist, and the leading intellectual of the Egyptian Muslim Brotherhood in the 1950s and '60s. Executed for treason.

R

Rabii, Amir Hussein: Air Force General, who later expressed his anger at U.S. General Robert E. Huyser, the deputy commander of U.S. forces in Europe. Huyser had been sent to Iran with the goal of persuading the military leaders not to mount a coup against the Shah's last Premier, Shapour Bakhtiar. Executed by firing squad.

Rabin, Yitzhak: Israeli politician and general; 5th Prime Minister of Israel, serving two terms in office, (1974-1977 and 1992) until his assassination in 1995. In 1994 Rabin won the Nobel Peace Prize together with Shimon Peres and Yasser Arafat. The first native-born prime minister of Israel,

Rafsanjani, Ali Akbar: President of Iran (1989-1997); later ran again for a third term in office, losing on the second ballot to Mahmoud Ahmadinejad in the 2005 election.

Rahman, Sheikh Omar Abdul: Founder of the country of Bangladesh and The Father of the Nation; later headed the Awami League, served as the first President of Bangladesh and then became its Prime Minister. Deceased.

Rajavi, Masoud: President of National Council of Resistance of Iran and the leader of People's Mujahedin of Iran (PMOI, also known as the MEK); a militant opposition organization active outside of Iran. After leaving Iran in 1981, he resided in France and Iraq. Since the 2003 invasion of Iraq he has not made any public appearances and is presumed to be either dead or in hiding.

Rainier III, Prince: Sovereign Prince of Monaco (1949-2005). Before his death, he was the world's second-longest reigning monarch with his fifty-six years of reign. Deceased.

Rainier, Princess Grace: American movie star; married Prince Rainier of Monaco in 1956. Mother of the current Sovereign Prince Albert II. Deceased.

Raskin, Marcus: A founder in 1963 of the Institute for Policy Studies, a Washington "Think Tank."

Reagan, Ronald: 40th U.S. President (1981-1989). Deceased.

Ribicoff, Abraham: Secretary of Health, Education, and Welfare under John F. Kennedy (1961-1962); longtime friend of Senator Kennedy, Ribicoff nominated his fellow New Englander for vice president at the 1956 Democratic National Convention and was one of the first public officials to endorse Kennedy's presidential campaign. Member of the House of Representatives from Connecticut (1949-1953), was a U.S. Senator (1963-1981). Deceased.

Rice, Condoleezza: 66th United States Secretary of State; the second in the administration of President George W. Bush to hold the office. The second woman (after Madeleine Albright in the Clinton Administration) and the first African American woman to serve as secretary of state.

Rice, Susan: U.S. Assistant Secretary of State for African Affairs (1997-2001); has been nominated by President Obama as Ambassador to the UN.

Rich, Marc: An international commodities trader. He created the spot market for crude oil in the 1970s. He fled the United States in 1983 to live in Switzerland while being prosecuted on charges of tax evasion and illegally making oil deals with Iran during the hostage crisis. After prosecution he was convicted of felonies related to tax evasion and illegal deals with Iran during the Iran hostage crisis. He subsequently received a presidential pardon from President Bill Clinton in 2001 during Clinton's last day in office.

Richardson, Elliot: Secretary of Health, Education, and Welfare; later Secretary of Defense and U.S. Attorney General under Richard Nixon, and Secretary of Commerce under Gerald Ford. Deceased.

Rickover, Hyman G.: Admiral in charge of U.S. nuclear submarine program. Deceased.

Rifai, Zeid: Prime Minister of Jordan twice (1973 to 1976 and 1985 to1989). His total time in the position was the longest in Jordanian history.

Robertson, Rev. Pat: Founded the Christian Broadcasting Network in 1960. Still hosts The 700 Club.

Robespierre, Maximilien: One of the best-known figures of the French Revolution; an influential member of the Committee of Public Safety and was instrumental in the period of the Revolution commonly known as the Reign of Terror, which ended with his arrest and execution in 1794.

Rockefeller, David: CEO, Chase Manhattan Bank (1969-1980); organized group to explore investments in Iran; helped gain permission for Shah to receive medical treatment in the U.S. in October 1979. Only surviving grandchild of John D. Rockefeller.

Rockefeller, Nelson: Forty-first Vice President of the United States (1974-1977), 49th Governor of New York, (1959-973). A descendant of one of the world's richest and best-known families, he failed repeatedly in his attempts to become president. Deceased.

Rogers, William: U.S. Attorney General under Dwight Eisenhower (1957-1961); Secretary of State under Richard Nixon (1969-1973). Deceased.

Roosevelt, Elliot: U.S. Army Air Corps officer and author; also the son of U.S. President Franklin D. Roosevelt (FDR) and his wife Anna Eleanor Roosevelt, the fourth of six children. Deceased.

Roosevelt, Franklin D.: Thirty-second U.S. President (1933-1945); died while serving his fourth term in office.

Roosevelt, Kermit "Kim": Grandson of Theodore Roosevelt; joined CIA following World War II; headed CIA operations in the Middle East; assisted in planning and execution of "Operation Ajax" to overthrow Prime Minister Mossadegh.

Roosevelt, Theodore (Teddy): Twenty-sixth U.S. President (1901-1909). Deceased.

Rostenkowski, Dan: Member of the U.S. House of Representatives (1959-1995); his political career was shattered in 1994 when he was indicted on corruption charges for his key role in the House post office scandal. He was forced to step down from all congressional leadership positions. In elections later that year Rostenkowski lost his seat and retired from political life.

Rubin, Gail: Known for her photographs of the wildlife and natural landscapes of Israel; began to work in Israel as a press photographer following a trip to the country in 1969. Murdered near Tel Aviv by Palestinian terrorists on March 11, 1978.

Rushdie, Salman: Author of *The Satanic Verse;* the novel caused great controversy for what many Muslims believed were blasphemous references. The book was banned in India and burned in demonstrations in the United Kingdom. The Ayatollah Ruhollah Khomeini issued a *fatwa* calling on all good Muslims to kill Rushdie and his publishers, or to point him out to those who could kill him if they could not themselves.

Rusk, Dean: Fifty-fourth U.S. Secretary of State; serving under both John F. Kennedy and Lyndon B. Johnson. Deceased.

Rustin, Bayard: Civil Rights Activist; counseled Martin Luther King Jr. on techniques of non-violent resistance. Deceased.

Rutherford, Guy: Alias employed by CIA operative Vernon Cassin.

S

Sadat, Anwar El: President, Egypt (1970-1981); Expelled Soviet advisors from Egypt; established friendly relations with U.S. and Shah; signed Camp David Accords, peace treaty with Israel; invited the Shah to spend last days in Egypt; presided over the monarch's funeral; assassinated in 1981.

Sadat, Jehan: Second wife of Anwar Sadat; served as first lady of Egypt from 1970 until Sadat's assassination in 1981. Jehan played a key role in reforming Egypt's civil rights laws during the late 1970s.

Sadiqi, Gholam Hossein: Minister of Post, Telephone, and Telegraph, Iran (1951-1952); Minister of Interior, Iran (1952-1953); mandated by Shah to form coalition government during final days of monarchy; efforts failed. Briefly considered accepting Shah's offer to become his prime minister; eventually rejected the offer when, among other things, Shah insisted on leaving Iran.

Salehi, Maj. Gen. Ataollah: A top Iranian military commander.

Salinger, Pierre: Press secretary to Presidents John F. Kennedy and Lyndon B. Johnson; later, chief European correspondent for ABC News. Deceased.

Saltzman, Bettylu: Political activist and community leader; her involvement in politics spans from 1969 to Barack Obama's 2004 campaign for the U.S. Senate. She served as Adlai Stevenson's Finance Director in 1982 and as director of Senator Paul Simon's office for Chicago and Northern Illinois from 1984-1988.

Sanjabi, Karim: Minister of Education, Iran (1951-1953); Minister of Foreign Affairs (1979); member of National Front; supported Mossadegh; Foreign Minister in Provisional Government; later resigned.

Sapir, Pinhas: Israeli politician during the first three decades following the country's founding; held two important ministerial posts, Minister of Finance (1963-1968 and 1969-1974) and Minister of Trade and Industry (1955-1965 and 1970-1972) as well as several other high-ranking governmental posts. Deceased.

Saunders, Harold H.: Assistant Secretary of State for Near Eastern and South Asian Affairs, U.S. State Department (1978-1981); Director, Bureau of Intelligence and Research (1975-1978); aided Secretary of State Vance to educate Carter on the Iranian crisis.

Scharansky, Anatoly: See Sharansky, Nathan

Schlesinger, James R.: Secretary of Defense (1973-1975); Secretary of Energy (1977-1979); attempted to limit arms sales to Shah; dispatched two advisors to Iran to advise Pahlavi and General Toufanian on ways to improve the military.

Schlossberg, Caroline Kennedy: American author and attorney; the daughter and only surviving child of U.S. President John F. Kennedy and his wife, Jacqueline Bouvier Kennedy Onassis.

Schmidt, Helmut: Became West German Chancellor in 1974, succeeding Willy Brandt; earlier served as the country's Defense Minister, then Finance Minister. Developed a close working relationship with France's President Giscard D'Estaing. Impaired by ill health, Schmidt's reign as chancellor came to an end in 1982.

Schultze, Charles: Chairman of Council of Economic Advisors during Jimmy Carter's administration.

Schwarzkopf, H. Norman, Sr.: Head of New Jersey State Police; hired by Iran to train Imperial Iranian Gendarmerie; help Shah remain in power during Mossadegh affair in 1953; father of General Norman Schwarzkopf, U.S. Commander during Operation *Desert Storm* in 1991.

Schwimmer, Adolf: Israel Aircraft Industry founder; secured a contract to overhaul Iranian airliners and American-made F-86 fighters.

Segev, Samuel: Free Press Middle East correspondent; he is based in Tel Aviv.

Segev, Yitzhak: General; military attaché in Tehran.

Selassie, Haile: Emperor of Ethiopia (1930-1974); introduced Ethiopia's first written constitution on 16 July 1931, providing for a bicameral legislature. Deceased.

Seurat, Michel: French writer; kidnapped and murdered by hostage-takers (1985) in Lebanon.

Shaefer, Col. T. E.: Commandeered an Iranian C-130 in a clandestine 1979 plot; flew into the town of Kapkan, Iran, exchanged 30 million rials for American hostages at an advance listening post, and transported them to safety.

Shafigh, Shahriar: Princess Ashraf's son, the nephew of the Shah; an Imperial Iranian Navy Captain, and the only member of the Dynasty who chose a military career; also the only member of Dynasty to stay inside Iran and keep fighting against the Islamic revolutionaries, up to the point when he had to flee in a small boat from the Persian Gulf to Kuwait under heavy-fire. After exile, he joined his family in Paris and began organizing a resistance movement inside Iran. He was assassinated in Paris on December 7, 1979, being shot twice in the head by a sniper wearing a motorcycle helmet.

Shafiq, Mohammad Musa: Afghan politician and poet; became Foreign Minister in 1971 and Prime Minister in December 1972. He lost both positions when Mohammed Zahir Shah was overthrown on July 17, 1973. Executed by the Soviets in 1978.

Shah, King Zahir: The last King (Shah) of Afghanistan; reigning for four decades from 1933 until he was ousted by a coup in 1973. Following his return from exile he was given the title "Father of the Nation" in 2002, which he held until his death.

Shah, Reza: Shah of Iran from December 15, 1925, until he was forced to abdicate by the Anglo-Soviet invasion of Iran in September 16, 1941. He overthrew Ahmad Shah Qajar, the last Shah of the Qajar dynasty, and founded the Pahlavi Dynasty. Deceased.

Sharansky, Natan: Former Soviet dissident, human rights activist, former Prisoner of Zion, Israeli politician and author. In March 1977 he was arrested, and in July 1978 convicted on charges of treason and spying for the United States, and sentenced to thirteen years of forced labor. After sixteen months of incarceration in Lefortovo prison, he was sent to a Siberian labor camp, where he served for nine years. Sharansky is chairman of the Adelson Institute for Strategic Studies at the Shalem Center. From March 2003 untilMay 2005 he was a minister without portfolio, responsible for Jerusalem, social and Jewish Diaspora affairs.

Shariatmadari, Ayatollah: Among the most senior leading Twelver Shi'a clerics in Iran and Iraq; known for his somewhat liberal views. Deceased.

Shari'ati, Ali: Noted as a founding father of the Islamic Revolution; associated with the LMI and Mujahedeen; arrested by the Shah's police in 1973; exiled to London in 1977; he died in Southampton of what his supporters believe was an assassination by the Shah's secret service (though it was ruled a simple heart attack by the British coroner).

Sharif-Emami, Jafar: Prime Minister, Iran (1960-1961; 1978); close advisor to Shah; President of Pahlavi Foundation; attempted to reach accord with clerics before overthrow of Shah, opposed by Khomeini; never able to establish order as Prime Minister in 1978; military government appointed.

Sharon, Ariel: Former Israeli Prime Minister and military leader; at the creation of Israel (and Haganah's transformation into the Israel Defense Forces), Sharon became a platoon commander in the Alexandroni Brigade. From 1958 to 1962 Sharon served as commander of an infantry brigade and studied law at Tel Aviv University; served as Prime Minister from March 2001 until April 2006, though the powers of his office were exercised by acting Prime Minister Ehud Olmert following Sharon's massive stroke on January 4, 2006.

Sharpton, Al Rev.: American Baptist minister, political and civil rights/social justice activist, and radio talk show host. In 2004 Sharpton ran for the Democratic nomination for the U.S. presidential election.

Shawcross, Lord Hartley: Resigned from Parliament in 1958, saying he was tired of party politics; was made one of Britain's first life peers on February 14, 1959, as Baron Shawcross. Deceased.

Shelton, Lou: Founder and head of the Traditional Values Coalition. The organization represents, by its estimate, over 43,000 Christian churches throughout the United States.

Shi, Qiao: Politician in the People's Republic of China; a recognized international studies expert within the Communist Party, he was at one time ranked third in the Communist Party leadership. He never rose to paramount power and retired in 1998.

Shomron, Dan: Thirteenth Chief of Staff of the Israel Defense Forces (1987-1991). Deceased.

Shukeiri, Ahmed: First Arab Chairman of the Palestine Liberation Organization (1964–1967); did extensive work at the United Nations between 1949 and 1963. The Camp David Agreement, the Egyptian-Israeli Peace Treaty, and the normalization of relations between Egypt and the Zionist state were considered by Al-Shukeiri as high treason towards the Arab and Palestinian cause. Deceased.

Shulman, Marshall: Information Officer for the U.S. Mission to the U.N., Special Assistant to Dean Acheson, and special advisor on Soviet affairs to Secretary of State Cyrus R. Vance. Deceased.

Sick, Gary: Iran Specialist, U.S. National Security Council (1977-1980); Naval officer stationed in Persian Gulf; assigned to National Security Council; closely involved with establishing Iran policies and in attempts to gain release of Embassy hostages.

Sickmann, Rodney: U.S. Embassy guard in Tehran; Marine Sgt.

Sklar, Holly: Op-ed columnist and author; edited the definitive book on trilateralism.

Smith, Howard K.: One of the major names in broadcast news for forty years; in 1960, he moderated the first debate between presidential candidates John F. Kennedy and Richard M. Nixon. Deceased.

Smith, Ron: An American energy specialist.

Sober, Sydney: Representative of the U.S. State Department.

Solana, Javier: Named Secretary General of the 10-permanent-member Western European Union in November 1999; was a physicist who became a political minister for thirteen years under Felipe González before serving as Secretary General of NATO (1995-1999).

Solzhenitsyn, Alexander: Russian novelist, dramatist, and historian; through his writings, he made the world aware of the Gulag, the Soviet labor camp system. For these efforts, Solzhenitsyn was both awarded the Nobel Prize in Literature in 1970 and exiled from the Soviet Union in 1974. Deceased.

Somoza, Anastasio: Officially the 44th and 45th President of Nicaragua (1967-1972 and 1974-1979). In 1979 Somoza resigned the presidency and fled to Miami. He was denied U.S. entry by Jimmy Carter, after which Somoza took refuge in Paraguay, where he was assassinated at the age of fifty-four.

Sorenson, Theodore: Special counsel and speechwriter for John F. Kennedy; selected by Jimmy Carter to head the CIA, but his name was withdrawn, so he was never confirmed.

Speck, Richard: A mass murderer who systematically killed eight student nurses from South Chicago Community Hospital in Chicago, Illinois, on July 14, 1966. The jury found Speck guilty and recommended the death penalty, but the United States Supreme Court declared the death penalty unconstitutional. Speck died in prison of a heart attack (1991).

Stalin, Joseph: General Secretary of the Communist Party of the Soviet Union's Central Committee from 1922 until his death in 1953. During that time he established the regime now known as Stalinism. He gradually consolidated power and became the de facto party leader and dictator of the Soviet Union.

Stassen, Harold: Best known for being a perennial candidate for the Republican Party nomination for president, seeking it nine times between 1948 and 1992 (1948, 1952, 1964, 1968, 1976, 1980, 1984, 1988, 1992) but never winning it. Also Governor of Minnesota three times and of Pennsylvania twice. Served in the U.S. Senate twice. Deceased.

Stein, Dr. Kenneth W.: Professor of Contemporary Middle Eastern History, Political Science, and Israeli Studies at Emory University; he was the first director of the Carter Center (1983-1986).

Stempel, John: Foreign Service officer who was stationed in Teheran; the Iranian Embassy's U.S. political officer.

Stephanopoulos, George: ABC News's Chief Washington Correspondent. Prior to joining ABC, he was a senior political adviser to the 1992 U.S. presidential campaign of Bill Clinton and later became Clinton's communications director.

Stethem, Robert Dean: U.S. Navy Seabee diver murdered by terrorists during the hijacking of the commercial airliner he was aboard: TWA Flight 847.

Stevenson, Adlai E.: Served one term as governor of Illinois and ran, unsuccessfully, for president against Dwight D. Eisenhower in 1952 and 1956. Ambassador to the United Nations (1961-1965). Deceased.

Stockman, David: Former U.S. politician and businessman, Republican U.S. Representative from the State of Michigan (1977–1981) and as the Director of the Office of Management and Budget (1981–1985). Stockman was elected to the United States House of Representatives for the 95th Congress and was reelected in two subsequent elections, serving from January 3, 1977, until his resignation January 27, 1981, to accept appointment as Director of the Office of Management and Budget under U.S. President Ronald Reagan.

Sullivan, William H.: U.S. Ambassador to Iran (1977-1979); favored a coalition government with departure of Shah and family from Iran; sought White House permission to contact Khomeini for approval to set up coalition; Carter rejected Sullivan's request; departed Tehran in 1979, before the Embassy take-over.

Sung, Kim Il: Leader of North Korea from its founding in early 1948 until his death (1994).

Swift, Ann: U.S. political officer in Tehran at the time of the students' attack in 1979.

T

Taheri, Amir: Iranian-born journalist and author.

Taleghani, Ayatollah Mahmoud: Iranian theologian, Muslim reformer and a senior Twelver Shi'a cleric of Iran; a contemporary of the Iranian Revolutionary leader Ayatollah Ruhollah Khomeini and a leader in his own right of Iran's Shi'a resistance movement against the pro-western, secularist Shah Mohammad Reza Pahlavi. Deceased.

Taraki, Nur Muhammad: His party, the PDPA, was eventually successful in overthrowing the Afghan monarchy and, after the prior president and his family were murdered in a coup, assumed authority as the next president of Afghanistan from 1978 until he was overthrown and thereafter murdered in 1979.

Tavakoli, Mohammed: Member LMI; aka, Mohammad Tavakoli; liaison between U.S. (or Tavassoli) Embassy and LMI (1978-1979); appointed mayor of Tehran under Khomeini.

Tehrani, Dr. Ahmad: Former Ambassador of Iran

Thatcher, Margaret: British politician; Prime Minister of the United Kingdom (1979-1990) and Leader of the Conservative Party (1975- 1990). She is the first and only woman to date to hold either post.

Tillich, Paul: German-American theologian. Deceased.

Tito, Marshal: Became president of Yugoslavia in 1953; he directed the rebuilding of a Yugoslavia devastated in World War II and the bringing together of Yugoslavia's different peoples. Deceased.

Tomseth, Victor: American Consul in Shiraz, Iran; one of the Americans held hostage by Islamic militants following the 1979 seizure of the U.S. Embassy. He also worked for the Department of State in Washington, D.C.

Torrijos, Omar: Dictator-like leader of Panama (1968–1978); negotiated the Panama Canal treaties with the United States, leading to Panama's eventual assumption of control of the canal.

Toufanian, Hasan: Vice Minister of War, Iran (1975-1978); procured arms for Iranian army; suspected of accepting a $28 million pay-off for expediting a contract with Grumman Aerospace; fled to the U.S. in 1979.

Truman, Harry S.: Thirty-third U.S. President (1945-1953); assuming office upon the death of Franklin D. Roosevelt. Deceased.

Tsafrir, Eliezer: Ex-Mossad agent in Iran; the Israeli intelligence organization's Beirut station chief in 1983 and 1984.

Turner, Stansfield: CIA Director (1977-1981); charged with "intelligence failure" in Iran.

Tzu, Sun: Chinese general and military strategist in 400 B.C.

U

Udall, Morris: U.S. Representative from Arizona (1961-1991). Brother of Stewart Udall, who was appointed Secretary of the Interior in the Kennedy administration. Deceased.

V

Vance, Cyrus R.: Secretary of State, U.S. Department of State (1977-1980); assisted in Camp David Accords negotiations; resigned after failure of U.S. Embassy rescue mission, which he opposed. Deceased.

Villalon, Hector: Argentine negotiator. A go-between for U.S./Iran negotiations to release Embassy hostages (1980); a shadowy Argentinean who was a confidant of Eva Perón in her heyday in the 1950s.

Volcker, Paul: Appointed as Chairman of the Federal Reserve by Jimmy Carter in 1979; reappointed to that post by Ronald Reagan in 1983. He left the Federal Reserve in 1987. Today, he is economic advisor to Democratic presidential candidate Barack Obama.

W

Waldheim, Kurt: secretary general of the United Nations (1972 to 1981); President of Austria from 1986 to 1992. Deceased.

Walid, Abu: Top lieutenant to Yasser Arafat; a senior leader of the Palestinian militant group Islamic Jihad, and a commander of the group's military wing, the Al-Qods brigades. He was killed by an Israeli air strike in Gaza City in 2006.

Wallace, George: 48th governor of Alabama; served four non-consecutive terms beginning in 1963 and finally ending in 1987. Also ran four times in presidential races. Deceased.

Wallis, Jim: Evangelical Christian writer and political activist; best known as the founder and editor of *Sojourners* magazine and of the Washington, D.C.-based Christian community of the same name.

Walters, Barbara: American journalist, writer, and media personality, who has been a regular fixture on ABC news programs; the first woman to co-anchor the network evening news, working with Harry Reasoner on *ABC World News Tonight*.

Walzel, Fred: Chief of the White House Branch of the Secret Service Uniformed Division during the Carter administration.

Warnke, Paul C.: Named by Jimmy Carter as Director of the Arms Control and Disarmament Agency; later served under Secretaries of Defense Robert McNamara and Clark Clifford. Deceased.

Washington, George: 1st U.S. president (1789-1797).

Weinberger, Caspar: American politician and Secretary of Defense under President Ronald Reagan from January 21, 1981, until November 23, 1987, making him the third longest-serving defense secretary to date. Deceased.

Weizman, Ezer: Seventh President of Israel; served a seven-year term (1993-2000). Before the presidency, he was Commander of the Israeli Air Force and Minister of Defense. Deceased.

Williams, John Bell: Became member of U.S. House of Representatives in 1946; Governor of Mississippi (1968-1972). Deceased.

Wilson, Woodrow: 28th U.S. president (1913-1921). Born in Staunton, Virginia. Grew up in South Carolina and Georgia. Deceased.

Wolfowitz, Paul: Former United States Ambassador to Indonesia, U.S. Deputy Secretary of Defense, and President of the World Bank; currently a visiting scholar at the American Enterprise Institute.

Woods, Tiger: Professional American golfer.

Woodward, Bob: Assistant Managing Editor of *The Washington Post*. While an investigative reporter for that newspaper Woodward, working with fellow reporter Carl Bernstein, helped uncover the Watergate scandal that led to U.S. President Richard Nixon's resignation.

Woolsey, James: Foreign Policy Specialist, former Director of Central Intelligence, and head of the Central Intelligence Agency (1993-1995). Undersecretary of the Navy (1977-1979).

Wright, Jeremiah, Jr.: Former Senior Pastor of the Trinity United Church of Christ (TUCC), a megachurch in Chicago. In early 2008, Wright retired after thirty-six years as the pastor of his congregation. Following retirement, his beliefs and manner of preaching were scrutinized when segments from his sermons were publicized in connection with the presidential campaign of Barack Obama, once a member of Wright's church.

X

X, Malcolm: American Muslim minister, public speaker, and human rights activist; became involved in the criminal underworld in Boston and New York, and in 1945 was sentenced to eight to ten years in prison. While in prison, Malcolm X became a member of the Nation of Islam. After his parole in 1952, he became one of the Nation's leaders and chief spokesmen. Tension between Malcolm X and Elijah Muhammad, head of the Nation of Islam, led to his departure from the organization in March 1964. After leaving the Nation of Islam, Malcolm X made the pilgrimage, the Hajj to Mecca and became a Sunni Muslim. Deceased.

Xiaoping, Deng: Prominent Chinese revolutionary, politician, pragmatist, and reformer, as well as the late leader of the Communist Party of China (CPC). Served as the *de facto* leader of the People's Republic of China from 1978 to the early 1990s. Deceased.

Y

Ya'alon, Moshe: Lt. General; Israel's Chief of Staff.

Yazdi, Ebrahim: Foreign Minister, Provisional Government (1979); Member LMI; Khomeini's unofficial representative in the U.S.; organized Islamic student associations; joined Khomeini in Paris as an advisor; elected to *Majlis* in 1980.

Yong-il, Kim: Current Premier of North Korea; appointed the premier by the 5th session of the 11th Supreme People's Assembly (SPA), replacing Pak Pong-ju.

Young, Andrew: Civil rights activist, former Congressman, and Mayor of Atlanta; the first African-American Ambassador to the United Nations.

Young, Don: Re-elected to the 110th Congress in 2006 to serve his 18th term as Alaska's only Representative to the House of Representatives.

Yousef, Ahmed: Chief political adviser to the Prime Minister of Hamas.

Z

Zahedi, Ardeshir: Iranian Ambassador to Untied States (1959-1961); Ambassador to the U.K. (1962-1967); Minister of Foreign Affairs (1967-1971); Ambassador to the U.S. (1973-1979); son of former Prime Minister Fazlollah Zahedi; former son-in-law of Shah; had close working relationship with Brzezinski; resides in Switzerland.

Zahedi, Fazlollah: Prime Minister, Iran (1953-1954); helped mobilize military in favor of Shah during Mossadegh affair; appointed prime minister to replace Mossadegh.

Zedong, Mao: Chinese military and political leader; led the Communist Party of China (CPC) to victory against the Kuomintang (KMT) in the Chinese Civil War, and was the leader of the People's Republic of China (PRC) from its establishment in 1949 until his death in 1976.

Zeevi-Farkash, Major General Ahron: Head of the Israeli Military Intelligence Directorate (Aman) (2002 to 2006); he previously served as head of the Technological and Logistics Directorate.

Zimmermann, Warren: U.S. Embassy political advisor in Paris; later served as the U.S. Ambassador to Yugoslavia from 1989 to the country's dissolution in 1992. Deceased.

BIBLIOGRAPHY

Abrahamian, Ervand. *Iran Between Two Revolutions*. Princeton: Princeton University Press, 1982.

Adams, Charles Francis, ed., *The Works of John Adams—Second President of the United States*. Boston: Little, Brown & Co., 1854.

Alam, Asadollah. *The Shah and I: The Confidential Diary of Iran's Royal Court 1969-1977*. New York: St. Martin's Press, 1993.

Aloni, Shlomo. *Arab-Israeli Wars 1947-82*. Oxford, England: Osprey Publishing, 2001.

Amuzegar, Jahangir. *The Dynamics of the Iranian Revolution*. Albany: State University of New York Press, 1991.

Anderson, Patrick. *Electing Jimmy Carter: The Campaign of 1976*. Baton Rouge: Louisiana State University Press, 1994.

Arjomand, Said. *The Turban for the Crown: The Islamic Revolution of Iran*. New York: Oxford University Press, 1988.

Ashcroft, John. *Never Again*. New York: Center Street, 2006.

Beck, Glenn. *The Real America*. New York: Pocket Books, 2005.

Bill, James A. *George Ball*. New Haven: Yale University Press, 1997.

Bill, James A. *The Eagle and the Lion: The Tragedy of American-Iranian Relations*. New Haven: Yale University Press, 1988.

Bourne, Peter. *Jimmy Carter*. New York: Scribner, 1997.

Brackman, Roman. *Jimmy Carter Provocateur-In-Chief*. Brooklyn: Deerfield Publishers, 1968.

Bright, Bill. *God is the Issue*. Peachtree City, GA: NewLife, 2003.

Brinkley, Douglas. *The Unfinished Presidency*. New York: Penguin Books, 1998.

Brzezinski, Zbigniew. *Power and Principle*. Toronto, Canada: McGraw Hill, 1983.

Butler, Keith. *Reviving the American Spirit*. Lake Mary: Front Line, 2006.

Carter, Jimmy. *Keeping Faith*. Fayetteville: University of Arkansas Press, 1983.

Carter, Jimmy. *Palestine Peace not Apartheid*. New York: Simon & Schuster, 2006.

Carter, Jimmy. *Our Endangered Values*. New York: Simon & Schuster, 2005.

Carter, Jimmy, and Don Richardson. *Conversations with Carter*. Boulder, CO: Lynne Rienner Publishers, 1998.

Chehabi, H. E. *Iranian Politics and Religious Modernism: the Liberation Movement of Iran under the Shah and Khomeini*. Ithaca: Cornell University Press, 1990.

Colmes, Alan. *Red, White & Liberal*. New York: HarperCollins, 2003.

Cooley, John. *Unholy Wars: Afghanistan, America and International Terrorism*. London: Pluto Press, 2002.

Corsi, Jerome. *The Obama Nation*. New York: Simon & Shuster, 2008.

Coulter, Ann. *Godless*. New York: Crown Forum, 2006.

Coulter, Ann. *Treason*. New York: Crown Forum, 2003.

Dayan, Moshe. *Breakthrough*. New York: Alfred Knopf, 1981.

Dershowitz, Alan. *Why Terrorism Works*. New Haven: Yale University Press, 2002.

Dumbrell, John. *The Carter Presidency: A Re-evaluation*. Manchester, England: Manchester University Press, 1993.

Eisenhower, Dwight. *Mandate for Change: 1953-1956: The White House Years*. Garden City: Doubleday, 1963.

Evans, Michael D. *Beyond Iraq: The Next Move*. Lakeland, FL: White Stone Books, 2003.

Evans, Mike. *Israel, America's Key to Survival*. Plainfield, NJ: Logos International, 1981.

Evans, Michael D. *Save Jerusalem*. Euless, TX: Bedford Books, 1995.

Evans, Michael D. *The American Prophecies*. New York: Warner Faith, 2004.

Evans, Michael, with Jerome Corsi. *Showdown with Nuclear Iran*. Nashville, TN: Thomas Nelson, 2006.

Evans, Mike. *Jerusalem Betrayed*. Dallas: Word Publishing, 1997.

Evans, Mike. *Jerusalem DC*. Bedford, TX: Bedford Books, 1984.

Evans, Mike. *The Final Move Beyond Iraq*. Lake Mary, FL: Strang, 2007.

Fardust, Hussein, and Ali Akbar Dareini. *The Rise and Fall of the Pahlavi Dynasty: Memoirs of Former General Hussein*. Bangalore, India: Motilal Banarsidass, 1999.

Farmanfarmaian, Manucher, and Roxane Farmanfarmaian. *Blood and Oil*. New York: Ransom House, 1997.

Fink, Gary. *Prelude to the Presidency: The Political Character and Legislative Leadership Style of Governor Jimmy Carter*. Westport, CT: Greenwood, 1980.

Freddoso, David. *The Case Against Barack Obama*. Washington, DC: Regnery Publishing, 2008.

Ganji, Manoucher. *Defying the Iranian Revolution: From a Minister to the Shah to a Leader of Resistance*. Westport: Praeger, 2002.

Germond, Jack W., and Jules Witcover. *Blue Smoke and Mirrors: How Reagan Won and Why Carter Lost the Election of 1980*. New York: Viking, 1981.

Gingrich, Newt. *Winning the Future: A 21st Century Contract with America*. Washington, DC: Regnery, 2005.

Glad, Betty. *Jimmy Carter: In Search of the Great White House*. New York: Norton, 1980.

Haig, Jr., Alexander M., with Charles McCarry. *Inner Circles: How America Changed the World*. New York: Warner Books, 1992.

Hannity, Sean. *Deliver Us From Evil*. New York: HarperCollins, 2004.

Harriman, W. Averill, and Elie Abel. *Special Envoy to Churchill and Stalin 1941-1946*. London: Hutchinson, 1975.

Hayward, Steven F. *The Real Jimmy Carter*. Washington, DC: Regnery, 2004.

Helms, Cynthia. *An Ambassador's Wife in Iran*. New York: Dodd, Mead, 1981.

Hunt, Col. David. *They Just Don't Get It*. New York: Three Rivers Press, 2005.

Huyser, Robert E. *Mission to Tehran*. New York: Harper & Row, 1986.

Ingraham, Laura. *Shut Up & Sing*. Washington, D.C.: Regnery, 2003.

Jones, Charles O. *The Trustee Presidency: Jimmy Carter and the United States Congress*. Baton Rouge: Louisiana State University Press, 1988.

Kaufman, Burton I., and Scott Kaufman. *The Presidency of James Earl Carter Jr.* Lawrence: University Press of Kansas, 2006.

Kapuscinski, Ryszard. *Shah of Shahs*. New York: Random House, 1992.

Kessler, Ronald. *Inside the White House*. New York: Pocket Books, 1995.

Khomeini, Imam Ruhollah, and Hamid Algar trans. and annot. *Islam and Revolution: Writings and Declarations*. London: Routledge & Kegan Paul, 1981.

Kipling, Rudyard. *Writings in Prose and Verse of Rudyard Kipling*. London: Charles Scribner's Sons, 1899.

Kirkpatrick, Jeane J. *Dictators and Double Standards*. New York: Simon and Schuster, 1983.

Kissinger Henry. *White House Years*. Boston: Little, Brown, 1979.

Kohlmann, Evan F. *Al-Qaida's Jihad in Europe*. Oxford, England: Berg Publishers, 2004.

Kupelian, David. *The Marketing of Evil*. Nashville: Cumberland House, 2005.

Ledeen, Michael, and William Lewis. *Debacle: the American Failure in Iran*. New York: Alfred A. Knopf, 1981.

Lekachman, Robert. *A People's History of the United States: 1492-Present*. Harper Collins: New York, 2003.

Lenczowski, George. *American Presidents and the Middle East*. Durham: Duke University Press, 1990.

Lewis, Bernard. *The Crisis of Islam*. New York: Random House, 2003.

Lilienthal, David. *The Journals of David E. Lilienthal: The Harvest Years, 1959-1963.* New York: Harper and Row, 1971.

Limbaugh, David. *Bankrupt.* Washington, D.C.: Regnery, 2006.

Lytle, Andrew Nelson. *"The Hind Tit," I'll Take my Stand.* New York: Harper & Bros., 1930.

Mackey, Sandra. *The Iranians.* New York: Plume Books, 1998.

Meese III, Edwin. *With Reagan: The Inside Story.* Washington, DC: Regnery, 1992.

Melman, Yossi, and Meir Javedanfar. *The Nuclear Sphinx of Tehran.* New York: Carroll & Graf Publishers, 2007.

Menashri, David. *Post-Revolutionary Politics in Iran.* London: Frank Cass, 2001.

Milani, Mohsen M. *The Making of Iran's Islamic Revolution: From Monarchy to Islamic Republic.* Boulder, CO Westview Press, 1994.

Miller, Nathan. *Star-Spangled Men: America's Ten Worst Presidents.* New York: Touchstone, 1998.

Moin, Baqer Khomeini. *Life of the Ayatollah.* New York: McMillan, 2000.

Montazam, Mir Ali Asghar. *The Life and Times of Ayatollah Khomeini.* London: Anglo-European Publishing, 1994.

Morris, Dick, and Eileen McGann. *Fleeced.* New York: HarperCollins, 2008.

Morris, Kenneth. *Jimmy Carter: American Moralist.* Athens, GA: University of Georgia Press, 1996.

Nahavandi, Houchang. *The Last Shah of Iran.* United Kingdom: Aquilion Ltd, 2005.

Naraghi, Ehsan. *From Palace to Prison.* Chicago: Ivan R. Dee, 1994.

Nasr, Vali. *The Shia Revival.* New York: Norton, 2006.

Nortin, Howard, and Bob Stresser. *The Miracle of Jimmy Carter.* Plainfield, NJ: Logos Books, 1976.

Pahlavi, Farah. *An Enduring Love.* New York: Hyperion, 1987.

Pahlavi, Mohammad Reza. *Answer to History.* New York: Stein & Day, 1980.

Pahlavi, Princess Ashraf. *Faces in a Mirror: Memoirs from Exile.* Englewood Cliffs: Prentice-Hall, 1980.

Parsa, Misagh. *The Social Origins of the Iranian Revolution.* Brunswick, N.J.: Rutgers University Press, 1989.

Parsi, Trita. *Treacherous Alliance.* New Haven: Yale University Press, 2007.

Pilevsky, Philip. *I Accuse: Jimmy Carter and the Rise of Militant Islam.* Dallas: Durban House, 2007.

Pollack, Kenneth M. *The Persian Puzzle.* New York: Random House, 2005.

Pryce-Jones, David. *Betrayal.* New York: Encounter Books, 2006.

Ramazani, R. K. *Iran's Foreign Policy 1941-1971.*

Reagan, Ronald. *An American Life*. New York: Simon and Schuster, 1990.

Roosevelt, Elliot. *FDR: His Personal Letters*. New York: Duell, Sloan and Pierce, 1947.

Rosenbaum, Herbert D., and Alezej Ugrinsky. *Jimmy Carter: Foreign Policy and Post-Presidential Years*. Westport, CT: Greenwood, 1994.

Ross, Dennis. *The Missing Peace*. New York: Farrar, Straus and Giroux, 2004.

Rubin, Barry. *Paved with Good Intentions*. New York: Oxford Press, 1980.

Ruppert, Michael C. *Crossing the Rubicon: The Decline of the American Empire at the End of the Age of Oil*. Gabriola Island, Canada: New Society Publishers, 2004.

Sadat, Anwar. *In Search of Identity*. London: Fontana, 1978.

Safa, Reza. *The Coming Fall of Islam in Iran*. Lake Mary: Strang, 1979.

Salinger, Pierre. *America Held Hostage: the Secret Negotiations*. Garden City: Doubleday, 1981.

Schaeffer. Francis A. *The Great Evangelical Disaster*. Westchester, IL: Crossway Books, 1984.

Sciolono, Elaine. *Persian Mirrors*. New York: Simon & Schuster, 2000.

Segev, Samuel. *The Iranian Triangle*. New York: Free Press, 1988.

Segev, Samuel. *Jimmy Carter, Foreign Policy and Post-Presidential Years*. Westport, CT: Greenwood Press, 1994.

Segev, Samuel. *The Moroccan Connection*. Tel Aviv: Matar, 2008.

Segev, Samuel. *The Road to Peace*. Tel Aviv: Masada, 1998.

Seliktar, Ofira. *Failing the Crystal Ball Test*. Westport: Praeger, 2000.

Shackley, Theodore. *The Third Option: An American View of Counterinsurgency Operations*. New York: Reader's Digest Press/McGraw-Hill Books, 1981.

Sharansky, Natan. *The Case for Democracy: The Power of Freedom to Overcome Tyranny and Terror*. New York: PublicAffairs, 2004.

Sharon, Ariel. *Warrior*. New York: Simon & Schuster, 1989.

Shawcross, William. *The Shah's Last Ride*. New York: Simon & Schuster, 1988.

Sheldon, Rev. Louis. *The Agenda*. Lake Mary, FL: Frontline, 2005.

Shogan, Robert. *Promises to Keep*. New York: Thomas Y. Crowell, 1977.

Sick, Gary. *All Fall Down*. New York: Random House, 1986.

Sick, Gary. *October Surprise*. New York: Random House, 1992.

Silver, Eric. *Begin: The Haunted Prophet*. New York: Random House, 1984.

Smith, Mark W. *Official Handbook of the Vast Right-Wing Conspiracy*. Lanham: Regnery, 2004.

Smith, Tony. *America's Mission: the United States and the Worldwide Struggle for Democracy in the Twentieth Century*. Princeton, NJ: Princeton University Press, 1994.

Sobhani, Sohrab. *The Pragmatic Entente: Israeli-Iranian Relations, 1948-1988*. New York: Praeger, 1989.

Somoza, Anastasio. *Nicaragua Betrayed*. Boston: Western Islands, 1980.

Sreberny-Mohammadi, Annabelle, and Ali Mohammadi. *Small Media, Big Revolution: Communication, Culture, and the Iranian Revolution*. Minneapolis: University of Minnesota Press, 1994.

Sullivan, William. *Mission to Iran*. New York: W.W. Norton, 1981.

Taheri, Amir. *Holy Terror: The Inside Story of Islamic Terrorism*. London: Sphere Books, Hutchinson Ltd, 1987.

Taheri, Amir. *Nest of Spies*. New York: Pantheon Books, 1988.

Taheri, Amir. *The Spirit of Allah: Khomeini and the Islamic Revolution*. Bethesda, MD: Adler & Adler, 1985.

Thornton, R.C. *The Carter Years: Toward a New Global Order*. New York: Paragon House, 2007.

Turner, Adm. Stansfield. *Burn Before Reading*. New York: Hyperion, 2005.

Turner, Stansfield. *Secrecy and Democracy*. Boston: Houghton Mifflin, 1985.

Vance, Cyrus. *Hard Choices*. New York: Simon & Schuster, 1983.

Viorst, Milton. *In the Shadow of the Prophet: The Struggle for the Soul of Islam*. Boulder, CO: Westview Press, 2001.

Walters, Barbara. *Audition: A Memoir*. New York: Random House, 2008.

Wells, David F. *No Place for Truth: Or Whatever Happened to Evangelical Theology?* Grand Rapids: Eerdmans, 1993.

Witcover, Jules. *Marathon: the Pursuit of the Presidency, 1972-7976*. New York: Viking, 1977.

Wilbur, Donald N. *Reza Shah Pahlavi: The Resurrection and Reconstruction of Iran, 1878-1944*. Hicksville: Exposition Press, 1975.

Williams, Paul L. *The Day of Islam*. Amherst: Prometheus Books, 2007.

Wright, Lawrence. *The Looming Tower*. New York: Random House, 2006.

Zahedi, Ardeshir, and Pari Absalti, comp. and ed. *Untold Secrets*. Houshang Mirhashem Publisher of Rah-e-Zendegi Journal, February 2002.

Zahedi, Dariush. *The Iranian Revolution Then and Now*. Boulder: Westview Press, 2000.

Zonis, Marvin. *Majestic Failure: The Fall of the Shah*. Chicago: University of Chicago Press, 1991.

E N D N O T E S

[1] Personal interview with Dr. Ahmad Tehrani, ambassador of Iran, June 12, 2008.

[2] One night in 1974, from a Cessna Citation aircraft, one of America's most famous citizens saw a UFO. There were four persons aboard the plane: pilot Bill Paynter, two security guards, and Governor of California Ronald Reagan. As the airplane approached Bakersfield, California, the passengers called Paynter's attention to a strange object to their rear. "It appeared to be several hundred yards away," Paynter recalled. "It was a fairly steady light until it began to accelerate. Then it appeared to elongate. Then the light took off. It went up at a 45-degree angle at a high rate of speed. Everyone on the plane was surprised. . . . The UFO went from a normal cruise speed to a fantastic speed instantly. If you give an airplane power, it will accelerate, but not like a hot rod, and that's what this was like." http://science.howstuffworks.com/ronald-reagan-ufo.htm. (Accessed August 2008.)

[3] Howard Norton and Bob Strosser, *The Miracle of Jimmy Carter*, (Plainfield, NJ: Logos Books, 1976), p. 93

[4] Andrew Nelson Lytle, "The Hind Tit," *I'll Take my Stand* (New York: Harper & Bros., 1930), p. 205

[5] Steven F. Hayward, *The Real Jimmy Carter* (Washington, DC: Regnery Publishing, Inc., 2004), p. 14

[6] ThinkExist.com; http://thinkexist.com/quotation/sometimes_when_i_look_at_all_my_children-i_say_to/213661.html. (Accessed February 2008.)

[7] Kenneth Morris, *Jimmy Carter: American Moralist* (Athens, GA: University of Georgia Press, 1996), p. 169.

[8] PBS *American Experience*; Timeline Jimmy Carter, http://www.pbs.org/wgbh/amex/carter/timeline/index.html. (Accessed December 2007.)

[9] Kenneth E. Morris, p. 140.

[10] Ibid.

[11] *New King James Version* (Nashville, TN: Thomas Nelson, 1982).

[12] Tilloch's quotation is cited in Gary Fink's *Prelude to the Presidency: The Political Character and Legislative Leadership Style of Governor Jimmy Carter* (Westport, CT: Greenwood, 1980), p. 9.

[13] Betty Glad, *Jimmy Carter: In Search of the Great White House* (New York: Norton, 1980), p. 108.

[14] *Merriam-Webster's Online Dictionary*, http://www.m-w.com/dictionary/existentialism. (Accessed January 2008.)

[15] Kenneth E. Morris, p. 180.

[16] Ibid., p. 178.

17 *American Experience:* Jimmy Carter, Part One;
http://www.pbs.org/wgbh/amex/carter/filmmore/pt.html.
(Accessed February 2008.)

18 Ibid.

19 Jimmy Carter's Inaugural Address, January 12, 1971; Carter Library archives.

20 *Time* cover, May 31, 1971.

21 *Cambridge Encyclopedia*, volume 45, Lester Maddox: Early Life, Life and Career,
Retirement; http://encyclopedia.stateuniversity.com/pages/13427/Lester-Garfield-Maddox.html.
(Accessed December 2007.)

22 Gary Fink, *Prelude to a Presidency: the Political Character and Legislative Leadership
Style of Governor Jimmy Carter* (Westport, CT: Greenwood, 1980), p. 19.

23 *American Experience: Jimmy Carter*;
http://www.pbs.org/wgbh/amex/carter/peopleevents/p_jcarter.html.
(Accessed December 2007.)

24 Gary Fink, p. 175.

25 Laurence H. Shoup, "Jimmy Carter and the Trilateralists: Presidential Roots," excerpted
from the book, *Trilateralism*, edited by Holly Sklar, South End Press, 1980.
http://www.thirdworldtraveler.com/Trilateralism/JimmyCarter_Trilat.html.
(Accessed May 2008.)

26 "President Jimmy Carter and the Killer Rabbit,"
http://www.narsil.org/politics/carter/killer_rabbit.html.
(Accessed April 2008.)

27 Stephen Hess, "Presidency: How do Historians Evaluate the Administration of Jimmy
Carter?" June 1978; http://hnn.us/articles/444.html.
(Accessed December 2007.)

28 Alexander M. Haig Jr., *Inner Circles: How America Changed the World*
(New York: Warner Books, 1992), p. 531.

29 *The Jeffersons*, American sitcom, January 1975-June1985, CBS.
http://www.answeringbell.com/Answering%20Bell/Songs/movin_on_up.htm.
(Accessed December 2007.)

30 "Turning Obama into Jimmy Carter," *The New York Observer*, February 25, 2008;
http://www.observer.com/2008/turning-obama-into-jimmy-carter .
(Accessed November 2008.)

31 Kenneth E. Morris, p. 191.

32 *Hamilton Jordan Original Strategy Memo for Jimmy Carter's Run for President*;
November 4, 1972; http://www.c-span.org/presidentiallibraries/Content/Carter/CarterStrategy.pdf.
(Accessed December 2007.)

33 Ibid.

34 Cited in Jimmy Carter, 2007 Schools Wikipedia Selection, http://schools-wikipedia.org/wp/j/Jimmy_Carter.htm. (Accessed June 2008.)

35 Jules Witcover, *Marathon: the Pursuit of the Presidency, 1972-7976*
(New York: Viking, 1977), p. 195.

36 Voice of America, *American History: Jimmy Carter Wins the 1976 Presidential Election*;
Transcript of radio broadcast, June 6, 2007;
http://www.voanews.com/specialenglish/archive/2007-06/2007-06-06-voa2.cfm.
(Accessed January 2008.)

[37] *Time*, "Candidate Carter: I Apologize," April 19, 1976,
http://www.time.com/time/magazine/article/0,9171,914056,00.html.
(Accessed December 2007.)

[38] Ibid.

[39] Central Intelligence Agency, CIA Briefings of Presidential Candidates, May 22, 1996;
http://www.gwu.edu/~nsarchiv/NSAEBB/NSAEBB116/cia/Chapter%205%20—
%20In-Depth%20Discussions%20With%20Carter.htm;
(Accessed March 2008).

[40] Admiral Stansfield Turner, *Burn Before Reading* (New York: Hyperion, 2005),
pp. 181-182.

[41] Peter Bourne, *Jimmy Carter*, (New York: Scribner, 1997), p. 250

[42] Patrick Anderson, *Electing Jimmy Carter: The Campaign of 1976*
(Baton Rouge: Louisiana State University Press, 1994), p. 93.

[43] Jimmy Carter, The Playboy Interview excerpt, November 1976,
http://www.arts.mcgill.ca/history/faculty/TROYWEB/Courseweb/JimmyCarterThe
PlayboyInterview.htm.
(Accessed December 2007.)

[44] *"The Foreign Policy Debate,"* October 3, 1976, Box 2, Special Files, Gerald Ford
Papers, Gerald Ford Library.

[45] *Time*, "Bitter, Not Better;" October 25, 1976;
http://www.time.com/time/magazine/article/0,9171,918434,00.html?promoid=googlep.
(Accessed January 2008.)

[46] Kandy Stroud, *How Jimmy Won*, January 1, 1997, pp. 425-6 (No publication
information available) Quote from
http://www.issues2000.org/Archive/How_Jimmy_Won_Jimmy_Carter.htm.
(Accessed January 2008.)

[47] Nathan Miller; *Star-Spangled Men: America's Ten Worst Presidents*
(New York: Touchstone, 1998), p. 25.

[48] Alexander M. Haig Jr., p. 532.

[49] History.com, This Day in History, 1977, "Carter Pardons Draft Dodgers,"
http://www.history.com/this-day-in-history.do?action=Article&id=123.
(Accessed January 2008.)

[50] Ronald Kessler, *Inside the White House*
(New York: Pocket Books, a division of Simon and Schuster, 1996), pp. 91-92.

[51] Charles O. Jones, *The Trustee Presidency: Jimmy Carter and the United States
Congress* (Baton Rouge: Louisiana State University Press, 1988), p. 1.

[52] Theodore Shackley, *The Third Option: An American View of Counterinsurgency
Operations* (New York: Reader's Digest Press/McGraw-Hill Books, 1981), p. ix.

[53] History News Network, "Presidency: How Do Historians Evaluate the Administration
of Jimmy Carter?" http://hnn.us/articles/444.html.
(Accessed December 2007.)

[54] PBS *American Experience*; Timeline Jimmy Carter,
http://www.pbs.org/wgbh/amex/carter/timeline/index.html.
(Accessed January 2008.)

[55] Ibid.

[56] Brainy Quote; http://www.brainyquote.com/quotes/quotes/g/geraldrfo179604.html.
(Accessed January 2008.)

[57] Peter Bourne, p. 421.

[58] Gary Fink, p. 163.

[59] Richard H. Rovere, "Letter from Washington," *New Yorker,* September 12, 1977; http://www.newyorker.com/archive/1977/09/12/1977_09_12_131_TNY_CARDS_000321461. (Accessed January 2008.)

[60] Bruce Bartlett, "Warriors Against Inflation," *National Review*, June 14, 2004, http://www.nationalreview.com/nrof_bartlett/bartlett200406140846.asp. (Accessed January 2008.)

[61] Burton I Kaufman and Scott Kaufman, *The Presidency of James Earl Carter, Jr.* (Lawrence: University Press of Kansas, 2006, Second Edition, Revised), p. 41.

[62] *Front Page Magazine,* "The Worst Ex-President," Jamie Glazov, May 6, 2004, http://www.frontpagemag.com/Articles/Read.aspx?GUID=CB7DA8C2-1DB1-4E8A-88B0-D03C8B5CA91A. (Accessed January 2008. (The quote was taken from an interview with Steven Hayward, the F. K. Weyerhaeuser Fellow at the American Enterprise Institute and Senior Fellow at the Pacific Research Institute. Mr. Hayward is the author of the book, *The Real Jimmy Carter: How our Worst Ex-President Undermines American Foreign Policy, Coddles Dictators, and Created the Party of Clinton and Kerry.)*

[63] Some Secrets of the British Royal Family, http://www.funtrivia.com/en/subtopics/Some-Secrets-of-the-British-Royal-Family-2321.html. (Accessed June 2008.)

[64] Alexander M. Haig Jr., p. 532.

[65] *New York Times*, Editorial, July 29, 1980.

[66] Institute for Policy Studies, http://www.ips-dc.org/projects/newinternat.htm. (Accessed January 2008.)

[67] U.S. Department of State, Foreign Aid and Human Rights (1976); http://usinfo.state.gov/infousa/government/overview/54.html. (Accessed August 2008.)

[68] Clair Apodaca, *U.S. Human Rights Policy and Foreign Assistance: A Short History;* Ritsumeikan International Affairs, Vol. 3, p. 64. (The paper was presented at the "Global Governance" project at a seminar held by the Institute of International Relations and Area Studies, Ritsumeikan University, March 8, 2004.)

[69] Ibid. pp. 66-67.

[70] John Drumbrell, *The Carter Presidency: A Re-evaluation* (Manchester, England: Manchester University Press, 1993), p. 181.

[71] Farah Pahlavi, *An Enduring Love* (New York: Hyperion, 1987), pp. 269-270.

[72] Manucher Farmanfarmaian and Roxane Farmanfarmaian, *Blood & Oil: A Prince's Memoir of Iran, From the Shah to the Ayatollah* (New York: Random House, 2005), p. 292.

[73] Asadollah Alam, *The Shah and I: The Confidential Diary of Iran's Royal Court 1969-1977* (New York: St. Martin's Press, 1993), p. 540.

[74] "Amir Taheri's Interview with Ardeshir Zahedi," cited in *Untold Secrets* by Ardeshir Zahedi, a compilation of original materials. Compiled by: Pari Abasalti, Editor-in-Chief, and Houshang Mirhashem, Publisher of Rah-e-Zendegi Journal, February 2002, p. 15.

[75] Manucher Farmanfarmaian and Roxane Farmanfarmaian, p. 266.

[76] Dwight D. Eisenhower, *Mandate for Change, 1953-1956: The White House Years* (Garden City, NY: Doubleday, 1963), p. 165.

77 "Heros and Killers in the 20th Century," Mohammad Mossadegh, Hero File, http://www.moreorless.au.com/heroes/mossadegh.html. (Accessed May 2008.)

78 White House Transcript, "Remarks at Millennial Evening: the Perils of Indifference," April 12, 1999; http://www.historyplace.com/speeches/wiesel-transcript.htm. (Accessed July 2008.)

79 Amir Taheri, "Iran and the U.S.: Who Should Apologize and Why?" (Cited in *Untold Secrets* by Ardeshir Zahedi; a compilation of original materials. Compiled by: Pari Abasalti, Editor-in-Chief, and Houshang Mirhashem, Publisher of Rah-e-Zendegi Journal, February 2002, p. 43.)

80 Personal interview with Dr. Parviz Mina, Paris, France, April 18, 2008.

81 Houchang Nahavandi, *The Last Shah of Iran*, translated from the French by Steeve Reed (France: Editions Osmonde, 2004), p. 97.

82 Barbara Walters, *Audition: A Memoir* (New York: Alfred A. Knopf, 2008), p. 201.

83 Houchang Nahavandi, p. 30.

84 Neil Farquhar, "Persepolis Journal; Shah's Tent City, Fit for Kings, May Lodge Tourists," *New York Times*, September 7, 2001; http://query.nytimes.com/gst/fullpage.html?res=9C06E6DB1039F934A3575AC0A 9679C8B63. (Accessed July 2008.)

85 U.S. Subcommittee Hearings 1973:507.

86 Henry Kissinger, *White House Years* (Boston: Little, Brown, 1979), p. 1261.

87 Ryszard Kapuscinski, *Shah of Shahs* (New York: Vintage Books, a division of Random House, 1985), p. 137.

88 Barbara Walters describes Ambassador Zahedi: "The ambassador was an imposing figure, tall and dark with a great head of hair, a prominent nose, a ready smile, and a glad hand for everyone. He was also smart, shrewd, and the Shah's most trusted adviser in the United States." She described the Iranian Embassy as "the number one embassy when it came to extravagance and just plain enjoyment…large parties with hundreds of guests, flowing champagne, mounds of fresh Iranian caviar, and a bulging buffet." Barbara Walters, *Audition* (New York: Alfred A. Knopf, 2008) pp. 248-249.

89 Personal interview with Ardeshir Zahedi, June 2008.

90 Ibid.

91 Asadollah Alam, p. 500.

92 National Security Archive, Memo from Henry Kissinger, July 25, 1972; http://www.gwu.edu/~nsarchiv/NSAEBB/NSAEBB21/03-01.htm. (Accessed April 2008.)

93 Mike Evans, *Israel: America's Key to Survival* (Plainfield, NJ: Logos International, 1981), p. ix.

94 Cited by Slater Bakhtavar, "Jimmy Carter's Human Rights Disaster in Iran," *American Thinker.com,* August 26, 2007; http://www.americanthinker.com/2007/08/jimmy_carters_human_rights_dis.html. (Accessed June 2008.)

95 Marvin Zonis, *Majestic Failure: The Fall of the Shah of Iran* (Chicago: University of Chicago Press, 1991), p. 60.

96 *New York Times*, April 20, 1979, p. 12.

97 Cited by Dariush Zahedi in *The Iranian Revolution Then and Now* (Boulder, CO: Westview Press, 2000), p. 155.

98 Asadollah Alam, p. 500.

[99] Ibid., p. 484.

[100] Dariush Zahedi, pp. 39-40

[101] Personal interview, Dr. Abdol Majid Majidi, Minister of Planning and Budget under the Shah, Paris, France, April 18, 2008.

[102] Jamie Glazov, "The Worst Ex-President," *FrontPageMagazine*.com, May 6, 2004, http://www.frontpagemag.com/Articles/Printable.aspx?GUID={CB7DA8C2-1DB1-4E8A-88B0-D03C8B5CA91A}. (Accessed January 2008.)

[103] Robert Shogan, *Promises to Keep*, (New York: Thomas Y. Crowell, 1977) p. 217.

[104] Carl Gershman, "The Andrew Young Affair," *Commentary*, November 1979.

[105] "Andy Young Strikes Again," *Time*, July 24, 1978; http://aolsvc.timeforkids.kol.aol.com/time/printout/0,886,946858,00.html. (Accessed December 2007.)

[106] Ibid.

[107] Clair Apodaca, p. 69.

[108] John Dumbrell, *American Foreign Policy: Carter to Clinton* (New York: St. Martin's Press, 1996), p. 17.

[109] Clair Apodaca, p. 79.

[110] Cited by Steve Farrell, "Jimmy Carter: Still on the Prowl," EnterStageRight.com, January 10, 2000; http://www.enterstageright.com/archive/articles/0100carter.htm. (Accessed December 2007.)

[111] Ibid.

[112] Edward Daley, "Jimmy Carter's Nobel Legacy," *The American Daily*, March 10, 2003, http://americandaily.com/article/1991. (Accessed January 2008.)

[113] J. Michael Waller, "China's Beachhead at Panama Canal, China to Control Panama Canal," *Insight on the News*, CNET Networks Business: BNET; August 16, 1999, http://findarticles.com/p/articles/mi_m1571/is_30_15/ai_55481519. (Accessed January 2008.)

[114] Robert Lekachman, *A People's History of the United States: 1492-Present* (Harper Collins: New York, 2003), p. 571.

[115] Steven F. Hayward, p. 102.

[116] Dr. Parviz Mina interview, April 19, 2008, Paris France.

[117] Comptroller General of the United States. "Iranian Oil Cutoff: Reduced Petroleum Supplies and Inadequate U.S. Government Response." Report to Congress, General Accounting Office, 1979.

[118] PBS: *American Experience: Jimmy Carter*, "The Crisis of Confidence Speech," http://www.pbs.org/wgbh/amex/carter/filmmore/ps_crisis.html, (Accessed June 2008.)

[119] PBS: *American Experience: Jimmy Carter*; http://pbs.org/wgbh/amex/carter/peopleevents/e_malaise.html; (Accessed January 2008.)

[120] Nathan Miller, p. 23.

[121] U.S. Senate Department briefing paper, May 15, 1977, Declassified. Document found in Archives in Chadwyck-Healy Volume, *Iran: The Making of U.S. Foreign Policy 1977-190*, Alexandria VA 1990.

[122] Asadollah Alam, p. 542.

[123] Ibid.

[124] CIA Report: Iran in the 1980s, pp. 1-3, Declassified. Archived in Chadwyck-Healy Volume, *Iran: The Making of U.S. Foreign Policy 1977-190,* Alexandria VA 1990.

[125] Manoucher Ganji, *Defying the Iranian Revolution: From a Minister to the Shah to a Leader of Resistance* (Westport: Praeger, 2002), p. 39.

[126] Annabelle Sreberny-Mohammadi and Ali Mohammadi, *Small Media, Big Revolution: Communication, Culture and the Iranian* (Minneapolis: University of Minnesota Press, 1994), p. 139.

[127] Confidential Document, U.S. Embassy to Secretary of State, "Opposition Views." January 1978. Declassified.

[128] Iran: Chronology of Revolution, 1978; http://ivl.8m.com/Chronology2.htm. (Accessed July 2008.)

[129] Eric Rouleau, *Le Monde,* "Khomeini's Iran", Fall 1980, http://www.foreignaffairs.org/19800901faessay8148/eric-rouleau/khomeini-s-iran.html. (Accessed February 2008.)

[130] U.S. State Department telegram Sullivan to Vance, April 25, 1978, Declassified. Archived in Chadwyck-Healey, *Iran: The Making of U.S. Policy 1977-1980,* Alexandria VA 1990.

[131] U.S. State Department Telegram Christopher to Sullivan, April 26, 1978, Declassified. Archived in Chadwyck-Healey, *Iran: The Making of U.S. Policy 1977-1980,* Alexandria VA 1990.

[132] Confidential Telegram, U.S. Embassy Tehran to Secretary of State, "Opposition lawyers capture Bar Association and plan closer scrutiny of political court cases," June 19, 1978. Declassified.

[133] Personal interview with Her Majesty Farah Pahlavi, March 28, 2008.

[134] William H. Sullivan, Dateline Iran: the Road not Taken; *Foreign Policy* No. 40, pp. 175-186.

[135] Zbigniew Brzezinski, *Power and Principle: Memoirs of the National Security Advisor* (New York: Farrar, Straus, Giroux, 1983), p. 252.

[136] Mohammad Reza Shah Pahlavi, *Answer to History* (New York: Stein and Day, 1980), p. 165.

[137] Ardeshir Zahedi interview, June 2008.

[138] Michael Ledeen and William Lewis, *Debacle: the American Failure in Iran* (New York: Alfred A. Knopf, 1981), p. 163.

[139] Ibid., p. 163.

[140] Ibid., p. 164.

[141] Cyrus Vance, *Hard Choices* (New York: Simon and Schuster, 1983), p. 316.

[142] Zbigniew Brzezinski, p. 357.

[143] Baqer Moin, *Khomeini: Life of the Ayatollah* (New York: McMillan, 2000) p. 149. The organization appears to have small, tightly-knit groups in Tehran and in several European and American cities. Its headquarters in the U.S. is reportedly in Houston, TX (per a telegram from the American Embassy, Tehran, to the Department of State, February 1, 1978, declassified).

[144] Ervand Abrahamian, *Iran Between Two Revolutions* (Princeton: Princeton University Press, 1982), pp. 466-467.

[145] Don A. Schance @ Tehran *Los Angeles Times* (Apr. 24, 1980) "New Soviet Links to Iran" p. 1: The Iranian government, in the words of Ayatollah Ruhollah Khomeini, has condemned both "Westoxification and Eastoxification."

[146] CIA intelligence memorandum, January 19, 1979, entitled "Iran: Khomeini's Prospects and Views."

[147] Ibid.

[148] Samuel Segev, *The Iranian Triangle* (New York: The Free Press, 1988), p. 117.

[149] Kenneth R. Timmerman, Insight on the News, "The Truth About Mahmoud Abbas," July 8, 2003; http://findarticles.com/p/articles/mi_m1571/is_2003_July_8/ai_104842031. (Accessed July 2008.)

[150] "On October 29, hijackers of a German Lufthansa passenger jet demanded the release of the three surviving terrorists...being held for trial. [Two] were immediately released by Germany, receiving a tumultuous welcome when they touched down in Libya and giving their own firsthand account of their operation at a press conference broadcast worldwide. In both ESPN/ABC's documentary *The Tragedy of the Munich Games* and in Kevin Macdonald's Academy Award-winning documentary *One Day in September,* it is claimed that the whole Lufthansa hijacking episode was a sham, concocted by the West Germans and Black September so that the Germans could be rid of the three Munich perpetrators. The view is that the Germans were fearful that their mishandling of the rescue attempt would be exposed to the world if the three Fürstenfeldbruck survivors had ever stood trial." http://en.wikipedia.org/wiki/Munich_massacre. (Accessed July 2008.)

[151] Ion Mihai Pacepa, "Russian Footprints," *National Review Online*; http://article.nationalreview.com/print/?q=NjUzMGU4NTMyOTdkOTdmNTA1 MWJlYjYyYZDliODZkOGM=. (Accessed June 2008.)

[152] Bartleby.com, Jimmy Carter Inaugural Address, January 20, 1977; http://www.bartleby.com/124/pres60.html. (Accessed April 2008.)

[153] "His Imperial Majesty Interview with Kayhan," *Kayhan International*, September 17, 1977.

[154] Cyrus Vance, p. 321.

[155] President Jimmy Carter, Presidential Directive/NSC-13, May 13, 1977; Declassified May 29, 1990, Jimmy Carter Library; http://www.jimmycarterlibrary.org/documents/pd13.pdf. (Accessed April 2008.)

[156] Asadollah Alam, p. 543.

[157] Cited by Gary Sick in *All Fall Down: America's Tragic Encounter with Iran* (Lincoln, NE: iUnvierse.com, Inc., 2001), p. 128.

[158] Joseph Kraft, "Letter from Iran," *New Yorker*, December 18, 1978; http://www.newyorker.com/archive/1978/12/18/1978_12_18_138_TNY_CARDS_000324558?printable=true. (Accessed January 2008.)

[159] U.S. State Department briefing paper for the President, November 8, 1977, p. 7, Declassified. Archived in Chadwyck-Healey, *Iran: The Making of U.S. Policy 1977-1980*, Alexandria VA 1990.

[160] David R. Farber, *Taken Hostage: The Iran Hostage Crisis and America's First Encounter with Radical Islam* (Princeton, NJ: Princeton University Press, 2005), p. 81.

[161] Ardeshir Zahedi interview, June 2008.

[162] Author unattributed, *Time*, "Greetings for The Shah," November 28, 1977; http://www.time.com/time/printout/0,8816,919138,00.html. (Accessed January 2008.)

[163] Ibid.

[164] *New York Times*, November 16, 1977

[165] Ibid.

[166] *Washington Post*, November 17, 1977, p. C6.

[167] Ibid.

[168] Ibid., p. A22.

[169] *Washington Post*, November 29, 1977, p. C1.

[170] "U.S. State Department briefing paper, W. Christopher to the President, December 12, 1977, Declassified. Archived in Chadwyck-Healey, *Iran: The Making of U.S. Policy 1977-1980*, Alexandria VA 1990.

[171] Ardeshir Zahedi interview, June 2008.

[172] Farah Pahlavi, p. 270.

[173] Farah Pahlavi interview, May 2008.

[174] U.S. State Department briefing paper, December 132, 1977, Declassified. Archived in Chadwyck-Healey, *Iran: The Making of U.S. Policy 1977-1980*, Alexandria VA 1990.

[175] Ibid.

[176] Ardeshir Zahedi interview, June 2008.

[177] Jimmy Carter, *Keeping Faith: Memoirs of a President* (New York: Bantam books, 1982), p. 277.

[178] William Shawcross, *The Shah's Last Ride* (New York: Simon and Schuster, Inc., 1988), p. 131.

[179] Pierre Salinger, *America Held Hostage: The Secret Negotiations* (Garden City, NY: Doubleday, 1981), p. 33.

[180] U.S. State Department document, Sullivan to Department, July 25, 1977, declassified. Archived in Chadwyck-Healey, *Iran: the Making of U.S. Policy 1977-1980*, Alexandria VA 1990.

[181] Farah Pahlavi, p. 279.

[182] Personal interview with Yitzhak Segev, May 28, 2008.

[183] Personal interview with Dr. Ahmad Tehrani, June 12, 2008.

[184] Ardeshir Zahedi interview, July 2008.

[185] Ibid.

[186] Mohammad Reza Pahlavi, p. 155.

[187] Fouad Ajami, "A History Writ in Oil," *New York Times*, Thursday, June 5, 2008; http://query.nytimes.com/gst/fullpage.html?res=940DE5DB1638F93BA35756C0A 96E948260&sec=&spon=&pagewanted=3. (Accessed June 2008.)

[188] Dinesh D'Souza, "Giving Radical Islam its Start," January 29, 2007, *Townhall.com*; www.townhall.com/Common/Print.aspx. (Accessed December 2007.)

[189] Mustafa Alani, "Probable Attitudes of the GCC States Towards the Scenario of a Military Action Against Iran's Nuclear Facilities," Gulf Research Center, 2004, p. 11.

[190] Ion Mihai Pacepa, "Russian Footprints," *National Review* Online August 24, 2006; http://article.nationalreview.com/print/?q=NjUzMGU4NTMyOTdkOTdmNTA1 MWJlYjYyZDliODZkOGM=. (Accessed June 2008.)

[191] Cited by William F. Jasper in "PLO: Protected Lethal Organization; Despite their terrorist track record, Yasser Arafat and the PLO are not only protected from punishment but are warmly welcomed at the UN," February 11, 2002; http://www.accessmylibrary.com/coms2/summary_0286-25029637_ITM. (Accessed June 2008.)

[192] Houchang Nahavandi, p. 77.

[193] James A. Bill, *The Eagle and the Lion: The Tragedy of American-Iranian Relations* (New Haven: Yale University Press, 1988), p. 204.

[194] H. E. Chehabi, *Iranian Politics and Religious Modernism: The Liberation Movement of Iran under the Shah and Khomeini* (Ithica: Cornell University Press, 1990) p. 12.

[195] Confidential Memo, U.S. Embassy in Tehran, "Student Unrest," October 1, 1977. Declassified.

[196] Misagh Parsa, *The Social Origins of the Iranian Revolution* (Brunswick, N.J.: Rutgers University Press, 1989) p. 172.

[197] Central Intelligence Agency National Foreign Assessment Center, December 21, 1978, "Opposition Demonstrations in Iran: Leadership, Organization, and Tactics." Declassified.

[198] Department of State Telegram, From the Embassy in Tehran to U.S. Embassies worldwide. Declassified.

[199] Ibid.

[200] Dr. Parviz Mina interview, Paris, France, April 18, 2008.

[201] Personal Interview with Uri Lubrani, May 2008.

[202] Cited by Dariush Zahedi in *The Iranian Revolution Then and Now* (Boulder, Co: Westview Press, 2000), p. 136.

[203] Ibid., p. 136.

[204] Ryszard Kapuscinski, *Shah of Shahs* p. 74.

[205] Jahangir Amuzegar, *The Dynamics of the Iranian Revolution* (Albany: State University of New York Press, 1991), p. 259.

[206] Chadwyck-Healey, *Iran: The Making of U.S. Policy 1977-1980*, Alexandria VA 1990, Organizations Glossary, p. 151.

[207] Misagh Parsa, p. 217

[208] Cited by Ofira Seliktar in *Failing the Crystal Ball Test* (Westport, CT: Praeger Publishers, 2000), p. 133.

[209] Mohammad Reza Pahlavi, p. 162.

[210] Mr. Parviz Mina interview, April 18, 2008, Paris, France.

[211] Michael A. Ledeen, *The War Against the Terror Masters: Why It Happened, Where We Are Now, and How We'll Win* (New York: McMillan, 2003), p. 12.

[212] Ardeshir Zahedi interview, June 2008.

[213] Department of State Telegram, From American Tehran, Declassified, Signed "Naas," August 17, 1978.

[214] Iran: Chronology of a Revolution, 1978; http://ivl.8m.com/Chronology2.htm. (Accessed July 2008.)

[215] Confidential telegram, From U.S. Embassy Tehran to Secretary of State, October 24, 1978. Drafted by GB Lambrakis. Declassified.

[216] Ardeshir Zahedi interview, June 2008.

[217] Houchang Nahavandi, pp. 194-195.

[218] Ardeshir Zahedi interview, June 2008.

[219] Charles Stuart Kennedy, "The Iranian Revolution: An Oral History with Henry Precht, Then-State Department Desk Officer," *Middle East Journal,* Volume 58, No. 1, Winter, p. 71.

[220] Strobe Talbot, Dean Broils, Parviz Raein, *Time,* "An Interview with the Shah," September 18, 1978, http://www.time.com/time/magazine/article/0,9171,916375,00.html. (Accessed March 2008.)

[221] Amir Taheri, *The Spirit of Allah: Khomeini and the Islamic Revolution* (Bethesda, MD: Adler & Adler, 1985), pp. 176, 199-200.

[222] Samuel Segev interview, May 2008.

[223] Rovshan Ibrahimov, "Israeli Pipeline: Ashelon-Eilat-The Second Breath," April 9, 2007, http://www.turkishweekly.net/comments.php?id=2564. (Accessed March 2008.)

[224] Fardust, Hussein and Ali Akbar Dareini, *The Rise and Fall of the Pahlavi Dynasty: Memoirs of Former General Hussein.* (Bangalore, India: Motilal Banarsidass, 1999), p. 217.

[225] Benjamin Weiser, "Behind Israel-Iran Sales, 'Amber' Light from U.S.," *Washington Post,* August 16, 1987, pp. 1, A-26-A28.

[226] R. K. Ramazani, *Iran's Foreign Policy 1941-1971* (Charlottesville: University Press of Virginia, 1975), p. 404.

[227] Trita Parsi, *Treacherous Alliance: The Secret Dealings of Israel, Iran, and the U.S.* (New Haven: Yale University Press, 2007), p. 63.

[228] The Old Testament books of Esther, Ezra, Nehemiah, and Daniel outline the historic ties between the Persians and the Jews.

[229] Cited by Benjamin Beit-Hallahmi in *The Israeli Connection: Whom Israel Arms and Why* (London: I.B. Tauris & Co. Ltd, 1988), p. 10.

[230] R. K. Ramazani, "Iran and the Arab-Israeli Conflict," *Middle East Journal* 3 (1978); p. 414-415.

[231] Gary Sick, p. 207

[232] Samuel Segev interview, May 2008.

[233] "The Islamic Republic of Iran," *Y-Net News;* August 1, 2006, http://www.ynetnews.com/Ext/Comp/ArticleLayout/CdaArticlePrintPreview/1,2506,L-3284215,00.html. (Accessed April 2008.)

[234] Mohamed Heikal, *Khomeini and his Revolution, Les Editions Jeune Afrique,* 1983, pp. 164-167 (Translated from French.)

[235] Trita Parsi, p. 44.

[236] Benjamin beit-Hallahmi, *The Israeli Connection: Whom Israel Arms and Why* (London: I.B. Tauris & Co. Ltd, 1988), p. 12.

[237] Yossi Melman, "Our Allies, the Iranian People," *Haaretz.com,* January 12, 2006, http://www.haaretz.com/hasen/spages/794384.html. (Accessed March 2008.)

[238] Uri Lubrani interview, May 2008.

[239] Ryszard Kapuscinski, *Shah of Shahs* p. 78.

[240] Samuel Segev, *The Iranian Triangle* translated by Haim Watzman (New York: the Free Press, 1988), p. 107.

[241] Personal Interview with David Ivri, May 20, 2008.

[242] James A. Bill, Foreign Affairs: Winter 1978/79, "Iran and the Crisis of '78," http://www.foreignaffairs.org/19781201faessay9896/james-a-bill/iran-and-the-crisis-of-78.html. (Accessed March 2008.)

[243] Arnaud de Borchgrave, "The Shah on War and Peace," *Newsweek*, November 14, 1977, p. 70.

[244] Sohrab Sobhani, *The Pragmatic Entente: Israeli-Iranian Relations, 1948-1988* (New York: Praeger, 1989), p. 101.

[245] Samuel Segev interview, May 2008.

[246] Elaine Sciolino, "Documents Detail Israeli Missile Deal with the Shah," *New York Times*, April 1, 1986.

[247] Samuel Segev interview, May 2008.

[248] NTI, Missile Overview, "Early Developments Under the Shah Pahlavi, 1977-1979," http://www.nti.org/e_research/profiles/Iran/Missile/index.html. (Accessed March 2008.)

[249] Ibid.

[250] Trita Parsi, p. 76.

[251] Mr. Parviz Mina interview, April 18, 2008, Paris, France.

[252] GeoCities.com, http://www.geocities.com/CapitolHill/7288/byeart.htm. (Accessed March 2008.)

[253] Sohrab Sobhani, p. 129.

[254] Trita Parsi, p. 32.

[255] Moshe Dayan, *Breakthrough* (New York: Alfred Knopf, 1981), pp. 106-107.

[256] Tehran Domestic Service, February 19, 1979, trans. in *Foreign Broadcast Information Service*.

[257] Henry Kissinger, p. 1261.

[258] Ardeshir Zahedi interview, June 2008.

[259] Pierre Salinger, p. 59.

[260] Donald N. Wilbur, *Reza Shah Pahlavi: the Resurrection and Reconstruction of Iran, 1878-1944* (Hicksville, NY: Exposition Press, 1975), p. 136.

[261] Ibid., p. 141.

[262] Cited by David Lilienthal in *The Journals of David E. Lilienthal: The Harvest Years, 1959-1963* (New York: Harper and Row, 1971), p. 234.

[263] James A. Bill, p. 137.

[264] William Shawcross, p. 85.

[265] *U.S. News and World Report*, March 6, 1961.

[266] David Lilienthal, pp. 257-258.

[267] Personal interview with Ahmad Tehrani, June 12, 2008.

[268] W. Averill Harriman and Elie Abel, *Special Envoy to Churchill and Stalin* 1941-1946 (London: Hutchinson, 1975), p. 282.

[269] Elliot Roosevelt, ed., *F.D.R.: His Personal Letters*
(New York: Duell, Sloan and Pierce, 1947), p. 48.

[270] Cited by Marvin Zonis in *Majestic Failure: The Fall of the Shah*
(Chicago: University of Chicago Press, 1991), p. 169.

[271] Defense Intelligence Agency Intelligence Appraisal, "Iran: Religious-inspired
Opposition," March 29, 1978. Declassified.

[272] James A. Bill, *George Ball: Behind the Scenes in U.S. Foreign Policy*
(Cumberland, RI: Yale University Press, 1998), p. 231.

[273] Gary Sick, *All Fall Down: America's Tragic Encounter with Iran*
(New York: Penguin Books, 1986), p. 193.

[274] Amir Taheri, *Nest of Spies* (New York: Pantheon Books, 1988), p. 90.

[275] Gary Sick, p. 195.

[276] George Ball, *The Past Has Another Pattern, Memoirs*
(New York: W. W. Norton & Co, 1982), pp. 456-457.

[277] T. D. Allman, "Reviewing Stand," *Harper's Weekly*, August 9, 1976, p. 20.

[278] David R. Farber, *Taken Hostage: The Iran Hostage Crisis and America's First Encounter*
(New Haven: Yale University Press, 2004), p. 67.

[279] James A. Bill, p. 88.

[280] The World, *BBC News*, "The U.S. and Iran, Part II—The Shah and the Revolution,"
October 26, 2004; http://www.theworld.org/?q=node/3567.
(Accessed May 2008.)

[281] Personal Interview with Marvin Kalb, May 2008.

[282] George Ball, pp. 460-461.

[283] Zbigniew Brzezinski, pp. 370-371

[284] Mohammad Reza Pahlavi, pp. 169-170.

[285] Uri Lubrani interview, May 2008.

[286] George W. Ball, "Issues and Implications of the Iranian Crisis," Declassified December
12, 1984; Princeton University Library, Seeley G. Mudd Manuscript Library,
Princeton, NJ.

[287] George Ball, *The Past Has Another Pattern: Memoirs*
(New York: W.W. Norton, 1982), pp. 458-459.

[288] James A. Bill, p. 168.

[289] George Ball, p. 435.

[290] Ardeshir Zahedi interview, July 2008.

[291] State Department Memorandum to file, Precht, December 12, 1978, Declassified.
Archived in Chadwyck-Healey, *Iran: The Making of U.S. Policy 1977-1980*,
Alexandria VA 1990.

[292] Dinesh D'Souza, "Giving Radical Islam its Start," Townhall.com, January 29, 2007;
http://www.townhall.com/Common/Print.aspx.
(Accessed December 2007.)

[293] Farah Pahlavi interview, March 28, 2008.

[294] Confidential Telegram, Secretary of State to American Embassy Paris, October 22,
1978, John Stempel. Declassified.

[295] Ardeshir Zahedi interview, July 2008.

[296] Memorandum of Conversation, Declassified, May 15, 1978, John D. Stempel, First Secretary.

[297] Confidential letter, Charles W. Naas, Minister/Counselor, September 6, 1978. Declassified.

[298] U.S. State Department Memorandum, Stempel to State, May 25, 1978. Declassified. Archived in Chadwyck-Healey, *Iran: The Making of U.S. Policy 1977-1980*, Alexandria VA 1990.

[299] State Department Telegram, Vance to Sullivan, November 30, 1978. Declassified. Archived in Chadwyck-Healey, *Iran: The Making of U.S. Policy 1977-1980*, Alexandria VA 1990.

[300] State Department Telegram, Stempel to State Department, December 3, 1978. Declassified. Archived in Chadwyck-Healey, *Iran: The Making of U.S. Policy 1977-1980*, Alexandria VA 1990.

[301] Ardeshir Zahedi interview, June 2008.

[302] Personal Interview with Dr. Abdol Majid Majidi, April 18, 2008.

[303] Central Intelligence Agency Intelligence Memorandum, 20 November 1978, declassified 28 October, 1985; obtained through Rice University, Houston, TX.

[304] Admiral Stansfield Turner, p. 180.

[305] Marvin Kalb interview, May 2008.

[306] John Simpson & Tira Shubart, History of Iran, "Lifting the Veil; Life in Revolutionary Iran," 1995; p. 4, http://www.iranchamber.com/history/articles/lifting_veil_life_revolutionary_iran.php. (Accessed May 2008.)

[307] Mir Ali Asghar Montazam, *The Life and Times of Ayatollah Khomeini* (London: Anglo-European Publishing Limited, 1994), p. 146

[308] Uri Lubrani interview, May 2008.

[309] William H. Sullivan, *Mission to Iran* (New York: W.W. Norton, 1981), p. 16.

[310] Cyrus Vance, p. 325.

[311] Mohammad Reza Pahlavi, p. 161.

[312] State Department Memorandum, Vance to Sullivan, December 28, 1978, Declassified. Archived in Chadwyck-Healey, *Iran: The Making of U.S. Policy 1977-1980*, Alexandria VA 1990.

[313] William Shawcross, p. 30.

[314] State Department Memorandum, Stempel to State Department, Declassified. Archived in Chadwyck-Healey, *Iran: The Making of U.S. Policy 1977-1980*, Alexandria VA 1990.

[315] Human Rights in Iran, Hearing before the Subcommittee on International Organizations of the Committee on International Relations, House of Representatives, Ninety-Fifth Congress, First Session, October 26, 1977, p. 14.

[316] Michael Ledeen and William Lewis, p. 71.

[317] Glen Reinsford, TROP, www.thereligionofpeace.com/articles/jimmycarter.htm. (Accessed June 2008.)

[318] Ardeshir Zahedi interview, June 2008.

[319] The Museum of Broadcast Communications, http://www.museum.tv/archives/etv/V/htmlV/vietnamonte/vietnamonte.htm. (Accessed July 2008.)

[320] Houchang Nahavandi, p. 242

[321] http://www.indymedia.org.uk/en/2008/01/388699.html

[322] BBC Persian Service Archives, program for the 65th anniversary of the Service, produced by Shahryar Radpoor.

[323] http://www.indymedia.org.uk/media/2008/01//388700.pdf

[324] Naraghi, Ehsan, Des Palais du Chah, Aux Prisons de la Revolution, *Editions Balland* 1991. Translated from the French by Nilou Mobasser.

[325] http://www.indymedia.org.uk/media/2008/01//388700.pdf

[326] Azarbardin interview, June 2008.

[327] Robert E. Huyser, *Mission to Tehran* (New York: Harper and Row, 1986), pp. 31-32.

[328] Charles Mohr, "Vance, in Iran, Asserts Stability Depends on Rights," May 15, 1977, *New York Times*, p. 3.

[329] *New York Times*, May 15, 1977.

[330] Ibid.

[331] *New York Times*, May 18, 1977.

[332] Ibid., April 6, 1977, June 7, 1977, June 8, 1977, July 13, 1977.

[333] Ibid., July 31, 1977.

[334] Ibid., June 20, 1977.

[335] Ibid., June 17, 1977.

[336] Ibid., November 6, 1977.

[337] Ibid., November 8, 1977.

[338] Ibid., December 14, 1978.

[339] Ibid., December 29, 1978.

[340] U.S. State Department Memorandum Stempel to State, September 25, 1978, Declassified. Archived in Chadwyck-Healey, *Iran: The Making of U.S. Policy 1977-1980*, Alexandria VA, 1990.

[341] Personal Interview, Valéry Giscard d'Estaing, April 2008.

[342] U.S. State Department Telegram Sullivan to State Department, October 1978. Archived in Chadwyck-Healey, *Iran: The Making of U.S. Policy 1977-1980*, Alexandria VA 1990.

[343] Barry Rubin, *Paved with Good Intention* (New York and Oxford: Oxford University Press, 1980), p. 220.

[344] Mir Ali Asghar Montazam, p. 169.

[345] Ardeshir Zahedi interview, July 2008. (Zahedi revealed to me that his memoirs and a plethora of documents are housed in the vaults of a Swiss bank. He has left instructions that none be published before his death.)

[346] *Washington Post*, January 16, 1979, p. A18.

[347] Farah Pahlavi interview, March 28, 2008.

[348] David Pryce-Jones, The Middle East Forum, "Betrayal: France, the Arabs, and the Jews"; http://www.meforum.org/article/1636. (Accessed on January 2008.)

[349] "How Iranian Workers Toppled a Dictator," June 30, 2006, http://www.workersliberty.org/node/6521. (Accessed January 2008.)

[350] Dr. Parviz Mina interview, Paris, France, April 18, 2008.

[351] Central Intelligence Agency National Foreign Assessment, January 12, 1979, "Iran: The Radicals in the Opposition." Declassified.

[352] Gary Sick, pp. 51, 60-61.

[353] CIA Letter to Sullivan, October 6, 1978, Declassified. Archived in Chadwyck-Healey, *Iran: The Making of U.S. Policy 1977-1980*, Alexandria VA 1990.

[354] Declassified U.S. State Department document, 11 November 1978, obtained through Rice University, Houston, TX.

[355] Cyrus Vance, pp. 327-328.

[356] William Shawcross, p. 23.

[357] Her Majesty Farah Pahlavi, p. 262.

[358] Ardeshir Zahedi interview, June 2008.

[359] Ibid.

[360] Charles Nelson Brower and Jason D. Brueschke, *The Iran-United States Claims Tribunal*, (Boston:Brill/Martinus Nijhoff Publishers, 1998) p. 345.

[361] Central Intelligence Agency National Foreign Assessment, January 12, 1979, "Iran: The Radicals in the Opposition." Declassified.

[362] Ardeshir Zahedi interview, June 2008.

[363] John Simpson and Tira Shubart, *Lifting the Veil* (Philadelphia: Coronet Books, 1995), p. 4.

[364] Ardeshir Zahedi interview, June 2008.

[365] Ibid., p. 331.

[366] Mohsen M. Milani, *The Making of Iran's Islamic Revolution: From Monarchy to Islamic Republic* (Boulder, CO: Westview Press, 1994), p. 116.

[367] Ardeshir Zahedi interview, June 2008.

[368] Farah Pahlavi interview, March 29, 2008.

[369] Ardeshir Zahedi interview, June 2008.

[370] Mohamed Heikal, *Khomeini and His Revolution*, Les Editions Jeune Afrique, 1983, (Translated from French), pp. 164-167.

[371] Interview with Shah of Iran, *Washington Post*, May 27, 1980, pp. 9-12, 1.

[372] William Sullivan, *Mission to Iran* (New York: W.W. Norton, 1981), p. 222.

[373] Jimmy Carter, Don Richardson, *Conversations with Carter* (Boulder, CO: Lynne Rienner Publishers, 1998), p. 158.

[374] Dante Alighieri Quotes, http://thinkexist.com/quotes/dante_alighieri/. (Accessed March 2008.)

[375] Michael Ledeen and William Lewis, p. 163.

[376] Jeane J. Kirkpatrick, "Dictators and Double Standards," *Commentarymagazine*.com; November 1979; https://www.commentarymagazine.com/viewarticle.cfm/Dictatorships—Double-Standards-6189?page=all. (Accessed January 2008.)

[377] *Washington Post*, October 31, 1978, p. A18.

[378] Ibid., November 8, 1978, p. A14.

[379] Ibid., January 8, 1979, p. A20.

[380] Dr. Abdol Majid Majidi interview, Paris, France, April 18, 2008.

[381] Alexander M. Haig Jr. with Charles McCarry, *Inner Circles: How America Changed the World* (New York: Warner Books, 1992), p. 538.

[382] Ibid., p. 538.

[383] Mohammed Reza Pahlavi, pp. 172-173.

[384] Lt. General Shapour Azarbarzin interview, June 2008.

[385] Dr. Ahmad Tehrani interview, June 12, 2008.

[386] Lt. General Shapour Azarbarzin interview, June 2008.

[387] Farah Pahlavi interview, March 28, 2008.

[388] Alexander M. Haig Jr., p. 536.

[389] Robert E. Huyser, p. 17.

[390] Michael Evans with Jerome Corsi, *Showdown with Nuclear Iran* (Nashville, TN: 2006), p. 3-4.

[391] Ardeshir Zahedi interview, June 2008.

[392] Mohammad Reza Pahlavi, p. 173.

[393] Alexander M. Haig Jr., p. 539

[394] Robert E. Huyser, pp. 146, 194, 205, 222.

[395] Jim Hoagland, "Carter Set to Tell European Allies He Fully Backs Shah," *Washington Post*, January 5, 1979, p. A5.

[396] Ibid.

[397] Extract from *Le Pouvoir et le Vie*, Part 3, Chapter 6, V. Giscard d' Estaing, 2006; translated in Paris for Dr. Evans with permission from Mr. d'Estaing in May 2008; and personal interview with Giscard d'Estaing, May 2008.

[398] Zbigniew Brzezinski, p. 295

[399] M. Parsa, p. 223.

[400] Cyrus Vance, pp. 336-337.

[401] Ibid., p. 380.

[402] Giscard d'Estaing interview, Paris, France, May 2008.

[403] Mohammad Reza Pahlavi, p. 171.

[404] Ibid., p. 172.

[405] Amir Taheri, *The Spirit of Allah: Khomeini and the Islamic Revolution* (Bethesda, MD: Adler & Adler, 1985) p. 228.

[406] Mir Ali Asghar Montazam, pp. 144-145.

[407] Daniel Johnson, "J'Accuse," *Literary Review*, http://www.literaryreview.co.uk/johnson_12_06.html. (Accessed June 2008.)

[408] Dr. Parviz Mina interview, Paris, France, April 18, 2008.

[409] Journal de 20 h, A2 October, 10, 1978. Video may be viewed online at http://www.ina.fr/archivespourtous/index.php?full=Khomeiny&genre=&chaine= &mode_document=&datedif_jour1=&datedif_mois1=&datedif_annee1=&action =ft&explorer_OK.x=4&explorer_OK.y=8&cs_page=0&cs_order=3

[410] Balta, Paul, http://www.clio.fr/BIBLIOTHEQUE/la_republique_islamique_diran.asp translated from the French by Dan Godzich.

[411] *Le Monde*, February 1, 1979 translated from the French by Dan Godzich

[412] Balta, Paul, http://www.clio.fr/BIBLIOTHEQUE/la_republique_islamique_diran.asp translated from the French by Dan Godzich

[413] "Une Guerre," ("One War"), ñditions des Arénes, Paris, 1997.

[414] Mohamed Heikal, *Khomeini and his Revolution*, Les Editions Jeune Afrique, 1983, (Translated from French), pp. 155-159.

[415] Cited by Houchang Nahavandi in *The Last Shah of Iran*, translated from the French by Steeve Reed (France: Editions Osmonde, 2004), p. 241.

[416] Personal interview with Charles Villeneuve, journalist, Paris, France, April 19, 2008.

[417] Giscard d'Estaing interview, April 2008.

[418] CIA Intelligence Memorandum: The Politics of Ayatollah Ruhollah Khomeini, November 20, 1978. Declassified. Chadwyck-Healey, *Iran: The Making of U.S. Policy 1977-1980*, Alexandria VA 1990.

[419] Mohamed Heikal, pp. 155-159.

[420] Lt. General Shapour Azarbarzin interview, June 2008.

[421] Samuel Segev interview, Jerusalem, Israel, May 15, 2008.

[422] Uri Lubrani interview, May 2008.

[423] Imam Khomeini, *Islam and Revolution: Writings and Declarations*, translated and annotated by Hamid Algar (London: Routledge & Kegan Paul, 1981), pp. 247-248.

[424] Jimmy Carter, p. 454.

[425] Discovery Channel, "Koppel on Iran," December 3, 1979, http://www.time.com/time/magazine/article/0,9171,948624,00.html. (Accessed January 2008.)

[426] Michael A. Ledeen, pp. 14, 20.

[427] Personal interview with Charles Villeneuve, journalist on Khomeini's flight to Tehran, Paris, France, April 19, 2008.

[428] Ardeshir Zahedi Interview, June 2008.

[429] William Shawcross, p. 134

[430] Charles Villeneuve interview, April 2008.

[431] William Shawcross, p. 26.

[432] Uri Lubrani interview, May 2008.

[433] Robert E. Huyser, pp. 293, 296.

[434] State Department Telegram, Vance to Sullivan, January 2, 1979, Declassified. Archived in Chadwyck-Healey, *Iran: The Making of U.S. Policy 1977-1980*, Alexandria VA 1990.

[435] *New York Times*, December 29, 1978.

[436] Ibid., January 7, 1979.

[437] Iran Politics Club, http://iranpoliticsclub.net/politics/hostage-story/index.htm. (Accessed May 2008.)

[438] *New York Times,* January 14, 1979.

[439] "Tearful Shah Leaves Iran," *Gulfnews* Report, January 17, 1979, http://archive.gulfnews.com/indepth/onthisday/january/10182356.html; (Accessed March 2008.)

[440] State Department Telegram to Sullivan, January 19, 1979. Declassified. Archived in Chadwyck-Healey, *Iran: The Making of U.S. Policy 1977-1980*, Alexandria VA 1990.

[441] Mohamed Heikal, pp. 188-191.

[442] William J. Daugherty, American Diplomacy.org; "Jimmy Carter and the 1979 Decision to Admit the Shah into the United States," http://www.unc.edu/depts/diplomat/archives_roll/2003_01-03/dauherty_shah/dauherty_shah.html. (Accessed March 2008.)

[443] Ibid., p. 170.

[444] Cyrus Vance, p. 336.

[445] Robert Huyser, pp. 274-275.

[446] Mohamed Heikal, *Iran: The Untold Story* (New York: Pantheon, 1982), pp. 145-146.

[447] Brainy Quotes, Alexander Haig, http://www.brainyquote.com/quotes/authors/a/alexander_haig.html; (Accessed March 2008.)

[448] Quoted in Fouad Ajami, *The Vanished Imam: Musa al Sadr and the Shia of Lebanon* (Ithaca: Cornell University Press, 1986), p. 25. (An old Shia saying attributed to the Imam Musa al-Jafar in 799; it was said by many that Khomeini matched this description.)

[449] Dr. Ahmad Tehrani interview, June 12, 2008.

[450] Houchang Nahavandi, p. 91.

[451] Mohamed Heikal, *Khomeini and his Revolution*, Les Editions Jeune Afrique, 1983, (Translated from French), pp. 188-189.

[452] Ardeshir Zahedi interview, June 2008.

[453] Department of State Telegram, Charles W. Naas, Director, Officer of Iranian Affairs, Bureau of Near Eastern and South Asian Affairs, Department of State, August 17, 1977.

[454] Lt. General Shapour Azarbarzin interview, June 2008.

[455] Gary Sick, p. 258.

[456] Tony Smith, *America's Mission: the United States and the Worldwide Struggle for Democracy in the Twentieth Century* (Princeton, NJ: Princeton University Press, 1994), p. 259.

[457] Mohamed Heikal, pp. 191.

[458] Jimmy Carter, p. 455.

[459] BBC World Service, "My Century…", Transcription, December 24, 1999, http://www.bbc.co.uk/worldservice/people/features/mycentury/transcript/wk51d5.shtml. (Accessed January 2008.)

[460] Lt. General Shapour Azarbarzin interview, June 2008.

[461] William R. Polk, "The United States and Iran: A Tragic Friendship," p. 6; http://www.williampolk.com/pdf/2007/The%20United%20States%20and%20Iran.pdf. (Accessed May 2008.)

[462] BBC; On This Day: 1979, "Exiled Ayatollah Khomeini Returns to Iran." http://news.bbc.co.uk/onthisday/hi/dates/stories/february/1/newsid_2521000/2521003.stm. (Accessed January 2008.)

[463] General David Ivri interview, May 20, 2008.

[464] *Newsweek*, February 12, 1979, p. 44.

[465] Wikipedia, William H. Sullivan, http://en.wikipedia.org/wiki/William_H._Sullivan. (Accessed April 2008.)

[466] Mohamed Heikal, pp. 188-191. (Translated from French.)

[467] Samuel Segev, *The Iranian Triangle* (New York: Free Press, 1988), p. 109.

[468] U.S. Congress, Committee to investigate the Iran-Contra Affair, 1987, p. 171.

[469] Eric Schechter, *C4ISR Journal,* January 4, 2007, "Desert Duel;"
http://www.c4isrjournal.com/story.php?F=2245036;
(Accessed April 2008.)

[470] Samuel Segev, pp. 110-111.

[471] Mohamed Heikal, *Khomeini and his Revolution*, Les Editions Jeune Afrique, 1983
(Translated from French), pp. 180-181.

[472] Jimmy Carter, *Keeping Faith: Memoirs of a President*
(New York: Bantam Books, 1982), p. 450

[473] Lt. General Shapour Azarbarzin interview, June 2008.

[474] Nadar Entessar, "Israel and Iran's National Security," *Journal of South Asian and Middle Eastern Studies* 4 (2004), p. 5.

[475] Ibid., p. 4.

[476] David Menashri, *Post-Revolutionary Politics in Iran* (London: Frank Cass, 2001), p. 266.

[477] Samuel Segev, *The Iranian Triangle* (New York: Free Press, 1988), p. 4.

[478] Gary Sick, *October Surprise* (Toronto: Random House, 1992), P.207.

[479] General David Ivri interview, May 20, 2008

[480] Don Hopkins, "The October Surprise: The Iranian Hostage Rescue Mission, and the 1980 Presidential Election," December 1998;
http://www.donhopkins.com/drupal/node/104.
(Accessed April 2008.)

[481] Gary Sick, p. 200.

[482] The Embassy capture will be chronicled in a later chapter in this book.

[483] Milton Viorst, *In the Shadow of the Prophet: The Struggle for the Soul of Islam* (Boulder, CO: Westview Press, 2001), p. 195.

[484] Ofira Seliktar, *Failing the Crystal Ball Test* (Praeger: Westport, CT, 2000), p. 128.

[485] Personal Interview with General Yitzhak Segev, June 2008.

[486] Extract from *Le Pouvoir et le Vie,* Part 3, Chapter 6, V. Giscard d' Estaing, 2006; translated in Paris for Dr. Evans with permission from Mr. d'Estaing in May 2008.

[487] James A. Bill, *The Eagle and the Lion: The Tragedy of American-Iranian Relations* (New Haven: Yale University Press, 1988), pp.289-284.

[488] Said Arjomand, *The Turban for the Crown: the Islamic Revolution in Iran* (New York: Oxford University Press, 1988), p. 190.

[489] Jihad Watch, "D.C. Imam Glorifies Khomeini, Justifies Suicide Bombing, Preaches Islamic Supremacism," http://www.jihadwatch.org/archives/015242.php.
(Accessed March 2008.)

[490] Ned Temko, "PLO ponders Iran," *Christian Science Monitor,* February 28, 1979, p. 4.

[491] Cyrus Kadivar, "Dialogue of Murder," January 11, 2003;
http://www.payvand.com/news/03/jan/1058.html.
(Accessed August 2008.)

[492] Samuel Segev, "Hameshulah Hairani," *Ma'ariv* (Tel Aviv), 1981, p. 68.

[493] Amir Taheri, *Holy Terror, The Inside Story of Islamic Terrorism* (London: Sphere Books, Hutchinson Ltd, 1987), pp. 95-100.

[494] Nadar Entessar, p. 6.

[495] Mohamed Heikal, p. 20-23.

[496] Cyrus Vance, *Hard Choices* (New York: Simon and Schuster, 1983), p. 345.

[497] Dr. Abdol Majid Majidi interview, April 2008.

[498] Margaret Talbot, "The Agitator, Oriana Fallaci Directs her fury toward Islam" *The New Yorker*, June 5, 2006; http://www.newyorker.com/archive/2006/06/05/060605fa_fact. (Accessed July 2008.)

[499] Ibid.

[500] Cited by Philip Pilevsky in *I Accuse: Jimmy Carter and the Rise of Militant Islam* (Dallas: Durban house Publishing Company, Inc., 2007), p. 126.

[501] Amir Taheri, Benador Associates, "America Can't do a Thing"; http://www.benadorassociates.com/article/8781. (Accessed January 2008.)

[502] Charles Stuart Kennedy, The Iranian Revolution: An Oral History with Henry Precht, Then-State Department Desk Officer, *Middle East Journal*, Volume 58, No. 1, Winter 2004, pp. 64-65.

[503] Ibid., p. 68.

[504] Jamshid Amouzegar served as Minister of Health, Minister of Finance and prime minister (1977-1978.) He was chastised as prime minister for not establishing a coalition with the traditionalists who backed the Shah.

[505] Ardeshir Zahedi interview, July 2008.

[506] U.S. State Department Memorandum Stempel to Sullivan, August 22, 1978, Declassified. Archived in Chadwyck-Healey, *Iran: The Making of U.S. Policy 1977-1980*, Alexandria VA 1990. Archived in Chadwyck-Healey, *Iran: The Making of U.S. Policy 1977-1980*, Alexandria VA 1990.

[507] U.S. State Department Memorandum Sullivan to Vance, August 29, 1978, Declassified.

[508] R. C. Thornton, *The Carter Years: Toward a New Global Order* (New York: Paragon House, 2007), p. 273.

[509] Chadwyck-Healey, *Iran: The Making of U.S. Policy 1977-1980*, Alexandria, VA 1990, U.S. State Department Memo, "A Comment on Terrorism in a Revolutionary Situation," February 28, 1979.

[510] Ibid.

[511] Walter Laqueur, "Why the Shah Fell," *Commentary*, March 1979; http://www.commentarymagazine.com/viewarticle.cfm/Why-the-Shah-Fell-6091. (Accessed January 2008.)

[512] Walter Laqueur, "Trouble for the Shah," *The New Republic*, September 23, 1978, pp. 12-21.

[513] William C. Rempel, *Los Angeles Times*, November 3, 1994, "Tale of Deadly Iranian Network Woven in Paris," http://www.shapourbakhtiar.com/article-tale-deadly-iranian.htm. (Accessed April 2008.)

[514] William C. Rempel, *Los Angeles Times*, November 3, 1994, "Tale of Deadly Iranian Network Woven in Paris," http://www.shapourbakhtiar.com/article-tale-deadly-iranian.htm. (Accessed April 2008.)

[515] Charles Villeneuve interview, April 2008.

[516] Dr. Parviz Mina interview, April 2008.

[517] Department of State Telegram, Declassified, October, 1978, From the American Embassy Paris to American Embassy Tehran., signed "Hartman."

[518] Mohammad Reza Pahlavi, *The Shah of Iran, Answer to History* (Briarcliff Manor, NY: Stein and Day, 1980), p. 182.

[519] Postscripts, "Iran: Imminent Threat or Paper Tiger?" November 1, 2007, http://notorc.blogspot.com/2007/11/iran-imminent-threat-or-paper-tiger.html. (Accessed April 2008.)

[520] Confidential Memo, American Embassy in Tehran, L. Bruce Laingen, Charge d'Affaires, to State Department, October 15, 1979. Declassified.

[521] Farah Pahlavi interview, March 2008.

[522] Denis Leary, Think/Exist.com; http://thinkexist.com/quotation/i_think_we_should_take_iraq_and_iran_and_com bine/203664.html.

[523] Lawrence K. Altman, *New York Times*, "Dr. Jean A. Bernard, 98, dies; Found Cancer in Shah of Iran"; April 30, 2006. (Accessed June 2008.) http://www.nytimes.com/2006/04/30/world/europe/30bernard.html?ex=13040496 00&en=9bb0bd1c47f2cffb&ei=5088&partner=rssnyt&emc=rss. (Accessed January 2008.)

[524] Farah Pahlavi, *An Enduring Love* (New York: Hyperion, 1987), p. 242.

[525] *Le Figero Magazine*, November 1979, Interview with Empress Farah Pahlavi, New York, NY.

[526] Pierre Salinger. *America Held Hostage: the Secret Negotiations* (Garden City: Doubleday, 1981) p. 15.

[527] Ibid., pp. 17-18.

[528] *Magazine VSD*, November 11, 1979. (Translated from French.)

[529] Ibid., p. 25.

[530] Mohamed Heikal, *Khomeini and his Revolution*, Les Editions Jeune Afrique, 1983, pp. 155-159. (Translated from French.)

[531] Uri Lubrani interview, May 2008.

[532] Samuel Segev, *The Iranian Triangle* translated by Haim Watzman (New York: the Free Press, 1988), p. 119.

[533] Find Articles, "Iran flexes its muscles: Iran has a grand plan to become one of the most influential countries in the region," *The Middle East*, May 2007; http://findarticles.com/p/articles/mi_m2742/is_378/ai_n25005917/print. (Accessed June 2008.)

[534] Princess Ashraf Pahlavi, *Faces in a Mirror: Memoirs from Exile* (Englewood Cliffs, NF: Prentice-Hall, 1980), p. 9.

[535] ABC News, Jimmy Carter Interview: Complete Transcript, This Week with George Stephanopoulos; April 13, 2008, http://abcnews.go.com/ThisWeek/Story?id=4641038&page=2. (Accessed April 2008.)

[536] "Carter: Obama will waste no time pursuing Middle East peace," Haaretz, http://www.hartez.com/hasen/objects/pages/PrintArticleEN.jhtml?itemNo=1036762. (Accessed November 2008.)

537 Cited by Mark Silverberg, featured writer, *The New Media Journal*.us; "The Strategy of Defeat"; December 27, 2007; http://www.therant.us/staff/silverberg/12272007.htm. (Accessed January 2008.)

538 Iran: Evaluation of U.S. Intelligence Performance prior to November 1978; Staff Report, Subcommittee on Evaluation, Permanent Select Committee on Intelligence, U.S. House of Representatives, January 1979.

539 Gary Sick, *All Fall Down: America's Tragic Encounter with Iran* (Lincoln: Penguin Books, 2001), p. 240.

540 Max Boot, "The End of Appeasement," *History News Network*, http://hnn.us/articles/1264.html. (Accessed June 2008.)

541 Cyrus Vance, *Hard Choices* (New York: Simon and Schuster, 1983), p. 374.

542 Mark Bowden, *The Atlantic.com*, "Among the Hostage-Takers"; December 2004, www.theatlantic.com/doc/200412/bowden. (Accessed January 2008.)

543 Stansfield Turner, *Burn Before Reading* (New York: Hyperion, 2005) p. 169

544 Ibid., p. 170

545 Farah Pahlavi, *An Enduring Love* (New York: Hyperion, 1987), p. 340.

546 Farah Pahlavi interview, March 28, 2008.

547 Ardeshir Zahedi interview, June 2008.

548 Cynthia Helms, *An Ambassador's Wife in Iran* (New York: Dodd, Mead, 1981), p. 181.

549 Farah Pahlavi interview, March 28, 2008.

550 Ibid.

551 Ardeshir Zahedi interview, June 2008.

552 George Lenczowski, *American Presidents and the Middle East* (Durham: Duke University Press, 1990) p. 200

553 *Time* editorial, "Anger and Frustration," April 14, 1980, www.time.com/time/printout/0,8816,923946,00.html. (Accessed January 2008.)

554 Sandra Mackey, *The Iranians* (New York: Plume, 1996) p. 29.

555 Lowell Ponte, "Carter's Appease Prize," *FrontPageMagazine*.com; http://frontpagemag.com/articles/Read.aspx?GUID=AED85BC7-49B9-41D6-9E60-CBB4EA2C73DB. (Accessed June 2008.)

556 Jimmy Carter, *Keeping Faith: Memoirs of a President* (New York: Bantam Books, 1982) p. 458.

557 Tehran Domestic Service, trans. in *FBIS*, November 8, 1979.

558 Hizb-i-Wahdat, FAS.org,, http://www.fas.org/irp/world/para/hizbi_wahdat.htm. (Accessed March 2008.)

559 Amir Taheri, *Holy Terror: The Inside Story of Islamic Terrorism* (London: Sphere Books, Hutchinson, Ltd., 1987), p. 206

560 John Cooley, Unholy wars: *Afghanistan, America and International Terrorism* (London: Pluto Press, 2002), p. 18.

561 Ibid., pp. 202-203.

[562] Perspectives of World History and Current Events, *Abdullah Azzam: The Godfather of Jihad*, http://ww.pwhce.org/azzam.html. (Accessed April 2008.)

[563] It seems ironic that the pilot who flew the Shah and his entourage from Tehran to Cairo later transported two Khomeini insiders, Abolhasan Bani-Sadr and Masoud Rajavi, to Europe when they fell out of favor with the Ayatollah. The pilot later became a member of the *Mujahedeen*.

[564] Stansfield Turner, *Burn Before Reading* (New York: Hyperion, 2005), pp. 172-173.

[565] General Yitzhak Segev interview, June 2008.

[566] Personal email correspondence with retired Marine Gunnery Sergeant John McClain, September 11, 2008.

[567] James A. Bill, *The Eagle and the Lion* (New Haven, 1988), p. 254

[568] Guide to Cyrus R. Vance and Grace Sloane Vance Papers, Yale University Library, Compiled by Mark Bailey and Staff of Manuscripts and Archives; http://mssa.library.yale.edu/findaids/stream.php?xmlfile=mssa.ms.1664.xml; accessed April 2008.

[569] Andre Fontaine, "Foreign Affairs: Transatlantic Doubts and Dreams," http://www.foreignaffairs.org, "According to the official version of history, CIA aid to the *Mujahedeen* began during 1980, that is to say, after the Soviet army invaded Afghanistan, 24 Dec 1979. But the reality, secretly guarded until now, is completely otherwise. Indeed it was July 3, 1979 that President Carter signed the first directive for secret aid to the opponents of the pro-Soviet regime in Kabul. And that very day, I wrote a note to the President in which I explained to him that in my opinion this aid was going to induce a Soviet military intervention." 19810201faessays8170/andre-fontaine/transatlantic-doubts-and-dreams.html. (Accessed February 2008.)

[570] Eighties Club; *The Daily News*, January 1980; http://eightiesclub.tripod.com/id95.htm. (Accessed January 2008.)

[571] Charles Alexander, "Carter's Farewell Budget," Time, January 25, 1981; www.time.com/time/printout/0,8816,954619,00.html. (Accessed August 2008.)

[572] Memo for President Jimmy Carter from Stuart Eizenstat, March 26, 1980, Box BE-13, Presidential Papers of Jimmy Carter, White House Central Files, Jimmy Carter Library.

[573] William Safire, *New York Times*, Essay, "The Four Eyes"; March 27, 1980; http://select.nytimes.com/gst/abstract.html?res=F6091EF9395C11728DDDAE0A9 4DB405B8084F1D3&scp=104&sq=&st=p. (Accessed January 2008.)

[574] Jack W. Germond and Jules Witcover, *Blue Smoke and Mirrors: How Reagan Won and Why Carter Lost the Election of 1980* (New York: Viking, 1981), pp. 190-193.

[575] *National Journal*, October 11, 1980, Cited by Steven F. Hayward, *The Real Jimmy Carter* (Washington: Regnery Publishing, Inc., 2004), p. 176.

[576] Burton I. Kaufman and Scott Kaufman, *The Presidency of James Earl Carter* (Lawrence, KS: University Press of Kansas, 2006), p. 240.

[577] Ronald Kessler, Ron Kessler's Washington, "An Odd President," *Newsmax*, July 2008, pp. 28-29.

[578] Ibid., p. 29.

[579] Ibid.

[580] Ronald Kessler, *Inside the White House* (New York: Pocket Books, a division of Simon and Schuster, Inc., 1996), p. 91.

581 Walter Isaacson, "A Vow to Zip His Lip", *Time*, October 20, 1980,
http://www.time.com/time/magazine/article/0,9171,951518-4,00.html;
(Accessed February 2008.)

582 U.S. Senate Committee on Foreign Relations, 1992, "The 'October Surprise' Allegations
and the Circumstances Surrounding the Release of the American Hostages Held in
Iran" (Washington: U.S. Government printing Office.) pp. 53, 7-8, 239

583 *Investors Business Daily*, Profile in Incompetence, Editorial Series, Part Two: "'Malaise'
Maestro," http://www.ibdeditorials.com/Special3.aspx.
(Accessed August 2008.)

584 *The American Experience*, PBS, Ronald Reagan Quotes,
http://www.pbs.org/wgbh/amex/reagan/sfeature/quotes.html.
(Accessed, February 2008.)

585 Hans F. Sennholz, "The Economics of Jimmy Carter," December 3, 2005;
http://www.lewrockwell.com/sennholz/sennholz10.html.
(Accessed August 2008.)

586 1980 Debate transcript, p. 13, www.debates.org/pages/trans80b.html.
(Accessed February 2008.)

587 1980 Debate transcript, p. 14.

588 Michael W. Miller, "Carter, Reagan Square Off in Debate", *The Harvard Crimson*,
www.thecrimson.com/article.aspx?refref=273013.
(Accessed February 2008.)

589 1980 Debate transcript, p. 22

590 Thomas A. Sancton, "The Hostage Drama", *Time*, November 3, 1980;
http://www.time.com/time/magazine/article/0,9171,924494-2,00.html.
(Accessed February 2008.)

591 The American Presidency Project, Jimmy Carter, November 2, 1980,
http://www.presidency.ucsb.edu/ws/index.php?pid=45443&st=&st1=.
(Accessed April 2008.)

592 Public Broadcasting System, American Experience: Jimmy Carter;
www.pbs.org/wgbh/amex/carter/peopleevents/p_oneill.html.
(Accessed February 2008.)

593 Cited by Steven F. Hayward, *The Real Jimmy Carter*
(Washington: Regnery Publishing, 2004), p. 191.

594 Jimmy Carter, *Keeping Faith: Memoirs of a President*
(New York: Bantam books, 1982), pp. 542-543.

595 Alaska History and Cultural Studies, Modern Alaska: ANILCA,
http://www.akhistorycourse.org/articles/article.php?artID=256.
(Accessed July 2008.)

596 Gary Sick, *All Fall Down* (Lincoln, NE: iUnvierse.com, Inc., 2001), p. 377.

597 Ibid., 397–398.

598 James A. Leggette and Michael W. Funk, "Ronald Reagan and the Opening Salvos in
the War on Terror," *American Thinker*, June 7, 2005,
http://www.americanthinker.com/2005/06/ronald_reagan_and_the_opening.html.
(Accessed February 2008.)

599 Daniel Pipes, *New York Sun*, "Reagan's Early Victory in the War on Terror," June 15,
2004; http://www.danielpipes.org/article/1888.
(Accessed January 2008.)

600 Ronald Reagan, *An American Life* (New York: Simon and Schuster, 1990), pp. 218-219.

601 Edwin Meese III, *With Reagan: The Inside Story* (Washington, DC; Regnery, 1992), p. 201.

[602] Bernard Weinraub, "U.S. Jets Hit 'Terrorist Centers' in Libya; Reagan Warns of New Attacks if Needed," *New York Times*, April 15, 1986, http://www.nytimes.com/1986/04/15/politics/15REAG.html. (Accessed April 2008.)

[603] Bernard Weinraub, "U.S. Jets Hit 'Terrorist Centers' in Libya; Reagan Warns of New Attacks if Needed," http://www.nytimes.com/1986/04/15/politics/15REAG.html. (Accessed February 2008.)

[604] "Anger and Frustration," *Time*, Monday, April 14, 1980, www.time.com/time/printout/0,8816,946,00.html. (Accessed January 2008.)

[605] Sean Hannity, *Deliver Us From Evil* (New York: Harper Collins, 2004), p. 62.

[606] "No Spirit of Camp David," *Time*, March 12, 1979; http://www.time.com/time/magazine/article/0,9171,948414,00.html. (Accessed August 2008.)

[607] Interview between Samuel Segev and former Israeli Mossad station chief in Tehran Eliezer (Geizi) Tzafrir, July 31, 2008; used by permission.

[608] Samuel Segev, *Jimmy Carter: Foreign Policy and Post-Presidential Years* (Westport, CT: Greenwood Press, 1994), p. 125.

[609] Ibid., p. 125.

[610] Ibid.

[611] Jimmy Carter, *Keeping Faith* (Little Rock, AR: 1995), p. 293.

[612] Shlomo Aloni, *Arab-Israeli Wars 1947-82* (Oxford, England:Osprey Publishing, 2001), p. 57.

[613] Samuel Segev, *Sadat - The Road to Peace* (in Hebrew) (Tel Aviv: Massada, 1998), pp. 30-32.

[614] Ibid., pp. 30-32.

[615] Samuel Segev, *The Moroccan Connection* (in Hebrew), (Tel Aviv: Matar, 2008), p. 138.

[616] Ibid., p. 167.

[617] Segev, *Sadat-The Road to Peace*, pp. 42-43.

[618] Segev, *The Moroccan Connection*, p. 166.

[619] Ibid., p. 177.

[620] Ibid., p. 178.

[621] Segev, *Sadat—The Road to Peace*, p. 45.

[622] Ibid., p. 46.

[623] Ibid., p. 46.

[624] Ibid., p. 47.

[625] Ibid., p. 48.

[626] Robert Burns, "To A Mouse," Standard English Translation, http://www.worldburnsclub.com/poems/translations/554.htm. (Accessed August 2008.)

[627] *Radio Cairo* (in Arabic), September 11, 1977.

[628] *Kol Israel* (in Hebrew), November 10, 1977.

[629] Interview with Senior Mossad official, Tel Aviv, August 2, 2008.

630 Segev, Sadat—*The Road to Peace*, p. 53.

631 Ibid., pp. 34, 71.

632 Maréchal Pétain, French prime minister, signed the French surrender to Hitler and the Germans. Northern France, with Paris, and the Atlantic coast came under direct German military administration. In Southern France, Marechal Petain formed a new government in the spa city of Vichy. The Vichy administration had little choice but to collaborate with the Germans. French authorities participated in the arrest and transport to the annihilation camps of 80,000 of the country's 330,000 Jews (about half of whom were French citizens). http://www.zum.de/whkmla/region/france/vichy.html. (Accessed August 2008.)

633 Ibid.

634 Ibid., pp. 74-75.

635 Ibid., p. 86.

636 Ibid., p. 104.

637 Ibid., p. 105.

638 Interview with Senior Mossad official, Tel Aviv, August 5, 2008.

639 Ibid.

640 IMRA, Zionist Organization of America, New York, N.Y.; November 30, 2006, http://www.imra.org.il/story.php3?id=31819. (Accessed April 2008.)

641 Dr. Laurence J. Peter, http://www.theotherpages.org/alpha-p1.html. (Accessed May 2008.)

642 Anwar Sadat, *In Search of Identity* (London: Fontana, 1978) pp. 364-364.

643 Israel and Judaism Studies.org; "The 1973 (Yom Kippur) War and the Camp David Accords"; http://www.ijs.org.au/The-1973-War-and-the-Camp-David-Accords/default.aspx. (Accessed February 2008.)

644 Copy of Menachem Begin's speech taken from the private papers of Dr. Michael D. Evans.

645 The text is in State Department, *American Foreign Policy 1977-1980*, p. 636-638.

646 Christopher S. Wren, *New York Times,* "Cairo Gala Draws a Glittering Crowd," September 28, 1979.

647 Serge Schmemann, *New York Times,* "A Separate Peace"; July 20, 1997; http://query.nytimes.com/gst/fullpage.html?res=9805E1DE1E39F933A15754C0A961958260&sec=&spon=&pagewanted=2. (Accessed February 2008.)

648 *The Presidential Campaign 1976*, 3 volumes, (Washington, DC: Government Printing Office, 1978), Vol.3, p. 313.

649 Israel Ministry of Foreign Affairs; December 18, 1975, "Toward Peace in the Middle East", Report of the Brookings Institution Middle East Study Group, December 1975; http://www.israel-mfa.gov.il/MFA/Foreign+Relations/Israels+Foreign+Relations+since+1947/1974-1977/144+Toward+Peace+in+the+Middle+East-+report+of+the.htm?DisplayMode=print. (Accessed February 2008.)

650 "Plane Talk on Capitol Hill," *Time*, May 8, 1978, http://www.time.com/time/magazine/article/0,9171,919599-1,00.html. (Accessed February 2008.)

651 Yehuda Avner, "The Day Jimmy Carter was Reduced to Silence," *Jerusalem Post*, September 11, 2003, reprinted at http://www.freerepublic.com/focus/f-news/980819/posts. (Accessed February 2008.)

652 *Jimmy Carter: Foreign Policy and Post-Presidential Years*, ed. Herbert D. Rosenbaum and Alezej Ugrinsky (Westport, CT: Greenwood, 1994) p. 162.

653 Shibley Telhami, "The Camp David Accords." Pew Case Studies in International Affairs (Washington: Institute for the Study of Diplomacy, 1992) p. 631.

654 Personal Interview with Ambassador Dore Gold, May 2008.

655 Cited by Serge Schmemann, *New York Times*, "A Separate Peace"; July 20, 1997; http://query.nytimes.com/gst/fullpage.html?res=9805E1DE1E39F933A15754C0A 961958260&sec=&spon=&pagewanted=2. (Accessed February 2008.)

656 Zbigniew Brzezinski, *Power and Principle* (Toronto, Canada: McGraw Hill, 1983), p. 276.

657 American Experience: Jimmy Carter, "Peace talks at Camp David, September 1978," http://www.pbs.org/wgbh/amex/carter/peopleevents/e_peace.html. (Accessed July 2008.)

658 Eric Silver, *Begin: The Haunted Prophet* (New York: Random House, 1984), p. 192.

659 Jimmy Carter, *Keeping Faith, President* (New York: Bantam books, 1982), p. 322.

660 *Time*, October 11, 1982.

661 Eric Silver, p. 193.

662 Michael D. Evans, *Save Jerusalem* (Euless, TX: Bedford Books, 1995), pp. 54-58. Used by permission of Bedford Books and Dr. Michael D. Evans.

663 *Der Spiegel*, Interview with Yasser Arafat, March 19, 1979.

664 *Al-Ahram Weekly Online*, Lessons of Camp David, Kaled Dawoud, September 25—October 1, 2003, Issue No. 657, http://weekly.ahram.org.eg/2003/657/eg3.htm. (Accessed March 2008.)

665 Barbara Walters, *Audition* (New York: Random House, 2008), p. 349

666 Nobel Prize.org, December 10, 1978; Presentation Speech delivered by Aase Lionaes, Chairman of the Norwegian Nobel Committee, on the occasion of the awarding of the Nobel Peace Prize for 1978, Oslo, December 10, 1978, http://nobelprize.org/nobel_prizes/peace/laureates/1978/press.html. (Accessed February 2008.)

667 Shapira, `Reflections on the Autonomy: The Camp David Accords and the Obligation to Negotiate in Good Faith', in Y. Dinstein (ed.), *Models of Autonomy* (1981) p. 285.

668 Tamar Sternthal, "*International Herald Tribune* Op-Ed Erases 20-Plus Years of Terror," http://www.camera.org/index.asp?x_context=2&x_outlet=139&x_article=751. (Accessed February 2008.)

669 Cited by William F. Jasper in "PLO: Protected Lethal Organization; Despite their terrorist track record, Yasser Arafat the PLO are not only protected from punishment, but are warmly welcomed at the UN," February 11, 2002; http://www.accessmylibrary.com/coms2/summary_0286-25029637_ITM. (Accessed June 2008.)

670 Ibid.

671 BBC, *On This Day*, October 6, 1981, http://news.bbc.co.uk/onthisday/hi/dates/stories/october/6/newsid_2515000/25158 41.stm. (Accessed January 2008.)

[672] Douglas Brinkley, *The Unfinished Presidency* (New York: Penguin Books, 1998) pp. 328-329 (Jimmy Carter to Yasser Arafat upon their first meeting.)

[673] Wikipedia; http://en.wikipedia.org/wiki/Blowback_(intelligence). (Accessed February 2008.)

[674] Hosea 8:7 (KJV)

[675] Samuel Segev, *The Iranian Triangle* (New York: Free Press, 1988), p. 4.

[676] Israel Shahak, "How Israel's Strategy Favors Iraq over Iran," *Middle East International*, March 19, 1993, p. 19.

[677] Global Research.ca; "After the National Intelligence Estimate on Iran: Let the Debater Begin," January 3, 2008, http://www.globalresearch.ca/index.php?context=va&aid=7722. (Accessed April 2008.)

[678] Samuel Segev, "Hameshulash Hairani," *Ma'ariv* (Tel Aviv), 1981, p. 98.

[679] Samuel Segev, *The Iranian Triangle* (New York: Free Press, 1988), p. 232.

[680] Council on Foreign Relations; State Sponsors: Iran; August 2007, http://www.cfr.org/publication/9362/#5. (Accessed February 2008.)

[681] "Proxy Power: Understanding Iran's use of Terrorists"; Brookings Institution; http://brookings.edu/opinoins/2006/0726iran_byman.aspx. (Accessed February 2008.)

[682] Iran Terror: List of Terror Attacks, July 19, 2005. (http://www.iranterror.com/content/view/38/56/. (Accessed February 2008.)

[683] *The 9/11 Commission Report*, Chapter 7, Section 3 (Washington: U.S. Government Printing Office, 2004) p. 240.

[684] Barnett R. Rubin, *The Fragmentation of Afghanistan: State Information and Collapse in the International System* (New Haven, CT: Yale University press, 2002) p. 180.

[685] The document has been declassified and is available through government channels. (Derivative CL BY 022367; declassified March 4, 2004. http://www.c-span.org/presidentiallibraries/Content/Carter/CarterAfghanistan.pdf/. (Accessed February 2008.)

[686] America Abroad Media, "America and Afghanistan: A Nations Rebuilding Interview with CIA officer Charles Cogan, http://www.americaabroadmedia.org/media/On%20line%20extra%20materials/A fghan-Cogan%20interview.pdf. (Accessed March 2008.)

[687] Lawrence Wright in *The Looming Tower: Al-Qaeda and the Road to 9/11* (New York: Vintage Books, 2006), p. 194.

[688] Cited in *Ghost Wars: The Secret History of the CIA, Afghanistan, and bin Laden, From the Soviet Invasion to September 10, 2001* (New York: Penguin Press, 2004), p. 51.

[689] Vincent Javert, Interview with Zbigniew Brzezinski, *Le Nouvel Observateur*, Paris, 15-21 January 1998, http://www.globalresearch.ca/articles/BRZ110A.html. (Accessed February 2008.)

[690] Declassified "Resolution of the CC of the CPSU" and "The CPSU on Events in Afghanistan, December 17-28, 1979, Top Secret," Handwritten document translated and declassified by Boris Yeltsin, 1993; http://www.alternativeinsight.com/Afghan_War.html. (Accessed March 2008.)

[691] Alexander Lyakhovsky, *The Tragedy and Valor of Afghan* (Moscow: GPI Iskon, 1995), pp. 109-112. http://www.gwu.edu/~nsarchiv/NSAEBB/NSAEBB57/r8.doc. (Accessed March 2008.)

[692] Alexander de Marenches with Christine Ockrent, *Dans le Secret des Princes: Perceptions et Actions* (Paris: editions Stock, 1986), pp. 211-214.

[693] CNN Cold War—Historical Documents: U.S. Memos on Afghanistan; Episode 20: Soldiers of God; http://www.cnn.com/SPECIALS/cold.war/episodes/20/documents/brez.carter/. (Accessed February 2008.)

[694] David Leigh and Richard Norton-Taylor, *The Guardian,* "House of Saud Looks Close to Collapse"; November 21, 2001, http://www.guardian.co.uk/world/2001/nov/21/afghanistan.socialsciences. (Accessed February 2008.)

[695] Cited in The American Empire Project, Book Review, *Blowback: The Cost and Consequences of American Empire,* Author: Chalmers Johnson, published by Metropolitan Books, 2004; http://www.americanempireproject.com/bookpage.asp?ISBN=0805075593. (Accessed February 2008.)

[696] Arnold Beichman, Hoover Institution, *Hoover Digest,* "Eight Years that Shook the World," http://www.hoover.org/publications/digest/4495741.html. (Accessed February 2008.)

[697] Ibid.

[698] Somalia Foreign Military Assistance, http://www.country-data.com/cgi-bin/query/r-12055.html. (Accessed March 2008.)

[699] Robert D. Kaplan, "Carter in Ethiopia: Revisiting one of the Nobelist's missed chances—former President Jimmy Carter," *National Review,* http://findarticles.com/p/articles/mi_m1282/is_21_54/ai_93370304/pg_2. (Accessed April 2008.)

[700] Gil Troy, "On Jimmy Carter's False Apartheid Analogy," George Mason University History News Network, December 18, 2006, http://hnn.us/articles/32916.html. (Accessed March 2008.)

[701] Douglas Brinkley, *The Unfinished Presidency* (New York: Penguin Books, 1998), p. 340

[702] Jimmy Carter, *New York Times,* "Needed: Middle East Peace Talks," January 2, 1991, http://query.nytimes.com/gst/fullpage.html?res=9D0CE5DF163EF931A35752C0A967958260&sec=&spon=&pagewanted=1. (Accessed March 2008.)

[703] "Iran, Hezbollah, Hamas, and the Global Jihad: A New Conflict Paradigm for the West" 2007; Brig. Gen. (Ret.) Dr. Shimon Shapira and Daniel Diker, "Iran's Second Islamic Revolution: Strategic Implications for the West", Jerusalem Center for Public Affairs; p. 41; http://www.jcpa.org/. (Accessed January 2008.)

[704] Mohammad Sahimi, "Iran's Nuclear Program: Part I, Its History," October 2, 2003, http://payvand.com/news/03/oct/1015.html. (Accessed March 2008.)

[705] James Earl Carter, Jr., State of the Union Address 1981; http://www.let.rug.nl/usa/P/jc39/speeches/su81jec.htm. (Accessed February 2008.)

[706] Bret Stephens, "How to Stop Iran without Firing a Shot"; May 15, 2006; http://www.opinionjournal.com/wsj/?id=110008382. (Accessed February, 2008.)

[707] Amir Taheri, "Reading Between the Lines", *Jerusalem Post*, May 13, 2006; http://www.benadorassociates.com/article/19490. (Accessed February 2008.)

[708] Michael Evans, *The Final Move Beyond Iraq: The Final Solution While the World Sleeps* (Lake Mary, FL: Front Line, 2007) p. 210.

[709] Cited by Mark Silverberg, featured writer, *The New Media Journal*.us; "The Strategy of Defeat"; December 27, 2007; http://www.therant.us/staff/silverberg/12272007.htm. (Accessed January 2008.)

[710] David Limbaugh, "Ashamed of America," *Townhall.com*, July 11, 2008, http://townhall.com/Columnists/DavidLimbaugh/2008/07/11/ashamed_of_america. (Accessed August 2008.)

[711] Nazila Fathi and Joel Brinkley, "U.S. Pursuing Reports that Link Iranian to Embassy Seizure in 1979," *New York Times*, July 1, 2005; http://www.nytimes.com/2005/07/01/international/middleeast/01tehran.html?_r=1 &oref=slogin. (Accessed May 2008.)

[712] "Iran, Hizbullah, Hamas and the Global Jihad: A New Conflict Paradigm for the West" 2007; Gen. (Ret.) Moshe Yaalon, "The Second Lebanon War: From Territory to Ideology", Jerusalem Center for Public Affairs; p. 16. (Accessed January 2008.)

[713] Jonathan Steele, "Lost in Translation," *Guardian,* June 14, 2006, http://commentisfree.guardian.co.uk/jonathan_steele/2006/06/post_155.html. (Accessed March 2008.

[714] Jewish Virtual Library, Jews of Iran, http://www.jewishvirtuallibrary.org/jsource/anti-semitism/iranjews.html. (Accessed April 2008.)

[715] Marcos Aguinis, "Death Wish", *La Nacion*; cited in Citizens in Defense of Defense; http://defendingdefense.blogspot.com/2006/05/children-advanced-in-tight-knit.html. (Accessed February 2008.)

[716] Edward Daley, "Jimmy Carter's Nobel Legacy", March 10, 2003, *The American Daily*, Phoenix, AZ; http://American daily.com/article/1991. (Accessed January 2008.)

[717] Lawrence Wright, *The Looming Tower: Al-Qaeda and the Road to 9/11* (New York: Vintage Books, 2006), p. 395-396.

[718] Ibid., p. 396.

[719] Serge Schmemann, *New York Times,*" A Separate Peace"; July 20, 1997; http://query.nytimes.com/gst/fullpage.html?res=9805E1DE1E39F933A15754C0A 961958260&sec=&spon=&pagewanted=2. (Accessed February 2008.)

[720] Barbara Walters, *Audition* (New York: Random House, 2008), p. 350.

[721] Cited by Lawrence Wright in *The Looming Tower: Al-Qaeda and the Road to 9/11*, pp. 54-55.

[722] Ibid., p. 46.

[723] Jay Tolson, *U.S. News and World Report*, Faith Matters: Cairo Journal Part II, March 7, 2008, http://www.usnews.com/blogs/faith-matters/2008/3/7/cairo-journal-part-ii.html. (Accessed March 2008.)

[724] University of Dayton, The Evolution of Terror, January 8, 2008, http://www.udayton.edu/News/Article/?contentId=8490. (Accessed March 2008.)

[725] Evan F. Kohlmann, *Al-Qaida's Jihad in Europe* (Oxford, England: Berg Publishers, 2004), p. 26.

[726] Rudyard Kipling, *Writings in Prose and Verse of Rudyard Kipling* (London: Charles Scribner's Sons, 1899), p. 273.

[727] John K. Cooley, *Unholy Wars*(Sterling, VA: Pluto Press, 2002), pp.41-43.

[728] Phil Gasper, "Afghanistan, the CIA, bin Laden, and the Taliban," *International Socialist Review,* November-December 2001, http://www.thirdworldtraveler.com/Afghanistan/Afghanistan_CIA_Taliban.html). (Accessed March 2008.)

[729] Michael C. Ruppert, *Crossing the Rubicon: The Decline of the American Empire at the End of the Age of Oil* (Gabriola Island, Canada: New society Publishers, 2004), -. 83.

[730] Tim Weiner, "Disclosure Urged for Secret Budget," *Time,* November 25, 2993, http://query.nytimes.com/gst/fullpage.html?res=9F0CE7DF153DF936A15752C1A 965958260&sec=&spon=&pagewanted=all. (Accessed March 2008.)

[731] John K. Cooley, *Unholy Wars*(Sterling, VA: Pluto Press, 2002), p. 226

[732] Alan Dershowitz, "Carter's Distorted World", AISH.com; http://www.aish.com/societyWork/arts/Carters_Distorted_World.asp. (Accessed February 2008.)

[733] The Carter Center, Theme Statement, http://cartercenter.org/about/index.html. (Accessed February 2008.)

[734] Habitat for Humanity; "Jimmy Carter and Habitat for Humanity", www.habitat.org/how/carter. (Accessed February 2008.)

[735] Jimmy Carter, *Our Endangered Values: America's Moral Compass* (New York: Simon & Schuster, 2005) p. 185.

[736] Douglas Brinkley, *The Unfinished Presidency: Jimmy Carter's Journey Beyond the White House* (New York: Viking, 1998), p. 293.

[737] Christopher Hitchens, Slate.com, "Peanut Envy," May 21, 2007, www.slate.com/toolbar.aspx?action=print@id=2166661. (Accessed January 2008.)

[738] Jonathan V. Last, The Claremont Institute, Book Review, Spring 2005, a review of *Malaise Forever: How Our Worst Ex-President Undermines American Foreign Policy, Coddles Dictators, and Created the party of Clinton and Kerry* by Steven F. Hayward; www.claremont.org/publications/crb/id.977/article_details.asp. (Accessed June 2008.)

[739] Kai Bird, "The Very Model and an Ex-President," *Nation,* November 12, 1990, p. 1.

[740] Chad Groening, *Associated Press*, "Pro-Israel group blasts Jimmy Carter over his support of HAMAS," http://www.onenewsnowcom/2007/06/proisrael_group_blasts_jimmy_c.php. (Accessed December 2007.)

[741] CNN, Glenn Beck Show, Guest Host Michael Smerconish, April 14, 2008, http://transcripts.cnn.com/TRANSCRIPT/0804/14/gb.01.html. (Accessed April 2008.)

742 "Barack Obama: The Black Jimmy Carter," January 28, 2008;
http://israelmatzav.blogspot.com/2008/01/barack-obama-black-jimmy-carter.html.
(Accessed November 2008.)

743 Ibid.

744 Ibid.

745 Ambassador Dore Gold interview, May 2008.

746 Personal interview with Professor Alan Dershowitz; Quoted by permission from
Professor Alan Dershowitz from an unpublished work. April 2008.

747 Simon and Schuster, Description of Jimmy Carter book, *We Can Bring Peace to the
Holy Land*, http://www.simonsays.com/content/book.cfm?tab=1&pid=648588.
(Accessed December 2008.)

748 Ibid.

749 Jerusalem Post, December 8, 2008, "Carter Arrives in Beirut to meet Lebanese
Officials,"
http://www.jpost.com/servlet/Satellite?pagename=JPost/JPArticle/ShowFull&cid=1
228728114042.
(Accessed December 2008.)

750 Yahoo! News, "Ex-President Carter says Hezbollah won't meet with him," December 9,
2008; http://news.yahoo.com/s/nm/20081209/pl_nm/us_lebanon_carter. (Accessed
December 2008.)

751 "Carter's New World Order," *U.S. News and World Report*, June 6, 1977.

752 Douglas Brinkley, *The Unfinished Presidency: Jimmy Carter's Journey Beyond the
White House* (New York: Viking, 1998), p. 400.

753 Ibid., p. 409.

754 Kim Il Sung, Killer File, http://www.moreorless.au.com/killers/kim-il-sung.html#kills.
(Accessed February 2008.)

755 Joshua Muravchik, *Commentary Magazine*, February 2007, "Our Worst Ex-President",
www.commentarymagazine.com/printArticle.cfm/Our-Worst-ExPresident-10824.
(Accessed December 2007.)

756 Ibid.

757 Neil King, Jr., "Cries in the Dark," *Wall Street Journal*, June 30, 2008;
http://online.wsj.com/article/SB121432276099000211.html?mod=googlenews_wsj.
(Accessed June 2008.)

758 Benjamin Shapiro, "Jimmy Carter: Emissary of Evil," *WorldNetDaily*.com, April 16,
2008, http://www.worldnetdaily.com/index.php?fa=PAGE.view&pageID=61724.
(Accessed April 2008.)

759 Fairness and Accuracy in Reporting, Jeff Cohen and Norman Solomon, "Jimmy Carter
and Human Rights: Behind the Media Myth," September 21, 1994;
http://www.fair.org/index.php?page=2263.
(Accessed February 2008.)

760 Edward Daley, *The American Daily*, "Jimmy Carter's Nobel Legacy," March 10, 2003,
http://americandaily.com/article/1991.
(Accessed January 2008.)

761 Jacqueline L. Salmon, *Washington Post*, "Baptists Uniting to Carve out a Moderate
Image," http://www.chron.com/disp/story.mpl/headline/nation/5488743.html.
(Accessed January 2008.)

762 Ibid.

[763] Erin Roach, *Baptist Press,* "Carter and Clinton Call for New Baptist Covenant," January 10, 2008, http://www.bpnews.net/bpnews.asp?ID=24745. (Accessed January 2008.)

[764] Mike Evans, *Jerusalem Betrayed* (Dallas: Word Publishing, 1997), pp. 87-88.

[765] Mona Charen, CBS News, *National Review* Online, "Jimmy Carter's Foolishness about Israel," December 16, 2006; http://www.cbsnews.com/stories/2006/12/15/opinion/printable2272275.shtml. (Accessed February 2008.)

[766] Alan Dershowitz, *The Huffington Post,* "The World According to Jimmy Carter," November 22, 2006, http://www.huffingtonpost.com/alan-dershowitz/the-world-according-to-ji_b_34702.html. (Accessed February 2008.)

[767] Eric Rozenman, *Pittsburgh Post-Gazette,* "In Rebuttal: Carter Can't See Straight," December 13, 2006; http://www.post-gazette.com/pg/06347/745588-109.stm#. (Accessed February 2008.)

[768] "Carter Board of Councilors Resignation Letter," January 11, 2007; http://www.foxnews.com/story/0,2933,243131,00.html. (Accessed February 2008.)

[769] Anti-Defamation League, "What the Experts are Saying: President Carter's Book", 2006; www.adl.org/carter/experts.asp. (Accessed December 2007.)

[770] Ibid.

[771] Ibid.

[772] Abraham H. Foxman, Anti-Defamation League, "Judging a Book by Its Cover and Its Content," www.adl.org/carter/carter_review.asp. (Accessed December 2007.)

[773] Available at www.cartercenter.org

[774] Ehrenfeld, Rachel, "Carter's Arab Financiers," *Washington Times* (21 Dec. 2006): A23.

[775] Chadwyck-Healy, *Iran: The Making of U.S. Policy 1977-1980,* Alexandria VA 1990, U.S. State Department Memo from U.S. Embassy Cairo to State Department, January 25, 1979.

[776] Ibid.

[777] Ibid.

[778] Jacob Laksin, "Jimmy Carter and the Arab Lobby," *FrontPageMagazine,* December 18, 2006, http://www.frontpagemag.com/Articles/Printable.aspx?GUID=D7B261EF-A52C-428E-9E5F-D6BBF5C49132. (Accessed March 2008.)

[779] Hamas Charter; http://www.mideastweb.org/hamas.htm. (Accessed March 2008.)

[780] Jimmy Carter, *New York Times,* "America can Persuade Israel to Make a Just Peace," April 21, 2002, http://query.nytimes.com/gst/fullpage.html?res=9C01E1DC133FF932A15757C0A9649C8B63&scp=2&sq=By+Jimmy+Carter&st=nyt. (Accessed February 2008.)

[781] Statement of Former President Jimmy Carter to the UN Human Rights Council, March 29, 2007; http://www.cartercenter.org/news/pr/humanrightscouncil_032907.html. (Accessed May 2008.)

[782] Nobel Peace Prize 2002, http://nobelprize.org/nobel_prizes/peace/laureates/2002/. (Accessed February 2008.)

[783] *Guardian* editorial, "Jimmy Carter Wins Nobel Peace Prize," October 11, 2002; http://www.guardian.co.uk/world/2002/oct/11/2. (Accessed February 2008.)

[784] Sean Hannity, *Deliver Us from Evil* (New York: Harper Collins, 2004), p. 93.

[785] Douglas Brinkley, *The Unfinished Presidency: Jimmy Carter's Journey Beyond the White House* (New York: Viking, 1998), p. 324.

[786] *New York Times*, "Carter Meets Arafat in Paris, Praises Him as Peacemaker," April 5, 1990, http://query.nytimes.com/gst/fullpage.html?res=9C0CE2DB133AF936A35757C0 A966958260. (Accessed March 2008.)

[787] Noel Sheppard, "Jimmy Carter on Al-Jazeera: 'I Wasn't Equating the Palestinian Missiles with Terrorism," http://www.newsbusters.org/node/10199. (Accessed March 2008.)

[788] Jay Nordlinger, "Jimmy Carter Apologist for Arafat," *National Review,* October 16, 2002, http://frontpagemag.com/Articles/Read.aspx?GUID=5A1AEC45-2FFD-456B-9CD9-0D50BF0F2F43. (Accessed March 2008.)

[789] Quote by PLO Chairman Yasser Arafat, http://learning.seriousgames.dk/quotes.aspx. (Accessed March 2008.)

[790] Douglas Brinkley, pp. 232-233

[791] "Jimmy Carter: The Malaise Speech," 1979, http://www2.volstate.edu/geades/FinalDocs/1970s&beyond/malaise.htm. (Accessed January 2008.)

[792] "Ex-U.S. President Jimmy carter has said Israel has at least 150 atomic weapons in its arsenal," BBC, June 2, 2008; www.globalresearch.ca/printarticle.php?articleId=9154. (Accessed June 2008.)

[793] Middle East Policy Council: Arab World Studies Notebook, http://www.mepc.org/workshops/musworld.asp. (Accessed July 2008.)

[794] Lance Morrow, "*The Lives of the Saint,*" *Time,* May 11, 1998.

[795] Jay Nordlinger, "There He Goes, Again," *National Review*, July 26, 2004, http://www.nationalreview.com/nordlinger/nordlinger200407262354.asp. (Accessed March 2008.)

[796] Jonathan Freedland, "I have moral authority," *The Guardian*, June 7, 2008. www.guardian.co.uk. (Accessed July 2008.)

[797] Ibid.

[798] Ibid.

[799] Joseph Lelyveld, "Jimmy Carter and Apartheid," The New York Review of Books," March 29, 2007, http://www.nybooks.com/articles/19993. (Accessed July 2008.)

[800] I Corinthians 13:1, New Living Translation © 1996 Tyndale Charitable Trust.

[801] Dennis Prager, "What makes a Liberal?", *World Net Daily.com*, August 2, 2003, http://www.worldnetdaily.com/news/article.asp?ARTICLE_ID=34041. (Accessed April 2008.)

[802] "Laurence Jarvik, Ph. D., "Ten Good Reasons to Eliminate Funding for the National Endowment for the Arts," Heritage Foundation, http://www.heritage.org/Research/Budget/BG1110.cfm. (Accessed March 2008.)

[803] Abraham Lincoln, Seventh and Final Debate with Stephen A. Douglas, Alton, IL, October 15, 1858, http://www.nps.gov/archive/liho/slavery/al11.htm. (Accessed April 2008.)

[804] Samuel Segev interview, May 2008.

[805] Geoff Winestock, *Wall Street Journal*, January 19, 2002, reprinted in The Arizona Daily Star, http://www.azstarnet.com/old_attack/indepth/wsj-egypt.html. (Accessed April 2008.)

[806] Peter Beinart, "Out of Egypt," *Wall Street Journal*, November 5, 2001, reprinted at www.norpac.net, http://www.norpac.net/media/norpac/outegypt.htm. (Accessed April 2008.)

[807] Benjamin Shapiro, "Jimmy Carter: Emissary of Evil," *World Net Daily.com*, April 16, 2008, www.worldnetdaily.com/indes.php?fa=PAGE.view&pageId=61724. (Accessed April 2008.)

[808] Aaron Klein, "France Admits Talks with HAMAS," *WorldNetDaily.com;* http://www.worldnetdaily.com/index.php?fa=PAGE.view&pageId=64724. (Accessed May 2008.)

[809] Ibid.

[810] Ibid.

[811] Norman Podhoretz, *CommentaryMagazine.com*, "A Response to Andrew Sullivan," November 19, 2007, http://www.commentarymagazine.com/blogs/index.php/podhoretz/1340. (Accessed April 2008.)

[812] "Carter-HAMAS Meeting comes on 25th Anniversary of Deadly Terror Attack," Fox News, April 18, 2008, http://www.foxnews.com/printer_friendlly_story/0,3566,351717,00.html. (Accessed April 2008.)

[813] "Carter-HAMAS Meeting comes on 25th Anniversary of Deadly Terror Attack," Fox News.

[814] "Rice says Carter was warned against meeting with HAMAS," Britibart.com, April 22, 2008, http://www.breitbart.com/print.php?id=D90708G80&show_article=1. (Accessed April 2008.)

[815] *International Herald Tribune*, "Jimmy Carter Visits Sderot, Rocket-battered Israeli Town," http://www.iht.com/articles/ap/2008/04/14/africa/ME-GEN-Israel-Carter.php. (Accessed May 2008.)

[816] Jeane J. Kirkpatrick, *Dictators and Double Standards* (New York: Simon and Schuster, 1983), p. 23.

[817] www.wisdomquotes.com. (Accessed April 2008.)

[818] Jimmy Carter, "Crisis of Confidence" speech, July 15, 1979, http://www.pbs.org/wgbh/amex/carter/filmmore/ps_crisis.html. (Accessed April 2008.)

[819] Jeane J. Kirkpatrick, Ambassador to the United Nations, Republican National Convention 1984, http://www.cnn.com/ALLPOLITICS/1996/conventions/san.diego/facts/GOP.speeches.past/84.kirkpatrick.shtml. (Accessed April 2008.)

[820] Lee May, "Reagan Blames Iron Triangle for Nation's Ills," *Los Angeles Times*, December 14, 1988, http://pqasb.pqarchiver.com/latimes/access/59880844.html?dids=59880844:59880844&FMT=ABS&FMTS=ABS:FT&type=current&date=Dec+14%2C+1988&author=LEE+MAY&pub=Los+Angeles+Times+(pre1997+Fulltext)&edition=&startpage=1&desc=Reagan+Blames+%60Iron+Triangle%27+for+Nation%27s+Ills. (Accessed April 2008.)

821 Dennis Prager, "What makes a Liberal?", *World Net Daily.com,* August 2, 2003, http://www.worldnetdaily.com/news/article.asp?ARTICLE_ID=34041. (Accessed April 2008.)

822 Sun Tzi, Chinese general and military strategist, 400 BC, http://www.quotationspage.com/quote/36994.html. (Accessed April 2008.)

823 Michael D. Evans, *Betrayed: The Conspiracy to Divide Jerusalem* (Dallas: Bedford Books, 2008) pp. 52-54.

824 Newt Gingrich, *Winning the Future: A 21st Century Contract with America* (Washington, DC: Regnery, 2005), p. 7.

825 Thomas Jefferson Memorial, northeast interior wall; http://www.monticello.org/reports/quotes/memorial.html. (Accessed June 2008.)

826 William Penn, http://en.proverbia.net/citasautor.asp?autor=15634. (Accessed November 2008.)

827 Isaiah 5:20, *New Living Translation,* Tyndale Charitable Trust, 1996.

828 William Jefferson Clinton, January 1998, "Sex, Lies and Impeachment," BBC News, http://news.bbc.co.uk/1/hi/special_report/1998/12/98/review_of_98/themes/208715.stm. (Accessed May 2008.)

829 Michal Lumsden, "God's Politics: An Interview with Jim Wallace," March 10, 2005; http://www.motherjones.com/news/qa/2005/03/gods_politics_jim_wallis.html. (Accessed June 2008.)

830 Cited by James D. Richardson in *A compilation of the Messages and Papers of the Presidents*, 1789-1897 (Published by Authority of Congress, 1899) from George Washington's Farewell Address, September 19, 1796. Vol. 1, p. 220.

831 Cited in Charles Francis Adams, ed., *The Works of John Adams—Second President of the United States* (Boston: Little, Brown & Co., 1854), Vol. IX, p. 229, from John Adams address to the military, October 11, 1798.

832 Patrick O'Hannigan, "We have a Pope," http://theanchoressonline.com/2006/09/15/oriana-and-rosie-two-women-of-the-left/. (Accessed July 2008.)

833 Jason Maoz, "When Rudy Booted Arafat," *JewishPress*.com, October 28, 2005; http://www.frontpagemag.com/Articles/Read.aspx?GUID=0A32F335-9197-4925-9EF4-71125E47F526. (Accessed April 2008.)

834 David Firestone, "The UN at 50: Arafat; White House Condemns Giuliani for Ejecting Arafat from Concert, *New York Times,* October 25, 1995; http://query.nytimes.com/gst/fullpage.html?res=990CE7D6163DF936A15753C1A963958260. (Accessed May 2008.)

835 Aleksander Solzhenitsyn, "A World Split Apart," address at Harvard Class Day afternoon exercises, June 8, 1978, http://www.columbia.edu/cu/augustine/arch/solzhenitsyn/harvard1978.html. (Accessed April 2008).

836 Bishop Keith Butler, *Reviving the American Spirit* (Lake Mary, FL: FrontLine, 2006), pp. 22-23.

837 Natan Sharansky, The Case for Democracy: The Power of Freedom to Overcome Tyranny and Terror (New York: PublicAffairs, 2004), 40–41.

838 Carol Iannone, "Homeland Insecurity," *New York Press,* October 16, 2001, http://www.nypress.com/14/42/taki/perspectives.cfm. (Accessed April 2008.)

[839] David Kupelian, *The Marketing of Evil* (Nashville: WND Books, 2005), p. 102.

[840] Michael D. Evans, *The Final Move Beyond Iraq* (Lake Mary, FL: FrontLine, 2007), p. 168.

[841] Michael D. Evans, *The American Prophecies* (New York: Warner Faith, 2004), p. 22.

[842] The Museum of Broadcast Communications, *NYPD Blue*, http://www.museum.tv/archives/etv/N/htmlN/nypdblue/nypdblue.htm. (Accessed April 2008.)

[843] Michael Evans, *The Final Move Beyond Iraq*, p. 35.

[844] The Barna Group, cited in "Christians Parent No Different than 'World,'" *WorldNetDaily.com*, March 3, 2005, http://www.wnd.com/news/article.asp?ARTICLE_ID=43128. (Accessed May 2008.)

[845] Cited by Shawn Macomber in "Jimmy Carter's Covenant," *The American Spectator*, February 1, 2008, http://www.spectator.org/dsp_article.asp?art_id=12675. (Accessed May 2008.)

[846] Francis A. Schaeffer, *The Great Evangelical Disaster* (Westchester, IL: Crossway Books, 1984), pp. 36-38.

[847] David F. Wells, *No Place for Truth: Or Whatever Happened to Evangelical Theology?* (Grand Rapids: Eerdmans, 1993), p. 136.

[848] Quoted by Mark Silverberg, "Jimmy Carter: The Untold Story," http://www.jfednepa.org/mark%20silverberg.jimmycarter.html. (Accessed August 2008.)

[849] Tysk News, March 20, 2000; http://www.tysknews.com/TyskWorks/the_liberal_left.htm. (Accessed September 2008.)

[850] Bruce Walker, "The New Jimmy Carter," *American Thinker*, March 19, 2008, www.americanthinker.com/2008/03/the_new_Jimmy_carter_.html. (Accessed June 2008.)

[851] Gregory D. Lee, "All Hail Obama, the Novice Messiah," *Townhall.com*, July 30, 2008; http://www.familysecuritymatters.org/publications/id.740/pub_detail.asp. (Accessed July 2008.)

[852] *Political Affairs Magazine*, April 8, 2008, http://www.politicalaffairs.net/article/articleview/6722/1/328/. (Accessed November 2008.)

[853] Ben Smith, "Obama advisor worries Israel supporters," *Politico*, September 12, 2007; http://www.politico.com/news/stories/0907/5783.html. (Accessed July 2008.)

[854] *Washington Post,* "Brzezinski Backs Obama," August 2, 2007; http://www.washingtonpost.com/wp-dyn/content/article/2007/08/57/AR2007082402127.html. (Accessed February 2008.)

[855] Barry Rubin, "The Region: Just be our Friend," *Jerusalem Post Online*, October 5, 2008, http://www.jpost.com /servlet/Satellite?cid=1222017466148&pagename=JPost%2FJPArticle%2FShowFull. (Accessed October 2008.)

[856] DiscovertheNetworks.org, Ploughshares Fund, http://www.discoverthenetworks.org/groupprofile.asp?grpid=7156&category=79. (Accessed August 2008.)

857 Ed Lasky, *American Thinker,* April 25, 2008,
http://www.americanthinker.com/blog/2008/04/obama_keeps_hiring_antiisraeli.html.
(Accessed August 2008.)

858 "Larijani, Iran Prefers Obama," YNetNews.com, October 22, 2008,
http://www.ynetnews.com/articles/0,7340,L-3611840,00.html.
(Accessed October 2008.)

859 Maamoun Youssef and Lee Keath, "Al-Qaeda No. 2 insults Obama with Racial
Epithet," Yahoo News, November 19, 2008;
http://news.yahoo.com/s/ap/20081119/ap_on_re_mi_ea/ml_al_qaida_obama.
(Accessed November 2008.)

860 David Limbaugh, "The Old Gray Lady's mind-numbing bias," *World Net Daily,* June
25, 2008, www.worldnetdaily,com/index.php?pageID=70471.
(Accessed August 2008.)

861 Con Coughlin, "Jimmy Carter pledged to reform U.S. Foreign policy…and look what
happened," *London Telegraph*;
www.telegraph.co.uk/core/content/displayprintablejhtml;jsessionid=P2LMBCVJR.
(Accessed July 2008.)

862 Amir Oren, "A crash course for Obama," *Haaretz.com*,
www.haaretz.com/hasen/spages/991086.html. (Accessed June 2008.)

863 Rev. Jeremiah Wright, "Confusing God and Government," transcript, Trinity United
Church of Christ, Chicago, April 13, 2003, *ABC News*,
http://abcnews.go.com/Blotter/Story?id=4719157&page=2.
(Accessed August 2008.)

864 E. R. Shipp, "Tape Contradicts Disavowal of 'Gutter Religion' Attack," *New York
Times*, June 29, 1984: A12.

865 Ibid.

866 Joan Vennochi, "Not quite the next JFK," *The Boston Globe*,
http://www.boston.com/news/globe/editorial_opinion/oped/articles/2007/01/18/no
t_quite_the_next_jfk/. (Accessed July 2008.)

867 Dick Morris, p. 89.

868 Ibid.

869 "Obama's Berlin Speech Plans Get Mixed Reaction in Germany." http://www.dw-
world.de/popups/popup_printcontent/0,,3473664,00.html.
(Accessed July 2008.)

870 Barack Obama Berlin speech transcript, July 24, 2008,
http://www.huffingtonpost.com/2008/07/24/obama-in-berlin-video-
of_n_114771.html. (Accessed July 2008.)

871 Robert Frost, "Mending Wall," http://writing.upenn.edu/~afilreis/88/frost-
mending.html. (Accessed August 2008.)

872 Ibid.

873 Dick Morris, p. 19.

874 Definition of Elitism, http://en.wikipedia.org/wiki/Elitism.
(Accessed July 2008.)

875 *National Journal Online*, "Biden's Senate Vote Record,"
http://www.nationaljournal.com/conventions/co_20080823_9669.php.
(Accessed August 2008.)

876 Hugh Hewitt, "Obama Picks Cliff the Mailman," *Townhall.com*; August 23, 2008,
http://hughhewitt.townhall.com/common/print.aspx.
(Accessed August 2008.)

JIMMY CARTER: THE LIBERAL LEFT AND WORLD CHAOS

[877] Ilana Mercer, "Not quite Muslim, not quite Christian," *World Net Daily,* August 1, 2008, www.wnd.com/index.php?fa=PAGE,view&pageId=71111. (Accessed August 2008.)

[878] Mark Krikorian, "Post Americans," *National Review Online*, June 22, 2004; http://www.nationalreview.com/comment/krikorian200406220944.asp. (Accessed August 20008.)

[879] The Editors on Barack Obama in Berlin on *National Review Online,* http://article.nationalreview.com/?q=MTE3ZTk0ZDc2ZGQ2MDc2NGU2Zjc3M TVmZGQ3YzdmM2Q=#more. (Accessed July 2008.)

[880] Marianne Means, "For different reasons, VP matters for both hopefuls," *Houston Chronicle*, July 31, 2008, Outlook B-9.

[881] Bruce Walker, "The New Jimmy Carter," *American Thinker*, March 18, 2008; http://www.americanthinker.com/2008/03/the_new_jimmy_carter. (Accessed November 2008.)

[882] George Will, "The Final Repudiation," *Newsweek.com;* http://www.newsweek.com/id/167572/output/print

[883] Charles Krauthammer, "Obama, the Charismatic New American Leader," Fox News Channel, November 4, 2008.

[884] Thomas Sowell, *Townhall.com,* "Pretty Talk and Ugly Realities," January 13, 2009; http://townhall.com/columnists/ThomasSowell/2009/01/13/pretty_talk_and_ugly_realities. (Accessed January 2009.)

[885] Jimmy Carter, *The Nation*, "An Unnecessary War," January 8, 2009; http://www.thenation.com/blogs/thebeat/395200/jimmy_carter_on_an_unnecessary_war. (Accessed January 2009.)

[886] "Syria, Iran must be involved in talks," *The Jerusalem Post,* January 15, 2009; www.jpost.com/servlet/Satellite?cid=1231950855500&pagename=JPost%2FJPArticl e%2FShowFull. (Accessed January 2009.)

[887] Ibid.

[888] Hilary Leila Krieger, "Obama to 'aggressively' seek ME peace," Jerusalem Post.com, January 22, 2009; http://www.jpost.com/servlet/Satellite?cid=1232643726975& pagename=JPost%2FJPArticle%2FShowFull. (Accessed January 2009.)

[889] Ibid.

[890] Ibid.

[891] Ibid.

[892] Ibid.

[893] Mideast Web Historical Documents, Hamas Charter: The Covenant of the Islamic Resistance Movement, Hamas; http://www.mideastweb.org/hamas.htm. (Accessed January 2009.)

[894] George Mitchell talks with Gwen Ifill about the Middle East, PBS Online NewsHour, May 2001, http://www.pbs.org/newshour/bb/middle_east/jan-june01/mitchell_5-7.html. (Accessed January 2009.)

[895] "Bill Clinton's policies may echo at hearing," Boston Globe, Boston.com, January 13, 2009; http://www.boston.com/news/nation/articles/2009/01/13/bill_clintons_policies_ may_echo_at_hearing/. (Accessed January 2009.)

[896] Jimmy Carter, *We Can Have Peace in the Holy Land* (Simon and Schuster: New York, NY 2009), p. 41

[897] Ibid, p. 41.

[898] Michael D. Evans, "Jimmy Carter's Myopia", *Washington Times*, January 28, 2009; http://www.washingtontimes.com/news/2009/jan/28/jimmy-carters-myopia/. (Accessed January 2009.)

[899] Jimmy Carter, *We Can Have Peace in the Holy Land* (Simon and Schuster: New York, NY 2009), p. 59.

[900] Ibid, p.101.

[901] Ibid, Introductory Page.

[902] Michael D. Evans, *Betrayed: The Conspiracy to Divide Jerusalem* (Bedford, TX: Bedford Books, 2008.) p.104.

[903] Jimmy Carter, p. 144.

[904] Ibid, p. 30.

[905] Michael D. Evans, p. 111.

[906] Michael D. Evans, pp. 1.

[907] Ibid, p.108.

[908] Jimmy Carter, p. 80.

[909] Mark Steyn, "Global Village Elders," *National Review Online*, http://corner.nationalreview.com/post/?q=YTFhOGRiY2IxOGE5NDNhMjhkNmNm ZGZiZGQ1MTc2NTY=. (Accessed January 2009.)

[910] Jimmy Carter, p. 180.

DR. MICHAEL D. EVANS is one of America's top experts on Israel and the Middle East. For over two decades he has been a personal confidant to many of Israel's top leaders.

Dr. Evans is an award-winning journalist and has been published in the *Wall Street Journal, Newsweek, USA Today, The Washington Times, The Jerusalem Post,* and newspapers throughout the world. He is a member of the National Press Club and has been covering events in the Middle East for decades.

Michael Evans is the author of eighteen books, including the #1 *New York Times* bestseller *The Final Move Beyond Iraq,* and *New York Times* bestsellers *Beyond Iraq: The Next Move* and *The American Prophecies.*

Millions around the world have seen his award-winning television documentaries on Israel based on his books. Dr. Evans is a top network analyst and is in constant demand. He has appeared on hundreds of network radio and television programs such as Fox, MSNBC, *Nightline, Good Morning America, Crossfire,* CNN World News, BBC, the Rush Limbaugh show, and others.

Michael D. Evans has spoken to over 4,000 audiences worldwide. In the past decade alone, he has addressed more than one million people per year at public events, from the Kremlin Palace in Moscow to the World Summit on Terrorism in Jerusalem.

"Mike Evans is a fighter for freedom in a world of darkening and narrowing horizons. In his devotion to Israel, Mike has consistently demonstrated the moral clarity necessary to defend Israel against the lies and distortions of its enemies." (The Honorable Benjamin Netanyahu, Prime Minister of Israel.)

"I have known Mike Evans for more than two decades. I consider him to be a great friend of Jerusalem and the State of Israel. He has always been there for us in our time of need, speaking out with courage and compassion. Mike Evans is a true Ambassador to Jerusalem representing millions of Americans." (The Honorable Ehud Olmert, Prime Minister of Israel.)

To contact Dr. Evans to speak at your event, please write

TIME WORTHY BOOKS, P.O. BOX 30000 PHOENIX, AZ 85046
or visit: WWW.TIMEWORTHYBOOKS.COM

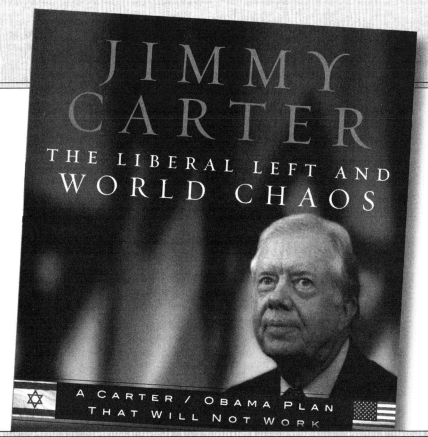